Revised Edition

HOUSEBUILDING

A Do-It-Yourself Guide

11

Revised Edition

HOUSEBUILDING

A Do-It-Yourself Guide

R. J. De Cristoforo
Updated by Mike McClintock

Drawings by
Richard J. Meyer,
W. Dave Houser
& the authors

STERLING PUBLISHING CO., INC.

NEW YORK

Library of Congress Cataloging-in-Publication Data

DeCristoforo, R. J.
 [Housebuilding illustrated]
 Housebuilding : a-do-it-yourself guide / R.J. DeCristoforo ; updated by Mike McClintock.
   p. cm.
 Includs index
 ISBN 0-8069-5521-X
 1. House construction--Amateurs' manuals.   I. McClintock, Michael, 1945-   II. Title

TH4817.3 .D412 2002
690'.837--dc21

                                                                                      2002070822

 10 9 8 7 6 5 4 3 2 1

Published by Sterling Publishing Co., Inc.
Originally published in hardcover by Grolier Book Clubs, Inc.,
Under the title "De Cristoforo's Housebuilding Illustrated"
copyright © 1977 by R.J. De Cristoforo
Distributed in Canada by Sterling Publishing
℅ Canadian Manda Group, One Atlantic Avenue, Suite 105
Toronto, Ontario, Canada M6K 3E7
Distributed in Great Britain and Europe by Cassell PLC
Wellington House, 125 Strand, London WC2R 0BB, England
Distributed in Australia by Capricorn Link (Australia) Pty Ltd.
P.O. Box 704, Windsor, NSW 2756, Australia

CONTENTS

9 INSTALLING CEILING JOISTS   187

10 FRAMING THE ROOF   197

11 ROOF SHEATHING   247

PREFACE

Building a house is probably the most ambitious project an amateur can undertake. It's a formidable assignment, like the challenge of climbing a mountain with peaks concealed by clouds. Yet amateurs have climbed mountains, and they have built houses. Like the sequence of steps in the climb, putting a house together is basically a matter of concentrating on the next nail. Maybe the overall task is intimidating, but it is just a long series of bits and pieces you would not hesitate to tackle if each were an individual project.

The prime factor is not whether you *can* get there, but whether you *wish* to. Determination and enthusiasm are priority tools.

However, don't think you can construct a house simply if you can saw a board and drive a nail. Even though this simplification may apply to the carpentry involved, it naively overlooks areas that require more than a hammer and a saw. You don't, for example, mix concrete with woodworking tools; nor do skills with those tools make you a plumber, an electrician, or an architect.

I state the above in a positive vein and for a number of reasons. For one, seeing the project in depth prepares you psychologically for the entire job, not just phases of it. For another, visualizing the complete assembly as a contribution of various crafts lets you organize a successful program without committing you to accomplish it all by yourself. This concept eases the mind of anyone standing on naked ground with only a dream. The builder who wants to do it all himself can. But builders who want to involve professionals or even other knowledgeable amateurs can do so while still making a contribution that leads to satisfaction and big financial savings.

Planning and mental preparation are an important part of housebuilding. You can make an excellent start by setting up an idea file—a collection of separate folders to contain (1) personal thoughts, (2) notes on existing structures and building details you have liked, (3) sketches you've made of floor plans, (4) tear sheets from publications showing artist's sketches of homes for which you can buy ready-to-use plans, (5) tear sheets of advertisements showing manufacturer's products in use, and (6) above all, catalogs by manufacturers that supply building materials and by associations that represent suppliers.

Since it's the purpose of catalogs and associations to give exposure to products and prompt their use, much of the available information contains enticing ideas you can use directly or modify.

One value of such a file is that it can acquaint you with the many types of house materials that are available. You may know in advance that you want wood siding. But what kind? Lumber, plywood, shingling? In each category there are choices and variables in relation to basic costs, appearance, and installation time. Some materials require finishing after installation; others stand as installed. Your reaction to initial cost should be influenced by follow-up requirements. A few more cents per foot for a prefinished product might be a more economical way to go, long range, than to pay less for an alternate material that requires painting now and painting again in later years.

With a good idea file and a book like this on hand you will be able to make critical decisions at leisure, not just in relation to materials but also concerning the scope of your physical involvement. I have seen and I've been involved in many successful amateur-constructed houses. Some, especially those designed as vacation or "second" homes, were erected from the first shovelful of soil to the last nail in the roof by the owner or his whole family. Other were examples of various group efforts; still others illustrated that the amateur can be both contractor and part builder. You can determine what parts of the job you wish to do and hire professionals to fill in.

The popularity of do-it-yourself activities has bred some companies that offer "finish-it-yourself" houses. The point where you take over is determined in advance. It might be after the frame is up or after the house has been closed in.

There are ways to go. You don't have to give up the dream of a custom home if the thought of doing it from scratch turns you off. You can take a middle road by providing all of the design but only part of the work.

In any case, if you are to be involved with house construction to *any* degree, or if you are just in the market for a finished home, or if you are happy where you are but wish to make changes, you should know what building construction is all about.

I have been guided in some areas by the fact that it is not the intention of the amateur to take up house construction as a career. Some suggested work procedures are not those used by pros, but they get you there with quality results and with minimum time devoted to preliminary study. My simplified explanation of the carpenter's square is a good example. The square is an ingenious instrument and has some highly complicated functions— but you need to know only the basic ones, so that's all I attempt to teach you. Besides, when you buy a good square, you get with it an impressive little booklet that tells all there is to know. So why repeat it here?

R.J. De Cristoforo

Revised Edition

HOUSEBUILDING

A Do-It-Yourself Guide

1

CODES, PERMITS, AND INSPECTIONS

Your house is your castle, and you should be able to build it or remodel it any way you please. There is a lot of room for variation in design and layout, but there are also a lot of rules. Basically, there are two types: building codes that control the details of construction, and zoning ordinances that control not only what you can build but where you can build it.

Codes used to be short and basic. Gradually, they have grown more complex, and now control almost all aspects of construction in great detail, and not just major structural components like the foundation and framing.

If you were familiar with old-time, stick-built construction that was common through the 1960s and into the 1970s, you'll find that codes, which are regularly updated, underwent a major change due to the energy crisis of the mid-70s. The result is that in an increasing number of regions there are now strict energy codes that govern the particulars of insulation and ventilation, the thermal quality of windows, and more. In the '80s and '90s, there was another major shift due to increased interest in a healthy environment in the home. Indoor air quality was thoroughly investigated as many houses built nearly airtight in the 1970s and 1980s had to be equipped with fresh-air exchangers and filtering systems. Unhealthy air in tight houses (and offices) even got a name: the sick-building syndrome. And along the way, some problems have cropped up with older building materials, such as asbestos in insulation and siding, and lead in pipes and paint, that were found to present serious health risks. Modern building codes take these and other health risks into account, including things like radon, a naturally occurring radioactive gas.

In many areas now, you also need special permits and/or special inspections, to make sure that the mechanical work (plumbing, electrical, and heating and cooling) is up to code. If you're building a large addition or a new house, you'll have to focus on the construction, of course. But there are a lot of technicalities to take care of before you get started.

ZONING AND VARIANCES

Zoning regulations control what you can do with your building site. The main categories are commercial and residential, but there are many subcategories. For instance, in one area you can remodel a large house into a two-family, but a few blocks away in a different zone you can't. Single-family houses on one street may need two acres of land, but only ¼ acre on another. In historic districts, your plans may have to be altered to include certain styles of windows, siding, and even paint colors.

For most owner–builders, zoning ordinances present two main constraints. They control the percentage of land that can be covered by buildings, and how the uncovered property can be distributed among front, back, and side yards. For example, the code may specify at least 100 feet of side yards, with a distribution percentage no greater than 80–20. That means the narrowest yard must be at least 20 percent of 100 feet—in theory, to prevent next-door neighbors from building nearly on top of each other.

The rules can box you in, but there may be a way out. It's called a variance, and each jurisdiction has its own, generally time-consuming procedure for granting one. Typically, you submit copies of your blueprints (including a detailed plot plan with survey information) to an appeals board, and present your case at a hearing after posting notices of the hearing up and down your street so neighbors have a chance to object. You can present the case yourself, relying as much as possible on facts and figures, or hire a real estate attorney to present a complex case where you anticipate objections from owners whose property abuts your own.

Variances are rarely granted just because you would like a larger house or a bigger garage. You're more likely to get one if your plan falls into one of three categories: if you're building or remodeling in a way that conforms to neighborhood standards—for example, if converting an attached garage on a street of houses with converted garages; if your plan oversteps a required proportion or minimum dimension by only a foot or so; and if there is no reasonable alternative to your plan, for example, if relocating a room from the side to the back of the house would require you to fill in a pond.

RULES OF THE ROAD

Most municipalities have codes modeled after one of four sets of rules called Model Building Codes. The following groups represent these codes: Building Officials & Code Administrators International, Inc. (BOCA); International Conference of Building Officials (ICBO); Southern Building Code Congress International, Inc. (SBCCI); and Council of American Building Officials (CABO). Yet more groups administer plumbing, electrical, and other specialty codes. Even for professional builders (and for subcontractors such as plumbers and electricians), the volume and complexity of these codes can be overwhelming. If you are building just one house, it is impossible to become fully familiar with all the codes, and you will have to rely on architects, engineers, and others at various times—and on the local building inspector throughout the project.

It certainly won't hurt to acquire a copy of the code, particularly the CABO One- and Two-Family Dwelling Code. It covers construction, electrical, mechanical, plumbing, and energy conservation, includes many illustrations, and generally is accepted as an option by municipalities that use one of the other three Model Codes (BOCA, ICBO, and SBCCI).

But even though building codes have the force of law, they are not absolutes. For one thing, the rules are applied in the field by inspectors who have different backgrounds and different ways of doing things. Some inspectors are sticklers for detail, such as how many nails you drive in a header, while others take a more overall view of the project. Some make an effort to deal with owner–builders who lack a lot of practical experience, while others seem to resent dealing with non-professionals

Another obvious variable is that houses are not the same. If you build an addition to match a 1950s-vintage Craftsman-style house, it may have 4-by exposed rafters and other structural systems that are quite different from the roof trusses now used in 90 percent of new houses.

On top of that, there are often several different ways to meet a code standard. A room full of do-it-yourselfers and professional builders might come up with a dozen different ways to get the same code-approved result using different materials and methods. For example, for most eastern states to meet year-2001 Dept. of Energy standards of R-18 insulation in walls (it used to be R-10), you can build with 2-by-6 studs that accommodate 5½ inches of fiberglass insulation. It's rated at about R-3.5 per inch and provides about R-19 in the wall. But you also can stick with standard 2-by-4s, fill the bays with fiberglass (total about R-12), and clad the frame with a dense urethane foam board to make up the difference.

Here's the catch. Even though there is more than one correct way to do things, if the inspector wants them one way as opposed to another, that's the way it has to be. It just doesn't pay to argue, or get on the wrong side of the person who is checking your work and approving the final Certificate of Occupancy that means your project is legal and livable.

Some building codes seem too strict, too detailed, and too limiting. After all, you should be able to decide that a row of porthole-style windows near the ceiling would look better in the new bedroom than larger, lower units a building inspector says you have to install instead. But there often is a good reason for the rule.

In this case, there are two. If a fire breaks out and blocks the door or the stairs to the first floor, you need a second way to leave the house—what building inspectors call a second means of egress. Typically, the windowsill can be no more than 44 inches off the floor so you can get over it easily, and the opening itself has to be at least 24 inches high and 20 inches wide. You may be athletic enough to climb over a higher sill and slim enough to slip through a smaller opening. But the somewhat roomy minimum size is set by code because someone else may have to get in—a firefighter wearing a bulky respirator backpack.

But bear in mind that there is no single set of dimensions or proportions to govern every type of house in every area of the country. There are several code authorities, but the one authority that counts is the local building inspector who checks your plans and visits the job site to be sure that what you put down on paper is what you're actually building.

CUSTOM AND NON-CUSTOM PLANS

When you hire a local architect, part of what you pay for is detailed knowledge of local codes and familiarity with quirks of the building inspection department. The same goes for a local structural engineer in the case where you draw up the basic plan in enough detail for an engineer to specify foundation depth, beam sizes, and other technical information required for a building permit.

In many jurisdictions, home owners can draw their own plans. A few building departments even provide local residents with generic, code-approved blueprints for popular projects such as building a deck. These often include tables for using different sizes of lumber for different spans so you can alter the generic layout to suit your site. However, for a complete house or major addition, you're likely to find that the inspector wants a full set of plans stamped with the seal of a licensed architect or engineer.

You also need to submit plans for approval when you want to assemble a house that comes in prefabricated parts, a log house in kit form, a complete part of a house such as a sunroom add-on; or build from plans out of a book. Even when so-called predesigned buildings and preapproved plans are sold with the assurance that they will satisfy building codes, there are likely to be areas where a local inspector will want some changes. You need to check these plans ahead of time because alterations needed to comply with local codes could defeat the economy of a kit system and turn the speedy, modular construction process into the slower, more traditional system of building one stick at a time. A precut log home might satisfy every structural requirement, for example, but fall short of local energy codes that are based on traditional stud walls filled with batts of insulation.

If you look at the fine print, many plans that promise code compliance contain qualifiers, for example, about modifying the foundation system for special sites and soils. Few buildings are so simple or so overdesigned that they can be plunked down anywhere, and changes often must be made to accommodate local conditions. It pays to check the plans with your local building inspection office and find out what alterations they will call for, and how much these will cost to make.

The point is that no matter what style of house you build or how experienced you may be with construction, final drawings must be reviewed by a building inspector before you can get a permit to start construction. That goes for plans you buy from a plan service, draw yourself, and those drawn for you by an architect or engineer.

CONTRACTORS AND CODES

Many homeowners–builders use professional contractors for some parts of the project, or to supervise a job where the home owner handles the interior finishing and other traditional do-it-yourself jobs. That makes sense because do-it-yourselfers don't have the heavy equipment or expertise to handle excavation work or or set large trusses, and don't have the licenses required by many local authorities to install the mechanicals, mainly the electrical and plumbing system.

Where it comes to codes and inspections, reputable contractors have no interest in cutting corners. They don't need the trouble that can accompany a corner-cutting reputation. And as a practical matter, inspectors become familiar with the work of local contractors. They know which ones need only a quick check, and save more time to examine jobs of a contractor who has tried to conceal violations in the past. Hire the wrong guy or bury violations yourself, and in most municipalities inspectors have the legal right to halt the job on the spot. They can require you to re-excavate foundations backfilled before footing depth was checked, remove drywall installed before wall framing was inspected, withdraw your permit, and levy stiff fines for severe or persistent violations.

You, or your contractor, may beat the system. But in the process you may bury a chronic maintenance problem, or worse yet, a structural fault or fire hazard. Some corners can be cut with less consequence, of course. The leading candidates are improvements, such as an extra bathroom, concealed so their added value won't raise your real estate taxes. Hidden improvements may be made with the proper materials and techniques and meet every code—except the one requiring a permit. But that one omission can cause legal and financial trouble if you decide to sell at some point, and the buyers and the building department discover that your current three-bath floor plan doesn't jibe with the two-bath description on record at the assessor's office. Worse yet, if your technically illegal addition happened to burn down, your home owner's insurance might not cover a replacement. If you need more reasons for going the permit route, bear in mind that inspectors routinely receive calls from neighbors near permitless jobs complaining about the noise, or piles of debris.

PERMIT REQUIREMENTS

"Will I need a building permit?" is a common question that homeowners ask when they're planning any major project. On a new house or large room addition, of course you'll need one.

Generally, any project that calls for a foundation, even piers for a deck, requires permit paperwork. But even when there is no new excavation, say, if you convert a garage or an attic to finished living space, you still need a permit because you're changing the original purpose of the structure. Joists in an unfinished attic, for instance, generally may be designed to carry a total load of 20 pounds per square foot, as opposed to joists in living areas that must be rated to carry twice that load.

In a nutshell, the complete permit and inspection process consists of assembling blueprints for your project, filling out various forms about the building's square footage and such, getting your permit approved (and paying a fee), having the inspector check crucial stages of the job on site and, finally, obtaining a Certificate of Occupancy (C.O.) when the job is done.

The best way to find out what information you need to provide to the building department is simply to ask them. There is no one rule. You may find that basic sketches with the key components labeled and sized are enough in a rural area with a small building department. In densely populated suburban areas, you generally need a complete set of blueprints. The full set typically includes a plot plan showing exact building locations on the site, which means you need accurate survey information to display the boundaries. Next up is a complete floor plan, and sometimes a similar print filled with details on the mechanical systems. Then there are four elevations (side views), and one or more pages of detail drawings, often shown as sections through the building, that cover crucial framing connections and other aspects of construction.

WORKING WITH A BUILDING INSPECTOR

Before you develop your plans too far, make a cordial first visit to the local building department to launch the relationship on a positive note. That's important because you don't want an adversarial inspection when it's time to check framing sizes and header spans before drywall is applied.

It's also important to realize just how different it is to deal with inspectors as opposed to contractors and other pros on the job. First off, you can't hire or fire a building inspector; you're stuck with the one the department assigns. The same goes for local codes, which are unlike everything else about a building project because you can't change them. There is no fussing or fudging the way there is with paint colors and trim details. If the building inspector says your foundation trench is too shallow, start digging. Inspectors have the final say on the size of main support girders, of course, and the locations of electrical outlets, the thickness of drywall, the height of railings, and just about everything else. And they can show up unannounced to tour the job and set you straight. It's not that you want to be bowing and scraping when the inspector pulls up, but it pays to be accommodating.

Obtaining a permit doesn't have to be an adversarial process. You can ask for a plan review, and follow up on the inspector's suggestion to increase the size of a girder or change a ventilation detail. Getting some sizes wrong on your plans is not a fatal error because getting a permit is not like a pass-fail test but more like an open-book exam. However, if your drawings have many mistakes that clearly demonstrate honest-to-goodness ignorance about structure and codes, the plans probably won't be approved. You have to know your own limitations in this area, and get professional help with your plans, if necessary.

Many inspectors report that homeowner–builders make the same kinds of mistakes, mostly errors of omission. Home-drawn plans often don't contain enough information to allow a full evaluation of the structure, they say. Even on plans that show foundation piers, support posts, girders, joists and other components, exact sizes and spans may not be specified. But they must be before a permit is granted. On major additions to existing homes, inspectors say that even a detailed plan for a new second story may not account for the extra load on the old foundation. But details that aren't caught in planning probably will be on-site, where you can expect at least four inspections: one to verify the depth of footings, one to examine framing, one to check mechanical systems, and one to make a final check before granting a Certificate of Occupancy.

The best bet is to plan the job as completely as possible, and visit your local building department for guidance. This is particularly important if you're planning anything even slightly unorthodox, such as a ground-source heat-pump system or a timber frame house clad with foam-filled stress-skin panels. As a rule, if you are obviously trying to do the right thing but don't have the expertise to fill in all the blanks, an inspector will help with the details and work with you on building the project.

KEEPING UP WITH CHANGES

Finally, you need to bear in mind that things change. That includes codes, of course, but also tools, techniques, and building materials. Sometimes a component that has been around for years suddenly undergoes a change, or is even banned.

One recent example is pressure-treated wood, which for decades has been used on decks, fences, and other types of construction, particularly anywhere wood is exposed to the weather or ground contact.

Due to increasing health concerns with arsenic, a component of the most common treatment, wood treated with CCA (chromated copper arsenate) is being phased out and will be banned by January 2004. An agreement between the Environmental Protection Agency and the wood-treating industry in 2002 eliminates all common residential uses of CCA-treated wood, including wood used in decks, play structures, picnic tables, landscaping lumber, fencing, patios, and walkways. As the CCA treatment is phased out, you'll have to use wood with alternative, non-arsenic treatments or naturally decay-resistant wood, such as redwood and cedar.

Luckily for owner–builders, drastic alterations in codes and materials are not common. But if your plans don't account for the latest changes, it's a safe bet that the local inspector will let you know about them.

2 BEFORE YOU BUILD

You need to consider all the regulations before you start construction, and do a lot of other planning as well. One crucial subject to investigate is the condition of the building site, including climate and soil. For example, you may need to conduct a soil test to find out if the house will need more than a standard foundation for support. If you're installing a septic system, you'll also need a percolation (perc) test to determine what kind of system you'll need.

It's crucial to know the average frost depth in your area—a figure that is available at the local building department. If the temperature drops anywhere near 32 degrees F. in your area, you'll need to place the footing (the support pad for the foundation on most houses) below the frost line. If you don't dig deeply enough, the foundation can crack from heaving when water in the ground freezes. Even the great weight of a concrete foundation can't withstand the force of heaving. With the footing below the depth of frost, the ground may move up and down but the footing and foundation will stay where you put them. This is such an important factor in construction that building departments normally call for a footing inspection to check the excavation depth.

Soil conditions and climate are only two of many factors that you need to consider. They vary widely across the country, and sometime even on sites only a few miles apart. That means a roof frame that is adequate in one area may prove inadequate where it must contend with heavy snow loads. Strong winds and freezing temperatures call for special considerations that do not apply where breezes are balmy and temperatures moderate.

To discover how your own ideas and needs might be met in a neighborhood, explore the area by car and on foot. You may find many different house styles, but a few common features that make sense. For example, in southern climates where there is a lot of sun and rain, many houses have a low-slope hip roof that allows for an overhang on all sides of the building. In northern climates, you'll find more steeply sloped cape roofs that more easily shed snow.

Talk to residents and pay a preliminary call on the building inspector. Chances are there will be literature available to spell out some of the design basics, such as how close to property lines you can build, how high the house can be, how high perimeter fences can be, facts about utilities, and so on. There will be more of such information available in incorporated areas than in outlying districts. But here too, it makes sense to discover what others have done in the same area. Learning from the experience of others is one way to minimize, if not eliminate, bad moves. Very few projects are accomplished without some redesigning done in retrospect. There is much camaraderie among owner–builders, whether the houses are close or separated by several acres. The sharing of skills, experience, and knowledge does much to speed the task and make it more enjoyable.

THE DREAM AND THE FACTS

You may have a castle in mind, but you need to keep a realistic view of cost and labor. Your physical contribution will decrease out-of-pocket costs, but material expenses, regardless of design, will be in direct ratio to the square footage of the plan. It simply requires more material to build a 6-cubic-foot box than a 3-cubic-foot box, assuming, of course, a similarity in structural design and materials.

The first home (which we assume to be a cave) was the absolute no-frills residence. There was no thought of a site that would be occupied by generations of the same family. The selection was for immediate needs, and aesthetics had nothing to do with the decision. This has been the case through much of man's history, and the familiar emphasis on comfort, scale, and appearance really doesn't go back so far. But the emphasis can change with ups and down in the economy. When times are tough, owner–builders concentrate on practical considerations. When times are good, houses have more frills and what real estate agents like to call amenities.

But it's always a good idea to plan a house for maximum utilization and minimum maintenance. Ideally, it would be nice to build a structure that could be made bigger or smaller to meet current needs. Some modular concept might still emerge whereby we might be able to build for today and later have a truck deliver a ready-to-attach add-on and then take it away after it serves its purpose. Mobile homes used to come close to such modular construction. They have given way to manufactured homes, and today almost one-third of new homes are built in a factory and shipped to the site partially assembled. But these homes generally are not for the owner–builder because almost all the building has been done.

But you can design a house to accommodate current needs, and build in the extra capacity you'll need to add on at a later date. For example, you can beef up the foundation to hold a future second story. The idea calls for a lot of planning in the initial construction if the end result is to appear unified and is to be achieved with minimum disruption. If you're considering future additions, pay special attention to the minimum setback and side yard dimensions required by local codes.

Another approach is to design for the future but finish for the present. For example, a couple might frame and close in a three-bedroom house but finish only those rooms that serve immediate needs. However, financing might be awkward because lenders may hesitate to provide money for a house that may not be finished for several years.

ROOF LINES AND SUCH

Consider the design of the house in relation to the ease or complexity of construction. If the house walls make a turn—with an L- or U-shape—rather than running in straight lines, you introduce construction complications. The gable roof, which is simply two slopes meeting at a high point called the ridge, is economical and comparatively easy to build until you choose to turn a corner. The junction forms a valley and the affected rafters require compound angles that take more time to cut accurately than the simple angles needed on the common rafters.

The low-slope shed roof is another option for the amateur who wishes to minimize construction intricacies. This is the way my family chose to go when we erected an addition for use as a studio (**2–1**). Building it against an existing garage saved material because we had one wall up to begin with. The idea should be considered by anyone wishing to build small now and add later. Shed and gable roofs like this one are often combined and are visually and architecturally acceptable.

2–1

Another option is to use roof trusses. About 90 percent of all new houses have them because they are less expensive and easier to install than individual rafters, even when the rest of the house is stick-built. Of course, on all but the smallest buildings you would need to hire a contractor with a crane to set them.

The point is, while you have almost limitless choices of styles and materials, you need to make practical decisions after considering a lot of options. The dream house may become a compromise but it need not become a nightmare.

BUILDING UP, OUT, OR DOWN

Assuming similar square footages of living area, building up is generally less expensive than building out. For example, a two-level square house with a given amount of floor space requires half as much foundation and roof as it would if built on a single level. Consider the single-level house in relation to three levels, or two levels plus a finishable attic. Of course, multilevel houses do break up the total square footage into separate blocks, which can reduce the feeling of spaciousness you might otherwise have. However, you can compensate by avoiding the tendency to make rooms mere closed-in boxes. Where possible, screen dividers can define areas and direct traffic without closing off space. A popular example is the area that serves as living room and dining room and, sometimes, kitchen. You can create an open, spacious feeling even though sections are defined by installing half walls, rails, planter boxes, and counters.

"Stacking" the living space also creates advantages with the mechanical systems, particularly plumbing and heating. It shortens the pipe and duct runs from furnaces, water heaters and air conditioners, which saves on the installation and on future utility costs. On a long horizontal run to a remote bath, for example, a lot of heat in water pipes or air ducts will be lost through the pipe and duct walls before it arrives.

"Building down" means a basement. In most cases, the only justification for a basement is its value as a living area, which includes spaces such as a workshop or a recreation room. If the basement is to become, as many do, a deposit area for all the stuff that won't fit upstairs, forget it. Doing without a basement will make housebuilding easier and a lot less expensive because you can eliminate a lot of costly excavation work.

THE ROOM AND THE SPACE

Somewhere near the beginning of the project must come the decision on how much space will be roofed over. There are two ways to go. One is to decide on the number and types of rooms you want and the size of each. The other is to arrive at a dollar-per-square-foot figure and decide how much you can or wish to spend. The second system seems wiser generally, even if you choose to work with an architect. One of the first questions he is likely to ask is how much you can afford. But bear in mind that per-foot costs can vary a lot. If most of the livable space is open, the costs will be low. That holds for other basic areas such as garages, too. Smaller, more complex spaces can drive up the costs, particularly extra baths that require a lot of mechanical work, fixtures, and tile.

Many houses are like the closets, cabinets, and drawers they contain: they waste space and materials. A walk-in closet is luxurious, but it does require traffic as well as storage space. A utility room may be nice to have, but if you think of it as so many dollars per foot to build and maintain, you may consider including a utility area in the garage instead. Also, there are modern laundry units that stack, and hot-water heaters that may be located under a counter. It's wise to use space that's already under the roof instead of adding new space.

A good way to economize on materials and labor is to view space in terms of actual requirements, and base your plans on real needs, not fantasies. Part of the fun of building for yourself is the challenge of design. Determine in detail what a room will be used for before deciding its shape and size. Quite often you can scale down in one area so you can expand in another. Your lifestyle must be considered, of course. Do you really need a family room *and* a living room? In most such situations that I know of, the living room has regressed to the status of an old-fashioned parlor that's used only for company.

You should view fad designs with a degree of skepticism. The oversize kitchen may prove a burden to those who use and clean it, and the conversation pit may only chop up floor space and require a lot of extra framing. If you realize that an elaborate but empty foyer will cost $100 per square foot, you may hesitate to be generous in that area.

LOWERING MAINTENANCE AND UTILITY COSTS

House designs today must give maximum consideration to heating and cooling requirements, and energy conservation in general. Some people do it to save energy and resources on a global scale; others to lower the ongoing monthly costs of running the house. Whatever the reason, it's important to install fuel-efficient systems that are highly rated. We'll get into it in more detail later on, but consider some of the recommendations for new houses from the National Association of Homebuilders. To save some of the nearly 50 percent of a typical home's utility bill that goes toward heating and cooling today, the NAHB says you should look for furnaces with an Annual Fuel Utilization Efficiency (AFUE) rating of from 80 percent for conventional furnaces to 94 percent for condensing furnaces. Look for a central air-conditioning unit with a Seasonal Energy Efficiency Ratio (SEER) rating of at least 12.

For heat pumps, which handle both heating and cooling, the NAHB suggests a unit with a Heating Season Performance Factor (HSPF) greater than 7 and SEER rating of at least 12.

(Units with SEER ratings up to 18 are available).These are 2002 guidelines that reflect ongoing improvements in fuel efficiency, but it's likely that efficiencies will increase even more in the future.

Regardless of the type of heating system you plan, the more you invest in insulation, the lower your long-range costs will be and the less demand you will be making on diminishing resources. Actually, efficient insulation is not just so many batts of fibrous material but a whole category of materials and design factors that includes weatherproofing, ventilation, the type of window glass, house orientation, and so on. To meet modern energy codes and keep utility costs low, you can build with 2 × 6s instead of 2 × 4s, or add foam board to the frame to increase overall R-values.

Glass is a major source of heat loss in any home, especially glass on a north wall. You do need windows, but there must be a compromise between floor-to-ceiling view windows on all sides of a house and the porthole concept. The placement of windows should be influenced by how the house is located on a site—which means, of course, that the house orientation should be determined in the first place with north, south, east, and west exposures in mind. The rules for glass, generally, are as follows:

- Keep window areas on the north wall to a minimum. The south wall can have more glass because you can benefit from the sun's heat in the winter. For protection from too much sun in the summer, you can work with greenery, window coverings, and overhangs. This applies to some degree to east and west walls also.
- Buying and installing double-pane windows that have high-performance glass sandwiching a gas-filled space (generally called low-e windows) cuts drafts and saves energy. This kind of investment often allows you to downsize heating and cooling equipment, as the energy-efficient windows help reduce heat loss in the winter and heat gain in summer.
- Try not to distinguish too strictly between view, light, and ventilation windows. The functions can often be combined to result in respectable savings in construction and materials.

THE HOUSE PLANS

There is a difference between knowing what you want and communicating that thought to the building inspector, the contractor, or the helper. Most people get around this by employing an architect, either for the entire job or for part of it. Having a stranger decide what your house should be like has negative aspects. Having someone work from your basic plans, doing the detailing and specifying structurally suitable sizes of materials, is something else. If you visit an architect cold, without having done considerable homework, the chances are that his point of view will predominate. To avoid this, it's wise to arrive prepared with floor plan sketches.

If you decide to work with an architect, it's best to visit several to discover which one will be most sympathetic with your scheme. Ideally, from the build-it-yourselfer's point of view, it should be possible to sketch your structural needs, wants, and shapes, and pay the professional to do the final plans so they conform to the building codes of the area. The pro, of course, will spot flaws and you can correct them before being told to do so by the building inspector. Remember that for large projects most building departments will require the stamp of a licensed architect or engineer on your plans.

What should interest the amateur is the variety of ready-to-use building plans that are often available for under $100. You can buy books that show hundred of plans featuring one basic design or another. You may think this is the same as giving someone else control over the design, but, on the other hand, it's possible you may find something that suits you to a *T*, or which can be modified. In any case, the more you consider professional designs, the more sophisticated your own design will become. This chapter shows a few examples, but the best bet is to send away for catalogs that show all that is available. Most such literature will tell briefly what the house is and show an artist's rendition plus a floor plan. Some organizations will even supply, for a small fee, itemized lists of materials, plumbing and wiring diagrams, and so on. Plans also are available from government agencies, such as the Department of Housing and Urban Development (HUD).

The rambling one-story house in **2–2** affords abundant space and considerable privacy. Note that entry to the garage is from the rear so the line of the house is uninterrupted by garage doors.

Available designs include multilevel homes like the one in **2–3**, which is designed to make the most of a steep, difficult site. Entry to the house is from the third, or street, level.

Traditional designs like the Cape Cod in **2–4** may be purchased also. The upper floor of this house can easily be viewed as a finish-later project.

Many designs for vacation or second homes are available. Some, like the one in **2–5**, start as a small basic unit to which you can add rooms at will until you end up with the completed plan. This plan, or something like it, makes a lot of sense for the person whose dream is to move permanently, someday, into the house he now escapes to on weekends and vacations. It should also appeal to a couple who want or can afford only the minimum now but have expansion in mind for the future.

No one should react negatively to the thought of working with ready-drawn plans. For one thing, checking catalogs doesn't commit you. For another, you can use one you like as the basis for doing your own thing. It's a lot cheaper to modify an existing plan than it is to have an architect draw one from scratch—and you will be more welcome in an inspector's office if what is under your arm resembles professional blueprints instead of doodles on a scratch pad.

2–2 RAMBLING ONE-STORY, PLAN 3301
(Hudson Home Guides)

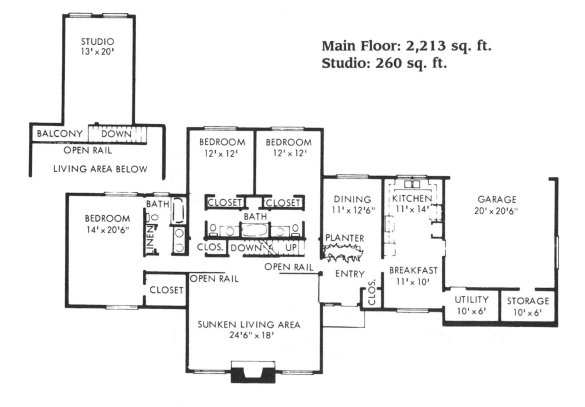

Main Floor: 2,213 sq. ft.
Studio: 260 sq. ft.

**2-3 TRI-LEVEL, PLAN 5004
(Hudson Home Guides)**

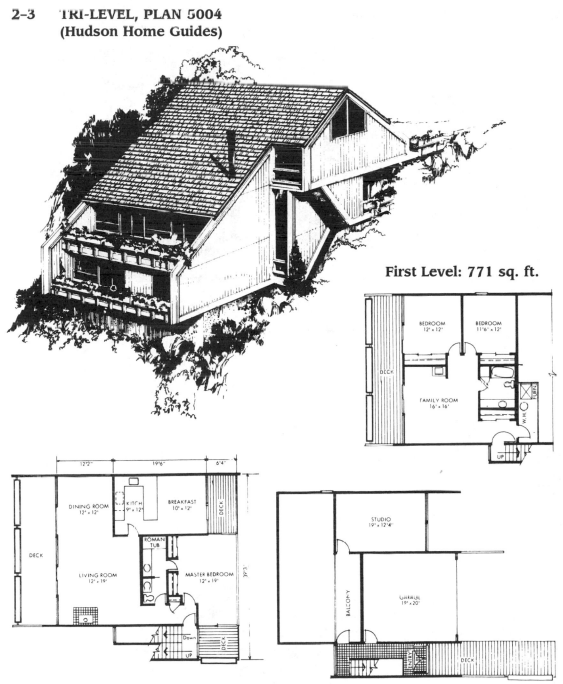

First Level: 771 sq. ft.

Second Level: 1,232 sq. ft.

Third Level: 565 sq. ft.

2–4 CAPE COD, PLAN 2238
(Hudson Home Guides)

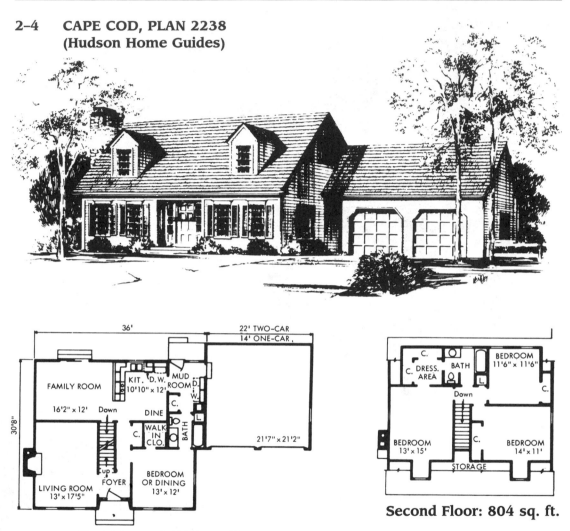

First Floor: 1,068 sq. ft.

Second Floor: 804 sq. ft.

SPECIAL IDEAS

Before deciding on your house design and how you will build it, check out some of the new, and not so new, ideas that are out there. There are many alternatives to the standard stick-built approach. For example, you could use prefabricated frames, roof trusses, or 24-inch modular framing with 2 × 6 studs. You can consider timber frames that combine old-fashioned joinery with energy-efficient stress-skin panels, or pole buildings, in which there

2–5   BASIC UNIT PLUS OPTIONAL ADDITIONS
(Western Wood Products)

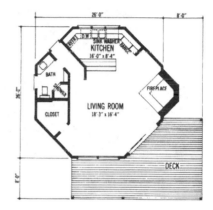

Basic Starter Unit: 556 sq. ft.

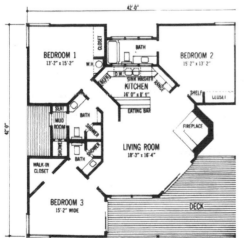

Completed Plan: 1,284 sq. ft.

is no conventional foundation and the structure is supported by pressure-treated poles sunk into the earth. And there are many kit houses, including post-and-beam frames, log homes, and other designs.

You may want to use a complete system, or a specialized component system such as the permanent wood foundation, which utilizes pressure-treated plywood and lumber instead of masonry for the foundation. This system has caught on in northern climates because it can be assembled in cold weather, which would otherwise interfere with pouring concrete.

There are special building systems and materials for sites where the house will be exposed to high winds, or fire, or even earthquakes. Many use steel studs and a variety of special connectors to reinforce the framing. And there are systems such as rammed-earth construction (compacted dirt and cement form the walls), cordwood masonry (walls are a combination of seasoned logs and mortar), and even houses built largely out of recycled tires or bales of hay. But anything out of the ordinary could cause you problems with local inspectors, particularly a system that uses unusual materials in unusual ways. If you're interested in a nontraditional system, be sure to check with the local building department ahead of time.

DO A DOLLHOUSE FIRST

A good way to see what the end result will be is to build a model. You can use stiff cardboard or thin foam board. Get yourself some tape, a sharp knife, a ruler, a pencil, and mock up your ideas. You can experiment with different floor plans, house shapes, and even sizes, and all you waste is cardboard.

Adopt a scale—say, ¼ inch equals 1 foot, which is the standard scale used on professional blueprints. If, for example, you are thinking of a 20 × 80-foot house, then your cardboard floor would be 5 × 20 inches. Play with the floor plan before you set up walls. If you like, you can carry this to the point of indicating furniture placement. Make items you can move around by measuring your own furniture and cutting pieces of cardboard accordingly. Color the furniture with crayon so it will stand out against the cardboard floor. It may pay to place the furniture before you consider partitions.

Make the roof of the model removable. Also check out the several house-planning software packages available for home computers. Many of them are easy to learn, and allow you to create many variations. Some of the more sophisticated programs even allow you to take a virtual tour through the building.

But building a true scale model in three dimensions is instructive. You can use the model to decide about orientation on the site. Draw the shape of the land on a sheet of paper, and indicate existing trees, slopes, and north, south, east, and west. Here, too, you can sketch in driveways, future gardens, utility areas, and so on. By working with dried moss, twigs, small branches, and the like, you can get a pretty good idea of what the final picture will be.

WORKING SAFELY

The easy way out on this crucial subject is to print a long list of do's and don'ts—the kind you find (and most people disregard) in product instruction manuals. In fact, many instruction booklets have a quick-start page because the manufacturers know you're not going to read the long list of 50 things not to do, particularly when most of them are things you know already, would never do, and don't need to be reminded about. And telling people they should use a tool safely, or work on a roof safely isn't much help. It may let the manufacturer off the hook, but safety is relative. Instead of burdening you with a list like that, we'll get to specific safety advice as the subject arises, for instance, some basic rules about using circular saws when it's time to start cutting lumber.

Overall, the most important safety rule is to use your common sense. If you don't have much experience with a tool or a specific trade, take the time to investigate the ins and outs, the tools, and the expertise you need. But it's worth mentioning a few items up front. For one thing, proper work clothes are important. Have a special uniform that fits you snugly and includes heavy, high, steel-toed shoes and a hardhat. There are areas of housebuilding where it makes plain sense to have someone help you lift things. Be sure any helper knows what's being done and how you plan to accomplish it.

Watch yourself when you get to upper areas where you may need to walk across open joists. Take the time to set down some scaffold planks as a temporary platform. Be aware that you can slide off a roof, trip over a board, or walk into a beam. Stack materials neatly and have a special place where you can deposit cutoffs.

Don't be careless when you find it necessary to construct a scaffold. It is a temporary thing, but your safety demands a structure that will not collapse. The design in **2–6** is typical. But don't make the amateur mistake of using dimensional lumber, such as 2 × 6s, instead of certified scaffold planks. Standard framing lumber isn't strong enough when laid on the flat.

You can, if you wish, rent scaffolds that are an assortment of pipes you assemble on the site, or a set of pump jacks. These attach to the building and allow you to raise and lower a scaffold to handle siding work. You can also use ladders fitted with ladder jacks and scaffold planks.

Sawhorses are important tools and may be used as bases for platforms and as benches

2–6

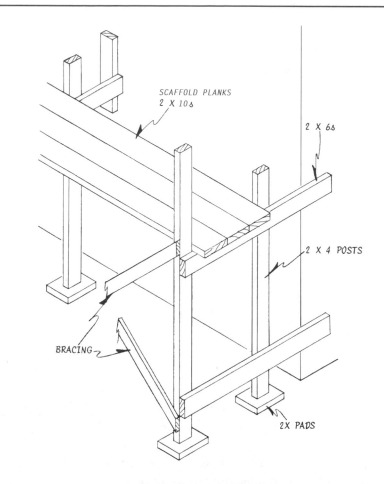

SCAFFOLD PLANKS
2 X 10s

2 X 6s

2 X 4 POSTS

BRACING

2X PADS

2–7

for cutting wood. Ready made brackets are good to consider since they can be used with various size legs to suit particular applications. The same brackets can be used to make a permanent sawhorse like that in **2–7**. Adding a shelf increases rigidity and gives you a place to put tools or boxes of nails.

Safety is the individual's responsibility. No set of rules will guarantee it. Being aware, always, that you can get hurt is probably the best precaution. Preview each phase of the job before you tackle it. Knowing what is ahead will prepare you for doing the job correctly and safely.

2–8 Commercial scaffolding such as this can help contribute to a safe working environment. (Photo courtesy of Bil Jax, Inc.)

3

THE HOUSE AND THE SITE

One of the surest ways to waste money, materials, and labor in house construction is to regard the site too casually, or to be so impressed with one feature that you become blind to practical considerations. Stories of people who became enamored of a storybook setting and were subsequently disenchanted by such prosaic things as the cost of putting in a road are not so rare. The moral is: hidden costs can upset your schedule and an otherwise sound financial program.

The question is not so much what can be done, but what you want to do and are prepared to pay for. Land that pleases you and is suitable for building without hidden costs is ideal. A land site should be approached with caution, if not suspicion; if possible, you should talk to a local builder and nearby residents.

Sometime during the thinking or building process, questions about access, water, power, zoning, and so on will have to be answered. The best time is before you buy. Seek out and calculate all costs carefully. Building on land with serious natural defects may be expensive enough to cause you to explore elsewhere.

SOME TYPICAL SITES

Five basic types of sites are shown in **3–1**. The site that is the least expensive to build on is usually flat topographically, and often flat aesthetically as well. A flat site needs little grading and excavation and does not require additional construction such as retaining walls or terraces. On the other hand, a flat site calls for careful investigation of drainage conditions, especially if it has hilly surroundings or is lower than adjacent properties.

A critical rule to remember is that there are two main threats to a house: fire, which can destroy a house quickly, and water (the much more common culprit), which eats away at a house over the years.

3-1

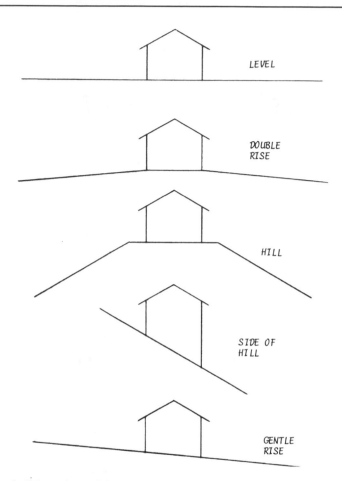

The best site of all is a rise. This provides an adequate view, natural air circulation, and good drainage that leads away from the building. Too much slope, though, and you might encounter problems with excavation, and situations requiring fill and retaining walls. Some hillsides can be very challenging from a design point of view. And when built on with minimum disturbance of natural grade, they often become prisons for the residents, since areas around the house are not level enough to walk on. Compensations take the form of expensive grading, which often destroys the naturalness of the site, or a system of decks for outdoor living.

It's okay to choose land that requires imagination to make it suitable as a homesite, but you have to think ahead. Be aware that extensive excavation, cutting access roads, and possibly importing fill are not easy chores for the average owner–builder. On the other hand, there is pole construction, a building technique that is suited to sloped sites and can be installed with minimum disturbance of natural surroundings.

Sites that are high above an existing street require steep driveways and front walks or steps. There are safety hazards here as well as additional construction expenses. Even in mild climates, rain can make such a driveway slippery. In snow country, the problem can be more extreme. Solutions take the form of lower-level garages and parking areas or switchback driveways, features that can add interest but inconvenience as well.

Sites that are below an existing street have problems too. There are still the driveway and entry-walk considerations, except now the pitch is down instead of up. Below-grade sites are also potential reservoirs, especially if existing gutters are not able to handle heavy rains.

TOPOGRAPHY

You won't have much enthusiasm for the project unless you can feel that the site is an asset—a piece of land with character and some natural advantages. The ideal would not be difficult to achieve if there were no concern for finances, reasonable proximity to schools, work, stores, and so on. Compromises should be accepted with grace and undiminished zeal, or else the project won't be worth doing.

My own present building site is a far cry from the view-lot we sought in the foothills of the Santa Cruz Mountains. We could get to such a lot, but only on foot. So we lowered our sights, literally, and settled for a three-acre chunk of property, as shown in **3-2**, that was almost a castoff because a county road had removed it from a large apricot orchard. The slope was more than we would have accepted on paper, and a quick look gave the impression that it was a natural drainage basin for surrounding terrain.

Upon closer examination, with open minds, we determined that we could correct obvious defects in a fairly straightforward manner. We wanted the house at the property's widest point, which also happened to be the area with the sharpest slope. But since a circular driveway was part of our plan, we figured that required grading could do two things—create the driveway and provide fill for a level area behind and along the sides of the house. Grading was planned carefully so there would be good drainage, a cut in the bank that would not require a retaining wall, and undisturbed ground for the house foundation, as shown in **3-3**.

Ultimately, the layout gave us adequate drainage away from all areas and enough soil from the grading to fill the gully and so create the entry driveway.

The plan work fine. During heavy rains we did have a small stream flowing at the base of the cut in the bank, but even though it was not a serious problem, we eliminated it by digging a trench and filling it with large gravel and a line of drain tiles.

The foundation area was still a slope, so we had to decide between full concrete

3–2

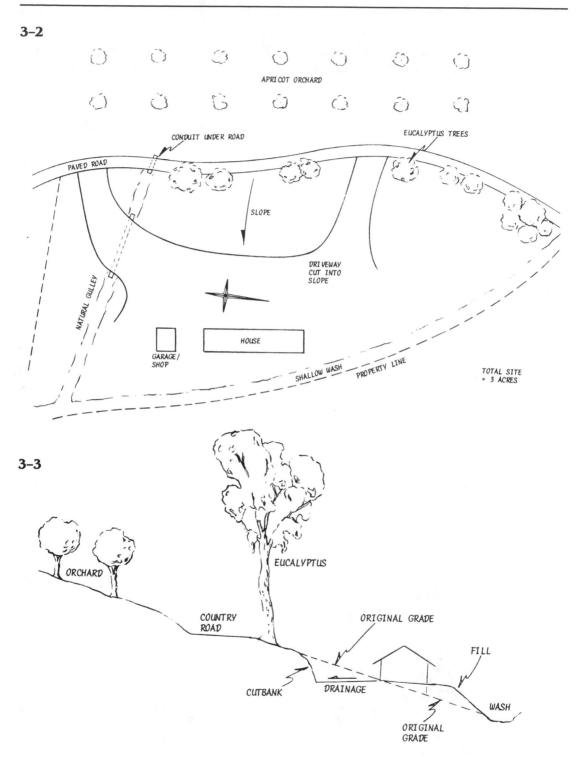

3–3

perimeter walls or a combination of concrete and wood. We made the latter choice, shown in **3-4**, mostly because I am more a woodworker than a mason, but either system would work. A split-level design of one kind or another would have been fine on our lot, of course, but that is not what we wanted.

3-4

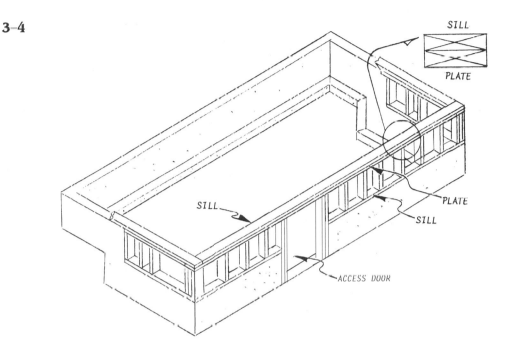

EXCAVATION ECONOMICS AND AESTHETICS

Make a close study of the characteristics of the site. Drainage, utility entrances, and grading all should be designed to preserve natural contours and natural growth as much as possible. Undergrowth and trees in the way of the house must be removed, but careless filling around, and injury to, well-located trees destroys valuable assets.

Grading is always simplified, and least expensive, when necessary cuts provide required fill. When civil engineers lay out the path of highways over changing terrain, they strive to equalize cut and fill. Ideally, they plan to excavate a hill to produce the amount of fill needed to fill in a valley. Expenses mount when excavated material must be hauled away from the site and when fill must be purchased and trucked in.

House sites do differ, yet there is enough similarity, generally, so a few examples can point up good excavation procedures. The two-level house in **3–5** is designed so the ground floor is at new-grade level. Material from the excavation is used to level front areas and as a fill at the rear for drainage.

On level ground you can use excavated material to raise the general grade, as shown in **3–6**. This actually reduces the amount of excavating you must do and provides drainage you might not have if you accepted the original grade.

A good example of minimum excavation is provided by the three-level design in **3–7**.

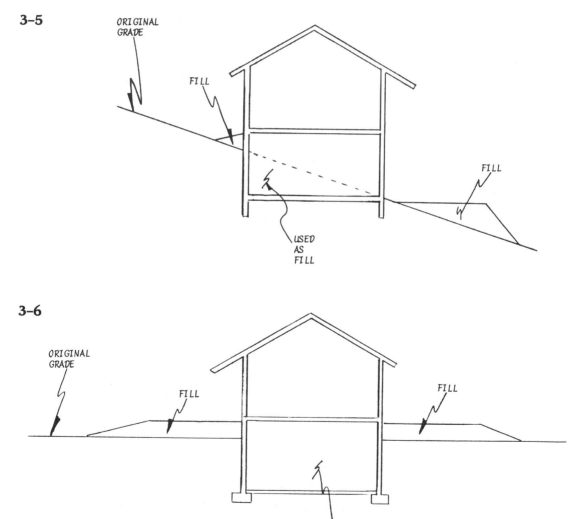

3–5

ORIGINAL GRADE

FILL

FILL

USED AS FILL

3–6

ORIGINAL GRADE

FILL

FILL

EXCAVATION PROVIDES FILL

3-7

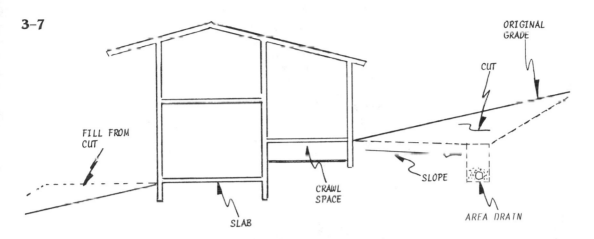

Note how the cut in the original grade is made to provide a drainage slope away from the house and how the removed material is used as a fill at the front. Another interesting feature is the use of both slab floor and crawl space.

In all situations where you have to excavate, scrape off, and save the topsoil, push it into a mound so you can spread it around the property after the building chores are done.

AREA DRAINS AND DRY WELLS

On a sloping location where your ideal site for the house happens to be in the line of a natural runoff, you'll need to make some provision for dealing with the water. We created what amounts to a small stream at the back of our house. You may need to install dry wells, which increase the water-holding capacity of a yard, or, better yet, an area drain.

A dry well might be 5 or 6 feet deep, 3 or 4 feet round, and filled with rocks or gravel. Because it is a lot less dense than solid dirt, it has a lot more water-holding capacity. That means it can serve as the destination for downspout drains, absorbing the flow like a reservoir, and gradually filtering it into the surrounding area. A dry well by itself also can solve puddling problems, say, in a low area of the yard, because it builds in more drainage capacity. To conceal the big hole filled with stones (or a concrete well), cover the top with a double layer of filter fabric (a tough mesh that's sold in many garden supply outlets); then cover the fabric with sod. The filter fabric lets water drain through, but keeps out a lot of the silt that can clog up the well.

To intercept a flow of groundwater and take the pressure off your foundation waterproofing, the best solution on a sloped site is to build an area drain, as shown in **3-8** on the high side of the house. It's basically the trench version of a dry well, say 3 feet deep

3-8

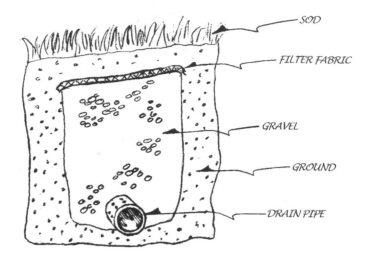

SOD

FILTER FABRIC

GRAVEL

GROUND

DRAIN PIPE

and a foot or two across, that collects water and diverts it to a release point where it can't get to the foundation. The trench can be lined with black plastic to keep out clogging dirt, covered with several inches of gravel, and then a length of perforated drainpipe to collect the water. You fill the trench nearly to the top with more gravel, and then add filter fabric under a concealing layer of sod.

SUMMARY OF DRAINAGE CONSIDERATIONS

A site that slopes up from an existing street usually provides good drainage toward runoff facilities. A site that slopes away from the street may have to be drained toward a rear yard or by a special underground pipe system to a storm sewer. A basement may not be advisable.

Check the topography of surrounding areas and study the directions of natural surface drainage. It's also wise to do some research on the possibility of subsurface drainage. City or county records might help here, but the surest way is to bore a few test holes so you can study the soil texture and look for accumulations of water. Negative results do not necessarily rule out the building site but they may point up the importance of storm-sewer locations, or the need for special construction techniques.

Always check established grades, such as streets, that you can't alter. These, plus any storm sewers that have been or will be installed, should be starting points when you investigate the drainage situation of your own site.

Level sites generally call for raising the existing grade, at the perimeter of the house at least, so surface water can be directed to a runoff point. The soil removed for a basement can be used for that purpose. Remember that drainage is, or should be, a community project. Your neighbors won't appreciate being inundated any more than you will.

HOUSE TYPE AND PLACEMENT

There are many variables and personal preferences that play a part in determining the type of house and its placement: available finances, codes, and so much more that it's impossible to provide all the answers. It is true, though, that no factor contributes as much to success as the right house for the lot. This can result from either of two approaches: Knowing exactly the kind of house you want and then searching for the ideal site; or falling in love with a site and designing the house for it.

Compromises should not reduce incentive. Often a design modification leads to a practical and satisfactory solution. Avoiding pitfalls may be more important than an artist's rendition of the ideal and picturesque homestead.

The small house will look even smaller if you set it like a box on a mound surrounded by steep embankments, as shown in **3–9**. But you don't have to increase square footage to make the house look larger if you design the garage as an extension. Construction costs will actually decrease because the driveway considerations will be similar and there will be no need for expensive retaining walls.

Try to plan for specific separations of outdoor areas while still making maximum use of the land. The more you reduce the length of a driveway, the less the project will cost. A garage or carport that utilizes an existing wall costs less to build. A detached garage, especially if it is far from the house, requires a long driveway, a walkway from garage to house, and extra costs for electrical work.

You might want to spread things out if the lot is large and especially if the site is elevated. A separate garage level can be made to avoid a steep driveway and ramplike entry steps to the house. But to avoid long flights of entry steps and a steep driveway cutting across contours that may require retaining walls, plan for something along the lines shown in **3–10**. Here you have an entry to the house from the driveway and close to the garage. You break up total elevation into two levels with minimum pitch for each. Also, when the house entry walk and driveway are combined, you leave an undisturbed area in front of the house.

In all situations, it's imperative to have an overall plan so you can decide on orientation of house and site to make maximum use of the most desirable features of each. **3–11** shows such a plan for a small lot.

3-9

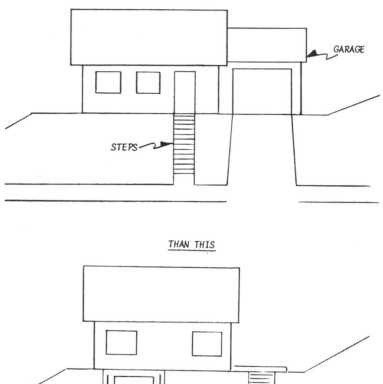

BETTER THIS

GARAGE

STEPS

THAN THIS

WALLS — — WALLS — STEPS

GARAGE

NATURE WILL COOPERATE, IF YOU LET IT

Study the features of the land before you draw the site plan. Any building will affect the environment and the landscape. The idea is to respect what nature has already established. Accept the terrain as a partner, and plan knowing you are making a lasting impact that should provide maximum comfort and economy for you with minimum harm to the area. If you can combine your needs with a good degree of reverence for nature, you have it made, and will profit. The effort you invest in planning the building and locating it will pay dividends in the form of enjoyable living and reduced energy demands.

3-10

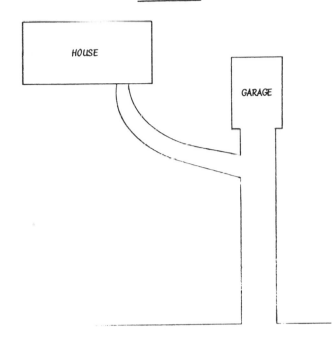

THIS IS GOOD

3-11 THE OVERALL PLAN AND WHAT TO CONSIDER

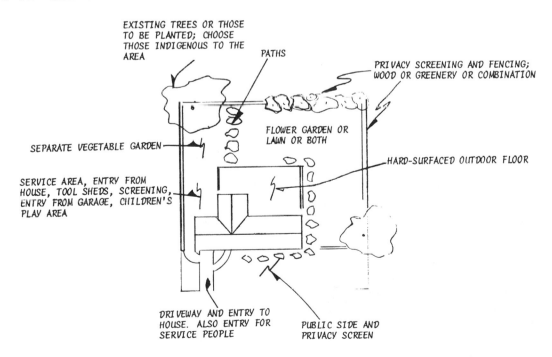

Privacy, views, wind directions, traffic convenience, and sun travel in winter and summer are the primary considerations:

1. Know how the sun travels over the building site (**3–12**). Bear in mind that hills, tall trees, and adjacent structures can affect sun and shade. This can be an important heating and cooling factor, especially if you add solar collectors at some time.
2. What about the view you want to look at and scenes you may wish to screen out?
3. Are there storms and cold prevailing winds in the winter? Day or night breezes in the summer?

A true study of orientation is a detailed science, one that would require a daily inspection of conditions of each site over a year's period. Yet there are basic considerations, as shown

3–12 SUMMER SUN

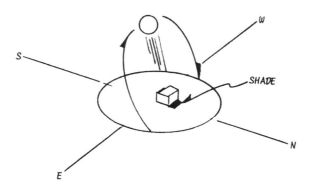

WINTER SUN

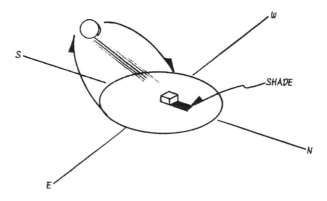

in **3–13**, and general rules to apply even though they are most applicable in the belt between 35 and 45 degrees north latitude (**3–14**). This belt includes the majority of the country's most populated places. When the house site is below this belt, taking advantage of summer breezes and seeking protection from intense sun heat are major considerations. When building above the belt, designing for protection from cold winter winds and getting the most from the winter sun are prime objectives.

3–13   SOME BASICS OF HOUSE ORIENTATION

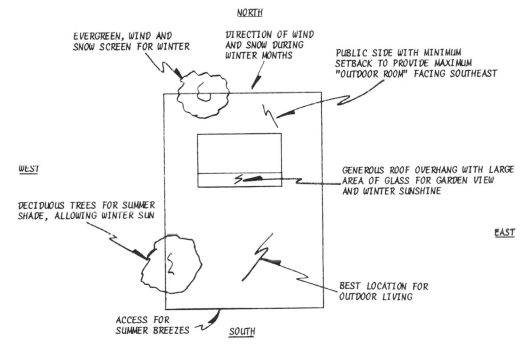

NORTH

EVERGREEN, WIND AND
SNOW SCREEN FOR WINTER

DIRECTION OF WIND
AND SNOW DURING
WINTER MONTHS

PUBLIC SIDE WITH MINIMUM
SETBACK TO PROVIDE MAXIMUM
"OUTDOOR ROOM" FACING SOUTHEAST

WEST

DECIDUOUS TREES FOR SUMMER
SHADE, ALLOWING WINTER SUN

GENEROUS ROOF OVERHANG WITH LARGE
AREA OF GLASS FOR GARDEN VIEW
AND WINTER SUNSHINE

EAST

BEST LOCATION FOR
OUTDOOR LIVING

ACCESS FOR
SUMMER BREEZES   SOUTH

3–14

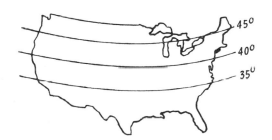

45°

40°

35°

WHAT TO CONSIDER

The summer sun is high overhead at midday and has an extended arc. In winter, there is a reduced arc and the midday sun is lower in the sky. The object is to protect from the overhead summer sun, but to capture as much of the winter sun as possible (**3–15**). Because of the sun factor, a southeast slope usually makes an ideal house site, but a south slope is also desirable. An east slope is better than a west slope. And a north slope should be avoided.

3–15

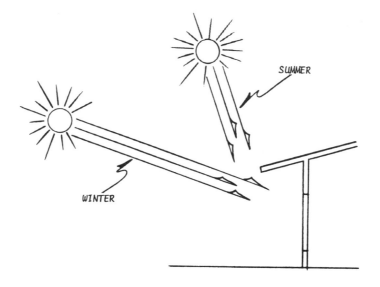

Roof overhangs make the most sense on the south side of a house. They may be used elsewhere for other purposes, but sun protection is achieved only when the exposure is generally south. West sides can be protected from the hot afternoon summer sun through the use of tall plantings or an attached garage.

A garage or tall evergreen trees, or both, can do much to screen the northwest direction and so provide protection against cold winter winds. Here you can also put topography to use; high ground to the north can serve as a screen too.

Open house designs are suitable in the south because they encourage circulation of summer breezes. Here, outdoor living can be enjoyed for a large part of the year, but overhead constructions should be incorporated to protect open and enclosed house areas from the summer sun.

You should design for a minimum of window area on the north wall. Large glass doors and windows are most suitable on the south side. Windows on the west side should get special protection against the hot summer sun.

Always remember that warm air will rise because it is lighter than cold air. Therefore, ventilation considerations generally should provide for cooler air to enter the house close to grade while warm air should be permitted to escape at a high point—at the ceiling or through the attic.

When you do the site plan, think of the lot as having three outside areas: one for your own outdoor living, one as a service area, and one as the public area. Defining these clearly and locating them in terms of convenience, livability, and privacy will contribute much to a satisfactory site development.

PRIVACY: ANOTHER GOAL

Privacy would not be difficult to achieve if you ignored all other factors and just put up solid walls and spent all your home time indoors. But today's lifestyles call for outdoor as well as indoor areas to relax, to eat, and to enjoy friends and recreation. Decks are a standard feature, and adding a deck is one of the most popular improvement projects. No house is so large that spreading living area to the outdoors won't be an asset, psychologically and in relation to house value. Often, providing for privacy also affords a good measure of protection from noise—noise from the outside or noise you make that might bother neighbors.

Success doesn't come by accident. It's achieved through the planning you do for the house and its surroundings. For effectiveness and attractiveness, you should have an overall plan that considers the shape of the house, its location on the site, subdivision of the yard, wood or masonry fences, greenery, and trellises. If, for example, you use a lot of glass in a wall because the rooms there will benefit from it, plan to shield the area so your privacy will be assured regardless of which side of the glass you are on. Don't forget there are such things as fast-growing vines and creeping plants you can grow on trellises. And there are fast-growing trees too. First check around to determine which plantings will do well in your area.

Your privacy goals can be combined with the private outlook, taking advantage of what is nice to look at and screening out what is bad. The view does not have to be a snow-covered mountain, a lake, or a river. It can be a low or high flower-bed wall, an attractive trellis, a garden waterfall, groups of trees or shrubs, and so on. Remember that your screening can also conceal eyesores on your own property such as areas designated for outdoor jobs, trash cans, or tool storage.

EXCAVATION BASICS

When you're thinking about the finished product, it's easy to forget about the dirt—great piles of soggy ground that have to be excavated before you start building.

Digging holes for a couple of deck piers is a job small enough to do by hand, even for a contractor. Anything bigger and most pros will bring in heavy equipment. But even a baby backhoe can chew up your yard. So before a driver accidentally bounces a bucket off a specimen tree, plan a route from the street to the site. Work with the contractor before any equipment arrives to mark the route with stakes. Make the effort to rope off untouchable areas (a clothesline hung with rags should do), and tie back tree branches that project into the path.

It's even more important to locate possible obstructions on an improved site. An experienced excavation contractor should take care of this for you, but it pays to double-check the location of underground utilities, particularly natural gas pipes—although in some areas all utilities are buried, including telephone, electric, and cable lines. Call your utility company before anyone starts digging. They generally will send out a representative to help you locate and mark underground lines. You also should locate and clearly mark the location of a water well, dry well, septic system, and underground piping.

It helps a lot to wait for a spell of dry weather when the ground is firm. If that isn't practical, consider taking the extra time and expense to protect the lawn by laying down a track of scaffold planks. They can distribute the tire load and prevent deep ruts. Another approach is to spread a track of crushed stone as a temporary driveway, and then scoop it up—most of it, at least—to use in a drainage trench against the new foundation.

On a small, fully landscaped site, every bit of dirt displaced by new construction may have to be carted away. That means more equipment (a dump truck), time, and mess running a bucket-loader back and forth to fill it, and, of course, more money. On larger sites, it's often possible to save at least some of this effort and expense by relocating the dirt on your own property. But even an excavation for a small foundation can produce a surprising amount of dirt—a pile as big as the new hole in the ground, of course, plus at least 25 percent more volume. That's because dirt in the ground is compacted, and freshly excavated dirt is aerated and broken into small clumps that take up more room.

If you don't have an obvious depression that would be more useful as level ground, consider raised flower beds, or step terraces that level a sloping yard. Some dirt can be recycled as backfill along the new foundation. But make sure that you use pure dirt instead of earth mixed up with debris from construction. Stray chunks of concrete blocks or bricks are okay, but not paper or wood—for two reasons. First, cellulose in any form is termite food that you shouldn't be spreading close to the house. Second, biodegradable material will gradually erode and cause excessive sinking in dirt around the building. That can create a water-catching trench and lead to leaks in the foundation.

FINAL CONSIDERATIONS

It is wise to know the capacity and the location of local facilities such as sewage and electric lines before you plan the house. In areas without public sewer and water systems, you still must consider electric and telephone lines, your own water supply, and your own sewage disposal. Building codes follow you most anywhere, and septic systems get a lot of attention. You may be required to have a septic tank of a certain size and a drain field of a certain length, and there may be restrictions on the location of the tank. Typically, local authorities require at least one perc test to determine the absorption rate of the soil. In some cases, you may have to alter the soil mix to provide adequate flow. Pay particular attention to this subject on a site near water (even a small pond), as codes are very strict about contaminating water supplies.

Local codes also may demand that utility lines passing through fill be specially supported and be made of special materials. This can increase expenses, and you may still have problems from fill settling. The length of underground lines can be controlled to a great extent by the house plan and its location on the site. It helps to use minimum setback from a street where community services run. Locating plumbing fixtures on that side will also reduce costs and labor. Blocks of plumbing can serve more than one facility—for example, two bathrooms; a kitchen and bathroom; a kitchen and utility room.

A single trench for both sewer and water lines can save money if local codes permit such an installation and if anti-contamination precautions are taken. The trench can be wider at the top area to supply a ledge for the water lines (**3–16**). Or you can cut into a minimum-width trench and provide a waterpipe seat as shown in **3–17**. The ledge height is variable for easiest connection to the supply source, as long as it is below the frost line.

Expensive fill and foundation walls may be required if drainage lines make it necessary to raise the house high above the natural grade. Changing the drainage situation or modifying the house to suit existing conditions may be a better solution.

Bear in mind that there is no such thing as a do-it-yourself connection to public water and sewer lines. In some jurisdictions, you may be able to handle the piping work in your house and even leading to the street. But the hookup plan must be approved (slope can be critical) and the connection generally must be made by a licensed plumber who is approved by the municipality to make these connections.

Overall, waste systems are tightly controlled by code because improper disposal can cause serious health problems. Here's just one example of the sweeping power of local

3-16   3-17

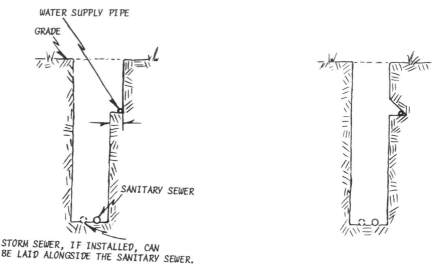

STORM SEWER, IF INSTALLED, CAN
BE LAID ALONGSIDE THE SANITARY SEWER.

inspectors in this field. If you have a well, and a water-quality test suggests that a neighbor's septic system could be contaminating the supply, inspectors can conduct a dye test in the neighbor's house. This consists of flushing a dye tablet down a toilet, and waiting to see if the garish yellow–green dye surfaces outside.

Through all this mechanical work and excavation, you'll want to save as many existing trees and large plants as possible. Trees are assets that will increase in value along with the house. Any time you must cut into the land for the house site or the driveway or a walk or whatever, scrape off the topsoil first and store it for use when construction work is complete.

Informal landscaping that makes use of indigenous greenery will be cheaper to do and easier to maintain than more formal schemes. Lawns do well on flat or rolling land, but they do require constant care and much water. When you add plants, be sure to research ultimate shapes and sizes and rate of growth. Groups of trees or shrubs usually have more visual appeal than overall coverage, although dense in-line arrangements are more effective as view and sound barriers. Check out local successful ground covers when you plant on embankments.

Obeying the rules that factor in house and location while keeping costs low and livability high will be easier on some sites, but a good balance is achievable just about anywhere. Each house and site will have problems. You may find it impossible to achieve absolutely everything you want—but as long as you study all the features and defects of the site in advance, and account for them as best you can in your plan, you can find the optimum solution.

4 LAYING OUT THE BUILDING SITE

We can assume that the lot has been professionally surveyed and that stakes marking property lines and corners have been correctly and legally established. A legal survey is part and parcel of acquiring a piece of land. There are true stories about sales with haphazard perimeters that resulted in construction that was later challenged and, in some cases, had to be moved. Removal may mean just a fence, or a greenhouse, or some new trees. But such problems can be avoided by having a professional survey. If there is a bank involved in your project, and there usually is, given today's land and building costs, they will insist on a survey even if you don't.

If you have the job done, it will not cost much more to have the surveyor establish the setback lines and place stakes to establish grade elevations. If you have already chosen house plans and decided house placement, he can set two stakes to show one side of the structure. From this point, you can just about work with a carpenter's level, a line level, a square, and a length of line to do other layout requirements. But it pays to know something about professional leveling instruments that you can rent, since they can be very helpful when laying out angles, establishing foundation heights, checking vertical corners, and so on, accurately and with minimum fuss.

There are many tools at your disposal. The traditional builder's transit will work, although many builders (and a lot of do-it-yourselfers) use more modern laser levels that project a beam of light against batter boards, story boards, and other markers. They can be valuable throughout your project—outside on siding, inside on trim, and even on odd jobs such as laying out tile. Instead of burying your layout lines with adhesive and working off your grid, lasers can project a beam on the surface of the adhesive that's easy to follow. Another old-fashioned but very worthwhile (and inexpensive) tool is the water level.

TRADITIONAL TRANSITS

Both the level and the level-transit are used to do surveying and land layouts, and to check ongoing construction work. Both tools are basically telescopes with built-in levels, read-out scales, and adjustment screws for leveling the instrument after it has been mounted on its tripod support. The telescope may be turned on its base so you can lay out or measure any angle on a horizontal plane. Because the line of sight through the scope is always a straight line, you can use the tool together with a leveling rod (**4–1**) to determine the difference in elevation between the point where the level is set up and the point on which the rod is placed. Leveling rods may also be rented, but many workers improvise by using one of the makeshift methods shown in **4–2**.

Hold a common level against one edge of the rod to be sure it is vertical. Needless to say, readings will be useless unless you take the time to set up the tripod correctly to begin with. Make sure the leg points seat firmly on or into the ground. Pick a site that won't be in the way as work progresses, where you can swivel to sight the four corners of the foundation. Work with the adjustable legs until the head of the tripod appears level. Check with a common level if you wish. Once the instrument is mounted, additional fine adjustments are made with the built-in screws.

Total or intermediate readings to find differences in elevations can be taken depending on where the rod is held. In **4–3**, the height of the scope, subtracted from the reading at A, tells the amount of change in grade at that point. A reading at B will tell the total change and can be used to determine the difference from point A.

It may be necessary to change the position of the scope when slopes are extreme, when terrain is erratic, or when long distances are involved (**4–4**). In such situations, be sure each scope position is prepared as carefully as the first one. This is the kind of site where a water level (see below) comes in handy.

To lay out angles or establish corners, attach a plumb bob to the screw or hook under the scope. Set the tripod so the plumb bob is positioned at the exact centerpoint of a stake that has been driven as a starting point. The centerpoint is usually a nail driven into the center of a 2 × 2 or 2 × 3 wooden stake.

With the instrument leveled and the plumb bob placed correctly, sight through the scope toward a rod at point B. Measure the correct distance with a tape, and by working with scope and rod, establish a stake and centerpoint (**4–5**). Then you can swing the scope 90 degrees, or whatever angle is needed, and take a second sighting to establish point C. Reposition the instrument at point C, and sight back to point A (**4–6**). Next, follow the same basic procedure to get point D. The job is complete if you are doing a rectangle or a square, but you may wish to position the scope at point D so you can sight to points C and B as a check.

4-1

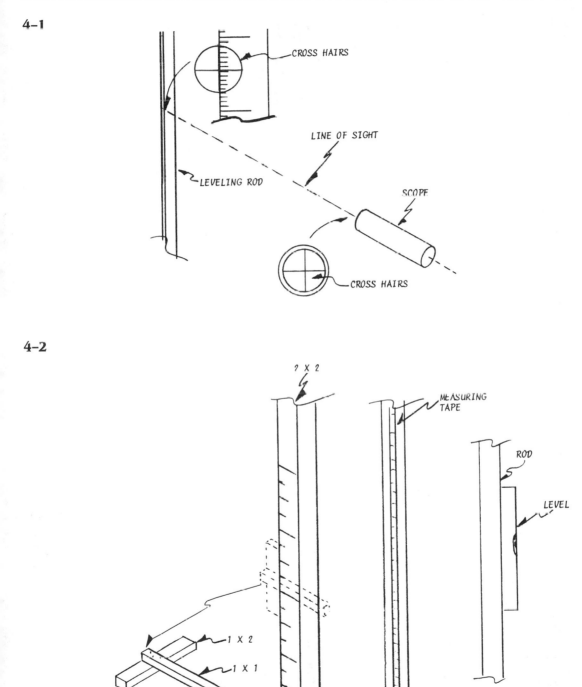

CROSS HAIRS

LINE OF SIGHT

LEVELING ROD

SCOPE

CROSS HAIRS

4-2

1 X 2

MEASURING TAPE

ROD

LEVEL

1 X 2

1 X 1

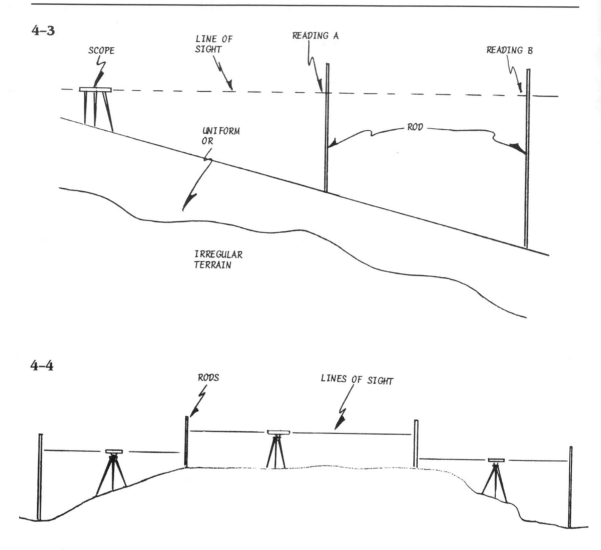

4–3

4–4

After corners are established, set up batter boards and lines to define excavation areas. From this point, it's usually fairly simple to work with a common level and a square to set stakes for small projections and any irregular shapes.

The procedure for laying out an L shape is much the same. As shown in **4–7**, the scope, set up at A, allows you to take sightings to establish points B and C. Then, sightings are taken from C to D, from D to E, and finally from E to F.

With corner stakes in, establishing grade stakes (for a footing) or the locating of better boards can be done more easily if the scope is set in a central location (**4–8**). This way distances will be fairly equal, and thus focusing changes will be minimized. Once the correct

4-5

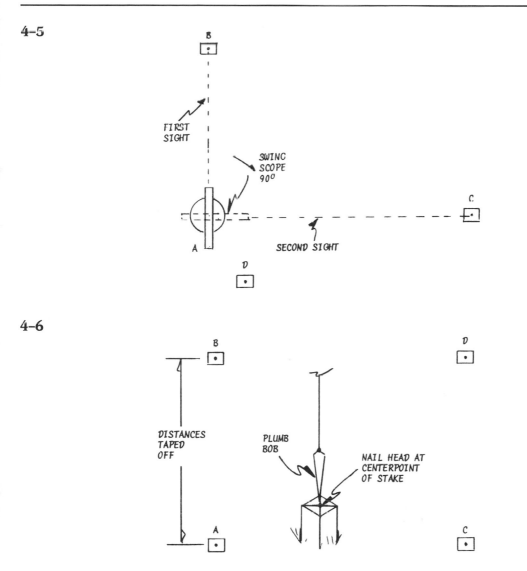

4-6

elevation is established at a control point, it can be transferred to all other points without your having to move the instrument. Grade stakes are usually driven to an approximate point and then adjusted to correct height while being checked with the level and rod.

The level and the transit-level work about the same way, but the transit-level has a vertical pivoting feature that can help you align a row of stakes (**4-9**) regardless of their height or to check the vertical accuracy of any construction (**4-10**).

When used for such purposes, the instrument should be leveled in the usual manner

4-7

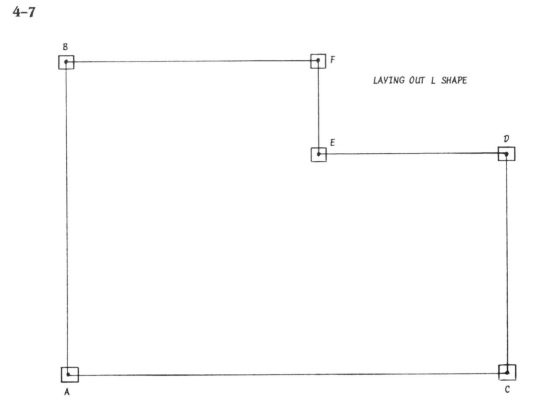

LAYING OUT L SHAPE

and then unlocked from its horizontal position. Pivot the scope both vertically and horizontally and establish a reference point along the vertical plane (if you are checking for plumb) or along a line (if you are establishing stake alignment). Then lock the horizontal position. Now, as you pivot the scope, all sightings will be on the same vertical plane. Vertical lines should be checked from two positions, the second position being 90 degrees to the left or right of the first one.

OTHER CONSTRUCTION LEVELS

Aside from a dome, and the unusual case where a house has curved walls, you need to build structures that are plumb, level, and square. For general work you can use a 4-foot carpenter's level, and a line level and mason's string for checking long spans. Carpenter's levels come in many lengths, but a 4-foot model is the most handy. To check surfaces longer than 4 feet, you can rest the level against a long, straight 2 × 4.

4-8

4-9

4-10

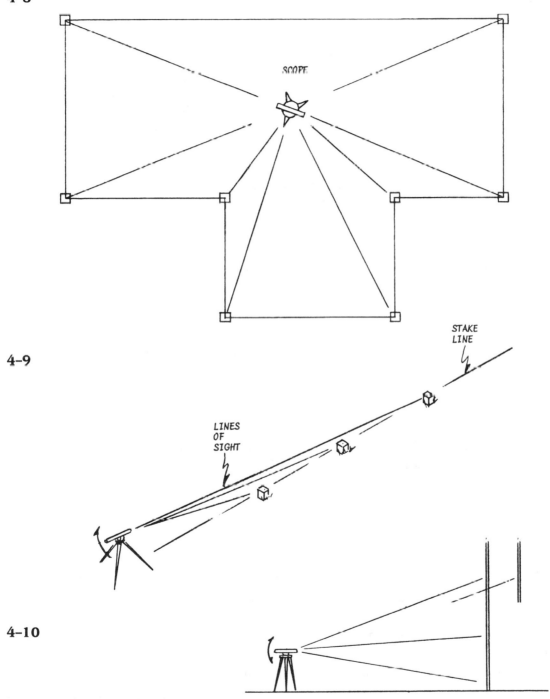

SCOPE

STAKE
LINE

LINES
OF
SIGHT

Some people have trouble reading the bubble in a carpenter's level, and use modern digital levels, which have battery-powered LED readouts and beep when they are level or plumb. The tools never go out of whack the way a spirit level can if you drop it, because you can reset them electronically. Some electronic levels also work as inclinometers to gauge slopes, and even the angles of rafters.

One of the most simple and inexpensive tools for leveling is also one of the most practical and accurate. The tool consists of a length of clear plastic tubing that you can buy in lengths long enough to suit your foundation layout. Fill it with water, raise the ends of the tube, and the water at each end will be level, as in **4–11**. Best of all, the tube can run up and down over rough terrain between corners, even down into a basement excavation.

It helps to color the water, and water-level kits generally contain a bottle of dye for this

4–11

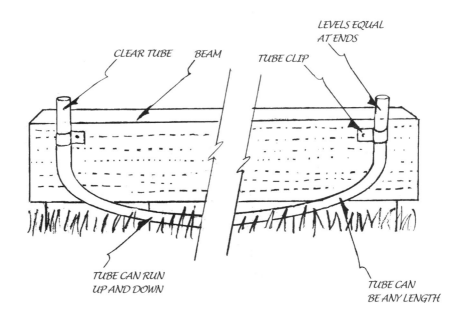

CLEAR TUBE   BEAM   TUBE CLIP   LEVELS EQUAL AT ENDS

TUBE CAN RUN UP AND DOWN

TUBE CAN BE ANY LENGTH

purpose. Kits also have clips for holding the tubing. Once you make sure there are no air bubbles in the line, the water at one end of the tube will be level with water at the other end, whether the ends are 10 feet or 100 feet apart.

Much checking can be done by working with a common level, a line level, and a measuring tape. The example in **4–12** is elementary, but it does serve to illustrate the procedure. Here a stake is set to establish the height of a footing. A line is stretched to a second

4-12

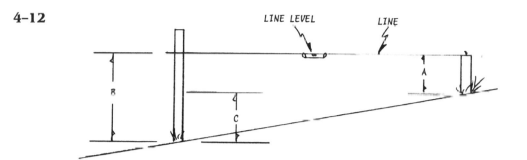

stake, which has been measured off an appropriate distance. The level will tell whether to raise or lower the line at the second stake. The differences between A, B, and C will tell the amount of change in elevation and will be guides that show heights of walls, or amounts of fill that may be required, or depths of excavations needed, depending on the design of the construction.

Much layout work involves the use of lines and the frequent tying and untying of knots. You can eliminate some of the knots if you attach an electrical terminal to the end of your line (**4-13**). The terminal can be slipped over a nail in a stake. From there, you can draw the line taut and tie it at the opposite end.

4-13

5

BUILDING THE FOUNDATION

There are many ways to build a foundation, but most designs call for concrete. You can use a concrete footing with either a poured concrete or concrete block wall on top of it to create a crawl space or basement. You can pour a concrete slab with a perimeter footing and save on excavation work. Concrete works because it is one of the most malleable building materials when it's ready to pour, and one of the strongest and most rigid once it hardens. The unusual combination makes it perfect for foundations, whether you need to pour a massive slab, a narrow footing, or a series of piers.

To contain concrete, masonry contractors use interlocking prefab forms. The do-it-yourself version is rough-surfaced plywood backed by 2 × 4s and braced so often and so sturdily that the sheets don't budge. The structure becomes rigid when each wall is independently braced with angled 2 × 4s pinned to stakes in the ground, and when the two walls are tied to each other with spacers. But before we get to the nitty-gritty details of forming and pouring concrete required for most houses, let's look briefly at some of the alternative systems.

ALTERNATE FOUNDATION SYSTEMS

Among several candidates other than concrete, you might be interested in wood foundations (pressure-treated), pole foundations, or foam-block systems.

Wood foundations used to be called the All Weather Wood Foundation System, a title that has been updated to the Permanent Wood Foundation (PWF). Wood foundations have caught on, mainly in cold climates, because concrete walls are replaced by pressure-treated wood. In a nutshell, the excavation is compacted and filled with gravel. Then a wide-grade board is installed to spread the load of the walls, and prefab sections framed with pressure-treated studs and covered with pressure-treated plywood are set in place.

When the walls are locked in place and braced, the exterior sheets are draped with plastic waterproofing and the foundation can be backfilled.

The PWF system offers quick assembly and no concrete work. The PWF approach dates back to the 1970s when it first began to gain popularity and code acceptance. It is widely used in Canada due to the shortened building season, and is typically installed by contractors who specialize in this approach and can provide a complete house foundation in one day.

Pole systems also eliminate a lot of excavation and concrete work. The idea is to plant a grid of treated poles on which you hang the house. Once the grid of 8- to 12-inch-diameter poles is joined by a network of bolted-on floor beams and rafters, it becomes even stronger overall than a stick-built house. The system was developed on the West Coast in the 1950s and 1960s, in part to reclaim hillside sites considered too sloped for conventional masonry foundations. You don't get a basement. But the system can make even steep sides buildable. As large poles are too unwieldy for a do-it-yourselfer to handle, poles typically are set by a crew and a crane. One big advantage with poles is that you get not only the foundation, but also the basic grid framework for the walls at the same time.

There are several proprietary foam-block systems on the market that generally follow the same approach. The idea is to stack a series of oversize, hollow, interlocking blocks made of dense foam; brace them; and then pour in concrete. The large foam blocks serve as the form for the pour, and also provide great insulating value that pays off when you create living space behind the foundation walls.

BATTER BOARDS AND BUILDING LINES

No matter what foundation system you use, you need to start by locating the building lines. After corner stakes have been established, batter boards, as shown in **5–1**, are set up 3 to 4 feet outside the marks. Batter boards are not always L-shaped. Straight ones are used in some circumstances and may be placed inside or outside the building site depending on the type of excavation needed; they are shown inside the site in **5–2**. The units do not have to be fancy but they should be firmly set, since you will be using them throughout the foundation work.

Use sharpened 2 × 4s for the stakes and 1 × 6s or wider stock for the ledgers (horizontal pieces). Work with a level when you set up the first set of ledgers and then with a line level to establish the height of others. Keeping all of them on the same horizontal plane will be an aid when you check depths of excavations, heights of footings, and so on.

Next, stretch the lines tightly between the batter boards and use a plumb bob to be sure the intersection of the lines is exactly over the established stake (**5–3**). Saw a shallow kerf

5-1

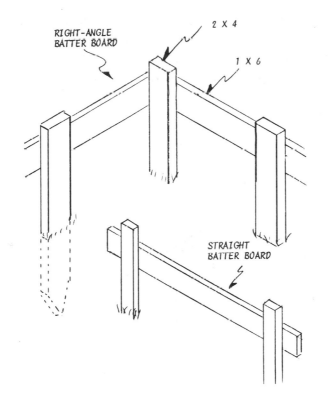

RIGHT-ANGLE
BATTER BOARD

2 X 4

1 X 6

STRAIGHT
BATTER BOARD

5-2

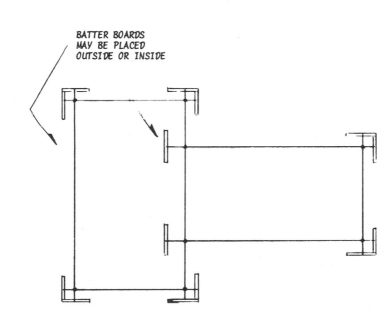

BATTER BOARDS
MAY BE PLACED
OUTSIDE OR INSIDE

in the ledgers as location points for the lines, and drive a nail so the strings can be secured. This way, when the lines have been removed for excavation purposes, they can be replaced accurately for positioning foundation forms, as shown in **5–4**.

Foundations that are out of square can cause many headaches throughout construc-

5–3

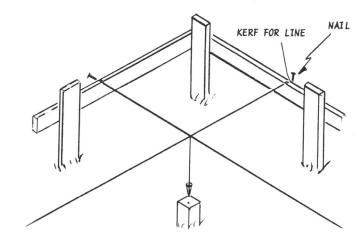

tion, so you want to be sure when setting up lines that corners form 90-degree angles. This can be done by using the 3-5–5 system based on the proportions of a right triangle. The hypotenuse will measure 5 feet if one leg is 3 feet and the other is 4 feet. You can use any multiples of these numbers so long as you stick to the same proportion. Therefore, you can determine if a corner is square by marking points 6 feet from the corner on one side and 8 feet from the corner on the other side, and then seeing if the distance between the points is exactly 10 feet. Doing this with tape is risky, however; accurate corners are easier if you take the time to make a check gauge as shown in **5–5**. The gauge can be used for other purposes also, such as to check plumb on vertical constructions. As a further check for square, measure the diagonals of rectangles and squares. If the corners of a square or rectangle are 90 degrees, the diagonals will be the same length.

THOUGHTS ON EXCAVATING

When little or no grading is required, you can set up batter boards and string lines immediately after topsoil has been scraped off. When the site is a slope, or the terrain is irregular, rough grading can be done before perimeter lines are organized. After batter boards

5-4

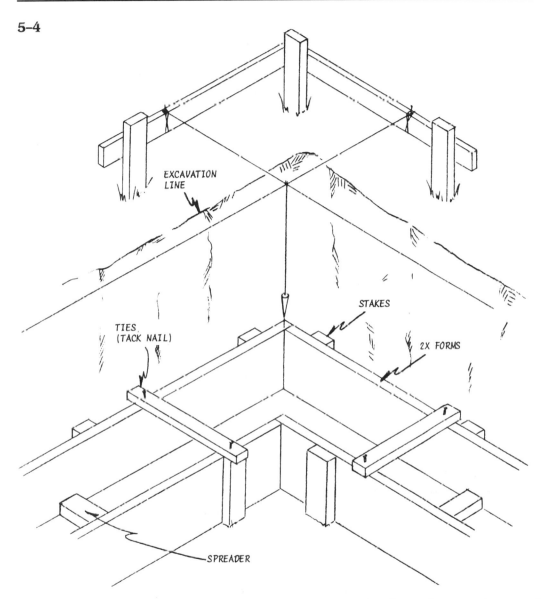

EXCAVATION
LINE

STAKES

TIES
(TACK NAIL)

2X FORMS

SPREADER

are established, temporary stakes can be driven to mark edges of excavations, and the building lines can be removed while work goes on.

If you are including a basement, excavate at least two feet beyond the building lines so there will bc plenty of room for the construction of forms for concrete, or for laying block. This extra digging isn't necessary if the house is to be on a slab or over a crawl space. Local codes will tell how deep to dig for foundations or footings so that bottom areas will be

5–5

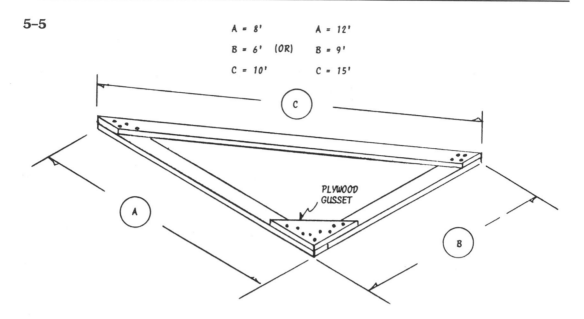

A = 8'   A = 12'

B = 6' (OR)   B = 9'

C = 10'   C = 15'

C

PLYWOOD
GUSSET

A

B

below the frost line. This is important to avoid the damage that can occur should water in the soil under a foundation freeze. Frost pressures can push walls upward and cause various types of damage that may be impossible to repair.

Excavation depths, which, of course, control foundation heights, are usually established by using the highest point of the building-site perimeter as a check point; all depth adjustments are made from there. All foundations, whether for basements, slabs, or crawl spaces, should extend above the final grade enough so that wood members of the house (studs, plates, trimmers, headers, etc.) are some distance from the soil. This distance, too, may be regulated by local codes.

Always control excavation depths so that footings and foundations can rest on undisturbed soil. Having to bring in gravel to fill to compensate for uneven digging can waste time and money, and may result in uneven settlement.

REINFORCEMENT FOR CONCRETE-MASONRY

The most common materials used to strengthen concrete and masonry constructions are steel bars (rebar), shown in a block wall in **5–6**, and welded wire fabric, shown in **5–7**. Both of the materials should be clean—free of scale, rust, and any foreign matter. The steel bars come in diameters up to ¾ inch, but ⅜- or ½-inch sizes are used for most home-construction projects. Use one-piece bars whenever possible; when the length or the design of the project doesn't permit it, overlap the bars and bind them with wire as shown in **5–8**. The

5–6

5–7

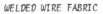

WELDED WIRE FABRIC

diameter of the bar has a bearing on the length of the overlap. Bars ¼ inch in diameter should be overlapped 1 foot, bars ⅜ inch in diameter should be overlapped 18 inches, and so on, increasing overlap by 6 inches for every ⅛ inch increase in diameter. It pays to use more than two ties for any overlap more than 12 inches. Plan the placement of bars for continuous runs around corners. If you can't, lap the bars at one or both ends as shown in **5–9**. Be generous with both the lap and the ties. Always use ties wherever bars cross (**5–10**).

The bars can be bent rather easily even though they are rigid and strong. Use a hacksaw to cut them to length by making a cut about halfway through the bar and then bending it sharply at the cut. Place bars so they will be midway, or better yet, in the bottom third of the pour. For example, if they are used in a slab, elevate them on pieces of stone so the concrete can flow under them. You can also use wire supports, called chairs.

Welded wire is used most often in slab work required for basement floors, full slab floors, patios, driveways, and the like. Overlap joints from 6 to 8 inches when you can't do the job with one whole piece as shown in **5–11**. The material tends to curl because it comes in rolls, but you can get rid of the curl by spreading it over a flat area and then walking on it. Use wire snips for cutting, but be careful; cut strands are apt to snap back at you.

Like the steel bars, wire fabric should be placed so it will be approximately midway in the pour, or in the bottom third. This can be accomplished with bricks or wire chairs, but many professionals place the fabric directly on the ground and then raise it with a rake or a wire hook as the concrete is being poured.

PLASTIC UNDERLAYMENT

Use a 6-mil-thick polyethylene sheeting to form a moisture barrier over a base of gravel before concrete is poured. The material is easy to cut and place, fairly cheap, and very effective with moisture control; there's no reason not to use it. You need to be careful during and after application not to pierce the plastic. Be very generous with overlaps and at perimeters. On a slab, for example, curl the sheet up and over forms. The excess is easy to cut away after the pour is complete.

RADON MITIGATION SYSTEMS

Among many possible health risks on your building site is radon, a naturally occurring radioactive gas that comes from the natural decay of uranium that is present in nearly all soils. Radon first came to widespread public attention in the 1970s. Testing procedures and remedies have improved since then, but the threat is still there. After extensive research in homes and long-term studies of miners exposed to radon, all major

5-8

5-9

5-10

5-11

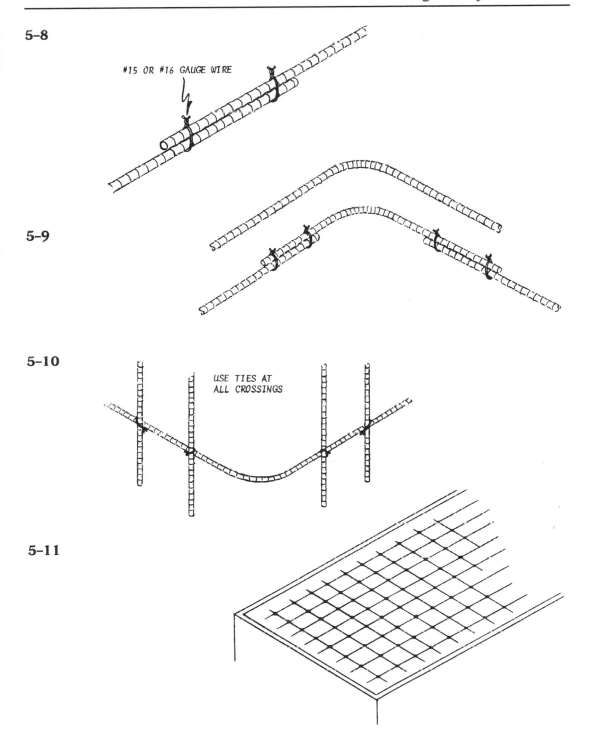

health organizations, including the Centers for Disease Control and Prevention, the American Lung Association, and the American Medical Association, agree that radon causes thousands of preventable lung cancer deaths every year. Some estimates range as high as 30,000 deaths per year, stemming from elevated radon levels in nearly one out of every 15 homes in the country.

Like the warnings on cigarette packs, the subject of radon carries a strong health advisory from the surgeon general. It says that indoor radon gas is a national health problem causing thousands of deaths each year, and that millions of homes have elevated radon levels. Homes should be tested for radon, says the warning, and when elevated levels are confirmed, the problem should be corrected.

There are different types of testing kits to use in existing homes. To check a building site, you need to call in a professional testing firm. The EPA recommends that you contact your state radon office for a list of these testers. You can locate state offices, and information about other radon programs and radon professionals on the EPA Web site.

Typically, the gas rises through the ground and into houses through cracks and other holes in the foundation or slab, for instance, where a sewer pipe exits the building. Once inside a modern, energy-efficient house that is built to retard air leaks, it can build up. Sometimes radon enters a home through well water, and in rare cases it can be emitted from some building materials. But the main problem is from gas rising through the ground under houses.

The amount of radon in the air is measured in picocuries per liter of air, which is noted as pCi/L. About 0.4 pCi/L of radon is normally found in the outside air. Indoors, the EPA estimates that the average radon level is about 1.3 pCi/L. Although the EPA says that any radon exposure carries some risk, the widely accepted threshold for making changes to a house, called the action level, is 4 pCi/L. With special sealants, vents, and other systems, elevated radon levels in most homes can be reduced to under 2 pCi/L.

If you are unlucky enough to be building on a site with elevated radon levels, one good solution is to install a slab-vent system. It consists of one or more lengths of large-diameter perforated plastic pipe laid in the gravel below the slab. Those pipes are connected to a vent pipe that runs up the foundation wall to an elbow and a short horizontal length that extends out of the house in a convenient location, say, in the space between floor joists, so you don't have to build an opening into the foundation. A very small fan housed in the pipe sucks air (including the radon gas) from the soil beneath the slab and out of the house. The system is very simple but effective because it gives the soil gas somewhere else to go—a path of less resistance—so it won't seep through cracks into your home. The EPA or your state radon office can provide details on radon mitigation systems.

THICKNESS OF FOUNDATIONS

Foundations do more than support the building—they protect against frost; guard against termites to some extent, if they are equipped with termite shields; may be designed to provide a basement; and can be constructed to resist minor shocks from earthquakes. Don't skimp on them just because they usually can't be seen once the building is complete and they stand between you and the fun part of the job. Local building codes specify minimum standards, but even if they don't, if you're haphazard about this important phase of construction, be aware that the house may tilt, floors may sag, doors may not open, and windows may jam. A good foundation is not difficult to plan or to build, and you can get expert advice about specifications merely by going along with the building codes.

When all parts of a concrete foundation are placed at the same time, it is called an integral foundation or monolithic pour. This is desirable in some areas because it is resistant to earthquake damage. **Figure 5–12** shows an integral foundation. However, even though the design is a one-piece unit, various parts should be viewed in relation to the jobs they must do. The main foundation, the part on which the house itself actually sits, for example, will require thicker and probably deeper walls and special footings. Other walls, like retaining walls needed for an outside stairway such as those shown in **5–13** and walls for a garage, can be thinner and may not even require a footing. Walls so designed are called trench walls and may be okay in your area to support light loads.

5-12

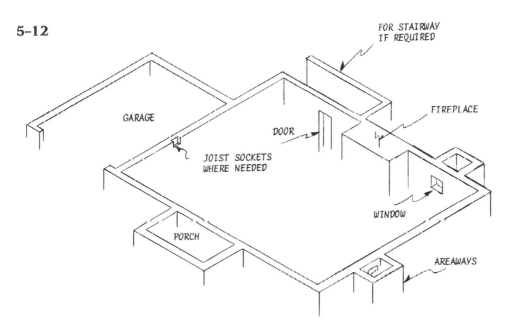

FOR STAIRWAY IF REQUIRED

GARAGE

FIREPLACE

DOOR

JOIST SOCKETS WHERE NEEDED

WINDOW

PORCH

AREAWAYS

Areaways, such as the one shown in cross-section in **5–14**, are often designed into a house foundation to provide light and ventilation for basement windows. They are thinner in cross section than load-bearing walls. Note that a sloped concrete floor and a drain are included in the design; these do not have to be part of the original pour. Actually, such features are often omitted and the light and ventilation problems are solved through good grading and the use of corrugated steel backstops (**5–15**).

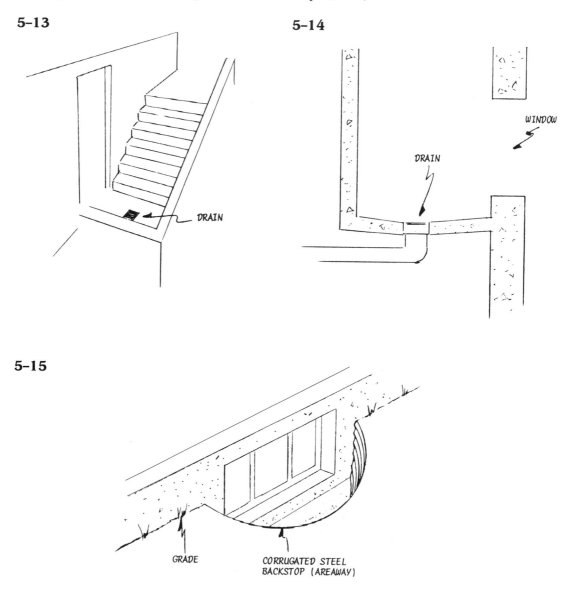

5–13

DRAIN

5–14

WINDOW

DRAIN

5–15

GRADE

CORRUGATED STEEL
BACKSTOP (AREAWAY)

5-16

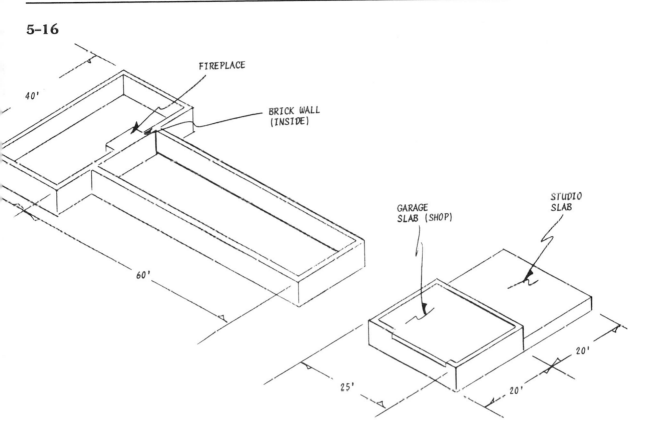

FIREPLACE

40'

BRICK WALL
(INSIDE)

60'

STUDIO
SLAB

GARAGE
SLAB (SHOP)

25'

20'

20'

Not all foundations can be so neatly integrated. In my own situation, shown in **5-16**, the garage and work areas are detached from the house so that we could have a breeze-way leading to a side entry and to a back patio. But wall height and thickness and footing considerations apply regardless. On some slope situations, and even fairly level grades if the idea conforms to a split-level design, the foundation itself can be stepped, as shown in **5-17**, and then filled in with wood materials.

Overall, good procedure calls for a detailed look at all of the foundation requirements. Even if the design doesn't permit a one-piece casting, formwork should permit a one-time pour. If you are building in or near an area with established building codes, you will have no problems getting correct specifications for a good foundation. If not, here are some guidelines. But remember that these guides may require further research, such as check-ing successful structures in the area, and that all foundations should provide for a depth that is below the frost line.

Foundations for a wood-frame house that does not include a basement should be at

5-17

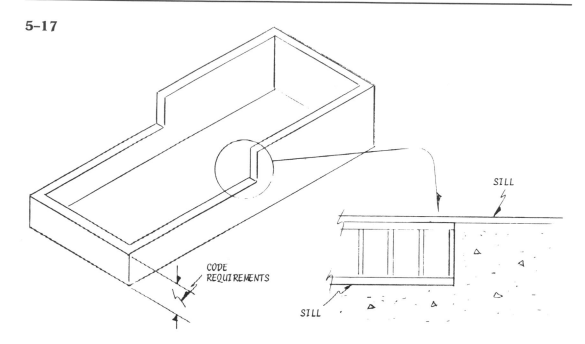

least 8 inches thick. With a basement, the minimum is 8 inches but should be increased to 10 inches if the walls are longer than 20 feet. A two-story wood-frame house with a basement calls for 10-inch-thick foundations that should be increased to 12 inches thick if the walls are more than 7 feet below grade. Minimum foundation thickness for two-story masonry walls should match the wall thickness, as long as the foundation depth is not more than 7 feet below grade. If it's more, increase foundation wall thickness to 12 inches.

Foundations only 5 inches thick will usually do for a porch, although it's generally more economical on both porches and decks to use girders supported by piers. Walls for areaways and exterior below-grade stairs usually must act as retaining walls, so some safety factor should be considered when determining wall thickness. A bit too much is better than too little; 6 inches will probably work for areaways, while 8 inches will be better for stair walls as long as they are not more than 10 feet long.

FOOTINGS

Footings carry the weight of the building and are always wider than the foundation so the load will be spread over a broader area. Soil conditions affect footing size and design, so codes should be checked before work is started. In typical residential construction, loads will be carried safely if the footing is designed along the lines shown in **5-18**. In most

5-18

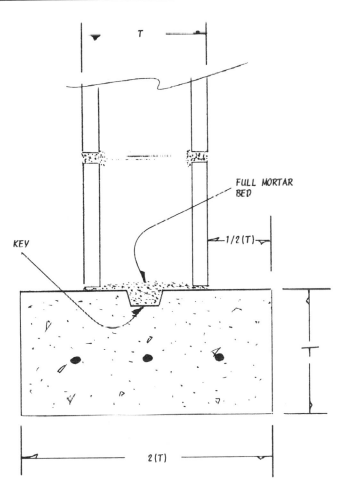

cases, the footing is at least 8 inches deep and 16 inches wide, while the foundation wall is 8 inches wide. However, the thickness of a footing should never be less than 8 inches.

The key shape is made by pressing a beveled 2 × 4 into the surface of the concrete after it has been poured and is being leveled. This key is not always included, but the safety factor a key provides is well worth the time required to make it.

Generally, a footing should be placed at least 12 inches below the frost line. This can vary anywhere from on grade to as much as 5 feet below grade depending on the locality—again, a check of local codes is in order.

Reinforcement rods are required in earthquake areas and wherever footings are placed on poor load-bearing soil, and they are recommended no matter where you build. Two ⅝-inch bars are normal practice in footings up to 12 × 24 inches, but this can vary; ½ inch bars may be acceptable, or three bars instead of two may be called for. The bars should be placed so they will be covered by at least 3 inches of concrete at all points. This is easiest to do with chairs, shown in **5–19**, which are made specifically for this purpose. The chairs may be spaced any distance as long as the bars are reasonably level.

5-19

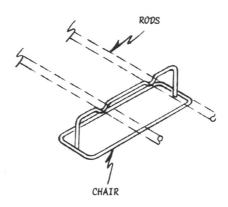

RODS

CHAIR

At this point, it is wise to consider the footings you may require for interior posts and bearing and nonbearing walls so that forming and concrete-pouring for them can be done along with the perimeter footing. It would seem reasonable to assume that the specifications of the perimeter footings can be guides for other types, but the soil conditions and the structural design of the house must be considered. Bearing posts, since they carry concentrated loads, and bearing walls will require huskier footings than non-load-bearing walls.

The designs shown in **5–20** illustrate typical construction procedures, but the thickness and depth of the footings should be determined after consulting with the building inspector. Such considerations apply to houses built on slabs and those with basements. In slab work, special footings are often provided for as shown in **5–21**. A square excavation in the ground is the form; reinforcement bars are included to supply strength to the single-pour casting.

Perimeter footings may also be designed as integral parts of the slab. This is the design I used when I poured a foundation for a studio addition on the back of the garage (**5–22**).

Houses built over a crawl space require supports between perimeter walls, but this is usually accomplished with precast piers that are set on footings a bit larger than the base area of the piers and from 6 to 8 inches thick (**5–23**). The supports are spaced in relation to the size of the beams that will support the floor joists.

5–20

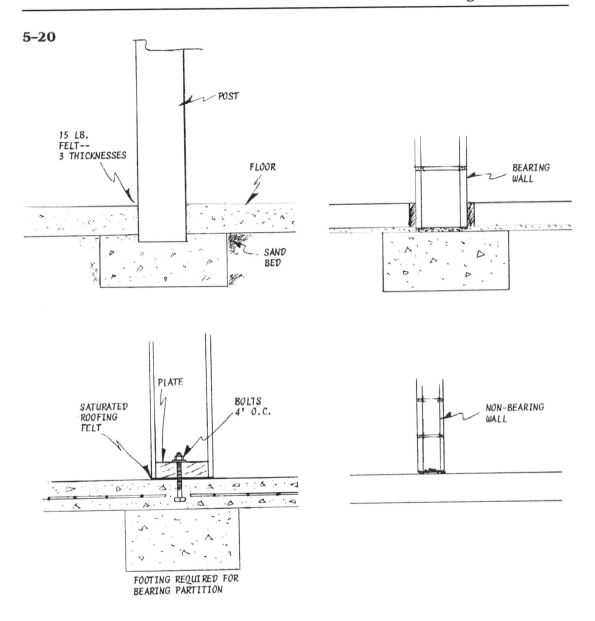

POST

15 LB.
FELT--
3 THICKNESSES

FLOOR

SAND
BED

BEARING
WALL

PLATE

SATURATED
ROOFING
FELT

BOLTS
4' O.C.

NON-BEARING
WALL

FOOTING REQUIRED FOR
BEARING PARTITION

FOOTING FORMS

Establish corners by dropping a plumb bob from the intersection of the lines stretched between batter boards (**5–24**). Drive one corner stake to establish the height of the footing and then work with a transit, carpenter's level, or a line level to set the height of

5-21

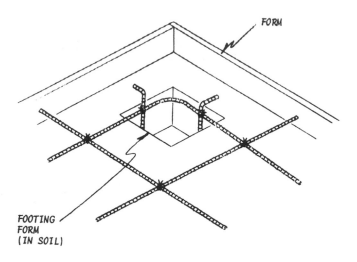

FORM

FOOTING
FORM
(IN SOIL)

5-22

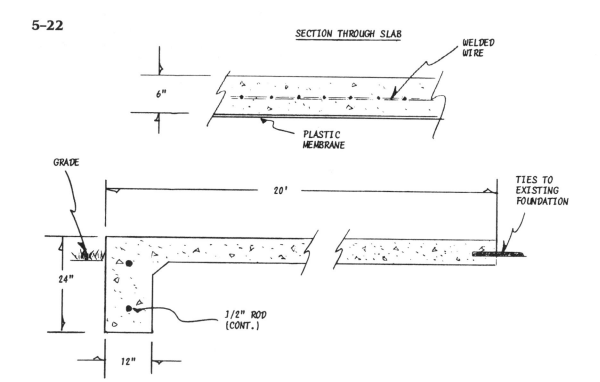

SECTION THROUGH SLAB

WELDED
WIRE

6"

PLASTIC
MEMBRANE

GRADE

20'

TIES TO
EXISTING
FOUNDATION

24"

1/2" ROD
(CONT.)

12"

5–23

5-24

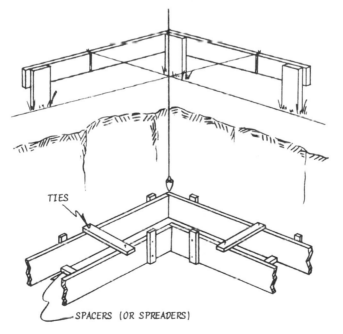

TIES

SPACERS (OR SPREADERS)

others. Stretch lines from nails in the stakes so you will know where the outside of the forms must be.

Either 1- or 2-inch boards can be used for the forms, the difference being that the thinner material will require stakes about 2 feet apart while the heavier material can be staked at 5–foot intervals. Use 2 × 2 or 2 × 4 pieces of wood, pointed at one end, as stakes. Attach form boards by nailing from the outside of the stakes, using regular common or box nails as long as you don't drive them completely, or double-headed (duplex) nails. The latter, shown in **5–25**, has one head that you drive, and a second head that remains exposed so nails are easy to pull when forms are removed. In all situations, remember that forms do have to be removed, and nails accordingly.

A good procedure is to set up outside form boards first, and then work with a carpenter's level to set the height of inside boards. Use precut spreaders between boards to maintain width and to avoid having to measure constantly; use ties across the top for strength during the pour. The spreaders are removed as the concrete is placed. Remember that if you pour from the chute of ready-mix truck, the force can overwhelm underbraced forms. It's wise to add extra braces where ready-mix concrete will be deposited.

THE CONCRETE

House-construction jobs require too much concrete for you to consider mixing it in a wheelbarrow or trough. In very remote locations, you could rent a mixer (some can be run with a gasoline engine), but the wisest procedure is to have concrete delivered to the site in a ready-mix truck, ready to pour.

5–25

DUPLEX HEAD

Many amateurs fear this professional method; they picture a mass of fluid stone and think the truck driver just wants to dump the load and run. Actually, the driver's knowledge will be a help and he will be aware that placement takes some time. Some ready-mix suppliers will make a surcharge if truck and driver are delayed an unreasonable amount of time in relation to the load they are delivering. But just figure that the extra charge, if necessary, is worth it if it eliminates a hand-mixing operation.

Another advantage of buying ready-mix is that the supplier will know, as well as anyone, the correct mixes for various types of work in that area. You might just get by with asking for a mix for a footing, for a wall, for a patio, or whatever. And there is always the building inspector.

Mixes are generally specified by three numbers, for example, 1-2-3, which means one part of portland cement to two parts of sand to three parts of gravel. A common mix for footings, foundations, and walls is 1-3-4. A mix of 1-2-2¼ is better for projects that will be exposed to extremes in wear and weather, while a 1-2⅕-3 mix is generally okay for walks, patios, and floors.

Your pour will be successful if you are ready for the material before you ask for delivery. Check all formwork and plan truck positions so the concrete can be poured directly into forms or, at least, with minimum transportation required. Have help and extra wheelbarrows on hand if they are needed. Be sure shovels and rakes are handy so the concrete can be spread and tamped to fill forms solidly. Lengths of 2 × 4s or 2 × 2s can also be used to tamp but, regardless of the tool used, don't overdo; you may move the gravel enough to destroy equal distribution. Tapping the outside of the forms with a hammer is another technique that helps settle the concrete and produce a smoother surface. When the forms are full, place a 2 × 4 across the top edges and move it to and fro to even the concrete. Keep a trowel handy so you can fill depressions and remove any excess.

Concrete must be allowed to cure before it is subjected to any stress even though you can remove forms after about two days. Curing means no more than keeping the concrete moist or taking steps to slow up evaporation. A frequent wetting with a very fine spray from a garden hose will do the job, and the applications can be minimized if you cover the project with a moisture-absorbing material such as burlap. The more modern approach is to cover the pour with plastic sheeting to retain moisture, or to use a curing compound that is sprayed or rolled on the concrete surface immediately after finishing.

Concrete work should not be poured in cold weather without special precautions. It should never be dumped on frozen ground, and if temperatures fall below 50 degrees you'll have to work with heated or treated mixes. Also, the temperature must be maintained for a period of time, which is one reason why many housebuilding projects start in the spring when there is temperate weather.

If the idea of doing the concrete work seems too challenging, just remember it is one phase of house construction that you can easily pass on to professionals. You can still do the formwork, planning and executing it exactly the way you want.

FOUNDATION FORMWORK

Forms for walls must be strong and braced enough to resist the tremendous pressures created when the concrete is poured. The pressures increase along with the height of the wall, so the higher the wall, the stronger the forms must be. Most forms for residential foundations can be made with 1-inch boards or ⅝-inch or ⅗-inch plywood as sheathing and 2 × 4 materials as studs. Because a considerable amount of money can go into the materials used to build forms, it's wise to think beyond the primary use and plan to use the material, after forms are broken down, as house sheathing, subflooring, joist bridging, and so on.

You don't have to be a master cabinetmaker to construct good forms, but they must be tight and smooth and correctly aligned. Joints between sheathing pieces must be tight enough to prevent cement paste from leaking through. Interior surfaces must not have projections that might lock pieces of the form to the concrete.

You can make forms for low walls, up to about 3 feet high, with boards or plywood, braced with 2 × 4 studs about every 2 feet (**5–26**). You can use this same design to go a bit higher, but more strength should be provided by using a closer stud spacing. Forms that are over 4 feet high should be reinforced further with wales, which are 2 × 4s or sometimes 4 × 4s placed horizontally along the studs (**5–27**). Notice that this particular form was constructed in a subgrade trench. In such situations, minimum trench width must provide room for work to go on.

Foundation walls that are above grade are often cast integrally with a footing that is contained by a trench formed in the earth, or forms are built over a footing that has been so cast (**5–28**). Notice that the bottom of the trench has been undercut to provide an adequate base that simulates the form of a separate footing. This approach is not advisable everywhere, so check local procedures before doing it. You'll find that it's best (and common) to pour concrete in forms.

In all situations, wire ties and spreader blocks as shown in **5–29** are used in addition to the ties across the top of the forms. The wire keeps the two sides of the form from spreading apart; the spreaders are gauges that maintain a uniform wall thickness. Pass the wire through holes that you drill on each side of the studs and then twist it with a screwdriver or something similar until it is tight. The best bet is to use a 1 × 2 spreader near each tie so you won't pull the form sides out of alignment because of excessive tightening. The

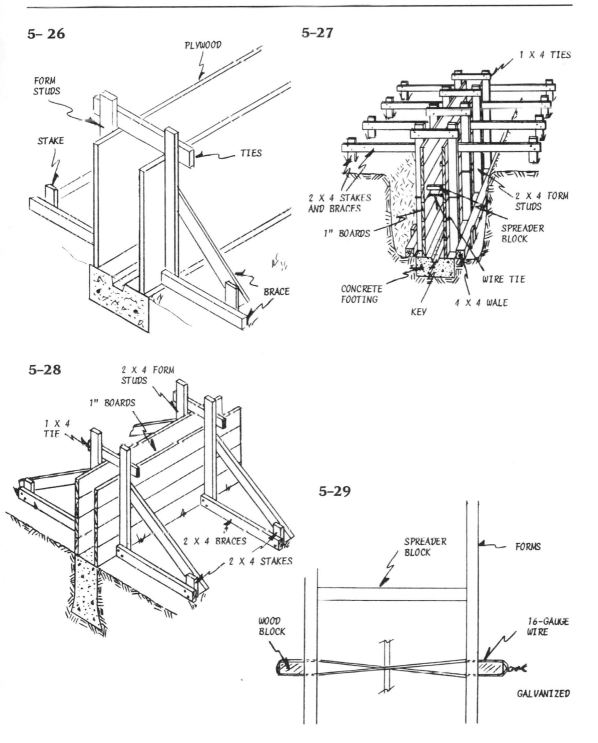

5- 26

PLYWOOD

FORM
STUDS

STAKE

TIES

BRACE

5-27

1 X 4 TIES

2 X 4 STAKES
AND BRACES

1" BOARDS

CONCRETE
FOOTING

KEY

4 X 4 WALE

WIRE TIE

SPREADER
BLOCK

2 X 4 FORM
STUDS

5-28

2 X 4 FORM
STUDS

1" BOARDS

1 X 4
TIE

2 X 4 BRACES

2 X 4 STAKES

5-29

SPREADER
BLOCK

FORMS

WOOD
BLOCK

16-GAUGE
WIRE

GALVANIZED

wire ties stay put until the forms are removed. Then, they are cut flush with the surface of the concrete. The spreaders are removed as the concrete is poured.

READY-MADE FORMS

Professionals work with reusable forms that are flexible enough for various types of constructions. Such products are usually available from concrete and masonry supply yards or other establishments on a rental basis. It pays to check out availability, because the forms can save time and may result in a better foundation. There have been amateur housebuilders who have purchased ready-to-assemble forms, or the hardware required for them, and then sold them after personal use. I know of one who retained the equipment, but rented it out to other builders and soon got more than his investment back.

The units that will be available in your area will probably conform to established foundation requirements. Forms needed for houses over crawl spaces will be one design, while those for basements or high foundations will be another. Some will be reinforced panels that you bolt together; others may be pieces of hardware that you use with sheets of plywood and 2 × 4s. You may find brackets, shown in **5–30**, and ties, shown in **5–31**, together with standard sheets of plywood. The plywood is drilled as shown in **5–32**. You can drill several sheets at a time if you stack them. The holes are ½ inch in diameter, drilled on 2-foot centers but with an edge distance of 1 foot. The standard drilling method produces eight holes in each sheet of plywood.

Shown in **5–33** are typical arrangements for a low and a high wall. Corners are turned as shown in **5–34**. If you're planning a brick veneer wall, remember that you need to form a support lip for the brick into the foundation. Some form systems are designed for this purpose (**5–35**).

FORM RELEASE

Wood forms can be separated from set concrete more easily and with less chance of damage to the concrete if they are treated with a release agent. A thin coat of engine oil applied with a brush or rags is an old standby, but more modern materials that are less messy and more environmentally friendly are available. These form releases may be purchased in bulk and applied with the type of insecticide sprayers that are used in gardens.

OPENINGS THROUGH CONCRETE

When window openings are required through the foundation, forms like those shown in **5–36** are installed between the walls of the foundation form. Size them to fit snugly

5-30

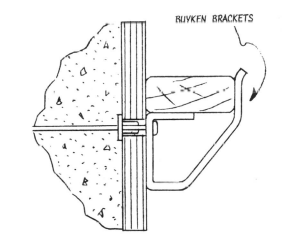

BUYKEN BRACKETS

5-31   ALLENFORM PLY-TIES

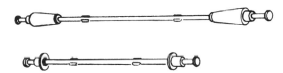

5-32   STANDARD DRILLING OF PLYWOOD

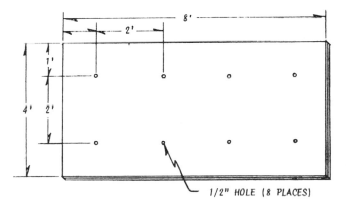

1/2" HOLE (8 PLACES)

5–33

CROSS SECTION OF TYPICAL 4′ WALL

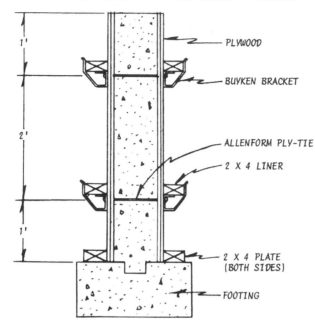

- PLYWOOD
- BUYKEN BRACKET
- ALLENFORM PLY-TIE
- 2 X 4 LINER
- 2 X 4 PLATE (BOTH SIDES)
- FOOTING

TYPICAL HIGH WALL

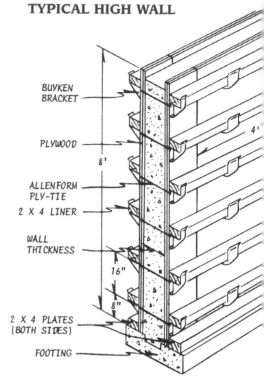

- BUYKEN BRACKET
- PLYWOOD
- ALLENFORM PLY-TIE
- 2 X 4 LINER
- WALL THICKNESS
- 2 X 4 PLATES (BOTH SIDES)
- FOOTING

5–34 TYPICAL CORNER DETAIL

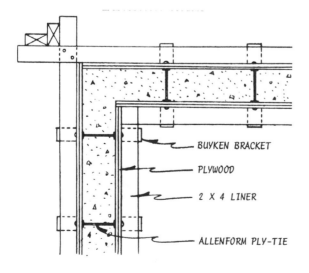

- BUYKEN BRACKET
- PLYWOOD
- 2 X 4 LINER
- ALLENFORM PLY-TIE

5–35 TYPICAL BRICK LEDGE DETAIL

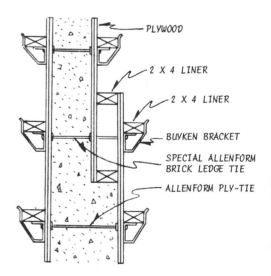

- PLYWOOD
- 2 X 4 LINER
- 2 X 4 LINER
- BUYKEN BRACKET
- SPECIAL ALLENFORM BRICK LEDGE TIE
- ALLENFORM PLY-TIE

against the main forms to prevent cement-paste loss. The keys can be beveled pieces of 2 × 2s, 2 × 3s, or 2 × 4s that will be locked into the concrete and used as nailing strips when window frames are installed (**5–37**). Door openings are done the same way except that form pieces are permanently attached to each other and actually used as jambs later on (**5–38**). Use good material and be very accurate when you make the frame, working with a level and a square when you install it in the form.

Keyed nailing strips may be utilized in other ways. The cast windowsill shown in **5–39**

5–36

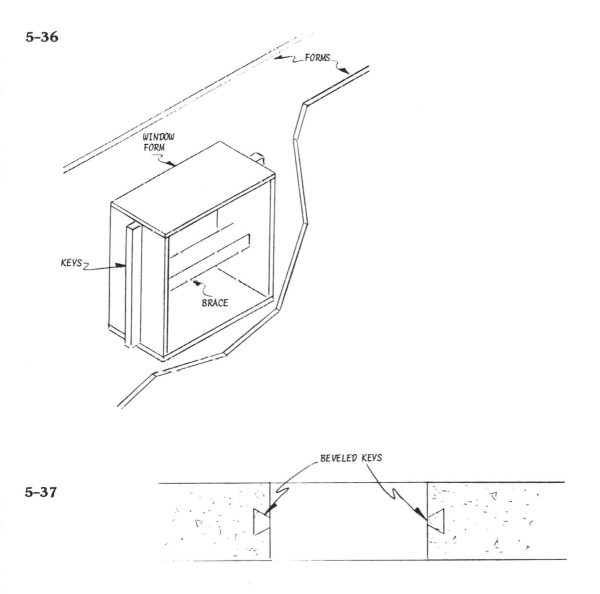

5–37

5–38

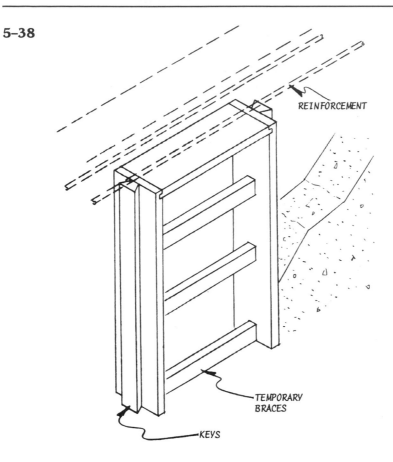

REINFORCEMENT

TEMPORARY
BRACES

KEYS

5–39

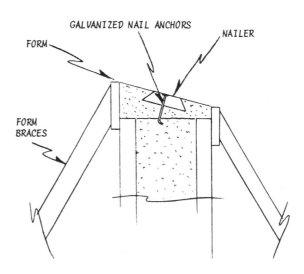

GALVANIZED NAIL ANCHORS

NAILER

FORM

FORM
BRACES

includes one so that wood members may be added later. Notice the forms and braces used for the special sill pour, and the nail anchors that help hold the key securely.

Ventilation openings through crawl-space walls are also made with preassembled forms. The form is U-shaped and sized to fit the screened vent that will be used (**5–40**). Pockets for beams that must span across foundation walls can be formed as shown in **5–41**, or simply with blocks of Styrofoam (**5–42**).

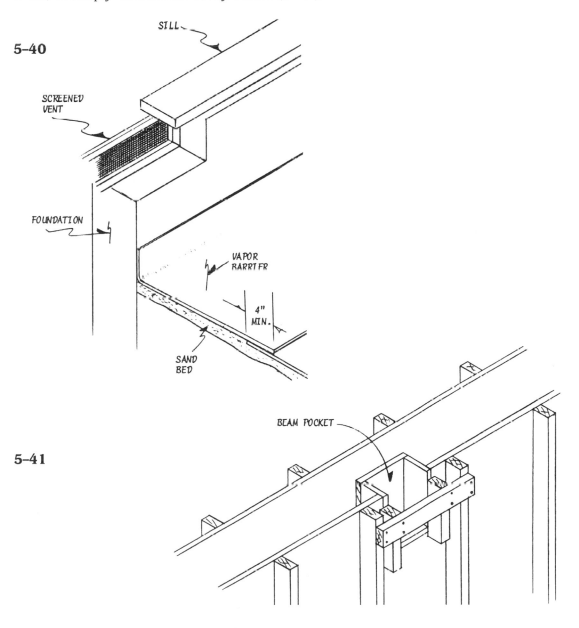

5–40

SILL

SCREENED VENT

FOUNDATION

VAPOR BARRIER

4" MIN.

SAND BED

BEAM POCKET

5–41

5–42

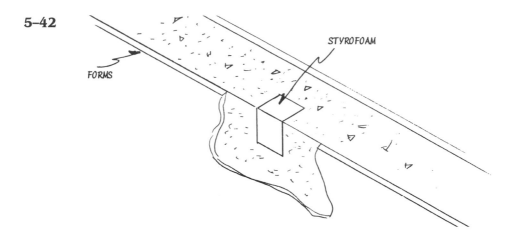

It's also wise to plan ahead for utility access, say, for a gas line, main waste line and other piping. Do this by inserting a plastic pipe through holes cut directly across from each other in the forms. Slide in the pipe (whatever diameter you need) and when the concrete hardens you can trim the ends flush.

WALLS OF CONCRETE BLOCK

Concrete blocks are available in various shapes and sizes that are especially suitable for foundation work and general house construction (**5–43**). They seem more appealing than poured concrete to the amateur builder because they eliminate form construction and permit a stop-and-go procedure. You can't quit in the middle of a foundation when pouring concrete.

All blocks are cast masonry units, but they may contain different types of aggregate. Sand and gravel or crushed stone are common, and the term concrete block, at one time, designated those materials specifically. Today, the term today often includes all units whether they are made with slag, cinders, shale, or whatever. Much of the weight of a block is in the aggregate. A dense and strong $8 \times 8 \times 16$ block can weigh 50 pounds, but a similar-size unit made with cinders or pumice may weigh half as much.

Both lightweight and heavyweight units are acceptable for many types of masonry construction, so your selection might be influenced by, in addition to weight, such things as texture, insulation factors, availability of types or shapes in your particular area, and, as always, how you must work to abide by local codes.

Generally, lightweight units do a better insulating job, but the hollow cores of all units may be filled with a granular insulating material. Both types do a better job of absorbing

5-43

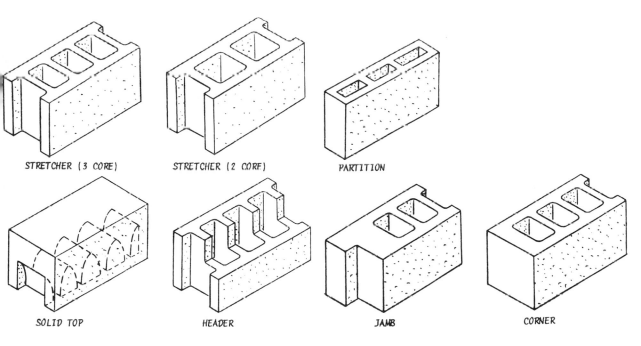

STRETCHER (3 CORE)   STRETCHER (2 CORE)   PARTITION

SOLID TOP   HEADER   JAMB   CORNER

sound than a smooth, dense wall of concrete, but in this area too, the lightweights are more efficient than the heavyweights.

Check out all special units and shapes that are available or that can be delivered to your site from outside the area. You may be able to incorporate some to facilitate a procedure or to end a job in a professional way. Specials include such units as headers that form a ledge as shown in **5-44**, caps that finish off the top of a foundation or any wall, and corner blocks with rounded edges for neat endings as shown in **5-45**.

TYPICAL SETUP

The organization of an all-block wall is shown in **5-46**. This one uses wide block on the foundation and narrower block at the level of the floor. There are several other ways you can build a block foundation. One of the most common is to top off the blocks with a sill that the floor joists rest on.

The installation of concrete drain tiles is often omitted in areas with very dry climates and where adequate subsoil drainage is guaranteed, but this seems unwise, especially when the wall is for a basement. Older drain systems used tiles with open joints covered by tar paper

5–44   **5–45   CORNER BLOCKS**

HEADER

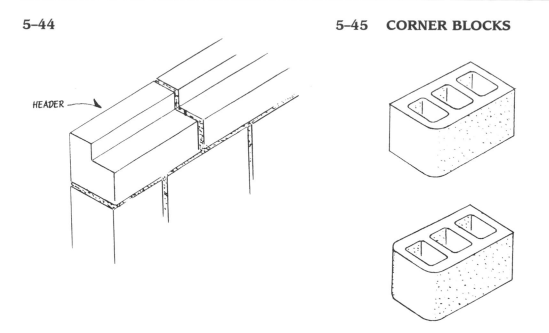

to keep out some dirt. The most basic drain system today uses perforated plastic pipe in gravel. The idea is that water flows down to the pipe through the porous gravel, and collects in the pipe, which should have enough slope to carry it away from the building. There are other, much more sophisticated systems for sites where groundwater may be a problem.

There are many ways to finish the earth side of the wall, and some that work in conjunction with the drains. The old-fashioned system used a parge coat of a 1–2½ mix of mortar applied in two coats to build up a total thickness of about a ½ inch. To apply the parge coat, first moisten the wall with a fine spray of water and trowel on a first, ⅕-inch-thick application of plaster. Allow this to partially harden and then rough up the surface a bit so you will have a good bond for the second coat. Professionals do the roughing up with a special scratch tool, but you can accomplish something similar by making random sweeps across the surface with a stiff-bristled broom.

Keep the first coating damp, but allow it to set up for about 24 hours before repeating the plaster application. Extend the parging to at least 6 inches above grade. Form a generous cove at the base of the wall so water can't collect near the wall-to-footing joint. Keep the second coating moist for at least 24 hours after application. The parge coat can be a single ½-inch-thick application of plaster, but in that case, keep the application moist for at least 48 hours.

Some builders waterproof simply by coating the foundation walls with hot tar. But this can eventually break down. Among the more modern waterproofing systems is an ingenious combination of materials and applications. First, the foundation is water-

5-46

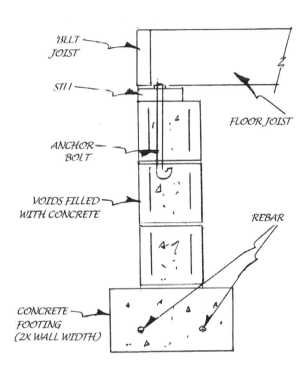

proofed with hot tar or elastomeric sheeting, which is similar to the modified bitumen used on flat and low-slope roofs. Generally, the foundation is rolled with a sealant-adhesive that the waterproof sheeting adheres to. Then blankets of coated wire mesh are fastened to the wall and covered by filter fabric before the excavation is backfilled. As groundwater approaches the foundation, it flows through the filter fabric (which keeps out dirt), enters the mesh, and drops down through the porous tangle to the foundation drain. With this kind of system, the foundation is not subject to hydrostatic pressure that can cause cracks and leaks.

MORTAR FOR BLOCK WORK

Correctly mixed mortar is necessary if masonry units are to bond as a strong, well-knit wall. Proportions of materials in mortars vary depending on the job to be done. Severe stresses and frost actions call for stronger and more durable mortars than you need for walls exposed to ordinary service. The table in **5–47** offers general recommendations, but these recommendations should be checked out for your area before being used.

5-47 MORTAR MIXES FOR CONCRETE BLOCK (BY VOLUME)

Work	Cement	Hydrated Lime	Mortar Sand
Average Projects	1 part masonry cement	None	2–3 parts
	1 part portland cement	1 to 1 parts	4–6 parts
Heavy-duty work—severe frosts, earthquake area, strong winds	1 part masonry cement plus 1 part portland cement	none	4–6 parts
	1 part portland cement	0–¾ part	2–3 parts

When mixing, follow the rule for concrete and mortar of blending all materials together in a dry state before adding water. Add enough drinkable water, gradually, to bring the mix to a plastic, workable state. A good mix will hold together but will spread easily. Stroke across its surface with a trowel to see if you get a smooth finish, which is one sign of a correct mix.

Don't mix more than you can use in about two hours. If the mortar stiffens because of evaporation, you can restore its workability by thoroughly remixing and adding a minimum amount of water. Mortar that becomes stiff through hydration should be thrown out. It's not easy to tell the difference between hydration and evaporation, so your best bet is to set a reasonable time limit in relation to how fast you work. You can always mix new batches of mortar as they are needed. All the precautions suggested for cold-weather work with concrete apply to block work as well. For safety's sake, it's best to do the job during temperate weather.

MORTAR JOINTS

The joints between blocks should be weathertight and neat. There is no need for anything but a flush joint, as shown in **5-48**, when the wall will be backfilled. This is done by cutting off excess mortar with the edge of a trowel and then running the point of the trowel along the line. The idea is to compact the mortar and force it tightly against the masonry.

Joints like the V, concave, raked, and extruded joints shown in **5-49** are often used in above-grade walls, but for appearance and sometimes for water-shedding. V and concave joints are the most popular since they look neat and do not form a ledge that might accu-

5–48

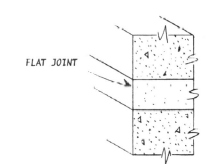

FLAT JOINT

5–49

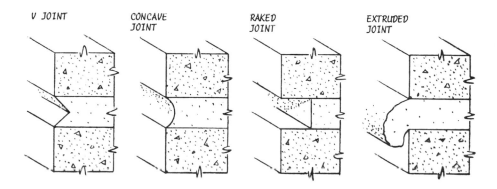

V JOINT   CONCAVE JOINT   RAKED JOINT   EXTRUDED JOINT

mulate water. The V joint can be done by working with a length of ½-inch-square bar stock, and a concave joint by working with a piece of ½- or ⅝-inch dowel stock or tubing.

Tool the joints when the mortar has become hard enough to retain a thumbprint. Do not attempt to move a block after the mortar has stiffened even partially. This will break the mortar bond and may create a water entry point.

LAYING BLOCK

Blocks are heavy, so stack them conveniently about the site to avoid excessive carrying. Handle them carefully to avoid damage to them and to yourself. Keep them covered, and use them dry and dust-free. If you have worked with brick, you know the units must be wet when placed. This does not apply to block.

A full mortar bed will cover all the web areas, while a partial one (face-shell mortaring) will not (**5–50**). For foundation work, use full coating. The procedures described here apply whether you are laying block on a footing, as in **5–51**, or on a slab.

Do a dry run first by placing the first course without mortar. Check for alignment and spacing so you won't have to make corrections after mortaring is started. On a long run you may be able to make some adjustments, design permitting, so you won't have to cut blocks to fill out a line. Now you can snap a chalk line to mark the footing.

Start at a corner with a full bed of mortar for two or three blocks. Furrow the mix with a trowel to get plenty of mortar along the bottom edges of the face shells. Place the corner block first and then add one or two others after you have applied mortar to the ends of the face shells (**5–52**). Use a level or a straight 2 × 4 as a straightedge to check alignment. Check both vertical and horizontal positions with the level.

If you have placed the blocks carefully, it won't require much more than tapping with the handle of the trowel to nudge blocks into proper position. All blocks should be placed carefully, but the first course and the corners deserve special attention. Starting right makes all that follows much easier. Lay the corners first and then stretch a line as an additional alignment guide and so you will have something against which you can check the height of each block (**5–53**).

5–50

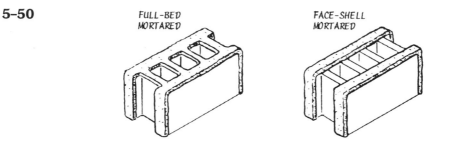

FULL-BED MORTARED   FACE-SHELL MORTARED

5–51

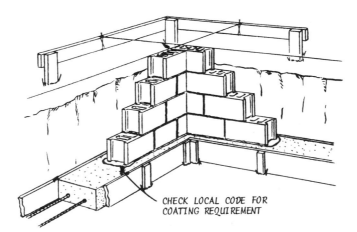

CHECK LOCAL CODE FOR COATING REQUIREMENT

5-52

5-53

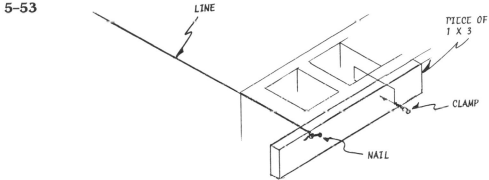

Build up the corners after the first course is complete. A story pole—often called a course pole—can be an accuracy aid for establishing masonry heights in each course. Such items can be rented, but one you make yourself as shown in **5-54** will do as well. Mark the vertical piece to designate masonry units and joints. This can be done with a pencil, or with different-width adhesive tapes; even tapes of different colors can be used to indicate special places like door or window openings.

5–54

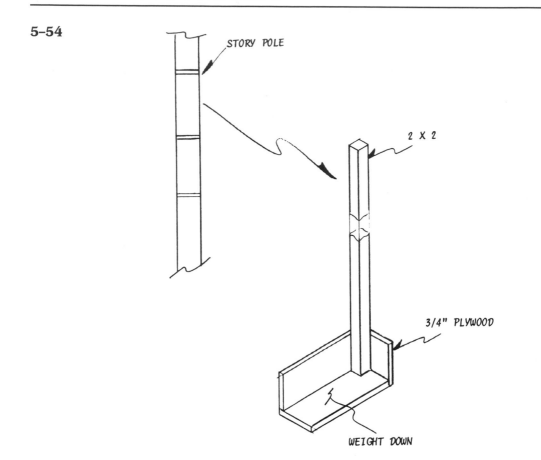

STORY POLE

2 X 2

3/4" PLYWOOD

WEIGHT DOWN

Build up the corners three, four, or even five courses high, but work constantly with a level, checking vertically, horizontally, and diagonally on each block and on the assembly as it progresses (**5–55**).

With corners up, you can fill in the wall between, working each course to a stretched line that you can hold in place as shown in **5–56**. If the wall is long and the line might sag, set up an intermediate block as shown in **5–57**. Hold down the flashing with another block.

Place each unit carefully to minimize jiggling that must be done to achieve alignment. If you work from the back side of the wall and tip the block a bit toward you, you'll be able to see the edge of the course below. This should help you to get a pretty accurate placement right off. The action should combine a slight roll to vertical position with a shove that puts the block solidly against the adjacent one. If you do this right, very little tapping with the trowel handle will be required to finish the placement (**5–58**). Be sure that you make

5-55

5-56

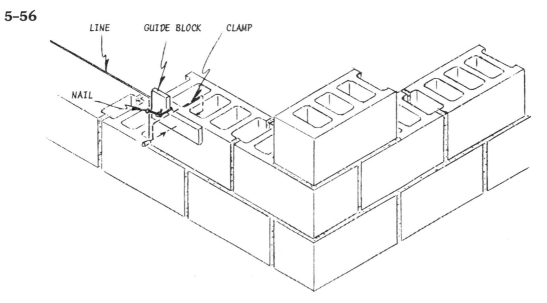

LINE   GUIDE BLOCK   CLAMP

NAIL

5-57

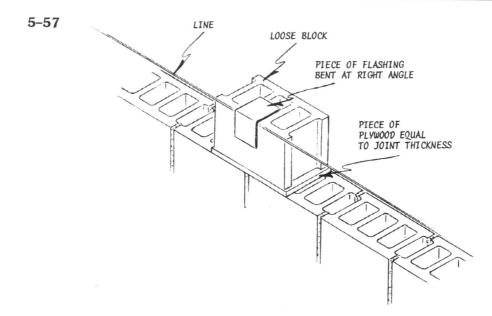

LINE

LOOSE BLOCK

PIECE OF FLASHING
BENT AT RIGHT ANGLE

PIECE OF
PLYWOOD EQUAL
TO JOINT THICKNESS

any block adjustment while the mortar is soft and plastic. If you move things after the mortar has stiffened, you'll break the bond, and that will cause problems later.

The closure block, the last unit in a course, gets special attention. Apply generous amounts of mortar to all four vertical edges of the block and to all edges of the opening (**5–59**). Lower the block carefully into position to be sure no mortar falls out. If you do lose mortar, which may cause an open joint, take the block out and repeat the operation after applying fresh mortar.

Tall block walls that are speedily erected and backfilled may require bracing for temporary support (**5–60**). The idea is to be sure the structure is knit solidly before stresses are applied.

The tops of foundation walls should be capped with a course of solid masonry units that will act as a termite barrier and also help to distribute loads. When solid blocks are not used, the cores in the top course can be filled with mortar or concrete. To do this, you must place a strip of metal lath in the mortar joint under the top course. The strip, which is just wide enough to cover the block cavities, forms a base for the fill you use in the top course.

REINFORCEMENT

Long walls, or walls subjected to above-average stresses, can be strengthened with pilasters. You can see in **5–61** how a typical design forms an interlock of units. In practice,

5-58

5-59

5-60

5–61

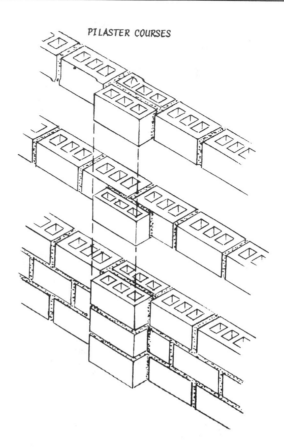

PILASTER COURSES

the design and size of the structure plus earth conditions must be considered when determining the need for pilasters and their size and frequency. Check codes; if such reinforcement is required, all units in the pilaster should have full mortar bedding.

Rebar is often used but, again, the need for it and the way it is used depend on local conditions. But it pays to place a ½-inch bar in each corner and to fill those cores solidly with mortar or concrete (**5–62**). If you anticipate this need, the bar can be embedded in the footing pour as a tie from wall to base. Often, especially on high walls and those that must withstand considerable pressures from slopes or backfilling, special reinforcement wire is placed in the joint of alternate courses (**5–63**).

CONTROL JOINTS

The purpose of control joints is to permit stress movements to occur without damaging the structure. Whether or not they are needed at all depends mostly on the length of the

5-62

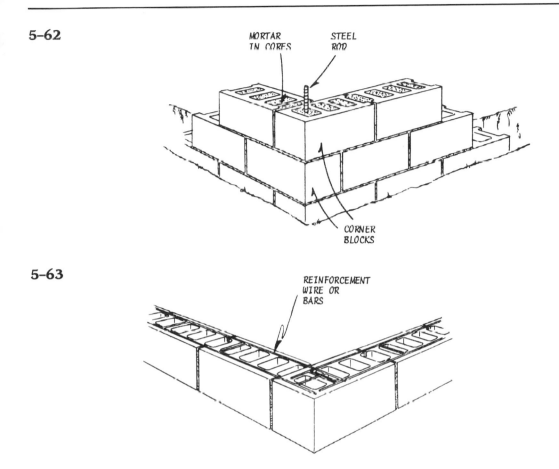

MORTAR IN CORES

STEEL ROD

CORNER BLOCKS

5-63

REINFORCEMENT WIRE OR BARS

wall. A basic stress joint is simply a continuous, vertical joint made by combining half and full-length blocks at the control point (**5-64**). Another type can be made with common stretcher block if Z-shaped metal ties are placed in alternate courses (**5-65**). The ties are narrower than the wall width and provide lateral support on each side of the joint. Offset jamb blocks, also reinforced with metal ties, may be used in similar fashion (**5-66**). A common procedure is to insert roofing felt into the channel of the block so that mortar can't bond the units together (**5-67**). Cut the paper so it will be long enough for the full length of the joint, and wide enough to span across it. Fill the channel with mortar to contribute lateral support.

There are also tongue-and-groove blocks that are available in half and full units (**5-68**). They provide much lateral support because of the way they are shaped. Such special shapes may not be available in all areas. Usually, control joints are incorporated every 25 to 30 feet.

5-64

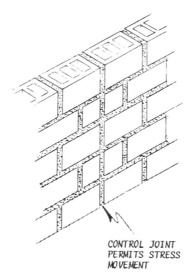

CONTROL JOINT
PERMITS STRESS
MOVEMENT

5-65

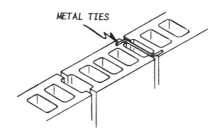

METAL TIES

5-66

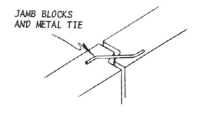

JAMB BLOCKS
AND METAL TIE

5-67

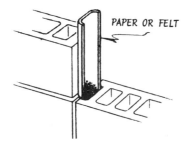

PAPER OR FELT

5-68

TONGUE & GROOVE BLOCKS

WALL INTERSECTIONS

Bearing walls should not be tied together with a masonry bond unless they occur at a corner. Let one wall terminate against the face of the other and include a control joint at that point. Tie bars, which supply lateral support, should not be spaced more than 4 feet apart vertically (**5–69**).

Nonbearing walls can be tied to other walls by using strips of lath or mesh across the common joint in alternate courses (**5–70**). If the nonbearing wall is to be constructed later, incorporate the ties in the first wall so they will be available when needed.

5–69

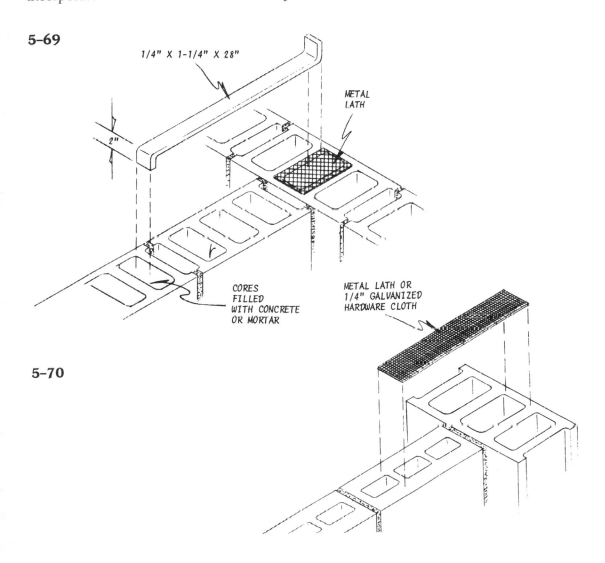

1/4" X 1-1/4" X 28"

2"

METAL
LATH

CORES
FILLED
WITH CONCRETE
OR MORTAR

METAL LATH OR
1/4" GALVANIZED
HARDWARE CLOTH

5–70

OPENINGS

Precast lintels, which do the same job that headers do in a wood frame, are often used to span the opening over doors and windows (**5–71**). Notice how the use of half and full units in this example produces a uniform appearance without the need to cut blocks. Make cast-in-place lintels by providing a temporary support frame or by including a permanent frame as you erect the blocks. Special lintel blocks, which can be filled with concrete and reinforced with steel bars, are available (**5–72**).

Frames installed as block work goes on can be locked in place with galvanized nails used as ties as shown in **5–73**. In such situations, be sure you use a level on the wood members as frequently as you do on the blocks.

Precast lintels, shaped to correspond with special jamb blocks, are often used over door and window openings for modular units (**5–74**). Channel blocks are used for windows that have steel or aluminum frames (**5–75**). The best bet is to lay up block on one side of the opening to the full height of the window. Place the window and align it by using wooden wedges, or whatever. Special wedges or fasteners to secure the window frame in

5–71

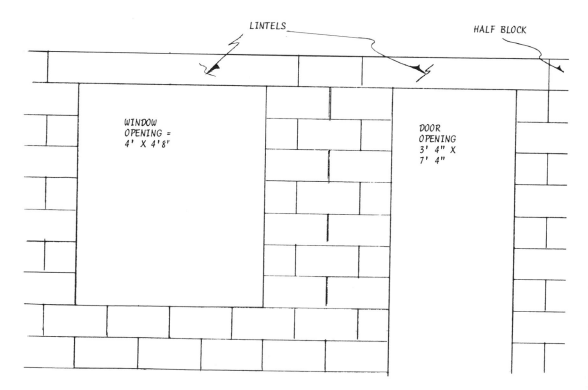

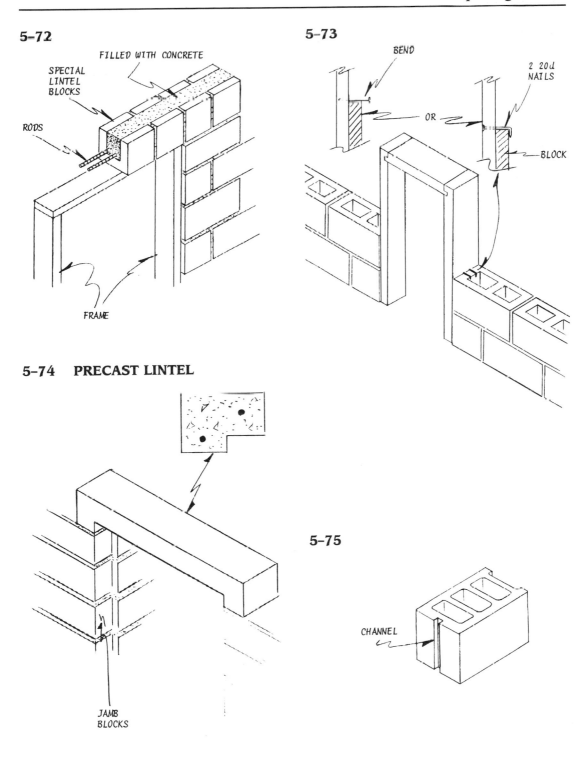

5-72

SPECIAL LINTEL BLOCKS

FILLED WITH CONCRETE

RODS

FRAME

5-73

BEND

2 20d NAILS

OR

BLOCK

5-74   PRECAST LINTEL

JAMB BLOCKS

5-75

CHANNEL

the channel are usually supplied by the manufacturer. You can also install steel channel to support blocks the way bricks are supported over the opening of a fireplace. You'll need to match the size and strength of the steel to the span and load on the wall above.

Sills may be cast in place, or can be precast units as shown in **5–76** that you bond to the masonry. In such cases, be sure you seal end joints completely by packing them tight with mortar or caulking (**5–77**).

Beam or girder pockets can be done by omitting a block from the top course—or a half block, if beam size permits—and then filling the opening with a solid block (**5–78**). Much depends on the size of the member to be supported. Sometimes it's necessary to do some block cutting to shape out a pocket. Two ways you can provide openings through block walls for crawl-space ventilation are shown in **5–79**.

5–76

5–77

5–78

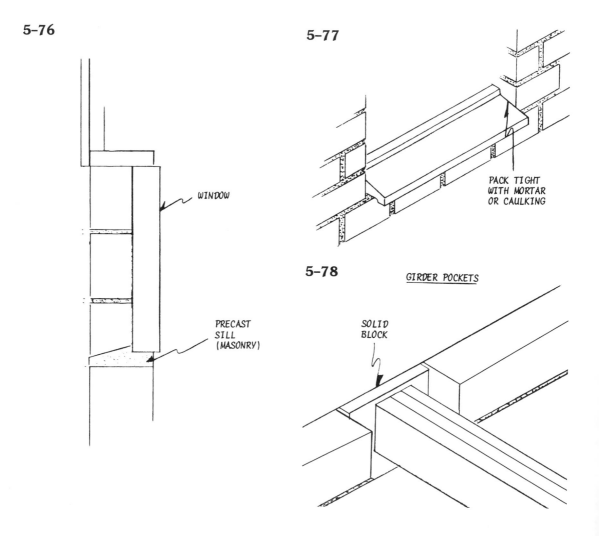

WINDOW

PACK TIGHT
WITH MORTAR
OR CAULKING

GIRDER POCKETS

PRECAST
SILL
(MASONRY)

SOLID
BLOCK

5-79

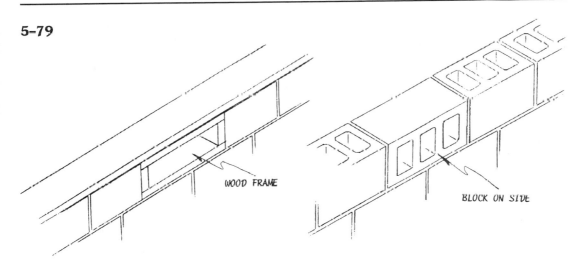

WOOD FRAME

BLOCK ON SIDE

ANCHOR BOLTS

There are several types of anchor bolts that are used to fasten the wooden sill, typically a pressure-treated 2 × 6, to the top of the foundation wall. The most common is hooked on one end and threaded on the other as shown in **5–80**. The bolts should be spaced following **5–81** pretty closely, but moving some an inch or two either way to clear a spot where a stud will be placed is okay. Or you could beat this problem by recessing the nut and cutting off any extra threads if the bolt happens to fall in the wrong spot. Generally, the amount of thread that extends above the sill is not critical as long as the nut can go on all the way with at least a ½ inch to spare. Placement of the sill is critical in slab work with integral footings where studs are attached directly to plates (**5–82**).

5-80

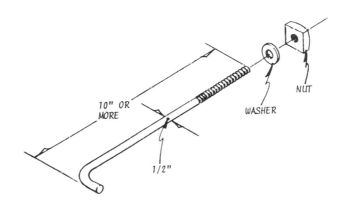

10" OR MORE

1/2"

WASHER

NUT

5-81

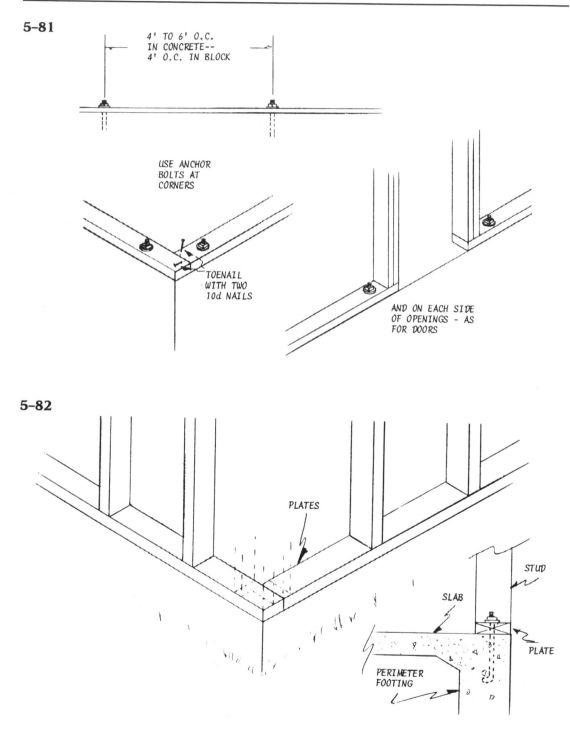

4' TO 6' O.C.
IN CONCRETE--
4' O.C. IN BLOCK

USE ANCHOR
BOLTS AT
CORNERS

TOENAIL
WITH TWO
10d NAILS

AND ON EACH SIDE
OF OPENINGS - AS
FOR DOORS

5-82

PLATES

STUD

SLAB

PLATE

PERIMETER
FOOTING

Whether you set anchor bolts in a concrete pour or mortar-filled voids in block, you need to keep them plumb and at the correct level as the mix hardens around them. One option is to make temporary holders that will keep the bolts centered, ensure correct projection above the pour, and suspend them vertically. You can make holders from scrap pieces of 1-inch wood, or use 2-inch material to simulate the sill. Drill holes to accommodate the bolt and tack-nail the wood to the top edges of the forms (**5–83**).

Anchor bolts in block walls are organized as shown in **5–84**. Positions are anticipated and a piece of metal lath is placed in the joint under the cores that will receive the bolt. Later, the cores are filled with concrete or mortar and the anchor bolt is embedded (**5–85**). When all the top cores of the blocks are to be packed, the metal lath should be installed the full length of the joint.

In all situations, be sure you do not tighten the nut until the concrete or mortar has hardened. It's also important to shield the exposed threads as you pour and until the sills

5–83

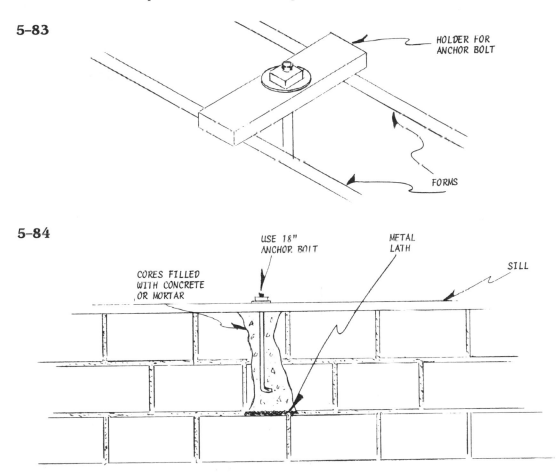

HOLDER FOR
ANCHOR BOLT

FORMS

5–84

USE 18"
ANCHOR BOLT

METAL
LATH

SILL

CORES FILLED
WITH CONCRETE
OR MORTAR

5–85

are attached. If concrete or mortar hardens on threads, you'll have to wire-brush them clean for the nuts to thread.

CONCRETE FLOORS

Slab-on-ground floors are the standard finish for basement floors. But they are desirable even in crawl spaces, although somewhat extravagant compared to a vapor barrier laid over several inches of gravel.

The slab design, which includes reinforcement requirements and drainage considerations, must be in accordance with local codes. Generally, you need to reinforce the pour with welded wire. In some areas, such as earthquake zones, you need to install ½-inch steel bars running the full length and width of the slab about 4 feet apart on centers.

Insulation and moisture controls are critical, and subgrades, typically soil covered by 4 or more inches of gravel, must be thoroughly compacted. The choice of a subbase often is based on what's available locally, such as gravel or crushed stone or slag, generally ranging in piece sizes from ½ inch to 1 inch so that there will be air spaces in the fill. These spaces have insulating qualities and reduce the capillary movement of moisture that might be present, or appear later, in the subsoil.

All mechanical installations such as heating ducts, pipes for radiant heating and water, and other utility entries should be completed and pressure-checked for leaks before the slab is poured. Water lines, when placed under a concrete floor, must be established in trenches that are deep enough to prevent them from freezing.

Drainpipes around a footing are a minimum precaution to prevent water accumulation under a slab. Soil that drains poorly usually calls for a granular fill and a special drain line leading to a positive outlet to carry away any water that would otherwise accumulate under the slab. If floor drains are used, the slab should be sloped accordingly, but with care to ensure a uniform slab thickness.

When there is the possibility of excessive water pressure under the slab, steel reinforcement to withstand the uplift pressure must be introduced. Often, such a slab is poured in two layers with a built-up bituminous membrane between them as a water block. The membrane consists of hot bituminous material and at least two layers of roofing felt. The membrane is continuous and carried up the foundation wall to the top surface of the slab.

Perimeter insulation is important to reduce heat loss from the slab to the outside. Rigid insulation, stable enough to resist wet concrete, is recommended. Thicknesses can vary and are often specified in relation to local temperatures and the type of heating to be installed.

Methods that provide for movement of the slab vary, but a common one is shown in **5–86**. The wood pieces are removed after the concrete has set and the groove is filled with a caulking compound. Perimeter nailers, if needed for work that comes later, can be installed as shown in **5 87**. The drawings in **5–88** are examples only and should not

5–86

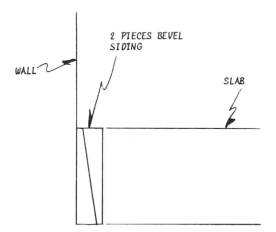

WALL

2 PIECES BEVEL SIDING

SLAB

5-87

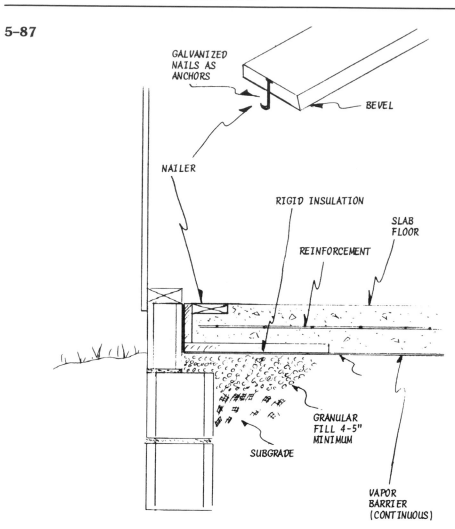

GALVANIZED NAILS AS ANCHORS

BEVEL

NAILER

RIGID INSULATION

SLAB FLOOR

REINFORCEMENT

GRANULAR FILL 4-5" MINIMUM

SUBGRADE

VAPOR BARRIER (CONTINUOUS)

be used as working drawings until they have been checked against local codes. The most common modern installation at joints between the slab and the foundation walls is backer rod, often covered by flexible caulk. This foam strip seals the seam while still allowing movement.

TERMITE PROTECTION

In regions where termite infestation is a problem, steps must be taken to block the termites between the ground and the wood (typically the sill) at the foundation. Never bury any

5 88   FOR VERY WET SOILS

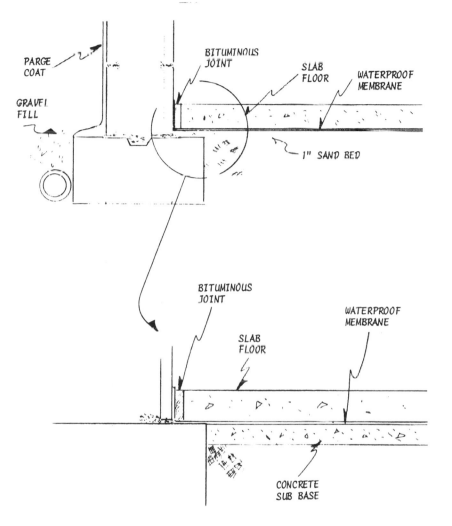

wood debris near a building, and make sure that you've cleared away grade stakes and footing forms. Place metal termite shields between the foundation and the sill for wall foundations. For slabs, a few inches of termite sand or diatomaceous earth on top of your vapor barrier should deter any termites from living underneath your floor. In some regions, the sand must be treated with an insecticide; consult with the building inspector. Bear in mind that in the most southern regions there are flying termites that can thwart typical ground-approach defenses.

6

FRAMING: GENERAL CONSIDERATIONS

Before we get into the details of putting together a solid house frame, it pays to think about what the frame will be made of.

Almost all houses are framed with wood. A small percentage use steel, which is formed into U-shapes that make hollow studs and joists. Steel takes longer to erect than wood, is less forgiving, generally more expensive, and reserved primarily for commercial structures and buildings with the most stringent fire codes. But if you are building in an area where the building will be subject to unusual stresses, including very high winds and possible earthquakes, steel is worth investigating.

Even with wood framing there are many choices. You can use dimensional 2-by lumber throughout the building, and build up large beams by nailing together several boards. But modern lumber, called engineered lumber, offers some interesting alternatives.

I-BEAM JOISTS AND COMPOSITE LUMBER

Some improvements in construction are really just cost-saving measures for the contractor who wants to use fewer materials and install them in less time. But plywood-web joists, often called I-beam joists due to the shape of two 2 × 4s on the flat separated by a piece of plywood, have some real benefits for owner–builders.

These and other types of modern, engineered timbers (**6–1**) work by using beefy material where it's most needed to carry loads and provide nailing for finished flooring above and a drywall ceiling below—near the top and bottom of the joist. But between the two heavier members, typically made of 2 × 4s, there is a sheet of plywood. That makes the timbers lightweight and easy to handle, and often less expensive than solid timbers. The lumber typically is available in sizes from 9½ to 16 inches deep.

6-1 (Photo courtesy of Georgia–Pacific.)

Another advantage is that the I-beam shape makes it possible to increase the span without increasing the depth of the joists as much as you would have to with solid lumber such as 2 × 10s. That can save you a few inches of headroom, or eliminate extra support posts in a basement. You could order single-piece, 32-foot-long, composite 2 × 10s, for example, that are strong enough to meet building codes when placed 24-inch on center with only one central girder support. Single pieces also can offer consistent quality and uniformity, compared to typical dimensional lumber.

The main drawback is extra time required at the ends of the joists, on most designs, because the plywood ribs don't provide a solid nailing surface. Where one of these joists meets another at right angles, you have to make the connection with special joist hardware designed for I-beams because the plywood webs themselves are too thin for nailing.

Where you need more strength and larger timbers, generally for girders that support rows of joists, you can use solid-wood beams (often at premium prices), assemble your own beams from 2-by lumber, or use a composite beam—another example of engineered lumber. There are several types of composites. *Glue-laminated beams* are made of lumber finger-jointed together in long lengths and joined with waterproof glue. *Laminated veneer lumber (LVL)* is made of wood plies assembled with glue into 1¾-inch thicknesses. *Parallel-strand lumber* is made up of small overlapping strips of lumber and glue, and is available in beams up to seven inches thick that can hold massive amounts of weight.

These engineered beams and joists are more often used on developments by crews of carpenters than on a house by an owner–builder. They take some getting used to. But the lumber is code-approved and well accepted by local inspectors.

LUMBER QUALITY

Whether you buy wood at an old-fashioned lumberyard or a brand new home center, the quality probably isn't what it used to be—for one reason: The rules that suppliers use to grade lumber haven't changed since a major revision was made in 1970—but the wood has. In the 1990s and into the 2000s, an increasing amount has been milled from young, fast-growing trees that are not as dense as the timber supply used even ten years ago. The younger trees have wider growth rings, are generally smaller in diameter, and yield a greater percentage of lumber with knots.

The decline in quality causes problems for professional builders and do-it-yourselfers alike. Contractors have to return more lumber than they used to, which is an option not always available to do-it-yourselfers. Year 2000 surveys by the National Association of Homebuilders indicate that some builders report an increase in callbacks due to popped drywall nails, open trim joints, and squeaking floors caused by framing that did not dry to a uniform and stable moisture content before it was installed. Complaints also come from framing subcontractors who have to pick through deliveries (returning as many as one in seven timbers), and still lose time bracing and straightening crooked studs.

With structural lumber such as 2 × 4 studs, you need to discard any lengths that are obviously heavier than the rest. The extra weight is due to extra moisture, and apart from obvious damage such as a long split, excessive moisture is the cause of most lumber problems. When the wood dries out in the walls of your house, moisture leaves spaces between the strands of wood grain. As the grain shifts into the cavities, the lumber shrinks (often unevenly), and can twist, warp, cup, and split. Framing lumber needs to be more stable—and should be because structural grades commonly used in construction are rated to contain less than 20 percent moisture. You may notice a grade stamp that says 19% MC (moisture content).

Ideally, your lumber should be true enough to install in a modular layout and stay where you put it. When it's not, try one of these maneuvers. When a series of joists or rafters aren't parallel because a few bow in or out along the run, straighten them out with a temporary brace at midspan. Duplicate the perimeter layout on a long board, bring any bowed timbers in line with your marks, and tack them there. Leave the brace on until you lock up the timbers with plywood (on roof rafters or floor joists), or with other surface boards on a deck.

When a stud or joist won't move in line with your square layout mark on an adjoining timber, a toenail may do. Drive a nail at an angle through the side of the board into the adjoining timber. This can apply just enough sideways force to shift it into place. For more leverage, attach a clamp near the end of the twisted piece and bend it into proper position for nailing.

To bring a bowed deck board into line, you can drive a chisel or flat bar into the supporting joist and use it as a level to pull the board into place. There are specialized, contractor-grade tools for this job, including an unusual cam-action, double-bar tool called the BoWrench (made by the Cepco Tool Company) (**6–2**). One of the bars has two pins that lock

6–2 (Photo courtesy of Cepco Tool Company.)

around the joist below, while the other bar uses a cam action to straighten the deck board above. The tool maintains pressure so you can let go of the handle to nail the board. If you need to shift a series of timbers, you'll probably need the force of a come-along. It consists of two cables with a ratchet-action winch between them. You can tie several boards together with bracing, hook on one cable (protecting the wood from its wires), and then anchor the other cable to the foundation, a braced corner post, or even a tree. When you crank the winch, the timbers hooked up to the first cable will gradually come into place.

A LOOK AT BASIC FRAMING TOOLS

A handsaw will work, of course, but a circular saw is easier and faster. A 7½-inch model is good for overall framing work. Smaller saws can't cut through a 2 × 4 in one pass, and larger ones are unwieldy. Use a combination blade for cutting with and across the grain; a blade with about 24 teeth is included with many saws.

When it comes to hammers, on most new construction work the pros use air-powered tools and shoot nails into lumber with a squeeze of the trigger. Air power is nice but impractical for most do-it-yourselfers. You need to buy the expensive tools to begin with, plus a compressor, and do all your work tethered to an air hose. It's generally better to use a basic 16- or 20-ounce claw hammer instead. It's maneuverable in tight spaces and light enough to use for more than a few minutes. Heavier hammers pack more punch—on misshits as well as on nails—but a big hammer with a straight ripping claw can be cumbersome in the confines of framing laced with pipes and wires. Try handles of fiberglass or steel with special inserts and grip rings and rubber sleeves—whatever feels best.

In tight spots where you don't have enough room to swing a hammer, use a drill and drive screws that have more holding power than nails. A corded drill will do, although an 18-volt cordless drill and a spare battery pack with charger offer more flexibility and enough staying power. Fit the drill with a screw-driving bit, or a boring bit to drill pilot holes for screws if you have trouble driving them. You can simplify the operation by using a quick-change accessory. It fastens into the chuck of the drill, and has a snap-in and snap-out sleeve that accepts boring bits and screwing bits. Another handy option is an extension sleeve that fastens into the chuck around a screw-driving bit. The idea is to fit the screw head onto the driving head of the bit, and then slip the sleeve over the screw so you can drive it in a straight line. The little gadget prevents the bit from jumping off the screw.

USING FRAMING HARDWARE

Most framing connections are held together with nails. They do a good job where you can drive them through the face of one board into the end grain of another—for example, when you nail a horizontal 2 × 4 onto the ends of vertical studs. Nails have much less holding power when toenailed—driven at a steep angle through the side of one board into another. On new framing work, most timbers can be face-nailed. But to make a secure connection that bears up under loads and conforms to codes, also install frame hardware.

The most common piece is a U-shaped metal bracket that fits around the end of a joist where it butts up against a second board, as in **6–3**. On the sides of the U-shape are flanges, perforated for nailing like the rest of the fixture, that rest against the second

6–3

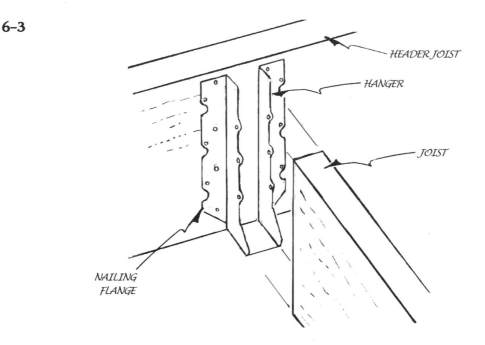

HEADER JOIST

HANGER

JOIST

NAILING
FLANGE

board. You can install the hardware where you need to nail a connection, and then fit the lumber into the bracket. If you're not sure exactly where the lumber will go, toenail it temporarily, then fit the bracket around the joint. Face-nail through the bracket into the first board, through the flanges into the second board, and the connection won't be able to shift.

There is similar hardware formed into shapes that wrap around almost every conceivable wood joint, including double-wide girders and angled rafters. Large manufacturers, such as Simpson Strong-Tie Co., offer hundreds of hardware configurations, including frame hardware designed specially to resist the excessive forces on houses located in areas with high winds or other loads. Bear in mind that hangers are generally required and not just an extra one where one horizontal timber butts at a right angle against a header joist.

TERMITES–YOU DON'T NEED THEM

Termites present a potential problem in most areas of the country. In some cases, they create very minor deterioration, while in others they can seriously damage the wood in your house. If you feel, as some do, that the dangers of termite damage have been greatly exaggerated, you might want to do some research in your area before taking any precautions. But be sure to check with your local inspector about termite shields and other possible requirements.

A common precaution is a continuous strip of 26-gauge metal placed as shown in **6–4** between the foundation and the sill. Let the shield extend from the foundation for about 2 inches at a 46–degree angle. Actually, this step is only a supplement to good construction.

6–4

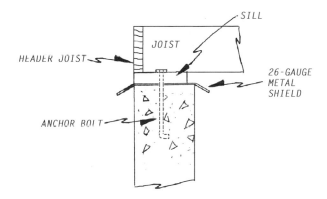

Shields alone may not be adequate. Because termites live underground, a logical procedure is to treat the soil under and around the house with a chemical that is toxic to the insects. You can have this done by licensed professionals, although some people would just as soon dispense with the use of toxic chemicals in and around their house. If you're interested in treatments, there are some alternatives, such as nematodes. You may have to search for a licensed pest control operator (PCO) who uses them instead of chemicals, but it's worth investigating.

Another approach is to use wood that has some natural resistance to termites, like construction-grade heart redwood, or more often these days, pressure-treated 2 × 6s for sills. The sill boards are important because they are the first pieces of wood above the masonry, which termites can't eat.

General anti-termite procedures call for keeping the work area clean of debris. It's important not to bury wood scraps when you backfill the foundation. Also, the sill and other wood members should be at least 6 to 8 inches above grade. A sign of termite activity is the earth tubes they build over nonwood materials to get from soil to food. You might check foundations frequently and take the necessary steps if you see such tubes.

INSTALLING SILLS

The sills, often called mudsills, are placed on the top of the foundation continuously around the structure and secured with anchor bolts, nuts, and washers. The usual material is 2 × 6 PT lumber, long enough, if possible, to run the full length of walls, although 2 × 8s are often used when the foundation is concrete block. Set the sill pieces against the anchor bolts and use a square to mark the locations of the holes you must drill. Make the holes about ¼ inch larger than the diameter of the bolts so there will be some play to make alignment of the sills easier.

The next step is to roll out a layer of sill insulation, and possibly install your termite shield. Special insulation rolls are available to fit foundations, and are an important energy-saving feature, particularly when the top of the foundation is rough, allowing air leaks between the sill and the masonry.

Place the sill pieces over the anchor bolts as they are drilled, but do not tighten the nuts until all pieces are placed and correctly aligned. The sills, in addition to being straight, should be level. Carpenters sometimes use wooden shims to fill depressions in masonry, but this is bound to leave openings between the foundation and the sill, even with an insulation barrier. It's better to do the job with mortar. Another common practice is to place a full bed of mortar on the foundation wall. This provides a good seal and the sill can be leveled without introducing other materials. Insulation should not be used as a means of leveling the sill.

Use large washers under all nuts. Walk around the foundation several times, tightening each nut an equal amount as you go. Adjoining pieces of sill, whether end-to-end or at corners as shown in **6-5**, should be secured by toenailing with 10d nails. Bear in mind that codes in some areas of the country may call for a sill thicker than the standard 2 × 6. Such sills can be solid material, in which case the anchor bolts provide sufficient security, or they can be built up by doubling 2-by material as shown in **6-6**. Use 10d nails to attach the upper piece, driving two nails at each end of each piece and spacing those between about 24 inches in a staggered pattern.

TYPES OF FRAMING

Before getting to the actual assembly of the house frame, it may pay to look at types of frames so you can preview the steps ahead and become acquainted with some of the

6-5

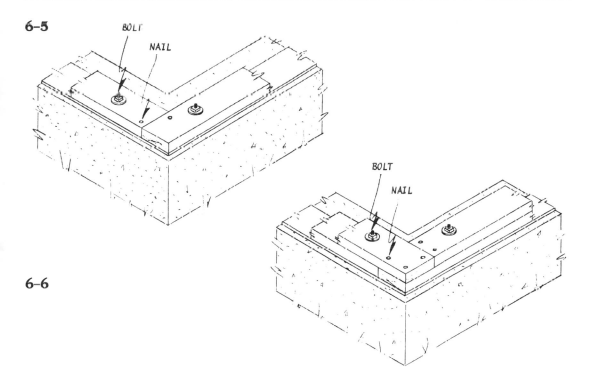

6-6

nomenclature. Platform framing is the standard today, while balloon framing was popular many decades ago. In both cases, the structural members have a nominal thickness of 2 inches, which actually is 1½ inches. This reduction in thickness also applies to widths. A 2 × 4 actually measures 1 × ½ × 3½ inches, and a 2 × 12 will be 1½ × 11½ inches, but there are small variations.

In platform frames, the floor frame consists of joists that span the foundation walls and have intermediate supports where they are required. We'll talk about bridging, openings through floors, and other factors later. Once the joist assembly is complete, it is covered with subflooring, as shown in **6-7**. At this point, you have a working platform and a solid structure on which to erect walls. It's the common system with carpenters because the platform becomes a large workbench on which wall-frame sections can be preassembled and then tilted into place.

The same floor-framing procedure is followed if the house has a second story, except that instead of the joists resting on a sill and foundation, they are supported by the studs and plates that compose the perimeter walls, as shown in **6-8**. With this system, you use the first platform to create a second platform.

The basic design of interior walls does not differ radically from the stud-and-plate arrangement of perimeter walls. Bearing partitions (generally, those that run at right

6–7

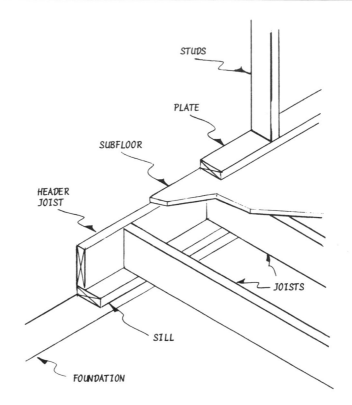

STUDS

PLATE

SUBFLOOR

HEADER
JOIST

JOISTS

SILL

FOUNDATION

angles to joists) are designed as shown in **6–9**. Note that the fire blocks (or fire stops), which do much to retard the spread of fire, also act as solid bridging to hold the joists parallel and plumb. Such pieces should be cut carefully so they will be uniform in length and have square ends.

In old-fashioned balloon framing, the studs run continuously from the sill to the plates, which support the roof rafters. Standard framing at the sill has the joists surface-nailed to the sides of the studs and includes fire blocks placed as shown in **6–10**. A design variation of this system is the T-sill, shown in **6–11**, which employs a continuous strip to serve as both a header and fire blocking. The subflooring is notched to fit around the studs as shown in **6–12**. Studs are notched at the second-floor level to receive a ribbon on which the joists will rest (**6–13**). The joists are placed so they can be nailed to the sides of the studs, and fire blocking is introduced as shown in **6–14**.

A bearing partition in a balloon frame is organized as shown in **6–15**. Framing over a crawl space, shown for a platform in **6–16**, does not differ from the methods already

6-8

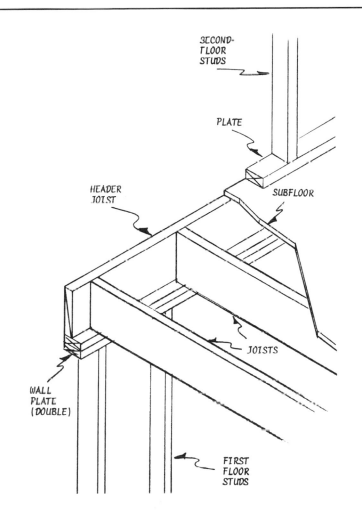

SECOND-FLOOR STUDS

PLATE

HEADER JOIST

SUBFLOOR

JOISTS

WALL PLATE (DOUBLE)

FIRST FLOOR STUDS

described; only the use of pier-and-post supports for beams or girders differs from similar components that may be needed when a basement is part of the structure. But very few balloon-framed houses have been built in the last 30 years or so, for good reasons: It takes too long, and the supply of very long and straight studs required basically doesn't exist anymore.

JOISTS

Joists are horizontal, structural components, placed on edge, which carry loads to girders and sills. They must be strong and stiff enough to carry loads over the span areas. The

6-9

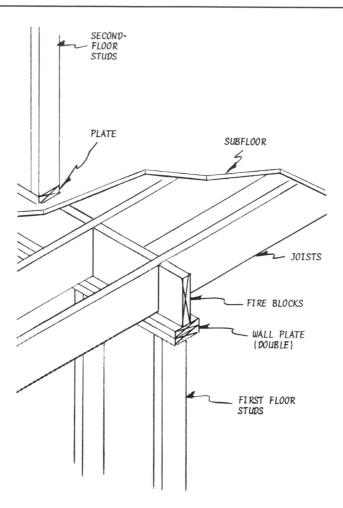

thickness, width, and spacing of joists together with sizes and spacing of subsupports (beams or girders) are determined by the load placed on them. That varies because structures with tile roofs, plastered walls and ceilings, and the like are heavier than structures with shingles, plywood walls, and acoustical ceilings.

It's important to remember that there is no one set of rules about lumber sizing. There will be a local building-code standard that has to be met. Joists in living spaces generally are required to carry a load of 40 pounds per square foot. Joists in an attic would need to meet the same standard for the space to become an area for living, but a lower standard, such as 20 pounds per square foot, for light storage. But whatever the standard is, there are several different ways to meet it. That's the complicated part of sizing joists—and rafters, headers, and other lumber that carries loads and spans open spaces. And that's

6-10

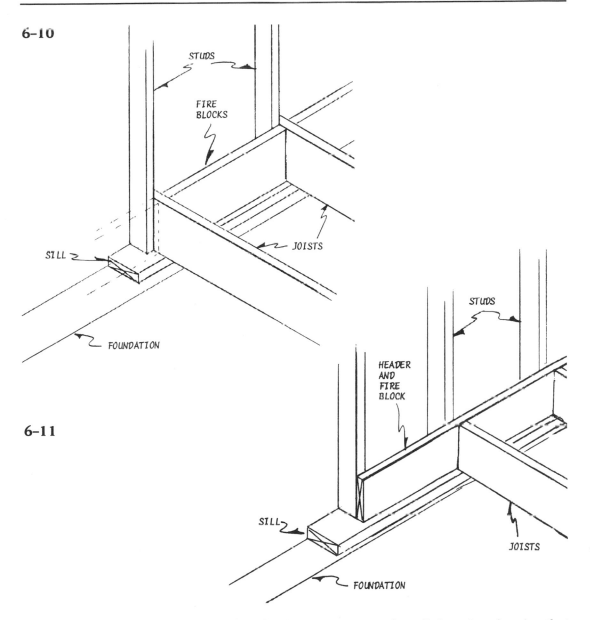

STUDS

FIRE
BLOCKS

SILL

JOISTS

FOUNDATION

6-11

STUDS

HEADER
AND
FIRE
BLOCK

SILL

JOISTS

FOUNDATION

why the local building department isn't likely to grant a permit until there is a drawing that shows each major component of the frame with a label about its size—whether you put the label there or the inspector does.

The size of the joist material is the biggest and most obvious factor because a 2 × 6 can't hold as much weight as a 2 × 10. Spacing also counts, because joists set 16 inches

6–12

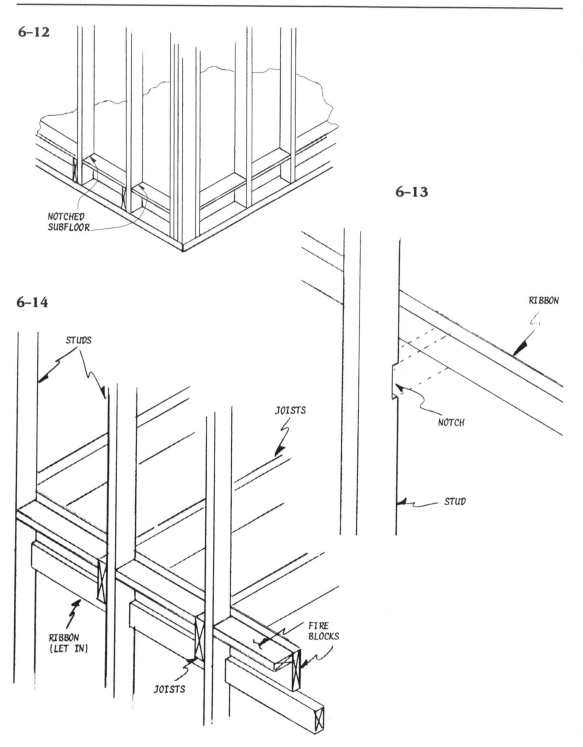

NOTCHED
SUBFLOOR

6–13

6–14

STUDS

JOISTS

RIBBON

NOTCH

STUD

RIBBON
(LET IN)

JOISTS

FIRE
BLOCKS

6-15

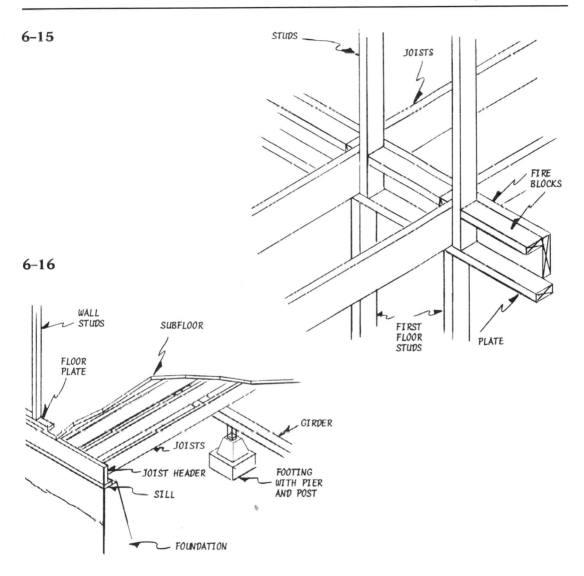

STUDS

JOISTS

FIRE BLOCKS

FIRST FLOOR STUDS

PLATE

6-16

WALL STUDS

SUBFLOOR

FLOOR PLATE

GIRDER

JOISTS

JOIST HEADER

FOOTING WITH PIER AND POST

SILL

FOUNDATION

on center can hold more weight than joists set 24 inches on center. If you cut the floor span in half by installing a girder at midspan, you can use smaller joists. If you want unobstructed space below the floor, you need larger joists. If you use engineered lumber, you'll need less of it because it generally provides more strength for the amount of wood used. If you use dimensional lumber, you'll find that one wood species is stronger and can span longer distances than another. Although the variations among different types of wood are shown on span tables, as a practical matter you'll be building with the type of lumber that's available locally.

If you're economizing, you can try to use the smallest possible size that codes allow. As a general guide with readily available lumber such as #2 Douglas fir, span limits still change with joist size and spacing to meet code for a 40-pound load per square foot. With spacing variations, for example, if you use 2 × 8s set 12 inches on center, you can span 14 feet, 2 inches. With 16-inch centers, the span limit decreases to 12 feet, 10 inches. With 24-inch centers, it decreases to 11 feet, 3 inches. With size variations, for example, if you use 2 × 6s on 16-inch centers, you can span 9 feet, 9 inches. Increase the size to 2 × 8s for a span of 12 feet, 10 inches, to 2 × 10s for a span of 16 feet, 5 inches, and to 2 × 12s for a span of 19 feet, 11 inches.

But for average-size rooms, it's generally a good idea to use 2 × 10 joists, and stick with them to maintain an even platform through the floor. Although you may need 2 × 12s or additional girders in larger areas, 2 × 10s offer several advantages. They provide ample room in the framing bays to run pipes, wires, ducts, and insulation where needed—for example, where the floor overhangs the foundation. Also, they provide a rigid floor with little or no flex that is suitable for almost any finish, including tile over an extra plywood underlayment. Although you can consult span tables as you work up your plans, remember that it's the local building inspector who has the final word on sizing.

GIRDERS, BEAMS, AND POSTS

Joists are supported where necessary between foundation walls by girders (also called beams). The ends of the girders rest on the foundation walls in the pockets provided for them, and they are supported at intermediate points with posts. The girders should bear a minimum of 4 inches on the foundation and should clear the walls of the pocket by ½ inch on both sides and the end.

The girders can be solid lumber, or they can be assembled by using pieces of 2-by material. **Figure 6–17** shows a 40-foot girder built up from six 20-foot pieces and a 24-foot girder built up from six 12-foot pieces. Both are three-piece girders that have three layers of 2-by boards. There is no reason why you can't work with other boards of standard lengths, but the joint design should follow what is shown in the examples. Drive 20d nails from each side (for a three-piece girder), positioning two near each end of each piece and spacing others about 24 inches apart in a staggered pattern. A two-piece girder is nailed the same way, but with 10d nails. For a four-piece girder, add a fourth board to the three-piece design with 20d nails. In all situations, the joint in a built-up girder should occur over a support post. Often a bolster, with a cross section that matches the girder's, is used between post and girder (**6–18**). It does help somewhat to distribute loads, but it is used mostly to provide a decorative detail.

In most situations, the cross-sectional dimensions of a wood post should match the

6–17

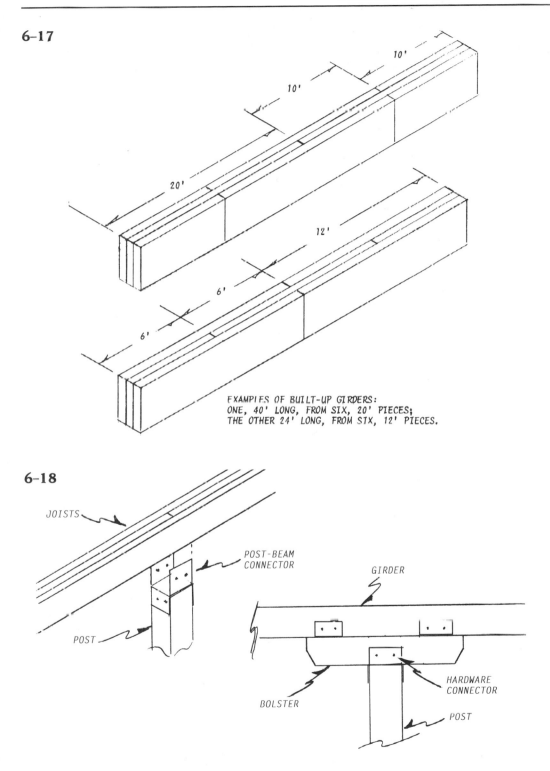

EXAMPLES OF BUILT-UP GIRDERS:
ONE, 40' LONG, FROM SIX, 20' PIECES;
THE OTHER 24' LONG, FROM SIX, 12' PIECES.

6–18

JOISTS

POST-BEAM
CONNECTOR

POST

GIRDER

HARDWARE
CONNECTOR

BOLSTER

POST

thickness of the girder. Thus, 4 × 4 posts are okay for a 4-inch girder, 6 × 6s for a 6-inch girder, and so on. In some areas, this general rule applies only when the post is not longer than 9 feet or smaller than a 6 × 6, so check.

Steel I-beams are sometimes used as girders but, like their wooden counterparts, cross-sectional dimensions and web thicknesses must be based on the load they will carry and the span. Generally, steel beams are so heavy that they require special handling and installation (aside from special ordering) so you are better off planning room sizes that can be handled with wood beams.

Supports for I-beams (and some wood beams) often take the form of Lally columns, many of which have a built-in adjustment for height (**6–19**). This can be an advantage when you are leveling, and even later should any sag occur. Lally columns may also be used under wood girders. They are locked to steel girders with nuts and bolts and to wood girders with lag screws. The top of a steel beam is usually set level with the foundation wall and a wooden pad is used on its surface as shown in **6–20** to set it level with the sill. Wood beams are organized so that top surfaces are level with the sill to start with.

Joists that must bear directly against steel beams can be attached as shown in **6–21**. It is not recommended that you notch the joists so they can rest on the beam's lower flange,

6–19

6–20

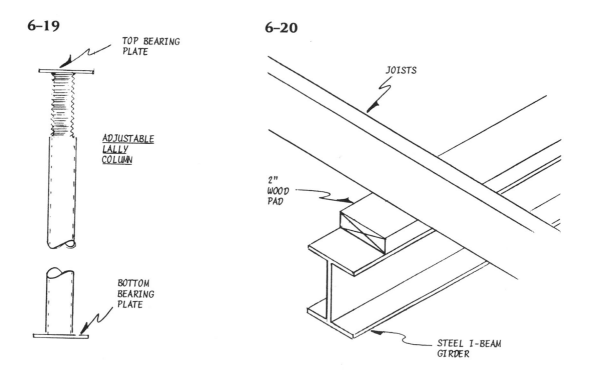

6–19: TOP BEARING PLATE / ADJUSTABLE LALLY COLUMN / BOTTOM BEARING PLATE

6–20: JOISTS / 2" WOOD PAD / STEEL I-BEAM GIRDER

6-21

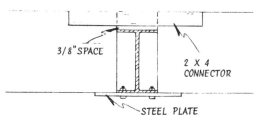

3/8" SPACE

2 X 4 CONNECTOR

STEEL PLATE

which does not provide good bearing. A common practice is to weld or bolt a steel plate to the bottom of the beam and to use a 2 × 4 connector across the top. Some clearance between the two materials is usually advisable as wood is more likely to undergo physical changes than steel.

With steel or wood beams, you may want to increase headroom clearance below by mounting the beam in the floor frame. That means the joists would butt into the beam, and be attached with hardware and nails as required by codes for joists.

POST SUPPORTS

Posts of steel or wood that support girders must have adequate footings so loads will be distributed over a broad, strong area. The method of securing the post to the footing, generally with galvanized hardware, should prevent any lateral motion.

Precast concrete piers, with wood blocks inserted at the top end, are sometimes used in a crawl space. The piers are set on a cast-in-place footing with a strong mortar used as a bond (**6–22**). Both the footing and the pier should be placed carefully to achieve level. To meet code, you probably will need to set the pin end of a U-shaped post anchor in the pier. The same type of pier may be used when a concrete floor is placed (**6–23**). The objection here is the appearance of the pier when a usable basement is part of the design.

A similar construction, with cast masonry you can form yourself or with ready-made forms, includes an anchor pin that seats in a hole drilled in the post (**6–24**). The pin can be a length of ½-inch, or larger, reinforcement rod or a bolt. In either case, it should penetrate the post a minimum of 3 inches. Forms you can buy for round concrete piers (or pedestals) look like large thick-walled mailing tubes. The pins are installed in the concrete as if they were anchor bolts. Steel posts and Lally columns are also set on footings. The bottom plate should be placed over bolts that are embedded in the footing pour, as shown in **6–25**.

Using galvanized post-holding hardware is the best solution (and likely to be required by code) wherever you set a wooden post between a footing and a girder. Posts that rest

6-22

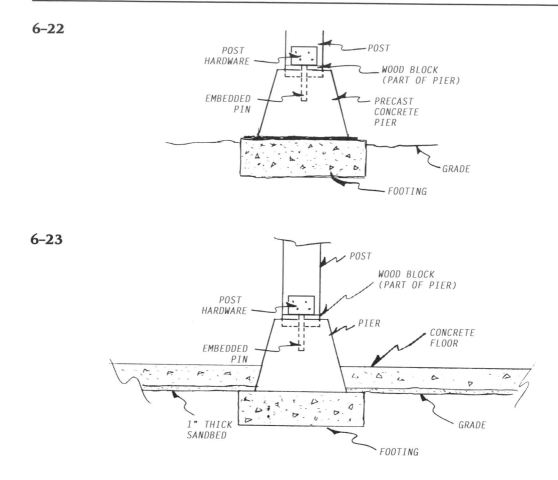

POST
HARDWARE

POST

WOOD BLOCK
(PART OF PIER)

EMBEDDED
PIN

PRECAST
CONCRETE
PIER

GRADE

FOOTING

6-23

POST

WOOD BLOCK
(PART OF PIER)

POST
HARDWARE

PIER

CONCRETE
FLOOR

EMBEDDED
PIN

1" THICK
SANDBED

GRADE

FOOTING

directly on a concrete floor are not uncommon, but the chances are they were an after-thought, installed when it became apparent that extra girder support was required. Special anchors, such as are shown in **6-26**, are often used to secure posts to an existing floor, although they are just as usable as inserts in a pour. Some have integral pins that you embed in the pour. Others fit over an anchor-bolt hole. Many of these anchors have built-in adjustments that provide some leeway in case you need to shift the posts into plumb. The bracket also keeps the wood off the masonry, which helps to prevent rot.

NAILING SPECS

At almost every location through the building frame, codes also specify the size and number of nails required. Situations vary, but most inspectors just don't have the time

6–24

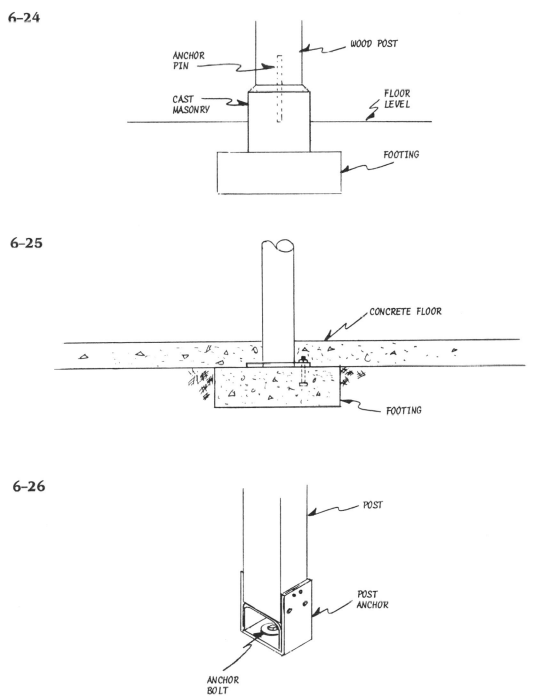

ANCHOR
PIN

WOOD POST

CAST
MASONRY

FLOOR
LEVEL

FOOTING

6–25

CONCRETE FLOOR

FOOTING

6–26

POST

POST
ANCHOR

ANCHOR
BOLT

to check the nails at every joint. For example, major codes call for two 8d nails at each end of bridging-to-joists connections; three 8d nails to toenail a joist to a sill; 16d nails 16 inches O.C. (on center) through soleplates into joists below; four 8d toenails or two 16d end nails to attach studs to soleplates. There is a spec for every nailing situation in a building.

You can consult nailing schedules as a guide. But as a practical matter, if you have no clue about what kind or how many nails to drive in a situation, you probably should not be building a house. Owner–builders generally are and need to be relatively experienced do-it-yourselfers who have a fair amount of construction experience. Bear in mind that almost all houses are built by professionals who do it day in and day out—and those new houses often have plenty of problems.

An inspector might be inclined to pay extra attention to an owner–builder job. But if he discovers joists toenailed to headers with no hangers, or only two 6d toenails between a stud and soleplate, you could be in for even more scrutiny. Those kinds of mistakes are so fundamental that even the most reasonable inspector will assume that there will be similar shortcomings throughout your project. As always, you should heed the advice of the inspector, for example, if he says that you should be driving more nails or using larger ones.

7

FRAMING THE FLOOR

Picture the floor frame as a large gridwork that is supported on the perimeter by the foundation and by girders, if needed, at intermediate points. The joists run parallel to each other and are boxed in by headers, which run across the ends of the joists, and by stringers, which are no more than terminal joists. Note that in different parts of the country there are different terms for parts of the frame. For instance, some people call the horizontal board at the base of a wall a sole-plate, others a shoe, and others a bottom plate. Their terms aren't right or wrong, just different names for the same thing.

Considerations for openings through the floor, special supports for partitions, whether joists run continuously or are pieced, and so on, affect the basic layout. On a typical floor frame such as in **7–1**, you'll see the relationship of various components. Two types of partition supports are shown along the center of the frame. The spaced-joist design is used when spaces are required for plumbing, heating, or electrical systems.

You could make the joist layout directly on the sills, but in platform construction, it's better to work by marking joist placement directly on the joist headers after they have been cut to correct length. Opposite headers can be butted edge to edge so you can draw lines across both at the same time. This is good practice that works on wall assemblies, as well. Place an X mark on one side of each line to show where the joists must go. When the joists are continuous, the X will be on the same side of each line, as shown in **7–2**; when joists are spliced, the X is marked as shown in **7–3**.

You can mark off the layout with a measuring tape. Most have highlighted marks at 17–inch centers as an aid. Another option is to make a marking jig such as shown in **7–4**. The pieces used between the 1-by stock should match the thickness of the joists. The regular joist spacing, usually 16 inches on center, should not be interrupted when other components are introduced. These pieces should be viewed as additions to the required joists.

Always choose the straightest pieces of wood you have as joist headers. Sight along an

131

7-1   EXAMPLE OF COMPLETED FLOOR FRAME

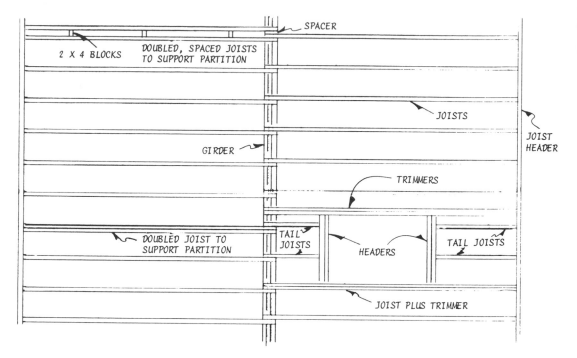

edge of each joist before you place it so you can discover if there is a bow. This process is called "crowning the joists." If there is one, always set the high edge, or crown, up so that the weight it carries will tend to straighten it rather than bow it further.

When it is necessary to double up on joists or headers or trimmers, work with 16d nails, at least at the start. Drive them straight through and then clinch them where they protrude. This will serve to pull the two pieces tightly together. Space the nails about 12 inches apart and maintain at least a 1-inch edge distance. You can also assemble them with 12d nails. If these are driven at an angle, holding power will be increased and the nails will not protrude. Both systems are shown in **7-5**.

NAILING JOISTS

A good procedure is to start with one joist header, toenailing it to the sill with 10d nails spaced 16 inches apart as shown in **7-6**. Keep the header as vertical as possible, but don't worry about absolute plumb because it will be plumbed when you add the joists, as long as their ends are square. Place the stringer joists, toenailing them to the sill as you did the

7-2   CONTINUOUS JOISTS

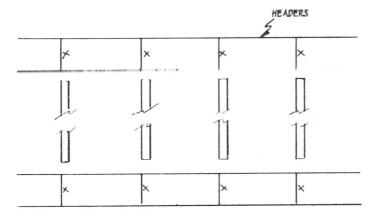

7-3   SPLICED JOISTS

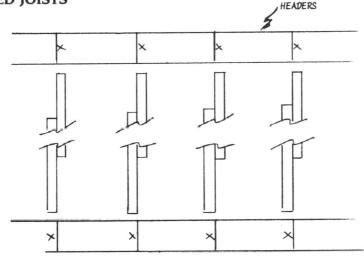

header and securing the stringer-to-header joint with 16d nails.

Place the joists in position, lock them in position with 16d nails, and then add the opposite joist header by following the same nailing schedule. Two critical considerations are the length of the joists and the squareness of their edges. If you allow variations to occur, contact points will not mate as they should, vertical surfaces will not be plumb, and gaps and irregularities will result in poor construction and cause more problems later.

Good nailing means good strength. The sizes and spacings specified here are common

7-4

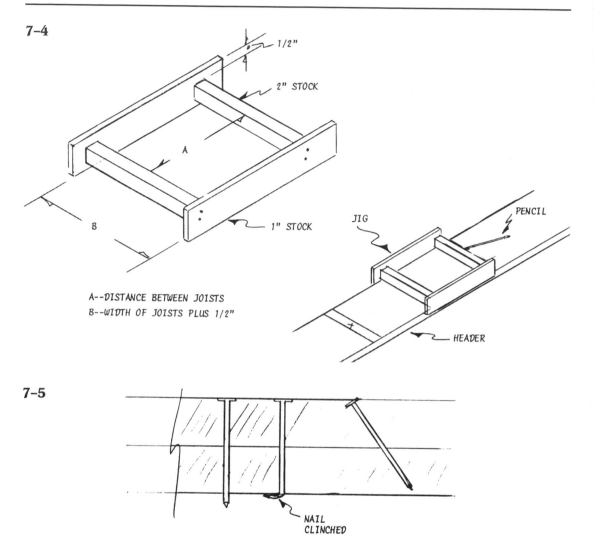

1/2"

2" STOCK

A

B

1" STOCK

JIG

PENCIL

HEADER

A--DISTANCE BETWEEN JOISTS
B--WIDTH OF JOISTS PLUS 1/2"

7-5

NAIL
CLINCHED

practice, but because the nailing patterns are so important and may vary depending on codes, it pays to do some checking. If you find that smaller or fewer nails are okay, you can save some time and money. Don't add more nails as a safety factor. Excessive nailing can cause splitting, now or when the frame is under stress. Too many nails can be just as bad as too few.

CIRCULAR SAWS

Long ago, power circular saws were used mainly by contractors who needed the speed of a spinning blade to save time and money on the job. But circular saws are almost as

7–6

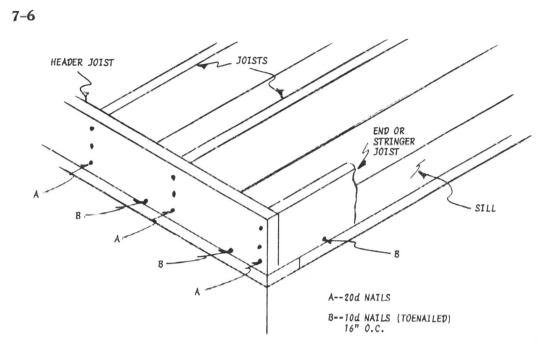

HEADER JOIST

JOISTS

END OR
STRINGER
JOIST

SILL

A

B

A

B

A

B

A

A--20d NAILS

B--10d NAILS (TOENAILED)
16" O.C.

common as electric drills today, and most do-it-yourselfers have one in addition to, and often instead of, a handsaw.

You can buy a reasonably good circular saw for under $50, and a very good one with more than enough power for home improvements and home construction for about $100. (You can spend much more, of course, but it isn't really necessary unless you plan on building houses for a living.) There are dozens of models, including huge, heavy saws with 10-inch-diameter blades that can slice through landscaping timbers, and midget models with four-inch-diameter blades designed to cut trim and flooring.

But two basic types offer the kind of overall versatility most do-it-yourselfers need: the standard, 7¼-inch corded saw, and the smaller, cordless version, generally called a trim saw, with a blade diameter of 5 to 6 inches.

If price is a prime concern, forget about cordless saws. They are compact, easy to handle in tight spaces, and slick. But they're expensive. While a good-quality 7¼-inch corded model rated at 13 amps with 2½ horsepower might cost $75 (including a carbide-tipped blade), a comparable, 18-volt cordless saw with charger, two battery packs and blade might cost $225 and up.

You don't get any extra power for the extra price. In fact, you generally get less. But in some circumstances, it's more convenient (and often safer) to be free of plugs and extension cords. If you're working outside, you don't have to worry about water seeping into plugs, or hooking into ground-fault circuit breakers. And you'll never become entangled in power cords. But corded saws are ready to go anytime, while if you forget to charge batteries on a cordless saw, you're stuck.

Another basic characteristic to consider is cutting capacity—how big a board the saw can cut in one pass, and, for cordless models, how many cuts it can make before running out of power. A typical 7¼-inch model can cut through 2¼ inches of material with the blade at 90 degrees, and 1¾ inches when the blade is tilted to 45 degrees for mitering. That means it can handle both types of cuts through a 2 × 4, which is actually 1½ inches thick. A typical cordless saw with a 5½-inch blade can cut through wood that is 1⅝ inches thick in one pass. It can't handle a 45-degree cut through a 2 × 4, but that's not a common cut. And if you're working with larger lumber, such as 4 × 4 posts, even 7¼-inch saws don't have enough blade depth to slice through in one pass.

Corded saws can keep cutting until your arms turn to putty. Cordless models have a limited fuel supply. But a good-quality, 18-volt-or-better model should be able to crosscut one hundred 2 × 4s on a single charge, depending, of course, on the hardness of the wood you're cutting. If you remember to keep the spare battery charged, a good cordless saw will probably have more energy to burn on a carpentry project than you will.

But even with a full charge, most cordless models just don't turn as fast as comparable corded models. The blade on a corded saw may spin at 5,000 rpm, while the blade on a cordless model may turn at 2,500 to 3,500 rpm. Speed isn't the only measure of cutting power. But motors that make blades spin faster generally have more force in the cutting action. You won't notice much of a speed or power difference on softwood like 1 × 6 pine. But you may notice the advantage of a corded power supply trimming a long row of floor joists.

Capacity and power won't matter much if you can't use the saw comfortably and safely. So after you check the performance numbers, heft several saws in the store to check weight and balance and test the hand holds, trigger, blade guard, and other controls. Almost all circular saws have the blade on the right and the handle on the left. Only one type (made by several companies), called a worm-drive saw, has it the other way around. But even if the standard lineup feels okay, you'll find quite a difference in handle and trigger positions. For many people, a high handle makes the saw easy to lift. But a lower handle nearer the back of the saw makes it easier to apply both control and force directly behind your cuts.

New saws will carry a long list of safety cautions. They may not mention the obvious— that you need to increase your safety awareness in general whenever you use high-speed power tools such as a circular saw, which has a sharp blade and can throw out chips of wood. Part of this awareness is setting up a safe cutting station where you are on solid ground and the wood you're cutting is adequately supported. Another aspect is wearing safety glasses. You also may want to wear hearing protection. The United States Occupational Safety and Health Administration (OSHA) recommends it when the noise level exceeds 85 decibels for an eight-hour workday. A typical circular saw emits about 110 decibels, but you're not likely to use one all day long.

If you're sensitive to dust, and whenever you cut pressure-treated wood, it's also wise to wear a dust mask. There are many types, but a disposable dust mask will do. You should look for a stamp of the National Institute for Occupational Safety and Health/Mine Safety and Health Administration (NIOSH/MSHA) on the mask approved for the work you're doing.

When you cut with a circular saw, or a chop saw that can be handy to trim boards to length, support the wood so that the saw blade won't bind. The cut should open, not close, as you run the saw across the lumber. Also beware of kickback, which can knock the saw out of your safe control. You can buy antikickback blades, which have modified tooth designs, but you can best reduce kickback by not rushing a cut and by stabilizing your work. In any case, it's wise to stand slightly off center and out of line with the cut, and to keep your hands away from the cutting area.

JOISTS OVER GIRDERS

Pieced joists are overlapped where they cross a girder, and solid bridging is installed between them (**7–7**). Typical nailing calls for the joist ends to be tied together with two 10d nails and for the joists to be tacked to the girder by toe nailing on each side with a 10d nail. The bridging, with nice square ends, is secured by toenailing along the ends into joists and along the base into the girder.

When the girder has been set higher than the sills to gain headroom below, the joists can be organized as shown in **7–8**. The ledger is a very important component here, so choose good, knot-free material and attach it securely with 16d nails. Cut the notch in the joist so there will be clearance over the girder. The place marked A is where bearing should occur, not at point B, which would cause splitting. The joists are toenailed to the girder and surface-nailed to each other with 10d nails. A better situation is to use girders and joists of the same size, which eliminates notching.

With the joists in line, a strip of wood is used as a tie across the ends of the joists (**7–9**). The tie should clear the girder by about ½ inch so that unequal shrinkage cannot lift the joist off the ledger. When you want the bottom edges of girders and joists to be flush for a smooth ceiling surface, you can butt the joist and carry its load in a joist hanger, also called

7-7

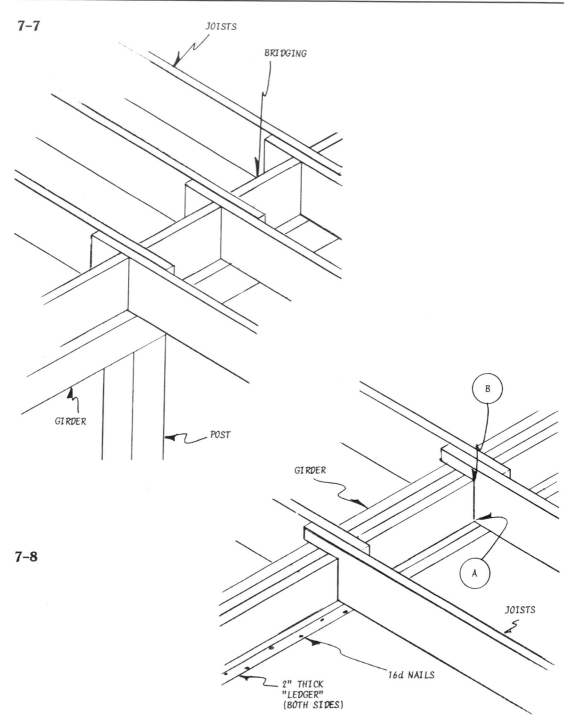

JOISTS

BRIDGING

GIRDER

POST

7-8

B

A

GIRDER

JOISTS

16d NAILS

2" THICK
"LEDGER"
(BOTH SIDES)

7-9   **7-10**

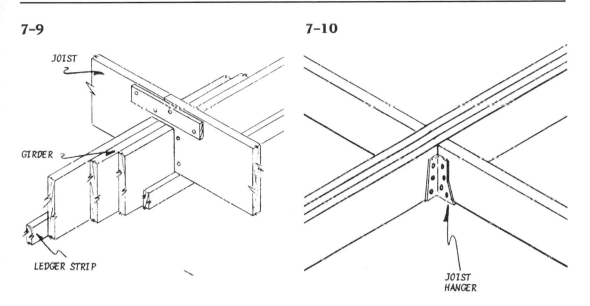

a stirrup (**7-10**). These are available in a broad range of sizes to suit this and other house-framing applications. Bear in mind that codes require hangers on all joist connections where there is not at least 1½ inches of bearing for the joist.

JOISTS UNDER PARTITIONS

Use doubled joists to provide support for any parallel-running partition wall (**7-11**). The joists can be spaced if you will need room in that area for plumbing or heating requirements. If so, use 2 × 4 blocks, as in **7-12**, spaced about 4 feet apart, as bracing for the joists. If you find that a block will interfere with a future installation, you may move it, but

7-11

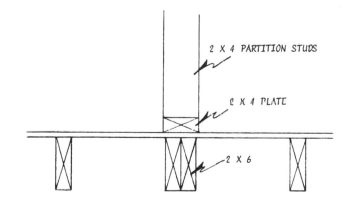

7–12

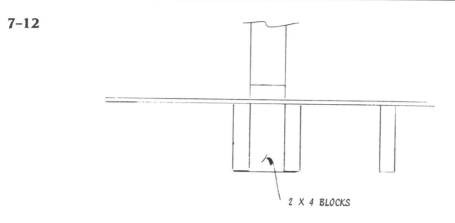

2 X 4 BLOCKS

don't reduce the number of blocks the 4-foot spacing calls for. In some situations, such as an opening through the floor for a heating duct, you can move a block to one side of the opening and add another on the other side. It's okay to add but not to reduce.

OPENINGS THROUGH FLOORS

Any opening through a floor frame must account for the strength that is lost when a regular joist is cut. A good system, together with nomenclature, is shown in **7–13**. The

7–13

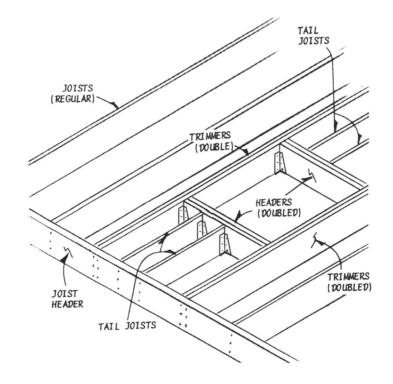

TAIL JOISTS

JOISTS (REGULAR)

TRIMMERS (DOUBLE)

HEADERS (DOUBLED)

TRIMMERS (DOUBLED)

JOIST HEADER

TAIL JOISTS

nailing schedule for the assembly can become confusing unless you anticipate it and approach the job step by step.

Start by installing the inside trimmers, nailing them in place as you would regular joists (**7–14**). Set them carefully to be sure they are parallel and correctly spaced. Cut the tail joists to correct length, making sure to allow for the thickness of the double headers. Clamp or tack-nail two of the tail joists to the trimmers as shown in **7–15** so they become gauges that position the first header correctly. Nail the first header in place with three 20d nails. Position and secure the tail joists by driving three 20d nails through the joist header and through the opening header. Add the second opening header by nailing through the

7–14

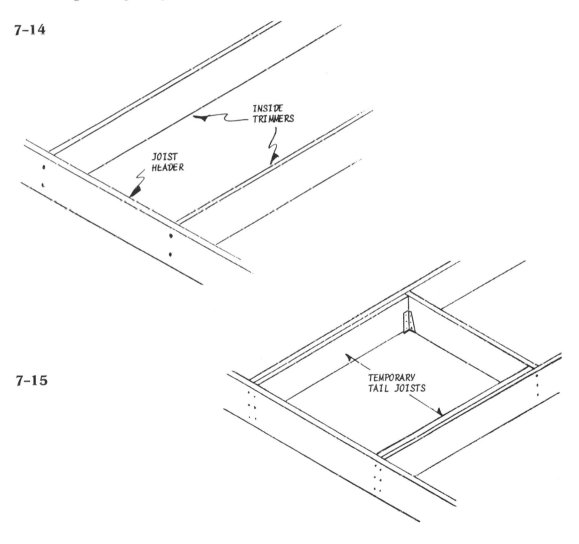

7–15

trimmers as you did for the first one. Bond the two headers together with 16d nails, staggering them and spacing them about 16 inches apart. Keep the nails a minimum of 1 inch away from edges. So far the assembly should look like that shown in **7-16**.

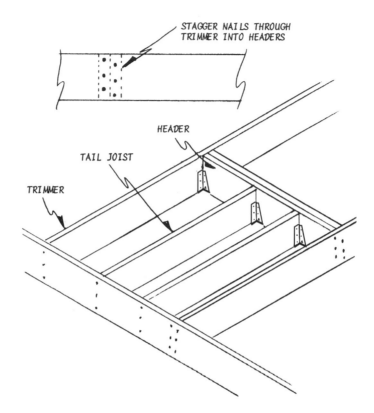

The other side of the rough opening is framed in the same way. Then the last step is to add the second trimmers. Use 16d nails spaced about 12 inches apart along the edges and staggered as shown in **7-17**. Maintain the usual edge distance of at least 1 inch. Joist hangers and framing anchors should be used when assembling trimmers, tail joists, and headers (**7-18**).

PROJECTIONS OUTSIDE THE WALL

Sometimes house designs call for floor extensions beyond the foundation walls. They may be needed for such things as porch floors, second-story overhangs or decks, or bay windows. If the run of the floor joists permits, they can simply be longer and cantilevered

7-17

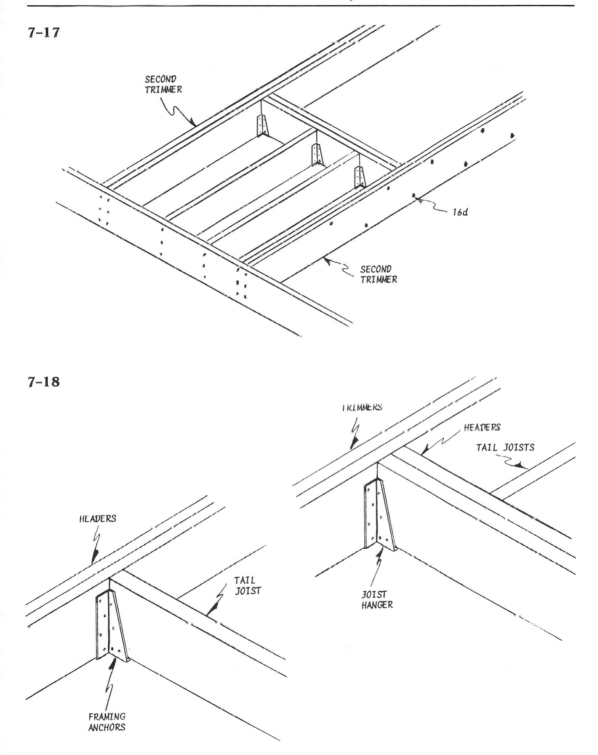

beyond the foundation as in **7–19**. A small overhang, as for a bay window, will probably not require additional support. If the overhang is wide, as for a porch or veranda, then supports outside the foundation wall will be needed. If the extensions are considered at the start, then substructures could be part of the foundation. If not, they can follow the pattern for joist support in a crawl space, as shown in **7–20**.

7–19

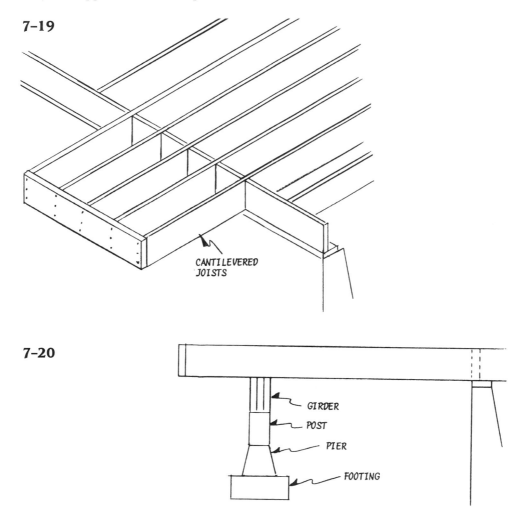

CANTILEVERED
JOISTS

7–20

GIRDER
POST
PIER
FOOTING

If the projection joists run at right angles to the floor-frame joists, then the regular joist against which their ends terminate must be doubled (**7–22**). A general rule for establishing the length of cantilevered joists is that the distance from the foundation wall to the doubled joist should be at least twice the length of the overhang. But this allowance can produce floors with too much flex. It's wiser to adjust the cantilever rule to project only one quarter of the length when the other three quarters are secured. Framing anchors must be used on such assemblies. Ledgers can be incorporated, as in **7–22**. But because the load (A) causes pressure upward against the joists, ledgers should be positioned along the top edges.

BRACING BETWEEN JOISTS

Bridging is commonly used between joists, although some argue it isn't necessary, and that good floor framing, adequately nailed, requires only the subflooring that follows to

7–21

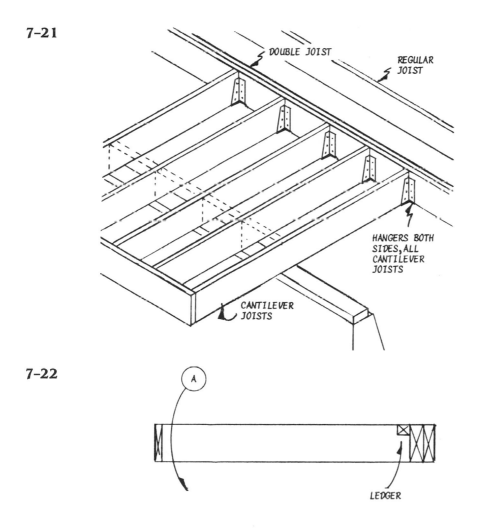

DOUBLE JOIST

REGULAR JOIST

HANGERS BOTH SIDES, ALL CANTILEVER JOISTS

CANTILEVER JOISTS

7–22

Ⓐ

LEDGER

keep members fixed and plumb. Most existing codes require it, so if only for that reason, it's included in most structures. A personal observation is that it doesn't hurt and it supplies an extra degree of rigidity. You'll probably find that the floor feels stronger once bridging is added.

The old-fashioned bridging system uses pieces of 1 × 3 or 1 × 4 lumber set between joists as shown in **7–23**. These should be spaced a maximum of 8 feet and should follow a straight line you can establish easily by snapping a chalk line across the top edges of the joists. In situations where you can't follow the 8-foot spacing, for example if the joists span 12 feet between foundation and girder, just place the bridging along a midpoint line.

Because many pieces of bridging are required, it pays to organize a system so you can cut them speedily and accurately. First, use a piece of the material as shown in **7–24** to mark the correct cut angles and length. Use this as a pattern for others if you are sawing

7–23   CROSS BRIDGING

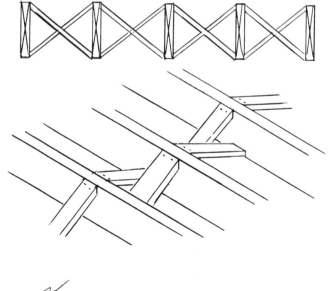

7–24

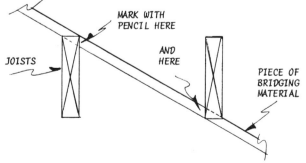

JOISTS

MARK WITH PENCIL HERE

AND HERE

PIECE OF BRIDGING MATERIAL

by hand, or as a gauge to set up a radial arm saw as shown in **7-25**. If you work with a portable saw, make a jig as shown in **7-26**. If you make the work-length stop and the saw guide long enough, you can cut several pieces at a time. Nail each piece of bridging at the top end with two 8d nails. Use the same size nails at the bottom ends, but do not drive them until the subfloor has been installed. If convenient, it's recommended that you do not secure the bottom ends of the bridging until after the finished floor is in place.

Bridging is easier to install if you use solid blocking between the joists. And nailing will be easier if you stagger the bridging as shown in **7-27**. Often, joist cutoffs can serve as bridging. The easiest installation of all is made with metal strapping. Each piece has nailing flanges on the end that make them easy to set in an X pattern.

CUTS THROUGH JOISTS

The load on a joist becomes more effective the closer it is to the center of a span. Thus, this area is the most critical point when it is necessary to cut a joist for plumbing or any

7-25

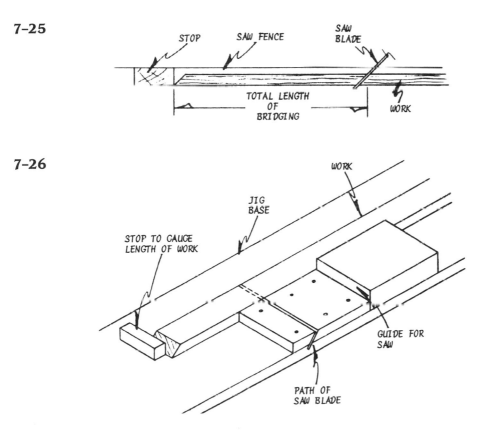

7-26

7-27

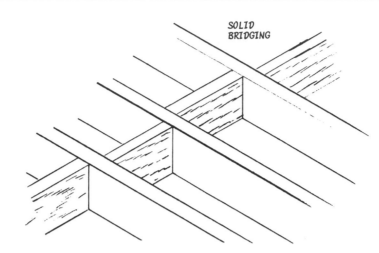

other reason. The midpoint of the joist across the width is a neutral axis where compression stresses end and tension stresses begin. The two are interrelated, but in essence compression will bend the joist and tension will crack it (**7–28**). This should be remembered whenever you cut a joist so you can compensate adequately with additional pieces. A hole bored on the neutral axis will have little effect on the strength of the joist as long as its diameter is not more than one-third of the joist's depth, although one-fourth or more is a safer ratio.

Bear in mind that a 4-inch-deep cutout in a 2 × 10 will reduce the strength of the joist below the cut to that of a 2 × 6; in a 2 × 6, a 2-inch-deep cutout leaves the strength of a 2 × 4 (**7–29**). This kind of over-notching can make joists inadequate to support their loads.

When large plumbing pipes are involved, it's preferable to hang them below joists. If that's not possible, you may be able to remove a section of the joist and support the

7-28

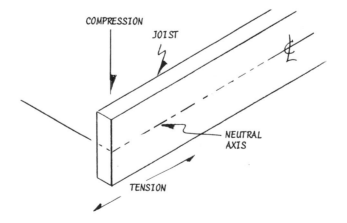

7-29

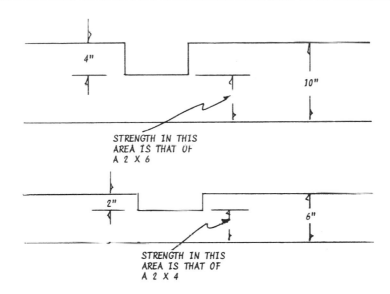

STRENGTH IN THIS
AREA IS THAT OF
A 2 X 6

STRENGTH IN THIS
AREA IS THAT OF
A 2 X 4

interrupted span with headers. In many cases, you also can strengthen the joist sufficiently by bolting on steel plates across the cut area.

In addition to the one third or, better yet, one-fourth safety factor for bored holes, you should avoid any cutouts in the middle third of the joist length, and keep hole cutouts 2-inches away from the top and bottom. If you need to cut notches, also keep them in the outer thirds of the span. Typical ratios for notches are a maximum of one-sixth of the depth when the notch is cut in the outer thirds and one-fourth when cut at the end. The actual sizes of notches will vary, of course, depending on the size of the joist. Never cut through the 2 × 4 pieces on truss-style joists. Many of these manufactured joists have properly placed punchouts in the plywood webs where you can run mechanicals.

ADDING THE SUBFLOOR

You can lay the subfloor immediately after the floor frame is complete. Subflooring used to be made of individual 1-inch T&G (tongue-and-groove) boards nailed at a 45-degree angle with the joists (**7-30**). Although there are other options, such as shiplap and end-matched boards, subflooring is almost always made out of 4 × 8 plywood sheets, which are widely available, easier to install, and cost less.

If you have access to old-fashioned subflooring, you can nail the boards at each joist crossing with two 8d nails. End joints for both plain and shiplap boards should occur over a joist (**7-31**). If you use subflooring that is tongued and grooved on both edges and ends,

7-30

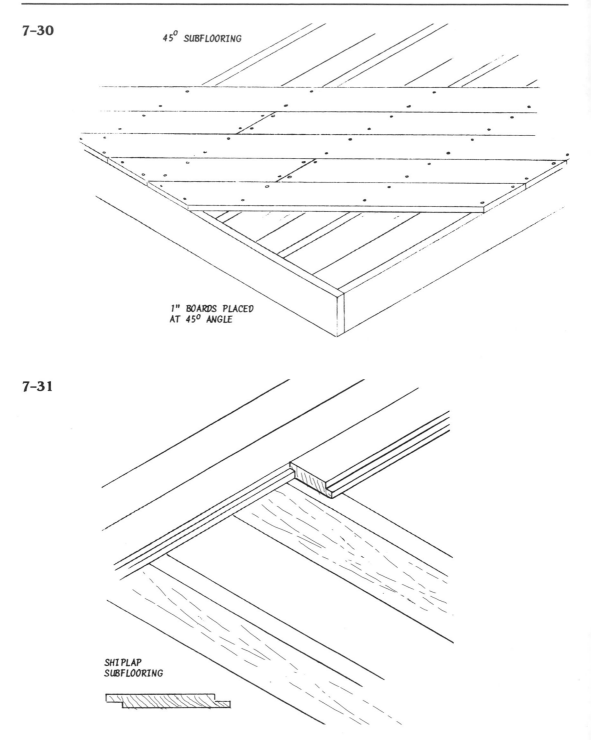

45° SUBFLOORING

1" BOARDS PLACED
AT 45° ANGLE

7-31

SHIPLAP
SUBFLOORING

then the end joints can occur anywhere (**7-32**). It's best to lay board subflooring without clearance between joints, although some manufacturers call for a ⅛-inch gap.

With sheet materials, you have several choices, including different types and sizes of plywood and the material frequently used by contractors and builders, called oriented strand board (OSB). This composite product started off as particleboard, which was made of sawdust-sized material and glue. The next generation was waferboard, a composite

7-32

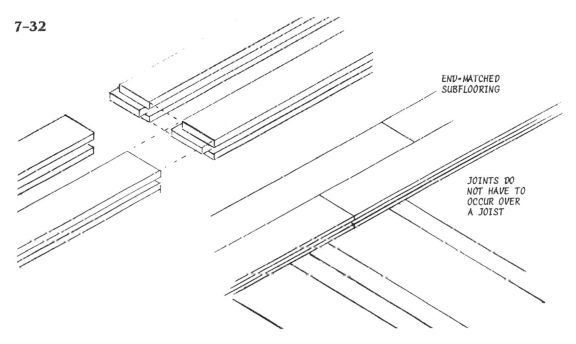

END-MATCHED SUBFLOORING

JOINTS DO NOT HAVE TO OCCUR OVER A JOIST

sheet made with larger pieces of wood. OSB is more highly engineered for strength with opposing strips of wood and can serve as subflooring and sheathing.

With plywood you have many choices, but the standard is either ½- or ⅝-inch-thick panels over joists set 16 inches on center. The sheets should be nailed every 6 inches at edges and every 12 inches in the field. Thicker panels are available to span larger framing bays. Special panels with interlocking edges also can be applied with adhesive and screws to serve over larger spans.

Place the sheets so the long dimension runs at right angles to the joists and so the joints will be staggered as shown in **7-33**. Some manufacturers recommend gaps between joints, which you can control with a strip of wood or heavy cardboard.

Nail with 8d nails following the pattern shown in **7-34**. Drive the nails so they will be centered in the joists and headers. Snapping chalk lines will help you achieve good

7-33

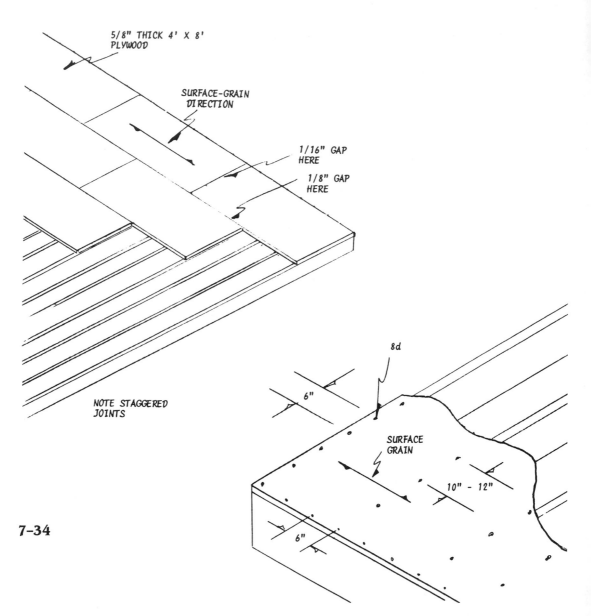

5/8" THICK 4' X 8' PLYWOOD

SURFACE-GRAIN DIRECTION

1/16" GAP HERE

1/8" GAP HERE

NOTE STAGGERED JOINTS

8d

6"

SURFACE GRAIN

10" - 12"

6"

7-34

nailing patterns. Drive nails only until they are flush with the plywood. Hammering beyond that will only cause dents in the subfloor. It's a good idea to plan the placement of sheets so that no piece will span less than three or four joists.

PLYWOOD FLOOR SYSTEMS

Over the years there have been several floor systems, often promoted by the American Plywood Association (APA), which grades plywood panels. Older configurations, such as the 2-4-1 system, call for T&G plywood panels that are usually 1⅛ inches thick and function as both structural subflooring and underlayment. Because the thickness of the panels provides considerable strength, codes may permit floor-frame designs with 2-by joists spaced up to 32 inches O.C., as shown in **7–35**, or application directly to 4-by girders spaced 4 feet apart, as shown in **7–36**. With 2 × 4 blocking placed 24 inches O.C. and toe-

7–35

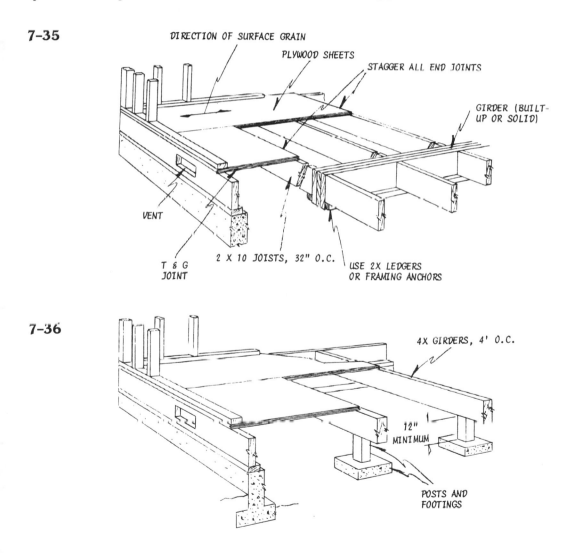

DIRECTION OF SURFACE GRAIN
PLYWOOD SHEETS
STAGGER ALL END JOINTS
GIRDER (BUILT-UP OR SOLID)
VENT
T & G JOINT
2 X 10 JOISTS, 32" O.C.
USE 2X LEDGERS OR FRAMING ANCHORS

7–36

4X GIRDERS, 4' O.C.
12" MINIMUM
POSTS AND FOOTINGS

nailed between girders, stiffness increases as much as 40 percent (**7–37**). This is reduced quite a bit if the blocking is spaced 48 inches. Blocking that is placed diagonally at an angle of 45 degrees will be easier to nail and will provide even more stiffness than straight blocking (**7–38**). The blocking will be most effective if it crosses panel joints at midspan.

Other variations use strongbacks, which are 2 × 4s placed flat and nailed or screwed to the bottom of the plywood sheets midway between the beams, as shown in **7–39**. For a low-profile floor with the oversize plywood attached directly to sills, the girders can be set

7–37

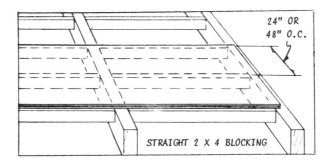

7–38

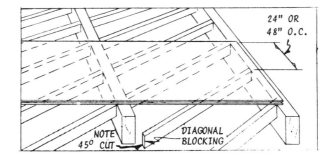

7–39

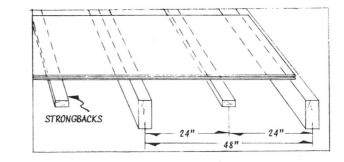

in pockets in a concrete wall as in **7–40**. You can also build masonry pilasters out from the foundation wall to support a main girder.

7–40

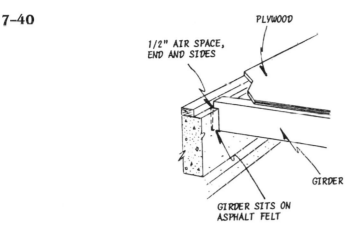

PLYWOOD

1/2" AIR SPACE, END AND SIDES

GIRDER

GIRDER SITS ON ASPHALT FELT

A variation of this approach, called the APA Sturd-I-floor system, employs panels with tongue-and-groove edges in a variety of thicknesses to meet code over different joists spacings. At standard spacing of 16 inches on center, the APA calls for $18/32$- or $5/8$-inch-thick panels. At 24-inch joist spacing, requirements increase to $23/32$- or $3/4$-inch-thick panels. Applying subflooring with glue and screws generally is worth the extra effort and modest added cost, as it tends to reduce or eliminate squeaks.

8

FRAMING THE WALLS

View wall frames as strong skeletons consisting of vertical and horizontal components that you lock together with nails. The wall framing supports upper structures such as ceilings and roofs, and also acts as a base on which you can nail outside and inside coverings, and in which you can place electrical wiring, pipes, heating ducts, insulation, and the like. The basic structure has three parts: a single horizontal member that rests on the floor, called a soleplate or shoe; vertical studs generally set 16 inches on center; and a doubled horizontal member across the top of the studs, called a plate. Within this basic design you need to add extra studs at corners and at partitions and openings, and headers to carry the loads of interrupted studs, mainly over doors and windows. A complete wall frame, with nomenclature, is shown in **8–1**.

You'll notice two different types of headers. The one-piece header, usually 4 × 10 or 4 × 12 stock, is used in some parts of the country where these oversize timbers are plentiful and cheap. Using solid headers reduces installation time, as compared to using built-up headers, and automatically establishes a common height for all openings with a minimum amount of measuring. Another important fact is that the 4 × 12 has enough strength to span just about any opening, so the chore of having to determine individual header sizes is pretty much eliminated except for special cases, such as unusual loads or an exceptionally long span.

In most areas, headers are built up from dimensional timbers that are more widely available and less expensive than 4-by lumber. The drawback is that a 2 × 10, for example, is only 1½ inches thick. Nail two together and you have a 3-inch-thick header, which is still ½-inch shy of the 3½-inch wall thickness. Across small door openings, some builders set the double header flush with the outside wall to help support sheathing, and simply bridge the empty space with drywall. But to provide complete nailing inside and outside, it's better to pack out the header and assemble the pieces around a piece of ½-inch-thick plywood. This makes the header the same thickness as the wall.

Figure 8–1 also shows an angled strip at the corner, called let-in bracing. This feature

157

8-1

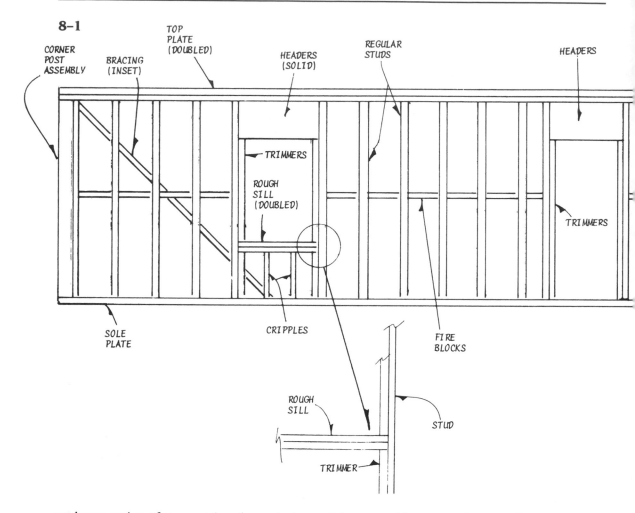

CORNER POST ASSEMBLY

BRACING (INSET)

TOP PLATE (DOUBLED)

HEADERS (SOLID)

REGULAR STUDS

HEADERS

TRIMMERS

ROUGH SILL (DOUBLED)

TRIMMERS

SOLE PLATE

CRIPPLES

FIRE BLOCKS

ROUGH SILL

STUD

TRIMMER

makes a series of strong triangles out of a wall frame and increases its overall strength and lateral stiffness. But it is left out of most homes today where modern sheathing (properly nailed) provides lateral reinforcement, and because the detail takes some time to install. You need to cut shallow recesses across many studs and break out the wood so the bracing lies flush with the studs. If you need to add extra stiffness to the frame, you can use the modern version of let-in bracing, which is an L-shaped strip of steel that's prepunched for nailing. Just snap a diagonal line across the studs, make one pass to create a kerf in each board, fit one side of the L shape into the kerfs, and nail the brace in place.

Within this overall framing scheme, procedures can vary region by region. Header treatment is one example. The placement of trimmers, often called jack studs, is another. Generally, trimmers at openings run down to the soleplate or shoe. Once they are installed at a door opening, the shoe is cut out to make way for a sill. But some carpenters cut the shoe between the last full-height studs, and run the trimmers down to the plywood sub-floor where the ends can be face-nailed into the cut ends of the shoe. This makes a clean, even-sided detail at door openings.

The different approaches spawn one of many common disagreements about framing details. (Remember, the building inspector automatically wins all arguments.) Some say the header bears on the trimmer, which must bear on floor framing, not on plywood between joists. On outside walls, there is no problem because the belt joist always provides some support. But there could be a case in partition walls where the trimmer rests on plywood between joists. There are two points in defense of this approach. First, trimmers are nailed to the adjacent full-height studs and transfer loads through the studs to the shoe. Second, partition walls generally are not load-bearing walls and simply divide up floor space. That means there is no typical building load on the trimmer, which is simply helping to support the ends of the header.

Also bear in mind that there are two basic approaches to wall framing. One is to set the soleplate, add the studs, which must be toenailed, and then the plates. The other is to frame the wall on the deck (the subfloor). This allows you to face-nail through the sole-plate and one plate. When the basic box is built, you tip up the walls, plumb them, brace them, and add the second plate. This system, once you get used to it, is faster and stronger, and eliminates most toenailing.

START WITH THE SOLEPLATE

Long pieces of 2 × 4 are placed flat and nailed along the perimeter of the subflooring as in **8–2**. Note that the staggered pattern will place alternate nails in either the joist header or a joist. Nails through plates that follow a stringer joist are not staggered but should follow the same 16-inch spacing.

Do not attempt, at this point, to make cuts in the plate where door openings occur. Instead, make the plates continuous and do the sawing after the wall framing is complete (**8–3**).

STUD SPACING AND LAYOUT

Studs are usually spaced 16 inches O.C., although there are designs (and in some areas, codes that permit it) that call for 24-inch spacings using 2 × 6s. Actually, some pros say that considerably greater spacing would still provide adequate strength, and the spacing of 16 inches (or 24 inches) is established more for accommodating sheathing materials

8–2

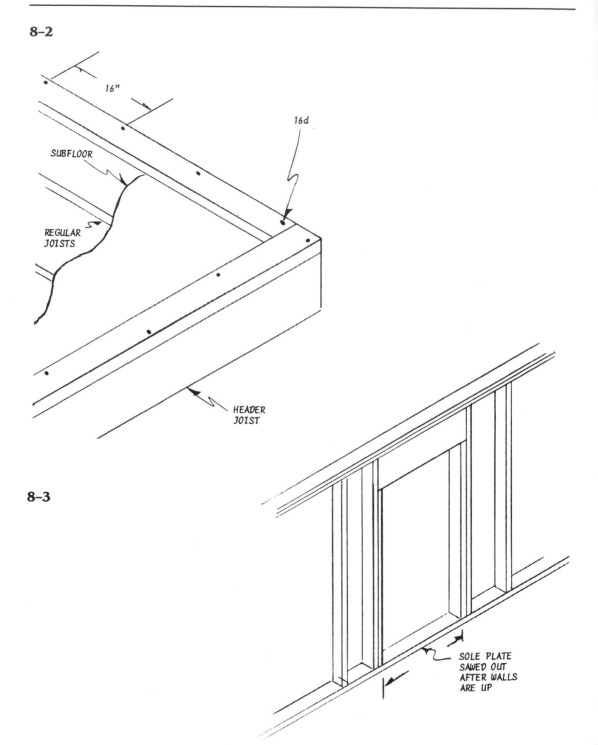

16"

16d

SUBFLOOR

REGULAR
JOISTS

HEADER
JOIST

8–3

SOLE PLATE
SAWED OUT
AFTER WALLS
ARE UP

than it is for support. The abbreviation O.C., of course, means on center, or the distance between the center of one stud and the center of the next one (**8–4**).

The spacing of studs must never be interrupted by the addition of other components such as cripples or trimmers. Regular studs may become cripples or even trimmers, or additional studs may be added to the basic structure, as shown in **8–5**, but when the wall is complete, you should be able to find a nailing surface every 16 inches.

8–4

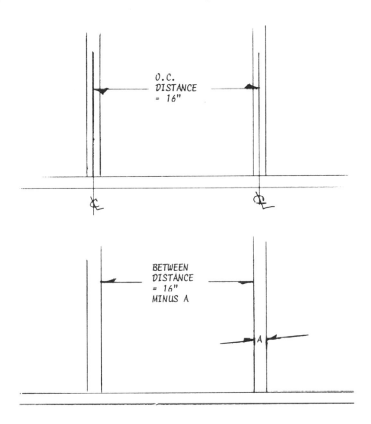

POSTS

Posts are assemblies of 2 × 4s that are used at corners of wall frames and where interior partitions join a perimeter wall. Designs can vary, and generally are based on how much material you want to use. The most solid posts used at corners have three full-height studs and blocks as spacers as shown in **8–6**. The sandwich forms an L shape to provide nailing surfaces (marked A and B) inside and outside on both walls.

8-5

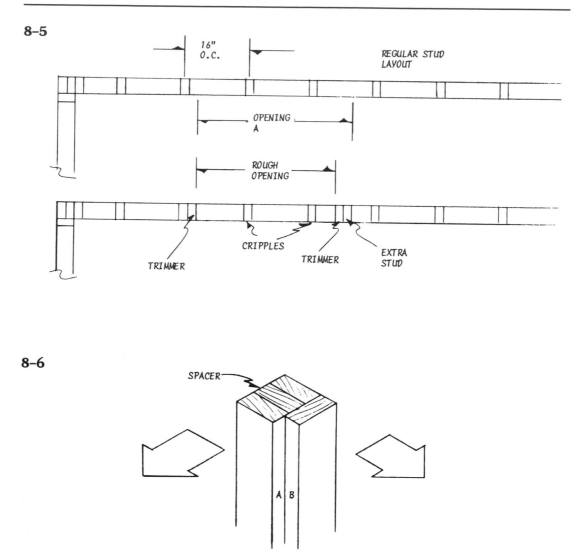

8-6

There are several other designs that use only two full-height studs. They are used mainly by builders because one stud saved per corner can make a difference on the lumber bill for a house, and even more so on the bill for many houses in a development.

ASSEMBLING POSTS

Be selective when you choose the material for post assemblies or for studs. A slight bow won't hurt because you can pull it back into line as you nail the studs together. But a major crook is something else (**8–7**). When such pieces are encountered during wall-covering procedures, the crown must often be removed with a plane to eliminate the high spot. It's better to cut such pieces into the shorter lengths required for blocking or braces.

8-7

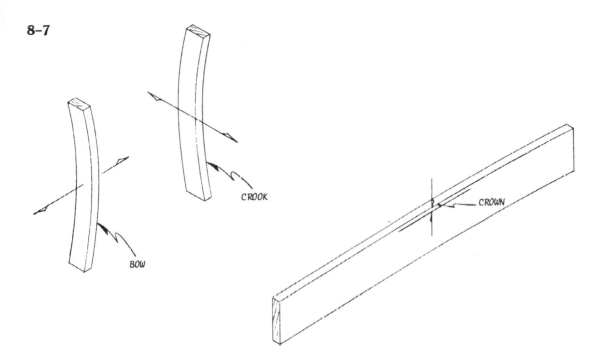

CROOK

CROWN

BOW

Assemble the basic corner post by nailing together two studs and three spacers (**8–8**), spacing mails about 12 inches apart and following a staggered pattern. When the post is for a corner, add a third stud as in **8–9**, driving 16d nails to join both studs and spacers. If need be, you can nail short pieces of 2 × 4 to posts to provide an additional nailing surface for baseboards (**8–10**). Another design for corner posts is shown in **8–11**. It uses three full-length studs but no spacers or blocking.

Solid connections must occur where partitions join outside walls, and the assembly must provide nailing surfaces. You can do this by using extra studs in the outside wall, spacing them with a third full-length stud, and then adding a fourth as shown in **8–12**. The regular studs in the wall may be used as part of this assembly if their location happens to work out. Partitions can terminate between regular studs if the opening is organized as shown in **8–13**. Attach the 1 × 8 board to each of the 2 × 4 blocks between the studs with 8d nails. This idea can be used anyplace between studs. It is not necessary for the partition to fall at the midpoint.

8–8

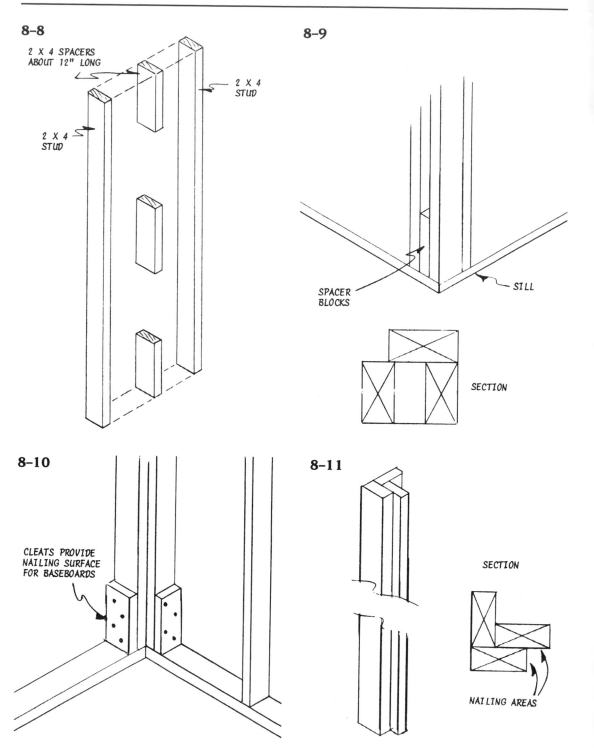

2 X 4 SPACERS
ABOUT 12" LONG

2 X 4
STUD

2 X 4
STUD

8–9

SPACER
BLOCKS

SILL

SECTION

8–10

CLEATS PROVIDE
NAILING SURFACE
FOR BASEBOARDS

8–11

SECTION

NAILING AREAS

8–12

8–13

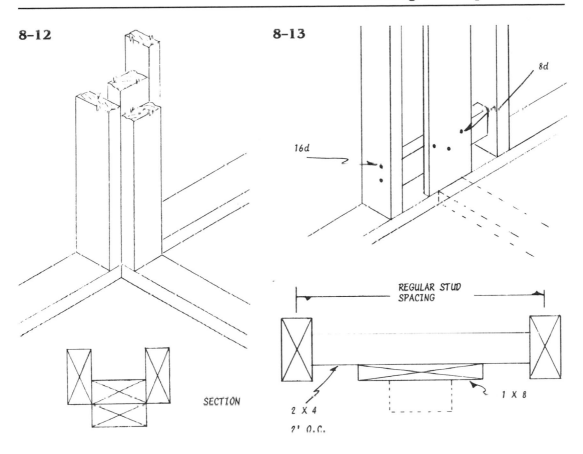

8d

16d

SECTION

REGULAR STUD
SPACING

2 X 4
2' O.C.

1 X 8

MARKING THE SOLEPLATE

You can locate studs with a measuring tape, many of which are specially marked for correct O.C. spacing of studs. But you may want to make a marking jig similar to the one we described for locating joists or to make a T-gauge (**8–14**). The T-gauge indicates spacing between studs and actual stud position. At any rate, the center of the first stud is 16 inches from a corner; other studs run 16 inches O.C. continuously. When you mark the soleplate, place the lower top plate alongside so layout marks can be carried across both pieces. Indicate studs by marking Xs (**8–15**). It's wise to get into the habit of marking all stud locations the same way, with what's called a step-ahead layout. You measure to the edge of the next stud in line, and then step ahead of the line to mark your X.

The next step is to show the positions of trimmers and cripples. The chances are that some studs will be eliminated because of door openings and others will become cripples

8-14

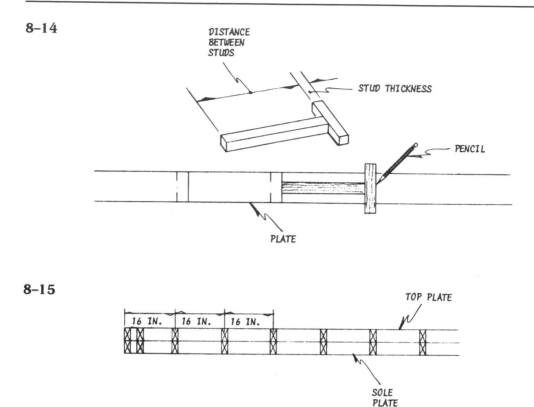

8-15

and, maybe, trimmers. As shown in **8-16**, mark the layout so you will know the role each piece will play.

The sizes of rough openings depend, of course, on the units you plan to install. In modern construction, doors and windows are purchased as complete assemblies that are just slipped into place. You can, for example, buy prehung doors that arrive already hinged,

8-16

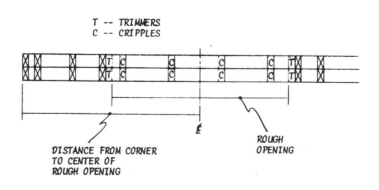

with holes drilled for hardware and with jambs in place. The manufacturer's literature will tell how large the rough openings must be. It isn't necessary to have the units delivered before you are ready for them, but you should know how to prepare for them.

Because wall frames will contain extra studs, trimmers, cripples, and headers, it's a good idea to mark where they are on the subfloor so you can locate them later, if necessary, after the walls are covered.

ERECTING THE STUDS

One approach is to toenail each stud to the plate with two 8d nails on each side (**8–17**). Some carpenters will drive just one nail on each side, but the most common practice (if you must toenail at all) is to drive two nails on one side and only one on the other. Four toenails at the base of a stud are too likely to cause splitting.

8–17

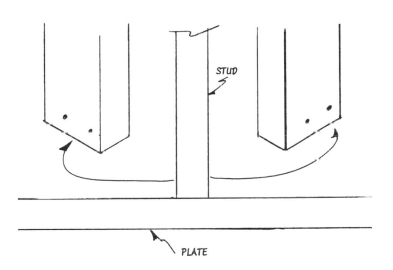

Toenailing can be a problem if you don't keep the stud firmly in place as you nail. The angle of the nail to the surface of the plate should be about 60 degrees, while the head-height should be about 1 inch (**8–18**). This makes driving easier and ensures sufficient penetration. This doesn't mean you must work with a protractor and a scale to place each nail, but you should strive for what is structurally correct even if you must practice a bit. Professionals do so much of this thing that they work by bracing the stud against their foot.

You can make a combination spacer and brace as shown in **8–19**. This is a piece of 2 × 4 as long as the distance between studs, less the thickness of one stud. Put it in place

8–18

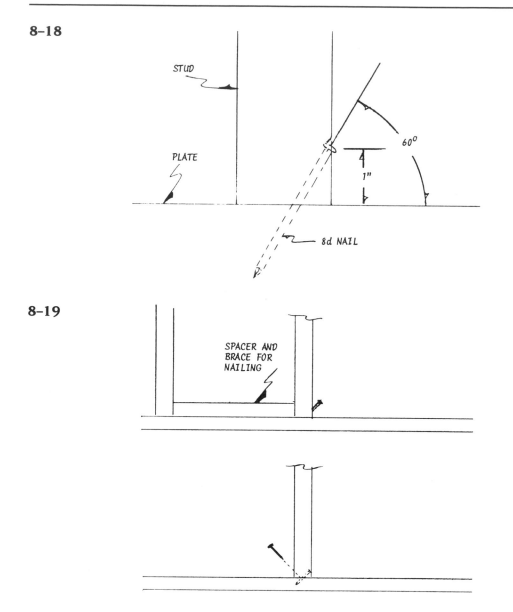

STUD

PLATE

60°

1"

8d NAIL

8–19

SPACER AND
BRACE FOR
NAILING

and step on it as you drive two of the nails. The nails on the opposite side will not be a problem because the stud will be firmly anchored. A more elaborate jig is shown in **8–20**. It does the job of the spacer–brace described above but includes two side pieces that work to keep the stud edges square to the plate. The clearance bevels at each end of the 2 × 4 are required so the jig can be tilted up after the first two stud nails are driven (**8–21**). The

8-20

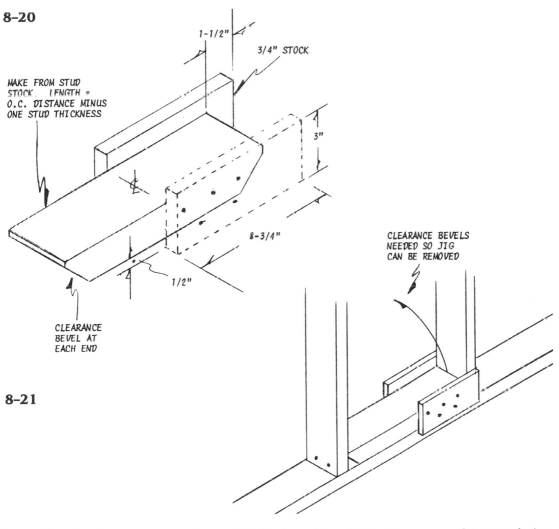

1-1/2"

3/4" STOCK

MAKE FROM STUD
STOCK. LENGTH =
O.C. DISTANCE MINUS
ONE STUD THICKNESS

3"

8-3/4"

CLEARANCE BEVELS
NEEDED SO JIG
CAN BE REMOVED

1/2"

CLEARANCE
BEVEL AT
EACH END

8-21

jig, or the simpler spacer, may be used at the top of the studs when upper plates are being installed, as well as at the bottom ends. But bear in mind that face-nailing is a better, stronger, and generally more practical alternative.

BUILDING TIP-UP WALL FRAMES

There are a few drawbacks to setting studs on soleplates one at a time. It's cumbersome to hold the stud and nail at the same time, for one thing, and toenailing often moves studs off their layout lines. Also, toenails don't have the holding power of nails driven through the face of the soleplate or top plate into the ends of the studs. You can solve these problems by using the system most carpenters use: Assemble the wall frame on the deck, and then tip it up into place.

First you mark the soleplate and top plate. Then you set one on edge, stand on it with one foot, set the first stud to the layout line (also on edge), step up to stand on it as well as to keep the boards from moving, and then drive two nails through the plate into the stud **8–22**. It may sound like a balancing act, but actually is quite easy once you get the knack. And when you have a few studs nailed in place, the frame becomes more solid and easier to work with.

8–22

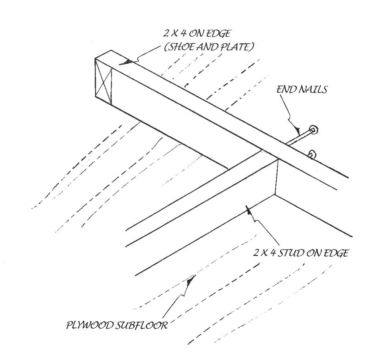

2 X 4 ON EDGE (SHOE AND PLATE)

END NAILS

2 X 4 STUD ON EDGE

PLYWOOD SUBFLOOR

You may want to assemble the full studs, tip up the wall, and then work on openings and other details. Some carpenters do all the framing, including headers and sometimes even sheathing, before tipping up the walls. For safety, tack a few 2 × 4 blocks to the outside of the floor to prevent the frame from slipping off the plywood platform as you raise it in place.

With a helper or two, you can safely erect walls without any mechanical aids. There are special jacks for this purpose, but if a stretch of wall is too long to tip with the muscle power you have on hand, build it in sections.

TOP PLATES

The top plates are two pieces of 2 × 4 nailed on top of the studs. The lengths are offset so the layers form lap joints over corners, as in **8–23**; where partition walls abut main walls, as in **8–24**; and where partitions intersect, as in **8–25**.

On approach is to surface-nail the bottom member, do so over a stud. End joints in the top member should be planned so they will be at least 4 feet away from those in the bottom piece.

On approach is to surface-nail the bottom part of the plate to each post and stud with two 16d nails. The top piece is secured to the lower one with 10d nails. Use two at each end and space those between about 16 inches apart in a staggered pattern. The assembly of the top plates should result in solid connections to all posts and studs and should be further strengthened by the interlocking action of the various pieces.

8–23

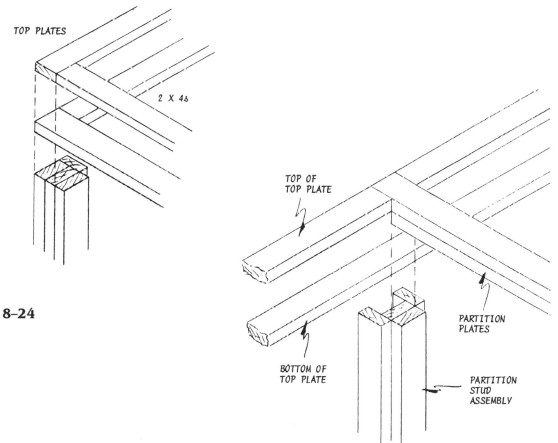

8–24

8–25

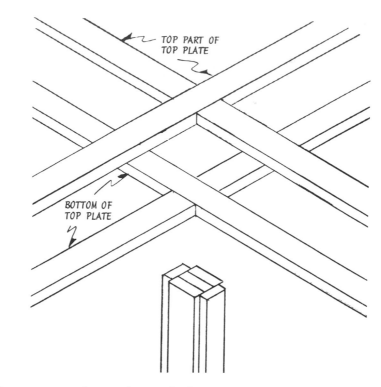

With the tip-up approach, you fasten the lower member of the top plate to the studs on the deck, which allows secure nailing instead of toenailing. Then you tip up the frame, and plumb and brace the wall. You'll need temporary braces in line with the frame to prevent lateral movement, and others tacked to blocks on the deck or to stakes outside the building to prevent the frame from moving in and out. When the frame is positioned and braced, you can nail on the second plate with overlapped corners. One twist on this approach that many carpenters use is to build, erect, and brace the frame with full studs, set the corner assemblies, and then add the second top plate.

HEADERS

Headers span across openings in a wall to supply support for the weight of upper structures. When a stud is cut or removed, particularly in bearing walls, a header is installed to compensate. All true headers rest on trimmers, so their total length must equal the width of the rough opening plus the thickness of two trimmers, usually 3 inches.

Built-up headers are made of two pieces of 2-by stock placed on edge with plywood spacers between to build up total thickness to match the width of other framing members.

The width of the header depends on the span and the load to be carried. To some extent, it also depends on the strength of the wood species you're using.

A header made of two 2 × 6s generally is rated to span 4 feet, 6 inches in a single story house, but only 4 feet in a two-story house. Doubled 2 × 8s generally can span 6 feet, 8 inches in single stories, but 4 feet, 5 inches with a second story. Two 2 × 10s generally can span 8 feet, 10 inches in one story; 6 feet, 8 inches in two stories; and 4 feet, 6 inches in three stories. Doubled 2 × 12s can normally handle spans of 10 feet, 12 inches with only a roof above; 8 feet, 10 inches with a second story above; and 6 feet, 8 inches with two stories above. As always, the building inspector may call for adjustments in these sizes, particularly if the house in general or the wall in particular is subject to extra or unusual loads.

Always use full studs, even if extra ones are required, at each end of the header. These, plus the trimmers, are good supports for the header but also provide a broad nailing surface for the inside and outside trim that comes later. You may want to double the rough sill for the same reason, even though a single 2 × 4 would do the job as far as strength is concerned. Any opening between the header and the top plate is filled in with cripples (**8–26**). These are toenailed to the header like studs.

Truss designs are sometimes used when the load above the header is unusually heavy or the span is excessive. Typical designs, such as those shown in **8–27**, are no more than cripples which are reinforced with diagonal, inset bracing.

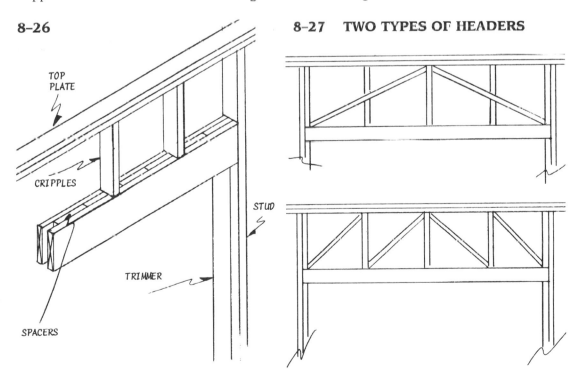

8–26

TOP PLATE

CRIPPLES

TRIMMER

SPACERS

8–27   TWO TYPES OF HEADERS

STUD

In a typical nailing pattern for a rough window opening, you nail the studs at each end of the header with four or more 10d nails, depending on the header's width. Trimmers and studs are nailed together with 10d nails spaced about 16 inches apart and following a staggered pattern. Toenail at the bottom end of the trimmers as if they were studs. Nail through the lower part of the sill into the cripples below with two 10d nails per cripple. Attach the upper part of the sill with 10d nails spaced about 8 inches apart and staggered. **Figure 8–28** shows a completed opening. One way to work when the frame is being tilted into place later is to break the trimmers at the sill line so the sills can be end-nailed through the stud (**8–29**).

An advantage of using full 4 × 12 headers throughout, as shown in **8–30**, becomes apparent when a span requires a header that is so large there is little room between it and

8–28

8–29

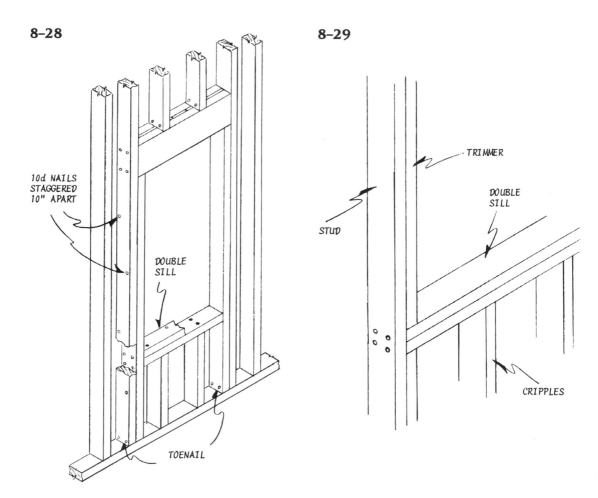

the top plate to install cripples. Many builders will then use full headers even though they might use other designs elsewhere. But there is a possible disadvantage to the full header. Some designers say that excessive shrinkage can occur in a full header and cause cracks above windows and doors unless wall coverings are applied with special precautions.

All door openings through bearing walls should have headers. When a header is not required, the opening is framed in simple fashion, as in **8–31**—enough to provide a base for jambs if a door is hung, or for trim if the opening is just a pass-through.

Walls should not be supported by fireplace masonry. Use headers as you would for any opening and provide at least two inches of clearance on all sides, as shown in **8–32**.

WALL BRACING

On most modern framing, plywood ties the components together. But you may want the extra strength provided by old-fashioned let-in bracing as well. The let-in type is usually made with 1 × 4 boards that fit snugly in notches cut in each crossed member of the frame

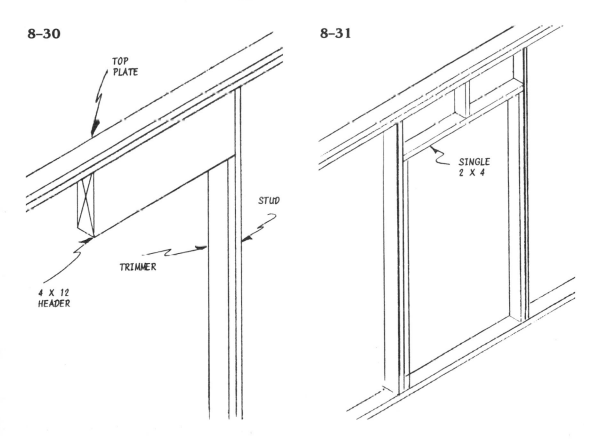

8–30

TOP PLATE

STUD

TRIMMER

4 X 12 HEADER

8–31

SINGLE 2 X 4

8-32

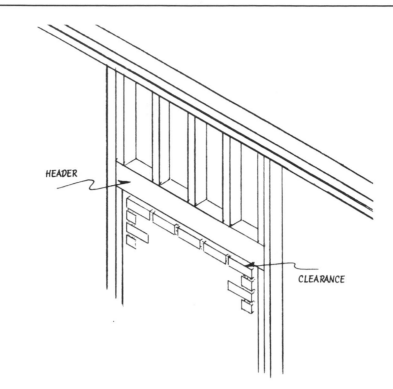

HEADER

CLEARANCE

(**8–33**). You can tack the brace in place, draw its outline across the frame members, make the side cuts as deep as the board is thick, and then clean out the waste material with a chisel. Attach the brace with three nails at each end and two nails at each crossing. Bracing application may vary to accommodate openings, as shown in **8–34**, and it can even take the form of a let-in ribbon (**8–35**).

Another option is inset bracing made with material that matches the cross-sectional dimensions of the studs (**8–36**). But installing these individual pieces calls for a lot of angular cutting and fitting.

In areas where buildings are subject to unusual loads and stresses, be sure to consult with the local building department about special bracing and additional frame-connecting hardware that may be required.

FIRE BLOCKING

These are 2-by pieces running horizontally in a wall frame to break air spaces and prevent drafts that would encourage fire to spread. They are crucial for fire safety, mainly by retarding the rate at which a fire can spread through framing cavities. But they also stiffen the

8–33   LET IN BRACING   **8–34**

8–35

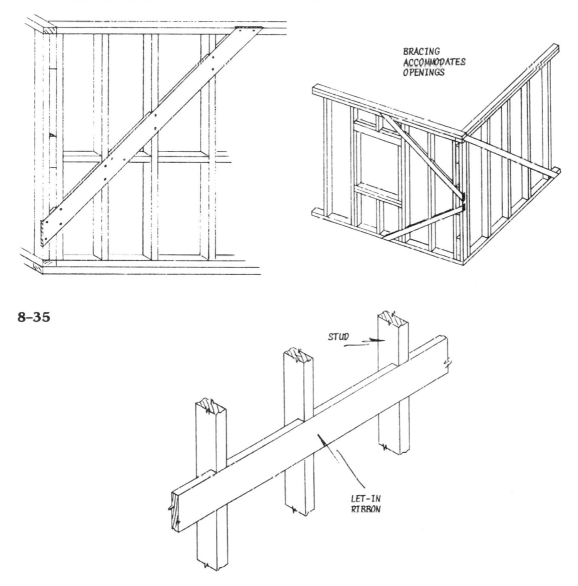

frame wall. The blocks may be installed on a line midway up the wall, or you can stagger them so they will be easier to nail (**8–37**).

Blocking can serve two purposes. A double line might be used, for example, to provide nailing surfaces for board-and-batten siding (**8–38**). In such cases, do not stagger the

8–36

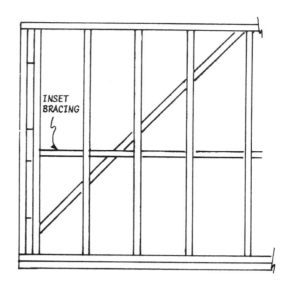

INSET
BRACING

8–37

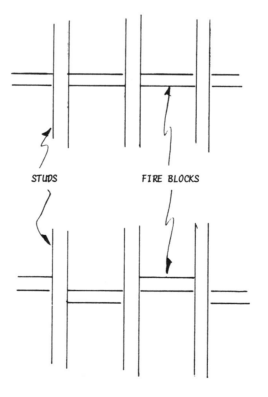

STUDS   FIRE BLOCKS

8-38

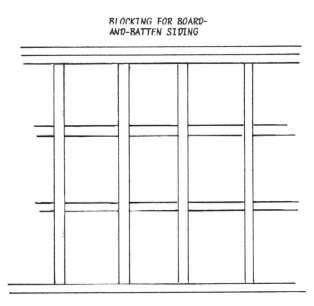

BLOCKING FOR BOARD-
AND-BATTEN SIDING

blocking because it would result in an unsightly nail pattern on the outside of the wall when siding is up.

In some applications, the blocks are called cats, and are required to stiffen and prevent twisting in long studs used to build high walls. If your plan calls for a room or area with ceilings higher than eight or ten feet, cats probably will be required. Even if they aren't, it's wise to install them to help reduce nail popping in drywall and other maintenance problems that stem from excessive movement in the frame.

PARTITIONS

Partition frames are erected after perimeter framing is complete. Usually, only those partitions that supply support for upper structures (bearing walls) are built at this point. Others that merely divide up floor space can be built after the roof is on and there is protection from the weather. For example, when the roof frame is made of trusses that require support from outside walls only, partitions can be built after the roof is complete. The idea is to make the structure rainproof as soon as possible.

Non-loadbearing partitions are organized just like outside walls, except that large headers and bracing are not needed. Like all walls, the designs must provide nailing surfaces for the wall coverings to be attached later. Although headers are not usually required in nonbearing walls, it's a good idea to include trimmers around all openings if only because of the broader nailing surfaces they provide for any casing and trim that will be used to finish the openings after walls are covered.

Like the soleplates in exterior walls, those for partitions are run continuously and sawed away at door openings after framing is complete.

SPECIAL WALL DETAILS

To increase insulation protection, make room for large waste pipes, and other reasons, you may want to increase the framing thickness in some walls, generally by using 2 × 6s instead of 2 × 4s for shoes, plates, and studs (**8–39**). Another approach is to build a double wall with staggered studs as in **8–40**. This will give you more room for pipes or you can weave soundproofing material in such a wall (**8–41**). Such soundproofing may be desirable when kitchen and living room, or kitchen and utility room, for example, have a common wall.

Anticipating what will come later gives you the opportunity to include other important construction details during initial framing stages. Openings may be required for heating ducts, and these must be framed to correct size and to provide strength. An opening between studs doesn't need more than a block set at the correct height. A wider opening means you must cut a stud. Codes may allow a single 2 × 4 crosspiece, but doubling up will provide greater strength and safety (**8–42**).

Bathtubs should have extra support blocks and special nailing strips placed horizontally for wall coverings that terminate at the tub line (**8–43**). Quite often, special consideration is given to the area under the tub, anticipating its extra load when filled with water. If a regular joist would interfere with the tub drain, it will not be too difficult to cut through and install headers as shown in **8–44**, with joists hangers as required by code.

Backings for wash basins or wall cabinets and even towel rods and such can be provided as shown in **8–45**. A wall-hung lavatory usually hangs on brackets and these require solid supports, often double 2 × 10s or larger beams as specified by the manufacturer.

A double row of studs, placed as shown in **8–46**, on an extra-wide plate, will provide unimpeded space so that pipes can run horizontally. Some contractors do this kind of thing to avoid the drilling that would be necessary with conventional stud placement.

Large waste vents that pass through plates can weaken the area considerably, so reinforcement, in the form of scabs, is used around the opening (**8–47**). Make the scabs from 2 × 4 stock and cut them long enough so they span across at least two studs.

Now is also the time to provide for some extra storage by using the wasted space in partition walls. Ideas for the recessing medicine chest shown in **8–48** are usable in kitchen and utility rooms for storing canned goods and the like. All you need at the framing stage

8–39

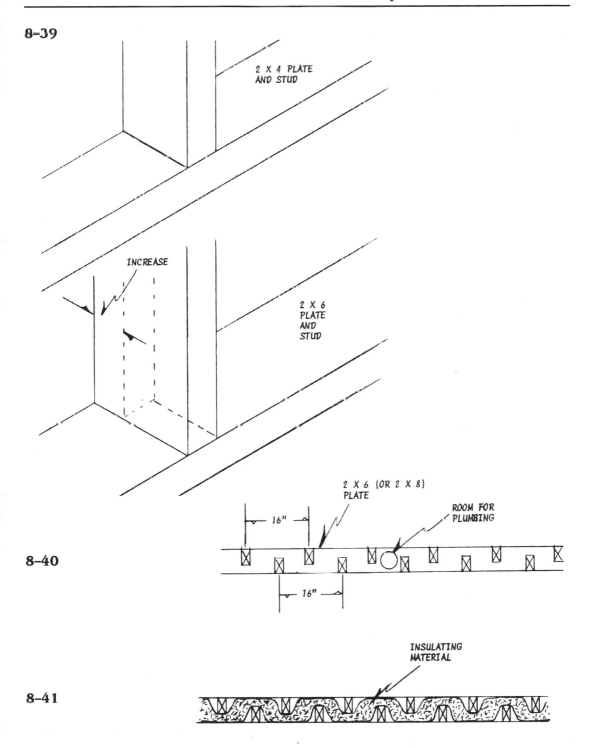

2 X 4 PLATE
AND STUD

INCREASE

2 X 6
PLATE
AND
STUD

2 X 6 (OR 2 X 8)
PLATE

ROOM FOR
PLUMBING

16"

8–40

16"

INSULATING
MATERIAL

8–41

8–42

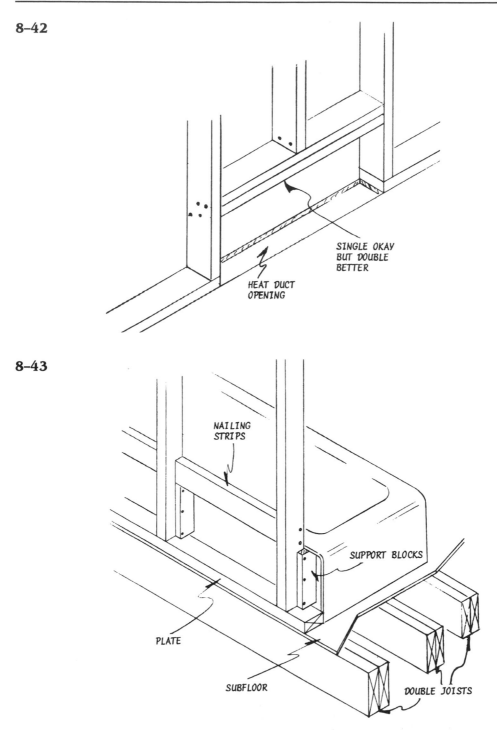

SINGLE OKAY
BUT DOUBLE
BETTER

HEAT DUCT
OPENING

8–43

NAILING
STRIPS

SUPPORT BLOCKS

PLATE

SUBFLOOR

DOUBLE JOISTS

are two pieces of 2 × 4 placed horizontally to indicate the top and bottom of the cabinet. You can line the interior and add the shelves later. Do the frame and hang the door after the wall covering is complete.

Among other spots where you'll need additional framing is the area around a prefab fireplace where clearance between wood and metal is specified by the manufacturer. Note that a header, when required, is supported by trimmers (**8–49**).

8–44

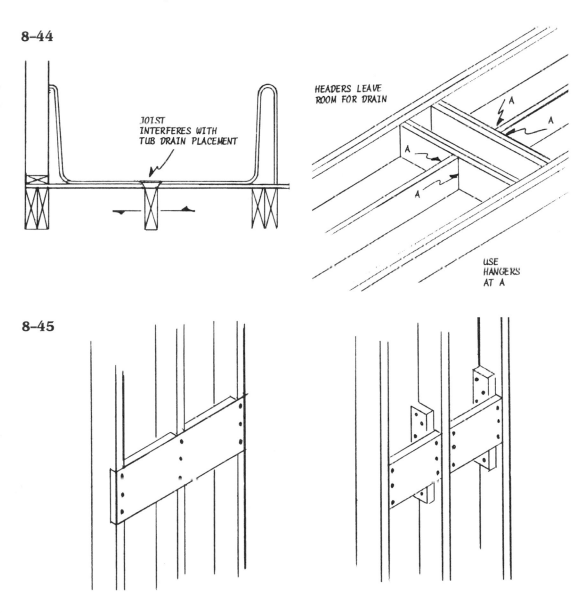

JOIST INTERFERES WITH TUB DRAIN PLACEMENT

HEADERS LEAVE ROOM FOR DRAIN

USE HANGERS AT A

8–45

8–46

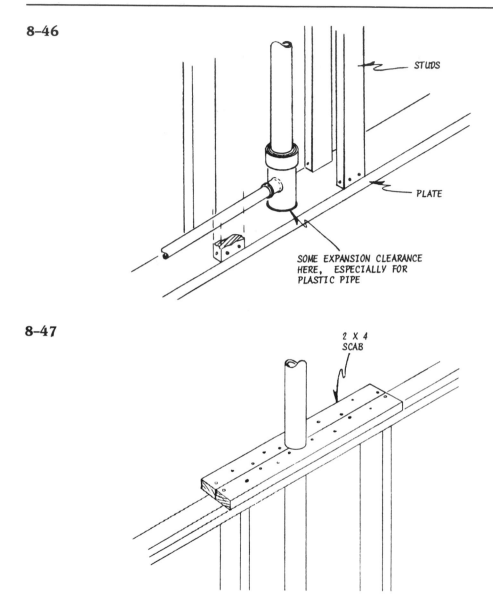

STUDS

PLATE

SOME EXPANSION CLEARANCE HERE, ESPECIALLY FOR PLASTIC PIPE

8–47

2 X 4 SCAB

Once the perimeter walls and partitions are up, it's a good idea to take some time and walk around the building to inspect the frame. You may need to make a few minor adjustments. You also may spot other areas where built-in bracing will pay off later on. For example, you can install horizontal 2 × 6s in bathrooms to anchor towel bars so you won't have to rely on molly fasteners. Also check all corners, including along the ceilings, to be sure that you have nailing for both wall and ceiling drywall.

8-48

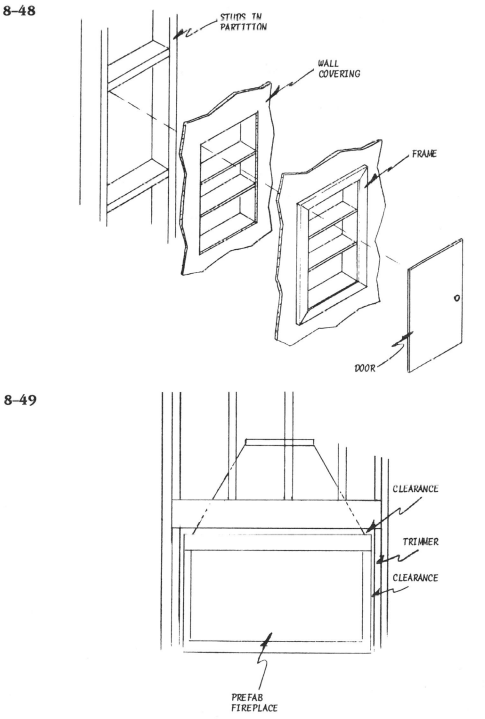

STUDS IN PARTITION

WALL COVERING

FRAME

DOOR

8-49

CLEARANCE

TRIMMER

CLEARANCE

PREFAB FIREPLACE

FRAMING HARDWARE

By using ready-made pieces of hardware like those shown in **8–50**, you could, at least in theory, frame an entire house without having to drive a single toenail. You'll find that the name of the piece often identifies its application. Rafter anchor, joist anchor, post base, and the like are typical. Some types come flat, so you can bend them to suit. But major manufacturers supply a tremendous variety of configurations. The examples shown here are just a few of the many available.

While hangers are common on joist installations, and required wherever a joist meets a girder without bearing, hardware generally is not required on wall frames except in special circumstances. For example, in areas subject to hurricanes and high winds, local codes may require tie-down hardware between components of the frame to resist uplift.

8–50   FRAMING ANCHORS AND HANGERS

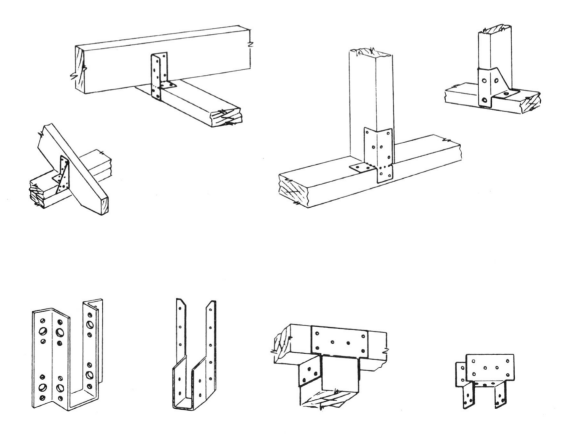

9 INSTALLING CEILING JOISTS

There are many possible sequences in construction. Some parts of a house have to be built ahead of others, of course. But some jobs, such as sheathing the wall frame, can be postponed in order to move on to the ceiling and roof. In general, you should plan to roof the house as quickly as possible, and then close in the walls. The drawback is that you have to leave many wall braces in place, which can complicate movement around the worksite. So you may want to do the sheathing work now to protect the building from the weather and stiffen the wall framing.

CEILING JOIST DESIGN

If you move directly to installing the ceiling joists, you'll find that their general layout is very much like floor joists, with a few wrinkles depending on the design of the building. If the ceiling joists on the first story are the floor joists on the second, all the rules apply, including the typical 40-pound-per-square-foot load requirement, using connector hardware at joints, and doubling up headers and trimmers at openings.

The design load generally is cut in half to 20 pounds per square foot if the ceiling joists become the floor of an attic not intended for living space. If you think you might remodel the space at some point, maybe to include an extra bedroom and bath, stick with the plan used on the first-floor joists.

Ceiling joists also act to some extent as ties between opposite walls and resist stresses that could push out the walls (**9–1**). All in all, it makes sense to be generous with ceiling joists instead of doing the opposite to save some money on material. Of course, local codes may make the decision for you.

Another option is to install trusses and use the bottom horizontal chords as the ceiling joists (**9–2**). You'll need to do a lot of planning when it comes to trusses, because they form

9–1

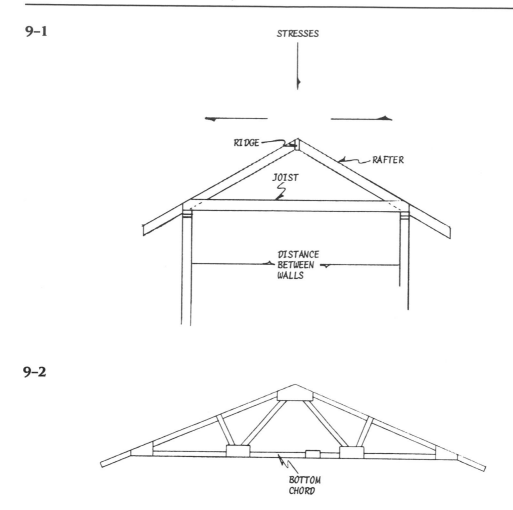

9–2

the ceiling line, roof, overhang, and other features all in one package. But the fabrication and installation is best left to pros. Most truss builders can offer many configurations: with or without overhangs, steep or low-slop, provisions for dormers, and more.

Yet another option (as it is on floor joists) is to use engineered timbers, such as I-beam joists with plywood webs between 2 × 4s. But whatever approach you take, plan to run joists across the narrower dimension of the wall frame so spans can be reduced—even if it means changing the direction of the runs. In the example in **9–3**, the long joists receive intermediate support from the bearing partition. Shorter joists are placed at right angles and are supported at each end on wall plates (**9–4**). Wall A should then be regarded as a bearing wall. The joists running across the wall can be one piece or made up of shorter pieces if they are overlapped or spliced at the wall (**9–5**). If possible, use single pieces that don't need laps.

9–3

9–4

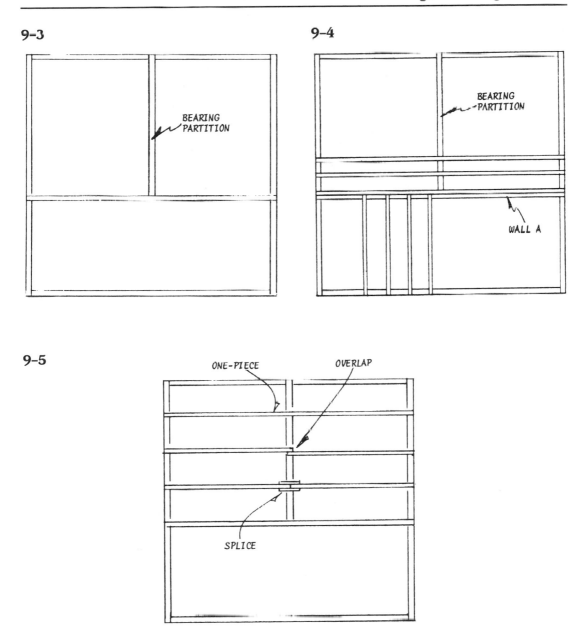

9–5

Another situation that calls for special joist considerations can occur when the roof has little slope (low pitch) and the joist run is parallel to the roof edge. Here, the roof slope may not make it over the outside joists, so shorter members are placed at right angles to the regular joists (**9–6**).

9-6

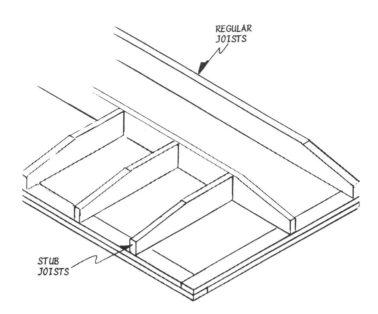

Using the same commonly available #2 Douglas fir species we used in the span guide-lines for floor joists on page 122, you'll find that the load reduction from 40 to 20 pounds per square foot allows smaller joists and longer spans. For example, at 40 pounds of design load for floor joists, 2 × 8s set 16 inches on center typically can span 12 feet, 10 inches. At a design load of 20 pounds per square foot, the same lumber and spacing typically can span 18 feet, 6 inches. Use 2 × 6s 16 inches on center to span 14 feet, 1 inch, and 2 × 10s to span 23 feet, 8 inches. As always, these guidelines may be changed by a building inspector when you are working with locally available lumber that has a different load-carrying capacity.

SPACING JOISTS

The spacing can vary but, as with studs, 16 inches O.C. is the standard. Because the dou-bled top plate of the wall frame supplies sufficient strength, joists, in theory, can be placed anywhere. But it makes some sense to set them over the stud positions as in **9-7**, as this will automatically determine the correct spacing and will establish a degree of conformity throughout the framing system. You can carry up layout marks from the studs by using a square, or work with one of the spacing gauges described previously.

It's a good idea at this point to preview placement of the roof rafters that will be added later. Preferably, these are placed to abut the joists so the two members can be nailed together solidly as well as to the plate (**9-8**). Any cut that is required at the end of the joist

9-7

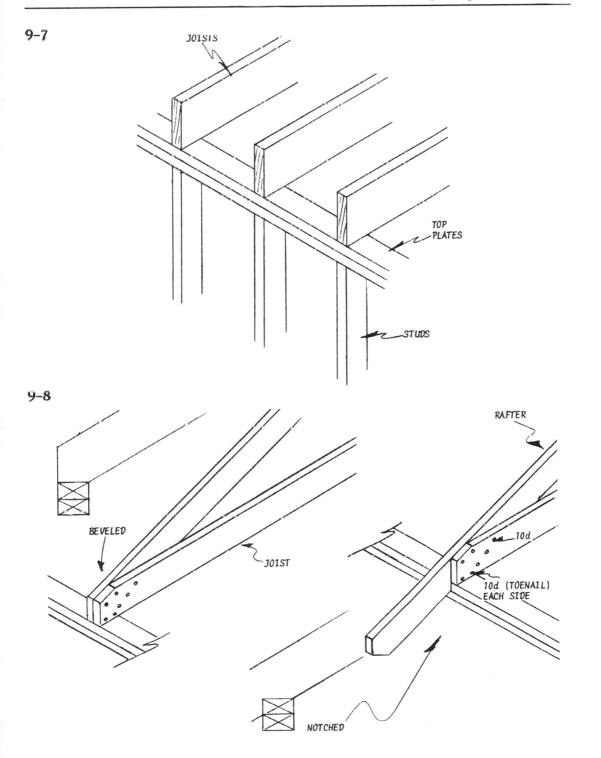

JOISTS

TOP PLATES

STUDS

9-8

RAFTER

BEVELED

JOIST

10d

10d (TOENAIL) EACH SIDE

NOTCHED

to match the slope of the rafters can be made before the pieces are placed, but most times the piece you must remove is small enough so you can do it easily with a handsaw or circular saw after the rafters are up.

NAILING THE JOISTS

Toenail the joists to each perimeter plate with 10d nails. In areas where high winds occur frequently, metal strap anchors are often added as shown in **9–9**, to provide more strength. Other types of ready-made framing anchors may also be used.

Joists that cross a partition are toenailed to the plate and 2 × 6 blocks can be added between them as shown in **9–10** to provide nailing surfaces for wall-covering materials.

9–9

9–10

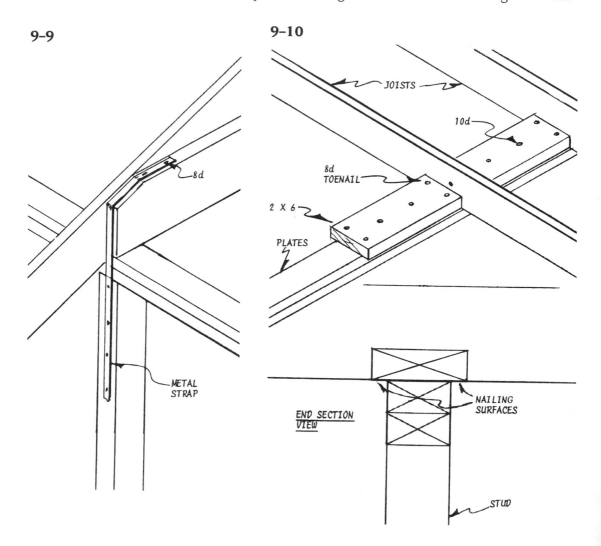

Pieced joists that overlap at a crossing must be tied together by surface nailing in addition to being toenailed to the plate (**9-11**). If the pieces are aligned, splice them at the joint by using 2-by material that is at least 24 inches long (**9-12**).

Partitions that are parallel to the joists must be tied in for rigidity and to supply nailing surfaces for other materials. Various procedures may be followed as long as they comply

9-11

9-12

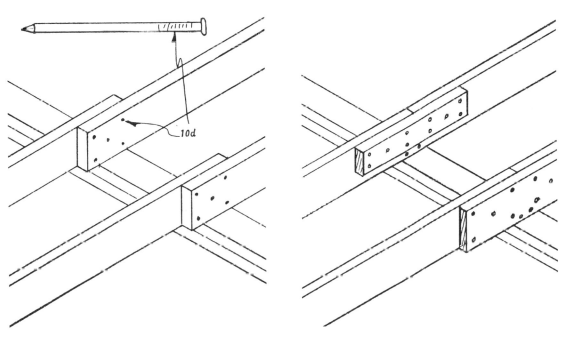

with the needs, but a fairly straightforward one, used often, is shown in **9-13**. Place the 1 × 6 (or 2 × 6)nailer first. (it's called a nailer because you nail drywall to it) centering it over the plate and securing it with 7d or 8d nails. Place the 2 × 4 blocks and toenail them as if they were joists before you drive the 16d nails at the ends. Work with a level to be sure the interior surfaces of the nailer and the joists are on the same plane.

If the room below will have an exposed beam ceiling, the joists are placed in standard fashion with suitable nailing blocks placed between them (**9-14**). When a hidden beam is used to support joists so there will be unbroken space below, as for a very large living room, the framing can be handled three ways, as shown in **9-15**. Using joist hangers is the preferred method, and typically required by code. It's also generally faster and easier to use hangers. If you do use ledgers, you may be able to rest the joists on them. If not,

9–13

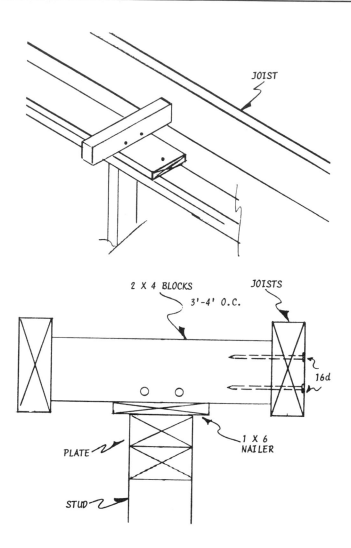

bear in mind that the depth of notches should be no more than one-eight the depth of the joist to avoid splitting and possible joist failure. Of course, a clear-span beam heading off the joists must be big enough to span the area safely without intermediate supports below.

Openings through a ceiling frame are handled like those through a floor. If the upper area will be nothing but an unused attic that requires only an access hole that isn't more than two or three feet square, you may be able to skip the trimmers and doubled headers. It's safer, and often required, to frame all openings using the double-up system.

9-14   9-15

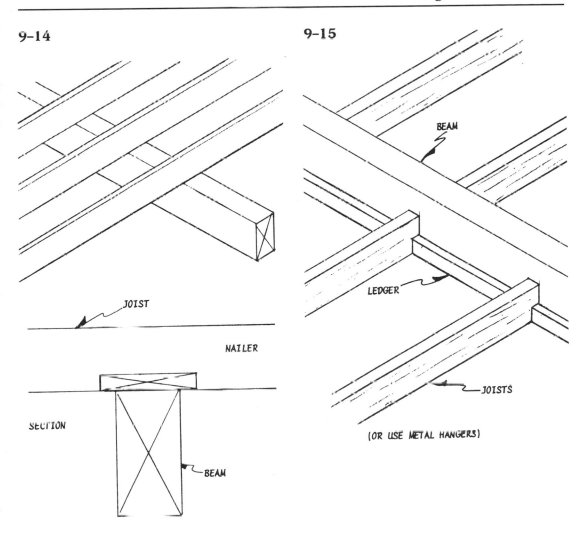

JOIST

NAILER

SECTION

BEAM

BEAM

LEDGER

JOISTS

(OR USE METAL HANGERS)

Local codes that relate to fire regulations may tell you what size such openings should be.

If you are considering anything like a prefab folding or disappearing stairway, information on the size of the rough opening required and possibly even the design of the framing will be furnished along with the unit. These larger openings will require double trimmers and headers.

10

FRAMING THE ROOF

I f you are afraid of heights, even one story off the ground, you don't need practical guidelines about when to work on a roof. It's scary and you're never going up there—end of story. But most owner–builders can handle the work if they stick to some basic safety guidelines.

On commercial jobs, OSHA requirements can include special fall-arresting harnesses that resemble mountain-climbing gear. Few contractors working on private homes encumber themselves with this equipment. But they do use safe scaffolding and certified scaffold planks (not dimensional lumber you happen to have on site) to hold themselves and their materials in place. The most complete scaffold systems generally are needed only when the framing is to be covered, first with sheathing and then with shingles. On roof framing, you'll be able to handle some of the work from within the building.

The safest roofs are walkable. That means they have such a gentle slope that you can walk around safely without scaffolding. Flat and low-slope roofs that qualify are obviously a lot easier for do-it-yourselfers to deal with. Of course, what seems walkable to one person may seem too physically taxing or even unsafe to another. Up to about a 30-degree slope, most people are fine. To find your own comfort level, which is really your safety level, there is no substitute for trying a test run—one step at a time, slowly and cautiously.

But even when a roof is not walkable, you can work on it with an assist from scaffold equipment. There are several types, which roofers use as standard equipment and do-it-yourselfers can rent. Pump jacks are used to support scaffold planks along the edge of a roof. This working surface can be raised and lowered on site-built posts running from the ground to roof level that are braced to the building. Normally used for siding work, they are handy on some roofing jobs requiring a wide working platform along the edge of the roof. (Be sure your equipment has the code-required back rail.) Without the jacks, you still might invest the time to build a fixed position platform of planks to hold materials and to provide a safe, flat transition between ladder and roof.

You can assemble a simple, though more rickety version of this platform by propping two extension ladders against the house and attaching an adjustable bracket, called a ladder jack, to each ladder between the ladder and the house to support scaffold planks. The system is safe enough but tends to sway, which can be unnerving. However, it allows you to plant your ladders on the ground, join them with planks along the roof edge, and gain a flat transition area plus storage space for some nails and tools.

To hold planks in a level position on a sloping roof frame, you can use adjustable scaffold brackets attached to the rafters (and later to the sheathing). The nails are driven through slotted openings in the base of the bracket. The idea is to drive nails almost all the way in, leaving just enough margin to slip the brackets up and off the nail supports when you have to move.

ROOF TYPES

Up to now, we've worked mostly by making square cuts across framing members and by using butt joints at connections. Unless you're building a flat roof, rafter work gets into angular cutting, the complexities of which are directly related to the design of the roof.

In a conventional gable frame you have angle cuts at each end of the rafter, one where it meets the ridge, and another where it is trimmed with a fascia. Your plan may call for a combination of roof styles where the main roof rafters are interrupted to form dormers (**10–1**). Parts of the building may have shed roofs with a single slope. Or you may want

10–1

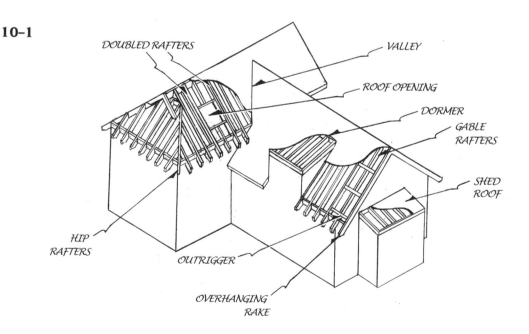

DOUBLED RAFTERS

VALLEY

ROOF OPENING

DORMER

GABLE RAFTERS

SHED ROOF

HIP RAFTERS

OUTRIGGER

OVERHANGING RAKE

the increased protection offered by a hip design with overhangs on all sides of the building. This design adds compound miter cuts to the puzzle of roof framing, which are more difficult to plan, lay out and install.

The shed roof, often called a lean-to roof, and the plain gable roof are examples of roofs whose framing members don't require more than simple miter cuts (**10–2**). In both cases, one angle applies regardless of where a cut is made in the rafters. As shown in **10–3**, on gable roofs with different slopes, the cuts at A, called plumb cuts, are parallel, and this may even be carried to the overhang end of the rafters if the design you choose is applicable (**10–4**). The parallel-cut factor applies to a shed roof even if it is along the lines of the plank-and-beam construction I used over my studio (**10–5**).

While a gable roof has simple exterior lines, it, or part of it, can be constructed to provide interest inside. For example, our living-room area is roofed over as shown in **10–6**, so we have exposed beams and roof decking there while other rooms have a conventional ceiling. Bear in mind that this design, which is generally reserved for timber frames and post-and-beam frames, causes additional work with insulation and ventilation. Most roofs today, by far, are basic gables with insulation and vent space between rafter bays, covered with plywood roof sheathing.

Gable or shed dormers are often added to plain gable roofs to break monotonous lines,

10–2

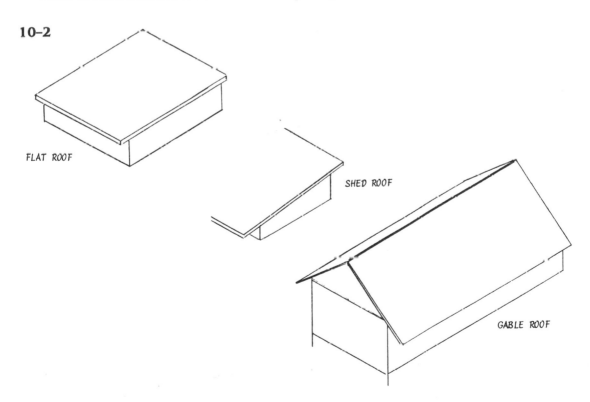

FLAT ROOF

SHED ROOF

GABLE ROOF

10–3

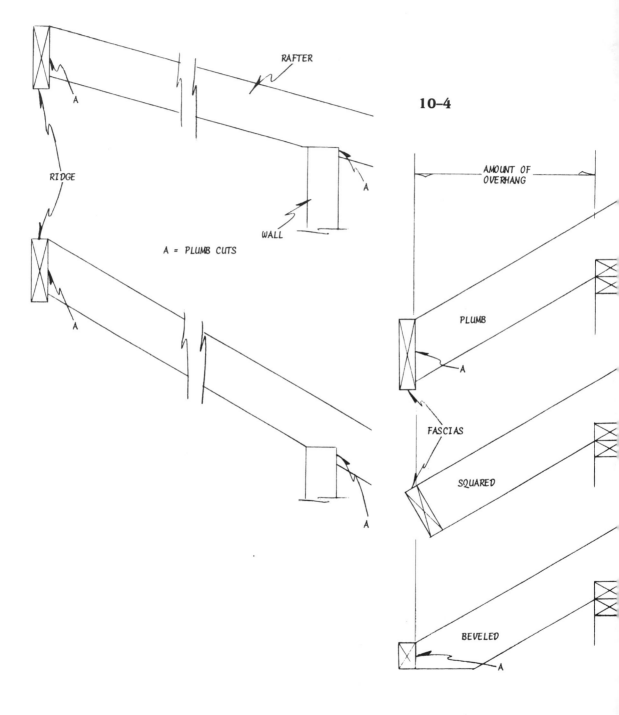

RAFTER

RIDGE

A = PLUMB CUTS

WALL

10–4

AMOUNT OF OVERHANG

PLUMB

FASCIAS

SQUARED

BEVELED

10–5

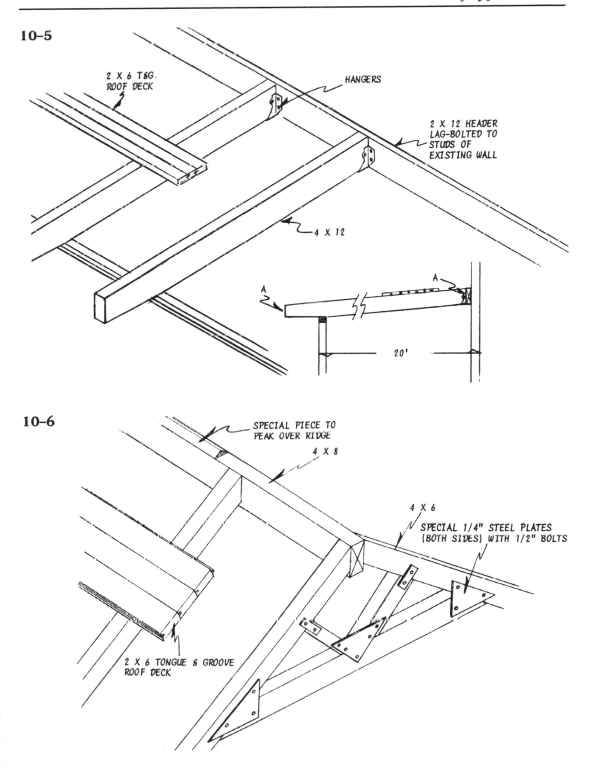

2 X 6 T&G.
ROOF DECK

HANGERS

2 X 12 HEADER
LAG-BOLTED TO
STUDS OF
EXISTING WALL

4 X 12

A

A

20'

10–6

SPECIAL PIECE TO
PEAK OVER RIDGE

4 X 8

4 X 6

SPECIAL 1/4" STEEL PLATES
(BOTH SIDES) WITH 1/2" BOLTS

2 X 6 TONGUE & GROOVE
ROOF DECK

as in **10–7**, or for the more practical purpose of providing light, air, and additional space to make attic areas more usable.

Examples of roof designs that get you into more complex construction procedures are shown in **10–8** and **10–9**. The hip roof is a popular design because its shape tends to hug the ground. It also provides protective overhangs on all sides of the structure.

The main difference between the gambrel roof and the gable is the break in the slope, which can be used advantageously at a second level to provide more headroom.

The mansard roof, like the gambrel, also has a double slope, but the second one is practically flat. The design will provide additional headroom for a second story.

10–7

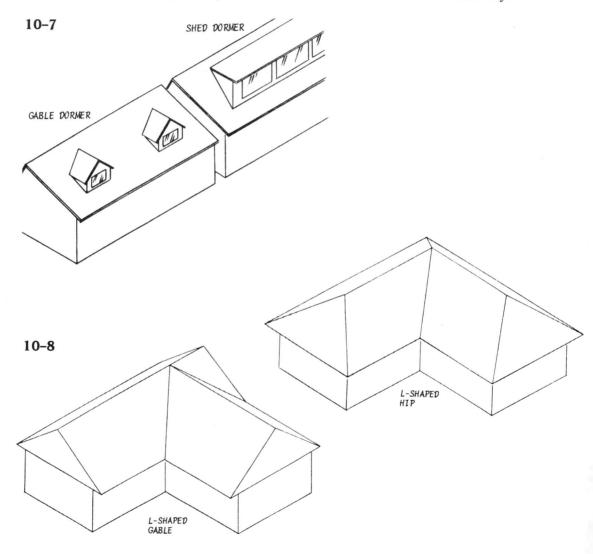

SHED DORMER

GABLE DORMER

10–8

L-SHAPED HIP

L-SHAPED GABLE

10–9

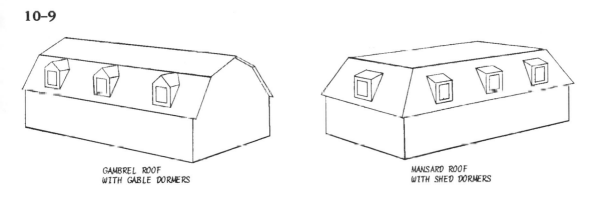

GAMBREL ROOF
WITH GABLE DORMERS

MANSARD ROOF
WITH SHED DORMERS

Roof framing may seem complicated, but it is well within the scope of the amateur. If it weren't, there would be no point in talking about housebuilding at all. Much of the geometry involved, for example, has already been done and is available in the form of printed tables and in the framing square, a measuring tool that is a math book in itself, when properly used. Also, there is no reason why the shape of components can't be picked up right on the job—the wall frames being the base to work from—or even by doing a large-scale drawing. It's often even possible to make a layout right on the subfloor.

It's wise to make one rafter, test it in place, and then use it as a template for others even when the length of companion pieces changes. Some designs require more thought than others, but the actual installation relies more on the builder's dedication than on encyclopedic knowledge or mysterious skills.

THE NAMES AND THE TERMS

Most roof-framing pieces are called rafters, but they are further identified by the part they play and their placement in the structure. The simplified top view of a roof frame for a T-shaped house in **10–10** includes several variations. Note that the common rafters, which play a part in most sloped-roof framing, run continuously from the ridge to the wall, and beyond if there is an overhang. Common rafters are used exclusively in a plain gable roof and are the easiest to cut and place because they need only simple angle cuts. A jack rafter needs a compound angle cut, at one end at least, because it connects to a hip rafter that is already set at an angle (**10–11**). This also applies to cripples where they connect to valley rafters, to the valley rafters themselves, and to hip rafters. Compare this with the way common rafters join the ridge board in **10–12** and you can quickly see the difference in the sawing required. (We'll talk about the collar beam later.)

The nomenclature and the various cuts needed in a common rafter are shown in

10–10   RAFTER TYPES (TOP VIEW)

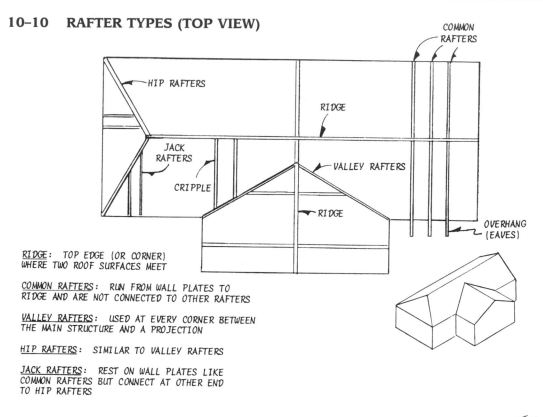

RIDGE: TOP EDGE (OR CORNER)
WHERE TWO ROOF SURFACES MEET

COMMON RAFTERS: RUN FROM WALL PLATES TO
RIDGE AND ARE NOT CONNECTED TO OTHER RAFTERS

VALLEY RAFTERS: USED AT EVERY CORNER BETWEEN
THE MAIN STRUCTURE AND A PROJECTION

HIP RAFTERS: SIMILAR TO VALLEY RAFTERS

JACK RAFTERS: REST ON WALL PLATES LIKE
COMMON RAFTERS BUT CONNECT AT OTHER END
TO HIP RAFTERS

10–11

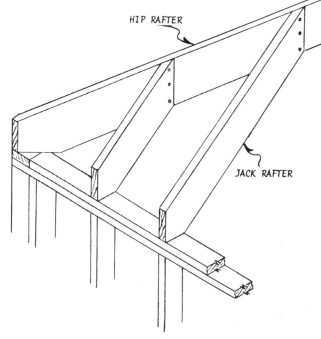

10–12. While the cuts arc simple, they should be made carefully so that the rafter will fit solidly against the ridge and snugly over the plate. The full bird's mouth is needed only when the rafter extends to form an overhang. You still need the seat cut if the rafter ends at the plate, but the plumb cut is made so the end of the rafter will be flush with the outside edge of the plate.

The run of a rafter is the distance from the centerline of the ridge to the outside of the wall. If the ridge is centered, as in **10–14**, then the run of all rafters is the same and equals one half the total span. The line length is the true linear dimension of the rafter between the points shown. Note that it is reduced by one-half the thickness of the ridge.

Bear in mind that you can use a mathematical approach to plan and cut your rafters.

10–12

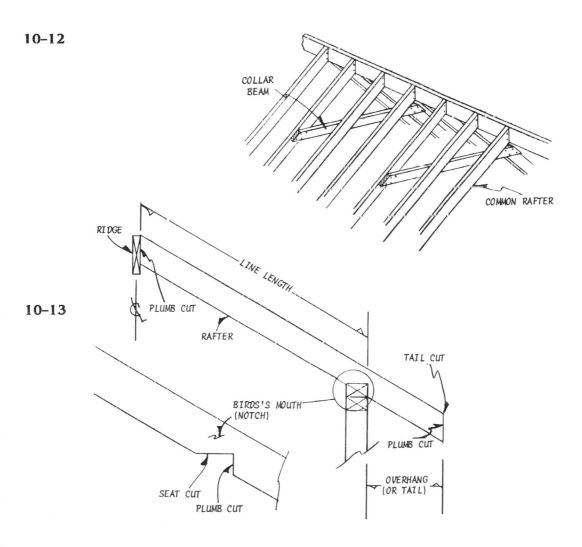

10–13

10–14

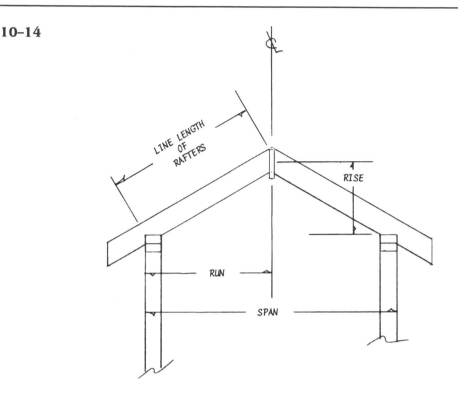

But there is another system that will appeal to people who don't take too well to math. It is to assemble a full-length rafter on a series of braces on the side of the building running from the outside wall to a well-braced ridge. You can adjust the braces to raise or lower the ridge and change the angle of the rafter. When you get the setup you want, you can mark the angle cuts at each end (the plumb cuts), and the bird's mouth cuts over the plate, and use that rafter as a template. You may wind up with a roof that is between standard slopes. But that doesn't really matter.

THE PITCH AND THE SLOPE

Both terms indicate the incline of a sloping roof. Pitch, as the ratio of the rise to the span, is a fraction derived by dividing the rise by the span. Remember, the span is twice the run (**10–15**). A 6-foot rise divided by a 24-foot span will have ¼ pitch. If the span is the same but the rise is 4 feet, the pitch would be ⅙ (**10–16**).

Slope is the incline as a ratio of the rise to the run expressed in inches per foot. If the incline increases 6 inches for every foot of run, the slope is said to be 6 in 12. If the increase is 4 inches, then the slope is 4 in 12.

10–15   PRINCIPAL ROOF-PITCHES

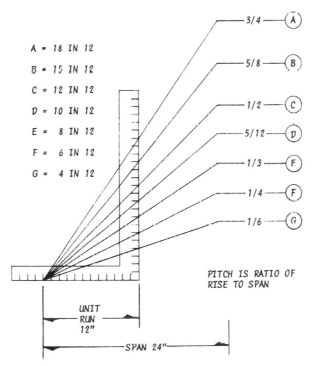

A = 18 IN 12

B = 15 IN 12

C = 12 IN 12

D = 10 IN 12

E = 8 IN 12

F = 6 IN 12

G = 4 IN 12

PITCH IS RATIO OF
RISE TO SPAN

UNIT RUN 12"

SPAN 24"

10–16   EXAMPLES OF PITCHES

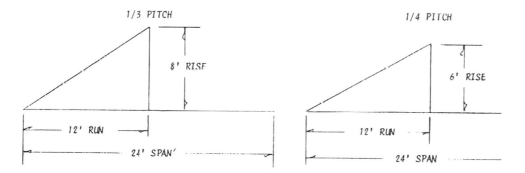

1/3 PITCH

8' RISE

12' RUN

24' SPAN

1/4 PITCH

6' RISE

12' RUN

24' SPAN

Roofs can range from no slope for a flat design, through slight slope for a shed, intermediate slope for a ranch or rambler-type house, comparatively sharp slope for a Cape Cod, to the extreme slope of an A-frame. While the slope of the roof is usually an architectural consideration, it can also be affected by the type of roofing to be used. This is not as critical today because modern roofing materials and newer methods of installation provide a great deal of leeway. For example, if you increase the thickness of the underlay material and decrease the exposure-to-the-weather distance of shingles, you can often get by with a lesser slope than might normally be required. By being very careful when you select asphalt and aggregate surfacing materials, you can lay a built-up roof on a slope. One modern roofing material, a rubbery sheet called modified bitumen, can handle both flat and low-slope roofs, and has largely replaced the old-fashioned built-up roof made of several layers of roofing material bonded with hot tar.

It is critical to consider the roofing ahead of time if you plan to use a heavyweight material such as slate or tile. In some high-wind areas, heavy roofing materials are standard. Concrete tiles, for example, weigh so much more than standard asphalt shingles that rafters that would suffice in one case will not meet code in another.

RAFTER SIZES AND SPACING

Rafters must support live and dead loads, and provide a skeleton to which you can nail covering materials. Because loads can vary with the weight of the structure itself, snow loads, wind pressures, and the like, the cross-sectional dimensions of rafters can vary as specified in building codes. Because rafters do not normally carry a heavy ceiling load, it's possible to use a wider spacing than the standard 16 inches prescribed for joists and studs. But 16 inches is standard, particularly if you intend to use standard 4 × 8 sheets of sheathing. Also, when rafters are spaced like the joists, each one can be tied to its companion joist as well as to the plate, as in **10–17**. If the spacing differs, some attempt should be made to tie in as many rafters as possible in similar fashion. This calls for some compatibility in the spacing, so some adjustment may be in order. This should not be done on the plus side and never so that spacing between rafters is irregular. The top view of a roof frame in **10–18** shows how the system works when joists are 16 inches O.C. and rafters are 24 inches O.C.

But the roof is a crucial part of the frame, and one where it pays to provide more strength than the minimum required by code. Using 2 × 8s instead of 2 × 10s may save some money in the short term. But in high winds or heavy snows—and when it comes time to reroof—the extra strength of larger timbers set 16 inches on center will pay off. Also bear in mind that other factors, mainly insulation, can wind up affecting rafter size. In some regions, particularly where there are strict energy codes, you may need to use a 2 × 12 instead of a 2 × 10 (even when a 2 × 10 would carry the loads), for example, so the roof has enough room for the required thickness of insulation, plus an inch or two between the top of the insulation and the bottom of the roof deck for ventilation.

10-17

10-18

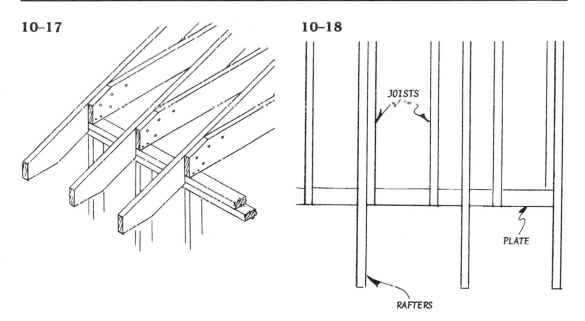

JOISTS

PLATE

RAFTERS

As always, there are many ways to meet your local codes, for example, by decreasing the spacing between rafters, using larger timbers, or, in the case of energy requirements, using dense insulation with a high R-value per inch. In areas where the house is subject to high winds, earthquake movement, or other exceptional loads, codes may call for exceptionally large timbers, special bracing in the roof frame, and tie down connectors.

There are so many variables that load requirements by code may range from 20 pounds per square foot over an attic storage space with no drywall and a roof covered with light-weight shingles, to more than twice that amount in full attics with a roof covered with heavy materials. As always, code requirements depend on the natural strength and grade of the wood species you are using. For example, in the case of a 30-pounds-per-square-foot load, rafter span tables will display many possibilities. Where 2 × 8 Douglas fir rafters graded Select Structural are spaced 16 inches on center, they could span 17 feet, 2 inches, while a Douglas fir 2 × 8 graded #2 could span 15 feet, 1 inch. There are different span limits for different types of wood.

Rafter spacing also has an impact. For example, with a light attic load of 20 pounds per square foot, #1 Douglas fir 2 × 12 rafters spaced 12 inches O.C. can span 28 feet, 7 inches. At 16 inches O.C., the same lumber can span 26 feet, and at 24 inches O.C., 22 feet, 8 inches.

Another wrinkle is that rafter tables (pages and pages of them to cover the many possible situations) may provide span information as a horizontal run—as though the rafter were a floor joist. You need to use a conversion factor (generally supplied with the tables) to determine the overall sloping distance of the lumber. This is one of the reasons why sizes on home-drawn plans are only estimates, and sometimes wrong. The local inspector may adjust the sizes due to several factors (lumber type, spacing, extra loads, and such) before granting the permit.

MAKING A COMMON RAFTER

If you view a half cross section of a sloped roof, you will see a right triangle whose altitude, base, and hypotenuse relate specifically to the rise, run, and rafter length of the structure (**10–19**). This relationship never changes, which is why you can work with a small right triangle that has a 12-inch base to represent the unit run and whose altitude equals the slope's rise per foot of run, as in **10–20**, to step off the length of the rafter. This is also

10–19

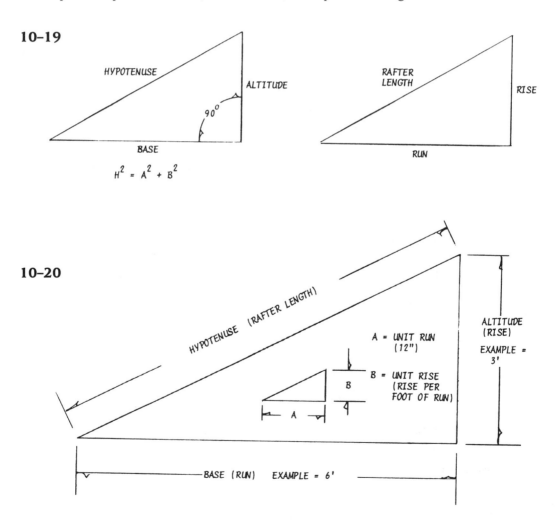

$$H^2 = A^2 + B^2$$

10–20

why the framing square is useful in rafter layout. Quality squares have stamped tables so you can actually calculate rafter lengths by reading the square, but that system is not often used, even by pros.

The squares are L-shaped and have a body (or blade) and a tongue (**10–21**). To step off the length of the pattern rafter, place the square as shown in **10–22** so the blade indicates the unit run (12 inches) and the tongue shows whatever the unit rise may be. Mark around the square with a pencil and repeat the procedure for each foot of run (**10–23**). The system works regardless of the amount of slope in the roof. The unit run dimension is constant; the unit rise depends, of course, on what the slope is (**10–24**).

10–21

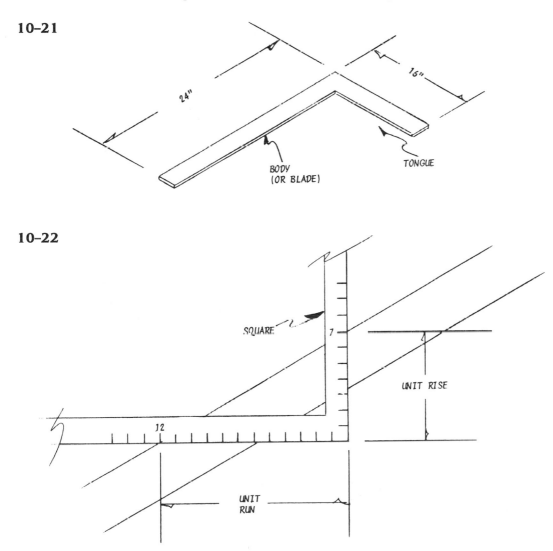

10–22

10–23

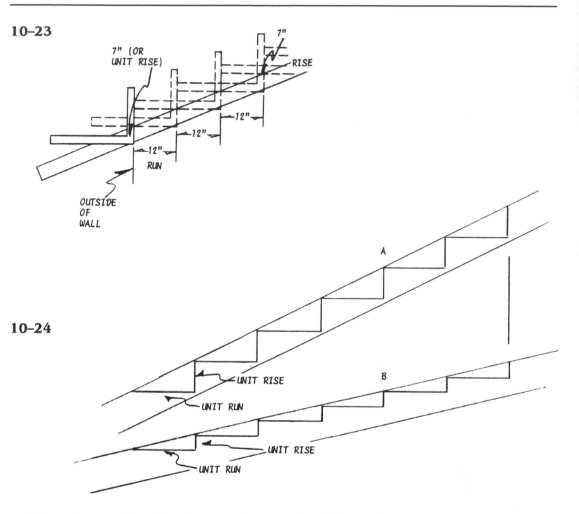

10–24

If there is an odd unit in the run—for example, if the total run is 10 feet, 6 inches—lay out the six inches at the ridge end of the rafter as shown in **10–25**. Notice that the position of the square in relation to the rafter remains as if you were marking for the full run and rise units, but the tool is moved toward the last layout mark A to set it for the odd 6 inches. All the vertical lines, including the last one marked, will be parallel.

Because the layout is made to the centerline of the ridge, the total length of the rafter must be reduced by one half the thickness of the ridge board.

The seat for the bird's-mouth is a horizontal cut that is about as long as the plate is wide (**10–26**). Lay out the overhang length of the rafter by starting from the line of the plumb cut. This may also be done with the square, but many carpenters just take a linear measurement with a tape.

10 25

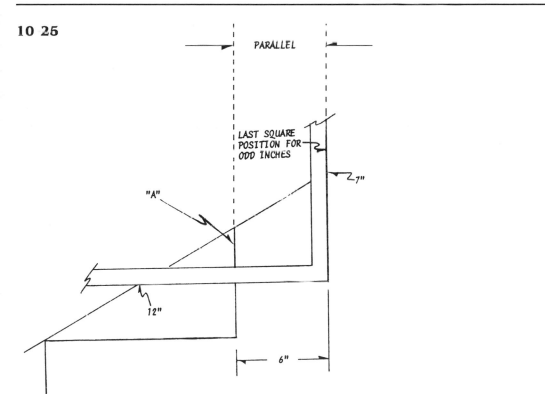

PARALLEL

LAST SQUARE
POSITION FOR
ODD INCHES

7"

"A"

12"

6"

10–26

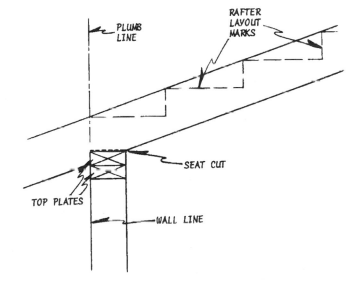

PLUMB
LINE

RAFTER
LAYOUT
MARKS

SEAT CUT

TOP PLATES

WALL LINE

WORKING WITH A TEMPLATE

The template shown in **10–27** simulates a framing square and is used the same way to step off the length of the pattern rafter. Make it from ¼-inch plywood, so it is a right triangle with a base equal to the unit run, with an altitude equal to the unit rise. If you make the triangle oversize to begin with, you can position the edge guide to provide the correct rise and run units. If there is an odd unit, mark it on the base of the template.

You can also make a full-size template. Here too, the project is a right triangle but its base and altitude are equal to the full dimensions of the rise and run. Make it with 1-by stock, braced for sturdiness, and use it as shown in **10–28** for a pattern rafter, or to mark

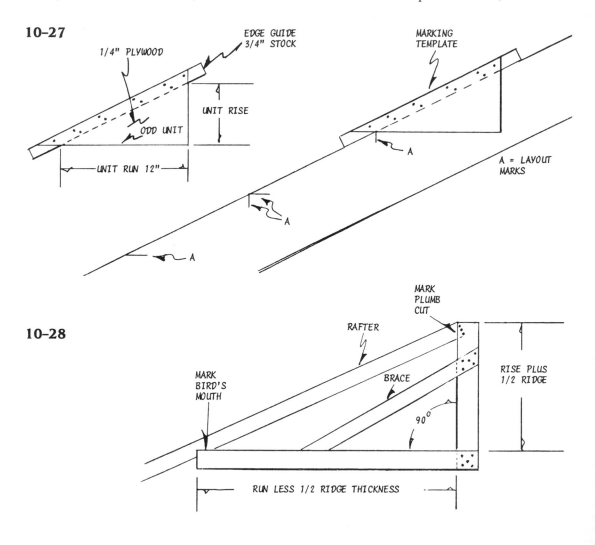

10–27

EDGE GUIDE
3/4" STOCK

1/4" PLYWOOD

MARKING TEMPLATE

UNIT RISE

ODD UNIT

A

UNIT RUN 12"

A = LAYOUT MARKS

A

A

10–28

MARK PLUMB CUT

RAFTER

MARK BIRD'S MOUTH

BRACE

RISE PLUS 1/2 RIDGE

90°

RUN LESS 1/2 RIDGE THICKNESS

all rafters. If you set it up sturdily across sawhorses, it can even be used as a cut guide. If you do the latter, it might be wise to make the altitude piece longer and just mark it for correct positioning of the rafter.

WORKING FULL-SIZE

This is a procedure that makes the most sense if it is done right after the floor frame and subfloor are complete. The idea is to use the platform as a giant drawing board on which you can place actual roof-framing material to mark lengths and cuts.

Snap a chalk line across the platform at right angles to the edges and then mark its center. From that point, erect a perpendicular and mark it to indicate the rise. Nail down thin sections of ridge-board and plate material as shown in **10–29**, and you can see that it is possible to get the true shape of the rafters. The idea will work even if the roof has different slopes; it's just a matter of where you position the simulated ridge.

10–29

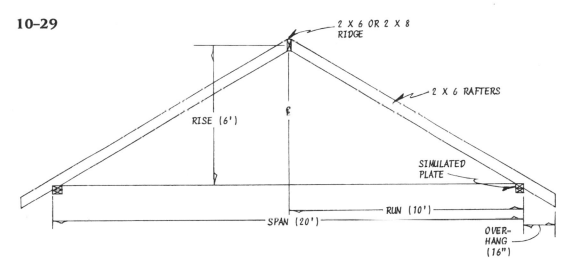

Working this way, you can even preassemble your own trusses. After the layout is made, nail down lengths of 2 × 4s to act as gauges for the placement of the truss components. Webs will have to be included, but the layout for them can be made just as it was for the rafters. Truss design is discussed later in this chapter.

Bear in mind that these are some of the several approaches that carpenters use. Many develop their own tricks of the trade, and some take shortcuts that eliminate most of the calculations. For example, if you know how much headroom you need in the attic, you can build a support tree at each end of the building and install the ridge at that height, including intermediate supports down to the deck as needed. Now you have the boundaries of the rafters established, and it is relatively easy to clamp or tack a rafter in position along one of the sidewalls and mark the cuts.

If the end wall and ridge are square to each other and each one is level, the rafter you mark for plumb cuts and seat or bird's-mouth cuts will serve as a template for the other rafters. No matter what approach you take, it's wise to test a rafter in place before you cut a lot of lumber.

CUTTING THE RAFTERS

How you cut the rafters depends, of course, on the tools you have available. The work can be done with a handsaw, but it will be tedious and time-consuming. It's better to work with a portable cutoff saw, or a radial arm saw, set up with side extensions to support long pieces. Special cutters are available for the saws so you can gang pieces and form the bird's mouth in a single pass.

Most owner–builders use a circular saw to make the plumb cuts and most of the bird's mouths. To avoid long overcuts at the right-angle pocket over the exterior wall, it's wise to finish the cuts with a handsaw. However you work, always use the pattern rafter, once you're sure it's the right size with the right cuts, to mark the other pieces. This is the way to avoid cumulative errors.

ERECTING THE COMMON RAFTERS

You won't need anything but common rafters if the roof is a plain gable. Even with other designs, the common rafters should be organized first so you can work from them to set up other components. The top ends of the rafters abut the ridge board, which, in a gable design, runs the full length of the structure. Where you can't possibly do this with one piece, plywood splices are used to join sections. It's a good idea to plan the length of the ridge pieces so the splice occurs midway between two rafters (**10–30**). Another option, in addition to splicing, is to join the ridge boards over a support post or bearing wall below.

Because the ridge board is used mostly as an aid in the erection and alignment of rafters, its thickness is not critical. Usually 2-by lumber is used to provide maximum support and nailing. At any rate, code always calls for the depth of the ridge board to be at least equal to the length of the cut in the rafter. **Figure 10–31** shows how a 2 × 6 rafter would mate with a 2 × 8 ridge, using actual instead of nominal dimensions. The upshot is that you can't use the same lumber for rafters and ridges on a sloped roof. Ridge lumber must be deep enough to cover the angled cut. On low-slope roofs, the angle will be slight

10–30

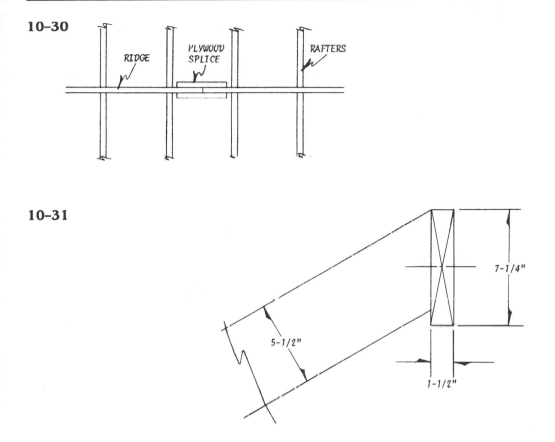

10–31

and the increase will be small. On a steeply sloped roof, the actual length of the plumb cut can be much longer than the depth of the rafter, and require a very large ridge board.

A good way to start setting up rafters is to make a few special supports that you nail temporarily to joists to hold the ridge board in correct position (**10–32**). They must, of course, be set on a common centerline and sized so the ridge height is correct.

Start by placing two end rafters so they are flush with the outside of the wall. Nail the first one through the ridge as shown in **10–33**, and attach its mate by toenailing as shown in **10–34**. Always add blocking or additional braces as needed to hold the ridge securely and prevent any sagging. Also, be sure to set the ridge (and the rafters) crown up.

Each rafter is secured at the plate with two 10d nails (toenailed) on each side (**10–35**). Some carpenters find that this leads to splitting, and use two nails on one side and a single nail on the other. If the rafter abuts a joist, the toenailing is done on each side of the assembly and additional 10d nails are driven through the joist into the rafter (**10–36**). Driving the nails through the rafter into the joist is also okay. Another option, which may

10–32

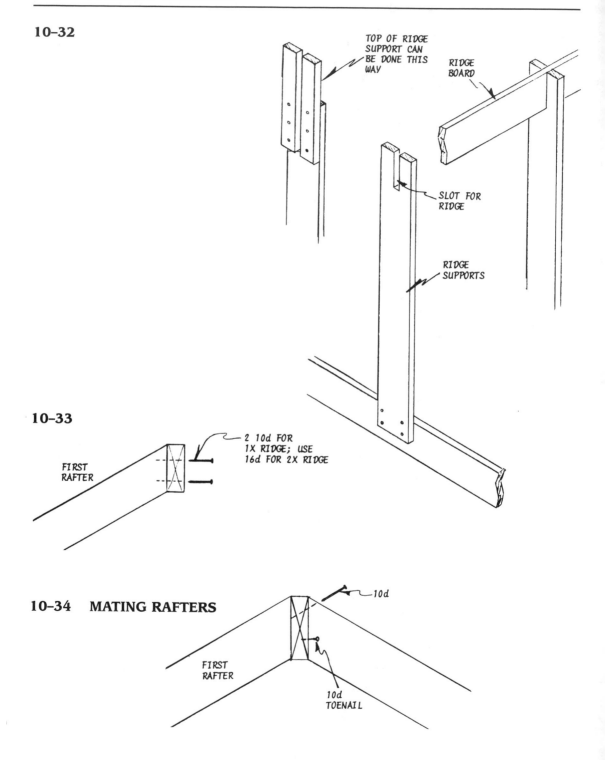

TOP OF RIDGE SUPPORT CAN BE DONE THIS WAY

RIDGE BOARD

SLOT FOR RIDGE

RIDGE SUPPORTS

10–33

FIRST RAFTER

2 10d FOR 1X RIDGE; USE 16d FOR 2X RIDGE

10–34 MATING RAFTERS

10d

FIRST RAFTER

10d TOENAIL

be required by code in your area, is to tack the rafters, and then fasten them permanently with framing anchors (**10–37**). You can follow the same procedure on every fourth or fifth rafter and then come back and fill in the ones in between. Yet another approach is to set up rafters at each end and then stretch a line across as a guide.

Bear in mind that there are other rafter framing plans, such as using a structural, 4-by ridge (often a select-grade exposed timber), and joining or lapping the rafters above it.

10–35

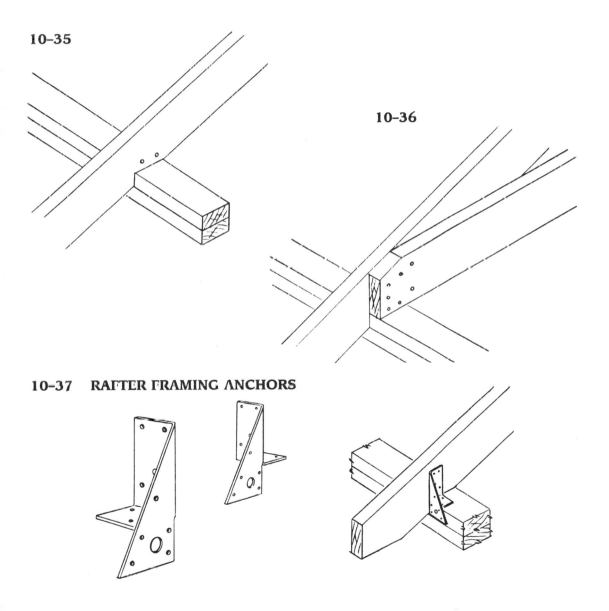

10–36

10–37   RAFTER FRAMING ANCHORS

BRACING THE ROOF FRAME

Rafters are connected solidly at the wall plates, and they lean against each other at the ridge to provide mutual support. But this arrangement imposes an outward thrust at the plate line (**10–38**). Unless you use trusses, or install sophisticated internal bracing (usually in combination with oversize wall frames), you need to counter this thrust with collar beams (**10–39**).

How great the thrust is depends on the slope of the roof. Much of the thrust is opposed by the joists, but collar beams generally placed in the upper third of the rafters

10–38

10–39

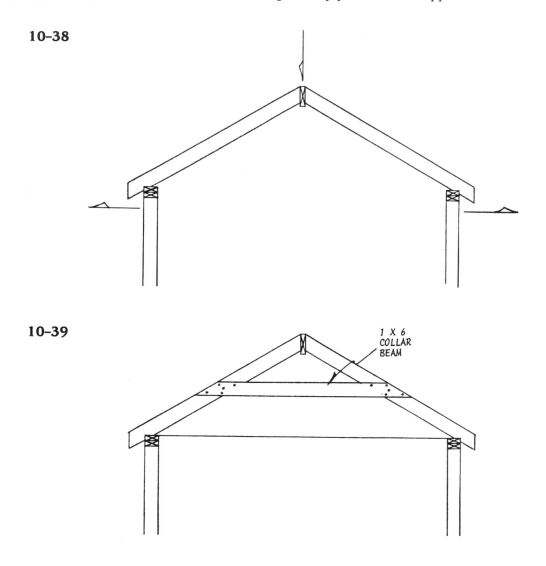

are desirable and likely required by code. Also consider that the ties will oppose the sag that can develop when the rafters are very long. In addition, because they reduce the span of the rafters, collar beams can make it possible to use lighter rafter material. Of course, these details should be checked before roof framing is started and, as always, against your local codes.

A common method is to use collar beams of 1 × 6 material and to place one across every third or fourth pair of rafters. A better method is to use one on every rafter, even though it takes a little more time and material. The reason is that the stiffening effect of collar beams is negligible except in relation to the rafters to which they are secured. Codes typically call for at least 1 × 4 material set 4 feet on center.

Collar beams are often located close to the ridge so they can be used as ceiling joists later when the attic space is made livable (**10–40**). In such situations the beams should definitely be placed across all rafters and should be 2 × 4 or 2 × 6 material, depending on the span. However, the nearer a collar beam is to the ridge, the less effective it is at resisting the sideways thrust of rafters.

10–40

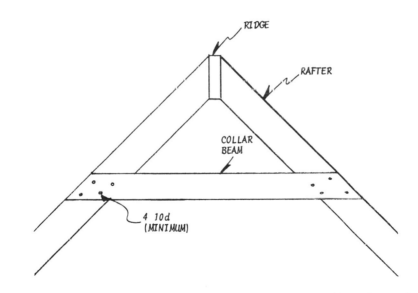

Another option that may be permitted by code is to use purlins—long pieces of 2 × 4 attached horizontally across the inside edges of the rafters (**10–41**). They can anchor diagonal braces when the rafter span requires additional support. The purlins are braced with lengths of 2 × 4 that rest on supporting partitions (**10–42**). The angle of the brace is not critical. The idea is to run from the midpoint of the rafter to a suitable support below. Even if this detail is permitted, bear in mind that the angled supports will chop up the storage

10-41

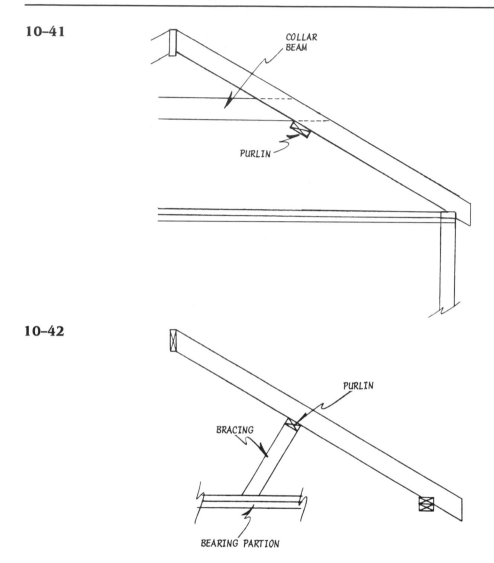

10-42

space, and pretty much eliminate remodeling for any living space. It's always wise to over-build, even above code requirements, so that you are not limited later on.

REINFORCING AN END WALL

An end wall that runs parallel to the basic roof structure does not receive the antithrust support that sidewalls get from joists and collar beams. A typical example occurs under sections of a hip roof. When necessary, ample strength is provided by running stub joists at right angles from a regular joist to the wall plate. The stub joists are nailed in place as shown in **10–43**, and may be reinforced further by using an anchor strap that is long enough to span three regular joists plus a good part of the stub joist. If a subfloor is planned, you can work with framing anchors to secure the stub joist to the regular joist. Regard the short pieces as regular joists when it comes to spacing, nailing, and the application of hangers.

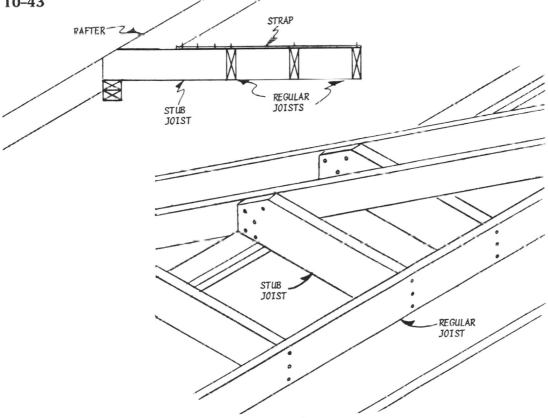

FRAMING AT THE GABLE ENDS

The opening between the plate and the end rafter is framed with studs that are notched at the top to fit the rafter (**10–44**).

The best way to proceed is to drop a plumb bob from the center of the ridge and mark the point on the wall plate. Because this is the place where attic vents are usually installed, you want to locate the positions of the first studs (right and left) to accommodate the opening you need. The best way to find the correct stud heights and cuts is to place a length of 2 × 4 at the point marked as #1 in **10–45**. Use a level to be sure the stud is plumb and then mark across it to show the top and bottom edges of the rafter. Do the same thing with

10–44

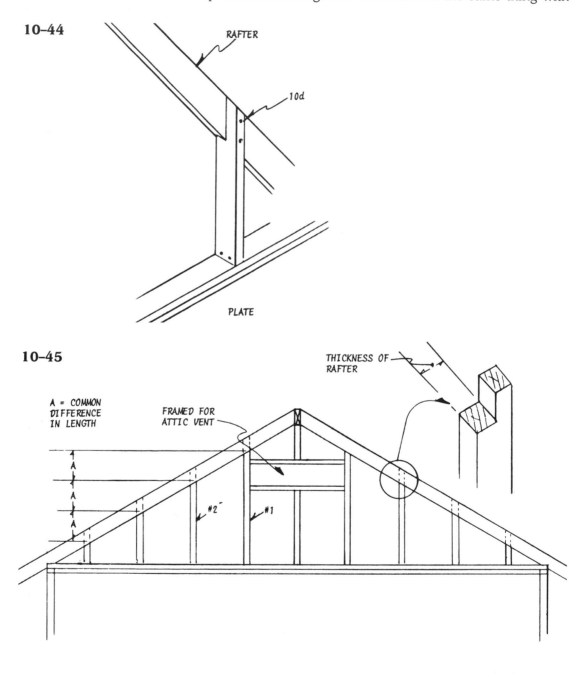

another piece of stock at point #2. The difference in length between these two pieces will apply to all others and, of course, the shape of the notches will be the same in each piece except that the direction of the angle will change, depending on whether they are used on the right or left side of the centerline. Put in the horizontal pieces for the vent opening before installing the two-piece center stud. Trimmers and headers are not required here, but you may want add them if you plan to install a powered vent with a fan.

FRAMING FOR A GABLE OVERHANG

Longer rafters provide for overhangs along sidewalls, but when the roof must extend at the ends, special framing is called for. There are various ways this can be accomplished, but a fairly straightforward one using lookout rafters is shown in **10–46**. The gable end is framed conventionally except that the studs are not notched for a rafter but are angle-cut straight across for a plate. This frame provides support for lookouts that travel up the slope like the rungs of a ladder.

10–46

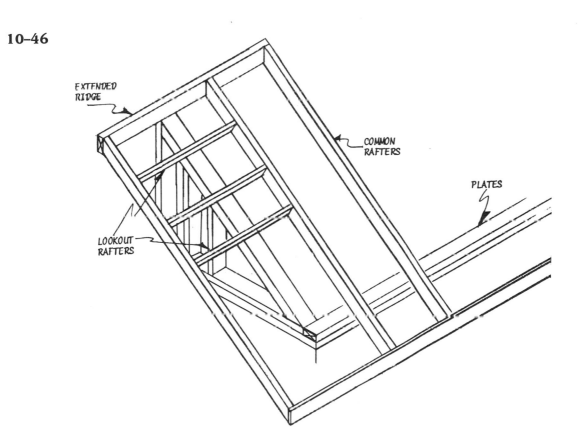

At the low end, the outermost rafter joins the extended fascia that runs along the plumb cuts of the rafters. At the high end, the outermost rafter joins the extended ridge board. Because both horizontal boards are cantilevered, you should not (and probably would not) have any splices near the end of the building. The cantilever rule of thumb is a maximum of two-thirds supported and one-third extended, although a proportion of one to four is sturdier than one to three. The entire assembly can be made following conventional nailing practices secured with framing anchors.

THE HIP RAFTER

If you slice vertically through a gable roof and then slope down from that point to the end wall, you have the form of a hip roof. A side view of the framing shows that a common rafter makes the connection between the wall plate and where the ridge of the gable ends (**10–47**). If you look down on the framing, you will see that the common rafter of the hip and the last common rafter of the gable form a 90-degree angle (**10–48**). The hip rafter is a diagonal that runs from the intersection to the corner of the walls (**10–49**). The length of the rafter and the cuts required can be calculated geometrically and by working with a framing square. They can also be determined by working right on the frame, a procedure that has much going for it, especially for the first-time builder.

Tack-nail a block at the corner of the walls to represent the height of the rafter where it crosses the plate. This is a common dimension and is easily picked up from the common rafters already in place. Drive a small nail at the intersection and at the corner of the height block and stretch a line between them. The line represents the center of the hip rafter, so you can measure it to find the line length and then add the amount of overhang. In situations like this, it's best to make the overhang longer than necessary and then cut to fit when you get around to installing fascia boards.

Use a T-bevel to find the vertical angle between the line and the intersection of the common rafters at the ridge. You can also do this by using a piece of stiff cardboard, pressing one edge into the corner and marking across the top of the line with a pencil. Transfer the angle you pick up to the rafter stock, as shown in **10–50**, and make a simple miter cut. This angle also applies to the plumb cut of the bird's mouth.

So that the end of the hip rafter will fit snugly in the corner, the miter cut is beveled on each side of the rafter's centerline (**10–51**). Another approach is to mark the line of the miter on both sides of the rafter and then set your saw blade to the correct bevel angle. Saw by following the miter-cut lines and you will have the correct compound angles that are called for (**10–52**).

The top edge of the hip rafter will be above those of other rafters. Because this would

10–47

10–48

10–49

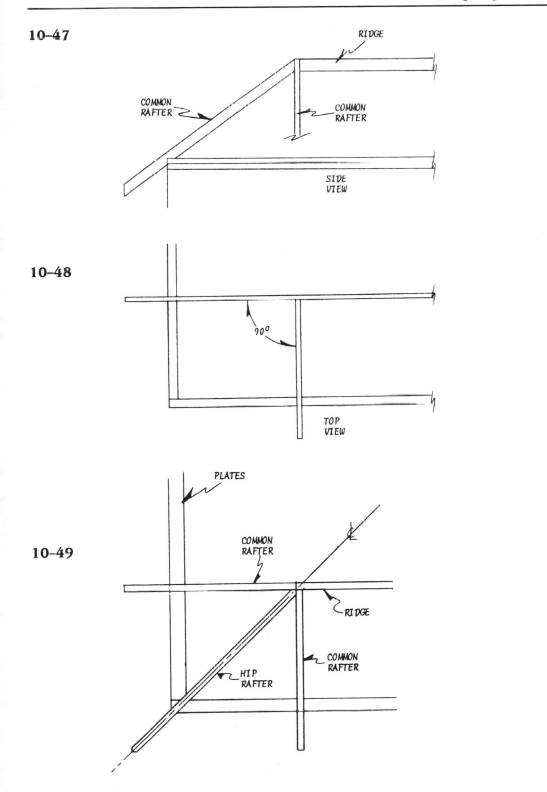

10–50

10–51

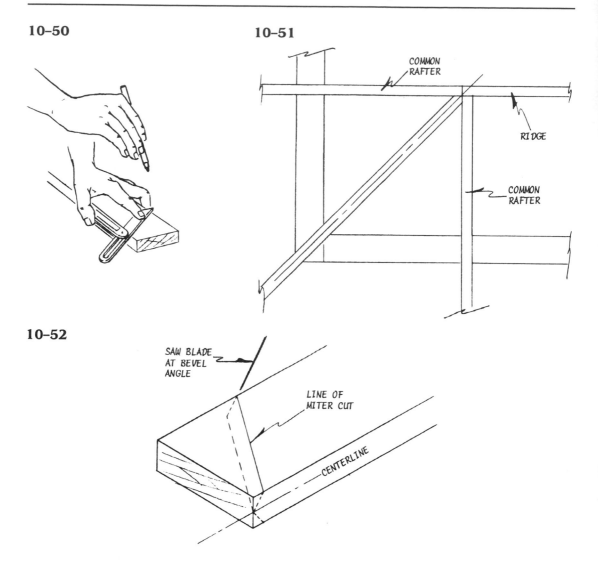

10–52

interfere with placing roof sheathing flat, it's a good idea to bevel those edges as much as necessary by working with a plane or a saw (**10–53**).

JACK RAFTERS

The jack rafters run parallel to the common rafter and span between the hip rafter and the wall plate. The form of the bird's mouth is just like that of the common rafters, but the end against the hip rafter requires a compound angle cut (**10–54**). If you view the assembly

10–53

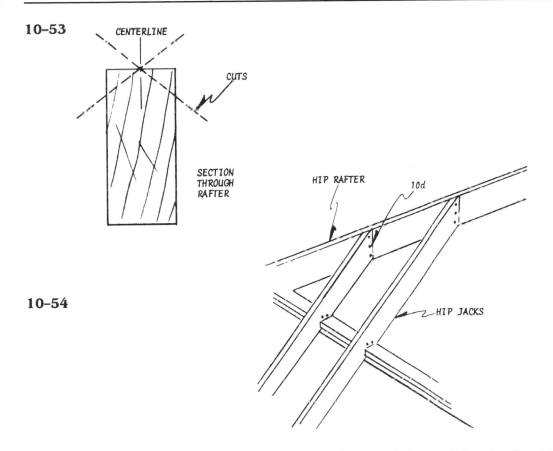

CENTERLINE

CUTS

SECTION
THROUGH
RAFTER

HIP RAFTER

10d

HIP JACKS

10–54

from both the top and the side, you will see the side or angle cut and the plumb cut that together form the compound angle (**10–55**). This accounts for the fact that the jack rafter joins the hip rafter at a figured horizontal angle and at a figured vertical angle.

Follow the same procedure we described for the hip rafter and you will be able to cut the jacks with a minimum of fuss. Stretch a line from the hip rafter to the wall plate to indicate the centerline of the first hip jack (**10–56**). Hold a short scrap piece of rafter material in the position shown in **10–57** and mark its end with a line parallel to the face of the hip rafter. Make the cut, and then use the piece of wood in the position shown in **10–58** so you can mark the line for the angle cut. This time, the line is parallel to the longitudinal run of the rafter. Make this cut, and the sample tells you the shape you need for all the jacks (**10–59**). (As always, test your cut in place.) The difference in length of all the jack rafters is consistent as long as they are equally spaced. Once you have cut the first two, you can apply the change in length to all the others (**10–60**).

It's a good idea to erect jack rafters in pairs so they will oppose each other to keep

10–55

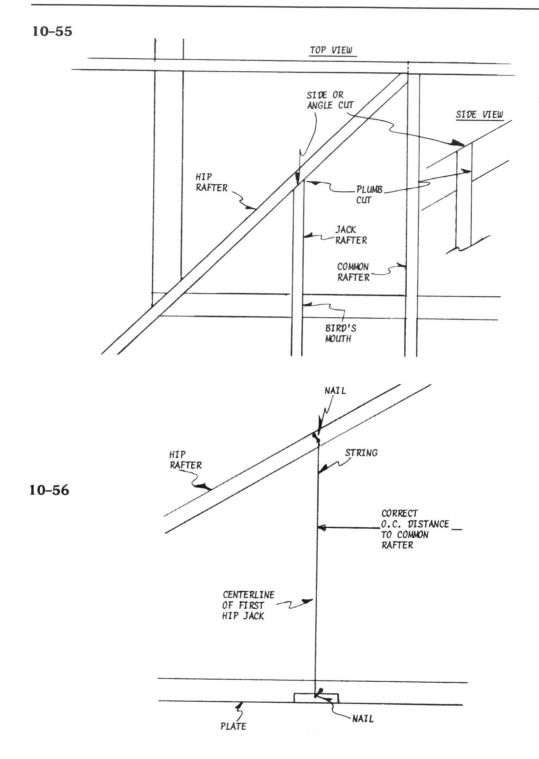

10–57

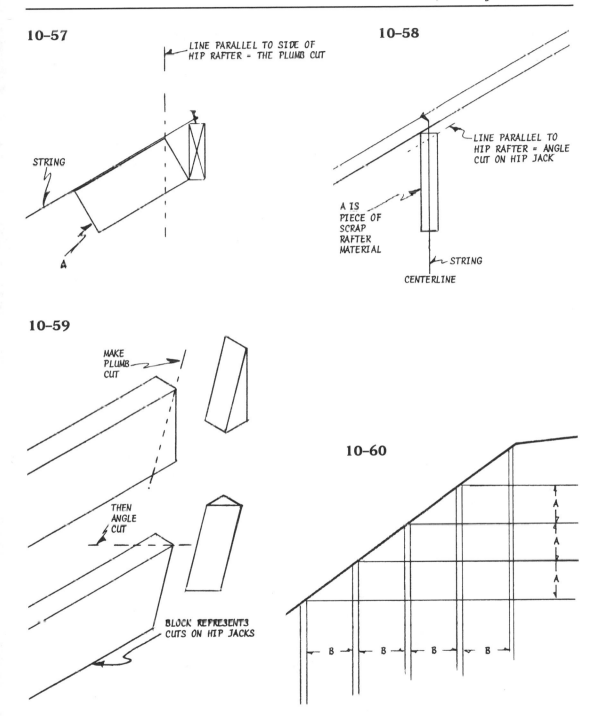

LINE PARALLEL TO SIDE OF
HIP RAFTER = THE PLUMB CUT

STRING

A

10–58

LINE PARALLEL TO
HIP RAFTER = ANGLE
CUT ON HIP JACK

A IS
PIECE OF
SCRAP
RAFTER
MATERIAL

STRING

CENTERLINE

10–59

MAKE
PLUMB
CUT

THEN
ANGLE
CUT

BLOCK REPRESENTS
CUTS ON HIP JACKS

10–60

A

A

A

B   B   B   B

the hip rafter from being pushed out of line. Start with a midpoint set, and then fill in with the others.

OTHER RAFTERS

All other rafters that may be required in a roof frame can be cut accurately following the on-job principles we have described for hip rafters and hip jack rafters. The valley rafter, in most situations, is almost a duplicate of the hip rafter. The difference between the two is told by the names. The hip rafter forms an outside corner; the valley rafter works the same way for an inside corner (**10–61**).

The shapes of the rafters at the end of the overhang are opposed. As you can see in **10–62**, they both form a V, but the one on the valley is inverted and a bit trickier to cut than the other.

Cripples are rafters that do not attach to either a ridge or a plate. They can connect, for example, between a hip rafter and a valley rafter, as in **10–63**, and are named specifically for their position in the frame. For example, they may be called a valley cripple jack or a hip-valley cripple jack. Because they span between sloping rafters, they require a compound angle cut at each end.

Valley jack rafters are brothers to hip jacks (**10–64**). They work in similar fashion, but

10–61   **10–62**

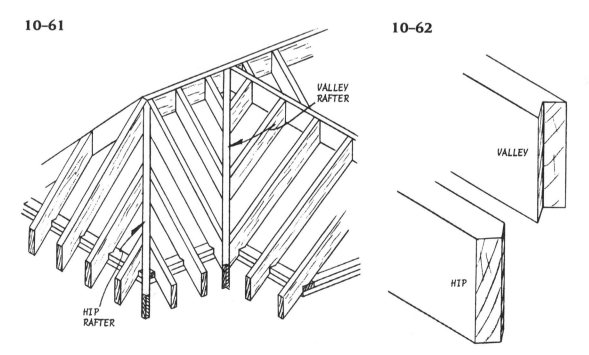

VALLEY
RAFTER

VALLEY

HIP

HIP
RAFTER

10–63

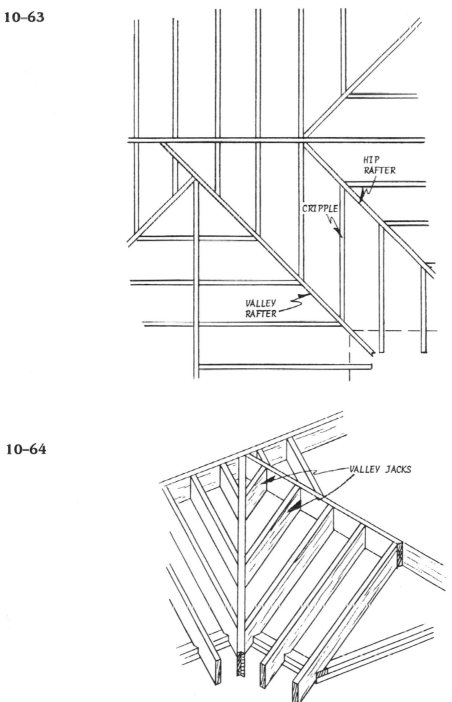

HIP
RAFTER

CRIPPLE

VALLEY
RAFTER

10–64

VALLEY JACKS

because they run from a ridge to the valley rafter, they require a plumb cut at the top end and a compound cut at the other.

SIZES OF SPECIAL RAFTERS

Hip and valley rafters, the latter especially, must often carry heavier loads than common rafters. Hip rafters that meet at a common point at the top get a good measure of support from each other and, if they are not excessively long, can safely be the same material as other rafters. In premium construction, valley rafters are often doubled or made of material two inches wider than the common rafters. Another reason for the extra width is to provide full bearing surface for the ends of the jack rafters after they are cut.

Whether these considerations will apply depends of course on your roof design. You might get a ruling on this detail from the building inspector, or, just as a safety factor, use heavier stock or double up for all hip and valley rafters.

GABLE AND SHED DORMERS

The gable dormer is so called because its roof design is the same as that of a regular gable roof and usually has a matching slope. Sometimes it's purely decorative but may combine its aesthetic value with a practical function such as providing attic ventilation. In the latter case, the front of the dormer would have screen-backed louvers and the whole assembly could be viewed as an add-on to the basic roof frame. It looks pretty from the front, but from the back you would see that it doesn't do much more than cover a hole through the roof.

Of course, a large dormer may also be designed to provide light and air for an attic room. In that case, its design would be more integrated with the basic roof framing. In low-slope roofs, dormers don't work very well because they don't add much headroom in the eaves. In a high-slope roof, however, you can gain a lot of walkable floor space under a projecting dormer. Of course, the proportions depend on the height of the ridge and over-all space in the attic.

The shed dormer is different because it can be incorporated to provide a lot more additional space inside. Its construction can be quite simple if you view its front wall as a vertical extension of the house wall and its roof as common rafters that have a different slope than the main roof. There is much leeway here in how much room you can pick up because the width of the shed dormer can run the full length of a gable design.

In both cases, the opening through the roof framing is reinforced with doubled rafters or trimmers and, where applicable, doubled headers between rafters. Study **10–65** and

10–66 and you will see that the framing procedures we have discussed in relation to walls and roofs apply to dormers as well. Remember that if you plan to use attic space for living, code requirements are different. Among many possible changes, you may need larger rafters to house more insulation, and a higher ridge to install code-approved collar ties and to maintain adequate headroom.

10–65

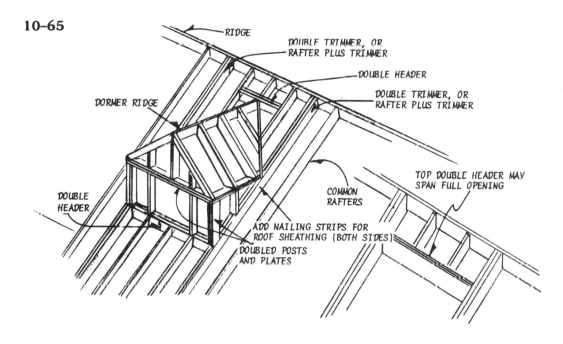

FRAMING A FLAT ROOF

A flat roof, or one with a slight slope, is easier to frame than conventional double-slope roofs. The design has always been with us, and its contemporary lines plus improvements in roof-surfacing materials and methods of application are making it more practical, at least in regions without heavy rain or snow.

The horizontal members, which, in this case, serve as both rafter and joist, are called roof joists. Because they must support both the finish roof and the ceiling, wider material than you would use for conventional joists and rafters is called for. You'll find that 2 × 12s set 16 inches O.C. are common. But the requirements of local conditions are, as always, an important factor to consider before making a decision. Generally, flat roofs are not a good idea in snow country for obvious reasons.

The framing, with due consideration for span support and the like, is done as if for a

10–66

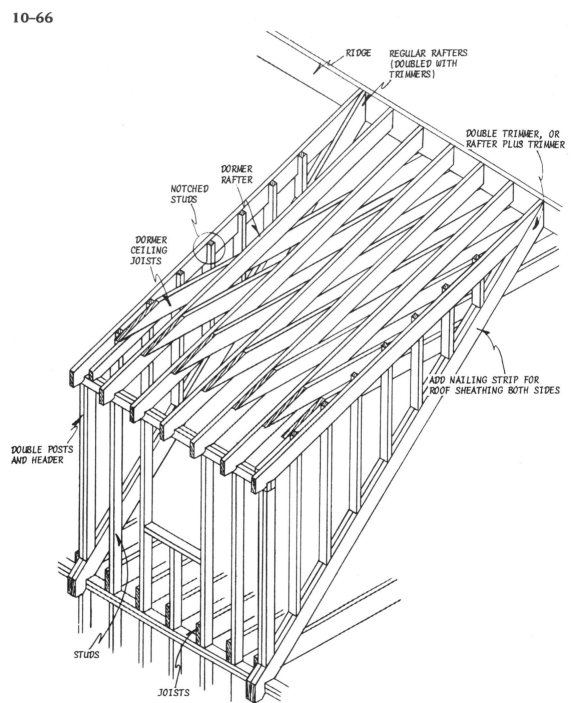

RIDGE   REGULAR RAFTERS
(DOUBLED WITH
TRIMMERS)

DOUBLE TRIMMER, OR
RAFTER PLUS TRIMMER

DORMER
RAFTER

NOTCHED
STUDS

DORMER
CEILING
JOISTS

ADD NAILING STRIP FOR
ROOF SHEATHING BOTH SIDES

DOUBLE POSTS
AND HEADER

STUDS

JOISTS

floor. But remember that the local building department may call for a design load even greater than the standard 40 pounds per square foot used for most floor joists. Overhangs are made by extending roof joists where possible and by using lookout rafters on other sides. The roof joists that support the lookouts are doubled to become headers. Conventional nailing can be used throughout with the addition of framing anchors as required by code.

Either of the two methods shown in **10–67** and **10–68** can be used to construct the

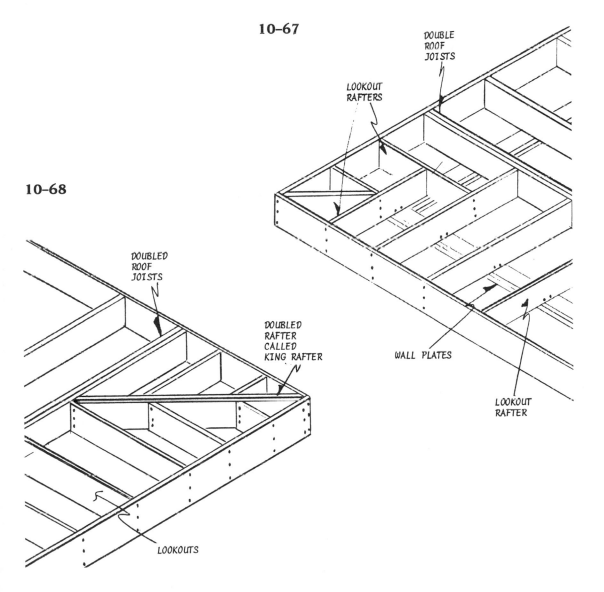

10–67

DOUBLE
ROOF
JOISTS

LOOKOUT
RAFTERS

10–68

DOUBLED
ROOF
JOISTS

DOUBLED
RAFTER
CALLED
KING RAFTER

WALL PLATES

LOOKOUT
RAFTER

LOOKOUTS

overhang framing. The doubled king rafter in **10–68** provides more support for deep over-hangs. As a design feature, in a rustic cabin with an open soffit area, for instance, the roof joists can be tapered in the overhang area (**10–69**). But you need level beam surfaces to build a boxed overhang with a plywood soffit with vents.

10–69

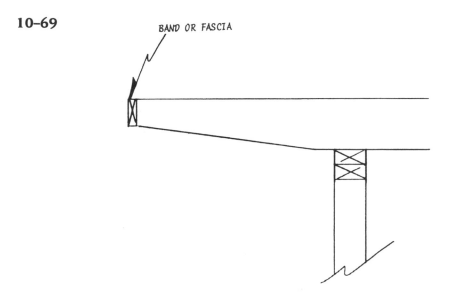

BAND OR FASCIA

CUTTING THROUGH RAFTERS

When you need to form an opening in the roof, use the same system that you use on floors (**10–70**). You need to account for the cut rafter (or rafters) by doubling up rafters along the sides of the opening, adding headers, and using frame hardware as required by code. You'll find that all headers and trimmers in the plane of the roof must be installed on hang-ers. If you make the opening after roof framing is complete, you'll need to provide tempo-rary support for the cut timbers. For example, you could set a couple of 2 × 4s across the underside of the rafters and brace them below, or just nail a couple of boards across the top of one cut rafter while you frame the opening.

You can frame small openings that do not require cutting merely by installing headers between regular rafters. In almost all cases, the headers are set plumb so their wide sur-faces are on a plane that is perpendicular to the ceiling joists. You can determine this easily just by dropping a plumb bob, or using a level.

Any opening you make for a chimney should include at least two inches of clear-ance on all sides. If you plan to install a prefab fireplace together with ready-made flue

10-70

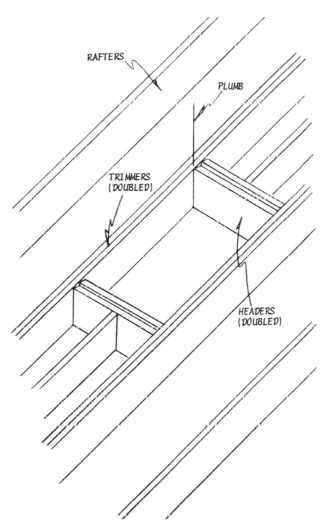

RAFTERS

PLUMB

TRIMMERS
(DOUBLED)

HEADERS
(DOUBLED)

section, check the specifications that come with the product to find pass-through requirements. Most triple-wall prefab pipe is mounted in a special bracket where it passes through framing.

FRAMING A ROOF WITH TRUSSES

A truss is basically a preassembled frame that does the job of conventional rafters and joists and makes it possible to span across outside walls without intermediate supports (**10-71**). Engineering has been refined and designs developed so applications can vary

10–71

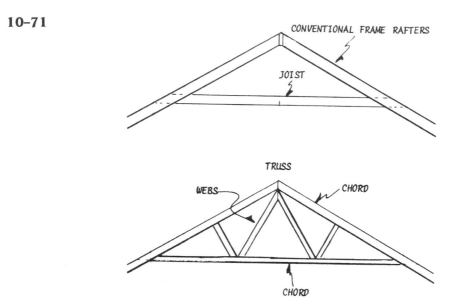

and spans can accommodate any residential application. In most cases, trusses can save time, material, and effort—and get the house covered up pretty quickly.

There are many types of trusses, but the basic designs for residential construction are shown in **10–72**. The king-post truss is the easiest to fabricate, but also the most limited in terms of span because the chord is supported only at the center. The W-type truss is used extensively, probably because the extra webs that support the chord permit greater spans than a king-post truss. The scissors-type truss is good construction when the house design calls for sloping ceilings. This can be general or limited to one or two rooms if you do the roof frame by, for example, combining scissors-type trusses with W-types.

The design of the truss and the materials used can't be arbitrary. Dead-load and live-load conditions must be considered as well as the span. But a truss manufacturer can build almost any configuration, including sets of trusses that nest into complex roof shapes, all conforming to local codes.

It's possible to build your own trusses, but not advisable. Among other reasons, you probably won't save any money (if your time has at least some value) because manufacturers are set up to produce trusses with uniform characteristics very quickly. If your house is anything more than a basic rectangle, you'll find it can be quite complicated to create the complex angles at valleys and hips. Also, if you do make them yourself, chances are you'll have to farm out the job of erecting them. So you might as well farm out the entire package. That way, an installer is responsible for the entire installation, and can't say that things won't work because of your assembly.

10–72

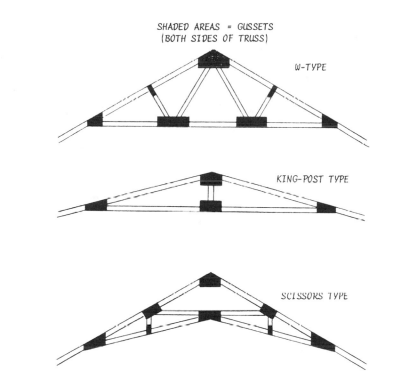

SHADED AREAS = GUSSETS
(BOTH SIDES OF TRUSS)

W-TYPE

KING-POST TYPE

SCISSORS TYPE

The example shown in **10–73** shows a typical W-type truss. It has 2 × 4 stock for the chords and webs with gussets made from exterior-grade plywood, which can be either ⅜ or ½ inch thick. The gussets might be thinner or thicker depending on strength requirements and the dimensions of chord and web stock. Some prefab trusses are supplied with different types and shapes of gussets, such as the metal plates in **10–74**. Still others have nails that are actually part of the plate. There are also special ring-type connectors and other connectors that fit into circular grooves you form with a special tool (**10–75**).

General guidelines for building your own trusses include applying gussets on both sides of the truss and attaching them with waterproof glue as well as nails. Assembled trusses must be handled carefully to avoid stresses that can cause distortion. Their strength is realized only when they are in a vertical position, and this is the way they should be carried and stored. If you must store them flat, be sure they get full-length support. Allowing the center or an end to carry the weight would result in distortion. If you carry them flat, have enough help at both ends and along the center. A common method of erecting them without a crane is to place them upside-down across the walls and then use long 2 × 4s at center points to tilt them upward. The connections at wall plates are made with framing anchors.

10-73

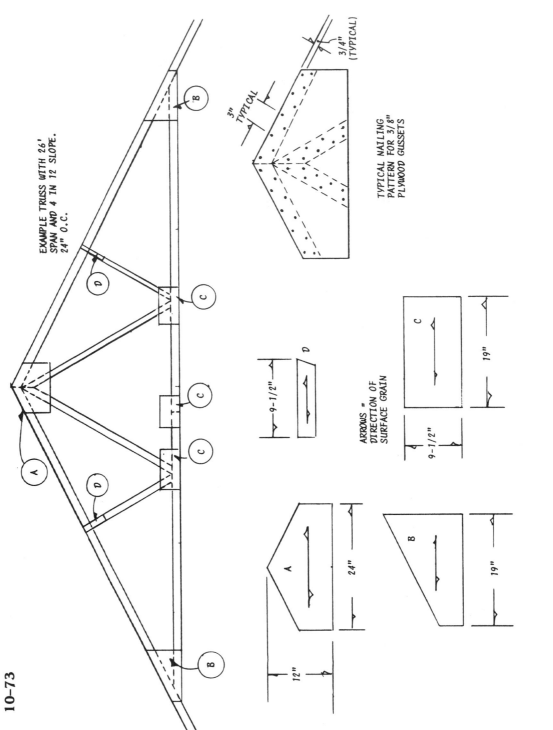

EXAMPLE TRUSS WITH 26' SPAN AND 4 IN 12 SLOPE. 24" O.C.

TYPICAL NAILING PATTERN FOR 3/8" PLYWOOD GUSSETS

3/4" (TYPICAL)

3" TYPICAL

ARROWS = DIRECTION OF SURFACE GRAIN

A — 24"
B — 19"
C — 19"
D — 9-1/2"
12"
9-1/2"

10–74

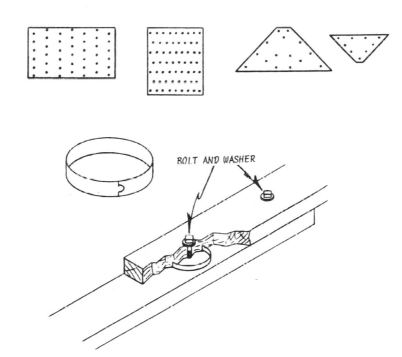

10–75

BOLT AND WASHER

GAMBREL ROOFS

Gambrel roof framing is similar to gable framing. The big difference is the break in the roof slope that occurs between the wall plate and the ridge (**10–76**). The angle above the break, in relation to a horizontal plane, is less than 45 degrees, while the one below is more than 45 degrees. Generally, the two work out as 30 degrees and 60 degrees. In the simplest gambrel design, if you bisect the point where upper and lower rafters meet, you'll find that the end cuts on the rafters are the same (**10–77**). This basic connection can be organized as shown in **10–78**, when it is the intention to provide a floor area that is free of posts and partitions. This design is often used for barn roofs.

Because the gambrel design is usually adopted to provide more headroom, the segmented rafters are usually made to sit around a doubled top plate supported by studs that will form a partition (**10–79**). The upper and lower rafters are notched to fit the plate. The cuts required are much like those for a bird's mouth—you have a plumb cut and a seat cut on each rafter.

10–76

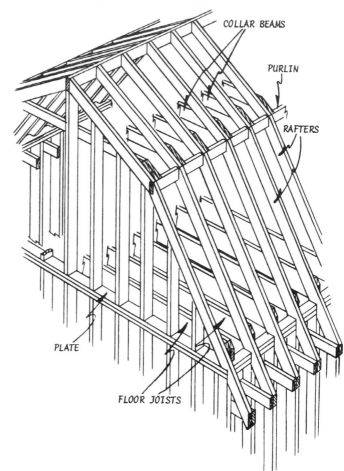

COLLAR BEAMS

PURLIN

RAFTERS

PLATE

FLOOR JOISTS

10–77

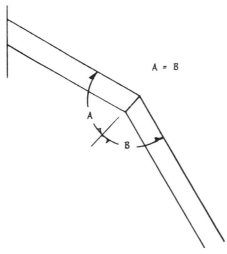

A = B

10-78

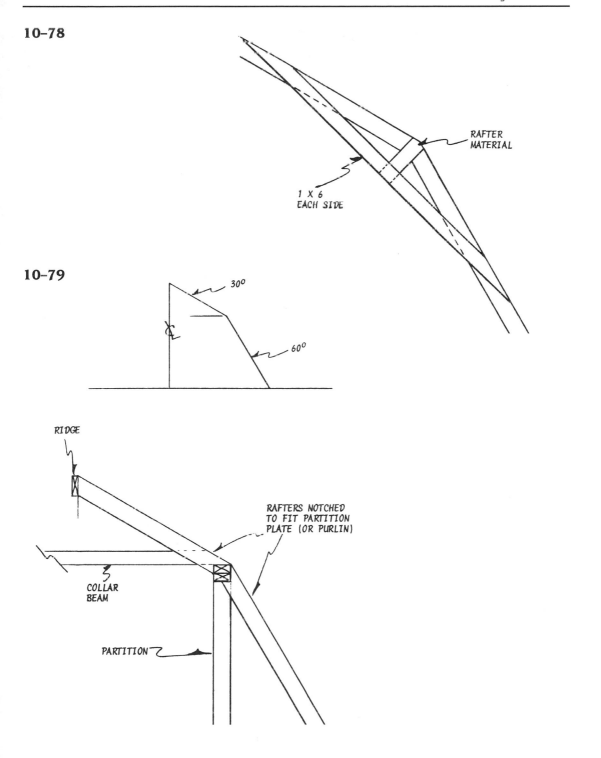

RAFTER MATERIAL

1 X 6 EACH SIDE

10-79

30°

60°

RIDGE

RAFTERS NOTCHED TO FIT PARTITION PLATE (OR PURLIN)

COLLAR BEAM

PARTITION

Collar beams can span across the partitions or they can be set higher (up to a point) to increase headroom. In this case, the ceiling would slope from the vertical plane of the partition to the horizontal plane of the collar beams. If you look at **10–79** again, you will see that the gambrel can be built like two roofs. One slopes from the wall plates to the break partition, and the other from the partition to the ridge. You can, if you wish, make the top part of the roof by working with small trusses that span the partitions.

11

ROOF SHEATHING

Before we get to the details of sheathing the roof, a few more words about safety. Even on one-story buildings, you'll need to be aware of heights as you work on the rafters, and on two-story buildings even more so. You may want to use an elaborate safety harness called an ascender rig, mandated by OSHA in professional workplaces. (Refer to Chapter 10.)

SAFETY FIRST

There are no statistics for owner–builder accidents during construction, but the National Safety Council reports that you're safer at work (on your house) than you are at home (in your living space) by a wide margin. The Council says that more than five times as many Americans die from preventable home injuries than from all work-related injuries. In addition to 27,000 deaths every year—the leading causes, poisonings and falls, claim over 15,000 lives—more than seven million people are seriously injured at home. The key word here is preventable. It means you can correct conditions that lead to accidents, mainly by using common sense, thinking out the situation before plunging ahead with the work, and always using modern ladders and scaffolding in a safe manner.

When it comes to ladders, there are many types for many situations. To receive a rating as a Household Type III ladder from the American National Standards Institute (ANSI), a ladder has to support an 800-pound load for one minute without buckling. This creates an extravagant safety margin, because Type III ladders carry a duty rating of only 200 pounds. Even extra heavy-duty industrial ladders (Type 1a) carry a duty rating of only 300 pounds.

But despite certification seals and prominent warning labels, more than 500,000 people a year are treated for injuries involving ladders. According to the Consumer Product Safety Commission (CPSC), most of the injuries are cuts, bruises, and fractured bones. But about 100,000 people receive emergency room treatment, and more than 300 people a year die from ladder-related injuries. Of course, this includes all types of ladder use in existing homes, and not just owner–builder use.

Although a fall from any height can be fatal, a report by the American Society of Safety Engineers indicates that 50 percent of people will die in a fall of eleven feet or more. That means you might have problems working on a ladder along the low edge of a roof. But the problems are more likely to be fatal working from an extension ladder on a second-story.

In many accidents investigated by the Bureau of Labor Statistics, either the person on the ladder or the ladder itself slipped. A slip can be caused by setting up a ladder on uneven ground, or at too steep or too shallow an angle. But in half of the ladder accidents, the Bureau found that workers carried materials in their hands as they climbed instead of raising them to an elevated workspace on a tether. This can contribute to slipping, and it violates two cardinal rules of using ladders safely: The ladder should always have secure, four-point contact with the working surface, and the climber should always maintain three points of contact with the ladder.

Metal stepladders and extension ladders that meet Underwriters Laboratories (UL) and ANSI standards have graphic labels warning about electrical hazards. But you can reduce the risk even further by following the CPSC advice and using a ladder that does not conduct electricity, such as a fiberglass or wood ladder, when working near overhead wires. If your ladder should start to fall into an electrical line, the CPSC offers these guidelines. Let it go, don't try to move it, but don't leave the ladder unattended. Have someone call the power company and ask them to cut off electricity to the line before you move the ladder. If someone is holding the ladder when it contacts the overhead line, never try to pull them away with your hands. Use something that does not conduct electricity, such as a long piece of dry wood or rope to push or pull them loose.

If you're buying ladders for your building project, check this list of tips that is based on recommendations of safety experts at Underwriters Laboratories (UL):

1. Look for the UL listing mark before buying a ladder.
2. Use a ladder that is long enough for the job at hand. Many accidents result from using a ladder that is too short.
3. Read the instructions, including the manufacturer's recommended limits on weight and height.
4. Use a nonmetallic ladder to reduce the possibility of electrical shock if the ladder will be used near electrical sources.
5. Inspect the ladder to make sure that it's in good condition without cracks or splits in the wood, or crimps in the metal.
6. Place the feet on a firm, level surface, not on rocks or boards. If you're using a

stepladder, be sure that the folding spreader is completely open and locked before placing any weight on the ladder

7. Don't carry equipment while climbing a ladder. Invest in a tool belt, or have someone raise the equipment to you.

8. Face the ladder climbing up and down and keep your body centered between both side rails.

9. Don't overextend your reach, and make sure you keep your weight evenly distributed.

10. Never try to move a ladder while standing on it.

11. Never stand on the top wrung of a stepladder or on the bucket shelf.

12. Read and follow the warning stickers for highest standing levels.

It's also important to wear nonskid shoes or boots while you're working on a roof. Shoes with slippery bottoms are out. Good types are made of leather, ankle-high, with rubber soles. Nonskid sneakers are a second choice. You may want to use a safety harness on a nonwalkable roof.

Professionals generally erect scaffolds on which they can store materials and stand when starting roofing work along lower edges. You could use dollied scaffolds such as shown in **11-1**, or a pump-jack system along the edge of the roof. If you make your own scaffolds, they must be secured to the house frame and covered with certified scaffold planks, not 2-by boards you use for joists or rafters.

On the roof itself, some pros simply nail down flat 2 × 4s to serve as foot braces. In that case, be sure the boards are nailed securely into the rafters (generally 16 inches O.C.) or through sheathing into rafters (**11-2**). The most common roofing system is called roof jacks. These small adjustable brackets are nailed through the sheathing into rafters, and support one or more scaffold planks.

It's important to remember that when you work on your own house, safety is up to you. There are hundreds of guidelines covering professional and commercial projects, and you may want to follow them, for example, by buying and using an OSHA-approved safety harness. On a roof of any slope, you should never be in an unstable position. If your setup raises the possibility of a fall in your own mind, you need a safer setup. And there is another obvious option: to turn over the roofing work to a contractor who has the equipment and experience to handle the job safely.

HOW ROOFING SHEDS WATER

Water flows downhill, and on a roof it should do so without interruptions that can cause dams that allow the water to slip under roofing materials instead of over them. This is why

11–1 DOLLIED SCAFFOLD

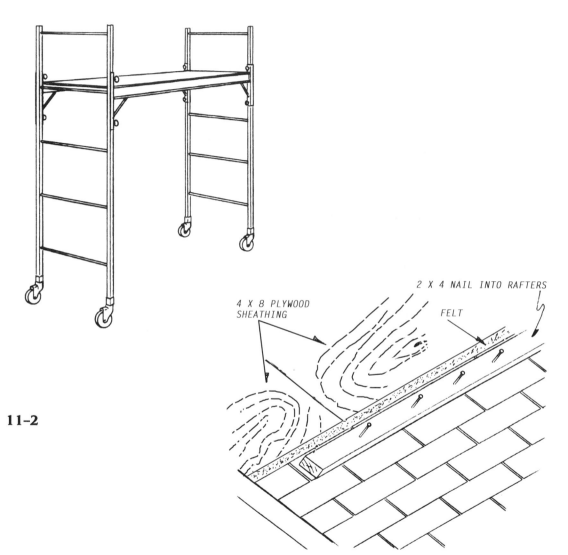

11–2

4 X 8 PLYWOOD SHEATHING

2 X 4 NAIL INTO RAFTERS

FELT

courses of roofing materials must always be lapped as shown in the lower part of **11–3**.

Exposure to the weather applies to all materials and is a phrase to take literally. It is always specified in inches. In the case of shingles, it is the distance from the visible edge of one course of shingles to the visible edge of the next course. As you can see in **11–4**, a short exposure can increase the thickness of the cover.

Head laps and side laps are shown in **11–5**. In each case, it's the amount of the lower

11–3

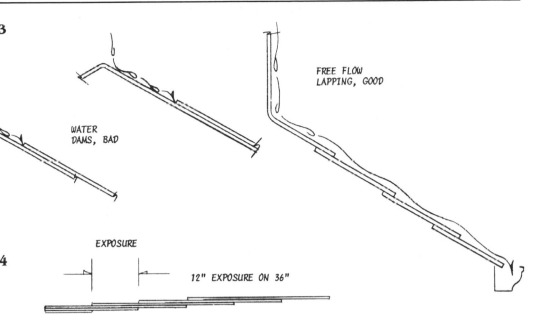

WATER
DAMS, BAD

FREE FLOW
LAPPING, GOOD

11–4

EXPOSURE

12" EXPOSURE ON 36"

EXPOSURE

18" EXPOSURE ON 36"

11–5

A

B

A = SIDE LAP
B = HEAD LAP
C = EXPOSURE

C

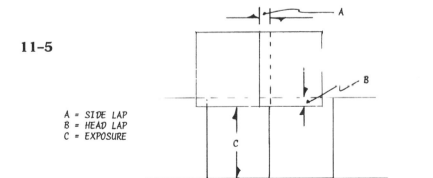

A

STRIP SHINGLE

B

C

shingle that is covered by the top one. Notice that in the case of the strip shingle shown, the head lap is measured from the top of the notch. There is no room for adjustment here. Nails are placed above the notches, called keys, and must be completely covered by the exposed tabs of the next course.

Roofing materials are purchased by the square. This indicates the amount required for 100 square feet of finished roof (**11–6**). Don't confuse the term with the actual square footage of the material itself.

On some materials, such as roll roofing, you can think of coverage in terms of roofing thickness as affected by the overlapping of the materials. It can be specified as single, double, or even triple coverage and is a measure of the weather protection so provided. Given a 36-inch-wide sheet of material, for example, short exposures provide more coverage than long ones.

Flashing is used on a roof wherever the regular placement of covering materials is interrupted. The cause can be a chimney, a valley, or a vent pipe. The flashing material can be similar to what is used to finish the roof, or it can be metals like copper, aluminum, or special alloys.

The cornice, also called the overhang, is a special construction that finishes and trims the underside of the area where roof and wall meet. There are various ways to accomplish this. Usually the design of the cornice includes considerations for ventilation of attic spaces.

Soffit refers to the underside of the cornice. In relation to a roof, it is the bottom of the

11–6

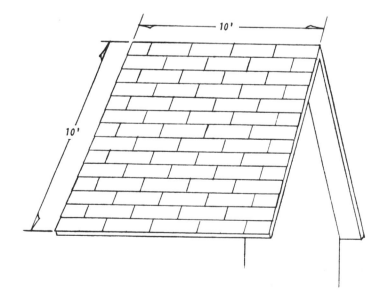

cornice, or, if there is no cornice, it can be the bottom of the overhang area covered by sheathing or docking.

SEEING THE ROOF AS A WHOLE

The roof consists of sheathing for support over the rafters and a surface covering that sheds water. But there are other components, including underlayment (felt paper), flashing, cornices and soffits, and gutters. All arc interrelated, and while there can be a step-by-step procedure, it is wise to check out all the factors before you take the first step. Some of the cornice work might be easier to do if basic pieces are installed along with roof framing. You might consider fascias and even some trim while you do the sheathing. Attaching the gutters might be simplified if you do it along with or immediately after the sheathing process.

A lot depends on the house design and the materials involved, but you can judge the logical next step or what jobs to combine if you see the complete picture beforehand.

Sheathing is installed over the roof frame to make it stronger and more rigid and to serve as a nailing base for the roofing material. The old-fashioned system of sheathing used individual boards joined over rafters with staggered joints (**11–7**).

In post-and-beam frames, you may use thick tongue-and-groove boards over the beams, which serve as sheathing, and are exposed along with the rafters to form a finished wood

11–7

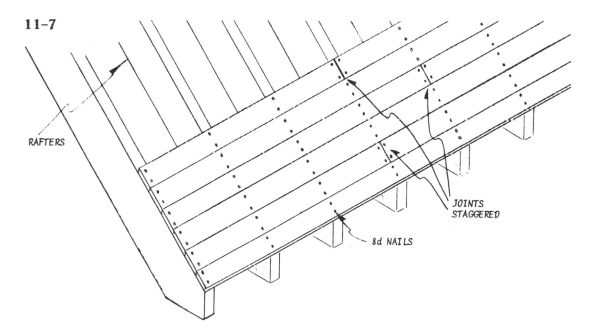

RAFTERS

JOINTS
STAGGERED

8d NAILS

ceiling. Aside from a few situations, boards have been replaced by plywood and composite sheet materials.

SKIP SHEATHING

One variation of board sheathing remains, called skip sheathing. It's still used sometimes under wood shingles and shakes (and some heavy roofing, such as concrete tiles) to provide a combination of support and ventilation under the courses. The spaced boards, generally 1 × 4s and sometimes 1 × 6s, must be placed to match the specifications of the shingles. That means the spacing of the boards must equal the amount that the shingle or shake will be exposed to the weather, regardless of how long the shingle or shake is. As the example in **11-8** shows, if the exposure is 5 inches, then the O.C. spacing of the boards

11-8

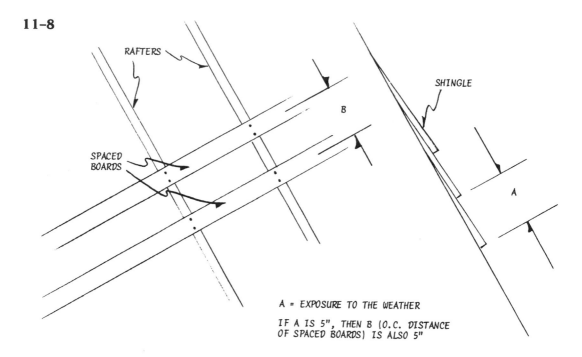

A = EXPOSURE TO THE WEATHER

IF A IS 5", THEN B (O.C. DISTANCE OF SPACED BOARDS) IS ALSO 5"

must also be 5 inches. A always equals B. The range of spacing generally is from about 5 inches for shingles and up to 10 inches for shakes.

There are a few points to bear in mind about this, by now, unusual sheathing system. First, you should check with the building inspector about the possible requirement for diagonal bracing across the rafters. In some regions, this will be required to make up for the diaphragm-type support provided by plywood sheets. You need to place the boards with staggered joints over rafters or trusses that cannot be spaced more than 24 inches apart. Drive two nails at each connection. If skip sheathing will support concrete tiles or other heavy roofing material, spacing typically is 12 to 14 inches. Due to the weight, however, you may need larger boards, or even 2 × 4s. Along the eaves, many roofers set several rows without spaces to provide more support for starter courses.

You can also use plywood covered with 1-by boards to provide ventilation. But many roofers now use a modern alternative to skip sheathing for wood shingles and shakes. It consists of a mat of porous, synthetic mesh (like a tangle of small wires) rolled out and tacked over felt paper and a conventional plywood roof deck. The mesh is stiff enough to provide support without compressing, which leaves a vent space under the shingles or shakes.

PLYWOOD SHEATHING

Today, the most common sheathing by far is 4 × 8 plywood or other composite panels such as sheathing-rated OSB panels. The sheets are easy to handle, relatively inexpensive, and go down fast. This is one of many areas where you are likely to find a difference between the minimal, cost-saving approach builders use and the way you might want to build your own house. Builders generally use the least amount of the least expensive material. For example, where codes permit, they will fasten $5/16$-inch plywood sheets on 16-inch O.C. rafters. You'll want to use $1/2$-inch-thick panels, or even thicker sheets if extra strength is needed for heavy roofing materials.

If you're interested in a minimal roof, you can use the thinnest allowable panels, and add blocking (**11–9**) or clips to support edges in the open spaces between rafters. But owner–builder common sense suggests that if you need special blocking or clips to support plywood edges and keep shingles from waffling, you probably could use stronger plywood.

Standard specs are for APA-rated panels (panels graded by the American Plywood Association) applied with staggered seams over at least three rafters with the long dimension perpendicular to the supports. Although the sheets will be quickly covered, you should use exterior grade (also called exposure 1 grade) panels. You should protect exposed edges, by, for example, installing flashing or J-channel on panels along the rakes and eaves.

Most manufacturers specify a $1/8$-inch space between sheets to allow for expansion without buckling, but gaps can be eliminated in dry climates. Attach sheets as shown in **11–10** with fasteners spaced every 6 inches at edges and every 12 inches in the field.

At valleys, hips, and other angled joints, sheathing joints should provide continuous support for roofing. This doesn't mean you must form compound angle joints at, say, valleys, such as those shown in **11–11**, but mating edges should be reasonably snug. You can opt for a persnickety ending at the ridge or just allow the sheathing edges to kiss (**11–12**).

11–9

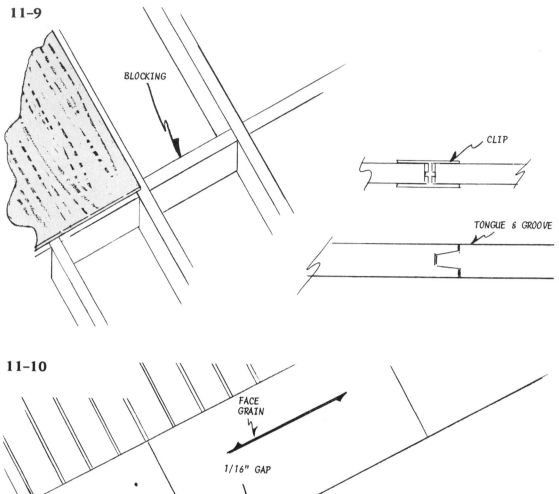

BLOCKING

CLIP

TONGUE & GROOVE

11–10

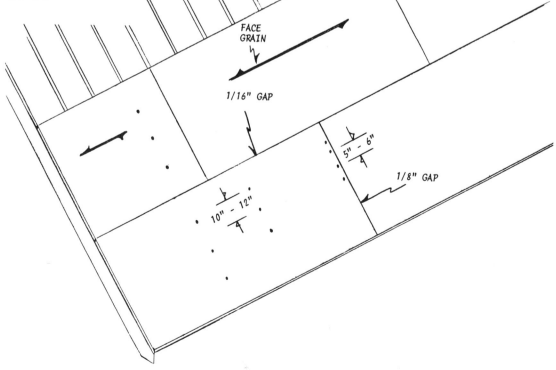

FACE GRAIN

1/16" GAP

$\frac{5" - 6"}{4}$

1/8" GAP

$\frac{10" - 12"}{4}$

11–11

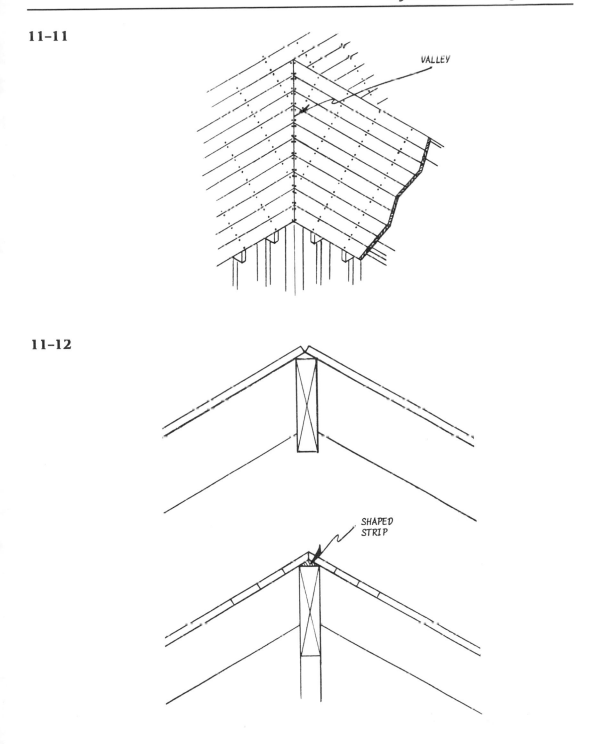

VALLEY

11–12

SHAPED
STRIP

BUILDING CORNICES

The cornice, also called the overhang, comes in many shapes and sizes. You'll want to build one that matches the style of the house, of course. To that end, you can carry rake trim around the eaves, and maintain other details at the cornice to make it blend in. But this area also serves other purposes. The overhanging structure protects building walls, includes a fascia board that ties together projecting rafters, and provides the main inlets for attic and roof ventilation. It's also an area that is prone to damage from roof leaks, particularly in northern climates where freeze-thaw cycles create ice dams along the edges of the roof.

OPEN, BOXED, OR CLOSED CORNICES

Some cornice components can be attached while roof framing is going on and before roof sheathing is placed. This applies especially to open cornices, which require nothing but the addition of fascia boards, as shown in **12–1**. The fascia is nailed directly to the ends of the rafters. Often it is allowed to project above the rafters an amount equal to the thickness of the sheathing (**12–2**). The advantages are that the finish roof then covers the joint and the

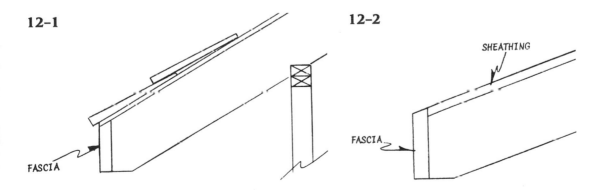

12–1

FASCIA

12–2

SHEATHING

FASCIA

fascia hides and protects the edge of the sheathing. To make a good transition between the roof and the fascia, rip the top edge to match the roof angle.

The fascia can become visible trim. In that case, end joints must meet at a rafter and should be spliced rather than butted. Inside and outside corners are best made with miters (**12–3**). It's a good idea to coat the mating edges of fascia joints, as well as those in other cornice areas, with a caulking compound. Apply the material generously so there will be ample squeeze-out, but remove the excess quickly to avoid stains. In many cases, precise carpentry is not required, and the 2-by structural fascia is covered with a 1-by trim board.

12–3

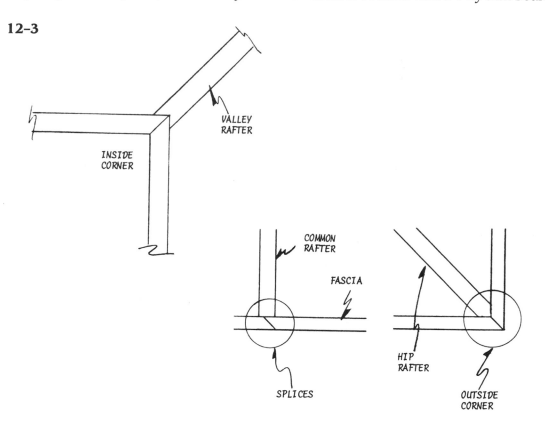

Wide overhangs, which are basically open soffits, can do more than serve as trim for the house. At my place, we extended the roof line for a good part of a large window area as protection from the sun and to make that outdoor area more usable, supporting the overhang with posts and beams, as shown in **12–4**. It became more a veranda than a simple overhang and we made the supports heavier than necessary simply for appearance;

12–4

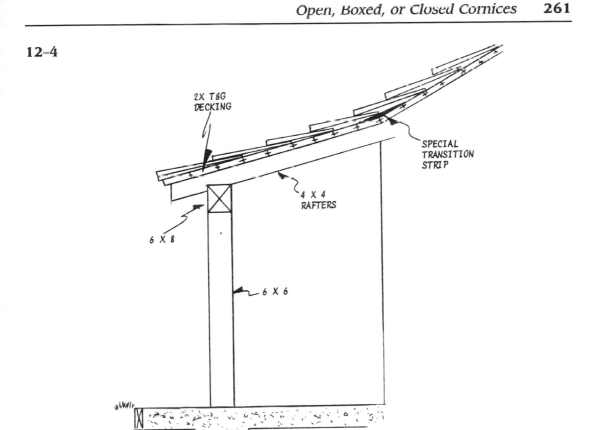

2X T&G
DECKING

SPECIAL
TRANSITION
STRIP

4 X 4
RAFTERS

6 X 8

6 X 6

nevertheless, the roof extension was open-soffit construction. The slope had to change a bit for headroom, so the regular roof rafters were stopped at the wall and others took off from there at the new angle.

The closed cornice can be simple in design and added after the roof and the house walls are complete. As shown in **12–5**, it may consist of just a trim board (called a frieze) and molding, or a plain board that you bevel on both edges to fit the corner. It's obvious that while this serves as a trim, the design doesn't afford much protection for the walls.

Another type of close cornice (also called a narrow boxed cornice) is shown in **12–6**. In this design, the rafter projections serve as nailing surfaces for both the soffit and the fascia. The amount of overhang available will depend on rafter size and roof slope. Note that wall sheathing has been installed and that the fascia is grooved to receive the soffit. The latter isn't always done, but it is premium construction and contributes considerably to weathertightness.

12–5

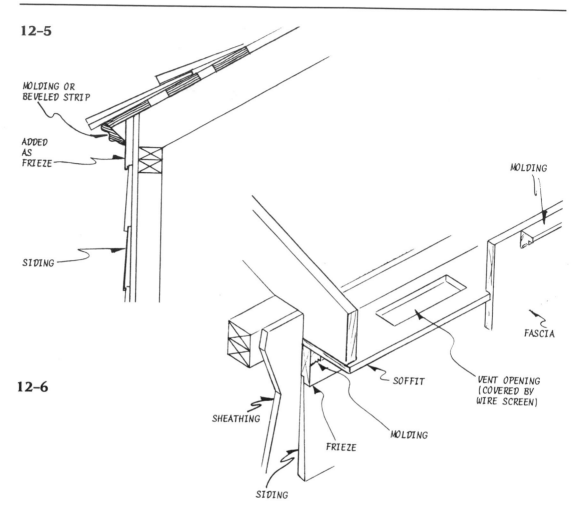

MOLDING OR
BEVELED STRIP

ADDED
AS
FRIEZE

SIDING

MOLDING

FASCIA

12–6

SHEATHING

SOFFIT

VENT OPENING
(COVERED BY
WIRE SCREEN)

MOLDING

FRIEZE

SIDING

THE BOXED CORNICE

Most boxed cornices include 2 × 4 lookouts that span between the wall and the end of the rafters, and serve as nailing surfaces for the soffits. The lookouts tie to ledgers nailed to the wall over sheathing. They may be butted and toenailed to the ledger, or they can be notched as in **12–7**. The width of the overhang is controlled by the extension of the rafters; the depth of the cornice increases in relation to the extension and the roof slope (**12–8**). The section through an elaborate cornice in **12–9** shows how you can gain bulk without increasing extension by using wider material for the lookouts and the ledger. Such installations require more time and more material, so be sure they are really desirable before you do them.

12–7

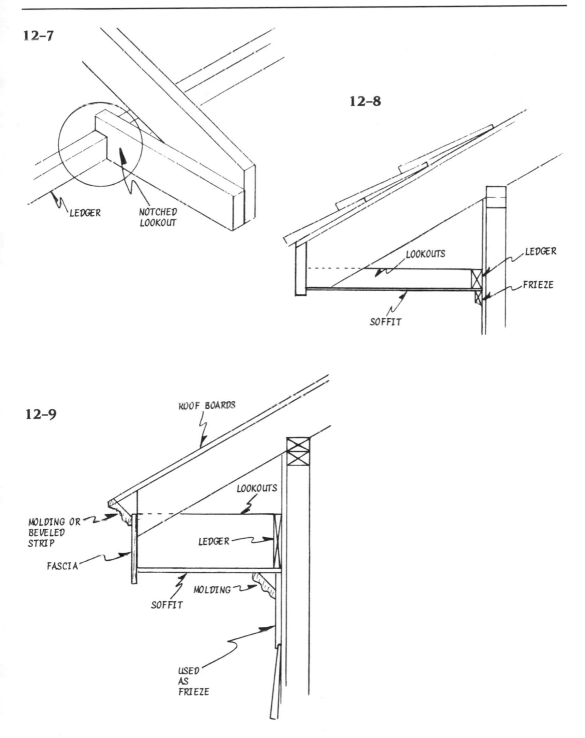

LEDGER

NOTCHED
LOOKOUT

12–8

LOOKOUTS

LEDGER

FRIEZE

SOFFIT

12–9

ROOF BOARDS

LOOKOUTS

MOLDING OR
BEVELED
STRIP

LEDGER

FASCIA

MOLDING

SOFFIT

USED
AS
FRIEZE

In all situations, it's a good idea to install the ledger first, positioning it by using a level between the wall and the end of the rafter and securing it by driving nails that will penetrate the wall studs. Place lookouts at each rafter, toenailing them at the ledger and surface-nailing them to the rafter (**12–10**).

Another type of boxed cornice does without lookouts, the soffit being nailed directly to the underside of the rafters (**12–11**). If you use a grooved fascia, it won't be necessary to

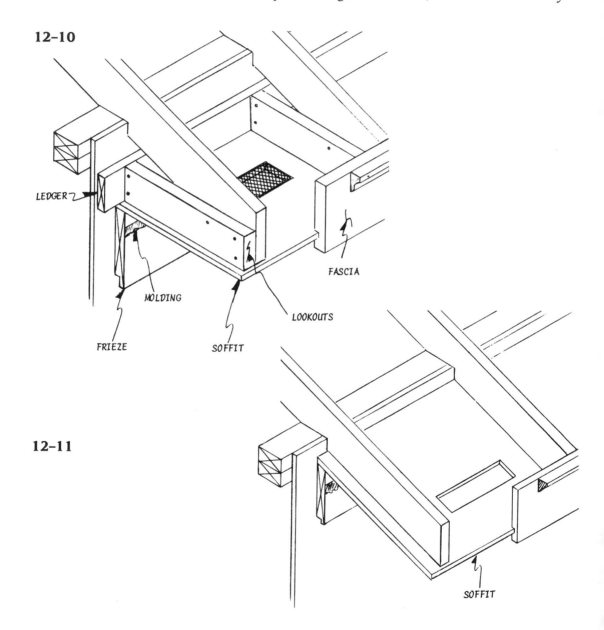

12–10

LEDGER

FASCIA

MOLDING

LOOKOUTS

FRIEZE   SOFFIT

12–11

SOFFIT

angle the cut if you pack the groove well with a caulking compound before you install the fascia. This will provide an effective seat to compensate for the extra-wide groove that will be needed. In all cases, the bottom edge of the fascia should be lower than the soffit by at least ½ inch so it will act as a drip to prevent water from getting into the cornice.

THE CORNICE AT A GABLE END

A close cornice doesn't require much more than a backup to move the fascia off the house wall. In a sense, the backup is another rafter, but since it substitutes for a frieze board, it should be regarded as trim and so should be a better grade material than you would use for regular rafters. A typical gable-end cornice is shown in **12–12**. Because there are a lot of joints here, premium construction calls for flashing strips that are placed before the finish roof is added.

A step between the close cornice and an extended one that permits a cornice up to about 8 inches wide, with a minimum of fuss, can be made using short lookouts to which the fascia is nailed directly (**12–13**). The molding is the final touch, ending the project decoratively and hiding the edges of the sheathing.

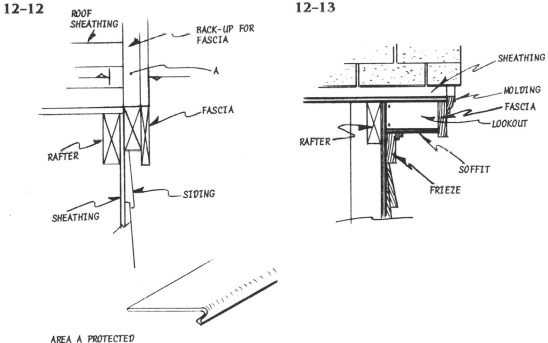

12–12

ROOF SHEATHING

BACK-UP FOR FASCIA

A

FASCIA

RAFTER

SIDING

SHEATHING

AREA A PROTECTED WITH SPECIAL FLASHING

12–13

SHEATHING

MOLDING

FASCIA

LOOKOUT

RAFTER

SOFFIT

FRIEZE

An open-soffit construction can be made merely by extending solid roof sheathing outboard to a fly rafter that ties in with the ridge at the top and the fascia board at the bottom. Wider overhangs are anticipated and provided for by incorporating lookout rafters in the basic roof frame as shown in **12–14**. Soffit material is attached directly to the underside of the lookouts and the fly rafter, and a fascia is added to cover the rafter and the edge of the soffit (**12–15**). For narrower overhangs where lookout rafters are not used, a nailer is attached to the wall so the inboard edge of the soffit may be secured (**12–16**).

Unlike the hip roof, where boxed cornices are continuous and similar around the entire structure, the gable roof requires what is called a return, where cornices along the side of the house meet those of the end wall (**12–17**). While there are many ways to design the return, a simple and practical one consists of widening the fascia at the end of the side

12–14

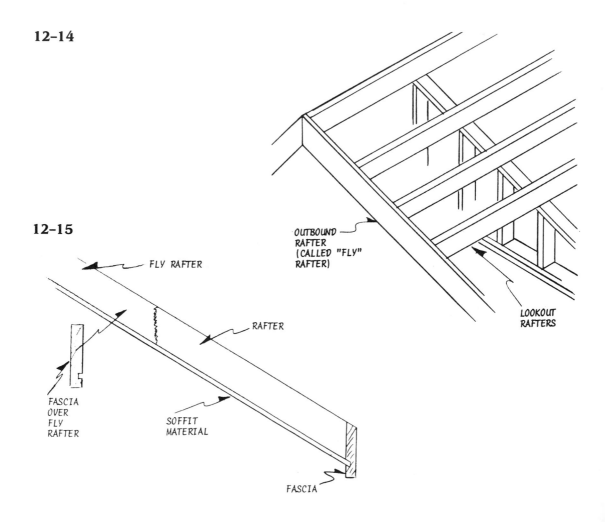

12–15

FLY RAFTER

OUTBOUND RAFTER (CALLED "FLY" RAFTER)

LOOKOUT RAFTERS

RAFTER

FASCIA OVER FLY RAFTER

SOFFIT MATERIAL

FASCIA

12–16

12–17

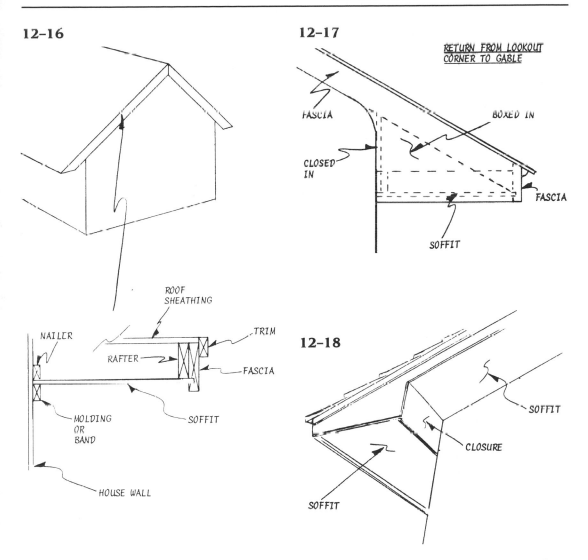

RETURN FROM LOOKOUT
CORNER TO GABLE

FASCIA

BOXED IN

CLOSED
IN

FASCIA

SOFFIT

ROOF
SHEATHING

NAILER

TRIM

RAFTER

FASCIA

MOLDING
OR
BAND

SOFFIT

HOUSE WALL

12–18

SOFFIT

CLOSURE

SOFFIT

cornices. It's not likely that this can be done with a single piece of material that is long enough to run from the ridge to the eaves or wide enough to cover the cornice. But do plan to use as few pieces as possible and to work so you get tight joints, preferably with a T&G arrangement at the mating edges.

The back of the side cornice is sealed with a piece of soffit material used as a closer (**12–18**). It will probably be easier to add this and the corner will be more weathertight if you do it before working on the fascia. Some of the many varieties of ready-made moldings that are usable to trim cornice and roof edges are shown in **12–19**.

12-19 READY-MADE MOLDINGS

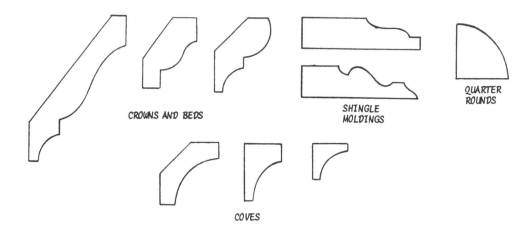

CROWNS AND BEDS

SHINGLE MOLDINGS

QUARTER ROUNDS

COVES

VENT REQUIREMENTS

To vent attic spaces, you need to let air in along the eaves and let air out near the peak. There are many ways to provide the outlets—for example, with large, triangular gable-end vents, with turbine or other roof-mounted vents, and with ridge vents, which is the most common system today. Inlets have to be built into the overhang. The system is designed to promote a flow of air that carries away moisture and prevents condensation problems.

There are dozens of ways to accomplish this. You can insert plug vents or rectangular vents between rafter bays. More commonly, builders install strip-grille vents that run continuously along the soffit. You also can install perforated aluminum or vinyl soffit panels instead of plywood to provide continuous ventilation (**12–20** and **12–21**).

Whatever approach you take, you need to provide a total vent intake area of not less than $1/150$ of the ventilated space. That's the starting point of most codes, and calls for some very large vents. But the rule generally applies only if the ceiling has no vapor barrier to retard moisture flow into the attic from the living space. With a vapor barrier installed on the warm side of the ceiling insulation, the ratio is reduced generally to $1/300$ of the ventilated space. It's much easier to meet this requirement—and sensible to install vapor barriers all around the thermal envelope of living space. Inspectors also are likely to grant you some leeway when the area of low inlets and area of high outlets are about the same.

Sticklers on vent and energy codes may want you to allow for the air reduction imposed by insect screening, which is sensible to install on the insides of all vents. The reduction of vent area is increased by a factor of 1.25 for $1/8$-inch mesh, and 2.0 for $1/16$-inch mesh.

12–20   (Photo courtesy of Lonestar.)   **12–21**   (Photo courtesy of Lonestar.)

ICE DAMS

When weather conditions are right, ice dams can form along the overhang like glaciers, clogging gutters and leaders, lifting shingles and twisting flashing, and eventually letting in a lot of water. There are two main causes that can combine to form thick dams that are nearly impossible to remove until the weather moderates.

The first is a series of freeze-thaw cycles—sunny days and cold nights, even sunny mornings and cloudy afternoons—that can ice up a thin blanket of snow. It begins to melt in the sun, which warms up the shingles even on a cold day, and then freezes when the sun goes down. In the same way an icicle drips and freezes, getting longer and longer, freeze-thaw cycles make a roof dam bigger and bigger. Once it takes hold and grows enough to block your gutter or downspout, the dam can hold more melting snow on the roof, and grow even faster.

The other cause is uneven roof temperature, which occurs to some degree even in new, heavily insulated buildings, and can create dams under a thick blanket of snow. These are the most damaging, often surprisingly large, and you may not spot them until the damage is done. Just a little heat radiating up through the roof will get things moving by melting the snow from the bottom up. That starts a trickle of water down the shingles, protected from freezing wind by the crusty-topped blanket. It traps air like a batt of insulation, and can keep the water running even in extremely cold weather—until it runs past the house wall onto the overhang where the temperature changes. There's no house underneath, and no heat, which makes the last few feet of roof stone cold. That's where the water freezes and forms a dam (**12–22**).

The best way to prevent damage is to build in protection. To let snow and ice melt from the top down and drain away, the main roof has to stay as cold as the overhang. In addi-

12–22

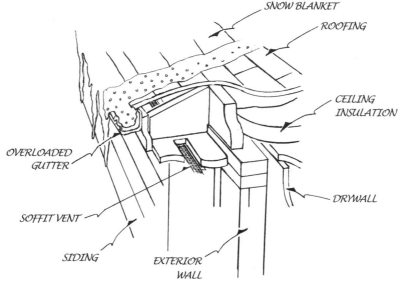

tion to insulation and a vapor barrier in the ceiling joists, you can accomplish this by adding insulation in or over the floor of an unfinished attic, and increasing ventilation with a combination of inlets and outlets.

To prevent dams from getting a foothold, and encourage ice and snow to slide off the overhang, you can install a continuous strip of sheet metal over the last courses of shingles. If this detail seems a little too rural (it's common on steeply sloped roofs in the northeast), you can dress it up by installing more formal and traditional sheets with standing seams. Metal edges work well, but may not look good.

If all else fails, there is one backup against ice-dam leaks: a rubberized membrane installed beneath the few courses of shingles on the overhang. It doesn't stop the problem, but it does control it. The membrane is made of rubberized asphalt and polyethylene in self-adhering sheets that bond directly to the wooden roof deck, and to each other at overlaps. When you cover it with shingles, the self-sealing membrane even closes around punctures from the nails. If water does back up and get through the shingles, it will stay on top of the membrane until it rolls off the roof into the gutter.

INSTALLING THE ROOF-DRAINAGE SYSTEM

During heavy rains, almost any house can be overwhelmed without roof drains that collect water, carry it to leaders, and on through underground pipes or other extensions away from the building. Without gutters, even light rain dripping off the roof will eventually wear a channel in the ground near the foundation that traps more water and increases the likelihood of leaks.

All drainage systems on sloped roofs, regardless of the materials used, consist basically of gutters and downspouts that work together to collect runoff water from the roof and direct it so it can't cause foundation seepage. Disposal methods depend on the amount of rainfall and snow in the area. When it is high, you must plan to avoid problems. When it is low or moderate, you can often make out merely by directing the water away from the foundation.

The size of the gutters depends on the amount of water they will receive, and this is affected by the area of the roof. Standardized guides say that a 4-inch gutter is the minimum and is usable for a roof that is not larger than 750 square feet. Use 5-inch gutters when the roof area approaches 1,400 square feet, and 6 inches thereafter. Downspouts that are 3 inches in diameter will do if the roof is under 1,000 square feet; use 4-inch downspouts if the area is greater. The size of the downspouts is of less importance than their number and location. One outlet for every 600 square feet of roof area is a minimum. A gutter run that is less than 20 feet can do with a single outlet at one end. Use an outlet at each end when the run is greater.

Don't figure the square footage of a roof on a horizontal plane. Figure its real area, including dormer roofs, overhangs, etc. All planes will collect water during any rainfall, especially if there is wind. The higher the ridge, the more true roof area there is and the faster water will be carried into the gutters. So if you have a very steep roof, you might plan to be more generous with gutter sizes, regardless of the roof area.

PLANNING THE INSTALLATION

The rule of thumb for gutter installations is to install them with a slope of about one inch per 10 linear feet of run. Practically no one does this because it seems wrong and looks bad. But slope is important because it helps to prevent clogs by encouraging the flow toward the leader exits. On segmented gutters (as opposed to seamless gutters), slope also helps to prevent water from coming to rest against overlapped seams and then leaking.

If you want gutters, there is no good solution for this problem, only a compromise. Install a sloped gutter on a 60-foot house, and it should drop 6 inches from one end to the other. The edge of the roof on many houses is not deep enough to accommodate this much drop. Also, the fascia is level, which can create a very noticeable discrepancy against a sloping gutter.

The compromise is to split the slope (and the discrepancy) in half. Do this by installing the high point of the gutter in the middle of the roof with the gutter sloping away in both directions. On long runs, this also fulfills a second rule of thumb about gutter installations, which is to provide a leader outlet every 35 feet. And in case one leader or outlet becomes blocked, at least some of the water that backs up can flow out the other end.

A typical layout is shown in **13–1**. There is no law that tells you where you must place a downspout, but appearance is a factor. Usually it's a good idea to locate them at the corners of a building and away from doorways. They can drop vertically from the gutters, but if the roof has an overhang they will be eyesores. It's better to use standard elbows so the downspout can be directed back to the house wall and tied there as inconspicuously as possible.

13–1

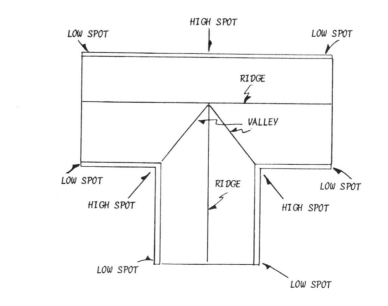

Ready-made gutter systems are available in various sizes, and in shapes that include half-round, K-style, and ogee. Materials include galvanized steel, copper, aluminum, and vinyl. The standard today is a seamless gutter. Though the designs and the method of hanging may differ, all gutter systems include the components that are necessary to make runs, turn corners, connect to downspouts, and so on (**13–2**).

13–2

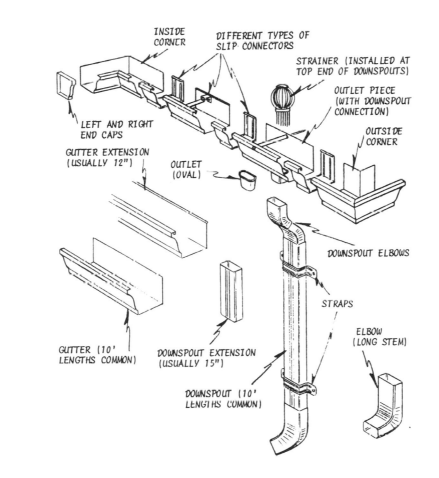

Some gutters are attached against the fascia and can be installed when the roof is complete. The easiest approach uses gutter spikes that pass through both sides of the gutter and are driven into the end of every other rafter (**13–3**). A sleeve, called a ferrule, fits inside the gutter (the spike goes through it) to keep the gutter from buckling.

Another type works with brackets that are installed against the fascia at alternate rafters (**13–4**). These may vary in design, and the manufacturer may suggest a different spacing, but basically the idea is to attach the brackets and then lock the gutters in place with a strap that is part of the assembly. Strap types work like the one shown in **13–5** and are installed after the roof sheathing is in place and before the finish roofing goes on. Other systems use a flange, or roof apron, which is attached to the edge of the roof over

13–3

SPIKE WITH SLEEVE

13–4

FASCIA BRACKET

13–5

STRAPS

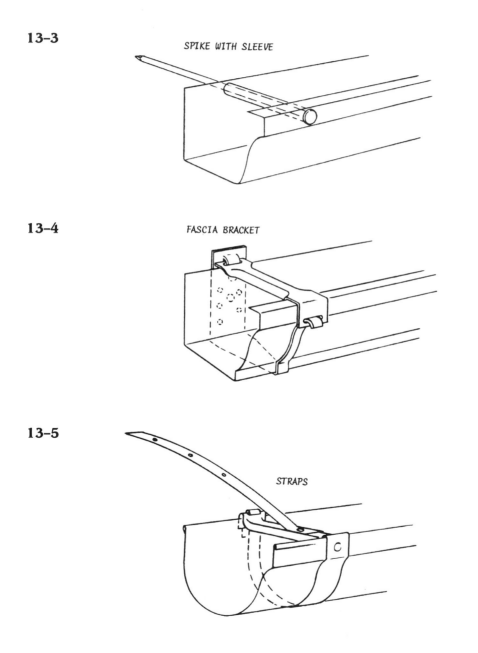

sheathing to act as a flashing (**13–6**). The designs can be one- or two-piece, with a lock connection between the flange and the gutter. The flange is attached with nails about every 12 inches. The hangers hook into a lip at the front edge of the gutter and are nailed over every other rafter.

Most segmented systems include slip connectors for joining sections of gutters (**13–7**). They are designed to grip without further attention except the addition of a caulking compound to waterproof the joint, but a wise extra step is to drill pilot holes and lock the joints with sheet-metal screws or pop rivets. The slip connectors are also used wherever the gutter turns a corner (**13–8**). Here, as with all connections, make the joints as smooth as possible so you won't create dams.

13–6

13–7

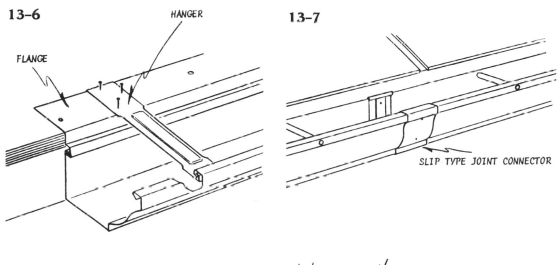

FLANGE

HANGER

SLIP TYPE JOINT CONNECTOR

13–8

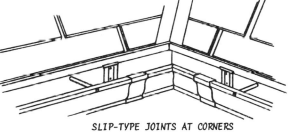

SLIP-TYPE JOINTS AT CORNERS

Install outlet sections at all downspout positions (**13–9**). End all runs with an end cap secured with mechanical fasteners plus a good amount of caulking (**13–10**). Downspout connections are made with elbows and, if necessary, short lengths of downspout extensions (**13–11**). Special straps are nailed in place to hold the downspout snugly against the house.

13–9

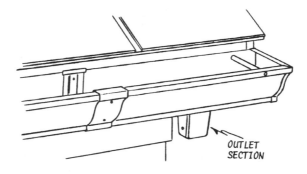

OUTLET
SECTION

13–10

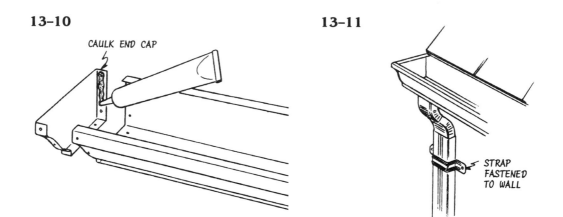

CAULK END CAP

13–11

STRAP
FASTENED
TO WALL

DOING THE JOB

A good place to start the installation is at the point that is farthest away from the downspout area. This can be at the end of a roofline so there will be a one-directional slope, or at a midpoint so the gutters will slope to both left and right. Drive a nail at the high point and then stretch a line to the other end, dropping it in relation to the slope you are using. Start placing gutters at the high point and run from there to the opposite end, or ends, attaching material so the top edge of the gutter follows the line. Downspouts will have to be installed after the house siding is up, but you may wish to preassemble parts so they will be ready when needed.

The metals involved can be cut easily with a hacksaw and a pair of metal-cutting snips. Be careful, though, and wear gloves, because cut edges are very sharp. Finish all cuts with a file or emery paper to remove burrs.

Vinyl materials may also be cut with a fine-tooth saw, but, as with metal materials, support the work solidly and keep the blade at a low angle. Vinyl gutter systems are assembled with a special cement provided by the manufacturer.

Bear in mind that seamless gutters automatically eliminate almost all joints that could leak. You have to order them because they are made to fit the house. A contractor takes measurements, and rolls aluminum through a former on his truck that transforms flat stock into a gutter shape.

GUTTERLESS SYSTEMS

Most roof drains require regular maintenance to work properly—nitty-gritty work scooping out slimy, decomposing leaves. If you skip this job in warm weather, clogs may lead to overflows and dripping as though you had no gutters. In winter, water can freeze, back up on the roof, get under shingles, cause leaks, and sometimes a lot of damage.

These built-in problems have spawned many gutter add-ons and replacements. Some consist of a simple plastic shield that covers almost all of the gutter to keep out debris. Others take the form of wire bulbs inserted over leaders that are supposed to stop debris that blocks water but let the water through.

Most of the gutter add-on products take one of two basic approaches. One is to cover the trough, generally with some type of screen or grate, so debris can't get in and cause clogs. What happens, typically, is that debris clogs on the screen or grate instead.

Another approach is to replace the trough shape with a so-called self-cleaning gutter. Most of these are louvers or otherwise perforated strips of metal that attach to the edge of the roof instead of a gutter. In fact, they are not gutters at all because they do not collect water, only disperse it. The slats or holes are supposed to break up the steady stream of water into smaller spurts that cause less erosion. But dispersers don't move water well away from the foundation, which is the main purpose of roof drains. They can't add any force to the flow, which generally drips straight down, unless there is a torrential rain—which would shoot well off the edge of the roof, in any case.

14 ROOF FLASHING

Every roof is interrupted by intersections of various roof planes or by house components such as chimneys, soil stacks, vents, or skylights. The joints that occur require special attention so water can't pass through them into the roof. The areas are treated by flashing, which is a procedure involving special materials such as galvanized metals, aluminum, or copper, sometimes in combination with roll roofing or a more modern roofing sheet material, called modified bitumen.

You may want to cut, shape, and install all your own flashing. But some components are quite complicated. For example, the combination of flashing, counterflashing, and cricket flashing between a chimney and a sloping roof may best be left to a professional.

You can assemble some of the constructions before the finish roof is applied; others are set with the final steps. The type and location of the flashing you need depends a good deal on how you are finishing the roof. But all the procedures are based on the water-flow principle in which roofing materials lap over one another. Water must drain over roofing material, not under it.

The most critical areas are at valleys, around chimneys, and anywhere a roof surface abuts a vertical wall. Of the three, the valley areas can cause the most problems. This is not hard to understand when you consider that valleys are depressions that collect water from various directions. Snow can lodge there and may become ice dams to interrupt the natural flow of water, which will then seek any weak point in the cover to escape. The slope of the roof is another factor. The less slope there is, the greater the danger of leakage.

Valleys can be closed or open. In a closed valley, shingles are woven across the joint and water flows on the roof surface. This requires some flex in the roofing material, and is used with asphalt shingles. On more common open valleys, which are suitable for all types of roofing, the shingles stop short of the valley, and the water travels along the valley trough.

There are some situations, especially with asphalt shingles, where you can use 90-pound mineral-surfaced asphalt roll roofing as the flashing material. This is applied as a double coverage, with the first piece about 18 inches wide and placed with the mineral side down, and the second piece about 36 inches wide and placed with the mineral side up (**14–1**). It's okay to use joints if the job can't be done with single pieces, but the top piece should overlap the bottom one by at least 12 inches and mating surfaces should be bonded with asphalt cement. A good application procedure is to nail down one edge of the

14–1

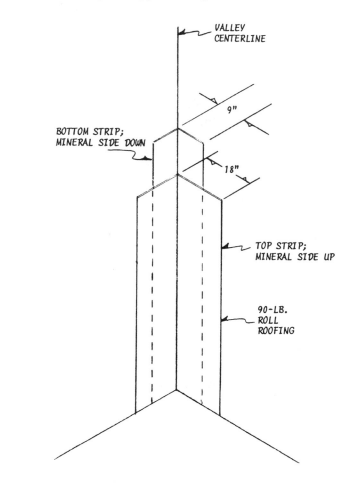

flashing and then fasten the other edge while the material is pressed firmly into the valley. Coat the edges of the first ply with a 3- or 4-inch-wide band of asphalt cement before you add the second ply. Use regular asphalt-shingle nails, but place them so they will be amply covered by the final roof material. Careful workers will coat those nail areas with cement before installing the shingles.

After the flashing is installed, it's wise to mark lines that will tell where courses of shingles should end. Start by snapping a chalk line to indicate the centerline of the valley. Then mark each side so you will know the width of the waterway. Most valleys have a uniform width for appearance. But in some cases, and particularly in very cold climates, drainage is promoted by increasing the flashing width toward the eaves. A typical valley is 5 or 6 inches wide at the tip, and can increase by $1/8$ inch per foot.

When you get to placing the shingles, the valley-end one in each course will be trimmed to follow the line you have established. Usually the top outer corner of the shingle is cut off at a 45-degree angle and the edge of the shingle is cemented to the flashing (**14–2**).

Valleys at gable dormers usually have short runs, so one-piece flashing is best. You may want to make a paper pattern for one side, which, when flipped, can be used for the opposite valley as well. The cut at C in **14–3** is a notch to permit flashing pieces to

14–2

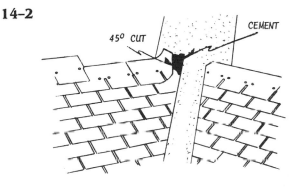

14–3

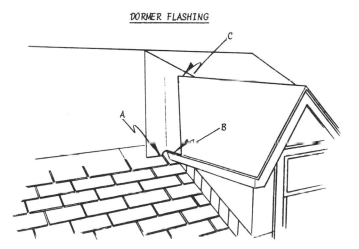

overlap at the ridge while the remainder lies flat on the roof. Edge B should extend beyond the eave of the dormer, while edge A should be long enough so at least 2 inches of it can lie flat on the roof. The corner between A and B should be cut as a curve so the flashing won't crack when pressed into the valley.

Valley flashing usually is made with metal. Start by checking the valley area carefully for any projecting nail heads. Premium construction calls for a layer of 30-pound roofing felt to be placed under the metal. You can also use heavier roll roofing. If joints are necessary, the top piece should overlap the bottom one by at least 6 inches.

Ready-made valley flashing with a splash rib or ridge running down its center is often used, and particularly when adjacent slopes have a different pitch (**14–4**). The purpose of

14–4

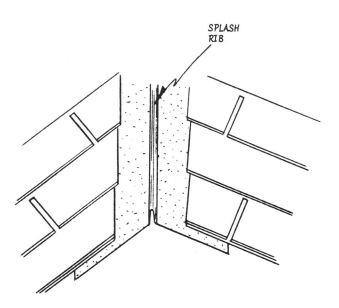

SPLASH RIB

the rib, or standing seam as it is often called, is to serve as a barrier so water flowing from one slope will not cross the valley and run under the roof cover on the other side.

Metal flashing also has folds along the edges to contain water and to provide an edge for flashing cleats—small metal strips made of compatible metal that grip the fold on one end and allow nailing to the roof deck on the other. You don't set nails in valley flashing.

Let valley flashing extend beyond the roof edge at least as far as the shingles. Generally, shingles extend at least 4 inches over each edge of the flashing.

AROUND CHIMNEYS

The joints between a chimney and a roof are waterproofed by using base flashing, step flashing, and counterflashing (**14–5**). On steep slopes or wide chimneys you also may need a water diverter, called a cricket or saddle, which is a large assembly of V shaped flashing that sends water to the sides of the chimney.

Because a chimney is established on its own foundation and the wood members around it are subject to expansion and contraction, the flashing must be installed in two opposing parts so movement can occur without breaking the water seal. If the installation is done correctly with sufficient laps, water will not be able to enter behind the flashings.

The base flashing is installed after the roof cover has reached the base of the chimney. Follow the pattern shown in **14–6** so the material can be folded to fit snugly around the chimney base. A similar piece, which is applied last, can be cut for the back of the chimney.

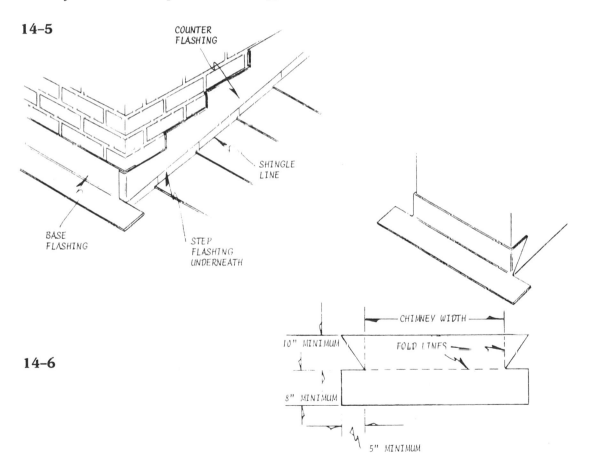

14–5

COUNTER FLASHING

SHINGLE LINE

BASE FLASHING

STEP FLASHING UNDERNEATH

14–6

CHIMNEY WIDTH

10" MINIMUM

FOLD LINES

8" MINIMUM

5" MINIMUM

The first piece of step flashing is placed as shown in **14–7**, while other individual pieces are set in position at the end of each course of shingles as shown in **14–8**. The pieces of step flashing are bent to form a right angle, with each leg 5 to 6 inches wide. The length should be at least 2 to 3 inches more than the exposure used on the shingles. Because the flashing is placed along with the shingles, you automatically get a good overlap at all joints (**14–9**). You can secure each piece with one or two nails along the top edge. Step flashing is not nailed to the roof, even though the nails will be covered by shingles.

Counterflashing is made with metal sheets or a single preformed piece. In each case, a flange at the top, as shown in **14–10**, must penetrate the mortar joint in the masonry at

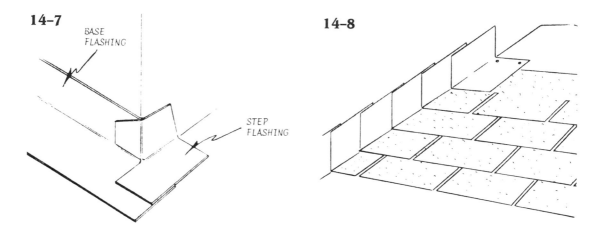

14–7
BASE
FLASHING
STEP
FLASHING

14–8

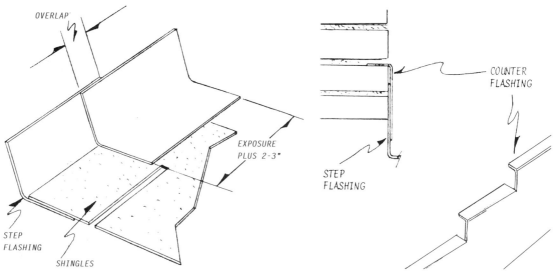

14–9
OVERLAP
EXPOSURE
PLUS 2-3"
STEP
FLASHING
SHINGLES

14–10
COUNTER
FLASHING
STEP
FLASHING

least one inch. Side flashing, which is stepped to conform to the slope of the roof, is often made by embedding separate sheets in the masonry joints and then bending them down over the step flashing when the mortar has set. This can be accomplished while the chimney is being erected.

If the chimney is already built, the mortar is raked out of the joints by careful work with a chisel and hammer, leaving a groove as shown in **14-11**. Then the joints are packed

14-11

with fresh mortar after the flashing is in place. The counter flashing at the front and the back of the chimney is made with straight pieces.

A SADDLE FOR THE CHIMNEY

A saddle, often called a cricket, is a gablelike construction on the high side of the chimney that is added to permit water to flow off more freely and for snow to have less chance of accumulating (**14–12**). This is quite difficult to make and should be installed only if the chimney is exceptionally wide or the climate is exceptionally wet. You probably will want to hire a metalworking contractor or roofer to make one. The construction may have a supporting frame (**14–13**), but generally is covered or made entirely of metal.

14–12

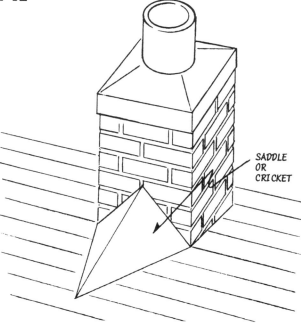

SADDLE
OR
CRICKET

14–13

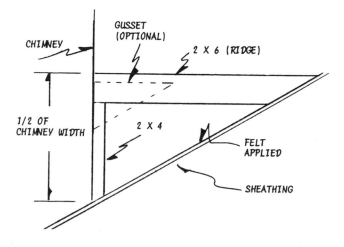

CHIMNEY

GUSSET
(OPTIONAL)

2 X 6 (RIDGE)

1/2 OF
CHIMNEY WIDTH

2 X 4

FELT
APPLIED

SHEATHING

FLASHING AT A VERTICAL WALL

You need this common flashing detail at the base of a partial second story or where dormers intrude. The sheets are installed following the procedure outlined for the installation of step flashing along the sides of a chimney, and is required wherever a vertical wall intersects a roof plane (**14–14**). In this case, flashing is shown in place before sheathing is applied. In most cases, you sheath first and flash second. The upper edges generally need only one nail placed high on the wall. The nails and upper edges are covered by siding.

You can easily make your own sheets by cutting from larger sheet materials. (You need to work carefully and with gloves because the edges can be very sharp.) It's often easier to buy precut sheets that are widely available.

14-14

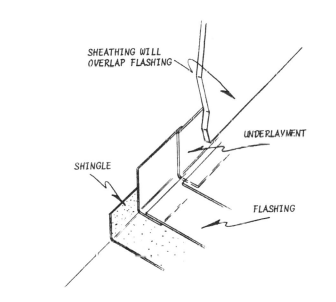

SHEATHING WILL OVERLAP FLASHING

UNDERLAYMENT

SHINGLE

FLASHING

FLASHING AT OTHER FITTINGS

Three other common flashing areas include the seams around skylights, roof vents and plumbing vent pipes. Skylight flashing is provided by the manufacturer, and often includes flashing and counterflashing.

On older roofs, pipes that protruded through the roof were flashed with a metal collar. Most of these installations eventually leaked and were sealed with tar—sometimes again and again.

Modern vent-pipe flashing is easier to install and longer-lasting. It has an aluminum base sheet like standard flashing that is set in roof tar below shingles on the high side of the pipe, and on top of shingles on the low side (**14–15**). The slick part is a flexible rubber gasket attached to the base that simply slides over the pipe to provide a neat, waterproof seal. Generally, this type requires no extra sealants or tape.

14–15   READY-MADE VENT-STACK FLASHING

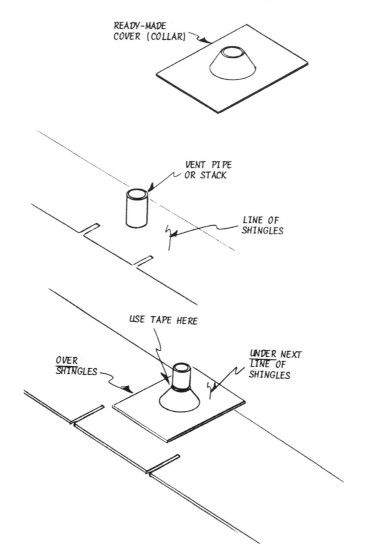

READY-MADE
COVER (COLLAR)

VENT PIPE
OR STACK

LINE OF
SHINGLES

USE TAPE HERE

OVER
SHINGLES

UNDER NEXT
LINE OF
SHINGLES

15

INSTALLING
FINISHED ROOFING

There are many choices for finished roofing, including some fairly exotic materials such as slate and terra-cotta tile that require special tools and expertise—and a heavy-duty roof frame to support the extra weight. For owner-builder projects, we'll stick to the basics, including asphalt shingles, wood shingles, and shakes, and both built-up and modified bitumen applications for flat and very low-slope buildings. We'll concentrate on asphalt shingles, which are used on four out of five new houses across the country.

ROOFING TERMS AND ESTIMATING

When you consider roofing you need to think about several factors, including cost, durability, and fire resistance. Generally, the least expensive is roll roofing. These overlapped sheets are not often used on houses, but more on utility buildings. As to durability, masonry roofs (such as concrete tiles) may last 50 years or more. But they are expensive, call for special framing, and are difficult to install. As to fire resistance, which is crucial in some regions, tile and metal are the best, although the thickest asphalt-based products, sometimes called dimensional or architectural shingles, receive high ratings as well. Wood roofs, obviously, are not as fire resistant, but they can be treated with fire retardants.

Thick shakes are very expensive and not used as much as they once were. When faced with reroofing, many home owners opt to remove them and install architectural asphalt shingles that have multiple surface layers which mimic the look of shakes instead. Asphalt shingles (today that means fiberglass-mat, asphalt-topped shingles) are relatively inexpensive, easy to lay, and come with warranties generally between 15 and 30 years.

We've covered some of the terms already. Remember that one square is 100 square feet of roof surface. To cover that area, you may need more of one type of shingle than another, depending on size and configuration. A square of standard 235-pound asphalt shingles is composed of three bundles, each containing 27 shingles.

Coverage refers to the number of layers of roofing protection provided. For example, standard modified bitumen for flat roofs provides one layer with narrow overlaps at seams. Dimensional asphalt shingles that look like shakes from a distance may offer many layers of coverage.

There are several ways to estimate roof surface area. The most obvious and reliable is simply to go up on the roof with a measuring tape. But remember to figure in extras—for example, four full shingles for every five linear feet of hip or ridge, or about 30 linear feet per square of shingles—to allow for some waste.

To save money and buy nails in bulk, figure to use about two pounds of standard, 1¼-inch galvanized roofing nails per square. To order 15-pound roofing felt that is applied beneath shingles and other types of roofing, remember that most manufacturers assume a 2-inch overlap and figure that one 432-square foot roll will cover about 400 square feet. However, the material is inexpensive, easy to install, and, with an 18-inch (half a roll width) lap that provides double coverage, adds extra protection against tears from the roof deck below and from leaks above. Using a minimal lap can add up to big savings for pros who use truck loads of felt every year. But on your own house or addition a few extra rolls makes only a marginal increase in cost. Installing double-cover felt is an inexpensive safety factor.

You also may encounter some confusion about asphalt versus fiberglass shingles. Many contractors say "asphalt" even though most shingles installed today are fiberglass. There is actually only a small difference in materials. Old-fashioned asphalt shingles have a base mat made of asphalt-saturated fibers. Modern fiberglass shingles have a base mat made of glass fibers. Both types are manufactured basically the same way, with asphalt coatings on both sides and a topcoat of mineral granules that improve fire resistance, resist brittleness from exposure to the sun, and add color. As a result, fiberglass shingles that cover the same area and provide the same fire rating as their pure asphalt counterparts are a bit lighter—about 225 pounds per square for a standard shingle, versus about 240 pounds for asphalt. Bear in mind that these shingles come in many weights. Heavier shingles generally have better fire ratings and last longer. But they cost more and there are fewer shingles per bundle.

ABOUT ROLL ROOFING

This inexpensive alternative to shingles for low-slope roofs consists of 36-inch-wide rolls that are 36 feet long. Although some sheets are covered with surface granules, the material is not often used on visible roofs of houses, but it is an option.

Like shingles, roll roofing may have an asphalt or fiberglass base, and in different thicknesses can weigh 55 to 90 pounds per square. Single-coverage rolls have a small overlap of only 2 to 4 inches over edge nails. The laps, and 12-inch starter roll, are sealed with cold-set asphalt adhesive. Double coverage offers more protection and durability due to more concealed nails, and a larger sealed overlap of about 16 inches (**15–1**). This application weighs 110 to 140 pounds per square.

Extra starter strips are often installed along the rakes. In valleys, lay an 18-inch-wide

15–1

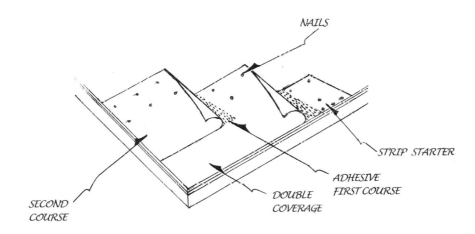

strip (mineral face down) under a full-width sheet, keeping nails to the outer edges. Run the cover sheet to 3 inches from the valley centerline.

Don't try to use roll roofing instead of built-up or modified bitumen roofing on a flat roof, even if you seal all nails and seams. Generally, you need at least a 2-in-12 pitch.

Overall, if you take a look at other houses in your area, you may find some roll roofing on a shed or the back of a garage that's hard to see from the street. But very few houses are covered with roll roofing.

ASPHALT SHINGLE ROOFS

The first asphalt shingles didn't last very long because they were made of rags. The fabric was saturated with asphalt and coated with mineral granules like modern shingles. It wasn't until the 1940's that the rag mat was replaced with cellulose. The next major improvement produced the lighter, stronger, fiberglass-mat shingles that cover most homes today. Some are rated to last 30 years or more. Four out of five United States houses are covered with asphalt shingles. Over 12 billion square feet are manufactured every year, enough for 5 million homes.

Asphalt shingles are available in several configurations and colors, including the standard three-tab shingle in different thicknesses, and laminated (architectural) grades with a textured appearance (**15–2**). You can also special-order shingles with zinc- or copper-coated ceramic granules to retard algae growth.

Like all shingles, asphalt shingles have a fire rating. The categories range from Class A, the highest rating, to Class C, the lowest. Although the rating varies according to shingle thickness (double-layer, laminated shingles have more resistance than single-layer shingles), most fiberglass-mat shingles have Class A fire ratings, and most organic shingles have Class C ratings. As a practical matter, you'll probably get fiberglass-based shingles whether you want to roof or reroof. Many suppliers don't stock anything else.

Most sloped roofs start with a layer of overlapped 15-pound felt paper stapled over plywood sheathing. When heavy felts impregnated with asphalt are coated with weather-resistant material and surface granules, they become roll roofing (**15–3**).

The minimum recommended weight for asphalt shingles is 235 pounds for the most common type: a rectangle with three tabs (**15–4**). They are overlapped as shown in **15–5** so that the keys are staggered.

15–2

15-3

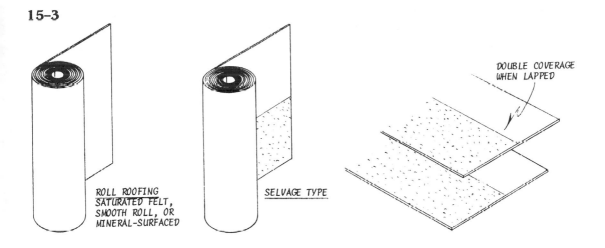

ROLL ROOFING
SATURATED FELT,
SMOOTH ROLL, OR
MINERAL-SURFACED

SELVAGE TYPE

DOUBLE COVERAGE
WHEN LAPPED

Individual shingles are available, as shown in **15-6**, which can be set down in standard patterns or used to create special effects, as long as the exposures and the laps recommended by the manufacturer are followed. Other types of individual shingles are designed to interlock when they are placed (**15-7**). But special configurations like this are not generally available or stocked at supply houses.

UNDERLAYMENT

A cover of roofing felt, usually 15-pound, is placed over the sheathing before shingles are nailed down. It provides additional weather protection for the roof, a barrier between the shingles and the wood, and keeps the sheathing dry until you get to the final cover. Rolls of 15-pound felt usually do a good job, but requirements can be affected by the type of shingles and the slope of the roof, so give some consideration to the recommendations of the manufacturer.

All underlayments should have a minimum 4-inch side lap and 2-inch top lap. They should be secured with the minimum number of staples or nails required to keep wind from blowing them off the roof until the final cover is in place. The laps at hips and across valleys should be at least 6 inches on each side of a centerline. In cold climates, codes may call for a 36-inch-wide strip of bituminous waterproofing.

Premium installations include metal drip edges along perimeters (**15-8**). These may be purchased ready-made, usually formed from 26-gauge galvanized steel and with the top flange 3 to 4 inches wide. Notice that the underlayment is placed over the drip edge at eaves but under it along slopes.

15–4

15–5

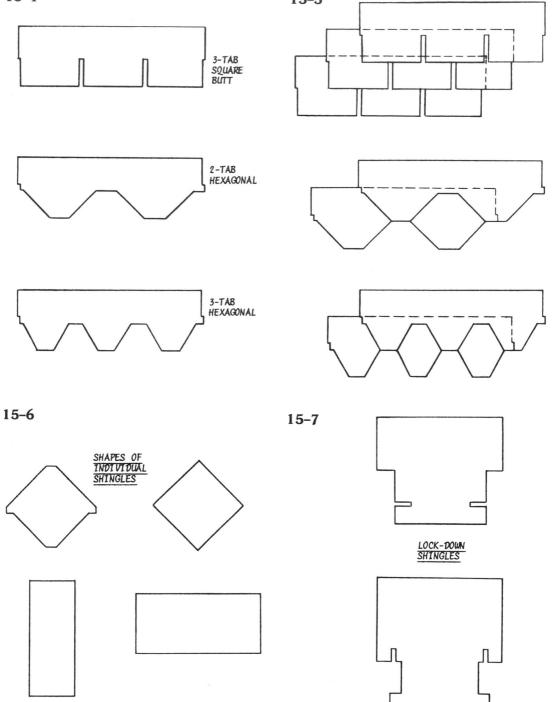

3-TAB
SQUARE
BUTT

2-TAB
HEXAGONAL

3-TAB
HEXAGONAL

15–6

15–7

SHAPES OF
INDIVIDUAL
SHINGLES

LOCK-DOWN
SHINGLES

15–8

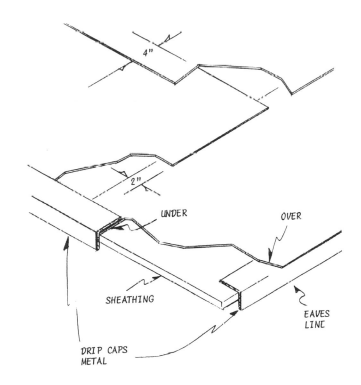

NAILING HOW-TO

Galvanized roofing nails have large head diameters to provide good holding power. Most owner installations are made with smooth-shank nails (**15–9**). The nail must be long enough to fully penetrate the sheathing. Typical nailing is four nails driven above the slots (including the half slots at each end) as in **15–10**. It's important to keep the nail shank perpendicular to the slope so the head won't tilt and cut through the shingle. Don't hammer so much that you sink the nail head into the surface of the material. If the nail doesn't hit solid sheathing, remove it, plug the hole with asphalt cement, and drive another nail close by.

A lot of nailing is required on jobs like this, so you might check out the possibility of renting power equipment. Tools designed specifically for the work, driving special roofing staples, are acceptable. Manufacturers of roofing covers can advise what type of staples can be used. The drawback is that you'll be tethered to an air hose supplying the tool from a compressor.

15–9

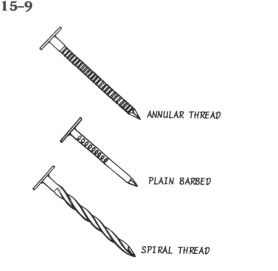

ANNULAR THREAD

PLAIN BARBED

SPIRAL THREAD

15–10

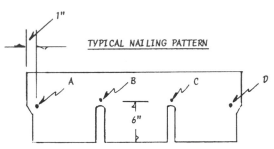

DOING THE SHINGLING

Start from one end of the roof, and dry-lay a course to check your spacing. Then you can adjust one way or the other for uniform placement and end cuts that do not fall, for example, in a slot area.

Use a starter strip under the first course of shingles to add bulk and to back up the slots. The starter strip should be 10 to 12 inches wide and can be cut from mineral-surfaced roll roofing that matches the shingles both in weight and color, or it can be made with strips of the shingling material placed so the slots point toward the ridge. That's the system most pros use—starting with a layer of shingles turned top for bottom.

Place the starter strip so it overhangs the roof edge a bit and secure it with nails spaced to be covered by the first course of shingles. Snap a chalk line across the starter strip so you will have a guide for the top edge of the first course of shingles. The first course and the following courses are placed as shown in **15–11**. Note that the layout aligns the slots in alternate courses.

Some roofers also set a row of shingles (face down) along the rakes. This extra layer tends to shift water back onto the main roof where it drains to the gutters instead of dripping off the rake ends. Overall, it's important to check shingle alignment regularly. You can measure up from the eaves at intervals and snap a guideline.

15-11

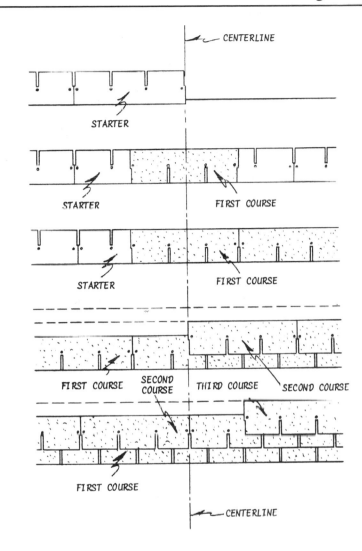

AT RIDGES AND HIPS

You can buy special shingles for use at ridges and hips, or use roll roofing cut to shape. But it's easy to make them by cutting tab sections of shingles (**15-12**). And using shingles will keep the color and exposure consistent. You simply use a utility knife to cut from the center of the keys at a slight angle across the covered portion of the shingle. When you install the tabs, the full-width tabs will line up and the angled section without granules will tuck inside the line to create a neat edge.

15–12

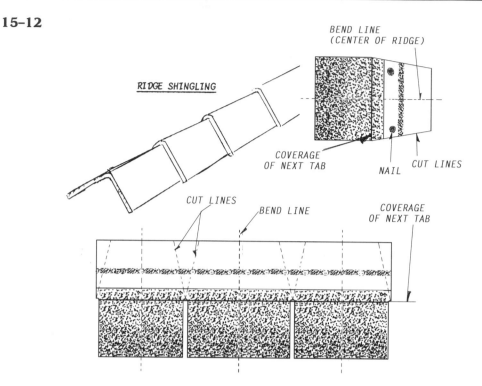

RIDGE SHINGLING

You set nails above the keys (partial keys in this case) where they will be covered by the next tab in line. Place them to deflect instead of catch prevailing winds, and spot roof cement over the final nails in a half tab that won't be covered. Pieces formed as hip and ridge covers should not be bent when they are cold or they may acquire surface cracks or even break. If you're working in cold weather, warm them in the sun or, if necessary, near a fire.

WOOD SHINGLES

Wood shingles are taper-sawed from decay-resistant species like cypress, redwood, and cedar, with cedar having the edge because of characteristics that include a low expansion and contraction ratio in relation to moisture content, a nice even grain, and a high impermeability to liquid. Unfortunately, wood does not resist fire too well, so wood shingles may not be allowed in some areas unless they have been specially treated with a fire retardant.

The traditional installation uses skip sheathing spaced to match the shingle exposure. Many roofers now use solid sheathing and a synthetic mesh mat (laid over felt paper) to provide needed ventilation.

Shingle lengths are 16, 18, and 24 inches, and each can be used with different exposures, depending on the thickness of the cover you want. You can see in **15–13** how the thickness increases as the exposure decreases. The correct amount of exposure depends on the slope of the roof. In most situations, the recommended exposure is as shown in the table in **15–14**.

15–13

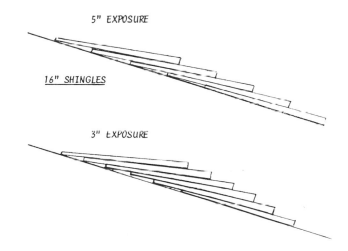

5" EXPOSURE

16" SHINGLES

3" EXPOSURE

15–14   EXPOSURE RECOMMENDATIONS FOR SHINGLES

Roof Pitch	Shingle Length	Exposure
4 in 12	16"	5"
or	18"	5"
steeper	24"	7"
less than	16"	3"
4 in 12 to	18"	4"
3 in 12	24"	5"
less than 3 in 12	NOT RECOMMENDED	

Note: Above exposures assume the use of No. 1 grade shingles.

Shingles do have to be cut, and while you can do this with a saw, the job will be faster and easier with a shingler's hatchet (**15–15**). This is a lightweight tool with two sharp edges and an adjustable gauge you can set to check exposure as you work.

You can also trim shingles with a utility knife, and even out crooked edges with a block plane. Do-it-yourselfers should stay away from the hatchet, and use a straightedge guide

15-15

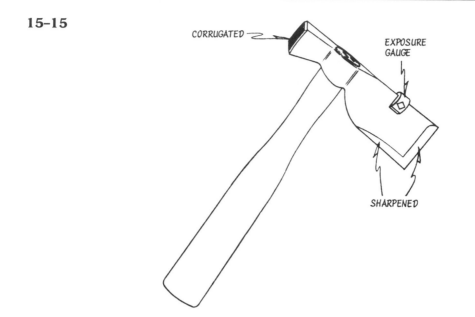

to score shingles with a utility knife, then snap them, and use a sharp block plane for final trimming.

Work only with rust-resistant nails, choosing sizes as recommended in **15-16**.

15-16   RECOMMENDED NAIL SIZES

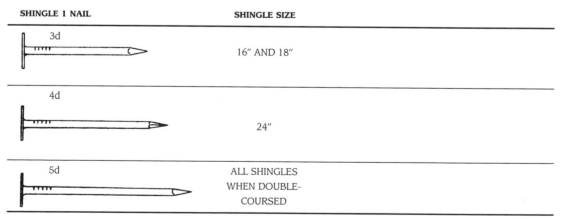

SHINGLE 1 NAIL	SHINGLE SIZE
3d	16" AND 18"
4d	24"
5d	ALL SHINGLES WHEN DOUBLE-COURSED

The shingles you get in a bundle will vary in width, but regardless, never use more than two nails per shingle, placed ¾- to one inch from the edge and so they will be covered by that same distance by the next course (**15-17**). Overlap shingles are shown in **15-18**.

15-17

15-18

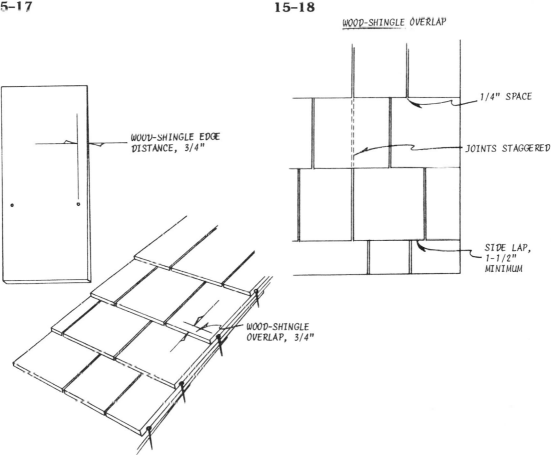

WOOD-SHINGLE OVERLAP

WOOD-SHINGLE EDGE
DISTANCE, 3/4"

1/4" SPACE

JOINTS STAGGERED

SIDE LAP,
1-1/2"
MINIMUM

WOOD-SHINGLE
OVERLAP, 3/4"

Note the ¼-inch space between that is needed shingles to allow for expansion that might otherwise cause buckling if the shingles were butted. Also notice that joints in adjacent courses are not on the same line. Maintain a side lap of at least 1½ inches between the joints in successive courses. Larger laps are better.

INSTALLING THE SHINGLES

Start with a double layer of shingles along the edge of the roof, letting them project enough to ensure that water will spill into the gutter (**15-19**). Often a cant strip is placed along the edges of a gable before the shingles are placed so water will flow more easily toward the eaves and not drip off the gable end (**15-20**). This is a difficult piece to make, but you can beat the system by using a length of beveled siding.

15–19

15–20

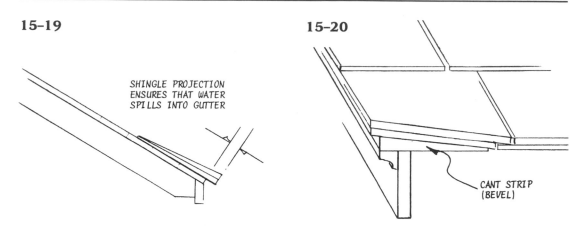

SHINGLE PROJECTION
ENSURES THAT WATER
SPILLS INTO GUTTER

CANT STRIP
(BEVEL)

Succeeding courses of shingles should be placed by following a chalk line that you snap, or by tack-nailing a straight piece of wood against which you can butt the courses of shingles you are nailing (**15–21**). It's wise to measure occasionally from the ridge or eaves to the last course of shingles, to keep the courses parallel. As you will discover quickly, you can't align the shingles along the tops because their lengths vary somewhat.

Courses that abut a valley should be started there, and with wide pieces of shingling. Make the angle cuts you will need very carefully so course ends will match neatly. Never end a course with a very narrow shingle. It's better to reduce the width of others in the same course so you can end with a wide piece.

Ready-made units which can be used to cover hip and ridge joints are available (**15–22**). Or you can make your own by beveling the mating edges of selected pieces of regular shingling. These are nailed together and placed with regular exposure, but with the

15–21

15–22

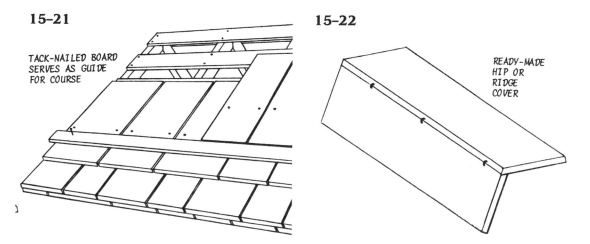

TACK-NAILED BOARD
SERVES AS GUIDE
FOR COURSE

READY-MADE
HIP OR
RIDGE
COVER

overlap moving left and right in alternate courses (**15–23**). Those on the ridge are placed so the open ends will not face prevailing winds (**15–24**). The first course in both hip and ridge covers is doubled and placed as shown in **15–25**. Be sure to attach the cover pieces with nails that are long enough to penetrate the sheathing, and place them so they won't be exposed to the weather.

15–23   **15–24**

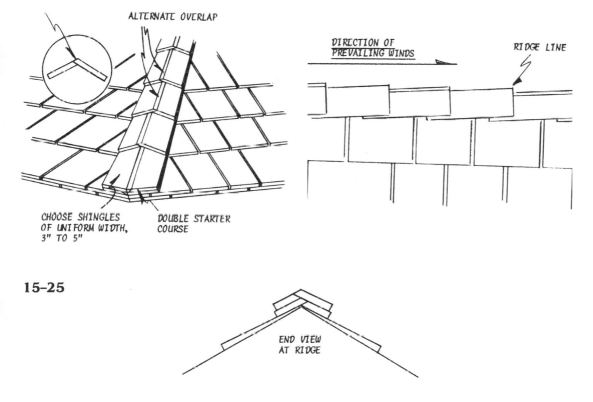

CUT BACK EDGE OF SHINGLES ON A BEVEL

ALTERNATE OVERLAP

DIRECTION OF
PREVAILING WINDS

RIDGE LINE

CHOOSE SHINGLES
OF UNIFORM WIDTH,
3" TO 5"

DOUBLE STARTER
COURSE

15–25

END VIEW
AT RIDGE

Two types of roof junctures are shown in **15–26** to demonstrate how to handle breaks in a roofline. The flashing should be galvanized metal (or copper if you can afford it) at least 8 inches wide, so 4-inch flanges will cover the roof slope and the area that follows. Be sure the flashing covers the nails in the last course of shingles. Notice that the new area begins with doubled starter courses.

On valleys, use sheets that will extend a minimum of 10 inches on each side of the centerline whenever the roof pitch is less than 12 in 12 (**15–27**). The extension may be reduced to 7 inches on steeper roofs. Lap the flashing by at least 6 inches on each side.

15–26

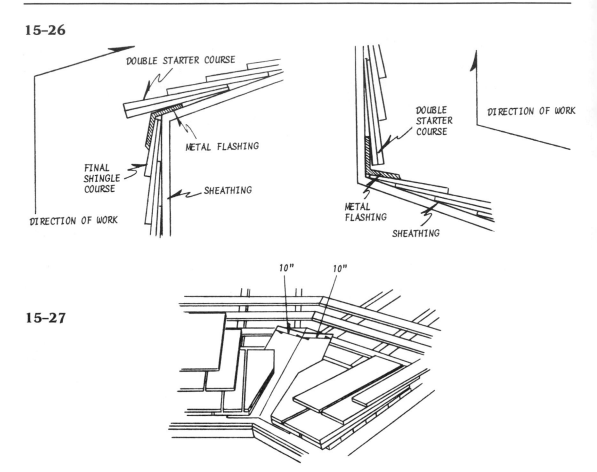

15–27

SHINGLES AVAILABLE AS PANELS

One option that saves time and trimming is to use panelized shingles, which are basically preassembled shingles bonded to ½-inch sheathing-grade plywood (**15–28**). The system lets you apply 16 shingles at a time together with sheathing, with nailing required only at the rafters.

The installation begins by nailing down special starter panels that are correctly positioned by placing a temporary starter strip across the rafters or by snapping a chalk line (**15–29**). Plywood clips can be used at all end joints in order to get a stronger underlayment (**15–30**).

A typical nailing schedule calls for two 6d box-head rust-resistant nails at each rafter, with one placed about 1 inch down from the top edge of the plywood and the other about 2 inches up from the lower edge of the plywood (**15–31**).

15-28

15-29

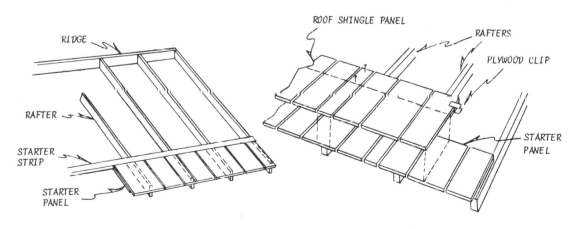

RIDGE

RAFTER

STARTER STRIP

STARTER PANEL

15-30

ROOF SHINGLE PANEL

RAFTERS

PLYWOOD CLIP

STARTER PANEL

Conventional flashing procedures apply generally, but a special design is recommended for valleys. Here, 1 × 6s or 2 × 6s are placed parallel to the valley rafter and so that top edges are flush (**15–32**). The idea is to supply a solid support for the flashing, which is installed in step fashion to protect the plywood from the weather (**15–33**). Hip and ridge units can be made by utilizing cutoffs from regular panels with a narrow piece of roofing felt used as an underlayment (**15–34**).

These shingle-panel systems generally are made for roofs with a 4-in-12 rise or steeper, and come with shingles or shakes.

15–31

15–32

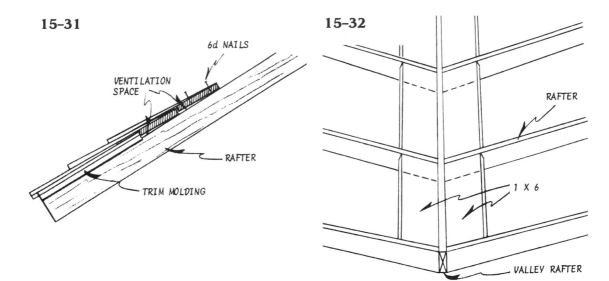

15–33

15–34

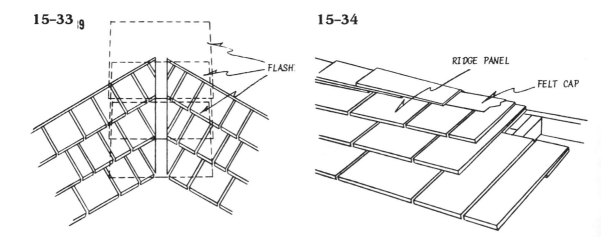

THE SHAKE ROOF

Roof covers made with heavy shinglelike pieces of wood go far back in the history of this country. Atlantic Coast colonists made them from various species of wood, including white pine, but today the emphasis is on red cedar, because of its fine grain, light weight, absence of pitch or resin, and natural resistance to decay.

Shakes are made in different ways, as shown in **15–35**. Resawn shakes are actually straight splits which are then cut on a band saw to get two shakes, each with a thin end

15–35

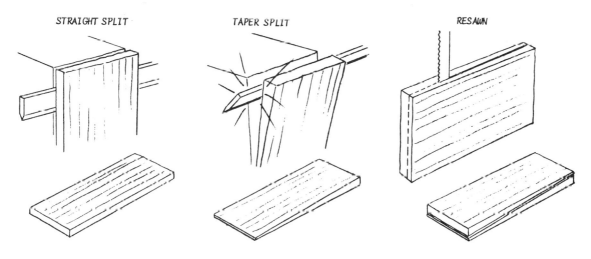

STRAIGHT SPLIT   TAPER SPLIT   RESAWN

and a butt end, and each with one sawn and one hand-split face. The multiple grooves that result from splitting act as channels that lead water off the roof. Also, splitting separates the wood fibers and leaves cell walls intact, so the shake absorbs little of the runoff. This is one of the main differences in cost and quality between thicker split and thinner sawn shakes. All quality shakes are made from the decay-resistant heartwood of the tree. The amount of sapwood in a shake is strictly controlled, usually limited to no more than ⅛ inch along an edge.

There are several variations in application techniques that include straight-line layouts and rustic designs, such as the random pattern in **15–36**.

15–36

BASIC APPLICATION OF SHAKES

Sheathing generally consists of spaced 1 × 6 boards matched to the shake exposure, as in **15–37**. The slope of the roof should be 4 in 12 or more, with a maximum exposure of 10 inches for 24-inch shakes and 7½ inches for 18-inchers. Premium installations often reduce exposure to achieve more coverage. Work with hot-dipped zinc-coated 6d nails unless the combination of shake thickness and weather exposure makes a longer nail advisable. The nail must be long enough to penetrate almost the full thickness of the sheathing. Use only two nails to a shake, placing them about 1 inch from edges and so they will be covered by 1 to 2 inches of the following course. Drive the nails only until the head meets the surface of the shake, but don't sink them (**15–38**). Leave a gap of about ½ inch between shakes and stagger the joints. All joints in one course should be offset at least 1½ inches from those in the following course.

15–37

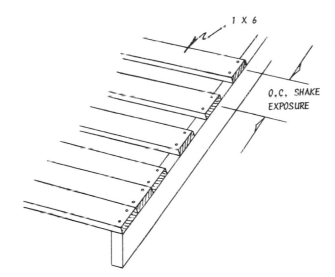

1 X 6

O.C. SHAKE EXPOSURE

15–38

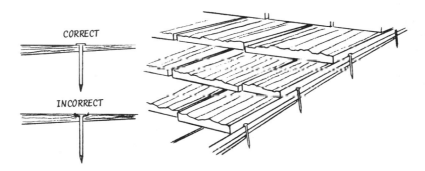

CORRECT

INCORRECT

DOING THE JOB

Start by placing a 36-inch-wide strip of 15-pound roofing felt over the sheathing along the eaves line. The starter course is always doubled, as in **15–39**, but may be tripled if you wish to bulk the edge. A cant strip may be placed on gable slopes (**15–40**). Nail on the cant strip before starting to nail shakes.

Courses of shakes are interwoven with 18-inch-wide strips of 15-pound roofing felt. Place the felt so its bottom edge will be away from the butt end of the course already in

15–39

15–40

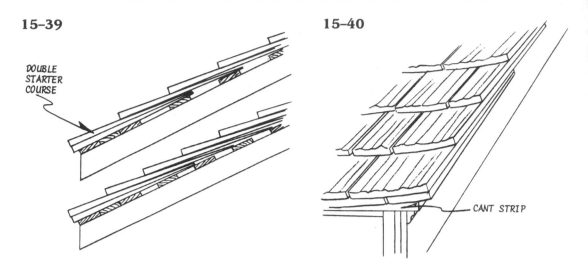

DOUBLE
STARTER
COURSE

CANT STRIP

place by about twice the weather exposure. This would be 20 inches if you are working with 24-inch shakes and a 10-inch exposure, so the felt would cover the top 4 inches of the shakes and also 14 inches of the sheathing (**15–41**).

Select large and uniform shakes when you get to the final course at ridge and hip lines. Place an 8-inch-wide strip of felt over the crown before nailing ridge or hip units (**15–42**).

15–41

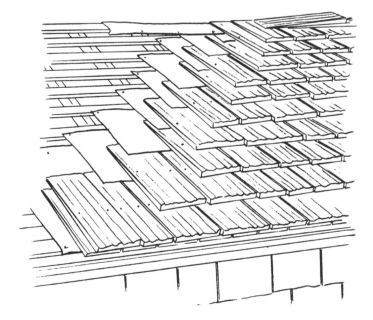

15–42

These units, which you can buy ready-made or assemble yourself using shakes about 6 inches wide, get the same exposure, given the roof shakes. As with shingles, the starter course for both hips and ridges is doubled and the crown joint moves left and right as the courses are placed (**15–43**).

Valley flashing should be 26-gauge or heavier, sheets that are at least 20 inches wide. Underlay them with roofing felt and use 6-inch head laps (**15–44**). Conventional base, step, and counterflashing is used around chimneys and other interruptions in the roofing.

Finally, because hand-split shakes are thicker than other roofing materials and tend to shed water runoff over a slightly wider zone, wider gutters might be in order. Use 5-inch gutters if the shakes are ¾ inch thick or less; 6-inch if the shakes are thicker. Most shake roofs do not require special treatments, but fungicidal chemicals can be used where heat and humidity prevail, to prevent moss, fungus, or mildew.

FLAT ROOFS

Old-style flat roofs were built up from as many as five layers of asphalt felt paper, each one sandwiched in a bed of molten tar, applied with the kind of labor-intensive steps builders

15–43

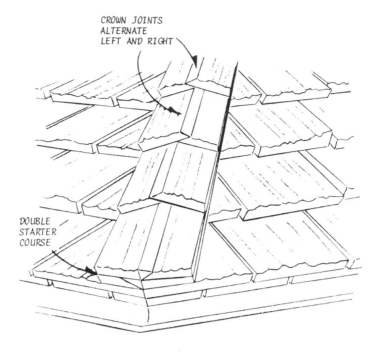

CROWN JOINTS
ALTERNATE
LEFT AND RIGHT

DOUBLE
STARTER
COURSE

15–44

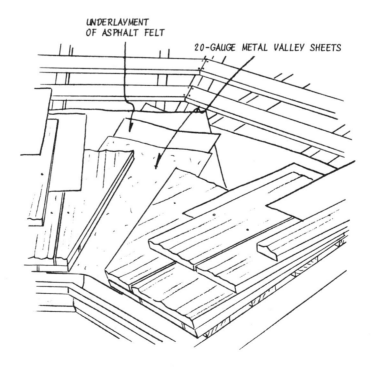

UNDERLAYMENT
OF ASPHALT FELT

20-GAUGE METAL VALLEY SHEETS

don't have the time or money for today. It's a heavy-duty, messy job that requires a tar kettle, among other things, and is not really a do-it-yourself project.

More modern flat-roofs are made with modified bitumen, which consists of rubbery sheets that do not require tar, even at the joints. Instead, they are fused by heating the material until it begins to melt, which effectively makes several sheets into a single roof surface where the joints are as waterproof as the full sheets. Pros use an oversize propane torch that looks a bit like a flamethrower. This is another specialized circumstance that signals the job is for experienced contractors. In fact, if you're not familiar with the proce dure you can light the sheets on fire.

The best recommendation for owner–builders is to leave both built-up and modified bitu men roofing to the pros. Even if you could gather all the equipment necessary to apply a built-up roof, you would have to bond the roofing panels to each other and to the deck with hot asphalt or pitch (**15–45**). This step is repeated several times as layers are added (**15–46**).

15–45

15–46

But if you want a flat roof, there are some steps you can take to prepare for a professional roof installation. One is to build up the perimeter of the roof with cant strips and drain outlets, as shown in **15–47**.

While most roofs are designed to shed water, flat roofs are built up around the edges to contain it and channel the flow to outlets. Large flat roofs also may be equipped with shallow channels to aid and direct the flow, generally called scuppers. These run from the drain outlet back into the roof several feet—maybe far enough to reach some of the low spots that don't drain completely.

In theory, flat, and nearly flat roofs are designed to hold standing water without leak-

15–47

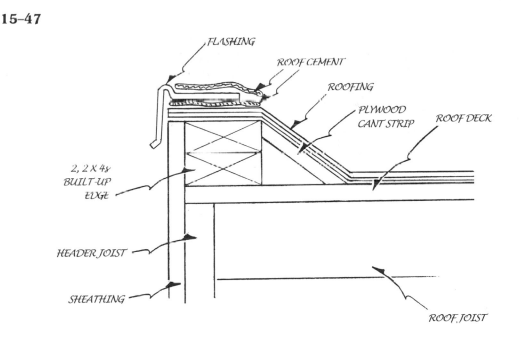

FLASHING

ROOF CEMENT

ROOFING

PLYWOOD CANT STRIP

ROOF DECK

2, 2 X 4s BUILT-UP EDGE

HEADER JOIST

SHEATHING

ROOF JOIST

ing. But low spots can cause problems, particularly in winter when the water turns to ice. Puddling can occur due to faults in construction, or because of gradual settling over time. In a flat roof, even a small sag in a rafter can create a low spot that won't drain.

SPECIAL ROOFING

There are several other roofing choices, such as tile, slate, and metal standing seam panels. These all last a long time but are very expensive and almost always require professional installation. Most are installed over skip sheathing, although some, such as standing seam panels, are fastened with a track-and-clip system installed over solid sheathing.

When it comes to cost, slate, for example, can run three or four times the price of asphalt on a basic Cape, and becomes exponentially more expensive on a complex roof that requires a lot of trimming around dormers and valleys. This material may even last 100 years. It is stone, after all—strong enough to stand up to foot traffic on patios—and used sometimes as a shim under wooden girders carrying extremely heavy structural loads. On top of that it's beautiful, whether you use one shade of gray, or a blend of gray, green, and red.

Individual pieces may be pint-sized compared to modern, multilayer asphalt shingles, but not nearly as flexible, and that makes slate difficult to work. Even gentle lifting pressure can cause cracking. A lot of breakage is common, even for some pros.

You generally need to use copper or brass nails, learn to chip tiles to size, and often rent a water saw to make inside corner cuts.

You also may want to check into clay tile, concrete tile, and metal panels. But if you are thinking about one of these special roofing systems, you need to anticipate the requirements for roof framing and sheathing. You may also need to adjust the angle of a low-slope roof since tile, for one, generally can't be used on a roof that has less than a 3-in-12 slope.

16

SHEATHING THE WALLS AND APPLYING SIDING

Wall sheathing is an exterior covering nailed directly to the framing. After it is applied, the only openings you will see are those left for doors and windows. The sheathing is a smooth, flat base on which you apply the final cover-siding, and it is strong enough so you generally don't need special bracing in the frame itself. In some areas, thick sheet-material siding (thicker than ½ inch) may be allowed by code to serve as sheathing and siding. Generally, sheathing is required.

Wall sheathing used to be made of individual boards. This is a nice system, but rarely used due to cost and installation time. The common materials are plywood, OSB, and even (in some areas) exterior grade gypsum sheathing. Owner-builders should stick to wood sheets.

Because the products vary in composition and come in different sizes, the type and length of nails and the nail spacing should follow the directions of the manufacturer or rating agency, which generally is the American Plywood Association (APA). Also check about spacing between panels, which typically is ⅛ inch. Local building regulations are written to cover the application, and may require special bracing in walls with many large window and door openings. Generally, you can use ⅜-inch panels on 16-inch centers and ½-inch on 24-inch centers. But it's wise, and customary, to stick with ½-inch material.

SHEATHING WITH BOARDS

In the rare case where boards are used for sheathing, you may find square edge boards, although shiplap or tongue-and-groove material will provide a much tighter cover. Random-length boards that are both side- and end-matched permit end joints to occur anywhere. Board sheathing can be applied horizontally, as in **16–1**, but only because it is easier and involves less waste than a diagonal pattern. This installation typically needs corner bracing.

317

16–1   HORIZONTAL BOARD SHEATHING

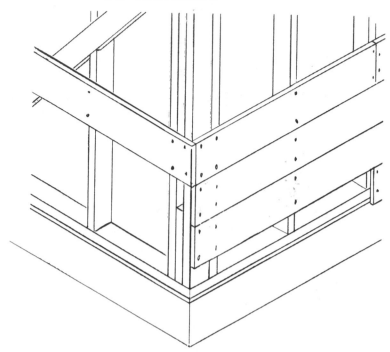

Nail horizontal boards to each framing member with two 8d nails. Use three 8d nails if the boards are wider than 8 inches. Attach diagonal sheathing by using three 8d nails at the corner post and two 8d nails at each stud (**16–2**). Add a nail at each place if the boards are wider than 8 inches. End joints, regardless of whether the boards are placed horizontally or diagonally, should occur at the midpoint of a stud unless the boards are end-matched. Stagger all joints, preferably by at least two stud spaces.

SHEATHING WITH PLYWOOD

Plywood and OSB are commonly used because they are less expensive and easier to apply. You can nail panels horizontally or vertically (**16–3**), depending on the situation. For example, you may find that vertical sheets cover the wall completely, and have no edges spanning between studs. But horizontal installations are stronger because more plies are oriented lengthwise, which betters braces the studs. This creates a stiffer wall that provides a better backing for materials such as shingles and stucco. To cover a full wall, including

16–2 DIAGONAL BOARD SHEATHING

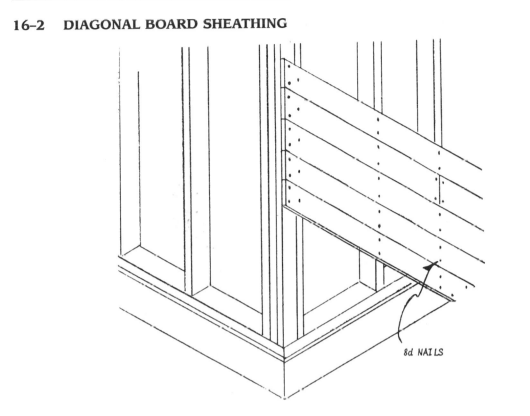

8d NAILS

the upper plates and the sill or rim joist, you may need to piece the sheathing, or special order panels that are available in 9- and 10-foot lengths.

When a horizontal application is advisable, you can include 2 × 4 nailing blocks in the wall frame to allow complete perimeter nailing. This can contribute enough anti-racking strength to make corner bracing unnecessary.

The sheathing can be attached with common smooth, annular, spiral-thread, or galvanized box nails. Nailing specs call for 6-inch spacing on the perimeter and 12-inch spacing in the field. Plan the installation so no piece of plywood will be shorter than the span across three studs. All vertical joints must be over a framing member and should be staggered.

SHEATHING AT THE SILL

There are several ways that, in theory, you could attach sheathing at the sill (**16–4**). It could end on the subfloor if the wall framing were set back to accommodate it (A). But this does not provide a tie between the wall and floor frames, and would need to be reinforced

16–3

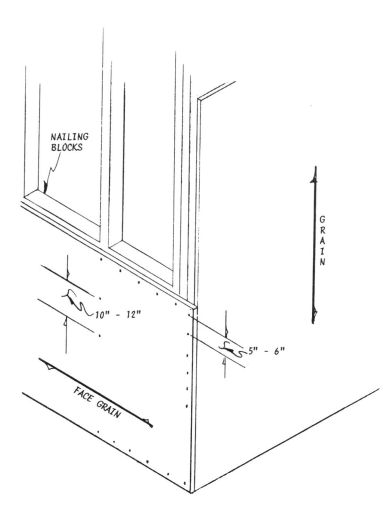

with anchor straps running vertically from the sill at, minimally, every other stud position.

A second situation has the sill and the floor and wall frames set back from the edge of the foundation the thickness of the sheathing (B). This does make a strong connection between framing components, especially when the sheathing is plywood or diagonal boards. But it's a bigger nuisance than simply setting the frames flush with the foundation and placing the sheathing so it extends a bit below the sill (C). This is the most common and practical system.

16–4

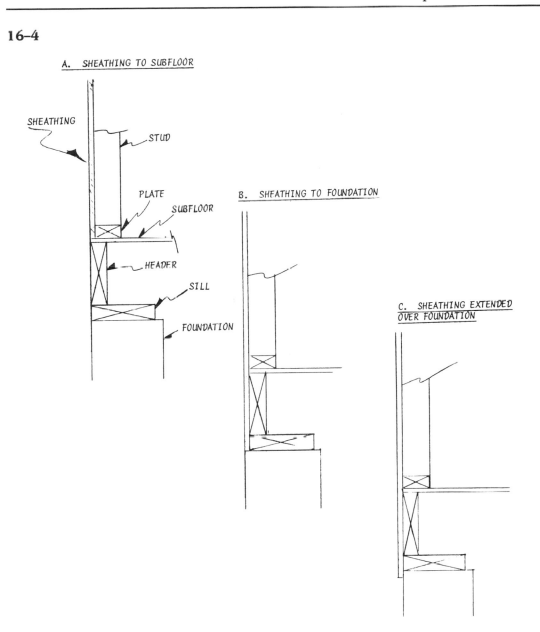

A. SHEATHING TO SUBFLOOR

SHEATHING

STUD

PLATE

SUBFLOOR

HEADER

SILL

FOUNDATION

B. SHEATHING TO FOUNDATION

C. SHEATHING EXTENDED OVER FOUNDATION

PAPER BARRIERS

The standard covering for sheathing has been 16–pound felt paper. It is still used to provide protection against the weather and air leaks. In fact, installations of stucco (**16–5**) and brick veneer (**16–6**) generally call for felt paper, and double layers in some locations.

16–5   PLYWOOD SHEATHING BEHIND STUCCO

16–6   PLYWOOD SHEATHING BEHIND BRICK VENEER

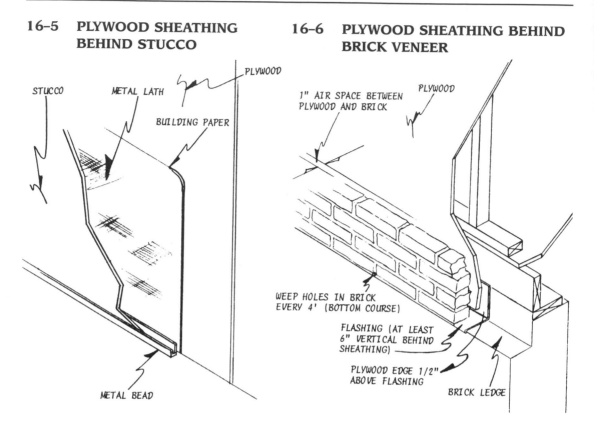

But modern energy considerations now call for a combination of vapor barriers inside (under drywall) and air-infiltration barriers outside (under siding). Both make life inside the house more comfortable and less expensive, and are worth adding to any new building.

Each barrier protects the house in a different way and in a different location. The barriers are not the same. Vapor barriers, typically plastic sheeting or foil, are designed to keep moisture produced inside the house from seeping into framing cavities where it can condense, rot wood, and soak insulation. In a typical household, there is more than enough moisture to cause problems—between 7 and 10 gallons generated every day from washing, cooking, and other activities.

Air-infiltration barriers are a fibrous weave designed to let out any moisture that does get into the wall, and prevent outside air from entering. The material works like a parka made of Gore-Tex, a fabric woven tightly enough to shed water in liquid form outside, and loosely enough to allow water in vapor form inside to escape. The large sheets are stapled over exterior plywood sheathing, and tucked in around the edges of windows and doors. Most of the barriers are white, with brand names plastered in huge letters every few feet.

Some builders leave out the air barrier—to save money, or because they think that one barrier can serve both purposes. If plastic sheeting under drywall forms a complete block against interior moisture, it figures that it would block incoming air as well. But it won't stop cold winter air until it passes through the wall insulation, and that would create cold spots, drafts, and possible condensation problems on the wall surface.

Other builders go to great pains to install nearly airtight drywall with special gaskets and coatings of vapor-barrier paints—an installation often called ADA, for Airtight Drywall Approach. It's one of several installations and combinations of materials that can control moisture and air leaks and temperature loss to varying degrees. But in most cases, using one air barrier and one vapor barrier offers the best overall return.

Air barriers should be stapled with overlaps of at least two inches. Work with a helper to smooth out the sheet and keep it level, and don't skimp on staples. A 1-inch-wide crown staple is recommended by Dupont for its product, Tyvek, although you can also use nails with large heads or nails with plastic washer heads. Directly over masonry, use a polyurethane- or latex-based adhesive.

During construction, an exterior house-wrap also can provide protection for the job because it goes up very quickly as soon as the house is sheathed. In the days or maybe weeks that follow before siding is installed, it will keep out most of the weather. Layers of old fashioned tar paper could do that job, too. But tar paper comes in 3-foot-wide rolls that leave many seams to tear in the wind, while house-wrap is wide enough to cover from foundation to roofline.

If you start a project and run into delays, don't worry about well-fastened house-wrap. The high-density polyethylene fibers are combined with an additive to resist the effects of ultraviolet light resistance, so you can leave the wrap uncovered for up to four months.

SIDING OPTIONS

If you add in the variations of size, shape, color and texture, there are hundreds of materials you can use for siding. But the choices boil down to six basic categories.

Wood shingles and shakes are easy to apply but very time consuming. Wood boards such as clapboard and board-and-batten siding cover more ground in less time. Panels come in many configurations from hardboard to plywood, some of which have exotic wood veneers. With large panels you can side a house quickly. Wood siding can be stained or painted, or sealed to show its wood tone and grain.

Synthetics include aluminum and the more common vinyl. These are easy to cut, and made to fit with complementary trim pieces. Masonry siding, which includes brick and stone, is generally more difficult to install and more expensive.

PANEL SIDING

All panels are exterior grade made with a fully waterproof glue. The common size is 4 × 8 feet, but 9- and 10-foot lengths are also available. The panels are surface-veneered with various wood species, but those most available are fir, redwood, and cedar. Surface patterns and textures also vary, as shown in **16–7**. There are many siding systems, such as Texture 1-11 plywood with shiplap edges and parallel grooves (**16–8**). It generally is available in ⅝-inch thickness with a variety of groove spacings and many surface textures.

Among many panel products, you're likely to find three that are widely available. *Surfaced panels* have a veneer skin that may be smooth, rough-sawn, striated or brushed. Mating edges are covered with trim. *Composite panels* are engineered panels that may

16–7

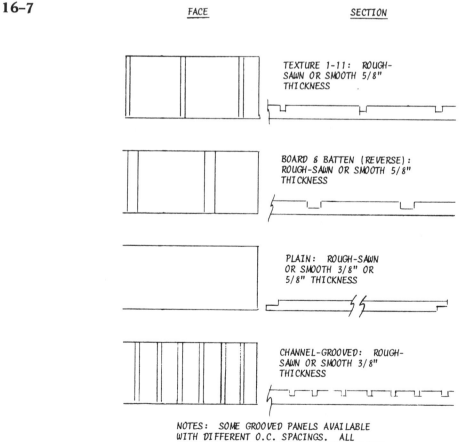

FACE   SECTION

TEXTURE 1-11: ROUGH-SAWN OR SMOOTH 5/8" THICKNESS

BOARD & BATTEN (REVERSE): ROUGH-SAWN OR SMOOTH 5/8" THICKNESS

PLAIN: ROUGH-SAWN OR SMOOTH 3/8" OR 5/8" THICKNESS

CHANNEL-GROOVED: ROUGH-SAWN OR SMOOTH 3/8" THICKNESS

NOTES: SOME GROOVED PANELS AVAILABLE WITH DIFFERENT O.C. SPACINGS. ALL PANELS AVAILABLE IN 4'X8', 4'X9', 4'X10'

16–8

include sawdust, wood chips, and other particles. There is no grain, so the panels are stable. *Grooved panels* generally have half laps along the grooved edge, which conceals the seam. Grooves may be narrow and close together, or very wide to resemble the relief pattern of board-and-batten siding.

INSTALLING PANEL SIDING

Panel installation, including spacing and nailing requirements, is specified by the manufacturer. But final installation details are up to the local building department. Sometimes this can be baffling—for example, where the manufacturer says you don't need sheathing and the local inspector says you do. You know who wins this argument. Builders who work in different jurisdictions, sometimes only miles apart across a state line, can come up against the same double standard. The point is that you need to check both the manufacturer's recommendations and the local code requirements, particularly if you are interested in a thin panel.

Generally, and always with grooved products, panels are installed vertically, as this permits complete perimeter nailing without having to add nailing blocks to the frame (**16–9**). Let all vertical joints occur over a stud, and remember to leave a gap between all panel edges where required. Over long runs, the accumulation of gaps between panels may require that you trim an occasional panel to keep its edge close to the centerline of a framing member.

16–9   PLYWOOD SHEATHING

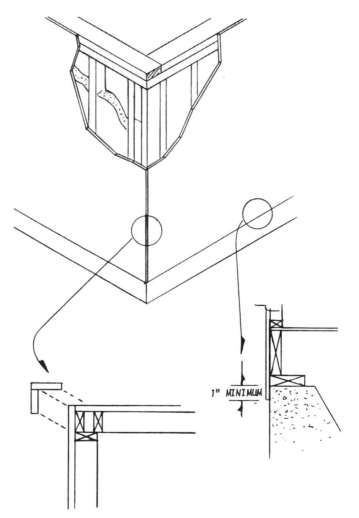

1" MINIMUM

Caulk the joints or treat the plywood edges with a water repellent. This isn't necessary if the edges are shiplapped or if the joint will be covered with a batten, but it's not a bad thing to do it anyway. Batten material can be plain strips of wood or molding (**16–10**). Attachment nails should pass between the edges of the plywood and penetrate the studs at least 1 inch.

If you wish to add some decorative detail to plain plywood siding, you can do so by

16–10

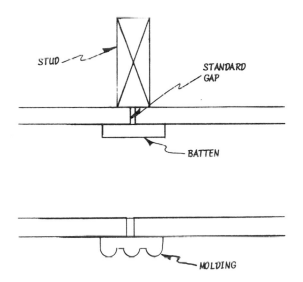

using batten material to form patterns like those shown in **16–11**. This is easier to do if the walls include sheathing. All nails should be long enough to penetrate the sheathing.

Shiplapped edges should also occur over a stud and join as shown in **16–12**. Some shiplapped edges are designed so the joint is a wide groove; others come together more tightly.

Outside corners deserve special attention to make them weathertight. You can build a neat, unobtrusive corner by using a rabbet joint, but one- or two-piece corner boards are more practical and easier to form (**16–13**). You can make the one-piece affair by sawing material that matches the siding or using a ready-made molding called a corner guard. If you do the former, the piece you cut out can be used to seal an inside corner. Notice that these illustrations do not show sheathing, which may be required.

It's a good idea to caulk the edges of panels that meet at an inside corner. A neat appearance results if you do the job carefully, but adding a corner, which can be a plain

16–11

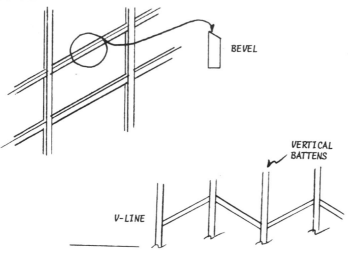

BEVEL

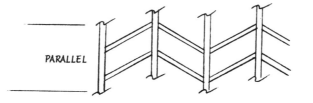

VERTICAL
BATTENS

V-LINE

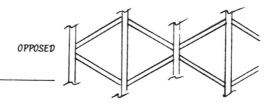

PARALLEL

OPPOSED

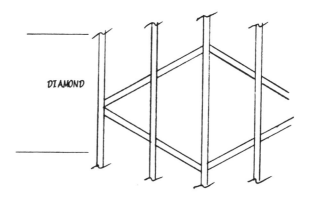

DIAMOND

square strip of wood or something like quarter-round molding, will complete the seal and make the panel joint less critical (**16–14**).

Horizontal joints should be backed up by nailing blocks placed between studs whether codes call for them or not, unless the frame has been covered with sheathing. The joints should be well caulked and may be covered with battens. A beveled top edge that will shed

16–12

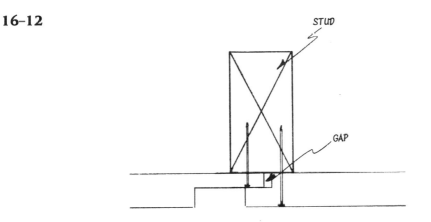

16–13   OUTSIDE CORNER TREATMENTS

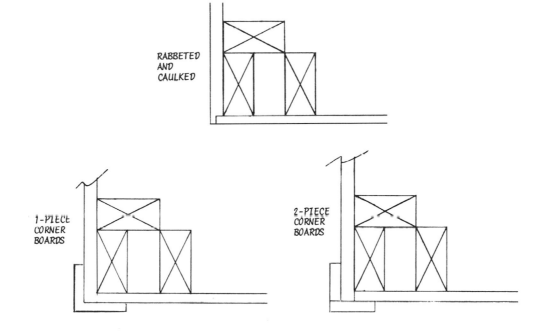

16–14 INSIDE CORNER TREATMENTS

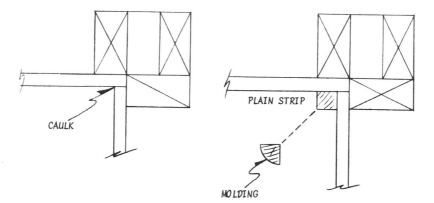

water, as shown in **16–15**, makes more sense than a square edge. Better yet, you can cut complementary beveled edges with the top panel overlapping the lower panel. Other options include installing flashing as shown in **16–16**, and using water-table molding that is more decorative (**16–17**).

16–15 BATTENS FOR HORIZONTAL JOINTS

16–16 FLASHING HORIZONTAL JOINTS

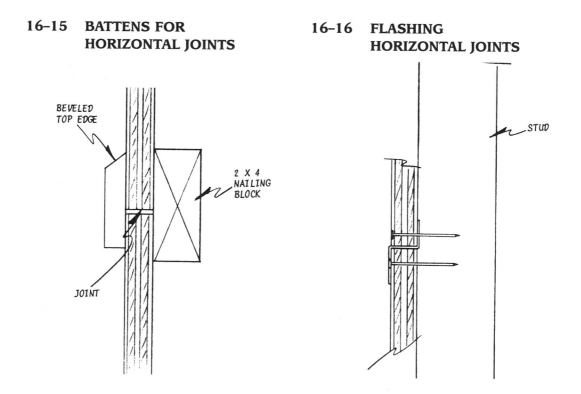

16–17   WATER TABLE MOLDINGS

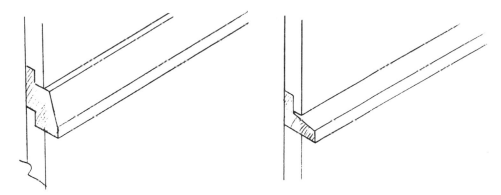

PLANK SIDING

Plank siding, which includes clapboard, consists of solid wood-boards that can be plain or shaped in various ways to create special effects. It is applied over sheathing. Most types are placed horizontally as in **16–18**, because the shadow lines, which are especially

16–18

prominent in bevel siding, help to lower the house profile so it seems closer to the ground. Most types of board siding are available in various wood species that include the western pines, cedars, and redwood.

There are numerous patterns, but those that have proved most popular are shown here together with some installation details. When the specifications say that a board has a smooth side and a rough side, it means that either side may be exposed to the weather, the deciding factor being whether you wish to have a natural or stained finish or a painted one. Common patterns are bevel and bungalow (**16–19**), Dolly Varden (**16–20**), drop, also called novelty siding (**16–21**), channel rustic (**16–22**), tongue-and-groove (**16–23**), and log cabin (**16–24**).

Board siding that is applied vertically is usually a shiplap or a tongue-and-groove type,

16–19   **16–20**

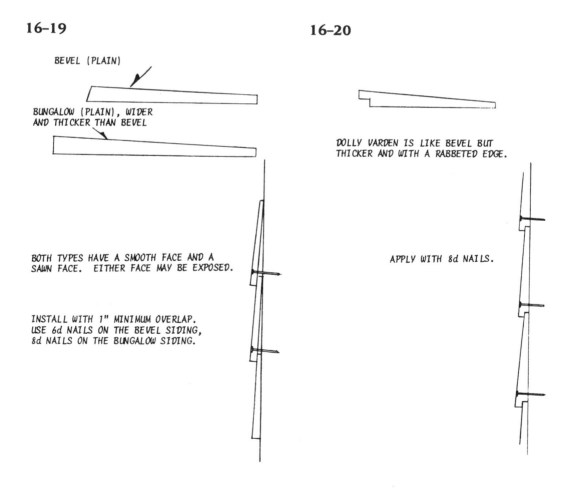

BEVEL (PLAIN)

BUNGALOW (PLAIN), WIDER
AND THICKER THAN BEVEL

DOLLY VARDEN IS LIKE BEVEL BUT
THICKER AND WITH A RABBETED EDGE.

BOTH TYPES HAVE A SMOOTH FACE AND A
SAWN FACE. EITHER FACE MAY BE EXPOSED.

APPLY WITH 8d NAILS.

INSTALL WITH 1" MINIMUM OVERLAP.
USE 6d NAILS ON THE BEVEL SIDING,
8d NAILS ON THE BUNGALOW SIDING.

16–21

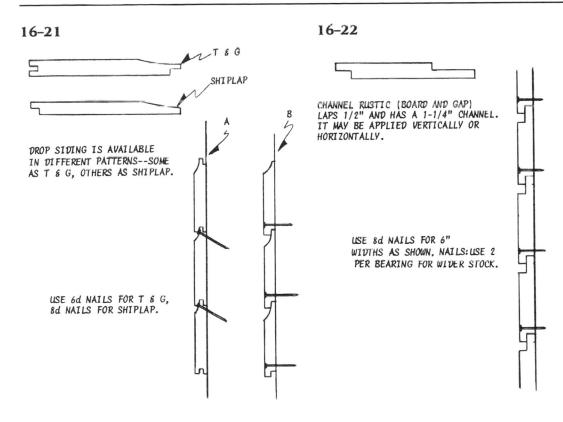

DROP SIDING IS AVAILABLE
IN DIFFERENT PATTERNS--SOME
AS T & G, OTHERS AS SHIPLAP.

USE 6d NAILS FOR T & G,
8d NAILS FOR SHIPLAP.

16–22

CHANNEL RUSTIC (BOARD AND GAP)
LAPS 1/2" AND HAS A 1-1/4" CHANNEL.
IT MAY BE APPLIED VERTICALLY OR
HORIZONTALLY.

USE 8d NAILS FOR 6"
WIDTHS AS SHOWN. NAILS: USE 2
PER BEARING FOR WIDER STOCK.

16–23

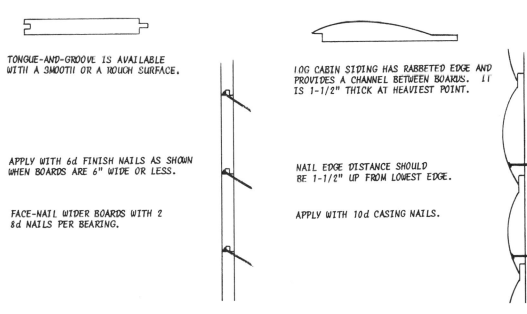

TONGUE-AND-GROOVE IS AVAILABLE
WITH A SMOOTH OR A ROUGH SURFACE.

APPLY WITH 6d FINISH NAILS AS SHOWN
WHEN BOARDS ARE 6" WIDE OR LESS.

FACE-NAIL WIDER BOARDS WITH 2
8d NAILS PER BEARING.

16–24

LOG CABIN SIDING HAS RABBETED EDGE AND
PROVIDES A CHANNEL BETWEEN BOARDS. IT
IS 1-1/2" THICK AT HEAVIEST POINT.

NAIL EDGE DISTANCE SHOULD
BE 1-1/2" UP FROM LOWEST EDGE.

APPLY WITH 10d CASING NAILS.

or plain boards that are applied in one of the ways shown in **16–25**, with two horizontal lines of 2 × 4 blocks placed between studs to provide nailing surfaces.

16–25   BOARDS

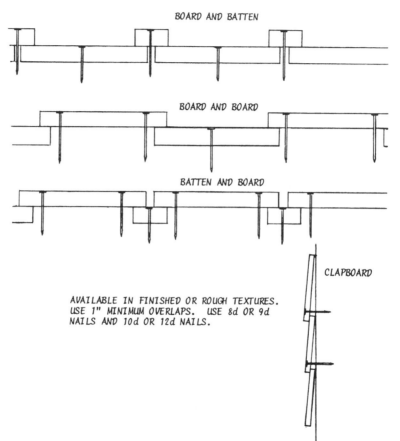

BOARD AND BATTEN

BOARD AND BOARD

BATTEN AND BOARD

CLAPBOARD

AVAILABLE IN FINISHED OR ROUGH TEXTURES. USE 1" MINIMUM OVERLAPS. USE 8d OR 9d NAILS AND 10d OR 12d NAILS.

   Wood board varies in thickness from ½ inch to 1½ inches, and runs in widths from 4 inches to 12 inches. There are hundreds of varieties when you consider wood type, size, shape and surface texture. If you have a special grade or wood in mind, spend some time with wood organizations' catalogs and be sure that your local supplier can get the wood— and at a reasonable price. Most lumberyards stock only a few of the many possible types.

   Redwood and cedar are probably the two most elegant, decay-resistant, and expensive types. But Douglas fir, larch, ponderosa pine and other species are also used. While solid wood may be the most aesthetically pleasing, you also will find board-type products made of hardboard. If they are under a few coats of paint you aren't likely to notice the difference. There are two basic types. One has splines that hook over the course below to allow blind nailing. The other fits with a rabbet along the bottom edge.

The table in **16–26** provides factors so you can determine the amount of material you need when working with different types of wood siding. To use it, multiply the square footage you must cover by the area factor.

16–26 COVERAGE ESTIMATOR

	NOMINAL SIZE	WIDTH		AREA FACTOR*
		Dress	**Face**	
SHIPLAP	1 × 6	5½	5⅛	1.17
	1 × 8	7¼	6⅞	1.16
	1 × 10	9¼	8⅞	1.13
	1 × 12	11¼	10⅞	1.10
TONGUE	1 × 4	3⅜	3⅛	1.28
AND	1 × 6	5⅜	5⅛	1.17
GROOVE				
	1 × 8	7⅛	6⅞	1.16
	1 × 10	9⅛	8⅞	1.13
	1 × 12	11⅛	10⅞	1.10
SANDED	1 × 4	3½	3½	1.14
4 SIDES	1 × 6	5½	5½	1.09
	1 × 8	7¼	7¼	1.10
	1 × 10	9¼	9¼	1.08
	1 × 12	11¼	11¼	1.07
PANELING	1 × 6	5⁷⁄₁₆	5¹⁄₁₆	1.19
PATTERNS	1 × 8	7⅛	6¾	1.19
	1 × 10	9⅛	8¾	1.14
	1 × 12	11⅛	10¾	1.12
BEVEL	1 × 4	3½	3½	1.60
SIDING	1 × 6	6½	6½	1.33
(1″ lap)	1 × 8	7¼	7¼	1.28
	1 × 10	9¼	9¼	1.21
	1 × 12	11¼	11¼	1.17

* Allowance for trim and waste should be added.

NAILS

Work with high-tensile-strength aluminum nails or galvanized nails that are mechanically plated. Hot-dipped galvanized nails are okay, but the degree of coating protection varies. Nail shanks should be ring-threaded or spiral-threaded and, preferably, have blunt points, since these are less likely to split the wood. To avoid splitting, it's wise to drill pilot holes at the ends of boards, particularly in thinner stock. Always check with the manufacturer for recommended fastening details, including nail type and spacing.

INSTALLING PLANK SIDING

There are five basic steps to installing horizontal board siding, applicable generally to both flat and beveled boards. One-story installations are started usually at the bottom of the wall, although it may be more convenient to do gable ends first, as in **16–27**, especially when scaffolding is secured to the house frame. Notice that here the siding was applied before the finished roof. This is often done with gables—frequently complete sheathing is done before the roof is finished or during the process. This adds rigidity and a good deal of weather protection to the structure right away.

First, apply your inside and outside corner boards, and other possible trim, such as a water-table base. You can use compound miter cuts and spend a lot of time with a block plane to make corner joints in clapboard, but these joints often don't stay closed. And they take a long time to make. It's easier (and often looks better) to install clapboard within a framework of trim that completely covers its end grain.

16–27

Second, establish a base level line and install a starter strip. You need a starter on any beveled board because there is no overlap in the first course. The starter strip (**16–28**), which can be a ripping from your siding, maintains the angle on the first course that all the other boards will have. You don't need a starter on flat boards that rest flush against the sheathing.

16–28

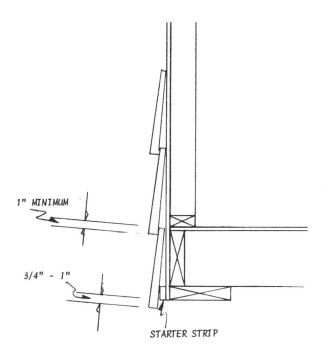

1" MINIMUM

3/4" - 1"

STARTER STRIP

Third, overlap the starter strip and install the first course. The extension of the first course below the starter strip provides a drip edge so water can fall free. Let all end joints occur over a stud, and stagger those in adjacent courses as far apart as possible. Make all end cuts very carefully so boards will butt tightly. Work with a fine-toothed saw to minimize tear out. Remember, these will be visible joints and, therefore, deserve special attention.

Fourth, add more courses, maintaining level and a uniform overlap. As work progresses, you may want to use a story pole to mark the courses. To make one, use a strip of wood that will reach from the soffit to 1 inch below the top of the foundation and mark it off in equal board-width spaces while allowing for overlaps. Another handy approach is to use a T-shaped spacing jig (**16–29**). You can carry this with you to make

16–29

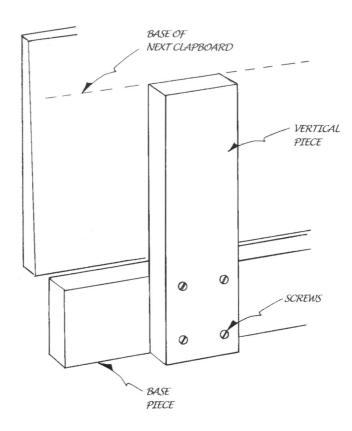

frequent checks. Periodically, you also should measure back to the base at several points along the wall.

Fifth, make cutouts as required to fit the clapboard around openings in the wall. Ideally, boards should fit against the top and the bottom of a window without large notches. Joints around openings are detailed in later chapters on doors and windows, but, briefly, siding should fit snugly against casings and over special drip caps, which are put in place as shown in **16–30**. Flashing should not be compressed or stretched.

To add a design feature, gable ends are often covered with a siding that runs perpendicular to what is used over the wall. The break between the two can be made weatherproof and attractive by using the same type of drip caps that are shown in **16–31**. Another approach is to place 1 × 3 furring strips over the studs or the sheathing of the gable so the siding placed there will project beyond what is used below (**16–32**). Notice that the bottom edge of the upper siding is beveled to serve as a drip edge.

16–30

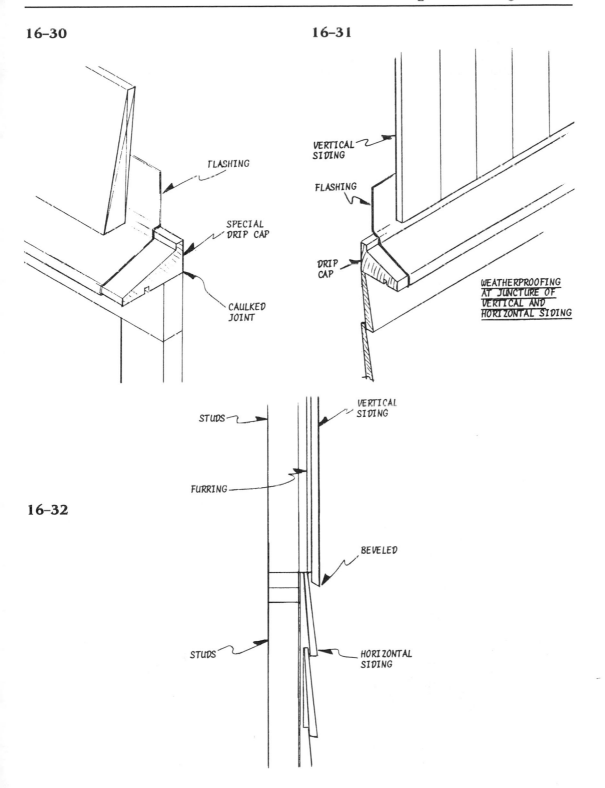

FLASHING

SPECIAL
DRIP CAP

CAULKED
JOINT

16–31

VERTICAL
SIDING

FLASHING

DRIP
CAP

WEATHERPROOFING
AT JUNCTURE OF
VERTICAL AND
HORIZONTAL SIDING

16–32

STUDS

VERTICAL
SIDING

FURRING

BEVELED

STUDS

HORIZONTAL
SIDING

CORNERS

There are many options on outside corners, depending on how you want the job to appear and the time you care to spend doing it (**16–33**). All siding, whether flat or beveled, can be mitered or butted against corner boards. Ready-made metal corners, because they go on quickly, are sometimes used (**16–34**), although they are somewhat commercial looking and heavy-duty for houses. For practical reasons, the job should be done with a min-

16–33

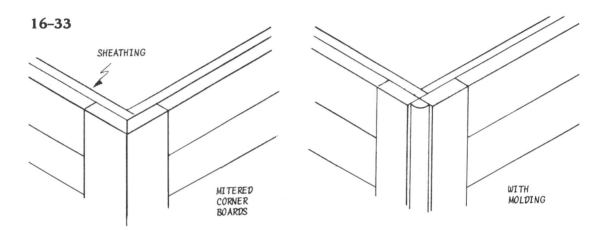

SHEATHING

MITERED CORNER BOARDS

WITH MOLDING

16–34

imum number of joint lines, but there is no reason why you can't do it your way as long as you remember that weathertightness is as important as appearance.

For inside corners, the most practical detail is a square corner strip against which the siding is butted (**16–35**). Basically the same idea applies when the siding ends against a vertical, such as a casing around a door or window (**16–36**).

16–35

16–36

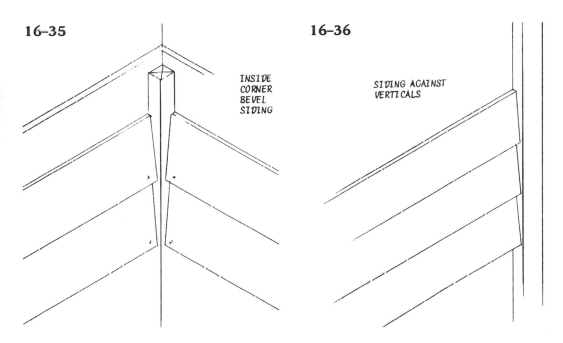

INSIDE
CORNER
BEVEL
SIDING

SIDING AGAINST
VERTICALS

In all situations, it pays to apply a caulking compound between mating surfaces. This should be done neatly, especially if the siding will be left natural or stained.

Premium construction calls for applying a prime coat of paint to the back surfaces of the siding before it is installed. If the finish will be natural or stained, then use a water repellent instead of the prime coat. A prime coat or a water repellent should also be used on outside surfaces as soon as possible after installation. Some siding, especially ply-woods, are available with basic protective coatings already applied.

HARDBOARD SIDING

Hardboards are manufactured products that resemble board siding. There are many choices. You can apply vertical or horizontal treatments with smooth or textured surfaces and in contemporary or traditional patterns. Most examples can be stained or painted or

16-37   SPECIAL METAL JOINT STRIPS

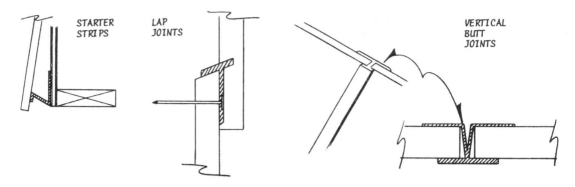

can be obtained prefinished in lap or panel form so that the job requires no attention after installation.

When prefinished siding is used, all marking and cutting should be done from the back surface to avoid marring the finish. Exposed nails are coated with a touch-up paint. Or special nails, color-matched to the siding—and driven in with a plastic-covered hammer-head (to preserve the color finish) —can also be used.

Some of the lap sidings include preshaped forms as starter strips and as seals for lap and vertical butt joints (**16–37**). Similar pieces are supplied so you can end inside and outside corners neatly (**16–38**). Other types are applied in more conventional fashion (**16–39**). Panels are applied over sheathing, unless codes allow direct application over studs (**16–40**). Joints and corners are done as shown in **16–41**.

16–38

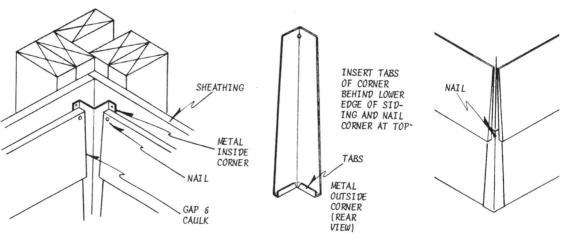

16–39

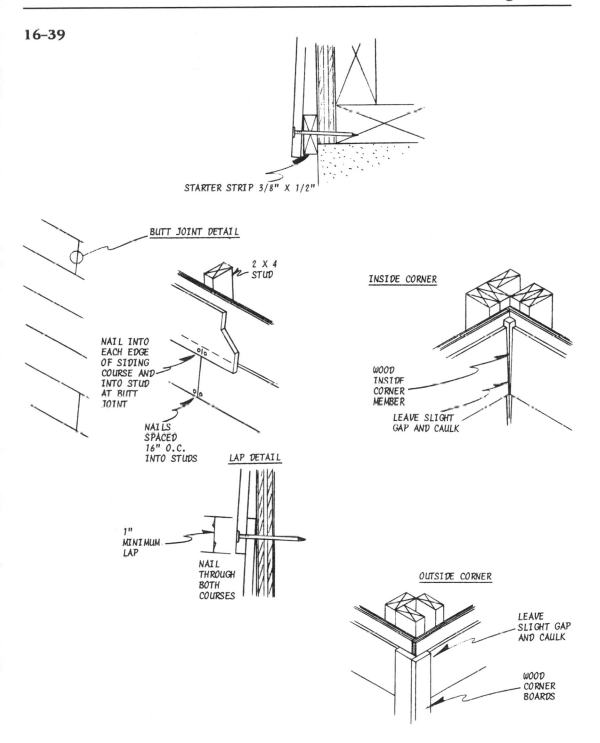

STARTER STRIP 3/8" X 1/2"

BUTT JOINT DETAIL

2 X 4
STUD

NAIL INTO
EACH EDGE
OF SIDING
COURSE AND
INTO STUD
AT BUTT
JOINT

NAILS
SPACED
16" O.C.
INTO STUDS

LAP DETAIL

1"
MINIMUM
LAP

NAIL
THROUGH
BOTH
COURSES

INSIDE CORNER

WOOD
INSIDE
CORNER
MEMBER

LEAVE SLIGHT
GAP AND CAULK

OUTSIDE CORNER

LEAVE
SLIGHT GAP
AND CAULK

WOOD
CORNER
BOARDS

Follow manufacturer's recommendations about leaving a slight gap where siding butts against trim. Don't force pieces together when you are doing a butt joint in a course. Fill all gaps with caulking. Color-matched caulking is available for use with prefinished siding

16–40

HARDBOARD PANEL OVER SHEATHING

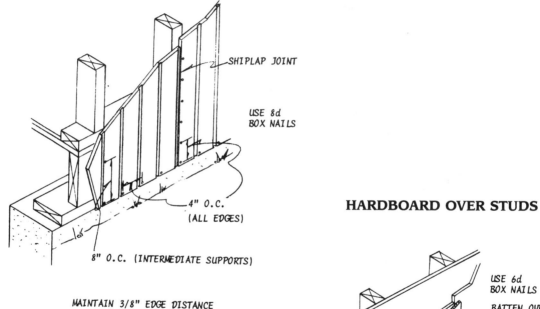

SHIPLAP JOINT

USE 8d BOX NAILS

4" O.C. (ALL EDGES)

8" O.C. (INTERMEDIATE SUPPORTS)

MAINTAIN 3/8" EDGE DISTANCE

HARDBOARD OVER STUDS

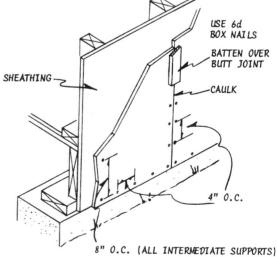

USE 6d BOX NAILS

BATTEN OVER BUTT JOINT

CAULK

SHEATHING

4" O.C.

8" O.C. (ALL INTERMEDIATE SUPPORTS)

MAINTAIN 3/8" EDGE DISTANCE

16-41

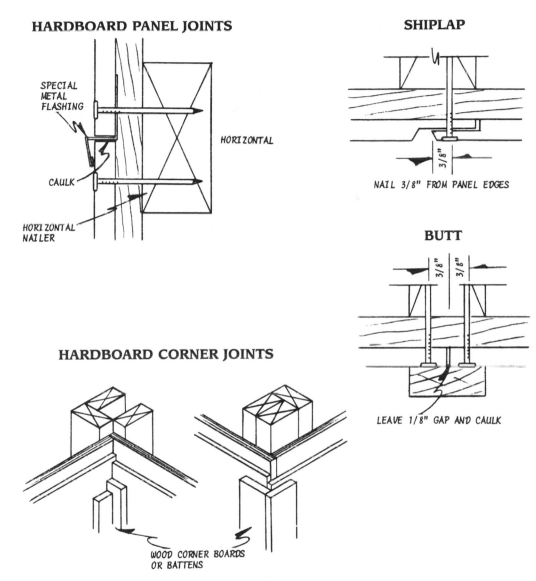

HARDBOARD PANEL JOINTS

SPECIAL METAL FLASHING

HORIZONTAL

CAULK

HORIZONTAL NAILER

SHIPLAP

3/8"

NAIL 3/8" FROM PANEL EDGES

BUTT

3/8" 3/8"

LEAVE 1/8" GAP AND CAULK

HARDBOARD CORNER JOINTS

WOOD CORNER BOARDS OR BATTENS

materials. Butt joints should always occur over a stud unless the wall is sheathed and you are using a system that includes butt-joint moldings.

Like most modern vinyl siding systems, some hardboard systems provide not only trim pieces to match the finish, but also matching soffit systems as shown in **16–42**, including aluminum fascia caps and roof edging.

16–42

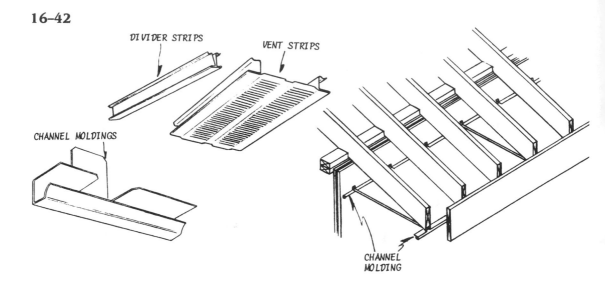

DIVIDER STRIPS

VENT STRIPS

CHANNEL MOLDINGS

CHANNEL MOLDING

SHINGLE AND SHAKE SIDING

You can side your house with the same type of shingles or shakes used to cover the roof or with special pieces whose edges have been trimmed so they are strictly parallel and whose butt ends have been sawed square. In addition, this type of shingle is available machine-treated so it has a flat back but a striated exposed surface. Most of the basic types are shown in **16–43**, but there are also fancy-butt shingles, shown in **16–44**, so the effects you can create are almost unlimited, ranging from more formal, symmetrical applications like those in **16–45** and **16–46** to the deep, rugged texture you get by working with regular shingles or shakes.

Premium-quality fancy butt shingles are packed in cartons that contain 160 pieces to cover about a third of a square. The shingles are 16 inches long and approximately 5 inches wide, and intended for concealed nailing with a 6-inch exposure to the weather. The nails are hidden by placing them a maximum of 1 inch above the butt line of succeeding courses. Widths do vary a bit, so spacing may have to be adjusted to maintain a desired pattern precisely. Exterior walls must be fastened over solid sheathing. If used indoors, as they often are for effect, they may be applied to spaced nailing strips. With different sizes and exposure factors, the amount of wall you can cover with the same amount of shingles varies quite a bit.

Regular shingles or shakes may be applied to solid sheathing with an underlay of felt paper. Use only as many nails or staples as you need to keep the paper in place until the

16–43   TYPES OF SHINGLES AND SHAKES

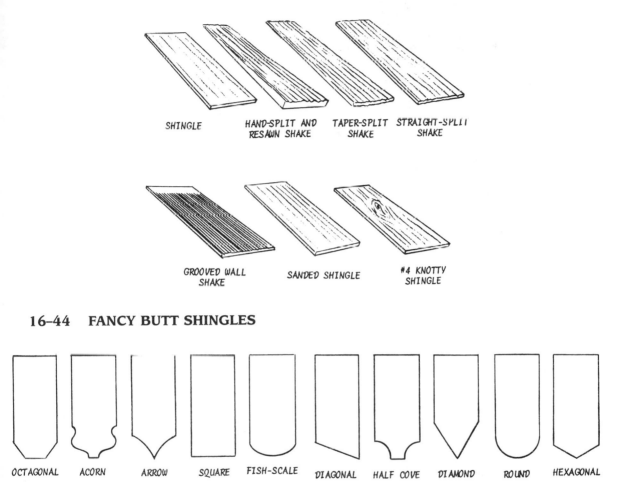

SHINGLE   HAND-SPLIT AND   TAPER-SPLIT   STRAIGHT-SPLIT
                   RESAWN SHAKE   SHAKE   SHAKE

GROOVED WALL   SANDED SHINGLE   #4 KNOTTY
   SHAKE   SHINGLE

16–44   FANCY BUTT SHINGLES

OCTAGONAL   ACORN   ARROW   SQUARE   FISH-SCALE   DIAGONAL   HALF COVE   DIAMOND   ROUND   HEXAGONAL

shingles are applied. When the cover is against open studs or over nonwood sheathing, nailing strips are installed (open sheathing) with spacing determined by the exposure of the shingles (**16–47**). The cover may be applied in a single course, as shown in **16–48**, in which case the exposure should be a bit less than half of the shingle length. For example, use 7½-inch exposure for 16-inch shingles, a 8½-inch for 18-inch shingles, and 11½-inch for 24-inch shingles. These suggestions apply for top-grade shingles. It's a good idea to reduce the exposure if you work with anything but a no. 1 grade.

Double-coursing, which is actually two layers of shingles—one placed directly over the

16–45

16–46

16–47

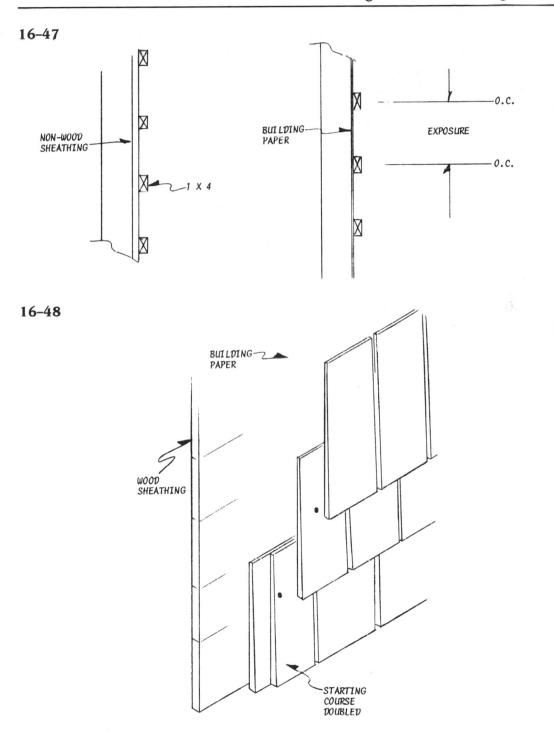

NON-WOOD
SHEATHING

1 X 4

BUILDING
PAPER

O.C.

EXPOSURE

O.C.

16–48

BUILDING
PAPER

WOOD
SHEATHING

STARTING
COURSE
DOUBLED

other, as shown in **16–49**—provides deeper shadow lines, a generally more solid appearance, and vastly increased protection from the weather. Although this approach is not often used, it allows you to increase the exposure: 12 inches is okay for 16-inch shingles, 14 inches for 18-inch shingles, and 16 inches for 24-inch shingles. With double-coursing, you can work with two grades of shingles—a quality material for the exposed course, but a no. 4 grade (often called under-coursing) for the bottom one. The top cover is placed so the butt end extends below that on the under course by about ½ inch (**16–50**).

You can place the shingles guided by a chalk line that you snap across the wall, but a more convenient method is to tack-nail a 1 × 2 guide strip on which you can rest the shingles as you nail them (**16–51**). You can also use the strip to lay out a series of shingles, and arrange them to provide the correct joint staggers.

Single-coursing doesn't differ from a roofing job except in the area of exposure, which we have already discussed. All nails holding one course should be concealed by the shingles in the following course. Use two nails to a shingle, with a ¾-inch edge distance, and

16–49   **16–50**

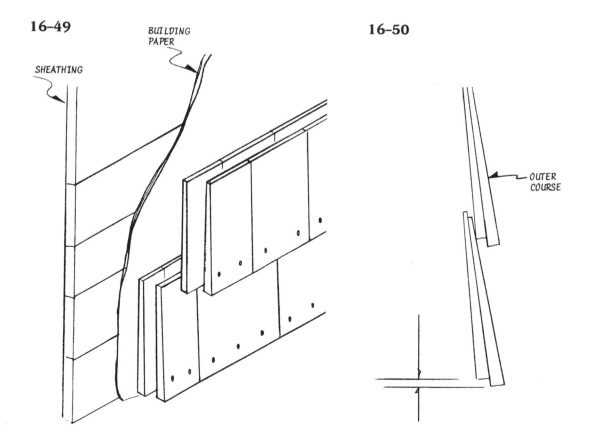

BUILDING
PAPER

SHEATHING

OUTER
COURSE

place them about 1 inch above the butt line of the next course. Use three nails if the shingle is wider than 8 inches, centering the third one between the first two.

Nails for all applications should be rustproof and long enough to penetrate the sheathing, or nailing strips if they are used; 3d nails are usually okay for single-coursing, and 5d for double coursing.

Always use two layers of shingles at the bottom of the wall unless you are double-coursing. Here, use a double layer of under-course shingles so the first line will actually be triple-thick (**16–52**).

16–51   **16–52**

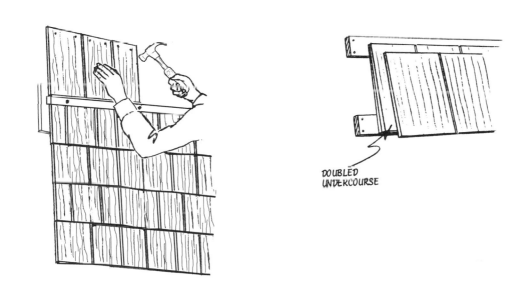

DOUBLED UNDERCOURSE

Space the bottom layer of shingles in all courses about ⅛ inch apart, but do not nail them in standard fashion. A single nail or even a staple placed somewhere near the top will do to hold the part in place until the top pieces are added. The final course can be set without spacing and secured with two nails having a ¾-inch edge distance and placed about 2 inches above the butt line (**16–53**). This, of course, results in exposed nails, so it's essential here to use a type that is rustproof and, preferably, has a small head. Be sure the nail is long enough to penetrate the sheathing.

Inside corners can be butted against a corner strip or woven by alternating how the course ends butt against each other (**16–54**). As shown in **16–55**, outside corners may also be woven or they can end in miter joints. Shingles that end against a vertical trim

16–53

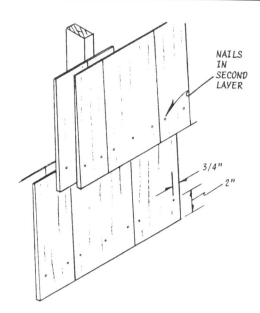

NAILS
IN
SECOND
LAYER

3/4"

2"

16–54   INSIDE CORNERS

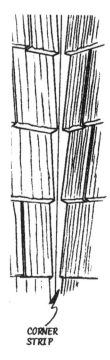

CORNER
STRIP

WOVEN

16–55   OUTSIDE CORNERS

WOVEN

MITERED

piece—around doors and windows—are just butted. A bead of caulking to cover the joint between trim and sheathing, under the shingle, won't hurt. Bear in mind that it's generally easier to fill up to a trim board than it is to shave pairs of shingles to make tight joints against each other.

You may be able to find panelized shingles that install in preassembled courses. Various constructions are used in the manufacture of the panels (**16–56**). The intent is to make them

16–56

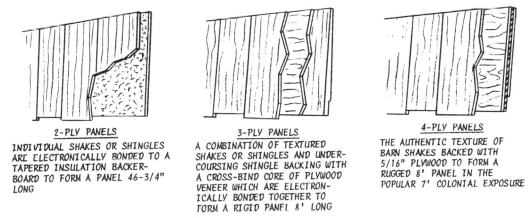

2-PLY PANELS
INDIVIDUAL SHAKES OR SHINGLES ARE ELECTRONICALLY BONDED TO A TAPERED INSULATION BACKER-BOARD TO FORM A PANEL 46-3/4" LONG

3-PLY PANELS
A COMBINATION OF TEXTURED SHAKES OR SHINGLES AND UNDER-COURSING SHINGLE BACKING WITH A CROSS-BIND CORE OF PLYWOOD VENEER WHICH ARE ELECTRON-ICALLY BONDED TOGETHER TO FORM A RIGID PANEL 8' LONG

4-PLY PANELS
THE AUTHENTIC TEXTURE OF BARN SHAKES BACKED WITH 5/16" PLYWOOD TO FORM A RUGGED 8' PANEL IN THE POPULAR 7' COLONIAL EXPOSURE

suitable for use directly on studs or over sheathing or nailing strips (**16–57**). Matching corners, as shown in **16–58**, and color-matched nails are part of the systems, so the job looks neat and the need to miter or weave around turns is eliminated. If the manufacturer's instructions suggest a 24-inch stud spacing, check this spacing against local codes.

VINYL SIDING

In the 1950s and 1960s, aluminum siding was the space-age material you were supposed to use instead of wood. Now it's vinyl, which is used on about 30 percent of new homes in the country, a figure that has stayed steady since 1995. There have been some improvements that make panels stiffer and more like real wood in appearance. And vinyl is easy to install over sheathing and a layer of house wrap. Installation speed is largely responsible for the material's success.

The basic products include clapboard with a plain face or with laps built in to simulate multiple courses. In the example in **16–59**, the fascias, soffits, porch ceiling, siding, and gutter system are all vinyl. The gutter system, shown more closely in **16–60**, can be used

16-57   PANEL SHINGLE APPLICATIONS

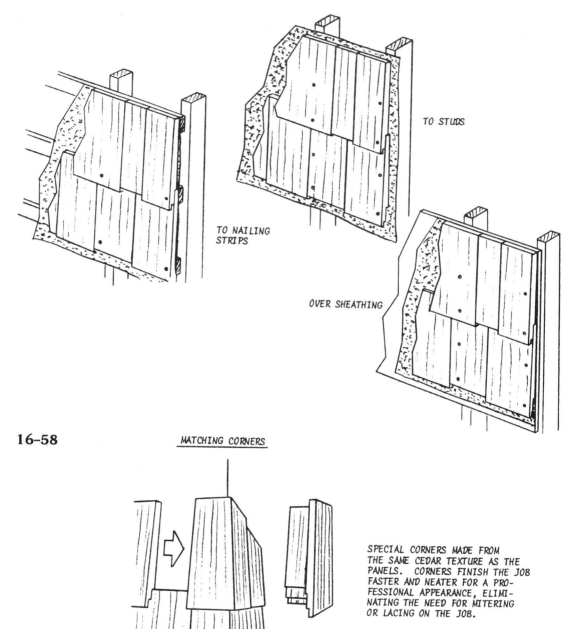

TO STUDS

TO NAILING
STRIPS

OVER SHEATHING

16-58

MATCHING CORNERS

SPECIAL CORNERS MADE FROM
THE SAME CEDAR TEXTURE AS THE
PANELS. CORNERS FINISH THE JOB
FASTER AND NEATER FOR A PRO-
FESSIONAL APPEARANCE, ELIMI-
NATING THE NEED FOR MITERING
OR LACING ON THE JOB.

16–59   **16–60**

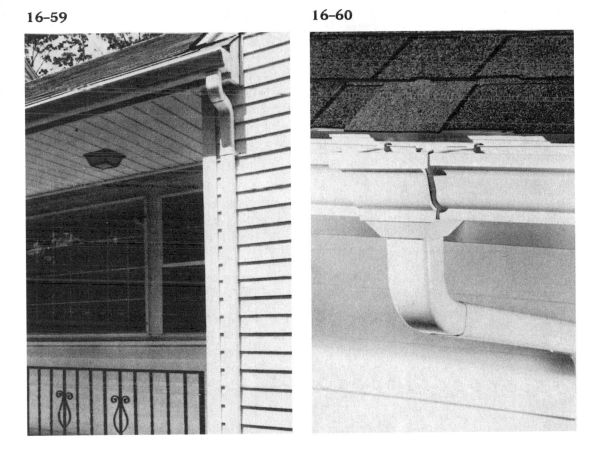

on any house design. Most manufacturers offer a wide range of trim pieces, and special-ties such as cornices, window trim, and panels that resemble fancy-cut wood shingles.

The overlaps in some panels can be staggered to look like butt joints in wood siding, and molded clapboard shapes can create the traditional shadow lines you expect from solid siding. From a distance, vinyl can fool you unless you spot the give-away polyvinyl glare. You may not be able to spot every vinyl-clad house from the street. But closer up there is no mistaking the rubbery-looking surface, even if it is embossed with grain patterns modeled from solid-wood siding, or tinted with brown streaks that are supposed to make PVC look like clear-sealed wood, but don't.

And if you touch it, vinyl bends because the standard siding is only $4/100$ of an inch thick—less than the space between $1/16$-inch marks on a ruler. That makes it easy to cut (you can use a shears instead of a saw), but whippy during installation.

The siding adds no structural value to the house; it simply clads the surface. In fact, the interlocking system is designed to hang somewhat loosely on partially driven nails, which can allow the panels to rattle in a stiff wind. It can't be fastened tightly because a typical length of PVC clapboard can expand and contract more than ½ inch during temperature swings from cool nights to hot days.

That's one of the reasons you can buy so many variations of off-white and beige vinyl, but not dark reds, greens, and blues. The lighter colors reflect more sunlight and keep the siding cooler. Dark colors would make sun-struck siding even hotter, and increase the chance of drooping, which actually is the first stage of melting. The problem is significant enough that the Vinyl Siding Institute, a plastics industry trade group, warns against storing the siding on blacktop pavement during unusually hot weather, or under dark tarps without air circulation. Lighter colors also help with fading, indirectly at least, because the bleaching effect of prolonged exposure to the sun would be more noticeable on a dark panel.

Early PVC siding was all vinyl. But to keep prices down and maintain popularity with cost-conscious builders, manufacturers have gradually diluted the mix with inexpensive fillers. The result is that in many vinyls today, only the top 20 percent of the siding contains the more expensive ingredients that increase weather resistance and ultraviolet light protection. For maximum durability, you can use thicker vinyl with reinforced joints. Standard thickness is .04-inch siding, but some companies offer .05 products, which may cost up to twice as much.

You also can strengthen a vinyl application by using panels with a rollover nailing strip. Standard panels have a small U-shape at the top, where the next panel hooks into place, and a single-thickness strip with perforated slots for nails. But some top-end products have a folded, double-thickness nailing strip and more material along the connecting seam. That makes the panels stronger and provides more holding power.

You need to fasten trim pieces securely, but don't drive the siding nails all the way in. Leave about 1/32-inch of space under the nail head, about the thickness of a dime. Center your nails in the horizontal slots provided in the nailing strip along the top of each panel. It will feel wrong when you're done (and you may hear some squeaking as panels shift in hot weather), but the siding should be loose enough to slide back and forth.

To remove a panel during construction (or to make repairs later on), you first have to separate its interlocking seam. The tool of choice for this job is called a zip-lock tool, although some pros get by with the claw of a hammer. Snake the zip tool's can-opener head up into the seam, pry out and down, and then slide the tool along the seam to unlock the entire length.

STUCCO SYSTEMS

In many parts of the country, new houses are finished in stucco, which can provide a house with an architecturally sleek, structurally hard, long-lasting, and weather-resistant shell. But the shell may crack.

Installation is generally not an owner–builder job. But you should be aware that problems can arise from movement in the building, such as gradual structural settling. When the foundation sinks unevenly, or new framing timbers shift as they dry out, the movement can create enough stress to crack rigid stucco walls.

Problems also can arise in the stucco itself. Fresh stucco (and a supporting masonry wall underneath) holds salt based components that can rise to the surface, burning off paint in the process. Although the alkalinity normally neutralizes in a natural curing process when exposed to the weather, initial deposits can create discoloration and cause cracking.

Even narrow cracks lead to trouble. They start the process of deterioration by letting in small amounts of water, creating more deposits, and eroding the wall structure underneath. That increases stress on the surface cracks, which open more and let in more water. In winter, freezing water can pop sections of stucco off the wall. Stucco doesn't need extra support over a solid masonry wall, but it needs metal lath and multiple layers over a wood frame (**16–61**).

16–61

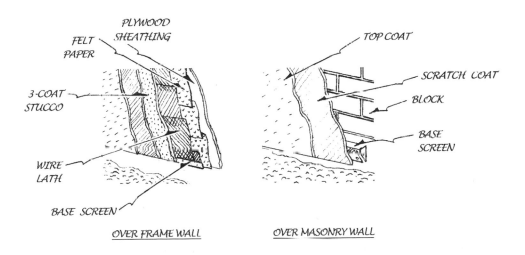

PLYWOOD
FELT SHEATHING   TOP COAT
PAPER
                                          SCRATCH COAT
3-COAT   BLOCK
STUCCO
                                          BASE
                                          SCREEN
WIRE
LATH

BASE SCREEN

OVER FRAME WALL   OVER MASONRY WALL

If you are considering stucco, be sure to look into potential problems with a stuccolike system called EIFS, which stands for Exterior Insulation and Finish Systems. In the late 1990s, some of these finishing systems were found to cause severe deterioration (from leaks and condensation) in the wooden frames of exterior walls. Problems have been widespread and very costly to repair. And the system itself is costly—about the same cost for installation as brick veneer.

Barrier EIFS typically consist of expanded polystyrene (EPS) foam board applied with an adhesive to OSB, plywood, or exterior-grade gypsum sheathing. A base coat of a cement/polymer mixture covers the foam board and provides a base for embedding a fiberglass mesh. Then a flexible finish coat in the desired color and texture is applied over the base coat. At this point, it appears that the most successful systems use a ribbed foam board, and make provision for draining away leaks and moisture so as to not become trapped and cause deterioration.

INSTALLING DOORS

After walls are sheathed, exterior doors (and windows) should be installed so that the house can be secured quickly and the final cover can coordinate with the frames and trim in and around openings. Interior doors can come later after walls are covered and, often, after the finish floor is down.

Almost all doors today are factory-assembled units that come to the site ready for placement in the rough openings. Some units, called prehung doors, are completely assembled. The door is hinged, hung in the frame, and may even have specified locksets installed. Unless you want an unusual door (manufacturers cover a wide variety of designs), this is the way to go.

Another possibility is to buy inexpensive flush doors and work on them, with moldings for example, so they become custom units (**17-1**).

17-1

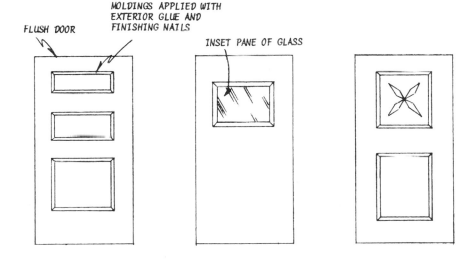

FLUSH DOOR

MOLDINGS APPLIED WITH
EXTERIOR GLUE AND
FINISHING NAILS

INSET PANE OF GLASS

Exterior doors are solid and are designed to be flush or paneled, often including lights, which are merely inset panes of glass (**17–2**). Most interior doors are hollow. The basic parts of these two basic types of doors are shown in **17–3**. There are also special decorator doors (**17–4**), which are available ready-made but have a custom-designed look that sets off the entrance. While most doors are made of wood, steel-clad doors

17–2

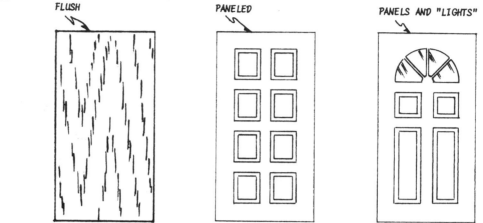

FLUSH   PANELED   PANELS AND "LIGHTS"

17–3

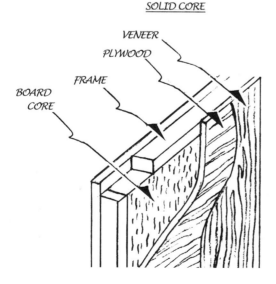

SOLID CORE

VENEER
PLYWOOD
FRAME
BOARD
CORE

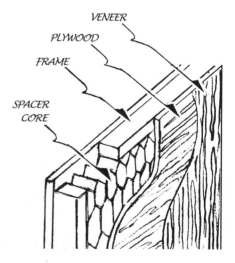

HOLLOW CORE

VENEER
PLYWOOD
FRAME
SPACER
CORE

offer several advantages: They have no grain and can't warp; and no wood fiber, so they can't rot. And because the core is filled with foam, they often are more energy-efficient than solid-wood doors.

Many times, utility entrances are made with simple doors and trim, while the main door and its setting include additional components that become architectural features. The detail doesn't have to be more than a cap with matching pilasters that you can make yourself (**17–5**).

Commercial caps in various styles are available ready to install (**17–6**) Most of them

17–4

can be purchased with matching pilasters. If you wish to do something more elaborate yourself, a basic construction scheme is shown in **17–7**. All such assemblies should be weathertight in themselves and at the connections wherever they are joined with the wall.

Utility entrances, especially those not protected by overhangs, can be finished as shown in **17–8**. View the top as a frame that will be finished to match the roof. The structure can be installed after the siding is up, but it will look less like an afterthought if you do it against sheathing. The latter procedure also permits adding adequate flashing along the top edge before siding is placed.

The main entrance door should be 36 inches wide and can be as much as 7 feet

17–5

17–6   COMMERCIAL CAPS

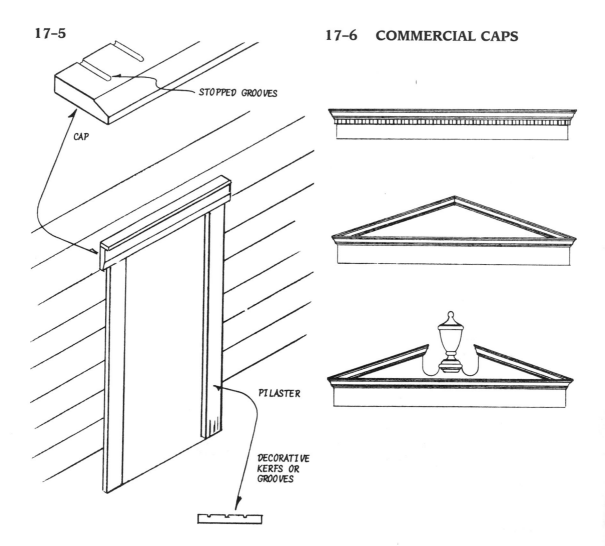

STOPPED GROOVES

CAP

PILASTER

DECORATIVE
KERFS OR
GROOVES

17-7

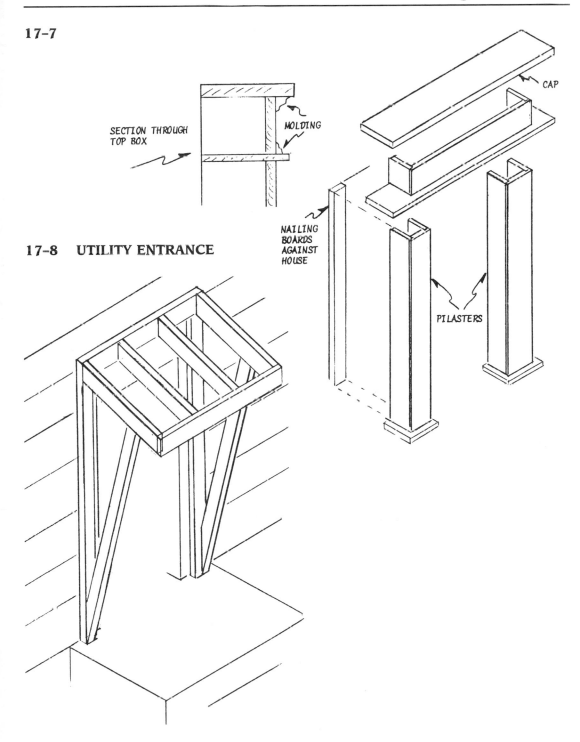

SECTION THROUGH TOP BOX

MOLDING

CAP

NAILING BOARDS AGAINST HOUSE

PILASTERS

17-8   UTILITY ENTRANCE

high, although 6 feet, 8 inches is standard. If you want a larger overall opening, you can buy complete units with sidelights and top lights. Other doors can be narrower, but don't go under 30 inches. Because all doors are passageways for furnishings as well as for people, there is nothing wrong with using the 36-inch width everywhere, with the exception of bathrooms.

THE FRAME

All frame installations must be made carefully so components will be plumb and square. A correctly installed door will remain open in any position, which will not be the case if the frame has a tilt. Door frames consist of jambs and stops, as shown in **17–9**, and, on exterior doors, a sill. Jambs and stops can be made from softwoods, but the sill, which must withstand considerable traffic, should be a hardwood such as oak.

17–9

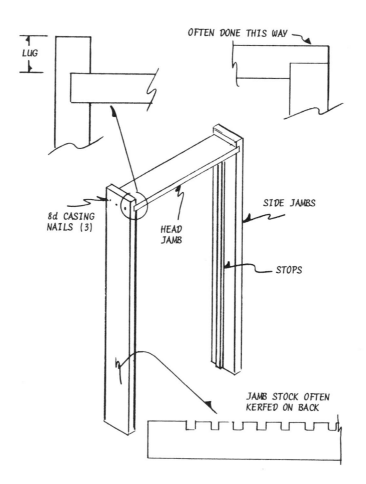

Jamb designs differ. Plain flat jambs made with ¾-inch stock are mostly for interior doors, while the other designs shown in **17–10** are for exterior applications. Jambs must be as wide as the total wall thickness so that the gap that will exist after the frame is installed in the rough opening can be neatly covered with trim (**17–11**).

Jambs come in standard widths to suit different designs. On exterior doors the material used is generally thicker than on interior doors, running from 1¼ inches up to 1⅝ inches,

17–10   EXTERIOR JAMB DESIGNS

PLAIN FLAT

SINGLE RABBET

SPLIT (ADJUSTABLE)

DOUBLE RABBET

17–11

JAMB

FINISH WALL

CASING

SET BACK

to provide more support for heavy doors and possibly screens or storm doors. Homemade types should resemble **17–12**. Rabbet cuts are made along both edges when it is necessary to accommodate more than the main door. Rabbet depth is ½ inch. The width of the inside rabbet equals the door thickness. The 2- or 3-degree bevel along the edges ensures a good fit for the trim.

17–12   HOMEMADE, ONE-PIECE JAMB MEMBER

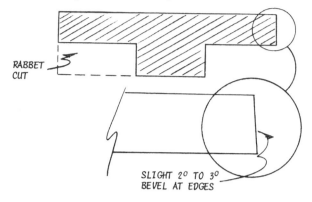

RABBET
CUT

SLIGHT 2° TO 3°
BEVEL AT EDGES

If you wish to make your own adjustable jambs for interior doors, you can do the job in either of two ways, as shown in **17–13**. But the best approach by far, even if you are an accomplished owner–builder, is to use standard, prehung units throughout the project, both for interior, hollow-core doors and solid exterior doors. This will save countless hours of hinge and lockset mortising, among other tedious and repetitive jobs.

17–13

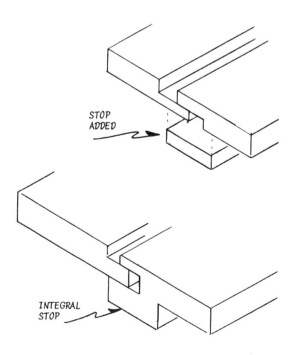

STOP
ADDED

INTEGRAL
STOP

One good tip is to leave on the diagonal brace that comes tacked to prehung units. It helps to keep the assembly square. Eventually, you will have to remove the brace. But leave it on as long as possible, including as you install the door, set shingle shims, and plumb the unit in the rough opening.

INSTALLING THE JAMBS AND STOPS

When you set the jamb (prehung or not) into the rough opening, use height blocks under the side jambs of interior installations if you are doing the job before the finish floor is down. This is to provide room under the jambs for the thickness of the final floor cover.

Work with a level to be sure the top jamb is horizontal and the side jambs are plumb. The frame is secured and adjustments are made by using opposing pairs of tapered shims (sections of shingles) between the jambs and the trimmers (**17–14**). To maintain the correct distance between the side jambs, use a length of wood as a spacer between the jambs

17–14

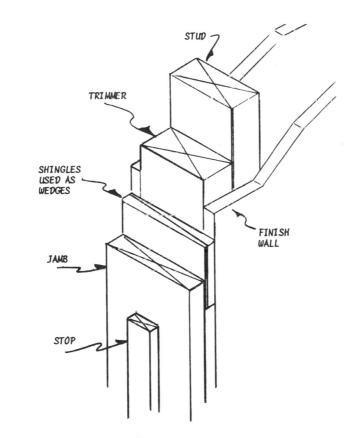

STUD

TRIMMER

SHINGLES USED AS WEDGES

FINISH WALL

JAMB

STOP

at the floor line. You should have three or four pairs of shims on each side of the frame, placing some of them so they will be approximately in hinge and lock areas. The head jamb, or the top edges of the side jambs, should not bear against the header.

As you increase the overlap of the opposing, wedge-shaped shims, you take up more of the gap left between the rough opening frame and the jamb. If you take up too much space and bow the jamb, simply back off the shims. After the shims are adjusted so the frame is rigid and straight, drive finishing nails that are long enough to penetrate through jambs and shims well into the trimmer. Place the nails so they will be hidden by the stops. Before you can add trim and finish the installation, you need to cut off the protruding ends of the shims. On exterior doors, stuff loose insulation into the gaps between shims to save energy and cut drafts before you close up the wall.

Stops are located to accommodate the thickness of the door and are installed as shown in **17–15**. Do the hammering carefully so you don't mar the wood. Sink the nail heads with a nail set so you can hide them with wood putty. Stops are supplied as part of a prehung door assembly. You can make your own by working with plain strips of wood or by using ready-made stop molding in various shapes (**17–16**).

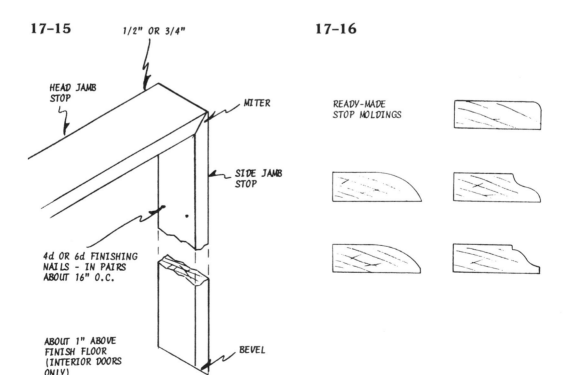

17–15

1/2" OR 3/4"

HEAD JAMB STOP

MITER

SIDE JAMB STOP

4d OR 6d FINISHING NAILS - IN PAIRS ABOUT 16" O.C.

ABOUT 1" ABOVE FINISH FLOOR (INTERIOR DOORS ONLY)

BEVEL

17–16

READY-MADE STOP MOLDINGS

INSTALLING THE SILL

There are various ways to install the sill for an exterior door. Much depends on whether its surface will be flush with the finish floor. Often the sill is rabbeted and it is secured directly to the subfloor so part of its width extends outside the house frame (**17–17**).

Custom-made sills might lie flat as shown in **17–18** and can include a small rabbet to accommodate the finish floor. This does leave a slight ledge, but it can be minimized, even beveled, so it will not be a tripping hazard.

17–17   **17–18**

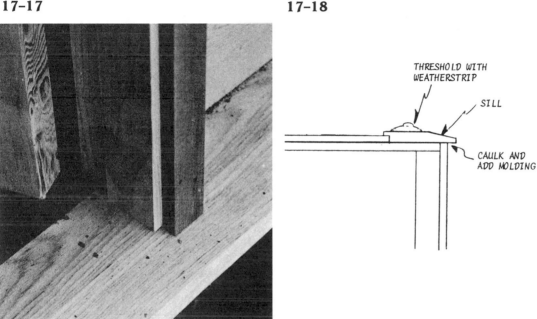

More complicated installations call for trimming the joist header (**17–19**). Add whatever reinforcement is necessary to support and supply perimeter nailing for the flooring. In such cases, the threshold, often a metal-and-vinyl one as shown in **17–20**, is placed to cover the joint between sill and floor.

The sill installation is critical because it must bear foot traffic and be weathertight and waterproof. Ready-to-install exterior door assemblies are available with complete weather-stripping, often an interlocking type, in place around jambs and at the sill. In such cases, the installation must be done in line with the design of the unit.

17-19

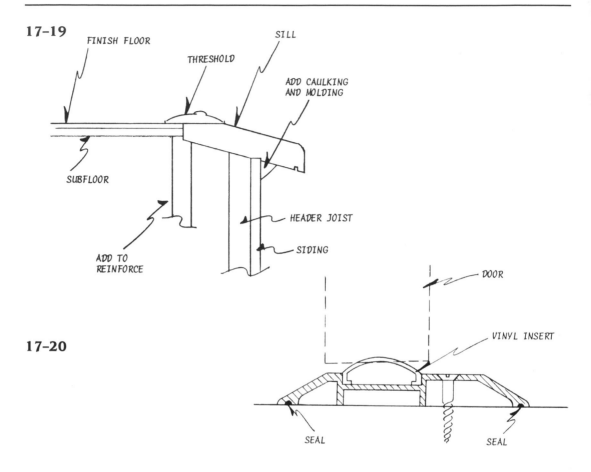

17-20

INSTALLING HINGES AND OTHER HARDWARE

Once you become really proficient at hanging a door, you might be able to mortise the hinges and lockset, and mount and adjust the door in a couple of hours. That doesn't count the time it will take to build and install the jambs. When you figure that it may take you longer than this to hang a door, times the number of doors in the house, you'll see why investing in prehung units makes sense.

If you want to hang them yourself, bear in mind that interior doors are usually hollow-core, and thinner and narrower than exterior units—1⅜ inches thick by 32 inches wide being fairly standard. That means they can be hung with two hinges instead of three. However, hinges do more than just let the door swing. They guard against distortion in addition to supplying support, and so a third hinge on all doors is a good safety factor.

Hinge locations and correct clearances are shown in **17-21**. You can work with loose-

17-21   HINGE PLACEMENT AND DOOR CLEARANCE

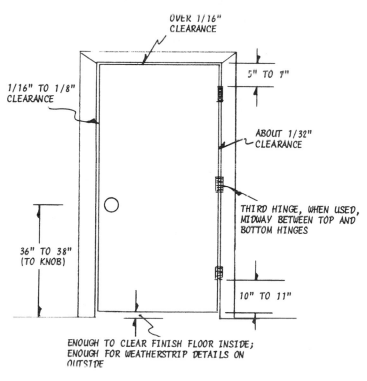

OVER 1/16"
CLEARANCE

5" TO 7"

1/16" TO 1/8"
CLEARANCE

ABOUT 1/32"
CLEARANCE

THIRD HINGE, WHEN USED,
MIDWAY BETWEEN TOP AND
BOTTOM HINGES

36" TO 38"
(TO KNOB)

10" TO 11"

ENOUGH TO CLEAR FINISH FLOOR INSIDE;
ENOUGH FOR WEATHERSTRIP DETAILS ON
OUTSIDE

pin butt hinges as shown in **17-22**, as they make it possible to remove the door after installation without having to take out screws. The size of the hinge goes along with the size of the door; see the table of suggested sizes in **17-23**.

17-22

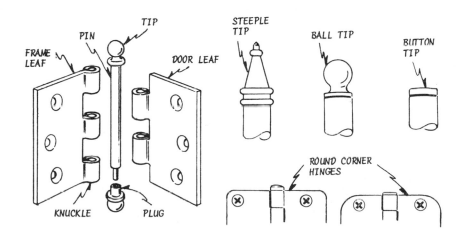

FRAME
LEAF

PIN

TIP

DOOR LEAF

STEEPLE
TIP

BALL TIP

BUTTON
TIP

ROUND CORNER
HINGES

KNUCKLE   PLUG

17–23 CHOOSING HINGES FOR DOORS

THICKNESS OF DOOR	WIDTH OF DOOR	SUGGESTED HINGE HEIGHT
¾" up to 1⅛" cabinet doors	up to 24"	2½"
⅞", 1⅛" screen or combination door	up to 36"	3"
1⅜"	up to 32"	3½"
	over 32"	4"
1¾"	up to 36"	4½"
	over 36 to 48"	5"
2"	up to 42"	5 or 6"

Some butt hinges (often called the "hand" of the door) are reversible, and some are not, so check how the door will operate and then decide, if necessary, whether you need right-hand or left-hand hinges (**17–24**). Also remember that some door locks must be chosen according to whether the door swings left or right.

17–24

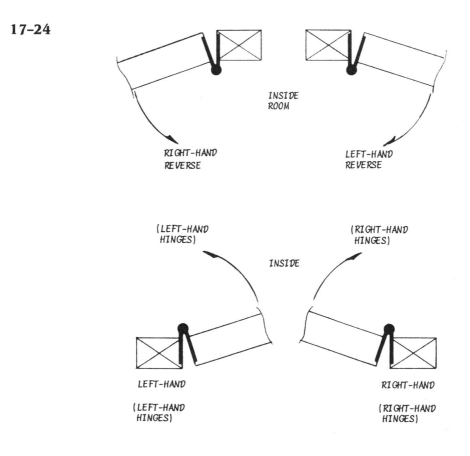

If you are installing the hinges, place the door in the frame and use shims to hold it there while you mark hinge locations on the door and the jambs. Use one leaf of the hinge as a pattern to mark its outline on the door edge, following the backset recommendations in **17–25**. Incise along the lines you have made by working with a sharp utility knife and then remove the waste with a chisel (**17–26**). The depth of the mortise should be just enough for the hinge to be flush with the wood. Follow the same procedure on the jamb, or, as some do, install the hinges on the door first and then prop up the door in the correct open position so you can trace the hinge outline on the jamb. In any case, the job

17–25   **17–26**

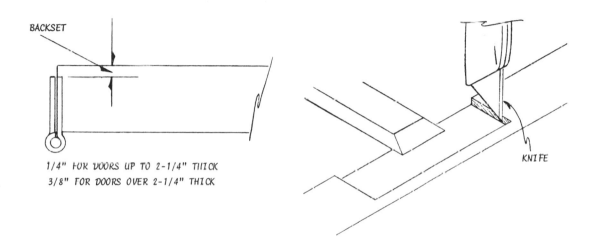

1/4" FOR DOORS UP TO 2-1/4" THICK
3/8" FOR DOORS OVER 2-1/4" THICK

should be done with precision so the hinges will seat correctly. The mortising can be done with a router driving a square-end bit. Special templates that almost eliminate layout work are available for use with a router.

Cylinder locks of the type shown in **17–27** are common in residential constructions. Notice that on exterior doors these days, it's customary to install a deadbolt, or a combination unit with both types built in. Cylinder locks require a large hole through the surface of the door, a smaller one drilled through from the edge, plus a mortise for the latch plate (**17–28**). The small hole can be drilled with a bit and brace, or you can use a portable drill. The large one requires a special bit, or you can use a hole saw and portable drill.

It's best to install the lock first so you can use it to mark the correct position of the strike plate on the jamb. The strike plate requires a cavity, which you can form by drilling overlapping holes for the strike box, and cutting a mortise for the strike plate (**17–29**). You can

17–27

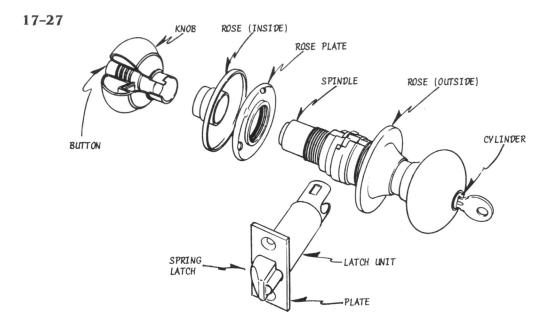

17–28   **17–29**

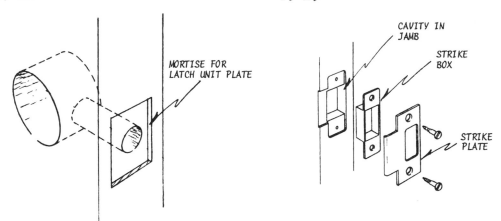

leave the lock hardware installed, but it's a good idea to remove it until after finish coats have been applied to the woodwork.

All lock sets come complete with installation instructions, and usually with cardboard templates to mark hole locations. Read all such instructions carefully before starting installations.

You will probably find it easier to install stops for interior doors after the doors are hung and the lock is in place. Work with the door closed and place the stops so there will be about ¹/₃₂-inch clearance between them and the door. Often the stop on the lock side is placed snugly against the door, since this will eliminate rattle.

INSTALLING DOOR TRIM

Trim, called casing, is used around doors to cover the gap that exists between the jambs and the walls. Two basic installations are shown in **17–30**. The miter joint is used more often; the butt joint can't be used on all types of ready-made casing but is a simple way to

17–30

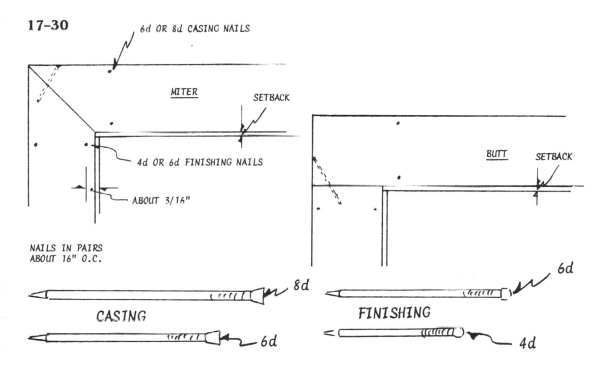

go if you decide to do your own trim. Homemade pieces can be simple, square-edged strips, or you can work on them to add the kind of detail shown in **17–31**.

There is much variety in the kind of casing material that is available ready to install. Some of the pieces shown in **17–32** are also used as baseboards. The material you use depends on the appearance you want. Simpler casing can blend in with the walls, while fancier casing highlights the openings.

17–31

17–32   CASING (ALSO BASEBOARD)

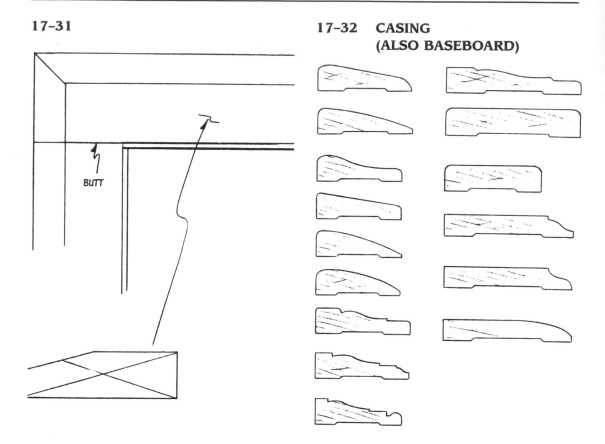

BUTT

DOORS THAT FOLD

Bi-fold doors come in styles that include solid or louvered panels (**17–33**). They are usually used on closets, but often are installed between open rooms to serve as dividers when needed. They look good, and they don't require as much swing room as regular doors do.

Most are available in two- or four-door designs with installation possibilities as shown in **17–34**. They are installed after the rough opening has been finished with jambs and trim, and all require special hardware that is placed following instructions that come with the kits (**17–35**). In essence, they are supported at the jambs by hinges or pivots and at the outer edge of each panel by a hanger that rides a track that is secured to the head jamb.

Folding doors include the accordion types, which are made by assembling many narrow panels of wood or other materials. They work, and are installed, pretty much like the bi-folds and are available in sizes to suit various openings. Because the panels are narrow and fold back on themselves, they require very little floor space when they are opened.

17–33   BI-FOLD DOORS WITH LOUVERED PANELS

17–34   TWO- AND FOUR-DOOR BI-FOLDS

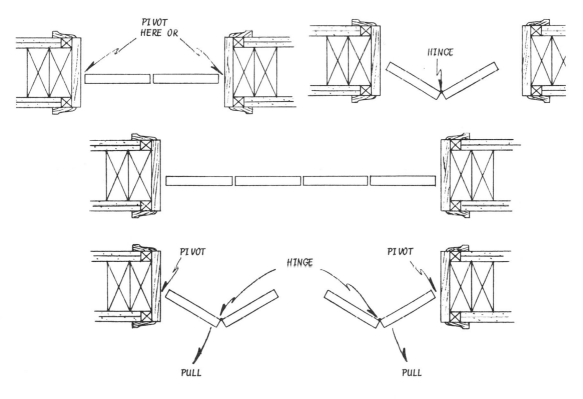

17–35   BI-FOLD DOOR HARDWARE

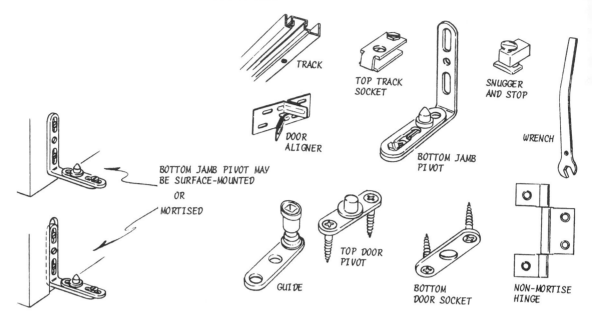

TRACK

TOP TRACK
SOCKET

SNUGGER
AND STOP

DOOR
ALIGNER

WRENCH

BOTTOM JAMB
PIVOT

BOTTOM JAMB PIVOT MAY
BE SURFACE-MOUNTED

OR

MORTISED

GUIDE

TOP DOOR
PIVOT

BOTTOM
DOOR SOCKET

NON-MORTISE
HINGE

SLIDING DOORS THAT BYPASS

These units hang from and move on double tracks that are usually installed against the underside of a conventional head jamb. Some tracks, like the one shown in **17–36**, have a built-in fascia; others are hidden by adding a trim strip after the installation is complete. It's also possible to get special head jambs in which the tracks are recessed so the top edge of the doors will be flush with the underside of the jamb. Like the bi-folds, hardware for sliding-door installations is available in kit form to suit various door thicknesses. A floor guide is included so the doors will remain perpendicular regardless of the hanging method (**17–37**). Good units will include an adjuster built into the hangers so the doors may be adjusted for correct height after they have been installed. The rough opening is framed conventionally and completed before the doors are hung. Bypass sliders do not require any swing space and are often used on closets and similar areas even though the design does not permit total access.

POCKET DOORS

These doors slide into the wall cavity. The space-saving design eliminates the normal swing of doors into the room, and works well as an entry off a narrow hallway, or as a set

17–36

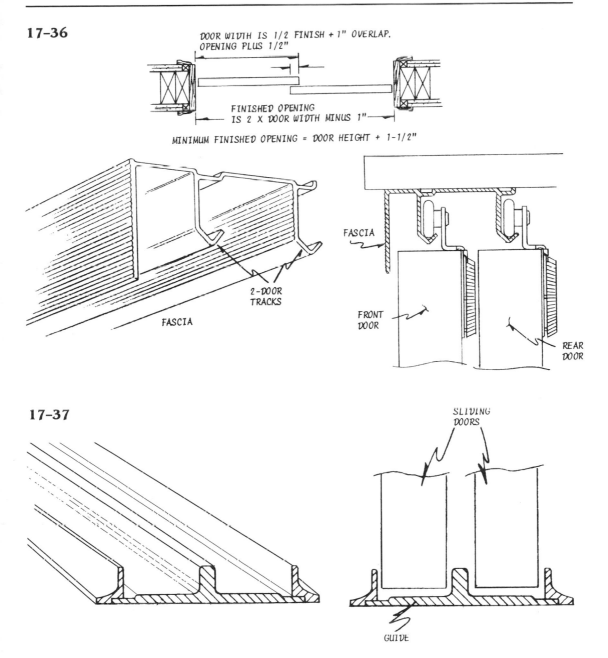

DOOR WIDTH IS 1/2 FINISH + 1" OVERLAP.
OPENING PLUS 1/2"

FINISHED OPENING
IS 2 X DOOR WIDTH MINUS 1"

MINIMUM FINISHED OPENING = DOOR HEIGHT + 1-1/2"

2-DOOR
TRACKS

FASCIA

FASCIA

FRONT
DOOR

REAR
DOOR

17–37

SLIDING
DOORS

GUIDE

of double pocket doors that serve as room dividers. This is the kind of thing you have to plan for in advance, buying preassembled units that you install as you erect the wall frame (**17–38**). You can view the job as you would a regular rough opening, except that it must be wide enough to accommodate the pocket as well as the door opening. Units are avail-

17–38

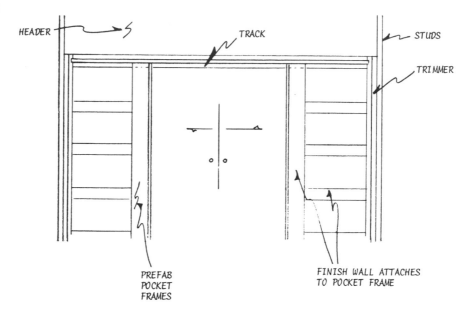

able in a number of standard sizes for double as well as single doors, with pocket frames made of steel or wood. Track and roller assemblies are much like those used on conventional sliding doors and include adjusters for door height and plumb. Good units will have silent-action rollers and will include rubber stop buttons inside the pockets so the doors will work without clatter.

But this design needs some special attention, particularly as many preassembled units are, frankly, somewhat flimsy. For one thing, the hollow cavities that house the door can't have full studs. Instead, the pocket-door frame is very thin, with small furring on each side to hold drywall. One result, at least in a bearing wall, is that you will need a header that spans the opening and the hidden pocket-door housing where full studs have been removed.

You also need to keep mechanicals out of the hidden cavity, and take care fastening drywall. The pocket frame isn't as strong as studs, and can't take pounding with a hammer. You should fasten the drywall with screws, and be sure the points don't protrude into the cavity.

CAFE DOORS

These units, though somewhat old fashioned, can be useful between a kitchen and a dining area, as they permit passage even though a person's hands are full. They do not provide much privacy, but enough to hide kitchen clutter from the diners. The doors can be simple or fancy and are hung on special pivot hardware that is attached to conventional jambs (**17–39**). Check the hardware you buy to be sure the bottom pivot includes a riser so that the doors can be held in an open position.

17–39

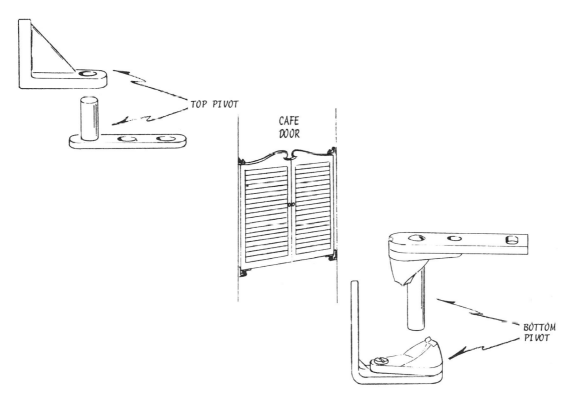

SLIDING GLASS DOORS

Sliding glass doors bring the outdoors in and provide easy access to a patio or garden. Factors to consider are thermal quality, built-in weathertightness, a security locking system, and, of course, the appearance you seek. Those made for residential use are framed with steel, aluminum or wood and are available in various stock sizes, generally up to 8 feet long and 8 feet high. It is important these days to check out the glass used and to spend more money if necessary for special insulating types, such as Low-E glass that will minimize heat transfer.

All units will include at least one fixed and one sliding panel (**17–40**). They are available with three panels (the center one sliding in one direction) and with four panels (the two center ones moving in opposite directions) as shown in **17–41**.

The size of the units and the dimensions of the rough opening will vary depending on the manufacturer, but the design of the opening will not differ from what is required for any door (**17–42**). You should, of course, have the specifications of the units on hand while you frame the wall. Some types require finish framing. Others are so complete, including sills, that you just slip them into place and secure and seal them, following the instructions that come in the package. In all cases, parts must be plumb and square if doors are to slide properly. Cross sections through the header, jambs, and sill of a typical installation are shown in **17–43**.

17–40

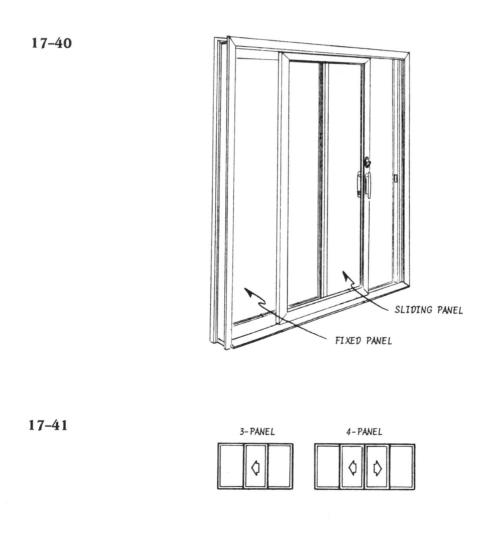

SLIDING PANEL

FIXED PANEL

17–41

3-PANEL   4-PANEL

17–42

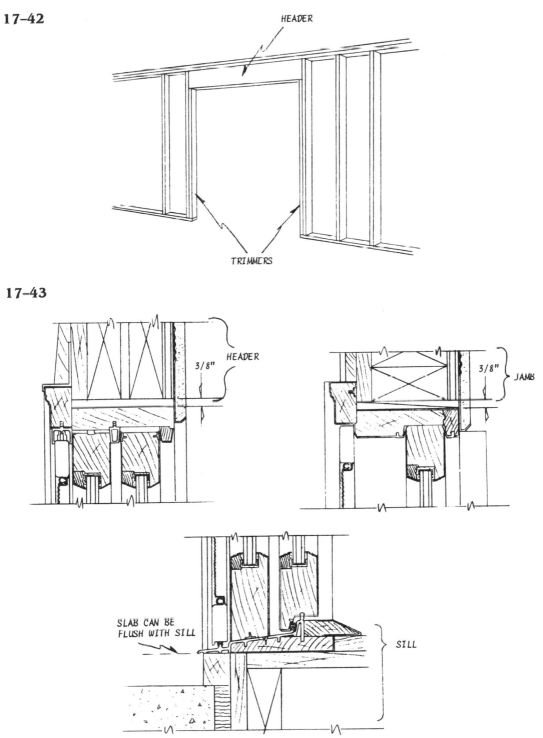

HEADER

TRIMMERS

17–43

HEADER

3/8"

JAMB

3/8"

SLAB CAN BE
FLUSH WITH SILL

SILL

It's a good idea to cover the installed door with plywood or some other material to protect the glass and frame from damage while other work is going on. The least you should do is place strips of masking tape over the glass so no one will try to walk through it.

GARAGE DOORS

Most modern garage doors will either swing up or roll up. Sliding bypass doors and hinged doors are much less practical. Segmented doors with automatic openers are most common. Rough openings are made in the standard fashion with substantial headers because of the wide openings (**17–44**). These may be the largest framed openings in the building, and require an exceptionally large header. On the other hand, if the

17–44

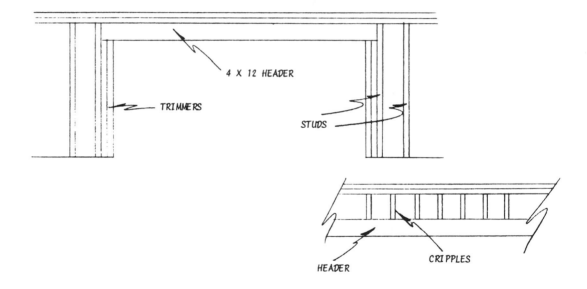

opening is under the cord of a roof truss where there is little load on the opening, a small header will do. You need to check the details of this wide opening carefully with the building department.

The opening is framed with side and head jambs just like those installed for regular exterior doors except that heavier material, usually 2-by stock, is used, and integral stops are not required. Inside jambs are often added as shown in **17–45**, when they are required to support track or other door hardware.

In the unusual case where you decide to make your own single-panel, tip-up door, the panel will be sheathed with plywood and reinforced as shown in **17–46**.

17–45

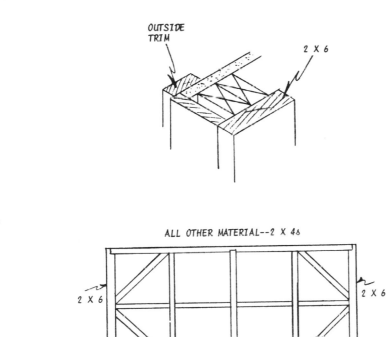

OUTSIDE TRIM

2 X 6

17–46

ALL OTHER MATERIAL--2 X 4ᵼ

2 X 6   *2 X 6*

GARAGE DOOR SAFETY

Since 1982, when the Consumer Product Safety Commission began keeping accident records, automatic garage door openers have caused many injuries and over 100 deaths. The figure was recently revised by the agency, and includes 46 children under the age of 15 who were trapped under closing doors.

If garage doors operated purely by gravity—that is, they had to be hauled open, and came crashing down to the floor when they closed—children might recognize the danger and steer clear. But when hundreds of pounds are counterbalanced with springs, it's understandable that a child could think of a garage door as one more almost toy-like piece of household equipment that operates effortlessly and by remote control.

Still, a garage door is the heaviest and largest moving object in most houses—and it is used more than any other entrance. It's the weatherproof route in and out when you come and go by car, and when children park their bikes. It's convenient because no one needs a key, just an access code, and even a small child can set the huge door in motion automatically. That may be the most convenient feature, but also the most dangerous.

Using a Remote Control

Manufacturers now pack illustrated labels that warn of entrapment with all garage door systems. But it's up to consumers to use door openers safely, tend to maintenance and repairs, and lay down operating rules for children. Instruction is crucial because in many households children regularly use the door without supervision—for instance, when they return from school before anyone else is home.

Manufacturers suggest that you keep portable remotes in the hands of adults, and that you install the permanent keypad at least five feet off the ground to keep it out of reach of small children. Along with the CPSC, they also stress consumer education and periodic safety checks that are detailed in a booklet available from all manufacturers called "Automatic Garage Door Opener Safety & Maintenance Guide."

Safety Systems

Due to the number of accidents and deaths, safety improvements have been made in automatic door openers. They are designed to meet an Underwriters Laboratories standard, which includes these four key provisions.

1. Garage door operators must reverse a downward moving door within two seconds after the door contacts a two-inch-high test block in the door's path.
2. Door operators must reopen the door within 30 seconds of the start of downward movement if the door does not fully close to the garage floor.
3. Once the door is moving down, it must stop, and may reverse, if the control button is pushed again. If the door is moving up, pushing the control button must stop the door and prevent it from moving downward.
4. Door operators must have a manually operated way of detaching the operator from the door.

Openers meeting these standards were phased into production in two stages. In 1991, all openers were required to have a reversing mechanism activated by contact. That means if the door hits something on the way down—your car or your head—it begins to open. In 1993, all openers were required to have the back-up safety of photoelectric cells. With this system, when a beam of light running across the opening between a pair of cells is broken—even if you pass safely under a closing door—the door reverses.

Checking Doors

If you're not sure about the safety of your door opener, you can conduct two tests. First, place a two-inch wooden block in the path of the door. If the door does not promptly reverse on striking the block, disengage the unit and call in a service technician to see if repairs are needed. If the opener does not have the reversing feature, the CPSC recommends that you disconnect the old opener and replace it with one meeting modern safety standards.

A second test, recommended by the CPSC and the National Safety Council, is designed to check door balance, which must be calibrated to prevent the door from moving too swiftly and with too much force. To conduct this test, disconnect the automatic opener release mechanism following manufacturer's instructions so you can move the door by hand. If the unit is properly balanced, you should be able to lift it with ease, and it should stay open three to four feet off the floor.

EXTRA DOOR SECURITY

Remember that while most building materials are designed to do one thing well, exterior doors have to be more versatile. They must resist cracking and warping even though they swing freely on hinges between conditioned air inside and unconditioned air outside. Mainly, they must be easy to open for the people who live there and almost impossible for the people who don't. To add an extra measure of security, there are some extra steps you can take during and after the installation to make a door and frame more durable.

A standard opening has double studs on each side. The inner stud helps to support the header. The outer stud runs past the header to the top of the wall frame. Although it's not generally added, you can strengthen the opening by adding a horizontal brace on each side at midspan. This easy-to-add extra is particularly helpful on sliding glass door installations where the closing side of the opening can take a beating. But extra braces will strengthen any opening, and can help to prevent twisting on the hinge side of heavy doors.

To strengthen the connection between the jamb and house wall, you can drive several long screws through the jamb into the nearest studs, particularly around the hinge and lock locations. This increases security by making it harder to pry the frame and release a latch or bolt from its keeper. It also makes the frame less likely to twist, and keeps the door better aligned.

Use screws at least 2 inches long that can reach through the jamb, the shimming space around the frame, and well into the wall studs. Drive the screws flush. (It will help if you drill countersink holes for the heads.) If you drive them too deeply, the jamb is likely to bow.

Once the jamb is joined more securely to the house wall, you can install the doorstop trim over the screws. With many hinges and keepers mortised into the jambs, you can accomplish a minor version of this extra reinforcing simply by replacing the relatively short screws often sold with the hardware with long screws. Don't use a screw so large that its head does not sit flush with the face of the hinge. That can cause the door to bind.

INSTALLING WINDOWS

Like exterior doors, windows should be installed just after walls are sheathed or otherwise prepared for siding. This is a satisfying stage of the job because you will be closing in the building. But there are many choices to make. The type and style of window you select has a major impact on the look of the house, of course. Your choices also have a great influence on energy-efficiency, comfort, ventilation, and the amount of natural light exposed to the living spaces. Also, windows must satisfy several important codes concerning safety, and sometimes other codes about energy efficiency.

There are many configurations, including double-hung (the most common) casements, sliding, awning, hopper, and fixed. There are also several relatively new types of glazing that take the place of single glass. And there are different material options, aside from the standard wood window. These include both metal and vinyl windows, and wood windows with weatherproof cladding on the exterior surfaces designed to eliminate periodic scraping and painting.

You'll find that modern windows are mass-produced to rigid standards that cover materials and methods of assembly and even the design of such details as drip caps and sills.

Wood is a very popular window material because it has natural insulating qualities and minimizes condensation. It may be painted to match any color scheme or it can be stained or finished in natural tones to match various sidings. Some of the units on the market, like the one in **18–1**, are provided with complete weatherstripping at the head, jambs, and sill to give a positive seal against the elements. Some are double-glazed systems that include aluminum-framed glass panels that can stay in place throughout the year and so eliminate the need for additional storm windows. Insulating glass and screen inserts are also available.

Wood windows are available with outside casing (trim) already attached, as in **18–2**, so that the basic installation can be made by nailing through the casing into the sheathing or the frame of the rough opening.

Because metal is strong and rigid, windows made of steel or aluminum generally have

18–1

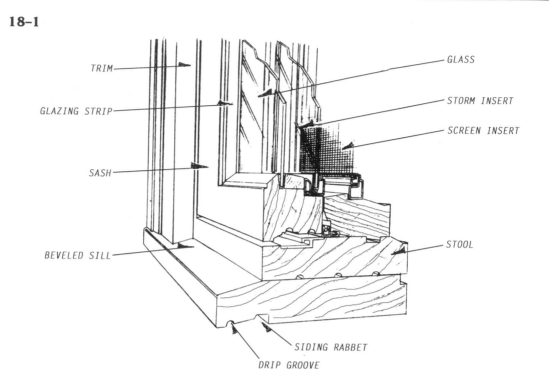

TRIM

GLAZING STRIP

SASH

BEVELED SILL

GLASS

STORM INSERT

SCREEN INSERT

STOOL

SIDING RABBET

DRIP GROOVE

18–2

WINDOW IN CASE

narrower framing pieces than those made of wood. But they do not insulate as well and often have condensation problems. For those who believe in wood construction but want the advantages of an exterior that does not require painting, there are clad windows with exteriors protected by factory-applied and factory-finished coatings (**18–3**).

The design of many windows eliminates the need for exterior casings to secure the window to the wall (**18–4**). The perimeter of the units is a predrilled installation flange that also acts as flashing. Attachment nails are driven through the flange (**18–5**).

18–3

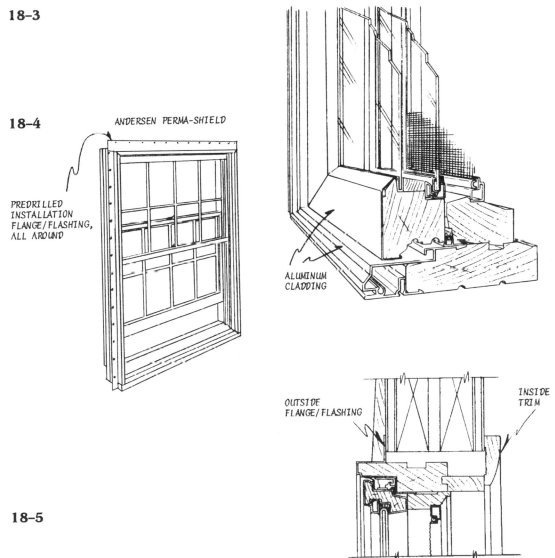

18–4

ANDERSEN PERMA-SHIELD

PREDRILLED INSTALLATION FLANGE/FLASHING, ALL AROUND

ALUMINUM CLADDING

OUTSIDE FLANGE/FLASHING

INSIDE TRIM

18–5

HEAD

WINDOWS CAN SLIDE, SWING, OR STAY PUT

Within the basic categories of windows that slide, swing, or are fixed, as shown in **18–6**, there is much variety in design and sometimes even in the method of operation. The double-hung window is a sliding type, but its two bypassing sashes move vertically. With the exception of the fixed window, it is probably the oldest design around, but it is still very popular and adaptable to many architectural schemes. At one time, the moving parts were held at a particular position through a system of cords and pulleys and counterbalancing weights that were hidden behind the side jambs. Replacing the cord or freeing a stuck weight was a real chore. Today the job of holding either sash at any position is done largely through friction designs or by spring-type hardware.

18–6

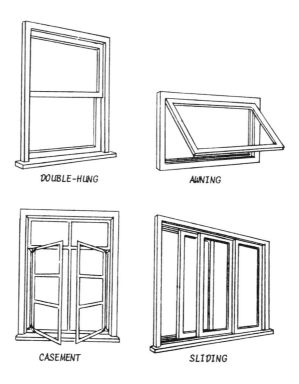

DOUBLE-HUNG

AWNING

CASEMENT

SLIDING

In addition to easier and surer operation, there are improvements in materials and features such as built-in weatherstripping, double glazing, and so on. Some units are made so the sashes can be removed, which solves the old problem of how to clean the exterior surface of the glass while remaining indoors.

A simplified cross section of a double-hung window is shown in **18–7**. Usually, and especially if the window is not under a protective overhang, a drip cap must be installed (**18–8**).

Sliding windows that move horizontally have two or more sash units. The most common designs are two-sash units with one or both of them being movable, or three-sash designs with the center one fixed. A common objection to the sliders has been a lack of security, but recent improvements include better locking hardware and built-in adjustable stops that can limit the distance a movable sash will open.

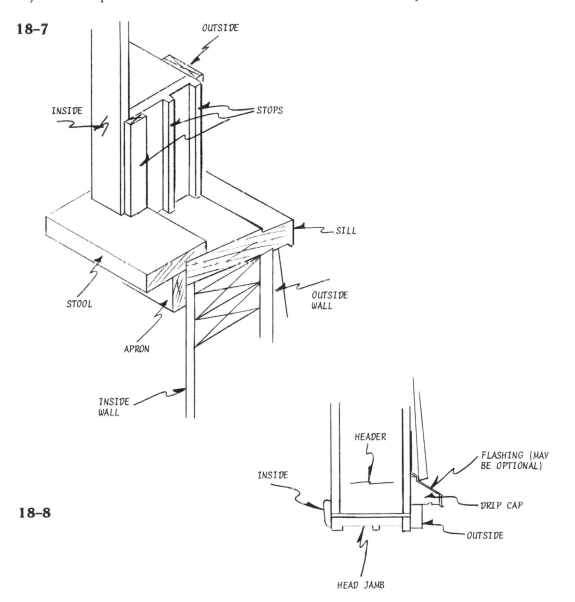

18–7

OUTSIDE

INSIDE

STOPS

SILL

STOOL

OUTSIDE WALL

APRON

INSIDE WALL

HEADER

FLASHING (MAY BE OPTIONAL)

INSIDE

DRIP CAP

OUTSIDE

18–8

HEAD JAMB

Casement windows have sashes that are hinged on one side like a door. They swing outward and may be adjusted by a crank or by a push bar that may be locked at any position. Because the movable parts swing to the outside, screens or additional storm sashes must be mounted on the inside. The design may be used throughout the house, but it is especially practical over a counter or similar object you must lean over to reach the window. Older units were difficult to make weathertight, but improvements in design and new weatherstripping materials have minimized the problem.

Do some thinking about the location of casement windows in relation to outside activities. They can cause a traffic problem if they open over a patio or porch or a path that is close to walls.

Awning windows are hinged like casements but along the top edge so they swing out and up. Some units are made with special hardware that provides a type of pivot action—the top of the sash moves down as you push the bottom outward. A practical feature of this concept is that units can be placed side by side to provide adequate light and ventilation, but close to the ceiling, leaving a maximum amount of wall space for placing furniture. Used this way, they can also provide greater privacy for a bedroom or a bathroom.

Often, awning windows are used in combination with fixed windows to provide necessary ventilation. Opening and closing mechanisms include the cranks and push bars used on casement windows, but some are designed so that such hardware is not needed. The outside-clearance consideration mentioned in relation to casement windows applies here as well.

Hopper windows look like awning types but are hinged at the bottom and designed to swing inward. They are most practical for installations near the ceiling. If placed low on a wall, they will obviously interfere with drapes and can cause traffic problems inside the room. With almost any type of window, you (on site) or the manufacturer can gang together assemblies, such as a fixed window with a casement or double-hung at each end.

ENERGY CONSIDERATIONS

About half the houses in the country still have single-thickness glass. But window technology has so outstripped single glazing that high-efficiency windows can pay for themselves long-term in reduced utility bills and increased resale value.

Single glazing may seem like a minor problem that creates a few drafts on cold days and occasional condensation problems. But single glass can lose enough energy to account for 10 to 25 percent of your heating bill. The Department of Energy reports that poorly insulated windows and doors nationwide waste about as much energy as we receive through the Alaska pipeline every year.

There are many more modern and energy-efficient options, including glass with heat-deflecting tints, and double-glazed low-emissivity (Low-E) windows with heat-resistant films and insulating gas instead of air between panes. With high-efficiency windows, there are several factors to consider:

1. *Low-E coatings.* Low emissivity is the crux of modern window efficiency. The term refers to the invisible metallic coating sealed between panes of glass and surrounded by an inert gas (typically argon) that is heavier and less conductive than air. The microscopically thin film reflects long wave heat energy back into the room but allows shorter-wave, visible light to pass through. It also blocks almost all ultraviolet light that bleaches wood and fades fabrics, and, to a lesser degree, reduces heat gain during the cooling season. Even leaky storm windows over single-thickness glazing will lower utility bills because heat passes through glass 10 to 12 times faster than it does through an insulated wall. But some double-glazed Low-E windows are manufactured with roughly the insulating value of 2 inches of fiberglass, and can reduce heating bills in cold climates by 30 percent or more. You're likely to pay at least 10 to 15 percent more for double-glazed windows with a Low-E film. But if a heating bill in a house with single glass were about $800, uncoated double-glazing would cut it by about $200, Low-E double glazing would cut it by about $280, and Low-E triple glazing would cut it by about $320.

2. *R-values and U-factors.* R-value is the familiar term for the thermal value of insulation—the higher the number, the better the insulating value. It's also used on windows, although the numbers are sometimes used to describe only the thermal resistance at the center of the glass, not the frame and overall energy efficiency. The inverse of the R-value, called the U-factor ($R=1/U$, if you want to do the math), is a better indicator of efficiency because it includes the spacer system between the glass and the frame, and the frame itself. Lower U-factors mean a greater resistance to heat flow and a better overall thermal value.

   Although there are some high-efficiency exceptions, window R-values typically range from 0.9 to 3.0, and U-values range from 1.1 to 0.3. To make valid comparisons, be sure that all U- or R-values listed by manufacturers are based on current standards set by the American Society of Heating, Refrigerating, and Air-Conditioning Engineers (ASHRAE), calculated for the entire window, including the frame, and compared among windows of approximately the same size and style.

3. *Reduced condensation.* One significant by-product of high-tech windows with warmer interior glass surfaces is reduced condensation. It's reduced the most on windows with what's called warm-edge technology—low-conductance spacers that reduce heat transfer near the edge of insulated glazing. When the temperature outside is 20

degrees F, for instance, single-glazing can sweat when the indoor air has only 20 percent relative humidity. But a double-glazed Low-E window exposed to the same outside temperature won't support condensation until the interior air has a nearly tropical 70 percent relative humidity.

4. *Spectrally selective coatings.* Optical coatings are the latest generation of Low-E technology that can filter out from 40 to 70 percent of the heat normally transmitted through clear glass without reducing transmitted light. No single type of coating is suitable for every application, and some houses may be most efficient with one type of glazing on sunny southern walls, and another type on shaded northern walls. Like other built-in energy-savers, windows that are this efficient can substantially reduce the initial costs of heating and cooling equipment in new construction because you need less capacity, and may qualify for utility rebates and other programs that aid in financing.

5. *Labeling.* Windows may carry several labels, including one for the Energy Star program of the United States Department of Energy that denotes overall efficiency. The most informative is the voluntary performance rating from the National Fenestration Rating Council, a nonprofit organization comprised of manufacturers, suppliers, builders, architects, code officials, utilities, and government agencies. It includes the U-factor, information on solar heat gain, and how much light gets through the built-in energy-saving systems. Bear in mind that local energy codes may require a minimum energy efficiency.

SIZES, TYPES, AND PLACEMENTS

Codes also may control considerations such as window size, type of glass, and placement. For example, most rooms have one door, which could be blocked by fire. That leaves the window as what fire inspectors call a second means of egress. As we mentioned in the first chapter, the windowsill typically can be no more than 44 inches off the floor so you can get over it easily, and the opening itself has to be at least 24 inches high and 20 inches wide. The requirements are based in part on people inside getting out, but also on the room needed for a firefighter wearing a bulky respirator backpack to get in. Bear in mind that egress also applies to baths and to habitable basements.

Many of the restrictions are not likely to impose any real limitations on your plans. For example, codes call for glazing to provide natural light on 8 to 10 percent of the wall surface. You'll generally want to have a lot more window area than that.

Glass type is also controlled in special circumstances, such as with requirements for tempered glass or safety glass near showers and doors. There are also limitations on large fixed-glass windows running nearly from floor to ceiling that someone might fall into or inadvertently try to walk through. Unless safety glass is used, you may need to install what amounts to a guardrail 34 to 38 inches off the floor.

Generally, standard windows supplied by major manufacturers and installed in line with widely accepted architectural norms will pass code. If you plan special glazings, very large window groups, or glazing in somewhat unusual locations, you should make a special check with the building inspector.

INSTALLING WINDOWS

If you do a good job on the rough openings, being careful with dimensions and making sure that sills and headers are horizontal and the trimmers are plumb, you will have no trouble placing the windows. Be sure, though, to check any literature that comes in the package just in case there are special directions that apply to the units you purchased.

Many units are shipped with temporary braces or spacers that guard against distortion. Let these stay in place during installation, but first make sure the units have not been damaged or thrown out of alignment despite the precautions. Cut 8- to 10-inch-wide strips of felt paper and tack them in place around the rough opening. If you use house wrap, apply it across the wall, cut the corners at openings, and tack it back into the frame.

Set the window unit in the rough opening from the outside so the exterior casing or the installation flange overlaps the sheathing (**18–9**). Because rough openings allow about 1 inch of extra space both vertically and horizontally, you have plenty of leeway to make sure the window is both level and plumb. The best bet is to rest the unit on the rough sill and then drive a nail partway at one of the top corners. In all cases, use rust-resistant nails that are long enough to penetrate framing members by at least 1 inch. Work with casing nails if you are attaching the window through exterior trim (casing) that is part of the unit.

Check with a level to be sure the window is in alignment both vertically and horizontally. If necessary, use shims to make adjustments (**18–10**). It's a good idea on wide windows to place wedge blocks at intermediate points to guard against any tendency of the sill to sag. When you are sure the window is placed correctly, drive nails at the remaining corners and then check all movable sash for easy operation before completing the nailing. Space nails through casing about 10 to 12 inches apart. The nailing pattern is already set if the unit has a predrilled installation flange. Attach flashing by nailing through the sheathing (**18–11**). Don't nail into the drip cap.

Caulking is usually applied after the siding is up, but it won't hurt to place a bead around the frame of the window right off. Stuff the open spaces around the window on the inside with insulation and then cover the areas with strips of vapor-barrier material (**18–12**).

18–9

SHEATHING   HEADER

ROUGH SILL

18–10

SHIM

18–11

SHEATHING

FLASHING

HEADER

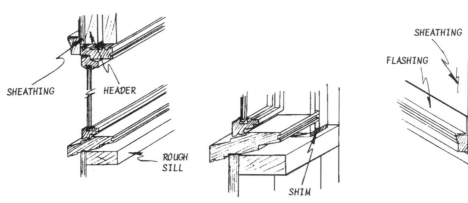

18–12

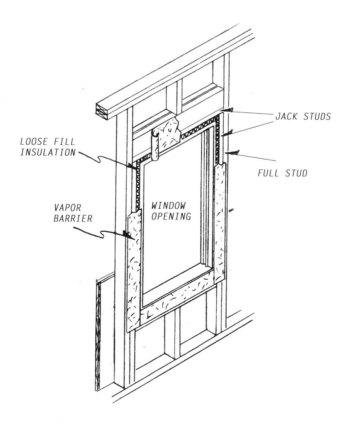

JACK STUDS

LOOSE FILL INSULATION

FULL STUD

VAPOR BARRIER

WINDOW OPENING

FIXED WINDOWS

Fixed units are windows that do not have movable sash. They are available already framed so you can install them as you would any window. This is often done in combination with units having movable sash that provide the ventilation; the entire assembly becomes a wide picture-window area. Fixed-glass windows, because they are usually on the large side, should be double-glazed (**18–13**). It's best to work with units of standard size; having such products made to order can be very expensive.

Large fixed units often are glazed on the site after the rough opening has been framed, as shown in **18–14**. The frames can be preassembled with one set of stops included, as in **18–15**, so they can be installed in the rough opening as you would any window unit. The frame can be made with heavy, kiln-dried material that is rabbeted to receive the glass, as shown in **18–16**. The glass should be set in a nonhardening glazing compound so there

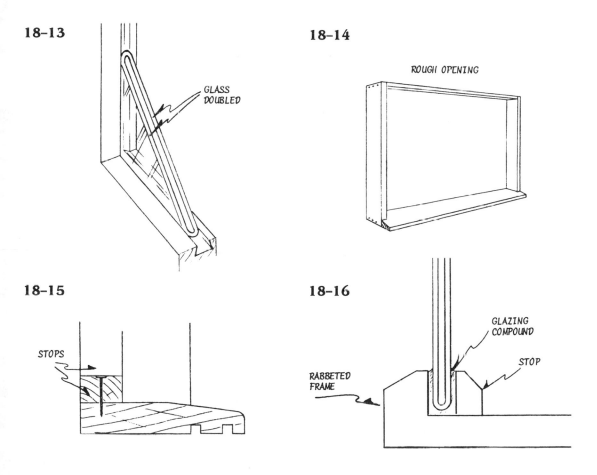

18–13

GLASS
DOUBLED

18–14

ROUGH OPENING

18–15

STOPS

18–16

GLAZING
COMPOUND

STOP

RABBETED
FRAME

will be no contact between the edges of the glass and the frame. Special neoprene spacers are available that clip to the edges of the insulating glass to maintain necessary clearances. Insulating glass can weigh as much as 7 pounds per square foot, so you want to use substantial material when you make a frame. Work with a dry, high-grade, warp-free wood; using waterproof glue in the joints is not a bad idea.

PLUMBING

The most sensible recommendation for the greatest number of owner builders is to leave the mechanical installations, including plumbing, to professional contractors. It's not that you won't be able to sweat copper-pipe fittings, or, where codes allow, make the very simple adhesive connections in plastic pipe. But planning the complete plumbing system for a modern house is a very complicated undertaking.

CONSIDERING CODES

Construction codes about framing are a lot to cope with, but on top of them you have plumbing codes, too. The most widespread is a fairly huge set of rules and regulations that represent the Uniform Plumbing Code (UPC). But there is a newer organization, called the International Plumbing Code (IPC), that could apply in your area. As always, you need to check with the local building department about the details of both the overall plumbing plan and the particulars of the installation.

Water generally comes from municipal systems, which means a water company and a meter. Similarly, wastes are delivered to a municipal sewer system. But many more rural homes get water from a well and deliver wastes to a septic system on the property. These two components are quite complicated just by themselves and are very closely controlled by inspectors. In this regard, you'll find that many codes concentrate on maintaining a healthy water supply, and segregating it from the waste drainage. The reasoning is obvious, as wastes can be harmful and even lethal, as they produce a variety of bacteria, which can cause severe health problems, and noxious methane gas, which can be explosive.

Just one of countless examples of code constraints is the limitation on air gaps to prevent a sink or tub full of dirty water from being siphoned back into the faucet where it would contaminate the water supply. To prevent this, there is a limit on the minimum distance (typically two times the spout diameter or at least 1 inch) between the end of the faucet and the overflow level (also called the flood line) of the fixture. Notice that even where in-ground pipes are concerned, codes call for separating these systems. You're likely to find that you can combine gas and electric service lines in one trench, for example, but not supply and sewer lines.

There are many code concerns outside the house (in addition to wells and septic systems). One of the most important is the distinction between wastewater and graywater. In most areas, there is only one main drain, which handles septic waste from toilets as well as sink water that may contain only a trace of soap.

Some codes allow you to split the drains so that septic wastes head to the sewer line or septic system, and graywater heads to its own system, often through a surge tank with an overflow line to the septic line. With minimal filtering, you may be able to recycle hundreds of gallons of graywater for watering landscaping.

Inside the house, the plumbing system must meet literally thousands of specific codes, which vary from one region to another. You may be allowed to use plastic pipe in one area and not in another, for example. The limitations may seem staggering. But in modern homes plumbing means a lot more than two pipes in for hot and cold water and one pipe out for drainage. The entire installation includes supply pipes, of course, but also what is called the DWV system, for drain-waste-vent.

This part of the overall system includes providing traps and vents for all fixtures (most toilets have their own built-in trap) to provide a water seal over the waste line and allow for smooth drainage. Without a trap, fixture drains would be open to the main waste line, and the potentially lethal sewer gases it contains. And to drain freely, wastes need to be replaced by air. Otherwise, you would get slow, halting drainage and lots of blockages.

There are many codes about drain lines, including minimum slopes designed to reduce blockages. You may find a minimum requirement of $1/16$-inch per linear foot. But most plumbers install drain lines with a somewhat steeper grade in the $1/4$-inch range. This is just one example of the complexities of modern codes, which call for different slopes with different diameter pipes—but not too much of a difference. The slopes are controlled because too little leads to blockages from wastes not flowing, and too much (generally $1/2$- inch or more per foot) leads to blockages from liquids moving too fast, leaving the solids behind.

And before you start plumbing the house, you need to size the system. For example, although water service often is through a $3/4$-inch pipe, a three-bath house generally calls for a 1-inch supply line. Among other codes, your region also may impose restrictions on fixtures, including such items as the flow rates of showerheads and the flush volume of toilets—one code change that has caused quite a few problems and a lot of controversy.

In many houses, plumbing also includes piping for natural gas. This is a crossover job.

On one hand, you may need a gas line for the water heater, which is obviously part of the plumbing system. Many of the tools and skills required for gas piping are similar to the ones you need for water plumbing, but piping for furnaces, for example, is generally considered part of the heating plan. The same goes for piping installed as part of a radiant-floor heating system.

Bear in mind that your locality may require separate inspections for the plumbing system. One of the first (if you need a septic system) is a perc test. This is designed to evaluate the soil so that the system can be designed to safely handle the expected drainage. Another is a pressure test to expose any leaks in the DWV system. In a typical test, the system is sealed, and pressurized to 5 or 10 psi; most hold the pressure for 15 minutes.

Granted, in some rural areas, you may be able to install a basic plastic pipe system without much trouble. But in many areas, these days, plumbing is controlled as closely as wiring, and you will need to be very familiar with accepted local practices to avoid a lot of scrutiny (and probably quite a few troublesome and possibly expensive starts and stops) by the inspector.

That means you have to consider the installation plans in this chapter as general guidelines. Details will vary for many reasons, including the type of pipe you are using. The upshot is that where mechanicals are concerned, there are enough codes to fill a large book—one for plumbing, another for electrical, and so on. That's one reason why it's best to leave the job to a licensed professional.

TYPES OF PIPE

There are many types of pipe. But several varieties that you may see in older homes, such as galvanized iron water pipes, are rarely if ever used today. In new houses, depending on codes, of course, you'll find plastic or copper, and sometimes a few pieces of cast iron.

Cast iron is a holdover from the days of using metal pipe at every location. Now it is sometimes used in 3- or 4-inch diameters for the main waste-vent line, often called the soil stack. It may also be used for the main sewer line that exits the foundation for the septic system or municipal sewer line. It is very strong, but heavy, difficult to cut, and even more difficult to fit. Traditional connections were made by stuffing the bell-shaped housings of connections with oakum, fitting a special collar around the housing, and then pouring in molten lead. If this does not seem much like a do-it-yourself job, you're right.

Today, most large-diameter vent and waste pipes are plastic. The first variety on the market was ABS, but now the standard is PVC, which is lightweight and very resistant to damage from heat or chemicals. The large-diameter pipes have tees, elbows, and other fittings, of course, and are easy to cut and fit. You can cut the plastic with a hacksaw or a tubing cutter, swab on an etching solution, then some liquid adhesive, and simply fit the pieces together. There is no pipe tape or pipe dope or solder as required with other systems. Some regions now permit PVC in place of cast iron, even where they do not approve CPVC, which is formulated to withstand the temperature and pressure of supply systems, for supply and drainpipes.

The other standard is copper, particularly for supply piping. Sweating joints does take some practice, but once you get it right it provides secure seals. Joints are brightened, coated with flux that draws solder into fittings, and heated with a propane torch so the solder melts and flows into the joint. Copper also is used with a chromed finish in some exposed supply lines, and in flexible tubing. Several years ago, when lead in drinking water was being investigated as a health hazard, it was found that lead in solder could contribute to the problem. Now, there is a safer type of material called tin-antimony solder.

BASIC SYSTEMS

By now you have the idea that the key is to know where and how to place and connect ready-made components so water will be directed to points of use or from points of discharge. Waste materials and water that are not consumed must be discharged, so drainage units are introduced. The discharge system and the pipes carrying incoming water should be viewed separately.

There can be situations where a third system of pipes is required, for example, when the house has a hot-water heating system. But the pipes carrying domestic hot water used in the kitchen, laundry room, or tub, and those that carry hot water for house heat are separate installations; water from one should not flow into the other, although in some modern hybrid systems, heat from one system is transferred to the other.

Fresh water enters the house under pressure through a single pipe, which may branch off in different directions but eventually arrives at a water-heating device. Here it divides and becomes two lines, usually running parallel to each other throughout the house. One line carries cold water, the other hot (**19–1**). At each point of use and at other critical places, the systems are interrupted with shutoff valves so you can stop the flow of water completely or at an isolated point.

The assembly of pipes that carry used water and wastes to a sewer system or your own septic tank is the discharge or drainage system. Those pipes that carry off used water are often called waste pipes, while the larger ones that carry off discharge from a toilet are called soil pipes.

Among the many complexities of venting is the distinction between wet and dry vents (**19–2**). Dry vents serve only to ventilate the line and do not carry wastes. Wet vents serve

19-1

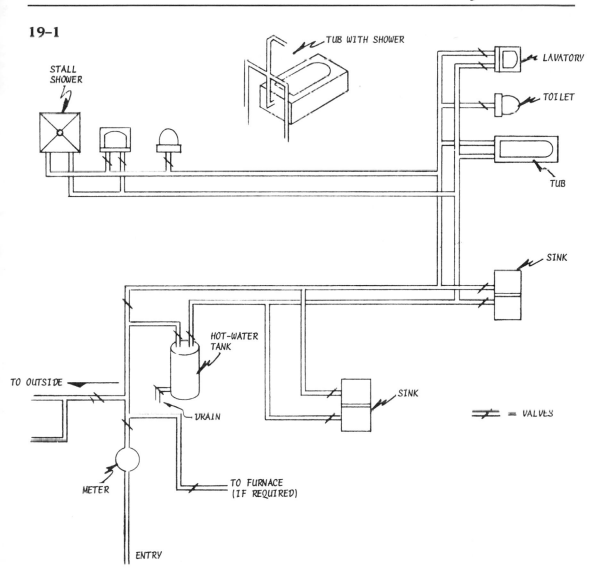

as vents for one fixture and as drains for another. Due to the double duty, a wet vent must be sized to handle all the fixtures it serves with larger diameters for more fixtures. The distance of the fixture to the vent is also taken into account. For example, even with a large, 3-inch-diameter vent pipe, you can have no more than 10 feet from the trap to the vent. With smaller diameters the distance decreases dramatically, down to 2½ feet with the smallest-diameter vent pipes.

Traps are included so sewer gases and odors won't enter the house. Traps are usually

19–2   WET VENT SYSTEM

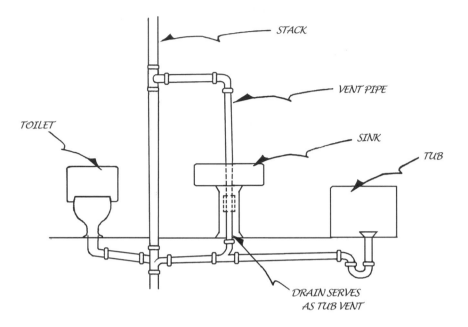

STACK

VENT PIPE

TOILET

SINK

TUB

DRAIN SERVES
AS TUB VENT

AUXILIARY VENT SYSTEM

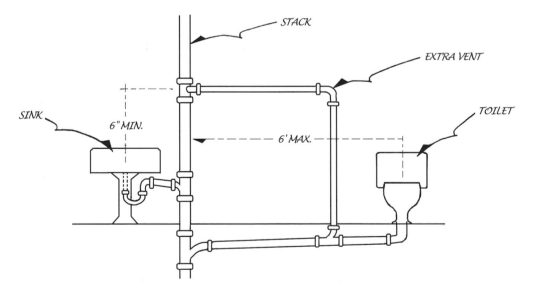

STACK

EXTRA VENT

SINK

TOILET

6" MIN.

6' MAX.

U-shaped connections that always contain water to form a seal between inside air and the air in the drainage lines (**19–3**). Toilets have built-in traps, and they work the same way. Whenever water runs down a drain, or a toilet is flushed, the trap water is replaced, so that it is always fresh and can't cause a problem.

19–3

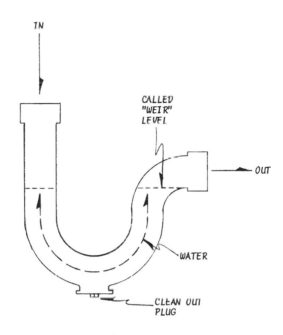

Trap design also is governed closely by code, mainly to prevent siphoning, which can remove the water providing the sanitary seal between the fixture and the sewer line. The main problems come from continuous S shapes where the tailpiece of a sink, for example, is connected to a U-shaped trap that is connected directly to another U-shaped drain. To work properly, the trap empties into an arm that extends to a vented drain.

Vents are part of a discharge system so gases and odors that can't break through the trap water will be able to escape. Venting also serves to maintain atmospheric pressure, without which the water in a trap could be siphoned off. With the sewer side of the trap lacking a vent, siphoning could easily happen if many different drains, or several inter-connected ones, were filled with water at the same time.

Vents for toilets are called main vents, while those that serve fixtures are secondary vents. Each vent must pass through the roof and be open to the air, unless the system is organized like the bathroom setup in **19–4** so that secondary vents will exhaust into a main vent which then passes through the roof. Remember that fixture location, vent-pipe diameter, and other factors can alter the basic installation.

19–4

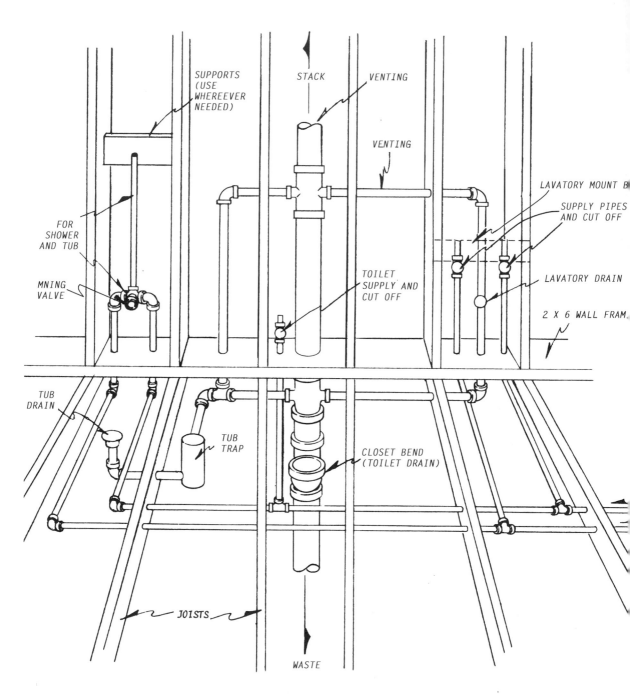

SUPPORTS
(USE
WHEREEVER
NEEDED)

STACK

VENTING

VENTING

LAVATORY MOUNT B

SUPPLY PIPES
AND CUT OFF

FOR
SHOWER
AND TUB

TOILET
SUPPLY AND
CUT OFF

LAVATORY DRAIN

MNING
VALVE

2 X 6 WALL FRAM.

TUB
DRAIN

TUB
TRAP

CLOSET BEND
(TOILET DRAIN)

JOISTS

WASTE

The DWV system also includes cleanouts, which are openings with removable plugs so that you can get to the insides of pipes should a blockage occur. The safest approach is to install one for each horizontal run. Among the codes you could encounter here, the UPC requires a cleanout at the upper terminal of horizontal branches and on any horizontal run longer than 100 feet. You also need a cleanout to provide access from the building drain to the main sewer line. Although cleanout locations sometimes are in tight spots, you need to provide at least 12 inches of clearance (by the UPC), though 18 inches or more for maneuvering room is preferable.

RECIRCULATING LOOPS

During the planning stage, you may want to add a few features that are not exactly standard. One of the most popular, particularly on houses with a big footprint that requires some long pipe runs, is a hot water recirculating system.

Making hot water represents only 15 to 20 percent of most utility bills. But the generally modest cost doesn't include the expenses involved in waiting for hot water to arrive at the tap—or the aggravation. And if you're on a municipal supply, the water meter clicks over as you wait. If you're on a well, waiting is even more costly in the long run because your pump runs more than it needs to.

The most thorough solution is a recirculating system. It requires a second pipe and some fittings to form a loop with the existing supply pipe, and a small pump that draws only a small amount of electricity to provide the circulation. Instead of standing in the pipe and losing heat until you open a tap, water constantly trickles toward the tap through the old pipe and back to the heater through the new pipe. When you open a faucet, the water is hot and ready for use.

Of course, it also helps to insulate the pipes and the heater. Easy-to-install, precut jackets for electric heaters are widely available and generally cost about $15 or $20. This insulation will pay for itself in energy savings within one year, according to the Department of Energy. Adding blankets on gas- and oil-fired heaters is somewhat more complicated, and you should ask a contractor or your local utility for instructions.

SEPTIC SYSTEMS BASICS

Many homes are constructed in areas where a municipal sewer line is not available and where you need a septic-tank system. When correctly sized for the house, properly installed and maintained, such a system will provide trouble-free service for decades.

As shown in **19–5** and **19–6**, a typical septic system consists of a subsurface, steel or

19–5   SEPTIC SYSTEM (TOP VIEW)

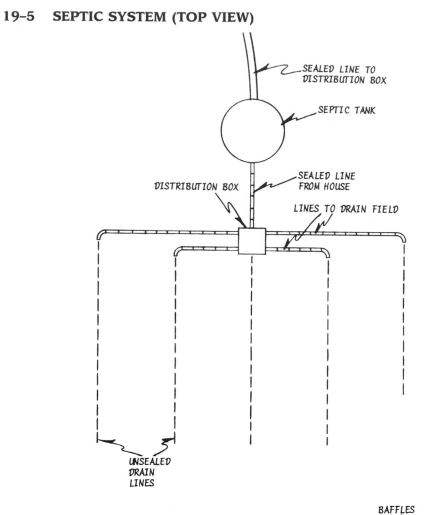

SEALED LINE TO
DISTRIBUTION BOX

SEPTIC TANK

DISTRIBUTION BOX

SEALED LINE
FROM HOUSE

LINES TO DRAIN FIELD

UNSEALED
DRAIN
LINES

19–6   STEEL SEPTIC TANK

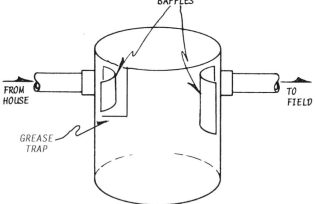

BAFFLES

FROM
HOUSE

TO
FIELD

GREASE
TRAP

concrete tank, which receives wastes from the house, and a subsurface drainage field, which is usually made of perforated pipe embedded in gravel. The drainage field disposes of the effluent from the tank. Waste from the house is carried to the tank by means of a sealed sewer line.

The tank is actually a settling tank designed to retain solids long enough for maximum decomposition to occur through anaerobic bacterial action. The matter that is not completely dissolved sinks to the bottom of the tank as sludge. There, it collects, filling the tank to a point at which it interferes with the tank's action and must be pumped out by professionals with special trucks designed for the job. Access sometimes is provided through a cover that has to be excavated (**19-7**). But more modern and convenient designs have an above-ground sealed stem where the cleanout truck hose can be inserted.

The overall system design is basically a tank with a system of branch pipes. The size of the tank and the number and lengths of pipes depends on the size of the house and the type of soil where the effluent will drain.

Tank capacity is noted in gallons. The minimum-size tank should not be less than 500 gallons, but even for a small house (two bedrooms or less), going to 750 gallons makes sense. Tank sizes go up as the number of bedrooms increases. This, of course, assumes there will be more people using the facilities. When you get to five bedrooms, the minimum tank size should be 1,250 gallons, or whatever local codes call for.

19-7   CONCRETE SEPTIC TANK

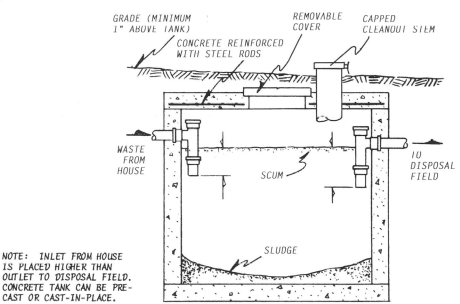

GRADE (MINIMUM 1" ABOVE TANK)

REMOVABLE COVER

CAPPED CLEANOUT STEM

CONCRETE REINFORCED WITH STEEL RODS

WASTE FROM HOUSE

SCUM

TO DISPOSAL FIELD

SLUDGE

NOTE: INLET FROM HOUSE IS PLACED HIGHER THAN OUTLET TO DISPOSAL FIELD. CONCRETE TANK CAN BE PRE-CAST OR CAST-IN-PLACE.

Effluent from the septic tank is only partially treated sewage and so is still in septic condition. Therefore, it must not be discharged to the surface of the ground, or directed to a stream, or used for irrigation purposes.

A good system calls for the effluent to flow through a sealed line to a distribution box (a small concrete box) so the liquid can be distributed among the number of drainage lines needed. The drain lines can be concrete or clay tiles or various types of pipe made of perforated fiber or plastic. The drain lines must not be watertight. The effluent is supposed to move out of the drain lines into surrounding soil where aerobic bacteria (those that live in the presence of air) complete the decomposition process and render the effluent harmless as it gradually drains down through the soil and rocks to the water table.

The total linear footage in the drainage/disposal field depends mainly on the moisture-absorption capability of the soil. A sandy-gravel soil will let water move more quickly than a clay soil and will let a septic system function efficiently with a minimum disposal field.

To determine the condition of your soil, you can perform a percolation test. You can conduct a basic perc test yourself by digging about 6 holes to the depth of the proposed drainage trenches over the area where the drain lines will be placed. Then fill the holes with water. After about 24 hours, add or remove water from the holes so you have about a 6-inch depth. At this point, you must determine how long it takes the water level to drop 1 inch. Based on this percolation test, you can consult charts in local codes to determine the number of square feet of absorption area per bedroom you will need.

Many local codes require that the percolation tests be conducted by health department technicians. They calculate the results and tell you how big the tank must be and how many feet of drain line you will need. Other code-controlled factors include distance between drain lines, between the tank and the house, and between disposal field and streams or wells that might be present, and so on.

Take advantage of any advice or planning aids you can get from city or county planning commissions and local health departments. Don't forget that the engineering or agricultural department of a nearby college or university may have done a soil survey of the area; this can help you select a suitable site for an absorption field.

PLANNING HOUSE PLUMBING

Building codes covering plumbing installations can raise some questions. The acceptance or rejection of plastic pipe is a case in point. The material is light, as durable as it has to be for the purpose, easy to cut, and requires only adhesive for connections. It's an ideal amateur plumber's product, which, justifiably or not, may be a main reason for some opposition.

Anyway, building codes should be checked out before you make plans and buy materials. And let's not forget that codes can be very educational, supplying data that will help you do the job correctly. In addition to types of materials, they cover such things as the sizes of pipes for various applications, the distance a fixture should be from a stack or a vent, the design of the venting system, and so on.

Generally, pipe sizes run along these lines: Water enters the service through a ¾- or 1-inch pipe. The main lines that deliver hot and cold water to points of use are ¾- inch; ½-inch branch lines take off from the main lines to fixtures and sometimes to appliances. There can be variations, with much depending on what you are going to install. The best bet is to know in advance the tubs, showers, toilets, and so on that you will be using. All such products come with installation instructions that will suggest sizes of connections and tell where the rough plumbing should pierce the wall, and, when necessary, the floor. The latter facts are critical, as you must know where to open up for toilet, tub, and shower drains and where to come through the wall with hot- and cold-water lines.

The main drains and vents in the DWV system that service toilets or groups of fixtures are 3 or 4 inches wide. Secondary vents that pass through the roof can be smaller, but check codes. Generally, toilets drain through 4-inch lines; showers through 2-inch lines; tubs, sinks, washers and the like through 1½-inch lines. Sewer lines are 4 inches. A good procedure is to plan the installation on paper, using the pipe sizes above, and then have your plan checked by the local plumbing inspector before proceeding.

There are two important points to remember. Fresh water enters the building under pressure, which should be enough to supply requirements at points of use while absorbing pressure losses caused by flow friction as water passes through pipes and fittings and by any vertical travel that might be in the system. Approximately 50 psi (pounds per square inch) is about average pressure for water supplied through a municipal system. This generally works out okay with the pipe sizes specified above. If pressure is lower (as from a well), you can compensate somewhat by using larger pipes, and, of course, by increasing the pressure in a sealed, pressurized storage tank.

The other important point has to do with the DWV system. Unlike the incoming water supply, which operates under pressure, the drainage installation uses gravity flow to exhaust its contents. That's one reason why larger pipes are used and why the system should be designed in a straightforward manner with runs as direct as possible, horizontal pipes sloped, and angular connections made so the gravity flow can function efficiently.

COPPER PIPE

Most amateur plumbers find copper tubing easier to work with than other materials. In some areas, special precautions must be taken to protect it. But overall, the desirable features outweigh the little problems.

Copper tubing is either hard or soft and available in various lengths, diameters, and wall thicknesses. The tempered type (hard) is rigid and is sold in 10- and 20-foot lengths. The soft version is flexible and comes in coils of 30, 60, and 100 feet. Often the rigid version of the product is called pipe and the soft material is called tubing.

Most types of copper fittings and connectors are designed for soldering and are called sweat fittings. The variety in sizes and shapes is extensive; some are shown in **19–8**. You can work with ready-made parts to suit any design. DWV copper pipe is also made for drainage systems. But the fittings, some of which are shown in **19–9**, are very

19–8

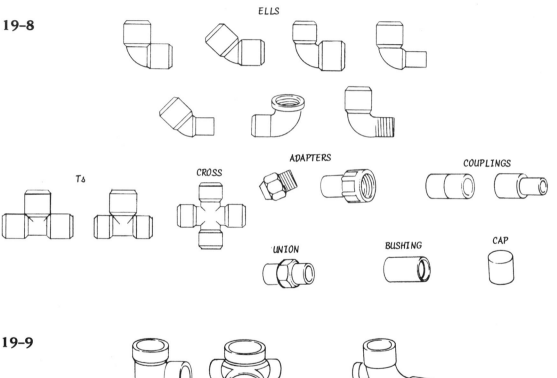

ELLS

Ts   CROSS   ADAPTERS   COUPLINGS

UNION   BUSHING   CAP

19–9

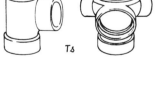

Ts   ELL

TRAP   Y   TURN

expensive, so the cost factor imposes limitations even though the simplicity of the soldered joints is appealing.

Soft-temper copper pipe (or tubing) is so flexible that it's possible, where codes allow, to make an entire run so that fittings are required only at the ends. Long, gentle curves are easy to form without special equipment, but tight bends, especially in short pieces, should be done with a special spring-type bender that will keep the material from kinking (**19–10**). These come in various sizes and are used by passing the tubing through them so the tool covers the bend area. You can do the actual bending over your knee, gently, or over a suitable curved surface. The bender is easy to remove if you rotate it as you pull it off.

Both types of copper pipe can be cut with a hacksaw or, for cleaner and more watertight joints, with a tube cutter, which is a smaller version of the pipe cutter (**19–11**).

19–10   **19–11**

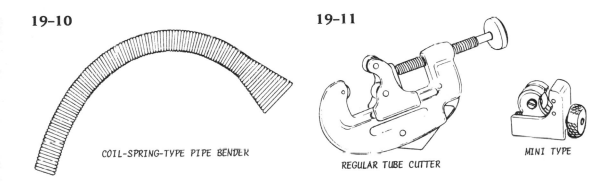

COIL-SPRING-TYPE PIPE BENDER

REGULAR TUBE CUTTER

MINI TYPE

Gripping the pipe in a vise is not good practice because the material is too soft to withstand much pressure. A better way is to rest the part on a flat surface and grip it firmly with your hand, or use a conventional miter box. The handle of the tube cutter, which is turned to bring the cutting wheel against the pipe, also supplies cutting pressure. This should be applied gradually, as excessive pressure can distort the pipe. Getting a smooth, clean cut is more important than doing it quickly. Most tube cutters have a triangular piece of metal attached that you use to remove burrs when the cut is complete. Hacksaw cuts can be cleaned with a smooth, round file.

SWEATING COPPER PIPES

All contact surfaces—the exterior of the pipe and the interior of the fitting—must be polished either with steel wool or a fine emery paper. There are also small, inexpensive steel-brush tool kits that make this job easy and quick. Check both the pipe and the fitting to be sure each is round and free of dents.

When installing runs, it's best to do all cutting, polishing, and fitting of joints first, and then move from point to point to do the soldering. Until you get the knack of measuring the pipe to allow for fittings, it's important to make dry runs to be sure that small errors in pipe lengths at fittings don't throw the run off of its target.

You seal joints with a propane torch, soldering flux, and solder. The important thing to remember is that the pipe and fitting are heated enough to melt the solder; the solder is not melted by the flame of the torch. Use a small stiff-bristle brush to coat all contact points with flux. Be a bit generous, as too much flux does no harm while too little can cause a poor joint. A typical soldering procedure is shown in **19–12**. Apply the flame to

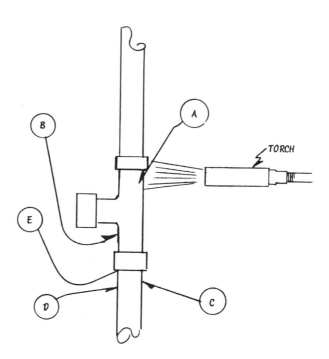

the heaviest part, usually the fitting (A), until it is hot enough for the solder to melt when touched at about point B. Then shift the flame to the pipe (C) but keep it about an inch away from the fitting. Heat the pipe until the solder readily melts when placed at about point D. When the parts are hot enough, press the tip of the solder against the joint (E), and capillary action will draw the solder to fill between pipe and fitting.

Hold the solder at that point until you see a full circle form around the joint. It's okay to keep applying heat for a few seconds longer, but don't overdo it or the solder may flow out. Don't touch the joint for a minute or so after the solder loses its brightness. Remember that the pipe and the solder, which can drip off the joint, are extremely hot and can cause serious burns. Wear safety gear, including gloves and safety glasses.

While standard copper supply pipes can be handled with sweat fittings, the flexible variety often is joined with flared fittings. This is convenient, involves no soldering, and provides joints that can be disassembled at any time with a pair of wrenches.

The flare is made after cutting and polishing the end of the tube (**19–13**). This is a critical procedure, as burrs, ridges, or ends that are not square will prevent a watertight seal. Don't use a reamer to the point where you bevel the inside edge of the tube. All you must do is remove burrs.

After it has been slipped through the flare nut, the tube is gripped in a die or flaring vise (**19–14**). The flaring tool, which has a threaded ram with a polished, cone-shaped tip, is placed on the die as shown in **19–15**. As you turn the ram, the cone bears against the tube and forms the flare. Use a touch of wax or oil on the cone and do the turning slowly. Check the flare carefully, and if it is flawed in any way cut it off and do the job over. Bring the nut up against the flare and put the fitting in place (**19–16**). Tighten it by using two open-end wrenches. In the case shown, the fitting serves as a coupling to join two lengths of tubing.

CAST-IRON PIPE

Cast-iron pipe is heavy and awkward to handle, but may be used for some parts of the DWV system. The ends are hub-shaped at one end (**19–17**), and joined so the hub is at the up side of a flow. Otherwise, solid wastes could lodge in the joint.

19–13

19–14

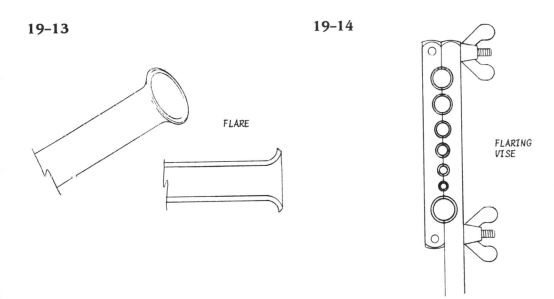

FLARE

FLARING VISE

19–15

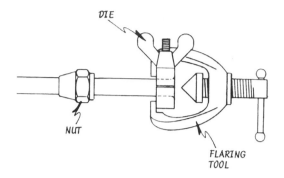

DIE

NUT

FLARING
TOOL

19–16

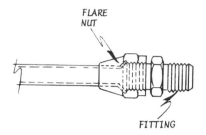

FLARE
NUT

FITTING

19–17

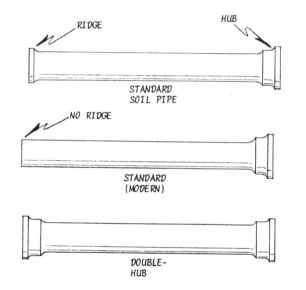

RIDGE   HUB

STANDARD
SOIL PIPE

NO RIDGE

STANDARD
(MODERN)

DOUBLE-
HUB

Like the other pipe materials, there are numerous types and sizes of fittings designed for cast-iron installations (**19–18**). Drainage fittings are designed to provide smooth inside surfaces so no shoulders can interrupt the passage of solid wastes (**19–19**).

To cut cast-iron pipe, rest it on a block of wood near the cut area. Use a hacksaw to form a slot about 1/16 inch deep completely around the pipe. Then work with a hammer or a light sledgehammer, tapping constantly as you rotate the pipe until it cracks along the slot (**19–20**). Another option is to use a cold chisel, tapping along the cut line until the pipe separates (**19–21**). The easiest approach is to rent a chain-tightened snap cutter.

19-18

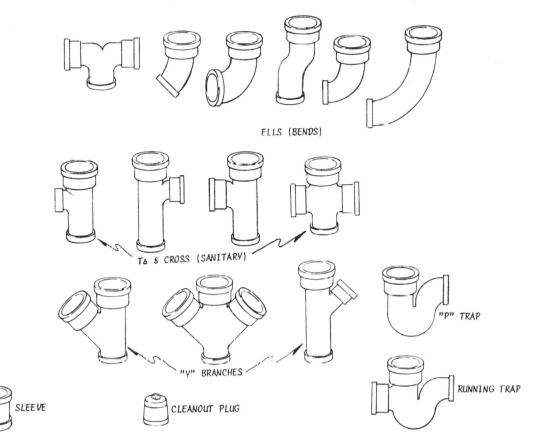

ELLS (BENDS)

T & CROSS (SANITARY)

"Y" BRANCHES

"P" TRAP

SLEEVE

CLEANOUT PLUG

RUNNING TRAP

19-19

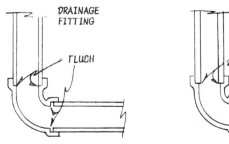

DRAINAGE
FITTING

FLUSH

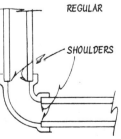

REGULAR

SHOULDERS

Cast-iron pipes are usually joined by caulking and leading in the connection. Fill the space in the joint with oakum, and then use an offset chisel, called a yarning iron, to force the oakum down tightly. Repeat the procedure, if necessary, until the space is about half filled. The remainder of the joint is filled with molten lead, which, when cool, is tamped down with caulking irons. An inside iron is used first, as shown in **19–22**, and then an outside iron, whose bevel is opposite the one on the inside iron, is used to tamp the outside edge of the lead.

The big job is melting the lead, but a plumber's furnace, which works with propane and includes a cast-iron pot and a ladle with a long handle, can be rented. Don't be careless

19–20   HOW TO CUT CAST-IRON PIPE

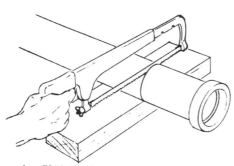

1. FORM 1/16-INCH SLOT ALL AROUND PIPE.

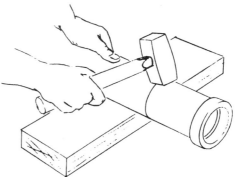

2. CRACK PIPE ALONG SLOT WITH HAMMER OR

19–21

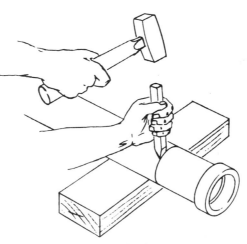

2A. USE A COLD CHISEL.

with molten lead. Wear leather gloves with long sleeves, and safety glasses or goggles. Pour carefully to avoid splatter. Don't pour lead if there is any moisture in the joint, as wetness can turn to steam, which can create enough pressure to explode the lead out of the joint. On angled runs, a joint runner contains the lead (**19–23**).

You'll find that the more commonly used connection today is a no-hub joint made with neoprene gaskets and stainless-steel sleeves. After the sleeves are in place, the clamps are tightened to secure the connection (**19–24**). It's as simple as that, and the joint can easily

19–22

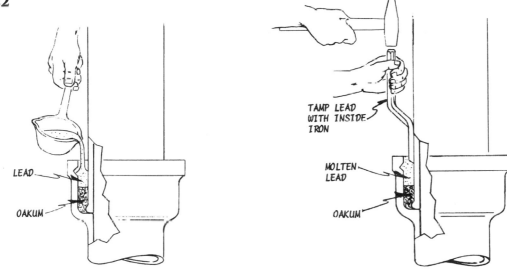

LEAD

OAKUM

TAMP LEAD WITH INSIDE IRON

MOLTEN LEAD

OAKUM

19–23

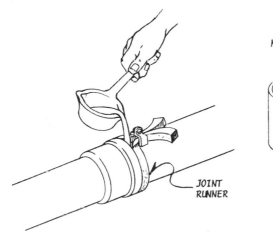

JOINT RUNNER

19–24

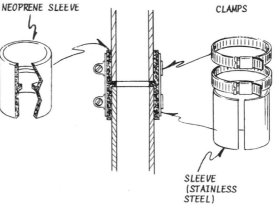

NEOPRENE SLEEVE

CLAMPS

SLEEVE (STAINLESS STEEL)

be opened for repairs or additions. This connection, often with double clamps on each side of the joint, also is commonly used on additions where a new, code-approved plastic system ties into an existing cast-iron line.

PLASTIC PIPE

Plastic is very easy to install, with one exception worth noting. There are likely to be some fixtures where you must install a metal valve with metal threads. Because you can't thread plastic pipe, you need to use an adapter, called a transition fitting, to join this connection to the plastic pipe system. Problems can arise if you make the assembly in the wrong order, and have to solder a metal connection near a plastic adapter that could deform from the extreme heat. One of the most common transitions is at a water heater where you need a fitting with female metal threads on one end and a female plastic pipe outlet on the other. You'll need Teflon plumber's tape on the water heater threads.

Connections at the hot-water heater must get special attention. For example, the heater's relief valve must coordinate with the water-pressure and temperature rating of the pipe. A quick check with local authorities will let you know if you can use plastic, and, if you can, how it should be installed.

The biggest benefit of plastic comes in the DWV system (**19–25**). It's much lighter and easier to fit than cast iron. Plastic is easy to cut with any saw that has fine teeth—a back-saw, hacksaw, crosscut saw, whatever. But you can also use a special tool that works much like those made for cutting metal pipe (**19–26**). Be sure that cuts are square and that you remove burrs from inside and outside edges. This can be done with a sharp knife or fine sandpaper.

Rigid plastic-pipe connections are made with a special solvent that literally welds the parts together. (You may want to use a prep solvent that basically cleans the surfaces and improves the bond.) The solvent works quickly, so you must be sure the parts fit and are aligned correctly. As with copper, it's wise to make a dry run first. Don't try to make a major adjustment after the solvent starts to set.

Read the instructions that come with the solvent very carefully. In all situations, contact surfaces should be dry and free of foreign matter, like oil or grease, that will prevent adhesion. Most instructions say to apply a thin coat of solvent inside the fitting and a heavier coat on the pipe. Use a brush that is wide enough to cover the joint area in a single swipe; you want to apply the cement quickly.

Put the pieces together immediately, using a short rotating action to join the alignment marks you made during the dry run. A good joint will show a bead of cement completely around the pipe at the fitting. Hold the parts tightly together for several seconds, and then wait for three or four minutes before doing more work in that same area. The instructions will tell you how long you should wait before conducting any watertightness tests.

19-25

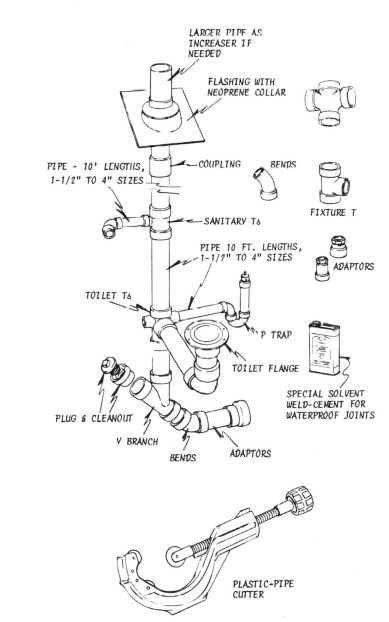

LARGER PIPE AS INCREASER IF NEEDED

FLASHING WITH NEOPRENE COLLAR

PIPE - 10' LENGTHS, 1-1/2" TO 4" SIZES

COUPLING

BENDS

FIXTURE T

SANITARY Ts

PIPE 10 FT. LENGTHS, 1-1/2" TO 4" SIZES

ADAPTORS

TOILET Ts

P TRAP

TOILET FLANGE

PLUG & CLEANOUT

SPECIAL SOLVENT WELD-CEMENT FOR WATERPROOF JOINTS

V BRANCH

BENDS

ADAPTORS

19-26

PLASTIC-PIPE CUTTER

THE PLUMBER AS CARPENTER

You should plan the plumbing system to minimize cutting of framing members, although some is inevitable. But once you've taken the trouble to build a strong frame, don't weaken it by chopping out large sections of joists and studs to make way for pipes. If possible, hang pipes below joists, or plan to run them in the bays between timbers. Of course, notching makes it a lot easier to install a pipe. With bored holes you have to snake the pipe through each joist or stud, and possibly make extra connections.

On holes, you'll need to leave at least ¾ of an inch of wood between the hole and the face of the stud, and 2 inches or more on joists. On joists, stay in the outer third of the span, and limit the hole diameter to at least one-quarter of the joists' depth, although one-sixth is a safer margin. If you need to make a bigger hole that would eat away most of a timber, you need a bigger timber. In a pinch, you may get away with strengthening notched joists with a 2 × 4 at least 4 feet long (**19–27**).

Overall, it pays to check the plumbing plan when you frame—for instance, to build an oversize partition at a bath to allow for a 4-inch vent pipe in the wall.

19–27

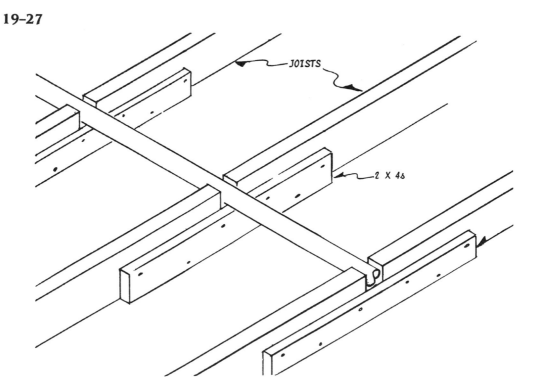

When pipes can run under or along joists, in a crawl space for example, notching will not be necessary, but the pipes should be supported at points not more than 10 feet apart with pipe clamps (**19–28**). Use copper clamps and nails with copper pipe. Any type of clamp can be used with plastic pipe, but it must fit loosely so that the plastic can expand. Also, plastic pipe should be supported at more frequent intervals of 4 to 6 feet.

The depth of notches cut in studs for pipes that run horizontally should be kept to a minimum—no more or less than the pipe needs. If you're running two pipes, stack them instead of burrowing more deeply into the stud. To protect wall-notched pipes from punctures during drywall, add metal covers over the notches as shown in **19–29**. Codes generally let this go if the pipe is at least 1¼ inches from the front of the stud. You may need to add additional studs placed as shown in **19–30**.

Closet bends, which are the connections that run between the floor flange of the toilet and the soil stack, can create problems because they are bulky (**19–31**). Whenever possible, position the bend between joists and use blocking and shims to support it and maintain its alignment (**19–32**). If the bend can be fitted by notching a joist, make the cut as small as possible and add compensating braces on each side.

If you must cut away a portion of a joist, then doubled headers, and, possibly, trimmers should be added for any opening through a floor frame (**19–33**).

Stacks, especially when they are made with cast-iron pipe, represent a considerable

19–28

19–29

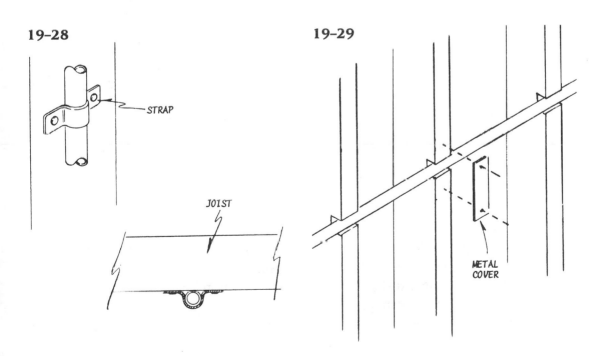

19–30

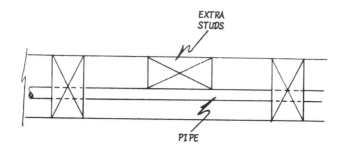

19–31

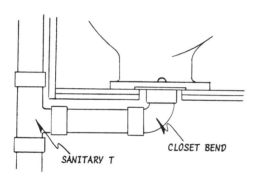

19–32

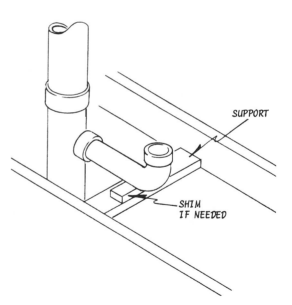

amount of weight that will rest entirely on the house drain unless intermediate support is provided. It's a good idea to transfer some of this weight to each floor frame that the stack passes through by installing additional frame pieces along the lines shown in **19–34**. Special braces that run between studs are available for large-diameter pipes. Horizontal runs of drain line in exposed situations (crawl spaces and basements) can be supported with special heavy-duty pipe straps (**19–35**).

All waste lines must be pitched toward the sewer pipe. A slope of about ¼-inch pitch

19–33

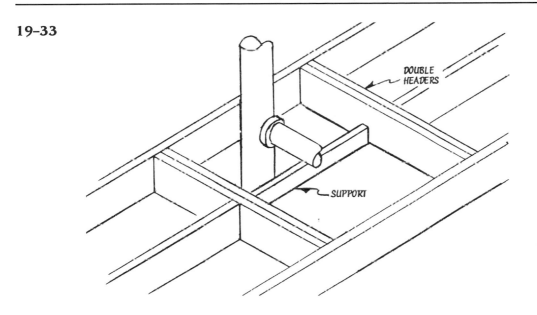

19–34

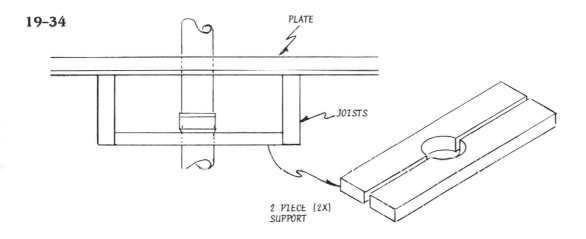

per foot of run allows waste to move most freely. At the other extreme, a pitch of 45 degrees or more poses no problems as the solids slide easily. If you can't make the run with the general pitch ratio of ¼-inch to a maximum of ½-inch per foot, you may be able to install the major part of the run using the ideal pitch and slope the remainder at 45 degrees (**19–36**).

19–35

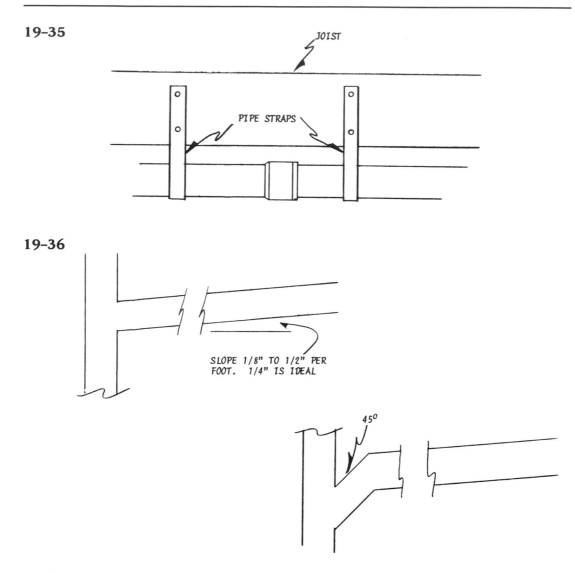

19–36

SLOPE 1/8" TO 1/2" PER FOOT. 1/4" IS IDEAL

45°

AIR CHAMBERS

A pipe-banging sound, generally called water hammering, can stem from air pockets in the pipe that create compartments of water that bump through the system instead of streaming through in a continuous flow. You also can hear rattling when a flow of pressurized water is stopped abruptly, for instance, by an automatic valve in a clothes washer cutting off the fill cycle. The force of the water can jar the pipe, and make quite a racket when the pipe vibrates against a wall stud.

To solve the problem of air pockets (after cutting off the water supply, of course), replace worn washers in faucets that allow air to be siphoned into the system when the faucet is closed. The most likely candidates are older fixtures, and faucets that drip.

To eliminate the banging, install what amounts to a shock absorber in the line (**19–37**) near the noisy pipes. The most basic is a length of pipe 18 to 24 inches long mounted

19–37

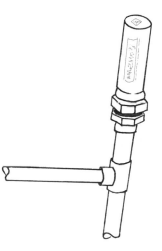

vertically in a T-fitting. The pipe is capped; it doesn't carry water anywhere. But the air filled section takes up some of the jolting force like a shock absorber on the wheel of a car. Modern devices have a gas-filled device, and generally a small bellows inside a fluid- or gas-filled chamber that provides more cushioning.

VENTING

As we've stressed already, in order for the drainage system to operate correctly it must be vented to admit air and to pass off sewer gases. There are many ways to design vent systems and many pros and cons for each. The principal guidance factor is to do it as simply and economically as possible while still staying within local codes.

The sketches that follow should not be accepted as architectural designs, but they can be the basis for a discussion with the local plumbing inspector. They may well need to be altered to suit your needs specifically and to satisfy local codes and practices.

Figure 19–38 shows a reasonable DWV installation for a two-story house. Notice that while the solid lines show how it can be done, the dotted lines indicate additional venting that local codes may call for. Notice that the sink trap at the right side of the figure does

19–38

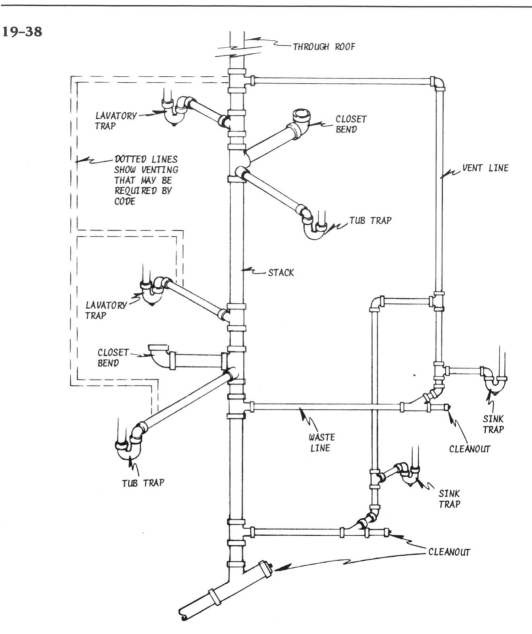

not indicate a vent for the fixture, which may be required, as shown above the lavatory trap slightly higher on the left side of the figure.

In the bathroom setup in **19–39**, both the tub and the lavatory will be back-vented to the main stack. Notice that the drain line is sloped toward the stack so water can flow out more readily.

19–39

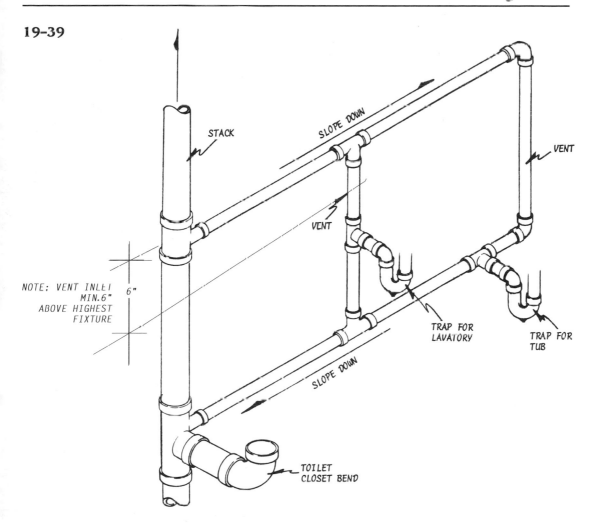

STACK

SLOPE DOWN

VENT

VENT

NOTE: VENT INLET MIN.6" ABOVE HIGHEST FIXTURE

6"

TRAP FOR LAVATORY

TRAP FOR TUB

SLOPE DOWN

TOILET CLOSET BEND

For a half-bath, you can do something along the lines shown in **19–40**. This is called wet venting and is not permitted by all codes, even though it makes for a rather simple installation. As shown in the previous figure, you probably will need a vertical vent extending up from the lavatory drain line as shown in the dry-venting system (**19–41**). If the alternate vent is permitted, codes typically call for it to be no less than 6 inches above the highest fixture.

A typical installation for a washing machine is shown in **19–42**. Notice the pneumatic anti-hammer devices on each line where pipe noise is most likely to result from the solenoid valves in the washing machine. The drain runs off to a main stack, which might also be the vent for the system, or the drain might be interrupted on the sewer side of the trap with a through-the-roof vent of its own.

19–40

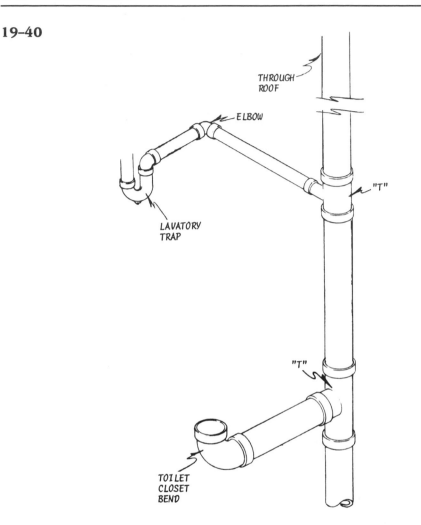

THROUGH ROOF

ELBOW

"T"

LAVATORY TRAP

"T"

TOILET CLOSET BEND

There is always the possibility that secondary vents, being smaller than main vents, will become clogged in snowy or wet and cold weather. For this reason, in some areas, the size of the vent pipe is increased where it passes through the roof (**19–43**).

PIPE INSULATION

Pipe insulation can keep cold-water pipes from sweating when the weather is hot and will reduce heat loss from hot-water pipes. The materials do not cost much and they help minimize maintenance costs. The job can be done in various ways, including spiral-wrap insu-

19-41

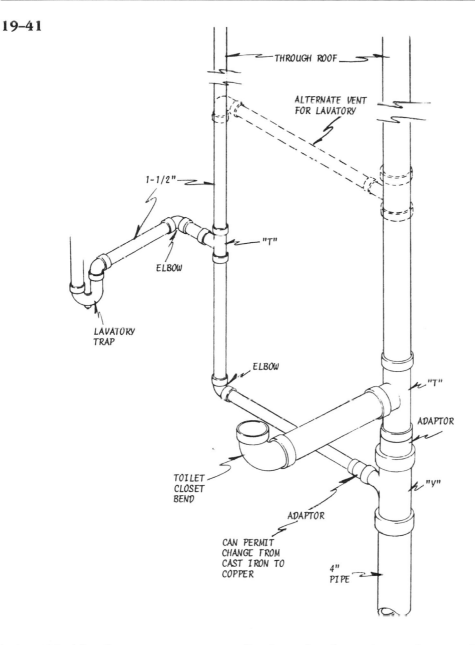

THROUGH ROOF

ALTERNATE VENT
FOR LAVATORY

1-1/2"

"T"

ELBOW

LAVATORY
TRAP

ELBOW

"T"

ADAPTOR

TOILET
CLOSET
BEND

"Y"

ADAPTOR

CAN PERMIT
CHANGE FROM
CAST IRON TO
COPPER

4"
PIPE

lation (**19-44**). The most common application (also the easiest and most effective) is to use snap-on foam tubes (**19-45**). They are available in flexible lengths and diameters to fit different size pipes. A special tape that you buy with the insulation is used to hold the pieces in place and to seal the joints.

19–42

19–43

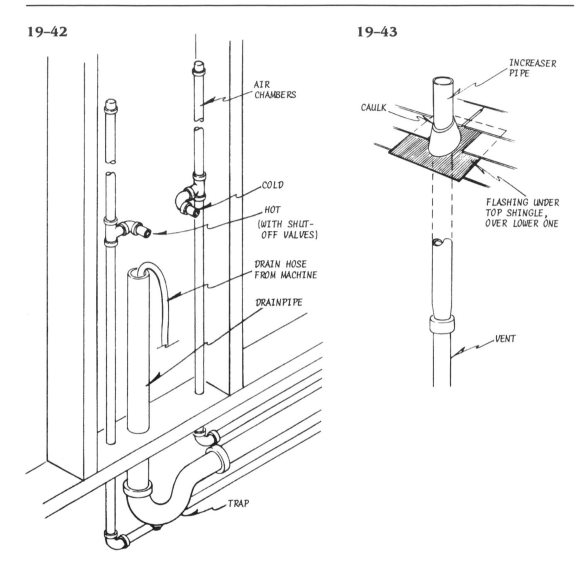

AIR CHAMBERS

COLD

HOT (WITH SHUT-OFF VALVES)

DRAIN HOSE FROM MACHINE

DRAINPIPE

TRAP

INCREASER PIPE

CAULK

FLASHING UNDER TOP SHINGLE, OVER LOWER ONE

VENT

LOW-VOLUME TOILETS

It may not seem fair to pick on one weak link in the codes, but low-volume toilets are an item you should know about. Home owners have talked about the problem since 1992 when the Department of Energy mandated low-volume flush toilets as a water conservation measure. The units are about the same size as older designs but use half the water— 1.6 gallons instead of 3.2 gallons per flush. Overall, replacing conventional toilets with

19-44   SPIRAL-WRAP INSULATION

19-45   FOAM-COLLAR INSULATION

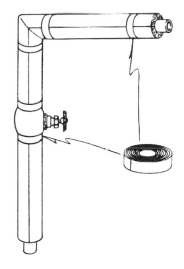

low-flow models has the potential to save up to 12,000 gallons a year in a typical household. But home owners and builders have had problems.

A recent nationwide survey of builders and home owners conducted by the National Association of Home Builders Research Center found that four out of five builders experienced problems with low-flush units. Most builders surveyed also said that they receive more callbacks on low-flush toilets than on anything else.

There are four common complaints: multiple flushes are needed to clear solids from the bowls; residue remains in the bowl even after multiple flushes; they clog easily; and they require more maintenance than 3.2-gallon models and cause more damage due to overflows. Although many builders said new low-flush units perform better than the first models, the NAHB survey found that 60 percent of builders and 28 percent of home owners experienced so much trouble that they contacted plumbers in what they described as futile attempts to solve the problems. While many of the reported service calls were under $200, nine percent cost up to $500 and more due to damage from overflows.

In the end, home owners are left to cope as best they can with the problems. Some try to adjust the fill mechanisms to increase the amount of water in the holding tank. Most revert to double flushing, which defeats much of the water-conservation potential of low-flush systems. This tactic may skew many of the surveys that show how much water low-flush units can save.

If you have a choice in the matter, there are three basic types of low-flush units to choose from, although one is largely commercial:

1. Gravity-tank toilets, the most common and inexpensive, have a bowl and a tank, and depend on the volume of water in the tank to flush wastes. In theory, they require water pressure of 15 psi.
2. Flushometer toilets, typically used in commercial buildings, have no tanks and are flushed with a hand level at a pressure-sensitive valve. They also depend on water pressure to flush wastes, but normally operate with higher water pressure.
3. Pressure-tank toilets, the other residential alternative, look like gravity models but have a secondary container inside the tank. It uses the pressure of water coming into the main tank to compress air trapped in the inner tank. The compressed air gives each flush a pressure assist to push out wastes instead of pulling them out with the siphon action of a gravity unit. This hybrid design normally operates with 25 to 35 psi of water pressure, and is roughly twice the cost of basic gravity units.

20 WIRING

The most sensible recommendation for the greatest number of owner–builders is to leave the mechanical installations, including the electrical system in particular, to licensed, professional contractors. This is the one area where it really makes sense to subcontract the work because even simple mistakes with wiring can be lethal (to yourself and the house in terms of a fire), while mistakes with woodworking, roofing, and most other trades only lead to extra maintenance and repair work.

It's not that you won't be able to strip a wire lead or connect a breaker. In fact, the tools and skills required for most wiring installations are very basic. The crux of the work is in the planning. And there are so many components and possible variables in a residential wiring plan that the job requires an extensive knowledge of codes.

Construction codes about framing are a lot to cope with, but in addition you have plumbing codes, and now electrical codes, as well. These are especially voluminous, and fill a book much larger than this one called the National Electrical Code (NEC), which is actually a registered trademark of the National Fire Protection Association (NFPA). This international nonprofit group, which publishes the NEC and other codes, is comprised of 75,000 members, including more than 80 national trade and professional organizations. It's not a do-it-yourself oriented group.

Bear in mind that electricians spend years on the job as apprentices, attending classes as well, and then must pass a difficult exam to receive a license. There just is no way for an owner–builder to leaf through pages of codes and absorb enough information to safely wire a modern house. That may sound discouraging, but it's the safest advice. And in some regions you'll have no choice because, as a practical matter, new house wiring must be installed by licensed electricians. Even your local utility company may refuse to bring power to the house if the inlet mast, generally called the service head, and main service panel are not installed to very precise specifications.

437

Local codes often allow an owner–builder to do some or even all of the work. But it must be done to the standards of licensed contractors whom inspectors are used to dealing with. Generally, there is much wider tolerance of owner–builder errors and omissions in general construction and carpentry than in electrical work. Electrical inspections tend to be technical and exacting.

A case in point is New York State, where electrical work is not overseen by the local building inspector, who is expected to know about foundations, framing, insulation, ventilation and roofing and more. Instead, you must apply for permits and receive inspection certificates from the New York Board of Fire Underwriters, which sends out its own inspectors who specialize in electrical installations. If you don't get the Board's certificate, you don't get the main building inspector's Certificate of Occupancy for the entire project.

Of course, you don't need a permit to make routine repairs, such as installing replacement switches and outlets and such. But in some cases you can't legally move an existing outlet or switch box without a permit. Also, you generally don't need a permit to work with low-voltage wiring where the risks of serious injury are minor compared to working with standard household voltages of 120 and 240. In New York, at least, the Board doesn't need to check your wiring on a low-voltage doorbell. The threshold typically is 25 volts or less. Anything more and you are in for the full treatment of paperwork and field inspections.

The upshot is that trying to wire your own house from scratch has many possible downsides, balanced only by saving the labor costs of hiring a contractor. (Materials are a wash, and contractors often get discounts at supply houses that are not available to one-time do-it-yourself buyers.) With this in mind, you'll find that the circuit plans and wiring diagrams in this section represent only a guide to some of the most common applications. You'll need to check your plans in detail with local inspectors.

For most do-it-yourselfers, it's enough to work safely with electricity as it applies to power tools on the job, a temporary service on a raw construction site, and the safe use of extension cords and other electrical construction equipment. So whether or not you participate in wiring the house to some degree, it's wise to start by familiarizing yourself with some of the most basic cautions that can help you avoid electrical hazards.

BASIC ELECTRICAL SAFETY

You may have felt the ominous buzz of electricity in your hand using an old power drill with worn wires outside in wet weather. Maybe you pulled on a frayed plug and experienced the arm-numbing and potentially lethal jolt of 110 volts. It doesn't happen very often because modern household wiring, appliances, and tools are designed to prevent shocks. There are many layers of protection, and it pays to know how they work—and how you can guard against problems that occasionally slip through the safety net.

1. Built-in shock protection. Safety is provided from the point where electricity enters the house, and through the network of wiring to fixtures it powers. At the service panel there is a main cutoff, typically a double toggle at the top of the box, that shuts off all power. Next in line are individual circuit breakers in rows beneath the main cutoff. Each controls a loop of wiring that services a specific part of the house. Some circuits feed several lights and outlets, others only a single appliance that uses a lot of electricity, such as a kitchen range.

    A severe electrical problem may trip the main breaker—the one you should trip if there's an emergency and you're not sure where the problem lies—although trouble normally is isolated and trips only the breaker on the problem circuit. Breakers provide the same function that fuses do in older homes, but they can be reset instead of replaced once you correct the problem that caused the trip. If you restore a breaker on a circuit that has a short in the wiring, it will immediately trip again, and again. You're still protected against shock, but repeated spurts of power across frayed wires can cause sparks and start a fire.

2. The next layer of protection is provided by grounded wiring. This is a key part of any wiring system that is required by code and cannot be omitted under any circumstances. Generally, grounds are connected between wires coming into a box (**20–1**) to the fixture the box serves, such as a switch or outlet, and to the box itself if it's metal (**20–2**). Most new installations today are made with plastic boxes with grounds connected in twist-on connectors only.

20–1   GROUNDING WIRES

20–2   RECEPTACLE GROUNDING

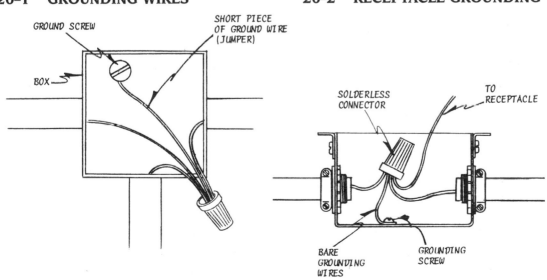

If you pulled two-wire cable through the framing you could hook up power to run the entire house electrical system with only a few exceptions, such as three-way switches controlling one light from two locations that require an extra wire. But an inspector would make you start from scratch with three-wire cable, generally called two-wire with ground, to link every fixture, switch and outlet back to a grounding rod.

Grounding is a crucial part of code-approved wiring because power flows through the path of least resistance, including your body if you happen to be touching part of the system when there is a problem. If power escapes from its normal path—when a loose wire contacts a metal switch box you may be touching, for example—you want it to travel through the grounding wire, which has less resistance than your body. The interconnected grounding system will carry the power all the way back to a grounding rod sunk deep in the dirt just outside the house where the power dissipates and does no harm. You can't have breaks in the ground chain. For example, where grounding is permitted on metal pipes, you need to install a jumper wire to bridge plastic fittings or a meter that would interrupt the grounding chain. Codes on grounding are exacting, down to the size of the grounding rod and how it must be buried.

3. More protection is provided by ground-fault circuit interrupters (GFCIs) at electrical outlets that are most likely to produce a shock because they are close to sources of water. They are more sensitive than standard breakers and trip instantaneously. GFCIs are required in all new baths, kitchen countertop outlets, laundries, garages, unfinished areas such as crawl spaces, and exterior outlets. GFCIs also are required in other circuits where contact with water is possible, such as a circuit powering a whirlpool tub, and to protect the temporary power setup on a construction site. This, now-standard safety device is available in many forms. It can be installed in the main service panel instead of standard breakers, in circuits instead of standard receptacles (the most common application), and as plug-ins to protect one tool or appliance.

4. Finally, some electrical appliances, including hair dryers manufactured since 1991, are equipped with devices such as appliance leakage current interrupters (ALCIs), or immersion detection circuit interrupters (IDCIs), which give extra protection against shock when an appliance is accidentally dropped in water.

Overall, this many layers of protection may seem to form a foolproof system. But there are a few trouble spots where the risk of electrical problems can escalate, particularly on a construction site, often without anyone knowing about it:

1. Extension cords. Check the UL label and you'll find that there are different types for different uses (inside versus outside, for instance), and cords with different wattage ratings. A standard household extension cord may be fine for a lamp with a 100-watt bulb. But plug it into a heater or a heavy-duty table saw and the cord can heat up and

start a fire. If you need to warm up a house under construction before the heating system is installed, the extension cord wattage rating should be 1.25 times the rating of the appliance, for example, 1,875 watts for a 1,500-watt heater. As you probably will be using many extension cords on a building project, you should be sure they are in good shape, and rated to provide both the power they will be carrying and the power required by the tool you're using.

2. Working on wiring. At any stage of any wiring job, you must be sure that the wires are not hot, i.e. not carrying any power. This is obviously not a problem when you're pulling cables. Once the system is wired back to the panel, however, there may be many times when you go back to install a special fixture or tap into the wiring system for some reason.

   You could trip the main breaker first, but that leaves the house dark, and creates other complications such as restarting major appliances. Generally, you can trip the breaker controlling the circuit you're working on. Some people plug a lamp into an outlet as a double-check. When the light goes out, the power must be off, they reason. But there are exceptions to what seems like a sensible on-off signal. Circuits may control wiring in a patchwork pattern. The upper outlet in a duplex receptacle sometimes is controlled by one breaker while the lower outlet is controlled by another. Sometimes power seems to be off at a wall switch, while an extra wire in the box from another switch is still hot.

Eliminate the risks two ways. First, make sure of the circuit layout by making a detailed map of the system (what controls what), and posting it at the main service panel. Second, after the correct breaker is tripped, double-check wires and outlets with a neon test light (**20–3**). These small, inexpensive devices have two metal leads. Hold them on the plastic behind the bare metal, and insert them into each side of the outlet—where the prongs on a plug go. If the power is off, the tester bulb won't light. You also may find it useful to use a simple outlet (receptacle) tester, which has three lights used in different combinations to indicate different conditions, or a multi-tester, which is a more complicated and expensive professional electrical analyzing tool. Always confirm with a tester that the power is off before you work on the wiring system.

20–3

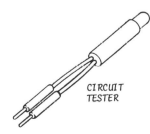

CIRCUIT TESTER

On a raw construction site, it's important to use grounded cords from a GFCI-protected temporary service feeding power to insulated tools. If the inspector doesn't fill you in about setting up the temporary lines, the local utility company will.

Finally, always work with materials that are tested and listed by Underwriters Laboratories. Such products are stamped or labeled with the UL identification so you know that they have been tested to meet accepted quality and safety standards.

POWER FLOW

Plumbing and electrical systems carry different materials that can't be mixed. But the two systems have some things in common. Both make an entrance through a main line (and often a meter), which then branches off to points of use with interrupters included in the layout so it can be shut down entirely or at isolated points.

The shutoffs in water line are operated manually with valves. Those in an old electrical system also are operated manually with fuses, but nowadays automatically with circuit breakers. You might view the incoming current as having to pass through a main gate before it can service smaller gates, which are the controls for branch lines in the form of individual circuits (**20–4**).

The larger the water pipe, the greater the flow of water. Similarly, the larger the wire, the greater the flow of current. Water flow is stated as so many gallons per minute, with pressure as pounds per square inch. In essence, the flow of electric current is stated as amperage, while the pressure is voltage (**20–5**). Wattage, which is a measurement of the total energy flowing in a circuit at a given time, is expressed by a combination: wattage = amperage X voltage.

As a rule (there are many exceptions to rules in electrical systems), black-insulated wires are always connected to black wires, white-insulated wires to white wires, and green-insulated or bare metal ground wires to other ground wires in addition to the fixtures, such as a metal switch box, that they ground.

Almost always, power flows in under pressure through black wires (hot wires) that are like water-supply pipes. In some situations, you may also use black wires with white markings or all-red wires, both of which are for hot lines carrying power at full voltage.

Just as depressurized water leaves through a drain line, electrical current flows back to the service panel through white wires that are neutral, or not pressurized, and at zero voltage. The ground wires (green or bare copper) form a chain of protection to carry power that escapes from this basic loop trying to make a short circuit, possibly through your body, back to a grounding rod.

20–4

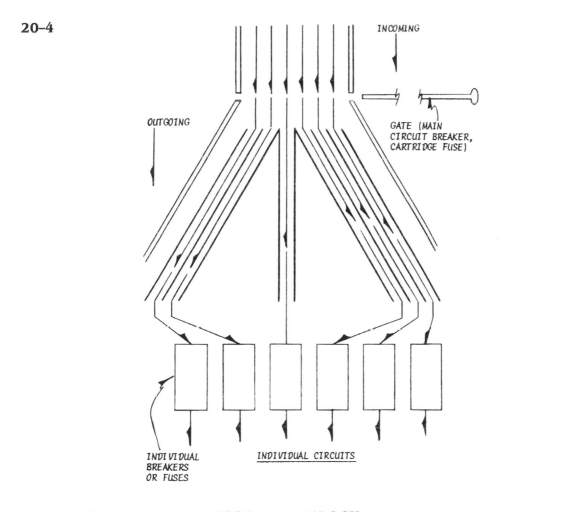

INCOMING

OUTGOING

GATE (MAIN
CIRCUIT BREAKER,
CARTRIDGE FUSE)

INDIVIDUAL
BREAKERS
OR FUSES

INDIVIDUAL CIRCUITS

20–5   WATER-PIPE/ELECTRIC-WIRE ANALOGY

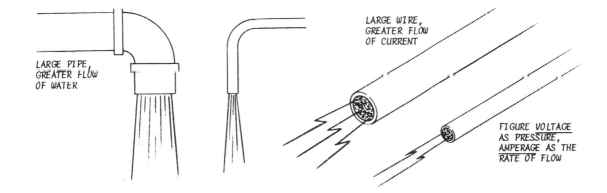

LARGE PIPE,
GREATER FLOW
OF WATER

LARGE WIRE,
GREATER FLOW
OF CURRENT

FIGURE VOLTAGE
AS PRESSURE,
AMPERAGE AS THE
RATE OF FLOW

TYPES OF WIRING

There are many types of materials used in wiring systems, but those acceptable by codes for conventional, residential installations are usually nonmetallic sheathed cable (commonly referred to by the trade name Romex), flexible armored cable (commonly called BX), and wires that are pulled through thin-wall or rigid metal conduit (**20–6**). Often, the

20–6   TYPES OF WIRING

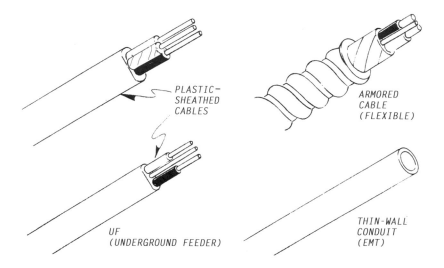

PLASTIC-
SHEATHED
CABLES

ARMORED
CABLE
(FLEXIBLE)

UF
(UNDERGROUND FEEDER)

THIN-WALL
CONDUIT
(EMT)

complete system may involve a combination of materials. For example, entrance wires may have to come through steel conduit while plastic-sheathed cable may be allowed anywhere inside. Generally, you'll use NM (nonmetallic) throughout the house, and conduit or UF (underground feeder) on some exterior lines. Remember that wire and cable type and size are closely controlled by code.

The number and the size of the wire is stamped on the insulation; for example, 12-2 means there are two #12 wires. If a ground wire is included, it is also noted. All wires are color-coded so you can identify them no matter where you make a cut. A two-wire cable will have a black and a white wire; with three wires, the colors generally will be black, white, and red. A ground wire, if it isn't bare, will usually have a green sheath. The different common sizes correspond to different uses (**20–7**), which can vary depending on the situation and the power requirements of the circuit or particular appliance. In most cases, standard interior circuits are run with NW 1½ G—that is, nonmetallic cable, which is flexible and

20-7   GROUNDING WIRE GAUGES, CAPACITIES AND USES

Gauge #	Capacity	Typical Use	
#6	60 amps, 240 volts	central AC; electric furnace	
#8	40 amps, 240 volts	electric range	
#10	30 amps, 240 volts	room AC; clothes dryer	
#12	20 amps, 120 volts	lights and outlets	
#14	15 amps, 120 volts	lights and outlets	
#16	10 amps, 24 volts	low-voltage lighting	
#18	7 amps, 24 volts	low-voltage bells, thermostats	

easy to install, containing two solid copper wires (one in a black sheath and one in white), plus a bare copper grounding wire.

Aluminum wire, which for a time was used as a replacement for copper, caused a lot of problems, including many house fires. Since 1971, codes call for outlets and switches to be marked CO/ALR, meaning their terminals won't tend to shift and loosen with aluminum wires, which was the cause of most aluminum wire problems. There are some situations where aluminum wire may be used, but you should stick to copper, which is likely to be standard practice in any case.

Some codes require that you use thin-wall conduit in several situations. (There is also stronger, thick-wall metal conduit and plastic conduit for some applications.) The hollow piping offers maximum protection for wires. But it's difficult to install, and then you have to pull all the wires you need through the pipe. It may be used indoors or out regardless of whether locations are damp or dry, for example, where an exterior line to an outbuilding leaves the house near the foundation and goes underground. But check to see if you must use a conduit heavier than thin-wall for an exterior application.

Although you'll find it commonly used in homes built through the 1940s, armored cable is not used much today, It sometimes is substituted for conduit where the nonflexible tubing would be difficult to install, or to connect permanently wired appliances.

WORKING WITH WIRES

Every type of cable requires different working techniques. The tools and methods you use on NM won't work on BX or conduit, at least not until you get to the wires. Stripping and attaching wires does require standardized methods.

With NM, you start with a cable ripper (**20-8**) that slices open the plastic sheath. You

20–8

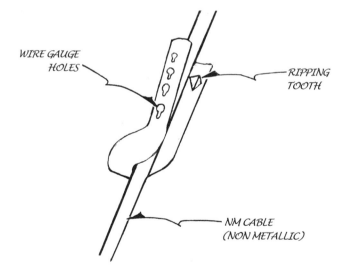

WIRE GAUGE HOLES

RIPPING TOOTH

NM CABLE (NON METALLIC)

generally rip 8 to 10 inches. Then cut away the excess sheath and paper wrapping inside with a cutting pliers. To strip the plastic sheath off each individual wire inside, use a wire stripper (**20–9**). A typical tool has cutting slots for different sizes of wire. When you put the wire in the right slot, the tool will slice through the insulation without cutting into the wire. If you do this job by hand, with a knife, for example, you are likely to nick the wire, which can cause breaks and lead to problems when you connect the bare lead to a fixture.

Wire ends should be looped to fit under a terminal screw and placed clockwise with the same rotation as the screw so the loop tends to close as you tighten the connection (**20–10**). The loops can be made with pliers only, but if you force a small piece of tubing over one jaw and then use the pliers as shown in **20–11**, you'll get uniform results.

Some receptacles have holes in the back, so you don't have to use screws at all. In this case, the stripped end is pressed into the hole, where it locks and makes the connection (**20–12**). Some of these items have a gauge stamped on the back so you can tell exactly how much of the wire should be bared. Inspectors have reported some problems with

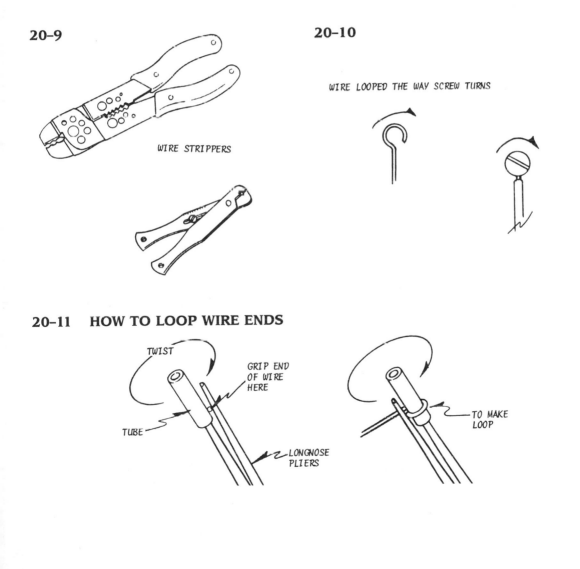

20–9

WIRE STRIPPERS

20–10

WIRE LOOPED THE WAY SCREW TURNS

20–11 HOW TO LOOP WIRE ENDS

TWIST

GRIP END OF WIRE HERE

TUBE

LONGNOSE PLIERS

TO MAKE LOOP

these connections, so you should be sure that back-wiring is allowed before you use fittings with this feature.

To make wire-to-wire connections, spiral together the stripped leads and twist on a wire connector (**20–13**), often called by the trade name Wire Nut. They come in various sizes, so you need to select the connector to fit the type and number of wires you are working with.

When you run NM cable, remember to drill holes at least 1½ inches back from the stud face so that drywall nails will not puncture the cable. If you notch or run wires closer for some reason, you must install protective nailing plates.

The main skill with BX is to cut the cable without cutting the wires inside. The basic

20–12   **20–13**

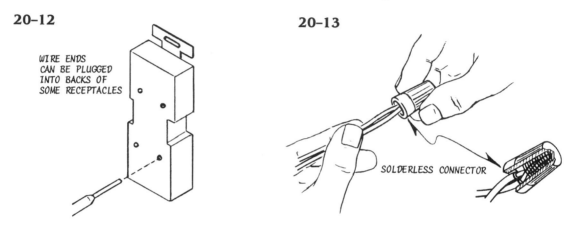

WIRE ENDS CAN BE PLUGGED INTO BACKS OF SOME RECEPTACLES

SOLDERLESS CONNECTOR

approach (**20–14**) is to hold the cable firmly and use a hacksaw at an angle to cut through one strip of the armor. All you want to do is cut through the thickness of the strip. Grasp the cable on each side of the cut and twist your hands in opposite directions so the armor will break and permit you to cut the wires. Repeat the procedure about 10 inches back from the cut end so you can remove the unwanted section of armor and protective paper.

There also are modern tools that make this job much easier. You simply slide the cable into the hand-held tool, lock down a screw on the cable, and press the handle to make your cut. A special plastic bushing, generally called an anti-short, must be inserted between the wires and the armor. Then the BX is fitted into a variety of metal connectors and secured with a screw built into the connector.

With metal conduit, you use a hacksaw. Bending the pipe to suit the installation is more difficult, and requires a special tool (**20–15**) to prevent crimping. To pull wires through conduit, you'll need a fish tape (**20–16**). The tape is strong but quite thin and flexible, so

20-14   CONNECTING ARMORED CABLE TO BOX

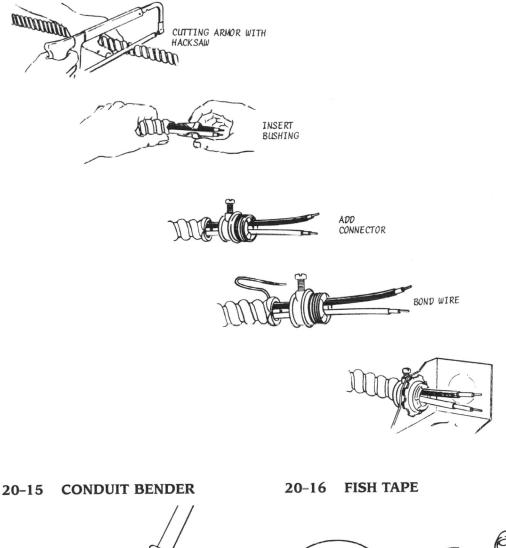

CUTTING ARMOR WITH HACKSAW

INSERT BUSHING

ADD CONNECTOR

BOND WIRE

TIGHTEN LOCK NUT

20-15   CONDUIT BENDER

20-16   FISH TAPE

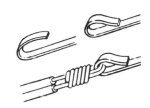

you can easily feed it through a run of conduit. Nevertheless, the job is best done with two people—one to feed the wires in at one end, the other to pull on the tape at the other end.

BRINGING IN POWER

The total amount of power in a house can vary widely, and you need to decide how much power to provide. In electrician's parlance, that means how big a service (**20–17**). The classic house of the 1950s had a 50-amp service. That denotes the amount of power supplied by the local utility company to the main breaker or fuse panel. In older homes, that power was split into only six or eight separate circuits. Today, to handle a standard load

20–17

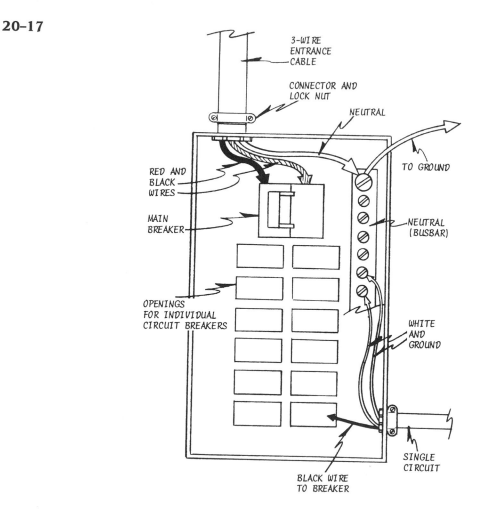

of modern appliances, even a modest-sized house needs at least a 100 amp service (150- and 200-amp services are common) and generally 16 or more circuits that distribute power evenly throughout the building.

Even small houses with electric heat often need 200-amp capacity, starting with the 16- plus circuit array, and another group of circuits (maybe 10 or more) to handle the heating equipment. To prevent overloads and balance the draw of power, houses with a combination of electric heating and air-conditioning may have those units on a separate 100- amp panel.

Ideally, every house should have a wiring plan matched to the building and the lifestyle of the people who live there. Problems can develop if the basic hardware can't handle the demand, or if it doesn't distribute power where you need it. That's the main reason that electrical codes mandate thorough and evenly spaced coverage with outlets and switches.

There are many codes about getting power from the street to the service, including tight restrictions on the service head, height and location of wires, and more.

DRAWING A PLAN

Don't try to work out your electrical system as you are actually installing the wires. Do it on paper first so you can make corrections with an eraser. The final diagram should be something you can present to the inspector. Professional drawings are neat because they are made with symbols and abbreviations to indicate runs of wire and wiring devices. There are many of these, and you can probably pick up a chart that shows them all, but the ones in **20-18** have been selected as being most applicable for a residential installation. Another way to go is to use an electrical-symbols template, which you can buy at most stores selling art supplies.

You can, if you wish, make a floor plan of each room on those sheets of paper you used to list electrical requirements. Then you can use the symbols to indicate where lights, outlets, and the like should go. You might even include wire runs to see what must enter the room to feed the equipment.

Eventually, you must produce an overall layout done on a floor plan that is drawn, preferably, to scale (**20-19**). This will be easier to do if you work on paper that has been squared so each square can represent an actual square foot of the house. If you wish to play safe, do the floor plan on the squared paper but the electrical layout on an overlay of tracing paper. Then you can make as many changes as you wish and, finally, add to the floor plan what you accept and what you will present to the inspector. **Figures 20-19** and **20-20** are not designs to follow but merely examples of working drawings you can display to an inspector for discussion.

20–18   WIRING SYMBOLS

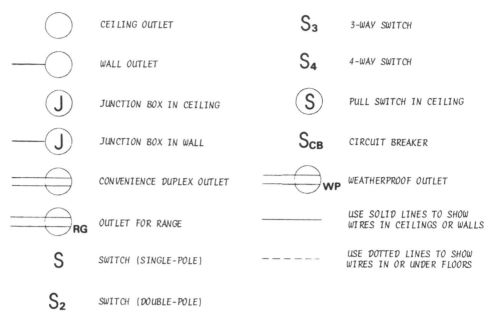

○   CEILING OUTLET S_3 3-WAY SWITCH

—○   WALL OUTLET S_4 4-WAY SWITCH

Ⓙ   JUNCTION BOX IN CEILING   Ⓢ   PULL SWITCH IN CEILING

—Ⓙ   JUNCTION BOX IN WALL S_{CB} CIRCUIT BREAKER

⊖   CONVENIENCE DUPLEX OUTLET   ⊖WP   WEATHERPROOF OUTLET

⊖RG   OUTLET FOR RANGE   ———————— USE SOLID LINES TO SHOW
                                                       WIRES IN CEILINGS OR WALLS

S   SWITCH (SINGLE-POLE)   - - - - - USE DOTTED LINES TO SHOW
                                                        WIRES IN OR UNDER FLOORS

S_2 SWITCH (DOUBLE-POLE)

20–19

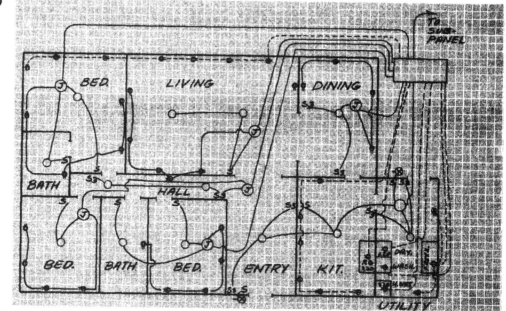

20–20   SAMPLE DO-IT-YOURSELF PLAN

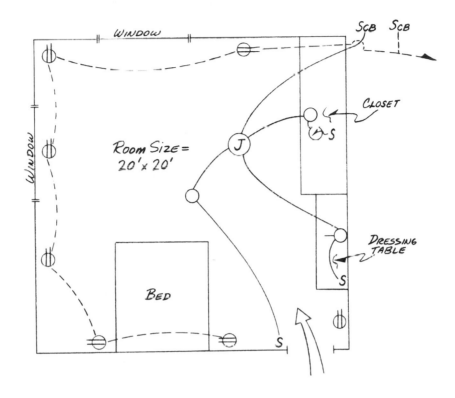

THE BASIC CIRCUIT

A circuit is a part of the electrical system with its own wires and its own circuit breaker that feeds a particular area of the house or, sometimes, a single appliance. Codes dictate the minimum number of circuits, based primarily on the square footage of the house and the expected load. The best plan is to overbuild, for example, by installing a service with room for additional circuits in the future that might serve a nonfinished attic, for example.

The smart way is to obey the codes as far as the mechanical installation is concerned but to plan the system to handle your needs. There are many advantages in having a considerable number of individual circuits. You can plan lights and outlets so no large area of the house will be in darkness should a breaker trip. With many circuits, the total load can be more equally divided so no one set of wires or breaker will have to carry more than it should. Voltage drop in each circuit will be less, so appliances and lights will operate more efficiently and power waste will be minimized. What you can carry on a circuit depends on the amperage capacity of the wire, which relates to wire size, and the ampere rating of the breaker.

SAMPLE WIRING DIAGRAMS

It's best to do the wiring after all boxes have been installed and you can plan the shortest routes for cable. Because the number of wires in plastic-sheathed cable is limited, there are situations where the run of the neutral wire is interrupted. This does not change the very important basic rule that the neutral wire must be continuous and never connected to a hot (black) wire. When an exception does occur, the white wire must be painted black at both ends of the connection so the strange use will always be evident.

The color of the terminals or lugs on receptacles, sockets, and the like will tell what wire must be connected to them. Hot wires go to copper or brass terminals, and terminals that are whitish in color receive the grounded neutral wire. Green terminals are for grounding wires. Ordinary switches have copper or brass terminals because they receive only hot wires. The common terminal on a three-way toggle switch has a special color to identify it. The diagrams that follow show installations with typical NM cable and a ground.

THE JUNCTION BOX

All connections that route power in different directions must be made in a junction box (**20–21**). Notice that black is connected to black, white to white, and that the grounding

20–21 BASIC JUNCTION

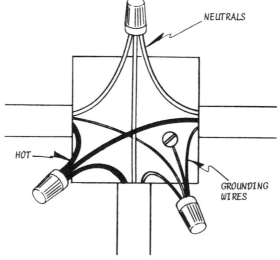

wires are continuous and also connected to the box. Pack the wires neatly inside the box after you have made the connections and then screw down the box cover.

The boxes must not be overcrowded, which sounds like simple and reasonable advice that would be easy to follow. But codes will dictate very precisely the number and size of the wires you can connect in a particular size box. Figuring out the limits can be a fairly complicated process if you're not used to what's allowed. Here's the drill. The NEC includes tables for different types of boxes with their available interior cubic inches, such as an 18-cubic-inch receptacle box. Then it lists every item that might be in the box, such as cable clamps, different types of cable, receptacles, etc., each by its own volume. You would need to add up all the items in the box by volume and compare the total to the allowable volume for the box to stay within code limits.

This is just one of many cases where lack of familiarity with codes can cost you a lot of time in research, or, worse yet, even more wasted effort when an inspector says you have to change the boxes or your overall circuit plan because the capacities are over the code limit. Your wiring could otherwise be perfect. But if the boxes were somewhat over-crowded with wires and connectors, you would have to pull out all your work and start from scratch.

LIGHTS

In some of these diagrams, you'll see it noted that the grounds are not shown. This is only to make the hot and neutral wiring more clear.

In every case you must, by code, install continuous grounds. For example, in the case of the first diagram of a wall switch controlling a ceiling light, the ground from the incoming cable would run to a connector. From the connector, there would be a short ground line to the metal box, the ground line running to the ground terminal of the switch, and a ground wire running to the fixture. This is typical of the grounding setup. You don't connect all grounds to a screw in a metal box. You "pigtail" to the box (if it's metal) from a connector where the grounds are tied together. Remember that the ground line is just as important as the wires carrying power, and must be installed according to code.

The wall switch in **20–22** controls a ceiling light that is located at the end of a run. The neutral wire must be coded with black at the points marked A because it becomes a hot wire. This is one of the neutral-wire rule exceptions.

In the situation in **20–23**, the current is entering at the switch. The black wire is broken to connect to the switch, but the white wire is continuous and therefore is not hot. **Figure 20–24** shows the same situation, but with grounding wires included.

A run that is interrupted to provide a switch that will control more than one light can be wired as shown in **20–25**. Here, because the neutral wire connects to the switch at one

20–22   WALL SWITCH/CEILING LIGHT

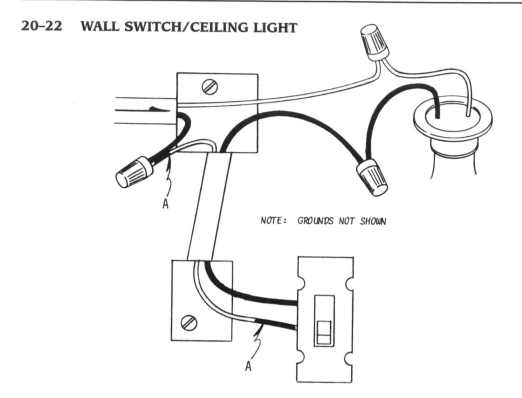

NOTE: GROUNDS NOT SHOWN

A

20–23   CURRENT ENTERING AT SWITCH

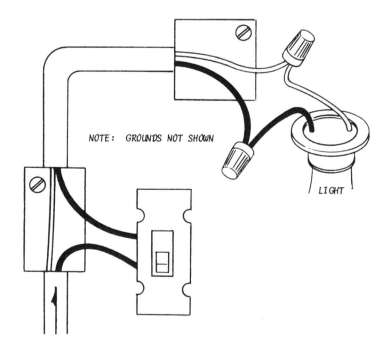

NOTE: GROUNDS NOT SHOWN

LIGHT

20–24

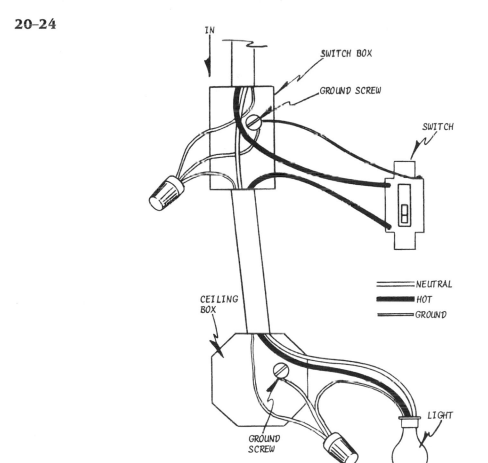

end and to a black wire at the other end, it must be coded black at the points marked A.

A run that is interrupted by a switch-controlled light is wired as shown in **20–26**. The neutral wire from the switch becomes hot; the current continues beyond the light.

The wiring is installed as shown in **20–27** when you interrupt a run to install a light that has its own switch. The current will still continue beyond the light.

The simplest kind of light to install is one that has its own switch and is located at the end of a run. It is shown in **20–28** both with and without grounding wires. Such fixtures may have screw terminals, in which case connections are made directly to the screws, or lead wires, in which case they are made by using solderless connectors to join wires.

If you wish to control a light from more than one location, which is code for some locations, you must work with special three-way switches. The idea is practical, for example,

20-25   ONE SWITCH FOR TWO LIGHTS

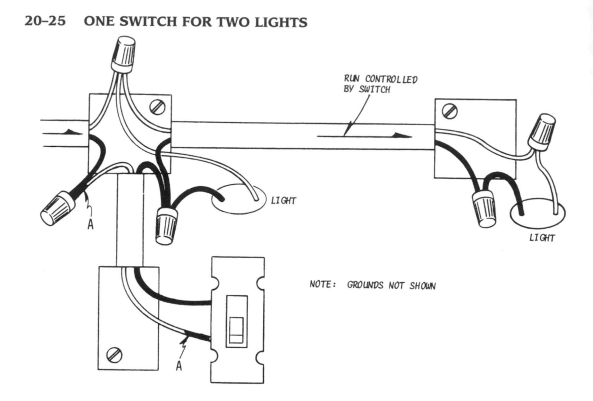

RUN CONTROLLED BY SWITCH

LIGHT

A

LIGHT

A

NOTE: GROUNDS NOT SHOWN

when you wish to control a garage light from both the house and the garage or a stairway light from both top and bottom levels.

The three-way switches look like ordinary toggle switches but they usually have three terminals, one of which is specially color-coded as the common terminal. Be sure you recognize which one it is, because it's an important factor in three-way-switch installations. A basic rule to remember is that the black wire from the current source goes directly to the common terminal on one of the switches. A black wire must also run from the common terminal of the second switch to the fixture, where it is connected to the fixture's black wire or brass screw, whichever is present.

The installation is made with three wires, the colors being black, white, and red. The wires at the fixture must always be black to black and white to white. The relative ease or complexity of the wiring depends a lot on where the current enters the installation. You have to work carefully and follow the colors.

20–26   INTERRUPTED RUN

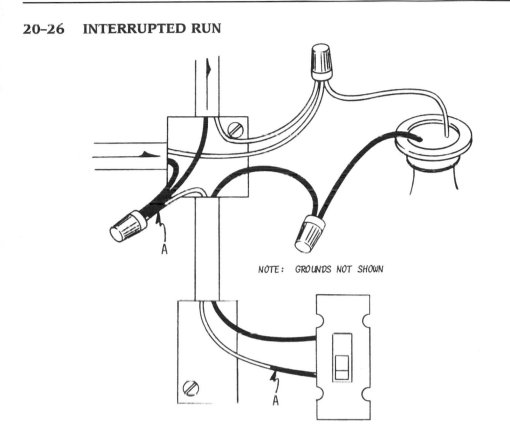

NOTE: GROUNDS NOT SHOWN

20–27   LIGHT WITH OWN SWITCH

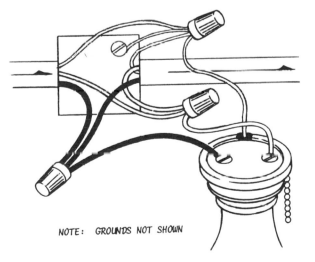

NOTE: GROUNDS NOT SHOWN

20–28 LIGHT AT END OF RUN

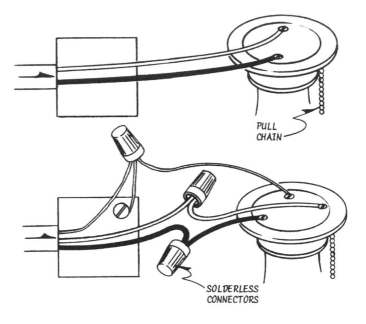

PULL
CHAIN

SOLDERLESS
CONNECTORS

RECEPTACLES (OUTLETS)

The wiring of routine receptacles is pretty straightforward, as shown in **20–29** with one receiving current from a junction box. The black wire goes to a copper or brass screw, the white to a silver terminal. You can add other receptacles on the same run by continuing the wires and making similar connections, as shown in **20–30**, which also shows how grounding wires should be installed. The grounding wires will be either green or bare and should be connected to the green terminal on the receptacle and make firm contact with a grounding screw in the box, itself. Remember that grounding is also required at outlets.

SPECIAL CONTROLS

Modern houses are loaded with electrical conveniences too numerous to mention. But there are a few special switches and controls you may want to include.

Timer switches can add convenience and save electricity. Generally, this switch is used to control fans in kitchen and baths so you can turn them on, and leave without turning them off. A timer mechanism built into the switch clicks down according to your setting, and shuts off the power automatically. The most practical application is in bathrooms, par-

20–29 BASIC RECEPTACLE

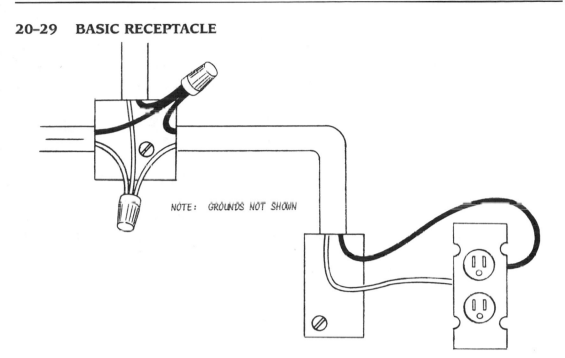

NOTE: GROUNDS NOT SHOWN

20–30 ADDED RECEPTACLE

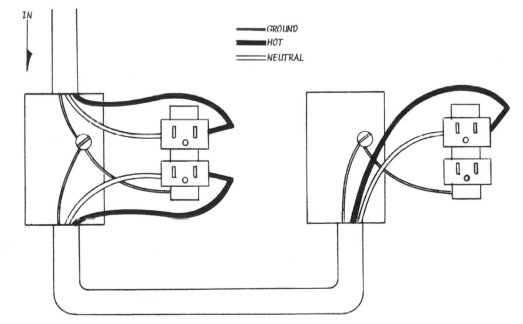

IN

GROUND
HOT
NEUTRAL

ticularly in winter. You step out of the shower into a warm, steamy room, and the last thing you need is a cool breeze. But the moisture will settle in grout seams and gradually mildew the wall unless you turn on the fan. A timer switch solves the problem. You can dry off comfortably, and set the fan to run several minutes and vent the moisture after you're out of the room.

Illuminated switches act as a guide to switch locations in dark rooms. Some have a small pilot light under the toggle; others have a toggle that emits a glow in the dark so you can't miss it.

You can always use standard toggles that click on and off, or a range of more modern units such as paddle switches, or silent switches without the click. If you decide to change a switch, make sure that it serves the same function as the old unit. A single-pole switch that controls a fixture from one location will most likely have three screw terminals: two for the power circuit and one for the ground wire. A three-way switch that controls a fixture from two different locations generally has three screw terminals plus the ground.

MODERN WIRING FOR ELECTRONICS

Eventually, you will be able to talk to your house and tell it what to do. Ovens will turn on, locks will lock, and you'll be able to control energy use, create custom home entertainment programs, and monitor home security all with one system. It will know who you are, where you are, and what you're doing because it will be in electronic touch with lights, appliances, thermostats, and your computer.

Although that kind of integration isn't here yet, many new houses have special cables built in to handle phones, computer lines, and other smart appliances. The industry is still evolving, and software programs that work with some computers won't work with others. Some appliances with built-in chips respond to programming over one kind of network, but won't recognize signals from another. Those are only some of the blind alleys you face as the basic phone line and modem are overwhelmed by the information superhighway. Another is waiting for the development dust to settle so you don't invest in the digital equivalent of an 8-track-tape system.

Along with personal computers, automated home systems have made exponential progress in the last decade—so much that by 2004, 40 percent of all new homes are likely to be prewired for advanced information services.

Maximum capacity comes from a system of dedicated cables, called structured wiring. It's the key to improving the speed and quality of all computer data transmission. Typical installations have three main components: a service-distribution box at one end, jacks and outlets at the other, and cables running between them.

The distribution box is the main interface with outside feeds, which can include telephone and cable TV lines, satellite signals, high-speed Internet access, and other lines. The signals wind up in specialized outlets in each room, or the one room you use as a home office. The cabling in between is where you can gain or lose the capacity to handle a deluge of data.

Capacity is plain language for bandwidth. Some electronic information, like your voice on a telephone line, requires only the narrow bandwidth provided by a standard, four-wire line called quad wiring. But if you want millions of bytes to flow instead of a few syllables, you need Category 5 wiring, which has eight conductors and more bandwidth. It's common now in electronic house installations, but about to be surpassed by Category 5 Enhanced, and then by Category 6, which should provide twice as much capacity as Category 5. That's in addition to RG-6 coaxial cable for video feeds. But as Internet speeds increase and home automation becomes more commonplace, even those cables will likely be surpassed by a Category 7 that doesn't exist yet.

The most reliable and versatile setup is called a star-pattern installation. With the star pattern, each line to each jack or outlet is connected back to the main distribution box. It's called a home-run circuit, and consumes a lot of cable. (To keep expensive incoming signals clear, data and power cables should be separated by at least 6 inches.) With the other option, called a daisy-chain installation (the way most phones are installed), cable runs from one outlet to another like a string of Christmas lights.

A fully connected new home can cost an extra $1,000 to $2,000, according to the Home Automation Association. But the cost can escalate depending on the cables you select and how difficult it is to weave them through the building.

HEATING SYSTEMS

To make a wise investment in your heating system, you have to compare alternatives before buying—to decide how much and what kind of warmth you'll get from a furnace fueled by gas, oil, or electricity. That's the most basic and common choice because almost all houses have conventional heating systems that distribute heat in water (through pipes to radiators) or air (through ducts to registers). But you may want to investigate an innovative system, such as a ground-source heat pump, a high-efficiency condensing furnace, or even a solar system.

BASIC FUEL COMPARISONS

You can number-crunch comparisons among gas, oil, and electricity by checking prices with local fuel suppliers and getting estimates on the different systems from local contractors. But don't forget to factor in basic, practical considerations. For example, gas will require a supply line from the street, while oil will require space for a storage tank.

Because all heat output can be measured in BTUs, you'll have a common denominator to make valid comparisons whether you're looking at oil, gas, or electricity. Remember that BTU input describes system capacity while BTU output is the usable heat a system delivers. On electric systems where there is no heat loss in combustion—at the power generating plant there is, but not in your house—the two ratings are the same. With oil and gas they are different because, although some gas units come close, neither fuel can be converted to usable heat with 100 percent efficiency.

It is more difficult to compare the cost of fuels used to produce BTUs, for example, kilowatt-hours of electricity and cubic feet of natural gas. You could use estimated monthly operating costs provided by contractors, fuel suppliers, and utility companies, or, to make your own unbiased judgment, convert the standard measure of each fuel to the common denominator of BTUs. Multiply the standard measure of gas, a cubic foot, by 1031 to find the BTU equivalent. Multiply the standard measure of electricity, a kilowatt-hour, by 3412 to find the BTU equivalent. Multiply the standard measure of oil, a gallon, by 139,000 to find the BTU equivalent.

HOT-AIR SYSTEMS

In central heating systems, heat is created at a central location and then delivered via ducts or pipes to points of use. The heat medium can be air or water.

A forced warm-air system is based on the fact that warm air, being lighter, tends to rise while colder air settles. Air heated by a furnace is blown through ducts that terminate at registers built into floors or walls. Return ducts (usually one in a central location) bring cool air back to the furnace, where it is reheated and recirculated. Among many codes governing heating systems, you need to place the return more than 10 feet from the main source of combustion.

Old-fashioned systems worked on gravity alone, allowing warm air to rise through ducts. Modern systems force air through the ducts with a blower. The blower moves the heated air from the furnace to registers, so distribution is equalized and can be controlled. There is a combustion chamber where fuel makes heat, and a heat exchanger where the temperature is transferred to a main plenum and on to the ducts (**23-1**).

21–1 FORCED WARM-AIR SYSTEM

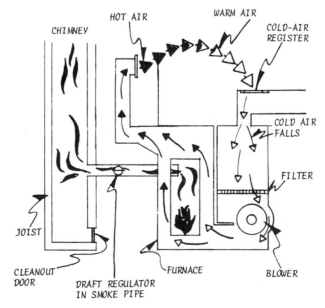

A forced-warm-air system can be designed with more than one blower or with special devices so the heated air can be directed to particular points of use, with each having its own thermostat. This allows you to have bedrooms that will be cooler than the kitchen or the living room.

Furnaces of various designs are available for different locations. A horizontal type that draws, heats, and then discharges air on a horizontal plane is especially good for an attic or a crawl space. Most systems have air intakes at the base and release hot air at the top. Bear in mind that in modern, energy-efficient houses that are tightly constructed, you'll need to duct in fresh air for combustion. There is also minimum clearance when it comes to locating the furnace.

Energy efficiency is listed on every modern appliance, so you can easily compare units. But typical delivery systems lose 20 to 40 percent of the heat they carry, according to the United States Department of Energy. It's lost directly through joints in ducts and by radiation through the walls of both hot-air and hot-water lines. But there are two kinds of loss. One is into unconditioned crawl spaces or attics—heat that eventually seeps outside. The other is into conditioned spaces like a finished basement—heat that warms a living space even though it doesn't come from a register or radiator.

It is practical to save heat squandered in unconditioned spaces by duct-taping seams to prevent air leaks. The next priority is to insulate lines feeding outlets that seem to emit less heat than others—even if they run through conditioned spaces. That gets the maximum amount of heat to registers and radiators far from the furnace.

You can also install fan-assisted ducts when insulation on a long run from the furnace won't preserve enough heat. A small fan can be installed at the end of the duct run below the register, and wired back to the main furnace fan. When the big blower starts pushing warm air through the system, the mini-blower starts pulling, and the underfed duct delivers more than its fair share of heat.

Another option is to install adjustable registers. Their louvers can be partially closed in warmer rooms, say, where windows let in a lot of sunlight. Or opened fully in colder rooms, where the windows are in shade. Also, the slats can be angled to direct air toward living areas—at seat level where the people are—instead of straight up to the ceiling. The effect is heightened by installing plastic scoops over registers.

Overall, forced-air systems provide the quickest response to thermostat changes. But they tend to create temperature swings in the living space that are more noticeable than the swings with hot-water heat supplied to radiators. You may feel a cool breeze when the blower first starts. But a well-designed system can be balanced to keep a relatively even temperature.

There are several modern twists on this basic system. One is to replace the standard furnace fan that blows air off and on with a continuous air circulation (CAC) system. These have variable-speed fans with a very low-speed cycle that runs all the time. This can eliminate the hot-cold variations you often feel in houses with hot-air systems, and more thoroughly mix the indoor air supply among all the rooms.

Another option is to install one or more thermostatically controlled dampers at strategic locations in the main supply ducts. This is the hot-air version of splitting the single loop of a hot-water system into controllable zones. The damper is a motor-driven panel mounted in the duct that opens and closes in response to thermostat settings. Increase the setting on the upstairs thermostat, for example, and the baffle will shift to deflect more warm air into the second-floor supply lines. You still have one furnace and fan. But with two or more automatic dampers you can send the heat where you most need it.

HOT-WATER SYSTEMS

In principle, air and water heating systems are quite similar. In modern, hot-water systems, furnace-heated water is pushed by small pumps through pipes to radiators, where much of the heat is transferred through the metal in the radiators and then into the room. There are many styles and sizes of radiators. You need to balance their heat transfer capability with the size of the room, and then supply the several loops of pipe in a modern system with enough hot water to do the job. When the water travels through the radiators and gives up most of its heat, it then returns to the boiler for reheating.

With hot-water systems, an older, single-loop design (**21–2**) is the most difficult to balance so that you get even heat throughout the house. Water leaves the boiler scalding hot and toasts the first few rooms it reaches. But by the time it's pumped upstairs and reaches

21–2   CLOSED WATER SYSTEM (SINGLE-LOOP)

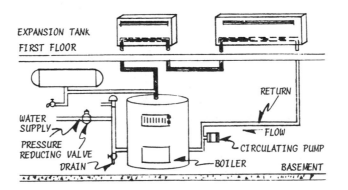

the most distant radiators, there may be very little heat left to give before the tepid water returns to the boiler. If only you could reverse the cycle and start with the cold rooms first once in a while. But after the supply is reheated it takes the same route, making warm rooms even warmer and barely maintaining the chill in remote areas.

Home owners in this situation have to move in groups between floors or play tag with the single thermostat. For someone staying up late on the first floor, a 68-degree setting is fine until the person upstairs calls down about freezing to death. But bump the setting to make it cozy upstairs, and the first floor broils.

The most economical solution would be to move the thermostat to a compromise area that exactly blended upstairs and downstairs temperatures. The problem is that most houses don't have one. Even in a central hall or stairwell, air is likely to be flowing from the warm area to the cold area and skewing whatever thermostat setting you dial in.

Within the limitations of a single-loop systems you may have more success by adjusting the radiators, allowing less water into the units in hot rooms, and keeping the valves wide open in cool rooms. But if the piping system takes the hot-water flow through each radiator, you can't partially close one valve without reducing the flow in the entire loop. If the piping system allows you to bypass a radiator, you might shut off one of two in a warm area to send more heat on to other rooms. You can improve on this somewhat primitive design by piping the system so you can bypass (or at least adjust the flow) at each radiator (**21–3**).

The better system that's now commonly used on houses is to split the single loop into at least two sections, generally, one for each floor (**21–4**). If your plan starts with a single loop, the main changes to the modern and more practical upgrade are a second pump near the boiler, and a new supply line leading from the new pump directly to the start of the second loop.

21–3   CLOSED WATER SYSTEM (SINGLE-PIPE)

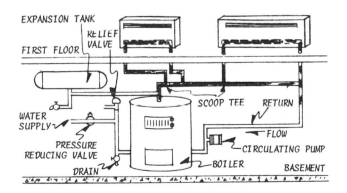

21–4 CLOSED WATER SYSTEM (SPLIT-LOOP)

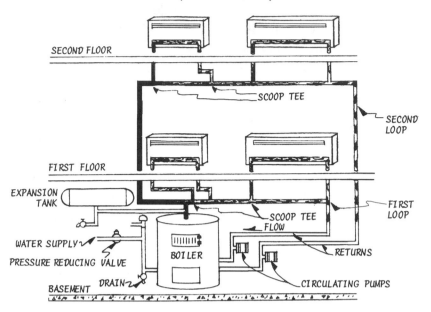

Each loop can have its own thermostat controlling its own pump. You can keep the first floor warm and the second floor cool during the day, and reverse the settings at night. Program two setback thermostats and you can warm up areas before you get there, and then save money by automatically cooling them down once you leave. But even without setback thermostats, this split-loop design will pay for itself in fuel savings because you won't be overheating one area of the house to make life possible without extra sweaters in another.

The most dramatic change in hot-water systems is a hybrid that can take many shapes. The basic system is called a condensing furnace (**21–5**). These furnaces have efficiencies of over 90 percent, which means that you get almost one dollar of usable heat for every dollar you spend on fuel, with only a few percentage points lost as exhaust.

The units are designed to milk so much heat from the combustion process that the exhaust is warm instead of hot. It seems improbable, like a car without an exhaust pipe, but the system works without a conventional masonry flue due to its high efficiency, which can be 95 percent.

In one version of this system, a large, heavily insulated tank of water is heated by the burner. Some of the water supplies kitchens and baths the way it does from a standard water heater. Another pipe carries hot water to a coil over the furnace fan where the water heat is transferred to air heat. (These systems also can be set up to deliver hot water for baseboard heating.)

21–5 CONDENSING FURNACE

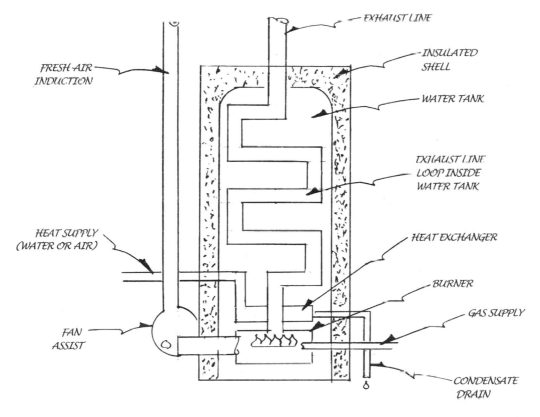

The most unusual feature is the system's internal exhaust. Instead of venting directly from the burner, it travels in a stainless steel pipe that coils through the water tank before exiting the unit. On route, the hot exhaust gives up most of its heat through the walls of the pipe into the water. When the exhaust reaches the end of the coil, it's cooled enough to vent the rest of the way outside through plastic pipe laid in framing bays. You don't need a conventional masonry flue, or even exhaust-rated triple-wall metal pipe. You generally do need a pipe to carry away the condensation produced in this combustion process.

Another variation on the basic hot-water system is the radiant pipe heating system. The essence of this approach is to pipe hot water through loops of flexible piping built into the floors (and sometimes the walls) of the house. You can dispense with all, or at least most, radiators, and the heat supplied is even and well distributed. The drawbacks are a high installation cost, and potentially major problems with even minor repairs. If a pipe loop springs a leak under a finished floor, for example, you'll have to rip surface materials (or even break up concrete) to fix the leak.

HEATING WITH ELECTRICITY

Electric-powered furnaces do away with the combustion process altogether. That means the system is easy to install and doesn't require a chimney or flue because there is no exhaust. The downside is that electric heat, though convenient, is generally the most expensive fuel—sometimes by far. Also, you will have to plan the installation as part of your electrical system, and bring in enough extra power to run the system.

The operation is very basic, and requires very little maintenance compared to combustion furnaces. Electricity is simply converted to heat when it moves through special conductors that resist the flow of current. The conductors (heating elements) become hot and transfer heat to the delivery system of forced hot air that blows through the house. You can also use electric baseboard heaters with different output ratings so they can be used for general heating or for supplemental purposes.

HEAT PUMPS

Heat pumps aren't new technology. But to many consumers their operation is just as confusing as it was when these combination air conditioning and heating appliances were introduced in the 1950s. Even today, manufacturers' sales information may say that heat pumps can extract heat from cold outside air to make a house warm inside in the winter. It seems impossible, but is accurate up to a point.

Basically, heat pumps are reversible air conditioners with a built-in, backup electric heater. Imagine a typical room air conditioner, nice and cool on the inside where a fan blows air over one set of pipe coils, but hot to the touch at another set of coils outside the house. Now imagine that as the seasons change and you want warm air inside instead of air conditioning, you simply swivel the room unit in the wall so the hot coils and warm air are inside. That's the basic idea, although with heat pumps you don't have to swivel the machine. The two sets of pipe coils stay in place and the flow of refrigerant between them is reversed. It's the refrigerant that handles the exchange of temperature as it passes through closed loops of pipes and valves, gaining and giving off temperature at different points. The ingenious idea of a heat pump is simply to reverse the basic operation as the weather changes. In summer, the heat pump runs like a conventional air conditioner. In winter, a reversing valve cycles the refrigerant in the opposite direction.

But heat pumps have limitations, and generally are recommended only for regions with moderate climates. You can use them anywhere, of course. But once the temperature outside drops toward freezing, the electric backup heater kicks in. Then you have what amounts to an electric (and expensive) furnace.

However, there are some interesting variations on this idea, including one of the most energy-efficient, though initially expensive installations: a ground-source heat pump that takes advantage of the temperature below ground.

GEOTHERMAL HEAT

Even a few feet below ground, the soil temperature is warmer than winter air and cooler than summer air. Combination heating and cooling systems that take advantage of this energy reserve (a mild 45 to 75 degrees F, depending on latitude) can take many forms. The common residential version, called a ground-source heat pump, uses the temperature to gain and lose building heat by sending liquid through underground pipes.

Ground source systems are more expensive than conventional heating and cooling equipment, by two or three times in some cases. But they are gaining favor—and financial backing from utilities and government agencies—because they are economical in the long run and do not burn fossil fuels. However, in many applications you can gain most of the temperature you need from the ground, but still require a small conventional system to reach the 68-degree comfort range.

According to the Department of Energy, the first residential ground-source heat pump was built in 1948—by an Ohio State University professor as a demonstration project in his own house. Now there are many rebate programs and other financial incentives that make geothermal heat pump systems more affordable. Many of the systems carry the DOE and EPA Energy Star label that can qualify for special loans with low interest rates and long repayment periods.

A typical system has three main components: an earth connection, a heat pump, and a distribution system (**21-6**). The earth connection is a long loop of pipes buried vertically or horizontally on site. The vertical installation is similar to a drilled well that offers enough room for the loop of pipes. The horizontal installation is generally called a race-track system. In both cases, water circulates in the sealed loop, absorbing heat in winter and giving off heat in summer.

The loop rises above ground and into the house, where temperature is exchanged in a heat pump. These appliances, working like reversible air conditioners, use the circulating water as a temperature transfer medium. Conventional ductwork is often used to distribute heated or cooled air through the building.

Geothermal heat pumps also can provide domestic hot water. Some systems use a component called a desuperheater to transfer excess heat from the heat pump's compressor to the house's hot-water tank when the system is operating. Now, more manufacturers are offering full-demand systems that use a separate heat exchanger to provide hot water even when the heat pump is not active.

The DOE estimates that an average geothermal heat pump system will cost about

21–6

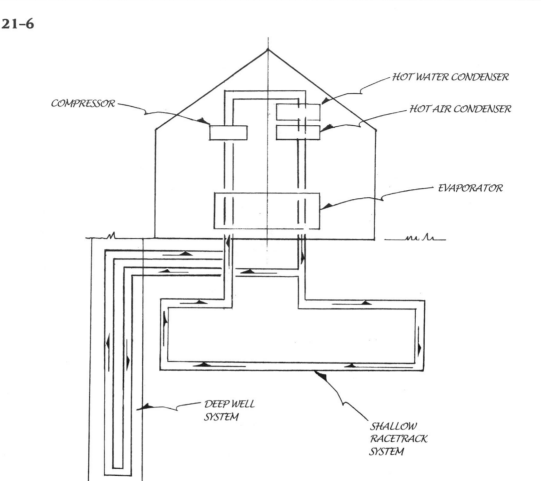

COMPRESSOR

HOT WATER CONDENSER

HOT AIR CONDENSER

EVAPORATOR

DEEP WELL
SYSTEM

SHALLOW
RACETRACK
SYSTEM

$2,500 per ton of capacity. That's $7,500 for a typical, 3-ton residential unit. The agency estimates that the extra $3,000 or $4,000 (compared to a conventional system) will add about $30 a month to your mortgage payment, but save more than that on utility bills.

CONSIDERING COOLING

One obvious advantage of installing a heat pump is that you get air-conditioning at the same time. You also can install a dedicated AC system, either a central unit or a few room units. If you're planning a forced hot-air heating system, you can use the same ducts to conduct cool air. But you can also install a separate duct system for cool air.

Back in 1970, about 35 percent of new houses nationwide had central air-conditioning.

By 1985, 71 percent had it. Of course, those figures included some areas of the country that never get very hot and muggy. In southern states, the figure is higher. In Washington, DC in the year 2000, for example, over 95 percent of new homes and 70 percent of all existing homes had central air.

There are many configurations, but the most common and practical is a split system with the heat dissipating coils mounted just outside the building. Another feature to consider is the space-saving option of small-diameter, flexible, high-pressure tubing instead of ducts. It can be snaked through the framing without causing as much disruption as conventional ductwork. And the outlets are smaller than conventional grills, ending in small, neatly trimmed holes that look more like a recessed ceiling light.

Most modern AC installations are zoned. This design approach offers the same kind of energy-saving control as zoned, or split-loop heating systems. Some large houses may be built with several zones, each with its own thermostat. But even two zones can save money long term, particularly in a two-story house. A downstairs, living-area zone kicks in before you get home from work, while an upstairs, sleeping-area zone calls for more cooling later on. The key is finding one or more locations to build what amounts to a fork in the road into your ductwork. The fork is a motorized damper controlled by a thermostat that modulates airflow the way a faucet controls water. Two major suppliers of zone systems, Carrier and Honeywell, estimate that temperature setbacks made possible by zoned ducts will cut cooling costs 10 to 30 percent.

On central systems with ductwork spread throughout the building, condensation can form almost anywhere—for instance, where 65-degree ducts run next to 120-degree water pipes. If ducts aren't separated from heat sources, particularly the oven-like air in unfinished attics, the combination can produce enough condensation to drip like a roof leak. When the hot-cold encounter is hidden in the framing, you may not see the effects until wood beams are rotting, and drywall on the surface becomes pulpy and spotted with mold.

Wherever ducts are accessible, make sure they are wrapped with batts of insulation, particularly where they run near heat sources such as hot-water pipes, kitchen stove fan ducts, water heater exhaust lines, and the hot air in attic or crawl spaces. Where complete wrapping isn't possible because ducts are tucked into spaces between beams, pack the framing cavity with loose fill insulation, and cover the top of the duct with a batt of insulation.

In more moderate climates where you can get by with one- or two-room units, there are many installation options. But the basic choice is making the unit removable by sticking it in a window, or building it permanently into the wall.

Basic site requirements are similar for both installations: a nearby outlet, and a spot where the exterior, heat-dispersing coils won't broil under direct sunlight. Also, it's nice to locate the humming, dripping box away from an entry, or a spot outside where you like to sit in peace and quiet. There is less chance of meeting all these design parameters with a unit whose location is controlled by existing windows; there is more choice with an in-wall machine.

Window units can be heavy—a big machine could weigh over 100 pounds—but they are easy to install. Manufacturers include adjustable panels and foam weatherstripping that surrounds the machine and fills the gaps between the metal case and the window frame.

In-wall units need a hole through the wall, but if you select a section that is free of pipes and wires, basic carpentry skills and tools will get you through the installation. If you pick a spot in a solid wall, you will have to build a header—a horizontal beam that picks up loads from studs that are cut short and carries them to the sides of the opening.

In most cases, you can save this slightly more complicated step by installing an in-wall unit beneath a window. It already has a header, and should have double studs running down each side all the way to the floor. You may have to make the air-conditioner space smaller than the window, which is easy, but you won't have to worry about supporting loads from above. Under a window is often a good choice for appearance, too. A metal box poking through a clean wall of siding will grab your eye. It's less noticeable under a windowsill, particularly if you take the trouble to trim the exterior of the conditioner the way the window is trimmed. Always follow manufacturer's directions for installation.

SOLAR AND PHOTOVOLTAIC SYSTEMS

Solar systems had a big boom in the 1970s as a result of the energy crisis. For a time, there were many financial incentives for development. But along with photovoltaic systems that convert sunlight directly to electricity, systems that require large collection panels on the roof haven't become mainstream. And in many houses that do use them, they provide supplemental energy, and often are backed up with a conventional system.

There are many types of solar systems, but typical installations have four components: collectors to harvest sunlight and convert radiant energy to thermal energy; storage to hold enough heat to last through the night or through periods of cloudy weather; a distribution system; and a backup system that will contribute heat when stored solar heat is exhausted because the sun has not been cooperating.

The collector is a heat-absorbing metal plate with an array of tubing that may be bonded to, or an integral part, of the plate. The heat transfer can be liquid or air. It passes through the collector, picks up the heat, and transports it to storage. A southern exposure for the collectors is optimum, but tests indicate that variations from due south do not cut efficiency much.

There are two basic ways to store the heat. If water is the heat carrier, then a large tank of water may be used for storage. Space heat can be extracted from the hot water by using a heat exchanger, which may simply be a series of finned pipes through which the hot water passes. If you force air over the fins, you get space heat (**21-7**). For hot water, you pipe the storage tank contents to points of use.

If air is the heat carrier, then the heat can be stored in a large insulated bin that is filled with rocks that range from about 1 to 3 inches in diameter. The idea is for the rocks to provide space for heat exchange while leaving sufficient passageways for air movement. Air from the bin, directed to points of use, provides space heating (**21-8**).

21-7   SOLAR LIQUID SYSTEM

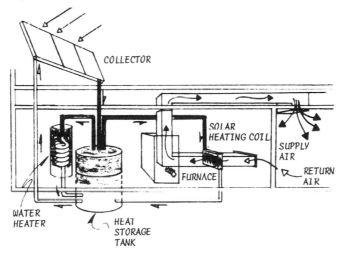

21-8   SOLAR AIR SYSTEM

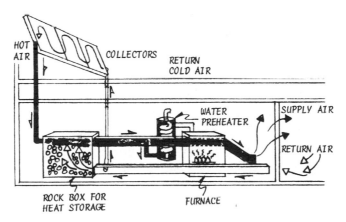

A backup system comes into play during long periods of inclement weather. That's the big drawback: without the sun, solar systems simply run out of energy. But even mainstream groups like the National Association of Homebuilders say that (in some regions at least), you should consider a solar water heater to reduce electricity costs. They also point out the possible benefits of other formerly off-the-grid systems such as photovoltaic panels that convert sunlight directly into electricity. The NAHB now promotes some of these systems because they are becoming a more attractive long-term investment for the new home owner as the average rates for utility-supplied power increase.

If you use an alternative system, be sure to check its installation with the building department ahead of time.

CONSIDERING ENERGY EFFICIENCY

Saving energy used to be a true do-it-yourself subject. If you didn't do anything about reducing your utility costs, no one else was around to help. The energy crisis of the 1970s (remember odd and even gas days?) changed all that.

Organizations that had never mentioned energy conservation started talking about it, and dozens of others sprang up to promote diverse energy systems from solar power to geothermal heat. Now there are hundreds of groups with varying agendas offering thousands of energy-saving suggestions. To give you just some of the many guidelines and suggestions, here is a look at recommendations from the National Association of Homebuilders (NAHB).

1. *Heating and cooling equipment.* To save some of the nearly 50 percent of a typical home's utility bill that goes toward heating and cooling, the NAHB says you should look for furnaces with an Annual Fuel Utilization Efficiency (AFUE) rating between 80 percent for conventional furnaces and 94 percent for condensing furnaces. Look for a central air-conditioning unit with a Seasonal Energy Efficiency Ratio (SEER) rating of at least 12.

   For heat pumps, which handle both heating and cooling, the NAHB suggests a unit with a Heating Season Performance Factor (HSPF) greater than 7 and SEER rating of at least 12. (Units with SEER ratings up to 18 are available.)

   Locate ducts within the conditioned space of your house, and minimize the length of duct runs. In homes with forced-air heating and cooling systems, you can seal duct joints with tape. If ducts must be installed in unconditioned spaces (attics and crawlspaces), seal the joint. During heating or cooling seasons, check and change air filters regularly. Dirty filters can reduce heating, ventilation, and air-conditioning system efficiency.

The NAHB also recommends programmable thermostats to help home owners automatically and efficiently match heating and cooling needs to their schedules. These units typically offer savings of 10 to 15 percent without compromising comfort, says the NAHB.

2. *Water heating.* To save some of the roughly 13 percent of a typical home's utility bill that goes toward water heating, the NAHB says you should buy an energy-efficient water heater and set its thermostat at between 115 and 120 degrees F. You also can install nonaerating, low-flow faucets and showerheads, and use clothes washers and dishwashers on energy-saver or water-saver settings.

SETBACK THERMOSTATS

Programmable thermostats are probably the easiest and least expensive way to save energy. And they work no matter what type of system you install. These units automatically adjust the furnace setting so you can reduce the heat overnight when you're asleep and during the day when you're not home. The program can return to a normal setting shortly before you return home or wake up.

There are sophisticated units at $200 or more that can react to light and adjust temperature based on occupancy. But a typical programmable thermostat has a touchpad where you enter times, dates, and other program commands that show in a small LED or LCD digital-readout window. Most can repeat two or more on-off times and temperatures for weekday and weekend schedules, although you can override the program anytime. Most units also have a battery backup so you don't have to reprogram the thermostat after a power failure.

Basic setback units, which have been around for decades, are widely available and cost from $30 to $100, depending on complexity. Use them to automatically turn down your thermostat 10 to 15 degrees F for 8 hours overnight and save from 5 to 15 percent a year on your heating bill, according to DOE estimates. If your heating bill is now about $500 a month ($3,000 over the area heating season), you could save $450—enough to pay for a $75 thermostat in the first month of operation.

To calculate combined savings for different day parts, figure up to one percent of your heating costs for each degree of setback over eight hours. If you're out of the house during the day, for example, you can duplicate the overnight setback and save up to 30 percent of your heating costs.

It is not true that reducing heat settings is pointless because it takes even more energy to reheat the house. The DOE reports that this misconception has been dispelled by years of research and numerous studies. You do need about the same amount of fuel to reheat a house as you save when the temperature drops, which makes the up-and-down temperature swing a wash. But you also save fuel between the time the temperature stabilizes at the lower level and the next time heat is needed. The longer your house remains at the lower temperature, the more energy you save.

The DOE also reports that many people mistakenly boost a thermostat above the final setting to make a house heat up faster. This has no effect because furnaces produce heat at a constant rate. A house will reach 68 degrees F in the same amount of time with the thermostat set at 68 as it will with the thermostat set at 88. And boosting could waste energy if you forget to turn down the setting.

22

CHIMNEYS FOR FIREPLACES AND WOODSTOVES

Home is where the hearth is, and has been for ages. At one time, a fireplace was a necessity because it was the only source of heat for warmth and cooking. It became less essential with the advent of more modern heating and cooking systems, so it became an option that's included in a house more for appearance and atmosphere than for utility.

One reason is that fireplaces are not very energy-efficient. The Colonial-era version, generally called a Rumford fireplace, had an opening extending high off the floor and a shallow back that was angled toward the room. This still is an effective design for radiating heat, but also very smoky. Most fireplaces in houses today have shorter openings, while the firebox itself is deeper. This traps the smoke, but most of the heat as well, which goes up the chimney instead of into the room. And as hot air escapes up the flue, outside air with a lower temperature is drawn into the room. People sitting within the radiation zone of the fire will feel its heat. Those who are farthest away may feel a cold draft. The net energy result may even be negative.

A conventional masonry fireplace is built like a box within a box. The inner lining of the firebox may be special firebrick, and the inner lining of the flue is usually clay tile. There is an airspace around these chambers, and an outer shell of masonry as well (**22–1**). The firebox is designed so that its sides splay outward while the upper part of its back slopes toward the room. The idea is to reflect the maximum amount of heat into the room. The smoke chamber serves as a funnel that directs smoke to the flue. There is a damper-controlled passage, called the throat, between the firebox and the smoke chamber. The smoke shelf is a barrier to downdrafts so they will eddy and be lifted upward by rising air currents. The flue carries off by-products of the fire. Its size in relation to the size of the firebox is very important if it is to carry off smoke the way it should.

Not all fireplaces include an ash dump, probably because construction is easier without one. It's a question of convenience; with an ash dump, ashes are dumped into a fire-

481

22–1

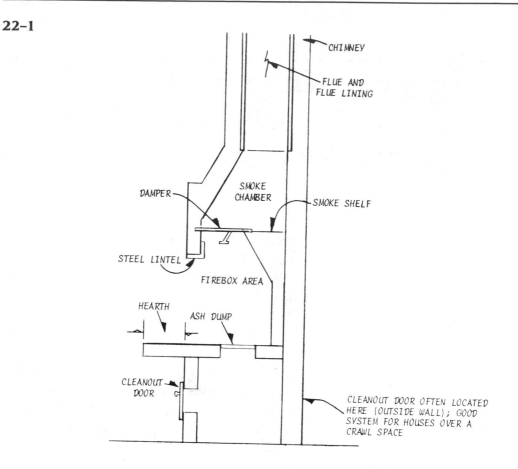

CHIMNEY

FLUE AND FLUE LINING

SMOKE CHAMBER

DAMPER

SMOKE SHELF

STEEL LINTEL

FIREBOX AREA

HEARTH

ASH DUMP

CLEANOUT DOOR

CLEANOUT DOOR OFTEN LOCATED HERE (OUTSIDE WALL); GOOD SYSTEM FOR HOUSES OVER A CRAWL SPACE

proof subchamber to be toted off when convenient. Without one, ashes must periodically be shoveled into a bucket and carried out through the house. It can be included by designing a raised hearth with an ash pit beneath (**22–2**). Or a ready-made steel lift-out box can be sunk into the hearth (**22–3**).

A well-designed and properly constructed fireplace is desirable because of its cheerfulness and charm, even if it provides only marginal auxiliary heat. In some situations, say in a small vacation cabin or an outbuilding, it might well be adequate as the only source of heat, especially in milder climates. And there are some modern options to the traditional masonry design that is costly and time-consuming to build. One is an improvement on the old vented fireplace design that circulates some room air around the firebox. Another is a gas fireplace, which simulates a real fire with the efficiency of a modern gas appliance.

22–2

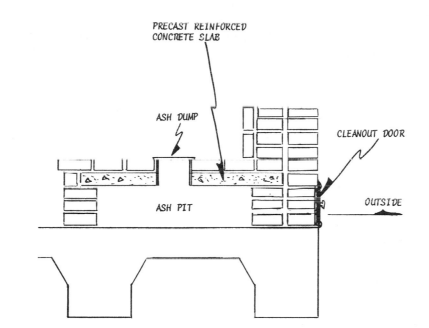

22–3

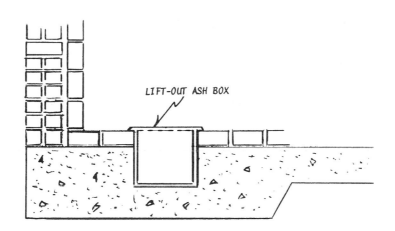

Even if you build a full masonry fireplace, you can reduce heat loss by designing the unit to include a convection system. This can be incorporated in a full-masonry installation by working along the lines shown in **22–4**. Cool air is drawn from the outside, passes through tubes in a special heating chamber, and is ejected into the room. Usually, however, the air inlet is located in the room close to the floor. This can be done by installing ductwork in the masonry or by building the project around prefabricated metal units, which are set in place and concealed with a construction of your choice (**22–5**). Bear in mind that codes are strict about fireplaces in general, and the possibility of mixing room air with exhaust gases in particular.

22–4

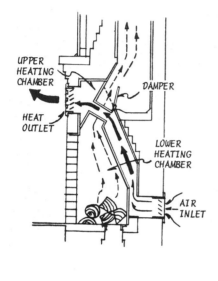

UPPER HEATING CHAMBER

DAMPER

HEAT OUTLET

LOWER HEATING CHAMBER

AIR INLET

22–5

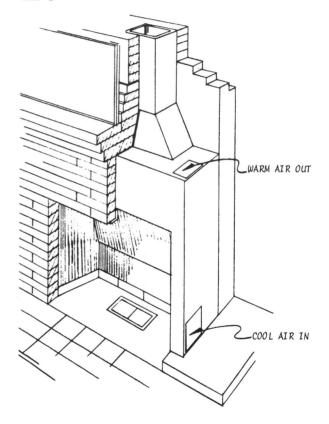

WARM AIR OUT

COOL AIR IN

BASICS OF MASONRY CONSTRUCTION

The masonry fireplace and chimney should be an independent structure that does not receive support from, or provide support for, other building components. This applies whether the unit is inside the walls or is part of an outside wall, as shown in **22–6**.

22-6

This means you need a concrete base, which may be poured along with the regular foundation that is capable of supporting the project so it won't settle or crack. Generally, the base, or footing, should be deeper than the frost line and 6 inches wider than the footprint of the chimney. In some soils you may need a larger, deeper, or specially reinforced footing, so check with local code officials before you start. Even when there is no subgrade frost line, the footing must still support considerable weight (about 130 pounds per cubic foot of brick), so you don't want to skimp on initial construction.

The size of a fireplace should be appropriate for the room it is in. A firebox width of 30 to 36 inches is okay for a room roughly 18 feet square. As a general guide, you can figure that the fireplace opening should be about 5 square inches per square foot of floor space. This formula is most applicable for small rooms; the ratio may be reduced in large rooms.

General guides say that the height of the opening should be about two-thirds to three-quarters of its width. The splay of the sidewalls and the height of the vertical part of the back wall are shown in **22–7**. There is a critical interrelationship in all dimensions of a fireplace, including the cross-sectional area of the flue. If the size of the flue is too small for the size

22–7

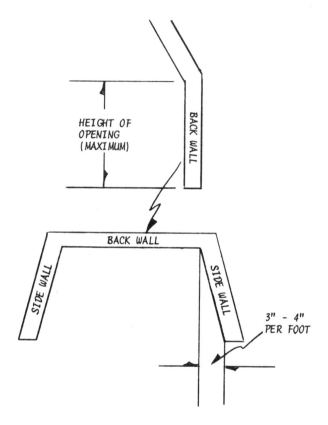

HEIGHT OF OPENING (MAXIMUM)

BACK WALL

BACK WALL

SIDE WALL

SIDE WALL

3" – 4" PER FOOT

of the opening facing the room, the fireplace will not be drafted correctly and will probably be smoky. A larger flue than necessary will merely result in too much downdraft and an excessively generous entrance for rainwater, unless you mount a chimney roof on top.

A fireplace proportioned to function efficiently can be designed by following the rules set forth in the diagrams and table in **22–8**, which were originated by the Majestic Company. Other tables may be available from the building department. There also are extensive tables in architectural books, such as the standard of design, called Architectural Graphic Standards. You have to use them carefully because altering one component, such as the flue size, changes the design size of another, such as the flue capacity.

22-8. FIREPLACE SIZING TABLE IN INCHES (KEYED TO DRAWINGS BELOW)

Finished Opening					Rough Masonry						
A	**B**	**C**	**D**	**E**	**F**	**G**	**H**	**I**	**K**		
Width	Height	Depth	Back	Throat	Width	Depth	Smoke Shelf Height	Smoke Chamber	Vertical Back	Inside of Brick Flue	Standard Flue Lining
24	28	16	16	9	30	19	32	11	14	8½ x 8½	8½ x 8½
26	28	16	18	9	32	19	32	11	14	8½ x 8½	8½ x 8½
28	28	16	20	9	34	19	32	11	14	8 x 12	8½ x 13
30	30	16	22	9	36	19	34	11	15	8 x 12	8½ x 13
32	30	16	24	9	38	19	34	11	15	8 x 12	8½ x 13
34	30	16	26	9	40	19	34	11	15	12 x 12	8½ x 13
36	31	18	27	9	42	21	36	11	16	12 x 12	13 x 13
38	31	18	29	9	44	21	36	11	16	12 x 12	13 x 13
40	31	18	31	9	46	21	36	11	16	12 x 12	13 x 13
42	31	18	33	9	48	21	36	11	16	12 x 12	13 x 13
44	32	18	35	9	50	21	37	11	17	12 x 12	13 x 13
46	32	18	37	9	52	21	37	11	17	12 x 16	13 x 13
48	32	20	38	9	54	23	37	15½	17	12 x 16	13 x 18
50	34	20	40	9	56	23	39	15½	18	12 x 16	13 x 18
52	34	20	42	9	58	23	39	15½	18	12 x 16	13 x 18
54	34	20	44	9	60	23	39	15½	18	16 x 16	13 x 18
56	36	20	46	9	62	23	41	15½	19	16 x 16	18 x 18
58	36	22	47	9	64	25	41	15½	19	16 x 16	18 x 18
60	36	22	49	9	66	25	41	15½	19	16 x 16	18 x 18

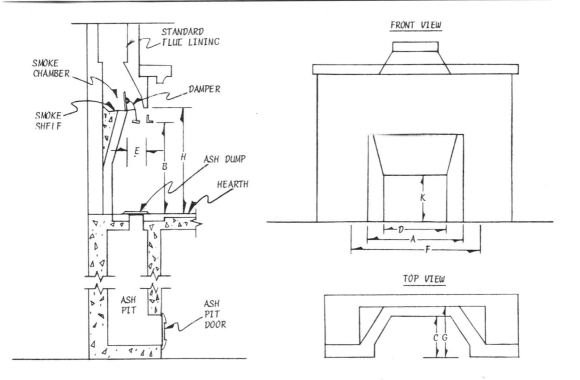

STANDARD FLUE LINING

SMOKE CHAMBER

SMOKE SHELF

DAMPER

ASH DUMP

HEARTH

ASH PIT

ASH PIT DOOR

FRONT VIEW

TOP VIEW

CONSTRUCTION MATERIALS

Brick is a good choice for fireplace and chimney construction because it is readily available. The units are light and you can pause at any time during the installation without losing anything, unless you mix too much mortar. The rule is to mix only as much as you can easily apply in an hour or so. Common brick, bonded with regular masonry mortar (1 part portland cement, 1 part hydrated lime, 5–6 parts sand), can be used for outer walls, but the firebox must be lined with special firebrick that is bonded with fireclay (**22–9**).

You will make more headway using concrete block to build the outer shell. In any case, you need to build the base first, work your way up to the damper, and then raise the outer walls and flues together.

Ready-made steel dampers of various shapes and sizes can be purchased to make construction easier and to increase draft efficiency (**22–10**). Be sure all brick joints are packed

22–9

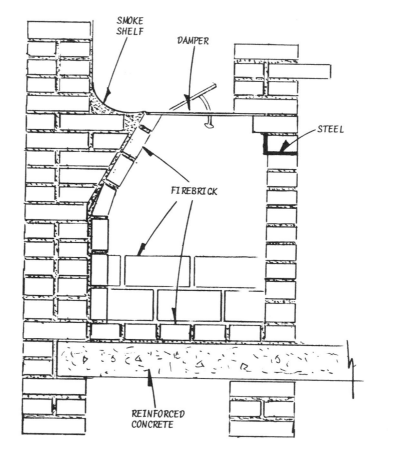

tight and are smooth. Loose, rough joints can let smoke escape where it shouldn't and can interfere with a smooth draft flow.

You can use any noncombustible material to frame the firebox and as a surface for a hearth that extends beyond the fire area. But any combustible trim material should be at least 6 inches away from the opening

CIRCULATOR AND PREFAB FIREPLACES

Prefabricated metal units like that shown in **22–11** are designed to fit into masonry or wood-framed enclosures. Specs vary, but the idea is that the manufacturer makes a double wall with an airspace between them, creating an exterior skin that can be placed close to combustible materials such as 2 × 4 wall studs. The units are hollow-core and have interior blades as shown in **22–12** placed to direct air over the hottest parts of the fireplace and to increase radiating-surface and heat-absorbing areas.

The products supply the radiant heat you get from any ordinary fireplace plus warm-air convection currents that can be directed into the room. This is accomplished with ductwork and inlet and outlet grills. How the grills are placed depends on where the fireplace is located. If it is outside a wall, the grills must be placed on the face side. If the fireplace projects into the room, the grills may be on the front or at the sides, or there can be a combination of front and side positions. The inlets should be close to the floor line, but the location of the outlets is optional, as shown by the sample installations in **22–13**.

Working with a prefab circulator doesn't restrict fireplace location. Actually, by using several units you can do back-to-back and end-to-end designs, so adjoining rooms can each have a fireplace (**22–14**).

But you need to observe codes that are strict about clearances, and be sure to use code-approved flue pipe. Typically, these units are triple-wall, and screw one onto another. Manufacturers offer special braces and a standoff that maintains required clearances where the pipe protrudes through the second floor and roof framing.

Prefabs come in many designs; a round-the-corner fireplace is shown in **22–15**. They do not require special foundations, and many are designed to permit zero clearance between them and wood-framing members. The actual installation doesn't consist of much more than boxing in the units as shown in **22–16** and then covering the framing with materials of your choice.

Some are made so multi-floor stacking installations are possible with venting occurring in a common chimney (**22–17**). Be sure to check local codes about the number and size of flues that may be allowed. You can't use a chimney to commingle the exhaust of a furnace or water heater as well as a fireplace. A great variety of elbows, brackets, special

22–10

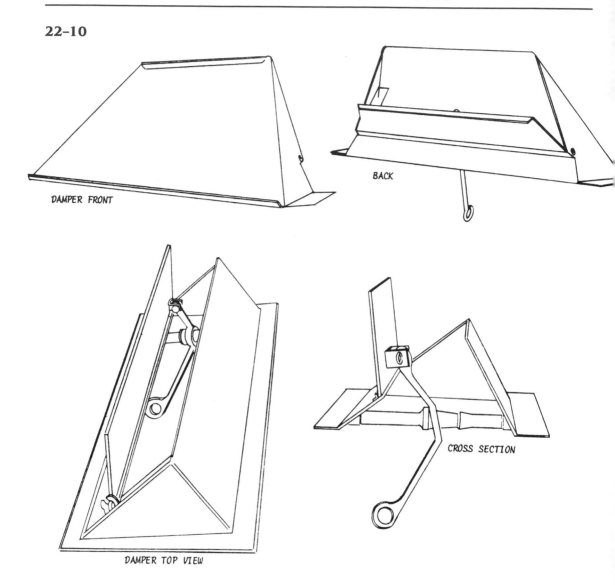

DAMPER FRONT

BACK

DAMPER TOP VIEW

CROSS SECTION

flashings, and other components are available. There are even tops of simulated brick patterns in a choice of colors (**22–18**).

CHIMNEYS AND FLUES

Both fireplaces and woodstoves are designed to contain flames in a masonry or metal chamber. But the lethal gases, sometimes stray embers, and other by-products of combustion are released up the chimney. Old chimneys were simply a hollow box made of

22-11

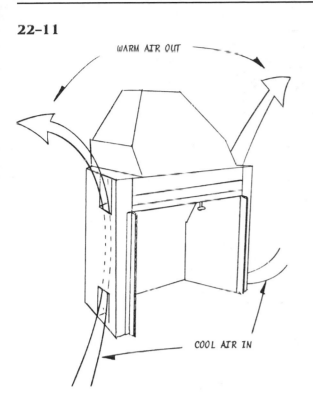

WARM AIR OUT

COOL AIR IN

22-12

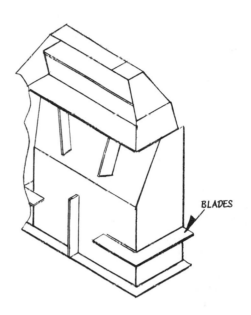

BLADES

22-13

GRILLS ON FACE

GRILLS ON SIDE

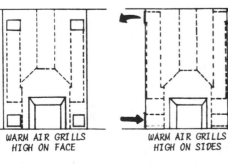

WARM AIR GRILLS
HIGH ON FACE

WARM AIR GRILLS
HIGH ON SIDES

GRILLS MAY BE CONNECTED
TO ADJOINING ROOM

22-14

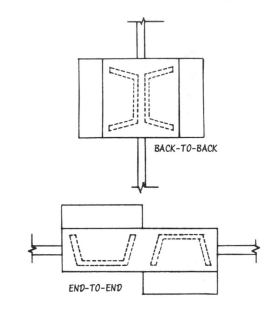

BACK-TO-BACK

END-TO-END

22-15

AROUND-THE-CORNER KIT

22-16

BASIC FRAMING OF KIT

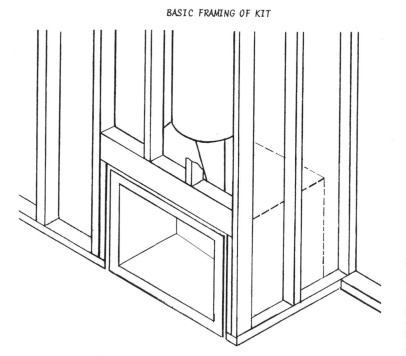

22-17

22-18

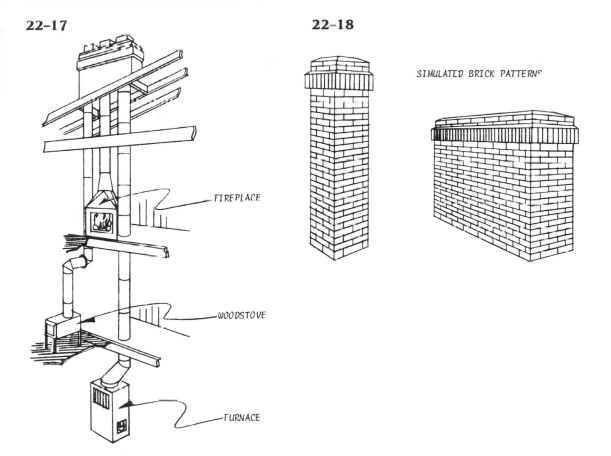

SIMULATED BRICK PATTERNS

FIREPLACE

WOODSTOVE

FURNACE

stone or bricks. Modern masonry chimneys with two layers of protection (an inner flue of hollow clay blocks, and a surrounding masonry structure) can safely channel out exhaust gasses. But they can't deal with the main cause of chimney fires, which is creosote.

This is a gummy residue of incomplete combustion that rises in smoke and sticks to the chimney walls. It's basically unburned fuel, which can reignite. If that happens, the deposits can burn, unseen, in the chimney and develop enough heat to crumble mortar and to crack clay flue blocks. If that happens, the fire can spread into the outer chamber of the chimney and work on its masonry walls. Beyond them is the tinder of studs, joists, flooring, and other combustible materials.

You can reduce creosote formations by burning dry hardwood instead of wet softwood. In woodstoves designed to keep a fire burning for a long time with a minimal draft, you can burn off some deposits by periodically running the stove with the door or draft gates open, mimicking the draw of a fireplace. Even then, the National Fire Prevention

Association recommends having chimneys inspected by a licensed professional chimney sweep once a year, or more often if the fireplace is used frequently.

Codes may permit installing more than one flue in a single chimney when exhaust systems are needed for more than one fireplace or woodstove. The constructions may differ, and it may be necessary to separate the flues by the width of a brick, as shown in **22–19**, or you may be able to use a clay tile flue of double construction, as shown in **22–20**.

If you need two flues and are permitted to install two adjoining liners so that only the wall thickness of the liners separates the flues, be sure to stagger the joints in the flue sections by at least 7 inches.

Chimneys are often made larger from some point below the roof frame. The technique, called corbeling, is practical because it reduces the width near the base that is required for the firebox. That means you need fewer bricks and blocks as the chimney rises above the

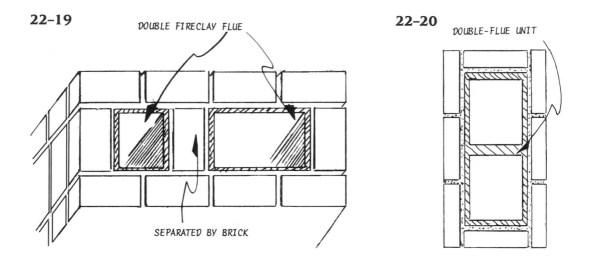

22–19   DOUBLE FIRECLAY FLUE

SEPARATED BY BRICK

22–20   DOUBLE-FLUE UNIT

firebox. The brick projection from course to course should not be more than 1 inch, and generally is less (**22–21**).

The chimney emerges from the roof through the rough opening you provided when you did the roof framing. Remember that combustible materials (wood framing members) must be kept at least 2 inches (consult your local codes) from the chimney walls. The gap should be filled with a noncombustible insulating material (**22–22**). The joint between the chimney and the roof is waterproofed by flashing.

The top of the chimney should be high enough above the roof to reduce exposure to the downdrafts that can occur when wind passes over the roof or nearby structures. The gen-

22–21

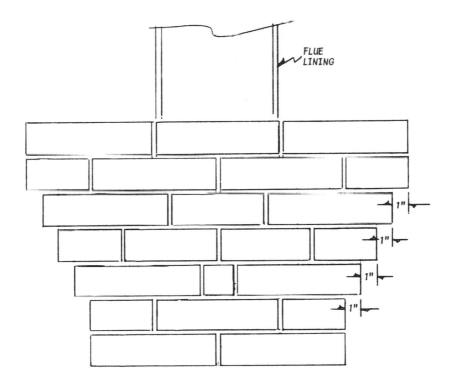

FLUE
LINING

1"

1"

1"

1"

22–22

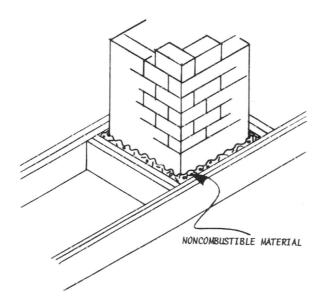

NONCOMBUSTIBLE MATERIAL

eral rule is for the chimney to be 2 feet higher than any ridge closer than 10 feet when the distance is measured horizontally. A flat roof calls for additional chimney height, as shown in **22–23**. Again, these dimensions can vary and are controlled by code.

Adding a cap such as is shown in **22–24** finishes the chimney nicely, but the cap has

22–23

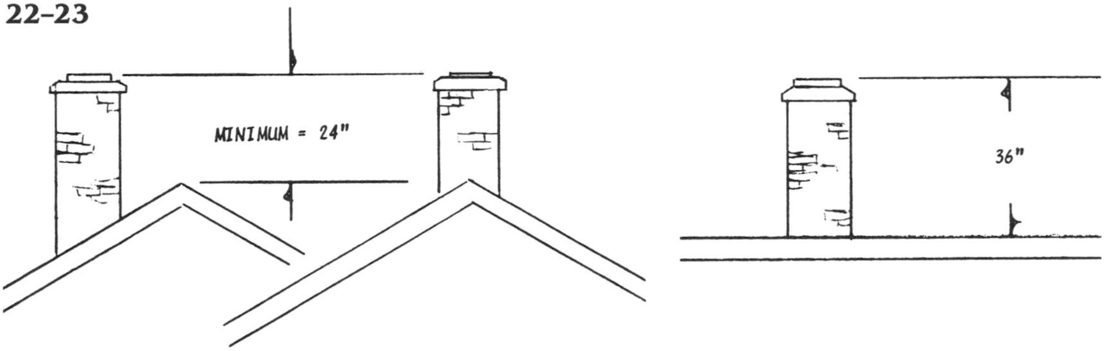

MINIMUM = 24"

36"

22–24

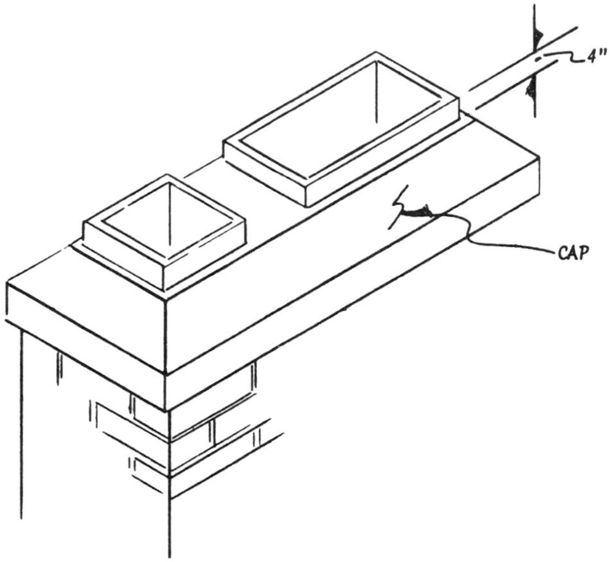

4"

CAP

practical functions as well. The sloping top deflects outside air upward, and this helps promote a good draft. The cap is easy to cast in place with mortar if you set up some temporary formwork (**22–25**). Let the cap extend beyond the walls of the chimney so that it will serve as a drip ledge. The ledge, plus the cap's slope, helps to drain water away from the chimney top.

22–25

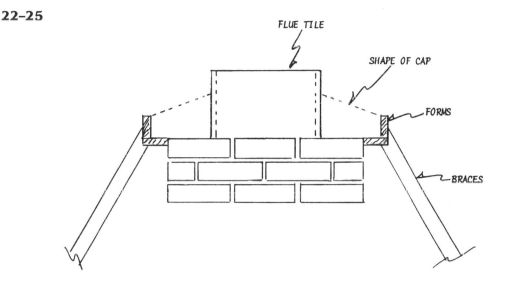

GAS FIREPLACES
===============

As charming as it is to burn real wood, for some people it's a hassle. Open-hearth fire-places may chug along for a while without puff backs or sparks, but then they need atten-tion—and a chimney sweep to clear creosote from the chimney, and an honest guy selling you seasoned hardwood that isn't laced with sappy new spruce you can't burn with a blowtorch.

In the slightly antiseptic world of smart houses with programmable lights you can turn on or off without flipping a switch, these nitty-gritty wood-burning problems have been solved by automatic gas fireplaces. Their popularity is growing.

In 1991, 380,000 stoves, fireplaces, and permanent logs fueled with natural and LP (Liquified Petroleum) gas were sold nationwide. According to recent figures from the Hearth Products Association, the annual sales rate is now over 10 million. There are models that fit in conventional chimneys, in freestanding islands, and snugly against walls even where there is no chimney. The hottest selling designs are freestanding units that look like wood stoves with gas logs inside.

Unlike open-hearth fireplaces, gas-fired units produce a predictable amount of warmth with ratings like a furnace—from about 20,000 up to 40,000 BTUs per hour. With a blower to increase warm air circulation, a large unit can provide supplemental heat for a 2,000-square-foot house.

And unlike conventional fireplaces that accumulate ashes and soot, gas-fired units require only minimal maintenance—generally the same kind of seasonal cleaning and tuning required for a gas furnace. Although gas units can be vented through a conventional fireplace flue, there are direct-vent and power-vent models that can route exhaust out the back of the fireplace directly through a firesafe thimble in an exterior wall to a ventilator hood.

If you already have a gas line in the house, running a branch line to supply the fireplace is relatively easy. Bringing a gas line in from the street could cost as much as building a chimney. If you aren't close to the gas-line grid, many models are available with LP gas.

It is difficult to compare the costs of operating a standard wood fireplace and a gas-fired model; there are too many variables like the quality and cost of wood. But many gas fireplaces burn at about 75 percent efficiency, which is comparable to a mid-efficiency furnace. The rating is well under the over 95 percent efficiency of a condensing, gas-fired furnace, but well over the roughly 50 percent efficiency of a typical open-hearth fireplace.

You'll get more warmth from a unit with a built-in fan that circulates heat, and better efficiency from a unit with an automatic damper that closes the flue to retain warm air when you're not using the fireplace. Modern gas units have another feature you can't duplicate with a wood fireplace: remote control. If you're in the mood for a fire, click, you get a fire. Some models even include built-in mechanisms to simulate the crackle of burning wood logs to make up for the eerie silence of high-efficiency flames rolling up from

22–26   GAS STOVE (Photo courtesy of Harmon Stove Company.)

ceramic logs. Remote control also lets you raise or lower thermostat settings from the couch, change the blower speed, and adjust the height of the flames.

One type of gas fireplace, called vent-free, is designed like a gas stove in your kitchen; it has no exhaust pipe. Whatever by-products of combustion it produces, including some carbon monoxide, you breathe in. Some vent free models burn cleanly at 90-percent efficiency. But some gas furnaces are even more efficient and they have exhaust lines. In a tight house, vent-free models also could cause excessive moisture buildup.

The lure is that you can put these units anywhere without building a chimney or breaking through the wall to install vent pipe. That could be risky, even though some of the model building codes that control construction standards nationwide do allow vent-free units. However, some local jurisdictions may contradict the code. If you want a vent-free unit, check with the local building department. Unlike vented gas fireplaces, vent-free units are equipped with an oxygen depletion sensor to shut off the fireplace if oxygen drops below a preset safety level—a sure sign that manufacturers see a potential risk.

CONSIDERING WOODSTOVES

The energy crisis of the 1970s made woodstoves popular home heaters. It also spurred manufacturers to make gains in energy efficiency, which has continued to increase over the last 30 years.

Early models were a bit primitive by today's standards. I remember a friend's mountain cabin in which the only source of heat was a potbellied woodstove. That cabin was warm, and if the stove top wasn't being used to cook something, there was always a pot of water on it that did a good job of humidification. I also recall an unheated two-car garage I used as a shop. At that time I bought a woodstove from a junk dealer for $15 and installed it with stovepipe for a flue. Although the garage was large, the woodstove heated it efficiently, and fuel consumption was less than the amounts of scrap wood that remained from projects.

Things have changed, and a modern, high-efficiency woodstove is an artful compromise that constrains a fire burning inside the house and lets it flourish at the same time. It carries dangerous exhaust gases outside but keeps heat inside. A good design lets you maximize heat and minimize emissions, but not automatically. To get the most out a stove, you need to understand and control the combustion process.

1. *The combustion cycle.* A typical combustion cycle has three basic stages. At first, the fire is tentative and not very hot because energy is consumed boiling water. In freshly cut logs, up to half the weight can be water. But even in seasoned firewood, about 20 percent of the weight is water. A lot of hissing and sizzling is a sign that the fire is producing steam instead of the heat you want.

In the second stage, fire temperature rises above the boiling point of water and the wood begins to break down, producing smoke instead of steam. In a hot fire fueled with a steady supply of oxygen (if you leave the doors or draft gates open), a lot of the smoke will burn and produce extra heat.

In a cooler fire (if you immediately close the doors and shut down the draft gates), a lot of the smoke will condense in the chimney as creosote. You lose the potential heat and run the risk that the smoke (as creosote deposits) will reignite and burn unchecked in the chimney.

In the third stage, most of the water and the hydrocarbons in smoke have vaporized. But about half the potential energy contained in the wood remains as charcoal. It burns cleanly without much smoke or flame, and churns out the kind of heat that cooks both you and the chair you're sitting in.

2. *Combustion efficiency.* Even in a deep, inefficient fireplace, you'll get more heat and cleaner exhaust burning well-seasoned hardwood than freshly cut softwood. But given the same fuel, what separates a modern stove from a fireplace is the ability to burn smoke before it enters the chimney. This milks more heat from the fire and dramatically cuts creosote deposits and polluting exhaust emissions.

Some stoves accomplish this with a catalytic combustor—a compact device made of a ceramic or metal honeycomb coated with platinum or palladium. A combustor reduces the ignition temperature of smoke so you can burn the unused fuel it contains. The main bonus is that you don't have to open the doors or draft gates to keep a combustor operating. It can increase heating efficiency and reduce emissions at normal stove temperatures.

Newer noncatalytic stoves increase efficiency by routing exhaust into a secondary combustion chamber. Smoke may be channeled around the firebox, reheated, and remixed with incoming air to ignite it before it escapes into the flue.

While an older model, such as a Franklin stove, may have about the same 50 percent energy efficiency as a fireplace, both catalytic stoves and noncatalytic models with secondary combustion chambers may have 75 percent efficiency.

3. *Setting the fire.* Before you install or operate a woodstove, be sure to check local building codes and the manufacturer's instructions. Codes are similar for the two basic types of high-efficiency stoves, but typical operating procedures are somewhat different.

With noncatalytic stoves, you should build a moderately hot fire to start with, and let larger logs ignite fully by running the stove with high draft settings for at least five to ten minutes. (The wood you use has a lot to do with the timing.)

It's tempting to close down the draft gates to extend burn time. But without enough air, logs will not ignite easily or burn completely. Greatly reducing the air supply and letting the fire smolder may also disable the secondary combustion system, which decreases efficiency and increases exhaust pollution and creosote deposits.

You generally need a fire of 1,000 to 1,200 degrees F to burn the pollutants in wood smoke, according to the Environmental Protection Agency, which can provide a list of certified stoves that meet modern emission standards. Temperature is difficult to judge even with a stove thermometer. But on some stoves you can see the secondary air inlets through a glass door and spot the darts of flame, called light-off, that indicate secondary combustion.

With catalytic stoves, you don't need as hot a fire to increase efficiency and decrease emissions. Generally, a catalyst will start burning smoke between 350 and 600 degrees F. It helps to buy a catalyst temperature monitor if your stove doesn't come with one. It allows you to monitor low-temperature smoke ignition and prevent damage to combustors that occurs with prolonged exposure to high heat in the range of 1600 degrees F. If the monitor shows a high temperature, you can change the draft path (it's generally called the bypass mode) so that smoke skirts the combustor and allows it to cool.

It's still a good idea to burn a robust blaze initially. But you should start the fire in bypass mode. This increases airflow initially and helps the fire get hotter faster. When the temperature rises, say, above 500 degrees Fahrenheit, you can switch the stove to catalyst mode. Once the catalyst is active, you can reduce the draft to extend burn time.

4. *Installation basics.* A woodstove, like a fireplace or a furnace, requires a flue—its own flue. You shouldn't plan to construct a fireplace chimney thinking you can cut into it someplace later and insert a stovepipe from a woodstove.

   Of course, you can also think about a woodstove instead of a fireplace, in which case you would construct a basic chimney/flue and provide for a smoke-pipe intake (**22–27**). Here, the lower part of the chimney should be solid masonry. A clean-out door can be installed just below the smoke pipe, but it doesn't seem necessary since removing the smoke pipe for cleaning, which you should do at least once a year, makes it easy to remove the soot that accumulates in the pocket merely by reaching through the pipe hole. You also can use specially insulated fixtures, called thimbles, to pass a stove exhaust pipe through a wood-framed wall into an exterior masonry chimney or code-approved prefab metal flue.

5. *Safety factors.* A minimum clearance is always required between a woodstove and a combustible wall. This will differ, depending on whether the stove is a radiating or circulating type. For the radiating type, which is simply a metal shell in which the fire is built, clearances may have to be as much as 36 inches. On the other hand, a circulat-

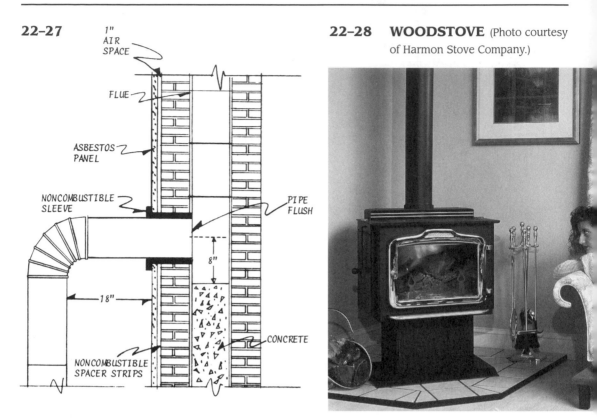

22–27

1" AIR SPACE

FLUE

ASBESTOS PANEL

NONCOMBUSTIBLE SLEEVE

PIPE FLUSH

8"

18"

CONCRETE

NONCOMBUSTIBLE SPACER STRIPS

22–28 **WOODSTOVE** (Photo courtesy of Harmon Stove Company.)

ing stove is a double-wall affair that creates an air chamber through which air circulates. It needs much less clearance for safe operation—in some cases, as little as 12 inches. But clearances can often by reduced by attaching a noncombustible material to the nearby wall. A relatively easy solution is to install a sheet of at least 28-gauge metal to protect the wall. This should be mounted on fireproof spacers so air can circulate between the wall or ceiling and the shield. Protection is also required under a stove if it is mounted on a combustible floor. You need to check local codes before building. As always, it's better to work with the inspector from the start than to risk having to make alterations later.

23

INSTALLING INSULATION

Energy codes have become increasingly important in new construction, and standards continue to rise. For example, a review of insulation requirements by the Department of Energy (DOE) in 2001 led to the first major overhaul in 10 years and standards that could be difficult to meet.

The DOE recommendation for attic insulation in many cold-climate states that was R-38, for instance, has been increased to R-49. (R-value is the standard measure of insulation effectiveness; the higher the number, the better.) To meet the new DOE guideline, you need to increase attic insulation by about 3 inches, which is easy enough to do in most new houses.

In walls, the old DOE guideline of R-10 has been increased to R-18. To meet that standard you need to add 2½ inches for a total thickness of 5 inches of fiberglass or mineral wool, which both have an R-value of about 3.5 per inch. The problem is that the wall cavities in standard construction are only 3½ inches deep and there isn't enough room. If this standard is code in your area, you need to use 2 × 6 studs, or apply an exterior layer of foam board.

The DOE recommendations are based in part on interviews with insulation installers across the country, and developed using a new analysis of building materials, techniques, and fuels to determine life-cycle costs for different types and amounts of insulation. The recommendations outstrip many existing local codes mainly for two reasons. First, some local codes haven't been updated to reflect new materials and installations. Second, local codes are to some extent market-driven instead of consumer-driven. Everyone involved wants buildings to be safe, of course, but there is resistance particularly among builders to sweeping changes that could add thousands to the cost of construction and make houses less affordable.

But the DOE recommendations (there are no federal building codes) will put pressure on regional and local code writers to upgrade existing regulations. Until they do, you can use conventional installations, or make alterations in your new construction or remodeling plans to accommodate more insulation.

EVALUATING INSULATION

There are many types of insulation. In fact, insulation (and the related subjects of ventilation and moisture control) has more twists and turns than most other components of a house. Since the mid-1970s, this subject has spawned all sorts of trick systems and proprietary products. Today, there is insulation in cans, plastic insulation that contractors blow into open framing cavities, and many other products and approaches. But almost all new residential construction and remodeling uses four basic types: batts, rolls, loose fill, and rigid foam boards (**23–1**).

The different configurations are best suited to particular locations. Batts are made to fit between studs. Rolls and blankets are better suited to fill the longer stretches between ceiling joists. These types are generally made of fiberglass or mineral wool. Loose fill often is blown into hard-to-reach spaces such as attics and finished walls to improve the insulation in existing homes. It may be made of fiberglass, mineral wool, or cellulose (basically recycled paper). All these materials have an R-value of about 3.5 per inch.

Some rigid foam board has a higher R-value per inch, generally from about R-4 to R-8. It's good for providing maximum thermal value in minimal or confined spaces, for instance, over foundation walls and concrete floor slabs. There are many types of foam board, including expanded and extruded polystyrene. They all come in sheets that can be nailed or glued over masonry and framing.

23–1

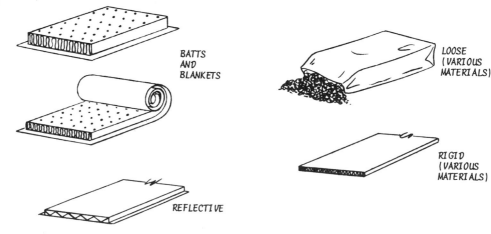

BATTS AND BLANKETS

LOOSE (VARIOUS MATERIALS)

RIGID (VARIOUS MATERIALS)

REFLECTIVE

No matter what type you use, you can measure its effectiveness using the common denominator of R-value per inch of thickness. Every insulator has an R-value, no matter what the insulation is made or how it's shaped. The math is simple: the higher the number, the more thermal value you get.

Batts may be most economical between 2× 4 studs in an exterior wall because they are manufactured to fit, and there is room for about 3½ inches of material. Multiply the depth of insulation by the R-value per inch (about 3.5 for cellulose), and you get a rating of about R-12. Foam boards, typically 2×8 or 4×8 sheets, are better suited to a wall surface—under new siding, for example.

Small differences in insulating value may seem insignificant, but the thermal envelope around the conditioned air space in your house has a major, long-term impact on fuel costs. In a typical American home, about 20 percent of the energy you buy goes for water heating, 10 to 30 percent goes for lighting and appliances, and the rest—between 50 and 70 percent of the total— goes for heating and cooling. Inadequate insulation and air leakage are the leading causes of energy waste in homes, according to the DOE.

You can compare different products and R-values on your own, of course. But you may want to take advantage of Web sites set up by the DOE (doe.gov) and Oak Ridge National Laboratory (www.ornl.gov). Log on, search for insulation, and receive a free online recommendation, whether you're building a new house or remodeling, to improve the building envelope, increase your comfort, and lower your utility bills.

On the DOE site, you can choose an insulation estimate for a new or existing house, select one of several types of heating systems and fuels, type in the first three digits of your zip code, and scroll down to a nearly instant solution. The zip-code computer program makes recommendations based on cost effectiveness using average local energy prices, regional average insulation costs, heating and cooling equipment efficiencies, regional climate factors, and potential energy savings for both heating and cooling seasons.

On a hypothetical existing house with a natural-gas furnace and central air-conditioning in the 200-zip area, for example, the DOE system produces recommendations of R-38 insulation in the attic, and R-11 for walls. The program suggests R-25 for floors over unheated spaces, R-11 for basement walls, and provides values for other insulation options, such as using insulation board sheathing under new siding.

On the Oak Ridge National Lab's site, you can navigate to their Whole Wall R-Value Calculation program to estimate the overall insulation values of different wall systems. For example, you can check the values of standard stud framing with batt insulation against structural insulated panels, a highly efficient wall system that consists of wood sheathing sandwiching a core of dense foam.

Before you get started with insulation, bear in mind that some people have reactions to handling the material, particularly fiberglass. You should protect against possible skin irritation when handling batts and loose-fill products. Cover up with a long-sleeved shirt with collar and cuffs buttoned, gloves, hat, safety glasses, and a disposable dust mask.

There are some modern products you may want to use, such as batt and blanket fiberglass encased in a sheer film that contains the fibers. This type can be very helpful if you have problems handling fiberglass.

BASIC APPLICATIONS

Batts of insulation may be installed by stapling its flanges to the sides of studs as shown in **23–2** to provide an air space or to leave the front edges of the studs uncovered. Professional installers of drywall often request this method because it eliminates the possibility of wrinkles and folds on stud faces that can occur when a job is done carelessly. Usually, though, and especially when the insulation has its own vapor barrier, the flanges are stapled to stud or joist edges as shown in **23–3** because this method provides a more

23–2

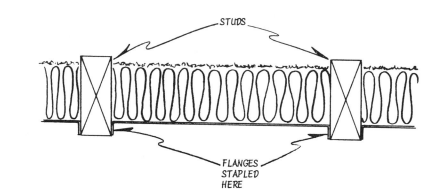

continuous seal. Use extra staples where necessary to be sure flanges lie flat and smooth. Some flanges you must make yourself, but this is just a matter of cutting the material longer than you need to fill a cavity and then removing a small amount of the insulation from the end or ends requiring a flange.

Thread insulation behind plumbing and electrical boxes. If gaps occur, use extra pieces of vapor barrier to cover them. If the insulation is behind a cold-water pipe, you can add a separate sheet of vapor barrier on the warm side of the room. (It's best to drape the entire thermal envelope with a vapor barrier.)

Ceilings can be insulated from below or from the attic. If the attic space is very tight

23-3

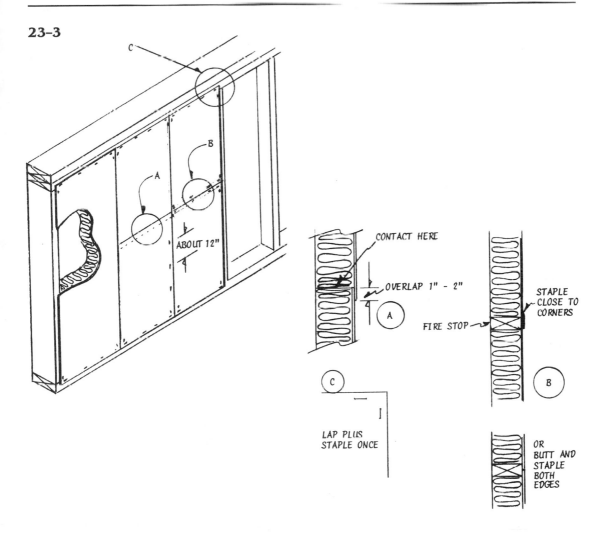

and you are working with blankets or batts, it will probably be better to work from below, doing the job along with the walls. Make sure that the insulation is carried over the top wall plates and that the corner joints are lapped, as shown in **23-4**.

If the ceiling is open, the insulation should be carried along the rafters as shown in **23-5**. Notice that it is necessary to leave an air space between the insulation and the roof sheathing. Don't neglect the gaps that exist around doors and windows. Fill the areas with insulation and be sure to provide an adequate vapor barrier (**23-6**).

Blanket insulation is easy to cut if you use a sharp utility knife and a straight piece of wood as a straightedge. Place the wood on the line of cut and then kneel on it to compress the material as much as possible. Then run the knife along the guide, more than once if necessary.

23–4

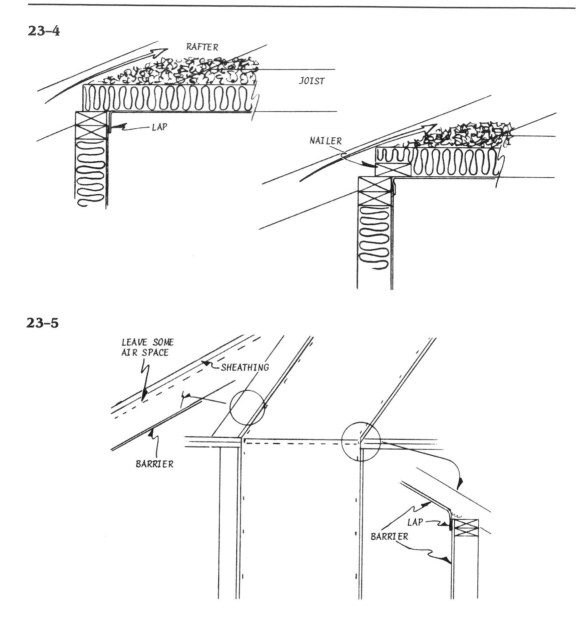

23–5

Although there are some products that combine insulation and vapor barriers, such as foil-faced batts, many pros use two applications. First, they staple up batts or blankets, generally filling the framing cavity in question. Then they drape plastic sheeting as a continuous vapor barrier over the insulated surfaces (**23–7**). The sheets should be overlapped by several inches, and trimmed carefully around windows and doors and electrical fixtures. The idea is to provide a continuous barrier to keep moisture from entering the framing.

This is important because moisture that works its way through the cavity, including the insulation, eventually will contact a cold surface (the inside of the sheathing in most cases), and condense. That water is then trapped in the wall, and can soak insulation and rot the framing.

23-6

23-7

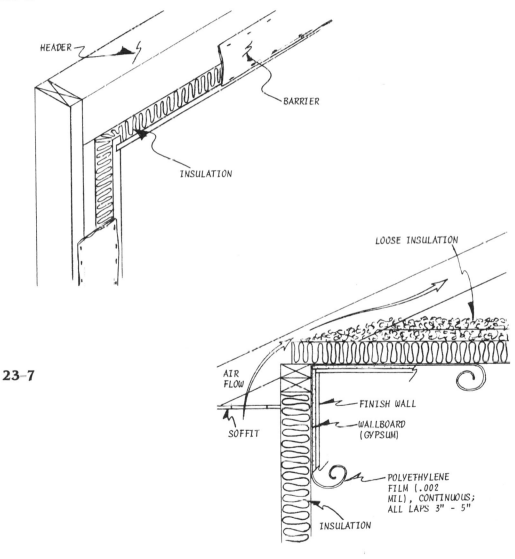

THE ATTIC IS CRITICAL

You can insulate attics with blankets or batts, or with loose fill, or by combining both as in **23–8**. If you use loose fill and the ceiling below does not have a vapor barrier, you can provide one by installing polyethylene film between the joists as shown in **23–10**. Be sure to use a retainer at all vent areas, but do not install it so it becomes a seal that will prevent airflow (**23–11**).

The modern way to do this is with inexpensive foam forms that you staple between rafters at the eaves. These air baffles provide a shallow tunnel for air under the roof and

23–8

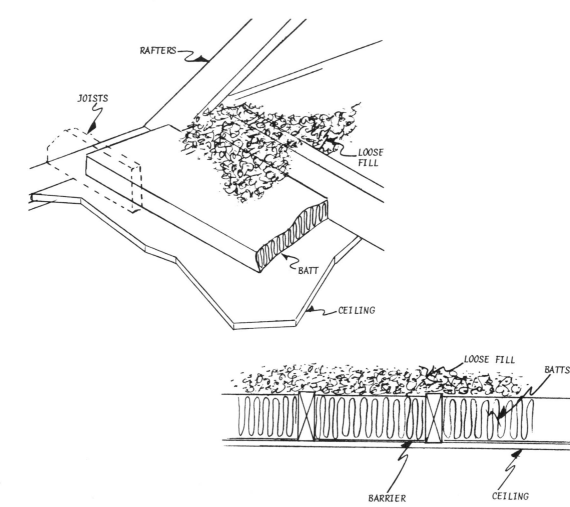

23-9   R-VALUES OF INSULATING MATERIALS

THICKNESS OF INSULATION REQUIRED FOR R-VALUE OF	WITH BATTS OR BLANKETS OF		WITH LOOSE FILL OF		
	Glass Fiber	Rock Wool	Glass Fiber	Rock Wool	Cellulosic Fiber
R-11	3½"–4"	3"	5"	4"	3"
R-19	6"–6½"	5½"	8"–9"	6"–7"	5"
R-22	6½"	6"	10½"	7"–8"	6"
R-30	9½"–10½"	9"	13"–14"	10"–11"	8"
R-38	12"–13"	10½"	17"–18"	13"–14"	10"–11"

prevent insulation from closing off required ventilation. If there are light fixtures recessed between the joists, it's a good idea to leave some space between the enclosure and the insulation (**23–12**). If the thickness of the insulation is greater than the depth of the joists, erect some headers at right angles to the joists to act as retainers and as a height guide (**23–13**). The spacing of the headers is not critical.

23-10

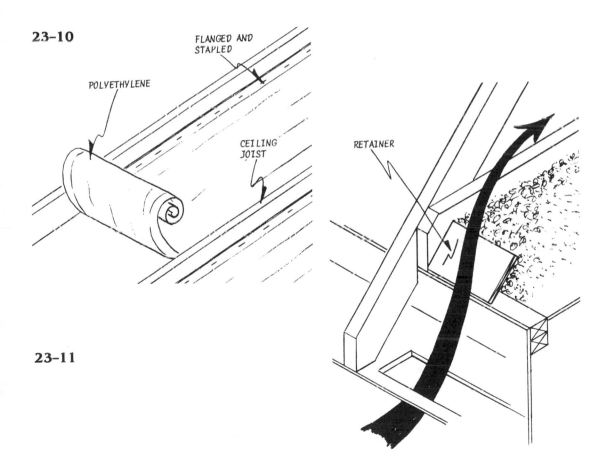

POLYETHYLENE

FLANGED AND STAPLED

CEILING JOIST

RETAINER

23-11

23-12

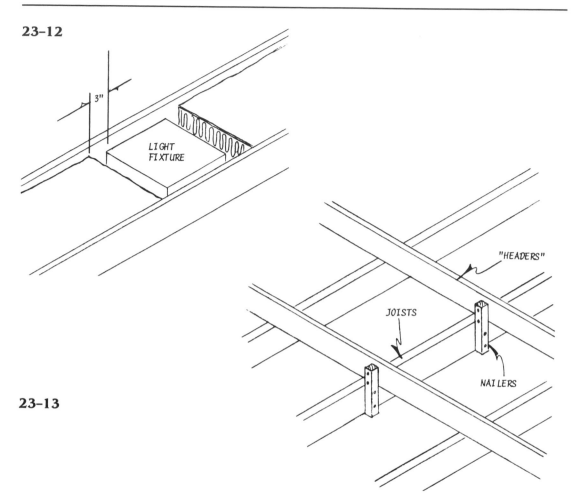

23-13

You can more than fill the area between joists, but limit the insulation at outside walls. Don't let material spill into the roof overhang and block air-intake grills. Remember that there's no point in insulating the overhang in any case because there is no heated living space below.

ATTIC VENTILATION

Attics are a special case because insulation by itself won't do. You need to provide ventilation as well. When it's a comfortable, air-conditioned 70 degrees F in the house despite a heat wave outside, the unconditioned attic may be baking at 125 degrees or more. You don't live under the eaves, so you don't feel the heat directly. But hot-head attics drive up cooling costs, shorten the lifespan of conditioning equipment, and can contribute to mold, rot, and other problems.

Insulation is part of the puzzle. The old rule of thumb was to fill the bays between ceiling joists. If you have 2 × 6 joists, for example, the bays can hold 5½ inches of insulation with a total R-value of about 20. To meet the new DOE standard for attic insulation in many cold-climate states of R-49, you would have to fill bays between 2 × 10s (for about R-33) and still add another layer.

Remember that you can't have a vapor barrier between layers; it will trap moisture in the insulation. There is only one place for a vapor barrier: directly under the drywall of the living space. Before you deal with vents, you also should add extra batts around any exposed air-conditioning ducts.

There are many types of attic vents, and many good places to install them. But one type in one place can't handle the job of keeping attic air close to the temperature of the air outside. You need a combination with about the same square footage of air inlet and air outlet.

You could install a huge vent in the roof, but not much hot air would flow out unless there were a way for fresh air to flow in and replace it. A large-scale mismatch of inlet and outlet area can even encourage leaks of conditioned air through cracks and other openings in the attic floor, which wastes energy and unnecessarily taxes your cooling system.

On the roof, you can install turbine vents that spin as hot air escapes and encourage the flow of more air. Another, less commercial looking option is a basic roof vent with a hood that keeps rain from entering (**23–14**). Both types require a rooftop installation where you have to cut back shingles and cut a hole in the plywood roof deck.

The most effective roof installation is a continuous ridge vent. It's the most widely used by far on new construction (**23–15**). The plywood roof deck is built (or cut back) short of

23–14   **23–15**

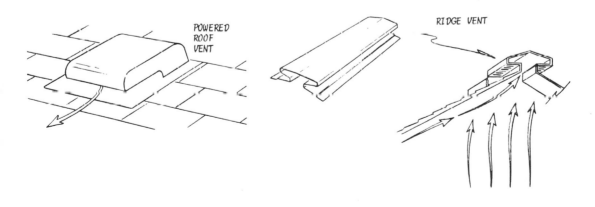

POWERED ROOF VENT

RIDGE VENT

the roof peak so that air can sweep up both undersides of the attic roof and out the vent. You can cover many ridge vents with shingles so that a ridge-vented roof looks about the same as a standard roof.

One of the most common outlet options is a gable-end vent (**23–16**). This louvered vent nestles under the roof ridge on the end wall of the attic. If you have two exposed gable walls, a louver (screened on the back to keep out insects) on each one encourages cross ventilation at the highest and hottest area of the attic. The venting area should be $\frac{1}{300}$ of the total square footage of the ceilings (with a vapor barrier) and twice that ($\frac{1}{150}$) without one.

There are four basic ways to bring air into the attic along the roof overhang, as shown in **23–17**. That's the best place for an inlet because cooler outdoor air will replace hotter attic air rising to the ridge.

Plug vents are small screened and louvered circles made of metal. Installing them is easy; there should be one per bay in the spaces between rafters. You cut a hole in the soffit (normally a flat piece of plywood forming the base of the overhang) and snap in a vent.

You can increase the vent area with the same approach by cutting large openings

23–16   GABLE VENTS

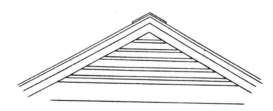

23-17

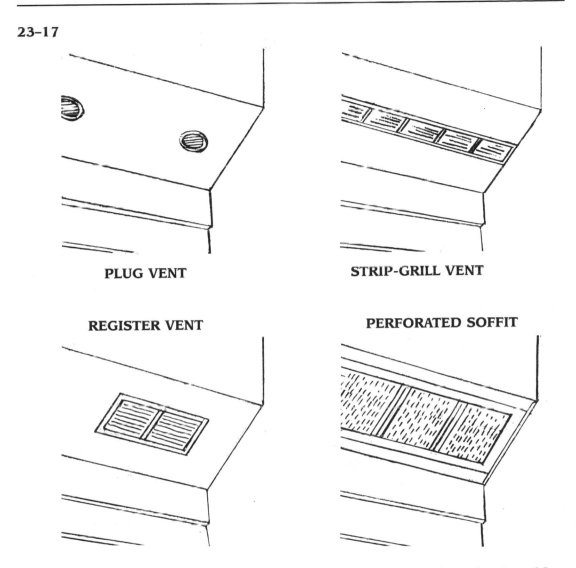

PLUG VENT   **STRIP-GRILL VENT**

REGISTER VENT   **PERFORATED SOFFIT**

between bays (or every other bay) and installing rectangular vents about the size of floor registers, although these can look a little clunky in an overhang.

A better option is to install a continuous strip-grill vent. It's only a few inches wide, but extends the full length of the overhang to provide a larger vent area and eliminate unvented dead spots. Use a circular saw to cut out a narrow channel of plywood and nail the strip grill into the recess. Another approach is to install the plywood soffit in two pieces around the strip.

You can also use perforated aluminum panels instead of plywood on the soffits. This venting system normally is used with matching aluminum siding and trim, but you can set the panels and trim the edges with wood.

THE CRAWL SPACE

You should restrict insulation to a thermal envelope around living spaces—in ceiling joists of the second story, in walls, of course, and in floor joists of the first story. The unfinished space below should be treated as part of the outdoors. But it is enclosed and can trap moisture, so it does need ventilation. Airflow is needed in particular with a dirt crawl space to deal with excessive moisture and odors that could build up and seep into the house.

The best approach is to pour a slab over the crawl-space floor. Next best is a vapor barrier (overlapped plastic sheeting or tar paper), covered with a bed of gravel. Both solutions allow you some access, say, if you need to fix a pipe or duct.

To insulate the floor, add batts or blankets (vapor barrier up) to fill the space between floor joists. Then nail sheets of foam board across the bottom of the joists where foam is allowed by code. If you don't need the extra thermal value, you can protect the insulation with wire mesh (**23–18**).

23–18

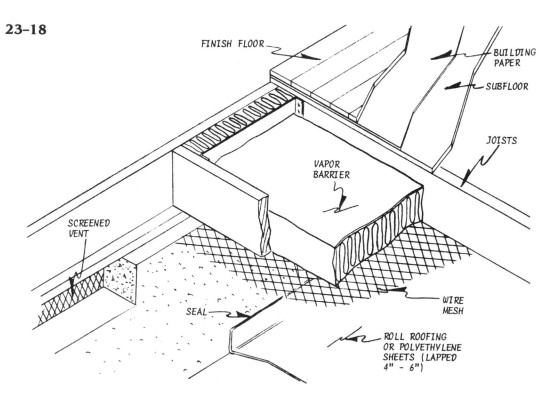

FINISH FLOOR

BUILDING PAPER

SUBFLOOR

JOISTS

VAPOR BARRIER

SCREENED VENT

WIRE MESH

SEAL

ROLL ROOFING OR POLYETHYLENE SHEETS (LAPPED 4" – 6")

The combination of 9½ inches of fiberglass insulation (the depth of 2 × 10 floor joists) plus a ¾-inch-thick, high-quality foam board, will provide an R-value of almost R-40, which is more than enough to buffer temperature between the spaces, even when the crawl space is ventilated with cold air (**23–19**). When you encounter bridging, cut the installation in one of the two ways shown in **23–20**. If you make straight rather than ragged cuts, use small pieces of insulation to fill in. It's also a good idea to cut pieces of insulation so you can fit them against joist headers (**23–21**).

23–19

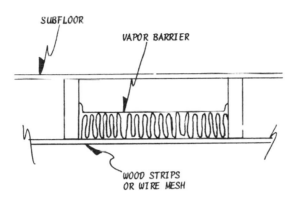

23–20

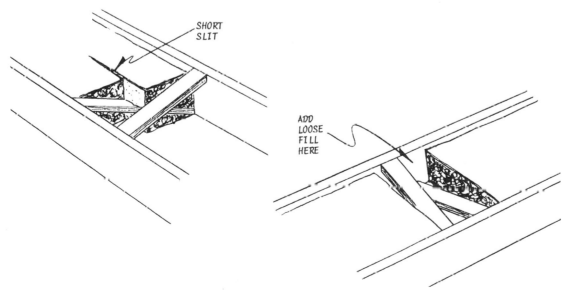

23-21

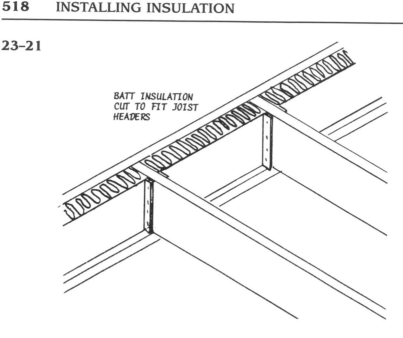

BATT INSULATION
CUT TO FIT JOIST
HEADERS

OTHER INSULATION LOCATIONS

There are many smaller areas where adding insulation in one form or another will pay off.

1. *Concrete slabs.* Most of the heat loss through a concrete slab occurs along the perimeter, so while the entire slab is poured over a continuous vapor barrier, a special rigid insulation is used only along the edges. This type of insulation, able to withstand contact with wet concrete, comes in thicknesses that range from 1 to 2 inches, so you can make a choice depending on prevailing temperatures and the type of heating you will use. The insulation can be installed in various ways (**23-22**). Extensions under a slab or vertically on a foundation wall should be at least 2 feet.

2. *Openings.* A good deal of heat can be lost through small openings that might be present around doors and windows. If heat can get out, then cold air, and dust and noise, can get in. The guards you can use against such infiltration come under the classification of weatherstripping (**23-23**). You'll find that modern windows and doors usually come equipped with efficient weatherstripping.

    If you need to add weatherstripping, one basic material is spring or cushioned metal strips that are nailed to jambs against the doorstops (**23-24**). When you close the door, the metal is compressed to form a seal. More sophisticated types are two-piece designs that interlock (**23-25**). Some are easier to install because they are surface-mounted. Others require a little more work but are neater since they are not visible when the door is closed. Some products, which include a type of built-in sealing strip, are made to be used in place of regular wood stops (**23-26**).

23-22

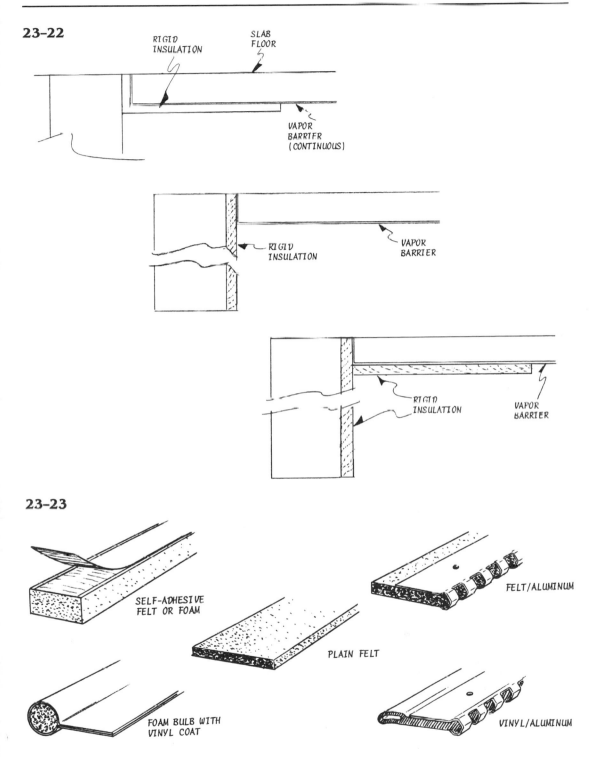

RIGID INSULATION

SLAB FLOOR

VAPOR BARRIER (CONTINUOUS)

RIGID INSULATION

VAPOR BARRIER

RIGID INSULATION

VAPOR BARRIER

23-23

SELF-ADHESIVE FELT OR FOAM

PLAIN FELT

FELT/ALUMINUM

FOAM BULB WITH VINYL COAT

VINYL/ALUMINUM

23–24

23–25

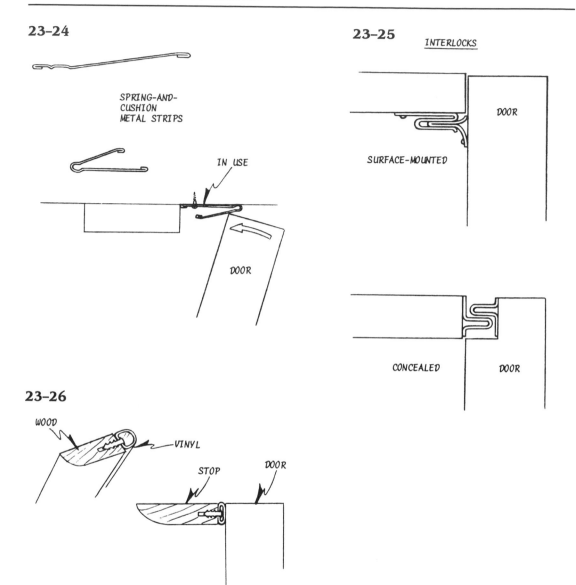

A widely used threshold is made of metal and includes a vinyl insert (sometimes a replaceable one) that presses against the bottom of the door (**23–27**). Another type places the vinyl on the bottom of the door and has an integral drip cap (**23–28**). Because the vinyl moves with the door, it doesn't take a beating by being walked on. An interlocking type is shown in **23–29**. Notice that the interlock element is nailed to the bottom of the door and that the door is rabbeted.

23–27

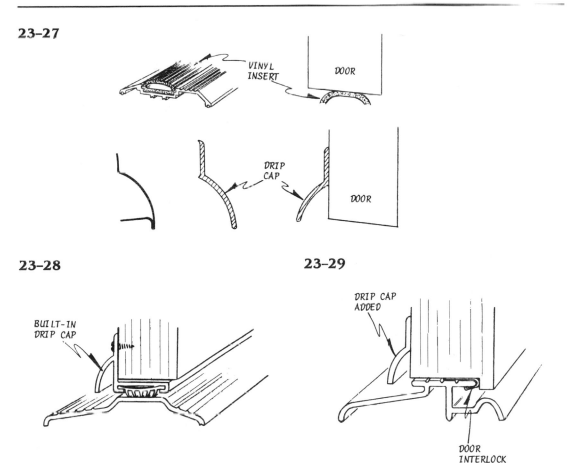

VINYL
INSERT

DOOR

DRIP
CAP

DOOR

23–28

23–29

BUILT-IN
DRIP CAP

DRIP CAP
ADDED

DOOR
INTERLOCK

3. *Electrical boxes.* Any wall puncture is a potential cold spot, and every house has dozens of them on exterior walls in the form of electrical switch and outlet boxes. On new construction and remodeling jobs, you can install plastic pans that guide insulation around and behind the boxes and make a positive seal with insulation batts and vapor barriers. You can also reduce drafts by fitting precut foam pads under the removable cover plates.

4. *Small openings.* Insulating foam in a can is an easy way to fill irregular gaps and cracks too small or too wet for loose fill. Where a pipe exits a foundation wall, or an air conditioner protrudes through siding, for example, just insert the nozzle and push the button. Foam comes out in a shaving-cream-like consistency, expands to fill irregular spaces you can't get to by hand, and then hardens to form an insulated, weathertight seal.

SOUNDPROOFING

Insulation is one of the best ways to reduce sound transmission in houses. Typically, builders install insulation only in exterior walls (and the envelope of floors and ceilings) for thermal protection. There are some other areas worth considering.

1. *Common walls.* You can combine many different layers of soundproofing materials for maximum effect, or only a few to make a modest improvement that minimizes the cost and time of the project. But in every case, it also helps to make the room acoustically soft. In a sparsely furnished room with bare hardwood floors and large glass doors, sound reverberates off the hard surfaces and sometimes even produces echoes. Soften the room with thick rugs on pads, heavy drapes, overstuffed couches (a huge sculpture of a sponge would be perfect), and the sound is significantly muffled.

    If you're starting from scratch with a new partition wall, you can incorporate batts of insulation and a layer of foam board on each side under the drywall. Working toward increasing levels of quiet (each with a small loss of floor space), you can use 2 × 6 studs instead of the conventional 2 × 4s. This allows you to pile extra insulation into the cavities between studs.

    But one of the most effective designs that is easy for do-it-yourselfers to build is a double stud wall. This builds in a complete disconnect by framing two walls set a hair apart. But the efficient approach is to use 2 × 6s on the horizontal members at the top and bottom of the wall, and staggered rows of 2 × 4 studs between them (**23–30**). You follow a standard 16-inch-on-center layout on both sides of the wall. But you stagger the installation so the row of studs flush with one side of the wall is set midway between the row on the other side. This makes one surface independent of the other.

    If you snake thick batts of insulation horizontally between the staggered studs, this

23–30

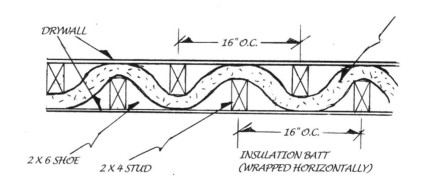

DRYWALL

16" O.C.

16" O.C.

2 X 6 SHOE

2 X 4 STUD

INSULATION BATT
(WRAPPED HORIZONTALLY)

assembly will stop most sound transmission. But you can take things a step further by covering each side of the wall with an inch or more of foam board, and caulking seams and edges before applying drywall.

The basic system is efficient because the overall framing depth is only 5½ inches. With an inch of foam on each side, plus drywall, overall depth is about 8½ inches, while a standard 2 × 4 wall with drywall is about half that size.

2. *Floors.* In music studios, floors often are raised on grids and sound-absorbing tiles that are basically upside-down versions of suspended acoustic ceilings. This ultimate disconnect from the vibrations that carry sound isn't practical in homes. But you can effectively deaden sound in floors by installing wall-to-wall carpet over a pad. (If squeaks are part of the problem, you can drive screws through the loose boards to keep them from shifting.)

It also helps to fill the framing cavities between floor joists with insulation. If the floor is above an unfinished basement, for example, you can staple thick batts of fiberglass or cellulose between the joists. You don't need batts that are faced with foil, or faced at all. But you might want to use insulation that is encased in a clear wrap to guard against the skin rashes and itching that some people get from handling loose fill insulation.

To build in even more sound protection, you can experiment with adding extra layers of sound-absorbing material. Dense foam board, for example, generally is rigid enough to support people and most furniture when it is laid under a pad and carpet. (You should check with your local building department to be sure the type of material you use conforms to fire codes; most foam, by code, must be covered with ½-inch drywall.)

Another relatively extreme option is to raise the floor on a series of 2 × 4s, called sleepers. This approach normally is reserved for elevating a finished floor surface over a concrete slab, but it can help in two ways. First, you can fill the 1½-inch depth between sleepers with extra insulation, which reduces sound transmission. Second, the sleepers generally are spaced 16 to 24 inches apart (and covered with a plywood subfloor), which helps to disconnect vibrations in the old floor from the new floor. The drawback with building up a floor—sometimes even with the inch or so of a thick pad and carpet—is that you may have to cut down doors that swing into the room.

3. *Ceilings.* You can add sound-deadening materials to ceilings the same way you add them to walls—for example, by stapling up a layer of foam board covered with ½-inch drywall. But the most efficient system is a dropped ceiling with acoustical tiles. The tiles themselves absorb sound, and the space above the tile grid can be filled with insulation.

The basic components of a suspended ceiling are L-shaped edge hangers that you fasten to the walls, long T-shaped main runners that you hang at right angles to the ceiling joists, and short cross-tees that divide the runners into a grid. The tiles, which are available in many different finishes and surface patterns, rest in the grid of supports. You can hang a grid very close to the existing ceiling, or leave more space if you can afford to lose the headroom, and add thick batts of insulation to dampen more sound.

4. *In-wall plumbing noise.* Several improvements can reduce noise from plumbing pipes. They are easy to make where pipes are exposed, for example, between joists in the ceiling of an unfinished basement.

   To keep supply pipes from rattling, mount them in plastic bushings, or insert a cushion such as a scrap of rubber garden hose between the pipe and the adjacent framing. If the problem is a gurgling sound from large drainpipes, wrap them in batts of insulation.

   If you're building a partition that will house drain lines, consider using 2 × 6s or 2 × 8s to allow more room for sound insulation. In a wider wall, a slick approach is to offset the pipes to the bathroom side of the partition, and pack more insulation on the side of the wall facing other living space.

24
COVERING WALLS AND CEILINGS

The most common wallcovering today is gypsum drywall. There are many types, but the standard for new construction and remodeling is a ½-inch-thick panel. Some suppliers don't stock anything else. Beefier, ⅝-inch-thick panels are not normally used in houses due to the extra cost and weight. What seems like a minor addition, only ⅛ of an inch, makes these panels surprisingly heavier and much harder to handle. Before we get into the nitty-gritty details of installing drywall, here are some things to consider in the planning stage.

1. *Panel size.* Standard sheets are 4 × 8 feet. Like plywood and many other building materials, it's a modular size that works with both 16- and 24-inch-on-center residential framing. Each one weighs about 55 pounds, and until you get the hang of it, a single sheet can be an unwieldy package and tough to maneuver in tight halls and stairwells. Two types of widely used special-purpose panels (one treated to retard fire spread, another to resist water damage), are even heavier, about 64 pounds each.

From the standpoint of handling, smaller sheets are best because they are easier to carry and install. You don't have to be a gorilla to get a grip at the balance point and trudge from delivery site to work site. Some suppliers making bulk deliveries can shuttle sheets into place even on second floors with maneuverable hoists mounted on delivery trucks. But from the standpoint of spackling and taping joints, which often takes more time than nailing panels in place, larger sheets are better because they cover more wall area and leave fewer joints. The right balance is to use the biggest sheets practicable—large enough to eliminate some seams and taping time, but not so large as to create major handling problems.

For example, if you're covering an 8-foot-high, 12-foot-wide room, you might be able to use two long sheets installed horizontally. Standard ½-inch-thick sheets can be ordered from most suppliers in 10- and 12-foot lengths. That configuration produces only one long horizontal seam to spackle—one that's easy to work on without scaffolding or ladders. But one 12-foot-long panel weighs about 86 pounds, and you'll need a direct, open route between the delivery truck and the installation site plus plenty of help moving them around.

Many do-it-yourselfers install panels vertically. It seems logical because panels are 8 feet long and most ceilings are 8 feet high. But that logic produces a floor-to-ceiling seam every four feet. Concealing them with tape and three coats of compound is likely to give you a backache from bending over, and you'll probably need a ladder or low scaffold to reach the top sections—up and down, again and again. So try the easier alternative: installing long sheets horizontally.

2. *Panel type.* On the manufacturing line, a soupy mix of pulverized gypsum and water flows like an endless pancake. It's wrapped with rough paper backing and a paintable paper surface, shunted through huge ovens to be baked hard and dry, and then trimmed to sheet size. These standard panels can be used on walls and ceilings in any room.

Two common variations are manufactured with qualities that improve panel performance in key areas: Drywall impregnated with fire-retardants, referred to as FC or fire-code panels, and panels treated to resist moisture, referred to as WR or water-resistant panels. Nothing can make gypsum fireproof or waterproof. But fire-retardant panels stay intact longer than standard panels when exposed to fire. They are generally required in rooms where fires are most likely to start, such as a furnace room.

Water-resistant panels include an asphalt mix in the gypsum core and a chemical additive in the surface paper. Sometimes called green board due to the color after treatment, they make sense in kitchens and baths.

3. *Cutting locations.* Wallboard is normally stacked in quantity on edge, on spacers leaning against some wall studs. That's where pros make most of the cuts instead of moving the sheet to a cutting table. When a crew of three guys gets $7 per sheet hung (that varies of course, but is a going rate for the year 2001), they like to handle each piece once—when it goes on the wall. In any case, find a safe spot to store the panels (generally on spacers on edge) until you need them.

MEASURE AND CUT

The easiest way to make straight cuts is to use a sharp knife with a straight piece of wood as a guide. Score deeply enough with the knife so as to sever the surface paper. Don't, as some do, separate the boards by pulling them apart. As shown in **24-1**, take the time to cut through the back paper after the board is snap-broken.

Openings will be neater if you drill holes at opposite corners and then make saw cuts in the directions shown by the arrows in **24-2**. You can use a keyhole saw or equip yourself with special saws made for the purpose such as the two in **24–3**. But with modern dry-wall saws, you can plunge-cut without drilling. Pros often use a small rotary cutter (like a hand-held router for drywall) to make cutouts. It can plunge through drywall, and closely follow the irregular outline of an electrical box—if you hold on with both hands and cut against the bit rotation so the powerful little tool doesn't take off on you.

24–1

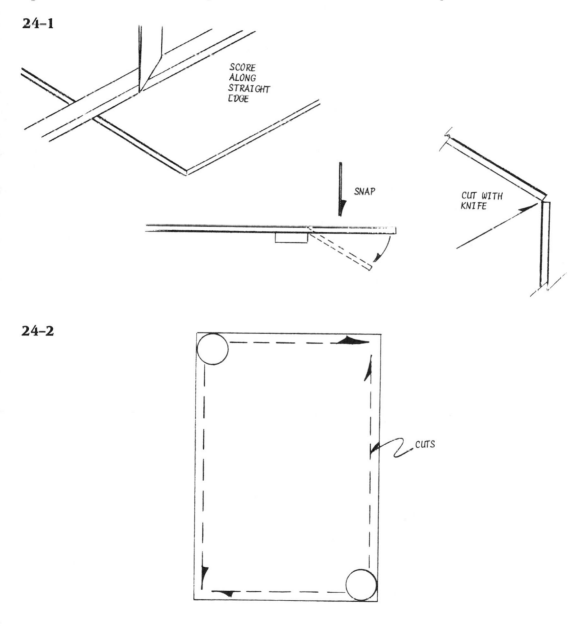

SCORE
ALONG
STRAIGHT
EDGE

SNAP

CUT WITH
KNIFE

24–2

CUTS

24–3

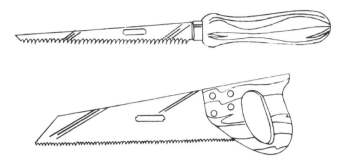

A standard tool to have on your belt is a straight-handled keyhole saw with a sharp tip to start a cut even in mid-board, and rough teeth to chew away gypsum. The saw takes longer than the router, but it's the more affordable alternative for do-it-yourself work, and easier to handle than a utility knife. Those razor-sharp tools are great for scoring sheets so they snap to the size you want. But it's difficult, and potentially dangerous, to use them to carve through interior cuts where a saw offers more control.

Even pros use a 4-foot-long metal T-square to guide the knife in a full-width cut through a sheet. You might get away with an uneven edge near a doorway where the discrepancy will be covered by trim, but you need a true edge at corners. To get a straight line without a T-square, clamp a straightedge in place. To trim the edge off a sheet, try this pro move: In one hand, hold the body of your ruler; in the other, your cutter against the end of the metal tape extended to the desired dimension. Keep your hands parallel, and drag the ruler along the manufactured edge of the sheet while the cutter digs in. Scoring the surface is enough to weaken the panel so you can snap it. Then trim the piece free by slicing through the paper backing.

INSTALLING GYPSUM BOARD

First check all framing surfaces for protrusions that could keep the panels from lying flat. Bowed studs can be replaced, or sawn partly through and then reinforced in a straight position. Every piece of supporting framework should be in the same plane. If part of a built-up ceiling beam or corner post sticks out, the sheet will ride over the ridge, and is likely to crack when you nail it home on the other side. Sometimes you can simply pound down an obstruction with a hammer. But when you encounter frame hardware that won't move, use a surface-forming rasp (like a small plane with a bed like a cheese grater) to carve a shallow seat for the obstruction in the back of the drywall that relieves the stress and prevents a crack.

You can attach drywall panels with nails or screws. Many professionals use screws, but if you go that way be sure to buy (or rent) an electric screwdriver with a built-in slip clutch that disengages automatically as soon as the screw head is seated. It's called a torque limiter. You can nail, of course—but screws go in faster; make neater, smaller dimples that are easier to spackle; and hold better than nails, which often cause problems with popout later on. It's really no contest, and you won't have any miss-hit hammer gouges to fill in. Nails generally are resin coated with a straight shank or one of annular-ring design. A drywall screw and both types of nail are shown in **24–4**.

Drive nails with a hammer that has a crowned head so the last blow will form a shallow dimple (**24–5**). Do not dimple so deeply that you break the paper. Hold the board firmly against the framing; don't depend on the nail to bring the board up tight. Start nailing at the center of panels and work out toward edges, using the nailing patterns shown in **24–6**.

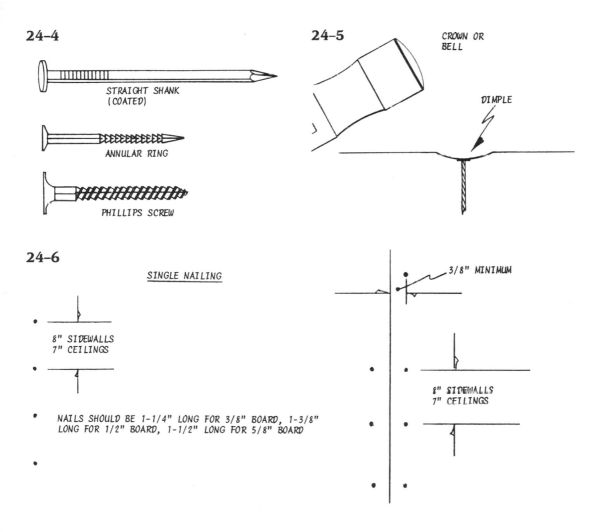

24–4

STRAIGHT SHANK
(COATED)

ANNULAR RING

PHILLIPS SCREW

24–5

CROWN OR BELL

DIMPLE

24–6

SINGLE NAILING

8" SIDEWALLS
7" CEILINGS

NAILS SHOULD BE 1-1/4" LONG FOR 3/8" BOARD, 1-3/8"
LONG FOR 1/2" BOARD, 1-1/2" LONG FOR 5/8" BOARD

3/8" MINIMUM

8" SIDEWALLS
7" CEILINGS

Whether you install sheets vertically or horizontally, the edge resting conveniently on the floor generally has to be raised a bit before you nail. At that point you're out of hands—but not feet, which you can use with a metal lifter—a wedge-shape that seesaws over a built-in wheel. Kick the lifter under the edge of the sheet, step down on one end, and the other end lifts the panel into position quite easily—with both hands still free for nailing.

On ceilings, if you don't have the luxury of helpers, you can still install big sheets overhead by yourself. It takes a lot longer, of course, but the job is doable with a deadman. The site-built version is a simple I-shape that's slightly shorter than the ceiling: a foot that rests on the floor, a wider hand that carries the sheet, and a 2-x-4 body in between. Nail a 2 × 4 support across the wall, keeping it ⅝ inch or so lower than the top surface of the plate. Place the sheet as shown in **24-7** and lift up the free end while bearing forward so the inboard edge will remain on the support.

The trick is to get one end of the sheet on the deadman, and keep it there while you climb a ladder carrying the other. On a big solo job, consider renting the mechanical alternative. It has a large horizontal frame to securely support a huge sheet, wheels so you can maneuver it into the perfect position—and the best part—a big crank that smoothly lifts the sheet and presses it against the ceiling while you stroll around underneath, driving in nails.

24-7

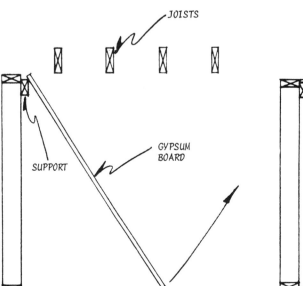

TAPING DRYWALL JOINTS

Standard finishing relies on three separate coats of joint compound, rolls of paper tape, and lengths of metal corner guard. Even if you leave a few gaps between sheets or pound some hammer marks into panels during the installation, finishing can erase the problems (**24–8**). Here is a breakdown of the applications.

24–8

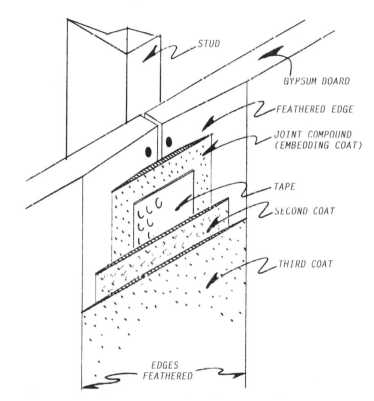

1. *Wall prep.* Before you apply any compound, check the wall surface to be sure the fasteners are fully seated. Do this by sweeping a wide metal taping blade across the wall surface. If a nail or screw head is slightly raised, you'll feel and hear the metal-on-metal contact. It's better to hit the nail now than later, when the blade will be loaded with joint compound and the contact will leave a ridge that disrupts the smooth surface.

   Also trim away any small tears of off-white surface paper or other loose edges that may have been damaged during delivery or installation. Use a utility knife to trim back paper neatly. The brown paper or hard gypsum surface you see underneath is easy to conceal with compound.

2. *First coats.* Every seam and fastener should get three coats of joint compound. Many pros get by with two because their sheet seams are tight and their fasteners are installed uniformly. This means they don't need as much compound as a do-it-your-selfer might, and sometimes get better coverage in two coats than do-it-yourselfers get in three (**24–9**). The joint compound is available as a powder that you mix with water, but it's better to work with a ready-mix that you can buy in 1- and 5-gallon cans. It saves time and work and assures you of a proper mix.

The best plan is to spread a layer of compound over the seams, set a strip of rein-forcing paper tape in the compound, and smooth the surface (**24–10**). It's best to get a set of broad-bladed tools made for this purpose (**24–11**). They're an inexpensive way to start the job right. Place the tape as shown in **24–12** as soon as the first layer of compound is down.

That's the first course. The trick is to spread an even layer of compound, and be

24–9

24–10

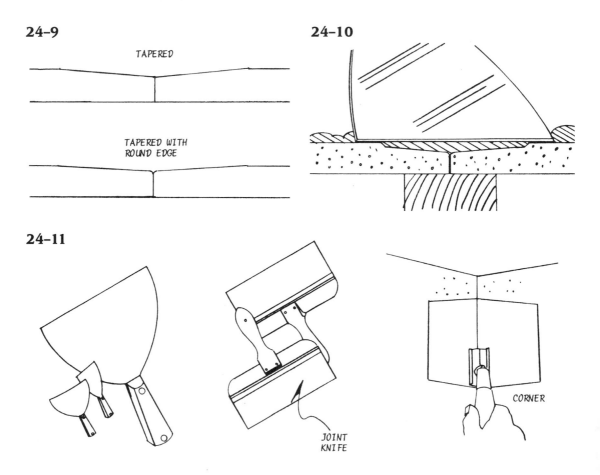

TAPERED

TAPERED WITH
ROUND EDGE

24–11

JOINT
KNIFE

CORNER

24-12

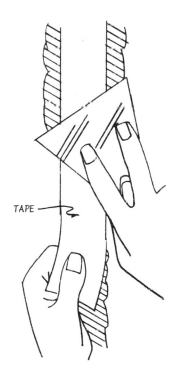

TAPE

sure that the paper embeds without any air pockets that can lead to bubbling. Moisture in the compound generally turns the paper darker as it embeds under your knife. So if you see a few light-colored spots, they probably are not yet embedded.

Before continuing with further coats, bear in mind that there are two kinds of seams. The long joints on panels generally are feathered to create a shallow V-shape when two sheets sit side by side. This built-in trough makes it easier to apply tape and compound without creating a noticeable bulge. But sheets also form full-thickness joints at the ends (and at some corners) that are not feathered. These are much more difficult to conceal. There are two ways to beat this problem. One is to install 4 × 8-foot sheets vertically so the full-thick ends will be concealed under trim. Another is to make the extra effort during delivery and application to use long sheets and install them horizontally, spanning wall to wall.

3. *Finishing coats.* If you have never taped drywall before, err on the side of adding too much compound, not too little. A bit of excess is easy to scrape away. You also can sand away excess compound once it hardens. But oversanding can scuff drywall paper near the joints and create rough surfaces. These can show up as dull spots even under two coats of paint. The preferable approach is to smooth out enough compound to cover both seams and fasteners, and touch up your work with minimal sanding before applying another coat.

The second coat should widen the first application and almost fill up the feathered joint (**24–13**). When it dries, you should no longer see the outline of paper tape over the joint. Again, do some light sanding where needed to smooth out any rough spots, using a 220- or 320-grit paper wrapped around a block of wood (**24–14**). A special sanding tool is available that allows you to reach any area of a wall or ceiling without standing on a stool or ladder (**24–15**). No matter what sanding you do, be careful not to rough up the paper surface of the wallboard.

24–13

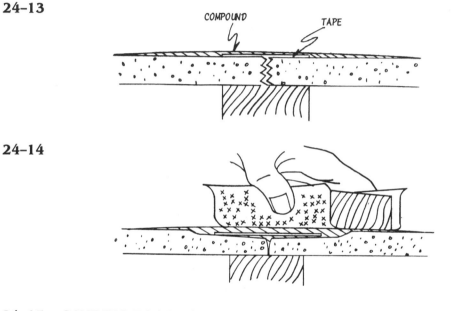

COMPOUND   TAPE

24–14

24–15   SANDING TOOL FOR CEILING

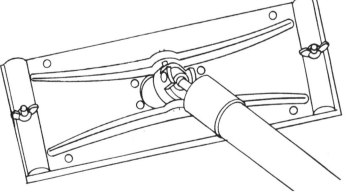

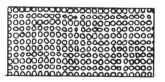

The third coat should be a soupy mix of compound that spreads easily and creates a smooth surface. You'll need a blade for this application that's wide enough to bridge the feathered joint. After yet another light sanding with fine paper, the wall should be smooth.

On inside corners, you can follow the same procedure of embedding and covering tape. But as you apply finishing coats, it's best to work on one side at a time so the edge of your blade doesn't disrupt the compound you've just smoothed. Fold the tape down the middle before placing it against the compound (**24–16**).

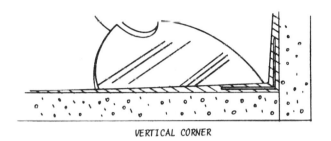

VERTICAL CORNER

On corners that are more easily damaged because they protrude into a room, apply metal corner guard instead of paper tape (**24–17**). Work with compound only, applying a minimum of two coats with total coverage extending about 4 or 5 inches away from the corner (**24–18**). The metal bead on the corner of the guard provides a guide

24-17

24-18

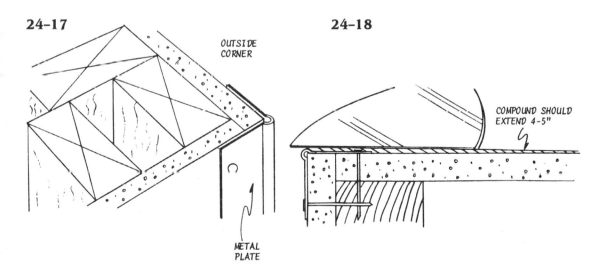

OUTSIDE CORNER

METAL PLATE

COMPOUND SHOULD EXTEND 4-5"

for your blade as you add compound that covers the nailing flanges of the guard. Drywall outlets that supply contractors also may carry a bullnose corner guard that forms a gently rounded corner, and flexible vinyl bead that serves the same purpose on curved corners over arches.

The nails or screws are easy to cover with a 4-inch knife and compound, applying only as much pressure as you need to fill the dimple (**24–19**). Apply a second coat after the first one dries and then do a light sanding job to finish up.

24–19

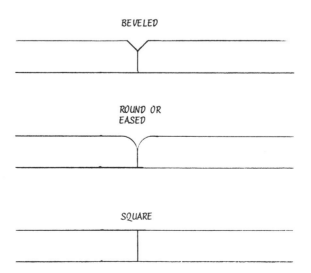

Prefinished gypsum wallboard does not require the joint treatments described above. Instead, the panels are attached with special color-matched nails. Various types of panels with edge-to-edge joints which may be left as is are available (**24–20**). Inside and outside corners and wall-to-ceiling joints are usually covered with special moldings.

24–20

BEVELED

ROUND OR EASED

SQUARE

PREFINISHED PLYWOOD PANELS

Using solid, natural wood may seem like the purest approach to paneling. But man-made panels, called sheet goods in the woodworking trades, have outstripped solid slabs of the real thing in just about every way lumber can be judged.

Unlike solid lumber that must be run through a thickness planer before you can be sure that all the boards are the same size, manufactured panels are uniform. They are also more widely available, and come in large 4 × 8-foot sheets. Also, solid wood with grain running in one direction is susceptible to swelling, shrinking, and all sorts of twisting. Even wood dried in a kiln may start to warp in humid weather. But panels are made like a seven-layer cake, some with as many as 13 laminations with grain running in opposite directions to prevent movement.

Another consideration is that solid woods in ¾-inch and greater thicknesses use up a lot of the dwindling supply of hardwood trees in the world's forests. Panels use that supply much more sparingly in very thin surface veneers—some only ¹⁄₄₀ of an inch thick. The space between the veneers is filled with more common wood, or even recycled fillers such as cardboard, so that panels generally cost a lot less per square foot than solid woods.

Among the many and confusing names for dozens of different types of panels, there are three basic types: plywood, fiberboard, and particleboard.

1. *Hardwood plywood.* These panels, which generally range from ¼- to ¾-inch thick, can have a surface in any number of wood species from plain, paintable birch, to the richest cherry or walnut. Underneath may be layers of common wood with alternating grain directions, a core of particleboard, or fiberboard (commonly called MDF for medium-density fiberboard)—both made from different preparations of compressed wood chips and fibers that lumber mills used to throw away.

   One of the most common types is called veneer-core plywood. A ¾-inch-thick sheet normally has seven plies with alternating grain. That makes the panels very stable, resistant to warping or twisting, and a good choice for general cabinetwork.

   Sheets with veneer glued over MDF or particleboard are called solid-core panels. With their reconstituted cores, they generally cost less than veneer core, but weigh more and don't hold fasteners quite as well.

   Lumber-core panels are made from a weave that includes solid-wood fibers to give the sheets great resistance to bending, such as when a long desktop is loaded with books and computer equipment. But lumber core is considerably more expensive than common veneer-core plywood.

   There are also a number of panels that combine thin layers of particleboard, fiberboard, and veneers in the core. These mix-and-match products generally cost less than veneer-core panels.

2. *Veneer grades.* A letter-grading system (A to E, for best to worst, and for most to least expensive) is used to rate the panel surface veneer. Panels with two visible sides, like those used on cabinet doors or bookcase uprights, get two letters. Panels also come with one good side and a serviceable, but not finished-quality veneer rated from 1 to 5 on the back, say, for the body (called the carcass) of kitchen cabinets.

   A is reserved for smooth-surfaced, knot-free, furniture-quality panels used with stain or a clear finish. B is, in theory, a less desirable surface showing more grain, knots, and other natural characteristics of the wood. C is for panels with some patched defects—wood plugs set by machine at the mill over gouges or voids. D and E panels have increasingly larger and more numerous patches.

3. *Exotic composites.* Some products incorporate special properties, such as bendability. Panels made with the grain of their layers all running in one direction, such as Wiggle Wood, or with saw kerfs cut into the back, such as Kerfkore, allow you to apply panels on curves. Some varieties can be bent to a radius of 1 inch.

   There also are lightweight panels that use a honeycomb or foam reinforcement layer between thin surface veneers, and panels assembled with waterproof glues to keep outdoor woodwork from delaminating.

4. *Formaldehyde-free panels.* The components of some panels are assembled with urea-formaldehyde glue, which can cause differing degrees of allergic reactions. Some people are very sensitive to residual fumes that outgas from new cabinets and furniture, although most people are unaffected. If this is a concern, there are formaldehyde-free alternatives. The small but growing variety of environmentally sensitive products also includes panels with wood veneers applied to cores of recycled materials ranging from old cardboard to soybean flour. Track down these sometimes difficult-to-find products through full-service lumberyards, or cabinet supply or custom furniture shops.

   Some panels are edge-matched to come together without a visible joint, or the mating might form a groove that is compatible with other grooves in the panel. Square-edge panels may be butted, or the joints may be finished in a variety of ways that can add some distinction to the installation. You can work with ready-made moldings or design your own dividers (**24–21**). It's possible too to find panels for which ready-made matching moldings are supplied by the manufacturer (**24–22**).

INSTALLING PLYWOOD PANELS

First check all studs to be sure none has developed a bow since the time of installation, and repair any bowing walls, by replacing the stud or cutting and reinforcing it (**24–23**).

Buy your paneling well before installation time and stand the individual pieces about

24-21

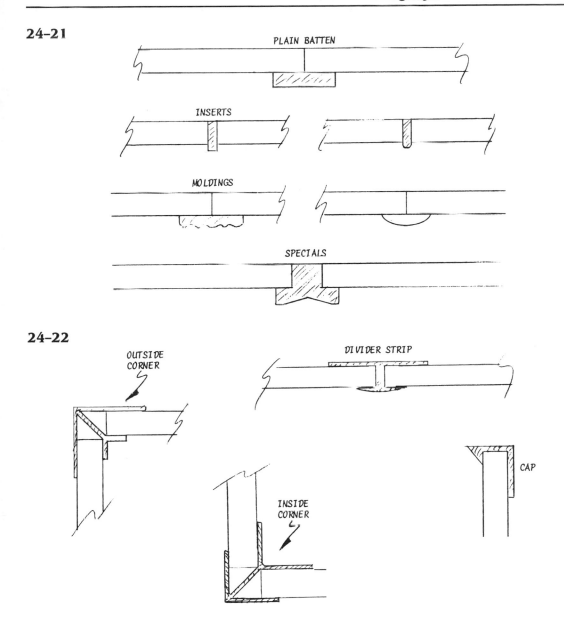

PLAIN BATTEN

INSERTS

MOLDINGS

SPECIALS

24-22

OUTSIDE CORNER

DIVIDER STRIP

INSIDE CORNER

CAP

the room so they will become acclimated. This is also the right time to plan the placement of panels to match tone and grain patterns. Plan the placement so the end panels on each wall will be about equal in width and not less than the space across three studs.

It's usually best to start the installation at a corner, cutting the panel, if necessary, so the outboard edge is plumb and falls on the centerline of a stud (**24-24**). Do the cutting

24–23

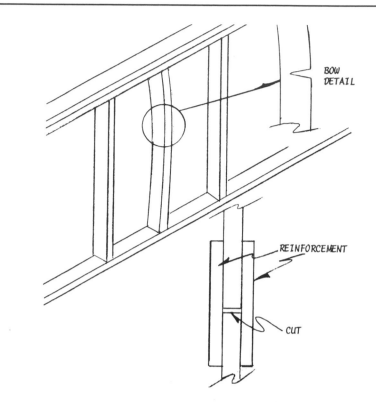

on the inboard edge of the panel, making sure that it conforms to any irregularities in the wall it abuts. The best way to do this is to hold the panel in place and use a pair of dividers or a compass as shown in **24–25**, in a process called scribing, to transfer the irregularity to the panel. Use a level at the opposite edge to be sure of plumb. Get this first piece placed correctly and all others will fall into place as they should.

Measure carefully when you need cutouts, but don't be so precise that the panels must be forced into place. Leave a gap at top and bottom (according to manufacturer's specs) to allow for expansion without buckling.

If you cut by hand, use a fine-tooth crosscut saw and keep the face of the panel up. If you work with an electric saw, either cutoff or saber, keep the face of the panel down.

Panels are usually secured with either color-matched nails or adhesives. In either case, follow the recommendations of the manufacturer as to nailing schedules or adhesive placement. With adhesives, it's usually suggested that a zigzag line of the material be applied to all contact points on the framing. The panel is pressed into place, pulled away from the wall to break the contact, and then returned to its original position. To firm the bond, go over the entire panel, hitting down on a length of 2 × 4 wrapped in some soft carpeting (**24–26**).

24–24

24–25

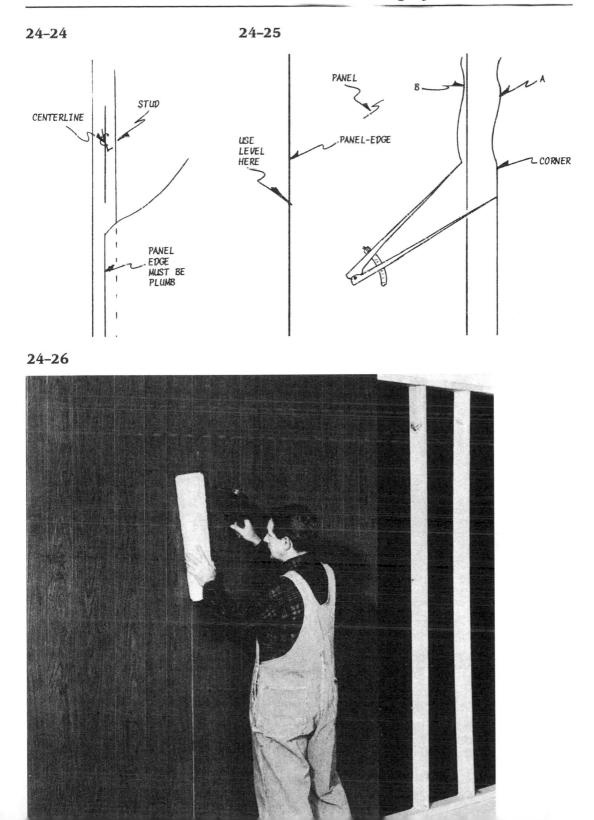

24–26

At corners and openings you can use moldings of your choice, or those that are specially made by the manufacturer to match the paneling (**24–27**).

HARDBOARD PANELS

What we said about plywood in relation to the wide range of designs, textures, and patterns that are available applies to hardboard paneling as well. In addition to realistic wood finishes (**24–28**), you can buy panels that look and feel like marble, stucco, brick, stone, and other materials.

Basic installation of hardboard paneling doesn't differ materially from plywood products unless you choose a type that is attached with special metal clips. If so, follow the instructions that are supplied with the product. Generally, panels are installed along the lines shown here: nailing directly to studs (**24–29**); nailing over an underlayment (**24–30**); attaching adhesive directly to studs (**24–31**); and attaching adhesive over a solid backing (**24–32**). Prefinished accessories in matching colors and wood grains are available for the final touches (**24–33**).

PLASTIC-FINISHED HARDBOARD

These are special hardboard panels with heat-baked modified-melamine finishes. Here too, choices run a wide range of simulated materials and textures that include rough-wood appearances (**24–34**), and high-gloss finishes that are suitable for kitchens and even bathrooms, shown in **24–35**. Some of these panels have tongue-and-groove edges that simplify fitting. Adhesive and special clips are used to attach the planks so there are no visible nails when the job is done (**24–36**). Bear in mind that the plastic finish on these panels is, in fact, a plastic replica of wood or some other material.

SOLID WOOD

If you want to install the real thing, you can use hardwoods such as birch, maple, and oak, or softwoods such as pine, cedar, or cypress. They can be ordered in a variety of sizes, although 1 × 6 or narrower boards generally have the right scale for a room. Another option is the type of joint between the planks—for example, shiplap, or tongue-and-groove, and the way the boards are positioned on the wall. Planks have the strength to span studs horizontally on the diagonal and vertically over horizontal furring strips.

Once you've settled those options, you'll still find a dramatic difference in the appearance and cost of planks (even for one kind of wood), depending on the grade you buy.

24-27

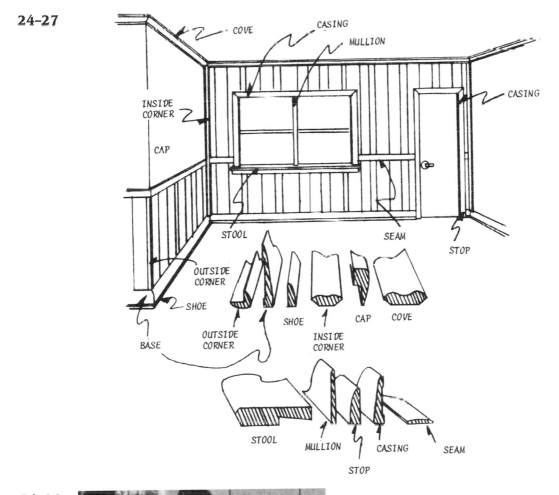

24-28

24-29

NAILS 8" O.C. AT INTERMEDIATE SOLID BACKING SUPPORTS

STUDS 16" O.C.

NAILS 4" O.C. AT JOINT AND ALONG ALL EDGES

NOTE: FOLLOW PROCEDURE FOR NAILING OVER OPEN FRAMING BUT USE SPECIAL 1-5/8" NAILS TO PENETRATE AT LEAST 3/4" INTO STUDS

24-30

NAILS 8" O.C. AT INTERMEDIATE SUPPORTS

STUDS 16" O.C.

NAILS 4" O.C. AT JOINT AND ALONG ALL EDGES

24-31

CONTINUOUS ADHESIVE BEAD 1/2" FROM ALL EDGES OF PANEL

16" O.C. MAXIMUM

INTERMITTENT 3" ADHESIVE BEAD 6" SPACE ON INTERMEDIATE STUDS

PANEL

MATCHING BASE MOLDING

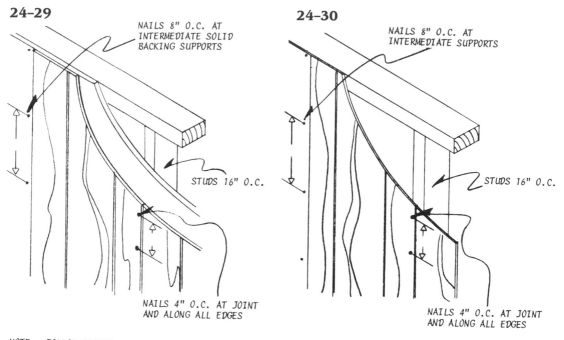

24-32

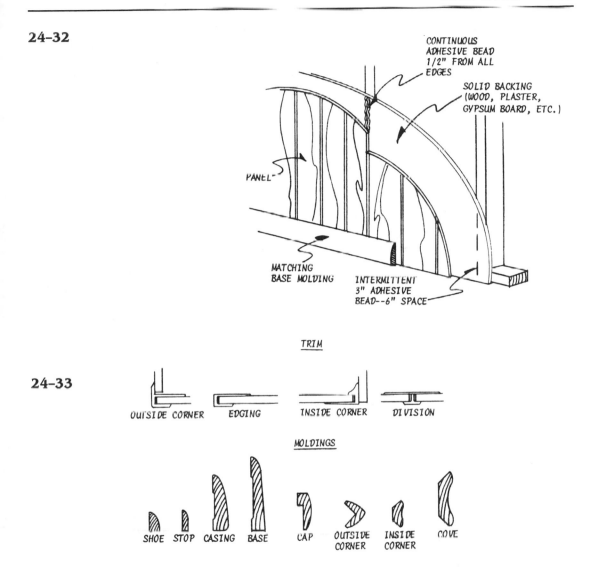

CONTINUOUS
ADHESIVE BEAD
1/2" FROM ALL
EDGES

SOLID BACKING
(WOOD, PLASTER,
GYPSUM BOARD, ETC.)

PANEL

MATCHING
BASE MOLDING

INTERMITTENT
3" ADHESIVE
BEAD--6" SPACE

TRIM

24-33

OUTSIDE CORNER   EDGING   INSIDE CORNER   DIVISION

MOLDINGS

SHOE   STOP   CASING   BASE   CAP   OUTSIDE CORNER   INSIDE CORNER   COVE

Although lumber grading is a nonstandardized quagmire for consumers (and some carpenters, too), here is a once-over. For softwoods, such as pine, there are three general categories for good-quality panel boards. Select lumber ranges from B or better, which has almost no flaws, to C, which has some natural flaws, and D, which has more flaws and some imperfections from milling. Finish lumber is the next category, followed by common board lumber.

For hardwoods, the grading system ranges from extremely expensive woods suitable for fine furniture called first and seconds, through common grades, which generally are

24–34

24–35

24–36

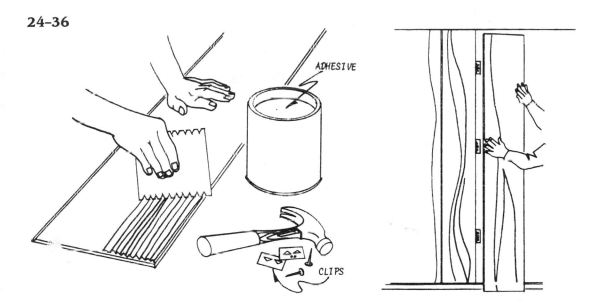

fine for plank paneling. To cut through the confusion, all you have to do is look at samples to see the kinds of imperfections each grade contains and how much more it will cost to use a grade without them.

All the grading systems have the same bias. They assume that clear wood without knots and grain variations is best. It's certainly rarer and more expensive than other grades but, to some, lacks the character of a less expensive grainy birch or knotty pine. If your paneling will have a clear finish such as polyurethane that enhances natural variations in the grain, clearer grades may look more subdued, uniform, and elegant. But if you plan to stain the boards, the appearance of knots and blemishes will be reduced instead of high-lighted.

You'll likely find that the most widely available are the interlocking tongue-and-groove types (**24–37**). If you use boards that are not more than 6 inches wide, you can blind-nail (**24–38**). Wider boards will probably require a nail or two between joints, and these will have to be set and concealed with a wood dough.

Plain, square-edge boards—as long as they are kiln-dried—are also usable, and you can do a board-and-batten or a board-on-board installation as you would for an exterior wall. Whatever you choose, be sure to store the boards in the room for as much as a week so they will become acclimated before you start to saw and nail. Use spacers between the boards so air can circulate (**24–39**).

The easiest but not the most popular installation is with the boards placed horizontally

24–37

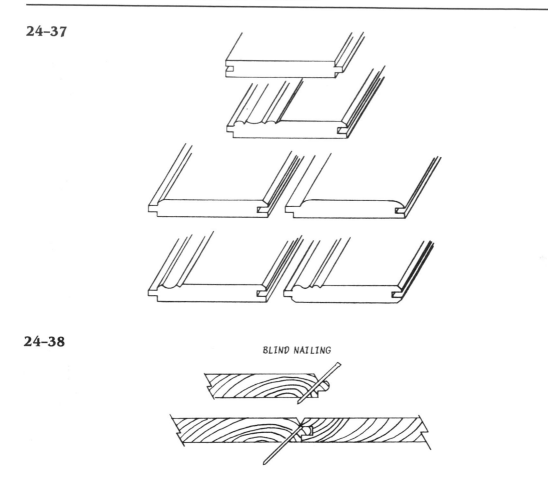

24–38

BLIND NAILING

so they can be secured to studs without the need for additional nailing surfaces (**24–40**). The job goes quickly, since a minimum number of cuts are required. A horizontal installation can make a room look longer, but will look its best only if the panel pieces are of uniform width.

A vertical installation calls for additional blocking between the studs (**24–41**). An alternative is to make a backing frame over the studs (**24–42**). Cut a slight relief bevel on the edge of the first board and install it so it will be perfectly plumb (**24–43**). If necessary, shape the inboard edge so it will conform to any irregularity in the wall it abuts, scribing the cut. Continue to add boards, but check occasionally with a level to be sure of alignment. Work carefully so board tongues will seat completely in mating grooves.

The bottom of the wall can be formed two ways, as shown in **24–44**. You can install a baseboard first and then cut the panels to form a tight butt joint, or cut the boards to

24–39

24–40

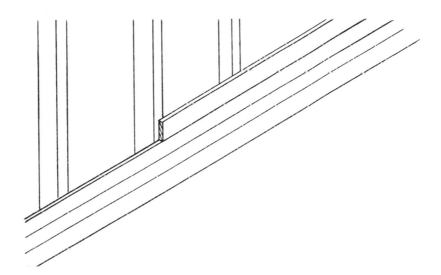

24–41

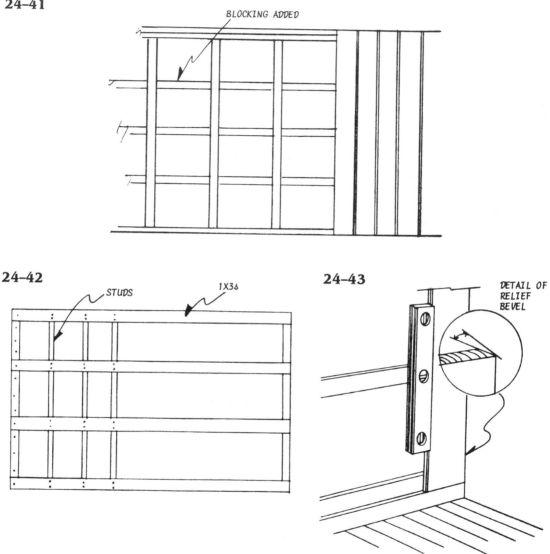

BLOCKING ADDED

24–42

STUDS

1X3s

24–43

DETAIL OF RELIEF BEVEL

extend almost to the floor and add a baseboard on the outside. The joint at the ceiling is easy to finish with molding of your choice. An example is shown in **24–45**.

If the paneling is horizontal and makes a turn, you can miter the corners. Careful work is called for, but you will get a tighter visible edge on outside corners if you overcut the miter just a bit (**24–46**). There are various ways to make inside and outside corners for both vertical and horizontal applications, as shown in **24–47**. A herringbone design forms an exciting pattern, as shown in **24–48**, but it is a very demanding type of installation.

24-44

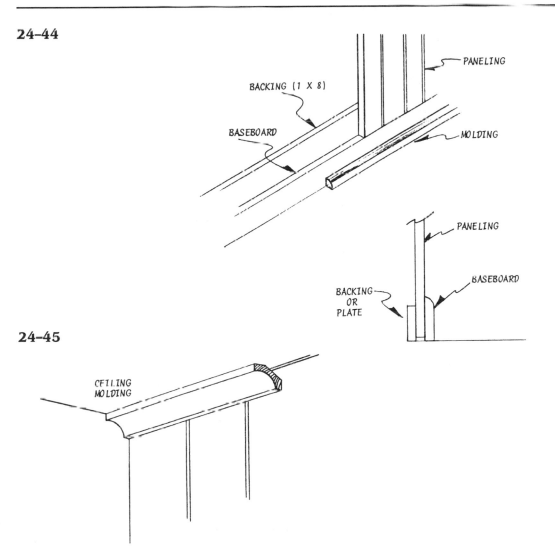

PANELING

BACKING (1 X 8)

BASEBOARD

MOLDING

PANELING

BASEBOARD

BACKING
OR
PLATE

24-45

CEILING
MOLDING

IMITATION BRICK OR STONE

There are many materials in this area. Some are made of plastic, others are thin slices of the real thing, and still others are combinations of crushed natural materials and bonding agents. They may be available as individual units or, in the case of bricks, for example, as panels; you install a dozen or so bricks at a time merely by driving a few nails.

Application methods differ depending on the product. Some require a wire-mesh installation over a solid backing to hold a special mortar, which in turn receives the brick

24–46

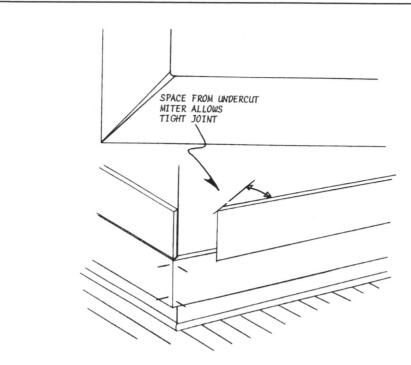

SPACE FROM UNDERCUT
MITER ALLOWS
TIGHT JOINT

24–47

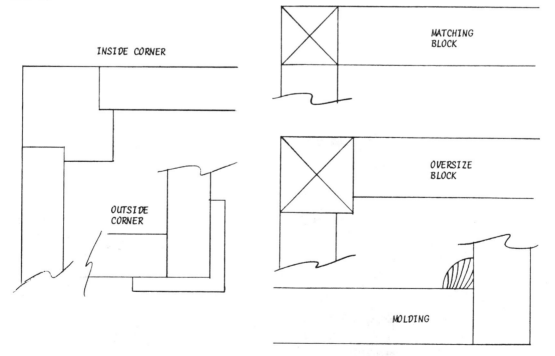

INSIDE CORNER

MATCHING
BLOCK

OUTSIDE
CORNER

OVERSIZE
BLOCK

MOLDING

24–48

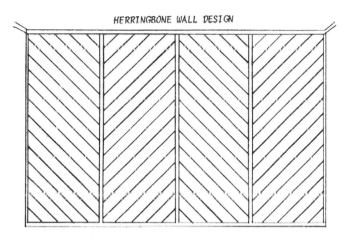

HERRINGBONE WALL DESIGN

or stone. Others will stick to a mastic that is applied directly to the backing. Where they may be used (indoors, outdoors, moisture areas, and so on) is also variable. Best bet is to check with manufacturers before making a choice. The following are just a few examples of what is available.

From a distance, plastic brick (**24–49**) and composites (**24–50**) may be difficult to tell from the real thing. Some can be used outside (**24–51**). One thing all these materials have

24–49

24–50

24–51

in common is that they are wall covers; they are not intended to be structural, load-bearing components.

CERAMIC TILE

Modern ceramic tiles are covered with uniform glazes, machined to consistent sizes, and hardened in temperature-controlled kilns. Combined with a dense grout, grid systems of tile resist wear better than most interior surfaces and should last as long as the surfaces that support them. The material does not burn, fade, or easily stain. But drop a heavy pot on a tile floor or crash a doorknob into a tile wall and you'll be faced with the tricky job of replacing one or two tiles without dislodging others. Of course, tile generally is used on floors instead of walls with the exception of some areas in kitchens and baths. On potentially wet walls, you should install cement-based backer board as an underlayment, not water-resistant drywall. On dry walls, you can tile directly over standard drywall.

The general procedure is to lay out the wall with equal partial tiles at the edges, and snap chalk lines as guides. Then spread the adhesive with a $3/16$-inch V-notch trowel (**24–52**), or

24–52

another notch size specified by the manufacturer. Don't cover more than a few square feet at a time until you gain some experience in placing the tiles. Many modern tiles have lugs that control the spacing of joints. If not, insert small plastic spacers.

Cuts will have to be made for fitting tiles and for providing openings for pipes (**24–53**). If the cut is irregular, you can work with tile nippers, breaking off very small pieces of tile until you achieve the shape you want (**24–54**). The secret here is not to break off large pieces that can cause cracks where you don't want them. The parts you break off can be quite sharp, so watch your hands, and wear safety goggles.

Make straight cuts with a snap cutter (you can rent one) or a tungsten-carbide-tipped tile cutter (**24–55**). A snap cutter keeps the tile square and works best. On large jobs, you also can rent a wet saw, which is basically a circular saw set up to cut tile.

Some sheets are filled with a special material, as suggested by the manufacturer, which is applied with a caulking gun (**24–56**). Smooth out the joint lines with your thumb or the eraser end of a pencil and then clean off excess material with a soft cloth dampened with denatured alcohol (**24–57**). Don't wipe across the joint, since any grout material left to dry on the face of the tiles will be difficult to remove later.

24–53

24–54

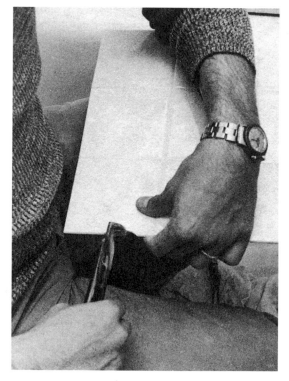

24–55

24–56

24–57

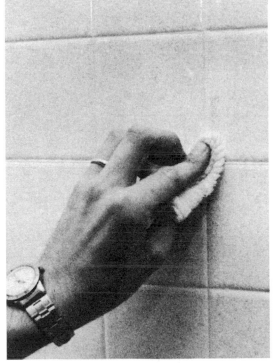

Most tile joints are sealed with grout, which you can apply generally the day after installation. Start by sweeping out the seams to clear debris and removing any spacers used to keep the tile seams even. Adhesive should be spread with a notched trowel that leaves uniform ridges. But if excess adhesive has bulged up in the joints, take the time to trim it out with a utility knife. Grout needs to fill the spaces between tiles.

Mix grout to a thick, soupy consistency following the manufacturer's directions, and use a sponge float or squeegee to work it back and forth across the joints. Use sweeping strokes on a diagonal to the grid pattern of tile to feed material equally into all seams. Don't try to force the grout in place by troweling in line with or directly into the seams. Instead, make several angled passes over the same area, first to fill the joints, and then to compact them.

When the grout sets up (the surface is firm but not yet hard), you can start to clean the surface. This process also requires many passes, but with a damp sponge, rinsing often to avoid respreading the grout residue. If you soak the sponge, excess water will dilute the grout and wash it out of the seams. Use a clean, damp sponge or cheesecloth pad to clear the final haze, which may not be visible until the surface dries completely.

FURRED CEILINGS

You can set ceiling tiles and planks, whether acoustical or purely decorative, over a furring system applied to the joists overhead. Whichever you use, some planning is in order so you don't end up with one of the two situations shown in **24–58**.

24–58

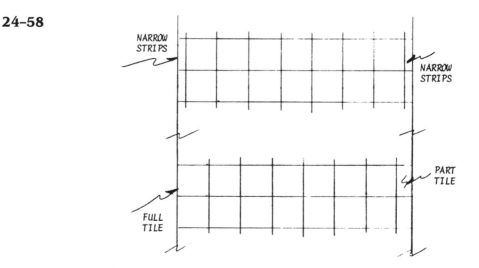

The solution is to mark intersecting centerlines of the room on the floor. Starting at the intersection, place a line of tiles on the floor and run them along both centerlines so you can see how the end tiles will fit. If the actual centerlines do not result in end tiles that are at least 6 inches wide, then shift the tiles so you will have a working centerline that will result in a more acceptable layout (**24–59**). The technique will work regardless of the size or shape of the tiles; rectangular tiles are shown in **24–60**.

24–59

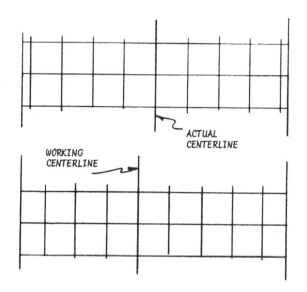

24–60

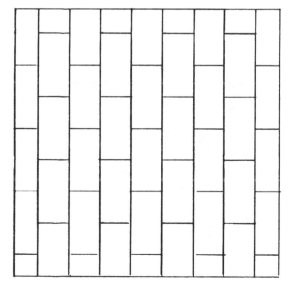

You can attach tiles or planks to 1 × 3 or 1 × 4 strips of sound wood (furring strips) that you nail directly to joists (**24–61**). The spacing of the strips depends on tile size, but measurements are always center-to-center. Use two 7d or 8d box or common nails at each bearing. Let end joints occur at a joist; fill in around the perimeter of the room as shown in **24–62**.

24–61

24–62

Check the furring for level, regardless of whether you are installing over a backing or directly to joists. When necessary, use thin pieces of wood as shims to make adjustments (**24–63**). When you are nailing through a backing, increase the length of the nails by ½ inch.

You can start the installation at the wall, being sure to cut the border tiles to correct width (**24–64**). Generally, it's wiser to work from the center out, and make the final cuts in partial tiles when the field is established.

You can nail the tiles, but the job is much faster and easier if you use a stapling gun. The patterns shown in **24–65** are pretty common, but check the literature that comes with the product you buy to be sure no special treatment is in order.

24–63

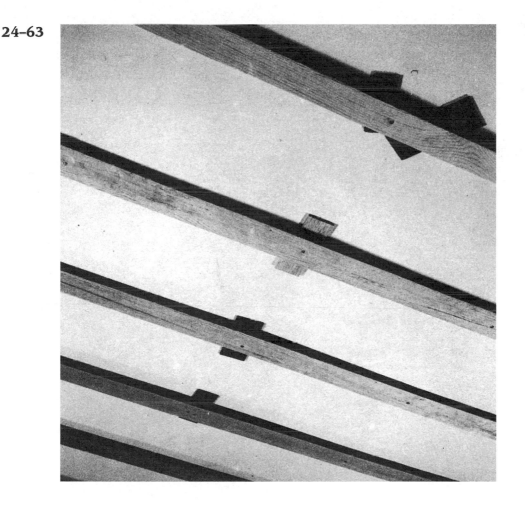

24–64

24–65

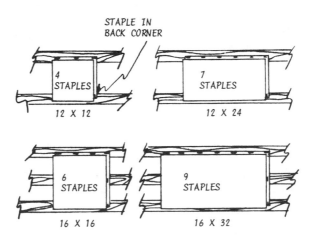

SUSPENDED CEILINGS

Suspended acoustical tile ceilings are standard in commercial buildings because they cover up pipes, ducts, and wires, provide easy access to the mechanical systems when needed, and dampen sound transmission. The system offers the same benefits in an unfinished basement (**24–66**).

The components include L-shaped edge hangers that fasten to the walls, long T-shaped main runners hung at right angles to the ceiling joists, normally from eye hooks and wires or proprietary hangers, and matching, 2-foot-long cross-tees that divide the runners into a grid. A variety of different panels can fit into this framework, which covers all the seams and eliminates trimming. Here is a look at the key steps in the installation.

1. *Planning ceiling height.* Normally you want the ceiling as high as possible. But it may be worth a loss of ceiling height to gain room for an extra sound barrier—for example, batts of insulation perhaps. To deal with pipes or ducts dropped below the joists,

24–66

pick a height that hides most of the mechanicals and requires only a minimum of extra furring or framing to box in obstructions.

2. *Planning the layout.* Because suspended ceiling grids are modular to accommodate 2 × 2-foot, or 2 × 4-foot acoustical panels, your initial layout should take this into account; adjust the grid to the room. To make a symmetrical installation, work from the midpoint out toward the walls. Find the midpoint by measuring the walls and dividing in half, or by stringing lines diagonally from corner to corner. The lines cross at the exact center.

It's helpful after measuring to draw out the ceiling plan on graph paper and pencil in the most economical and balanced grid. You could design a grid that has a long runner along the midline between two walls. But if this system leaves very small panel sections along the edges, try a grid where the midline that splits the room in half also divides the center row of panels. Make sure to balance the grid in both directions; then double-check your plan on paper and with strings on the ceiling. Observe the old carpentry adage: Measure twice, cut once, and you won't waste time reinstalling part of an unbalanced grid.

Working from your plan measurements, buy edge pieces, cross-tees and runners, generally sold in 8- and 12-foot lengths, that can be easily trimmed to fit with a tin snips. If you need a longer run, buy the next most economical section, which interlocks to form a continuous support. Because you are working from a balanced layout of main runners, the system has enough flexibility to accommodate hanger wires at holes normally predrilled every 3 inches, and cross-tee pieces at locking slots that are prepunched in the runners every 6 inches.

3. *Installing edge strips.* Using horizontal chalk lines snapped at equal heights off the floor as a guide, nail or screw edge strips to the wall studs on frame walls with 6d (two-inch) nails (**24–67**). Over masonry walls, use masonry nails and wear an eye

24–67

shield as the nails are hardened and can cause unexpected hammer rebound, or split off small pieces of masonry. At inside corners, butt one edge strip against the other. If the room has jogs or partitions that create outside corners, cut the strip long and make a 45-degree miter to create a neat joint.

4. *Installing runners and cross-tees.* Snap chalk lines across the existing ceiling or exposed joists to mark the location of the main runners. To be sure of your layout and to check the grid for square, stretch strings where the runners and cross-tees will be located; then check several string intersections with a carpenter's square. If you stretch the strings tightly to make sure they are level from wall to wall, they will serve as a leveling guide as you adjust the hook eyes and wires on the main runners later on.

   To start with, place the main runners so that their prepunched slots for crosspieces align with your strings or chalk marks. To support the runners, insert a hook eye into a joist about every 3 or 4 feet (check the grid manufacturer's exact directions); then loop 18-gauge hanger wire through the eye and secure the end by wrapping it around itself several times, twisting it with a pliers. Loop the other end through the hole in the main runner directly below and secure its end the same way.

   If you have trouble keeping a runner level with its guide string, secure the wire ends through the eye hooks and just loop the hanger wire through the runner holes temporarily. Then make final, minor adjustments in the wire length before twisting it tight. Some systems use special clips, as in **24-68**, but lengths of wire may be used,

24-68

and in fact may be called for. With the hangers up, the main grid runners are put in place (**24–69**). Then you can start placing tiles, using short, interlocking cross-runners as dividers (**24–70**).

24–69

24–70

Once the main runners are suspended, you simply snap the connecting cross-tees into their slots. No hanger wires are needed on the short lengths. Then comes the easiest part of the job, removing your string guides and installing the panels, tipping each one at a slight angle up and through the grid, and then letting it down into place on the frames.

EXPOSED BEAMS

Unlike construction lumber today that is sawn to shape out of a workable wood such as fir, early Colonial beams were hand-hewn from oak trees. Bark was peeled with a chisel the size of your arm, called a slick, and the tree was squared off into a beam shape with oversized axes. When hardwood was plentiful and labor was cheap, the massive framing members were mortised and tenoned, assembled with pegs into structural works of art, and promptly buried under clapboard and plaster.

Parts of the beams sometimes protruded from the ceiling or were left exposed under second-story floorboards. But as house interiors became more finished, the rugged-faced timbers were considered too rustic to remain exposed and were completely concealed or boxed in with finished boards. Either way, rough-hewn or smooth-clad, exposed ceiling beams are an architectural feature that harks back to simple, solid construction, and a look that still attracts owner–builders and remodelers.

Some manufacturers offer ready-made, lightweight beams of wood, hardboard, or plastic. Most are available in channel form to reduce weight and provide a passageway in which you can install plumbing or wiring. Those of wood or hardboard are nailed to 2 × 4s or 2 × 6s, which are first attached to joists, preferably with lag bolts; those of plastic are secured with zigzag lines of adhesive that you squeeze from a tube.

To do your own thing, you can attach 2 × 4 or 2 × 6 false beams across joists before placing the ceiling (**24–71**). This requires pretty accurate fitting and additional nailing surfaces, so if you wish to work this way it will be better to form rabbets in the beam before you attach it (**24–72**). Another, easier way is to attach the beams after the ceiling is installed (**24–73**).

If you do this with solid stock, limit the thickness to 2 inches and make the attachment with lag bolts driven into every other joist. Sink the lag bolts in counterbored holes that you then plug with dowel to get a pegged effect. You can also make the beams like long U-channels, using ½- or ¾-inch stock to reduce weight. In **24–74**, a ¾-inch-thick nailer is attached across the joists first and the box beam is secured to the nailer. One idea you might check out is using baseboard or casing molding as the sides of the beams (**24–75**). You can get some interesting architectural effects without the need for elaborate equipment.

24-71

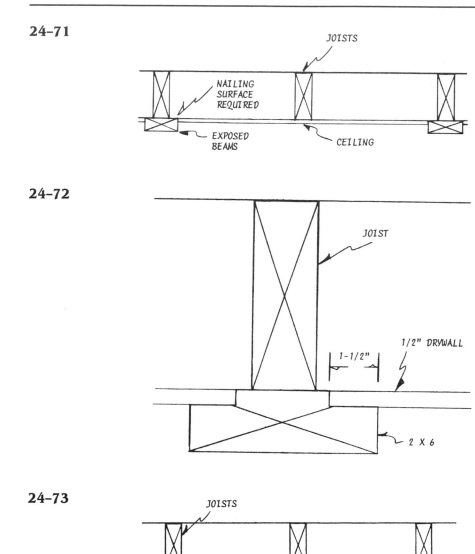

24-72

24-73

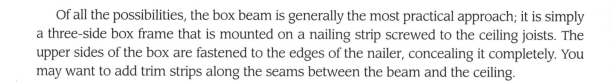

Of all the possibilities, the box beam is generally the most practical approach; it is simply a three-side box frame that is mounted on a nailing strip screwed to the ceiling joists. The upper sides of the box are fastened to the edges of the nailer, concealing it completely. You may want to add trim strips along the seams between the beam and the ceiling.

24-74

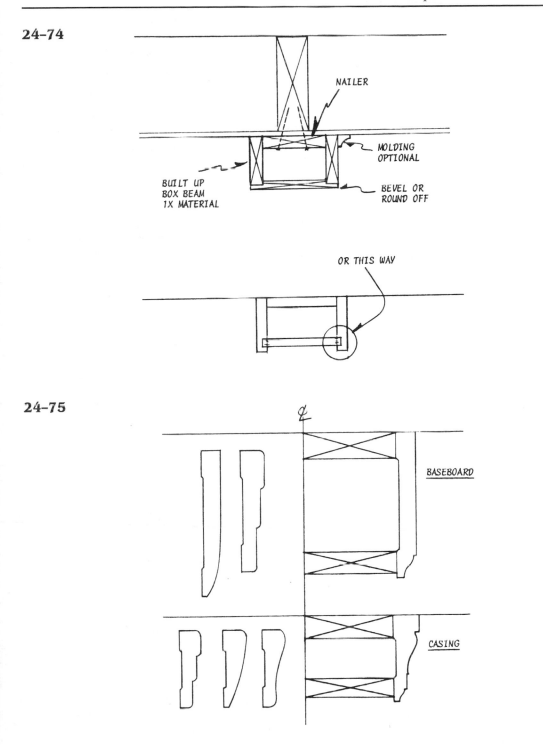

NAILER

BUILT UP
BOX BEAM
1X MATERIAL

MOLDING
OPTIONAL

BEVEL OR
ROUND OFF

OR THIS WAY

24-75

BASEBOARD

CASING

It pays to do all the assembly and finishing jobs on a workbench. When you mount the beam, you won't need to do any sanding or staining that could mar the existing ceiling. You can use 1 × 6 pine that is easy to cut and rout, or larger boards, depending on headroom and how much beam you want to show below the ceiling.

To make a finished-looking box, you should miter the lower corners and assemble the boards with glue plus biscuits or finishing nails. Set up the corners in a square position and clamp them that way (usually overnight) until the glue sets. Butt joints are easier to make, but they expose strips of rough end grain. This isn't a problem if you plan to paint the beam. If you plan to stain it, the end grain of pine will absorb more colorant and look darker than the smooth faces of the boards.

Once the box is framed, you also can use a router to create elegant grooves, beading strips, and other decorative details along the lower corners. You should test the pattern on some scrap lumber, and different finishes, too.

25 BUILDING STAIRWAYS

The construction of a stairway can be simple or complex, with much depending on where the unit is located. Service or utility stairs—those coming from a basement or into an attic—can be basic and easy to assemble, especially if they are hidden; a necessary but purely functional element. In the case of an attic, the means of access can often be greatly simplified by installing a ready-made folding unit that pulls down when needed (**25-1**). It does its job efficiently and does not consume floor space. On the other hand, visible main stairs are often architectural fea-

25-1

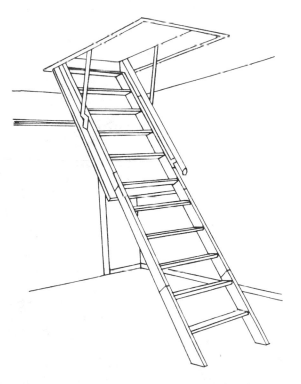

tures, as in **25–2**, and deserve the attention and the quality of construction you would ordinarily apply to a fine piece of furniture.

But before we get into the details of stair planning and construction, which can get quite complicated, bear in mind that almost all builders subcontract this work to stair-building specialists. This generally does not apply to prefabricated units (**25–3**), which include fit-together models such as circular stair kits. It does apply to almost all wooden units.

Once the opening for the stairs is completed and the floor elevations are established, the subcontractor comes on site to take measurements, and returns later with a complete

25–2

staircase. These specialists generally can give you a very competitive rate, and turn out the work very quickly. They can handle straight runs, of course, but also stairs with multiple runs and landings, and stairs with exotic woods and trim details.

Also, stairs are subject to many codes, which a stair builder is familiar with. On winders, for example, you need to maintain a 10-inch tread width at a 12-inch diameter from the narrow end of the converging tread. Limits like this can make layout a little tricky. Generally, the most important codes require a grippable handrail at 34 to 38 inches off the stairs, 6 foot, 8 inch minimum headroom, and at least a 3-foot walkoff. Tread width is gen-

25-3

erally 36 inches or more, tread depth 10 inches, and riser height a maximum of 7 feet, ¾ inch. Considering how complicated it can be to fit stairs into two-story framed openings following these and other guidelines, it becomes clear why (even for pros) subcontracting out this work is the way to go.

Stairways can be open or closed (**25–4**). The open design in **25–5** shows a wall barrier, but a railing, of course, can be used just as well. The wall idea does have an advantage, because it provides a surface for decorations such as pictures or plants.

25–4

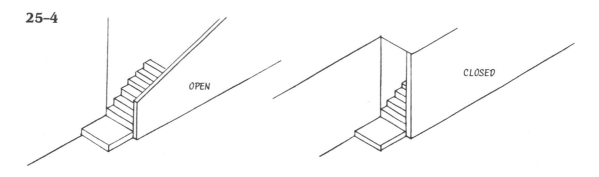

Stairways that are straight runs are the easiest to build, but often, for aesthetic or practical reasons, the run is broken by a landing, which is a platform that permits a directional change. When a landing is included, and space permits, it can be designed attractively so it makes a contribution to pleasant surroundings (**25–5**). You can actually gain much by being a little more generous with space than a basically practical solution would demand.

25–5

Winder-type stairs are used when space is very tight, but they can be unsafe because of the narrowness of the treads at the convergence point (**25–6**). When they must be used, the major design consideration should be to maintain a uniform and safe tread width along the normal traffic line, which is usually about 15 to 18 inches from the narrow end. One way to do this is to have the convergence point of the winders outside the construction rather than at the corner (**25–7**).

25–6

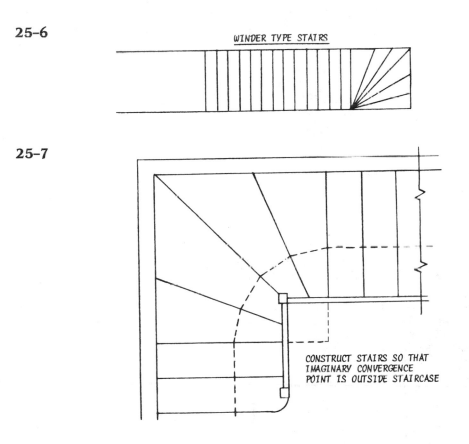

WINDER TYPE STAIRS

25–7

CONSTRUCT STAIRS SO THAT
IMAGINARY CONVERGENCE
POINT IS OUTSIDE STAIRCASE

THE FUNDAMENTALS

The steps have a tread and a riser and are supported by sawtooth stringers that decide the slope of the project (**25–8**). Headroom, rise angle, and all the other factors must be considered when doing initial planning so that the stairway will be safe and convenient to use. The relationship between the tread and the riser is critical and some guides have been established that relate to what you might call the average climbing stride.

25-8

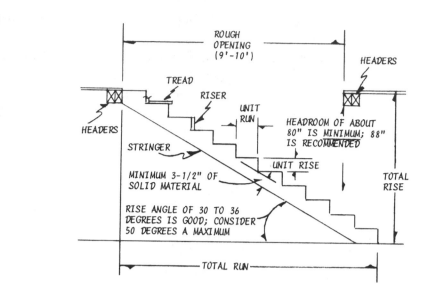

If you study **25-9**, you will discover the importance of applying all three of the rules. For example, using a riser of 4 inches and a tread of 14 inches, rule #2 results in 18 inches which, apparently, is acceptable. But check with rules 1 and 3 and the result is far from the ideal. 2(4) plus 14 = 22; 4(14) = 56.

25-9.   STAIR TREAD AND RISER GUIDELINES

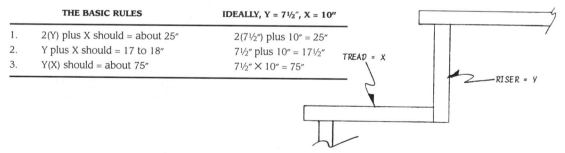

	THE BASIC RULES	IDEALLY, Y = 7½″, X = 10″
1.	2(Y) plus X should = about 25″	2(7½″) plus 10″ = 25″
2.	Y plus X should = 17 to 18″	7½″ plus 10″ = 17½″
3.	Y(X) should = about 75″	7½″ × 10″ = 75″

To use the ideal figures would mean having to design around the staircase so total rise and total run would be suitable. This isn't always possible, but you should try to work within reasonable tolerances, and, as always, it's crucial that your design conforms to code.

For a main stairway, risers can change from 6½ inches to 7¾ inches, treads from 10½ inches to 11 inches. You can see that the range does permit adjustments, so you can fit a stairway in available space without sacrificing safety. As riser height increases, fewer riser treads are required. The fewer treads there are, the less space is required for the stairway. That's why attic and basement stairs are sometimes built without regard for safety, which is poor thinking. Excessively high risers and narrow treads should be avoided, and are not likely to pass a building inspection.

A WAY TO PLAN

Divide the total rise, say 9 feet, by 7. The answer, in this case, is 15.429, but only the whole number is used to tell the number of risers that will be required if each is to have an approximate height of 7 inches. Divide the total rise (108 inches) by the number of risers (15) and you get the actual individual riser height of 7³⁄₁₆ inches. Work with rule #2 of **25-9** and you will see that a tread about 10 inches wide is compatible with the riser height. Because the number of treads is always one less than the number of risers, multiply 10 by 14 to find the total run. Adjustments can be made by changing the riser and tread dimensions as long as you don't violate the basic rules.

You can see why it is wise to consider a stairway installation when you are doing the house framing. Changing the height of a ceiling to accommodate a flight of steps might be a bit extreme, but it is no trouble to plan the length of the rough opening so that it will accept a stairway you can design with a minimum of fuss.

The table in **25-10** shows riser-tread relationships for installations of various heights that you can use as a planning guide.

25-10. TREAD AND RISER RELATIONSHIPS

TOTAL RISE	NUMBER OF RISERS	RISER HEIGHT	NUMBER OF TREADS	TREAD WIDTH
7'-8"	12	7²¹⁄₃₂"	11	9" to 9¾"
8'-0"	13	7 ³⁄₈"	12	9½" to 10"
8'-4"	14	7⅛"	13	10" to 10½"
8'-9"	14	7½"	13	10⁵⁄₁₆"
9'-0"	15	7³⁄₁₆"	14	10" to 10½"

THE CONSTRUCTION

The stringer, sometimes called the carriage, is the main structural member and should be made of strong rigid material, generally 2 × 12s. If you view the profile of a straight-run flight, you will see that it is a right triangle, the hypotenuse representing roughly the length of the stringer. You can pick this up on the job merely by stretching a line from the top to the bottom of the stairs, but add a foot or so to this to find the length of the stringer material to start with.

Another way is to make a full-scale layout of one or two tread-riser cuts and then multiply the bridge dimension, shown in **25–11**, by the number of risers. Add a foot or so to

25–11

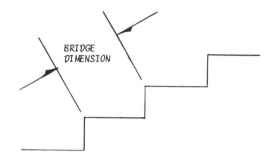

BRIDGE
DIMENSION

the result and you will have a good stringer length to start with. All stairway material should be kiln-dried and warp-free. Hidden stringers or those used in a basement don't have to be pretty, but visible ones on a main, open stairway should be carefully selected for appearance as well as strength.

Usually, stringers are notched to form a sawtooth pattern that supplies a nailing surface for each riser and tread. The pattern can be laid out by using a square as shown in **25–12**, or by making a special template and using it as shown in **25–13**. The latter method minimizes the possibility of error.

25–12

10"   7"   TREAD   RISER

25–13

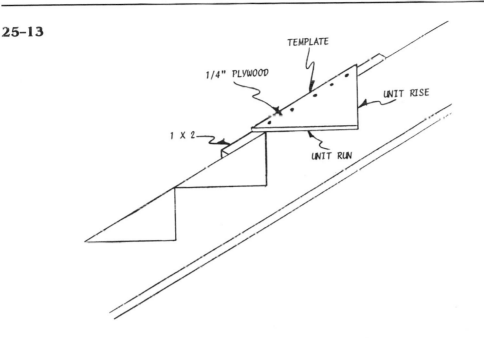

The cutting can be done entirely with a handsaw, or you can use a power cutoff saw, moving as far as possible into the cut and then finishing with a handsaw. Similar stringers can be clamped together so that two (or three) can be notched at the same time. If sawing through such thicknesses bothers you, then form one and use it as pattern to mark the others. The cut stringers should look like those in **25–14**.

25–14

A CUT STRINGER

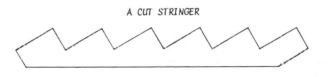

A widely used type of stairway (usually prefab or shop-built) is called housed construction and consists of stringers, risers, and treads that are assembled with glue and wedges as shown in **25–15**. This is top-quality work and when correctly installed results in a handsome stairway that is strong, dustproof, and squeakless. This kind of thing can be done on the job, but not without a router and a special adjustable template that serves as a guide for forming the tapered grooves.

Open-type stairs (no riser boards) are often used in basements or outdoors. Here, stringers can be formed by using cleats to provide tread support. A more sophisticated way

25–15

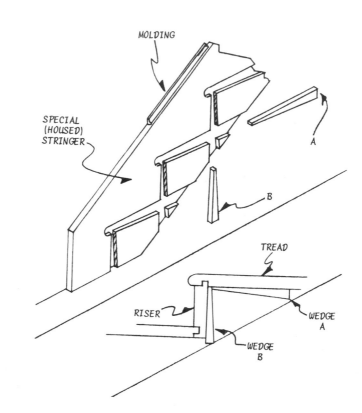

is to form dadoes in the stringers. As **25–16** shows, riser boards are easily added if you wish to close in the steps.

Open stairs can also be made as shown in **25–17**, which presents the opportunity to be a bit more creative. But don't let your imagination run to the point where you neglect the safety factors or code requirements.

TREADS AND RISERS

Stair treads are strongest if they are made of hardwood or a vertical-grain softwood. Flat-grain softwoods are not really suitable for a main stairway unless you plan to use an additional cover material such as carpeting.

Tread material with the front edge already shaped as a nosing is available in thicknesses that may be $1\frac{1}{16}$ inches or $1\frac{1}{8}$ inches. If you make your own, the nosing can be shaped in any of the ways shown in **25–18**.

The nosing contributes to appearance, but it should never extend beyond the riser more than $1\frac{1}{2}$ inches or it will become a tripping hazard. Actually, the wider the tread, the

25-16

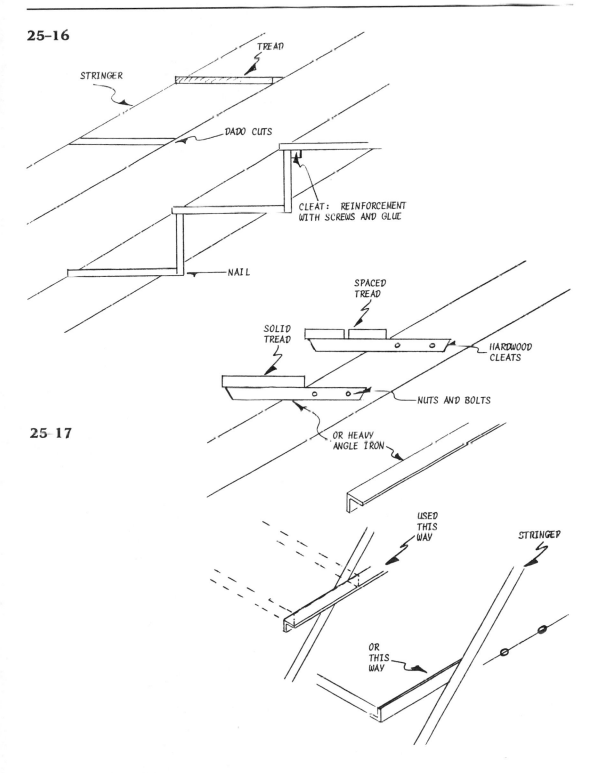

STRINGER

TREAD

DADO CUTS

CLEAT: REINFORCEMENT
WITH SCREWS AND GLUE

NAIL

SPACED
TREAD

SOLID
TREAD

HARDWOOD
CLEATS

NUTS AND BOLTS

25-17

OR HEAVY
ANGLE IRON

USED
THIS
WAY

STRINGER

OR
THIS
WAY

25–18   SHAPES OF TREAD NOSINGS

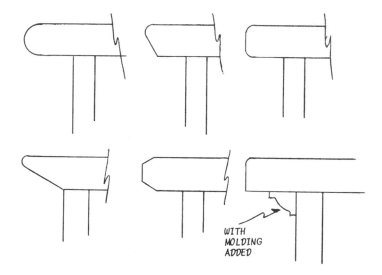

less nosing you will need. The width of the nosing is not included when you are doing the initial dimensioning.

Risers can be ¾ inch thick and should be made of tread-matching material unless you plan to cover the stairs. Good construction, when butt joints are used, calls for the bottom end of the riser to mate with the back edge of the tread as shown in **25–19**. If you use screw-reinforced glue blocks at the top of the riser, the job can be done without visible nails. Another way to do the job, which takes some time but results in premium quality, is to use dado and rabbet joints as shown in **25–20**.

25–19   **25–20**

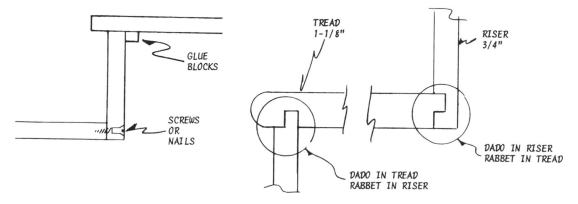

INSTALLATION

Framing for a straight-run stairway is shown in **25–21**, and framing for a stairway with a landing in **25–22**. Two stringers are sufficient for minimum-width stairs, but use three on wide stairs or if you wish to add more strength and firmness.

25–21

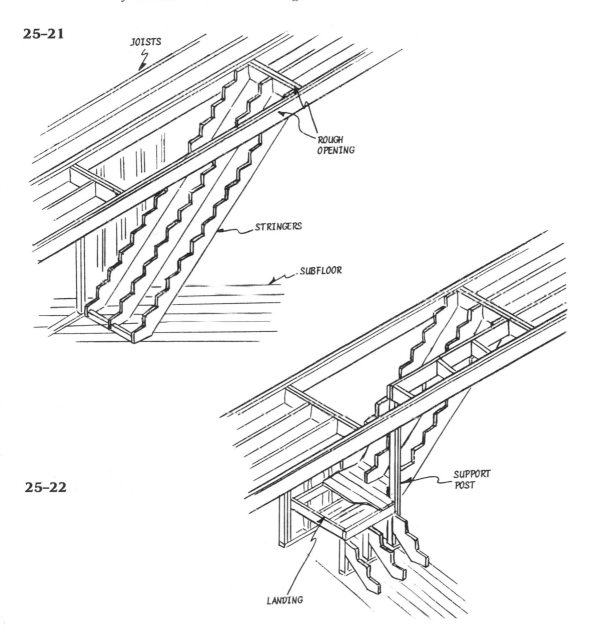

25–22

Stringer attachments at the top end can vary considerably, with much depending on whether the top tread will be flush with the finish floor. If it will be, you can add considerable strength while making installation easier by notching the stringers and including a support ledger (**25–23**).

25–23

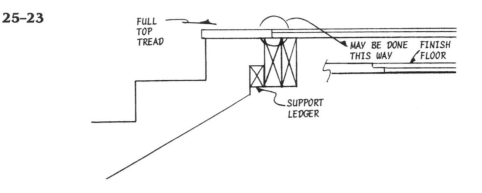

If the top tread is below the finish floor, which is common, and generally the way subcontractors provide stairs, you can use either of the methods shown in **25–24**. Such attachments are especially important on an open stairway. On a closed stairway, the outboard stringers are securely spiked to the wall frames, which results in a very strong installation.

25–24

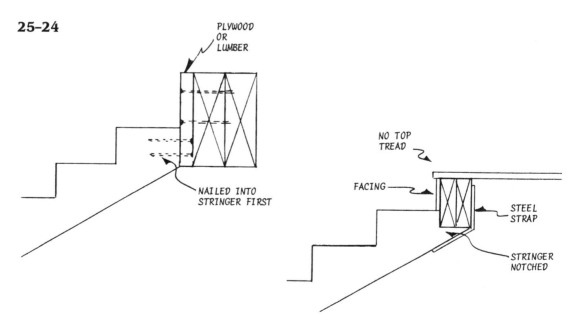

The attachment at the bottom is much simpler because it doesn't require more than braces, which, if possible, are nailed through the subfloor into joists. Figure **25–25** shows the stringer braces and also some of the finish work.

25–25

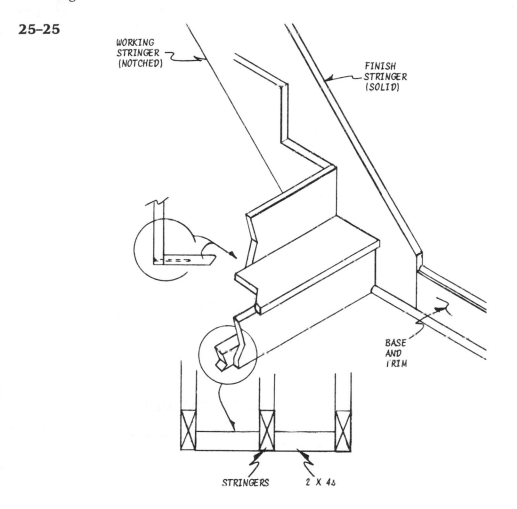

WORKING STRINGER (NOTCHED)

FINISH STRINGER (SOLID)

BASE AND TRIM

STRINGERS   2 X 4s

THE BALUSTRADE

Stairways that are open on one or both sides should be lined with safety rails consisting of newel posts, handrails, and intermediate posts or balusters. Often this functional assembly is emphasized as an architectural feature. But modern codes also limit the spacing between balusters. The 4-inch maximum may seem restrictive, but is designed largely to prevent small children from sticking their heads through and becoming stuck.

Structurally, the newel post at the bottom of the stairs is quite important. Often it passes through the floor and is bolted or spiked to a framing member (**25–26**). If a framing member is not conveniently located, you can always add a header between joists.

25–26

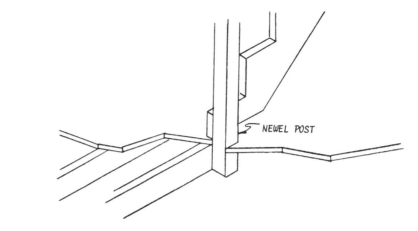

NEWEL POST

Other ways are to secure the post to the outside of the stringer, as in **25–27**, or to notch it so it straddles the stringer, as in **25–28**. You can, of course, make your own balustrade components by working with clear kiln-dried stock and doing the assembly as shown in **25–29**.

25–27   NEWEL POST SECURED TO OUTSIDE OF STRINGER

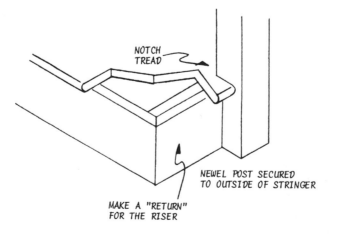

NOTCH
TREAD

NEWEL POST SECURED
TO OUTSIDE OF STRINGER

MAKE A "RETURN"
FOR THE RISER

25-28 NEWEL-POST-SECURED STRADDLING STRINGER

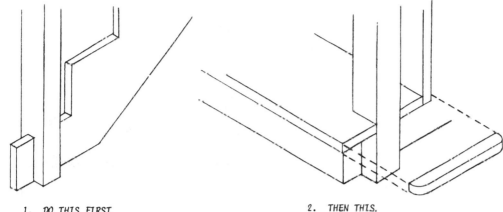

1. *DO THIS FIRST.*

2. *THEN THIS.*

25-29

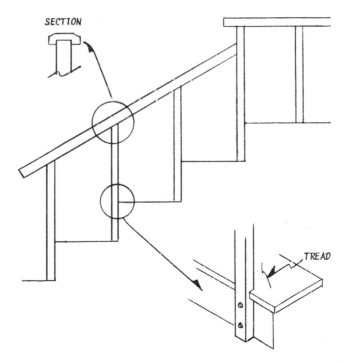

SECTION

TREAD

Handrails need to be placed 34 to 39 inches above treads and landings (**25–30**). On wide, open stairs and on closed stairs, stock handrails are often used. These are easily attached to walls by using ready-made brackets designed for the purpose (**25–31**).

25–30

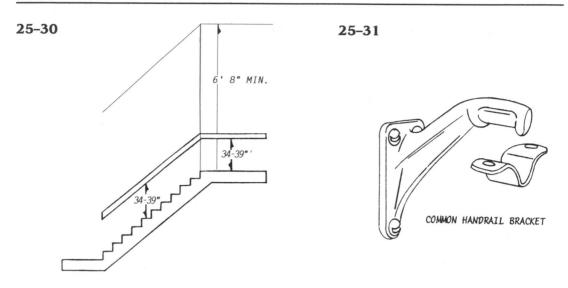

25–31

COMMON HANDRAIL BRACKET

A few examples of other factory-made parts are balusters (**25–32**), newel posts (**25–33**), complete sets of components for balustrades of various designs (**25–34**), and decorative pieces such as brackets (**25–35**).

25–32

25–33

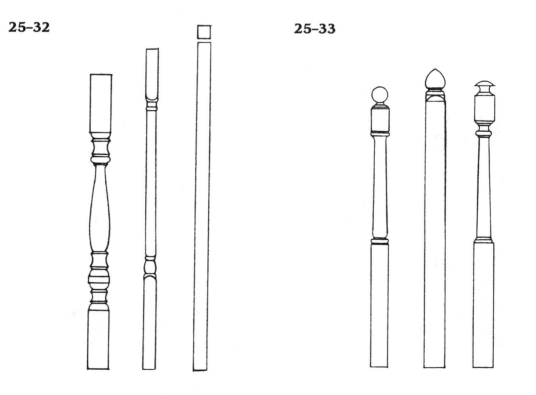

25–34

25– 35

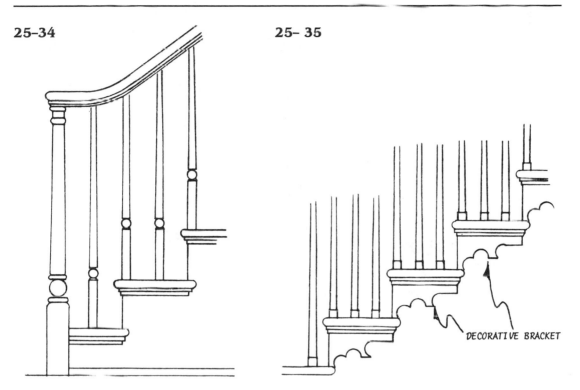

DECORATIVE BRACKET

26 INSTALLING FINISHED FLOORS

The durability and the appearance of wood amply justify its time-less popularity as a flooring material. Today it is available in many forms for flooring, generally classified as being strip, plank, or block. Modern versions of strip and plank may be installed with either nails or adhesives. Blocks, which produce a parquet floor, are usually placed with adhesive. All types are available prefinished so that the job is complete as soon as the material is down. (If you use prefinished flooring, this should be the last installation on the job.) Woods, patterns, and finishes are so numerous that the only way to make a proper choice is to visit a flooring supply house and see the wide range that's available.

Strip flooring is basically of two types. The more complex version has an interlocking tongue-and-groove arrangement on all edges and ends (**26–1**). Technically, it is described as being side- and end-matched. The undercut on modern products is provided so the

26-1

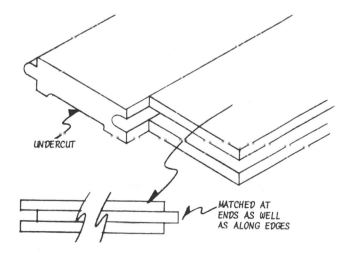

UNDERCUT

MATCHED AT
ENDS AS WELL
AS ALONG EDGES

pieces are more likely to stay flat and remain stable even if the subfloor is less than perfect. Nails are driven at an angle through edges so they are concealed.

Square-edged strip flooring, as the name suggests, is simply narrow lengths of wood butted edge to edge and end to end (**26–2**). Here, surface nailing is required and the flooring chore is extended because you must set and conceal the nails with a wood putty. Plain boards are rarely used these days, with the exception of a house where you are trying to recreate a Colonial style with wide pine boards.

Plank flooring comes in random widths and can be either solid boards or laminated (**26–3**). The material is available with false pegs already in place or is designed for surface attachment with screws or nails driven through counterbored holes, which are then filled

26–2   SQUARE-EDGED STRIP FLOORING

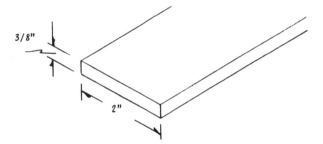

26–3   LAMINATED TONGUE-AND-GROOVE PLANK FLOORING

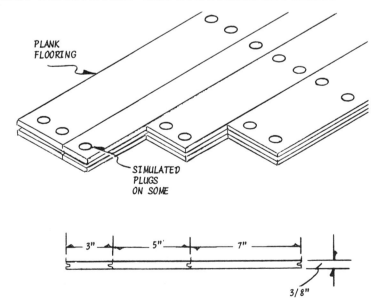

with plugs. While some of these products merely simulate the kind of floors you would expect to find in old Colonial homes, others are the real thing, for example, solid oak planks with authentic walnut pegs.

There are many choices in block flooring, both in patterns and in sizes. Some are assemblies of small, solid pieces of wood. Others are laminations, and still others resemble short pieces of strip flooring that are edge-joined into square blocks (**26–4**). Some manufacturers add a polyethylene foam pad on the back to soak up noise and cushion the

26–4

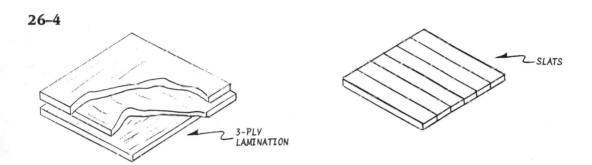

floor somewhat. Many of the modern versions of both plank and block flooring are designed for adhesive application on wood or directly to concrete.

But the most common wood installation in new houses is strip-oak flooring—a standard and widely available material made of ¾ x 2¼ inch boards set in random lengths so the ends overlap row to row.

UNDERLAYMENTS

An underlayment is a ¼-to ½-inch-thick layer of plywood, hardboard, or particleboard that you may have to place over the subfloor, depending on the type of material used for the finish floor (**26–5**). In some situations, such as ceramic tile installations, you need underlayment for additional rigidity. In other cases, the idea is to provide the smooth surface that's needed under resilient materials such as linoleum, vinyl tile, and carpeting. It may be necessary to add an underlayment for thin wood flooring, but it is not necessary under thick strip or plank flooring.

A point to remember if you use different-thickness floor coverings in various rooms is that you might be able to end up with a uniformly even floor throughout the house by compensating with underlayments of various thicknesses.

Recommended underlayment grades of plywood have a solid surface backed with

26-5

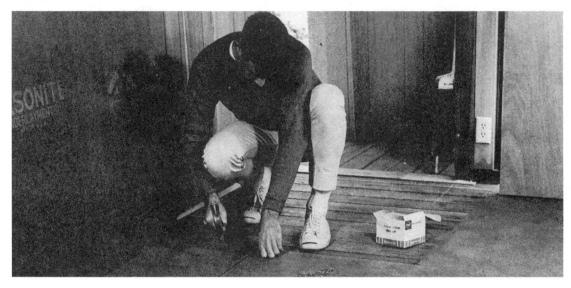

inner ply construction that resists deformations caused by concentrated loads. A typical installation is shown in **26-6**.

Place panels so that the surface grain will run across joists and end joints will occur over a framing member. Stagger end joints, and plan for all joints to be staggered in rela-

26-6

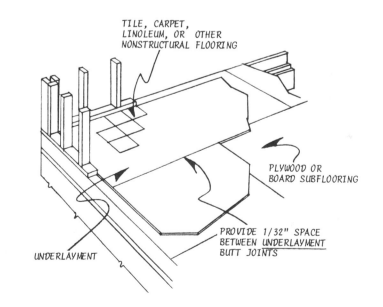

TILE, CARPET, LINOLEUM, OR OTHER NONSTRUCTURAL FLOORING

PLYWOOD OR BOARD SUBFLOORING

PROVIDE 1/32" SPACE BETWEEN UNDERLAYMENT BUTT JOINTS

UNDERLAYMENT

tion to those in the subfloor. Space nails 6 inches apart along edges, 8 inches apart in the field. Check the installation carefully to be sure all nail heads are flush and no unevenness has occurred at joints. Use a few extra nails wherever you think they are needed; do some sanding if nails have raised splinters or if sawed edges are rough. There's no taboo against filling all joints with a wood putty. The installation instructions on some sheet flooring will require it to prevent small changes in level from showing up as creases in the sheet surface.

Hardboard underlayment is manufactured from wood fibers that are bonded under heat and pressure to form panels that are dense, durable, and grainless. Most have one coarse-sanded surface designed to increase adhesive bonding qualities. Installation doesn't differ from that outlined for plywood except for the specifics shown in **26-7**.

Particleboard is a panel of wood particles bonded with special additives under heat and

26-7

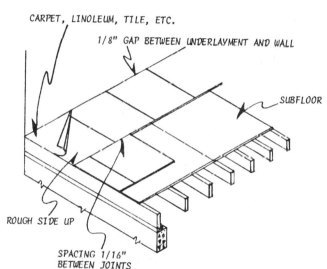

CARPET, LINOLEUM, TILE, ETC.

1/8" GAP BETWEEN UNDERLAYMENT AND WALL

SUBFLOOR

ROUGH SIDE UP

SPACING 1/16" BETWEEN JOINTS

compressed to a uniform density. It is flat and grainless, and while it is strong, it should be carefully handled to avoid damage to edges. Usually it is recommended that a vapor barrier be placed between it and the subfloor. A typical installation is shown in **26-8**.

All underlayment material should be placed immediately before the installation of the final cover. If there must be a time lapse, take steps to protect the underlayment from physical damage and moisture, generally by rolling out inexpensive pink-colored building paper and taping the joints.

26–8

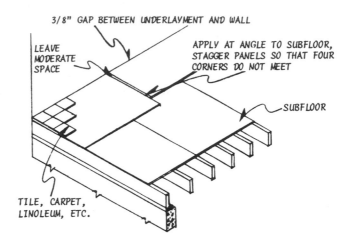

3/8" GAP BETWEEN UNDERLAYMENT AND WALL

LEAVE
MODERATE
SPACE

APPLY AT ANGLE TO SUBFLOOR,
STAGGER PANELS SO THAT FOUR
CORNERS DO NOT MEET

SUBFLOOR

TILE, CARPET,
LINOLEUM, ETC.

STRIP-OAK FLOORING

The standard oak floor is set so the ends overlap row to row. The edges are held in tongue-and-groove joints, and fastened with a machine that sets nails in the joints as the boards go down so you don't see any trace of fasteners on the surface. In a typical installation you load the machine (you can rent one) with nails, set the guide on the edge of a board, and pound down on the setting head of the machine with a heavy hammer. The process is hand-powered, but guides the nail at exactly the right angle. It's the only way to do the job reasonably, and one that the pros all use.

As to materials, some suppliers produce variations on the basic configuration, including narrower planks, and end-matched boards that interlock on all four sides. There are also prefinished materials, and a recent trend to dress up plain oak floors by laying border strips of contrasting cherry and birch (there are about 30 species of hardwood flooring to choose from), and highlighting floors with hardwood medallions. The details can dress up the price, too, with a single two-wood rose medallion at about $250, and borders starting at $10 to $15 per linear foot.

But all installations should be saved until the end of your construction job so the wood won't be damaged, and won't swell or twist before heating and cooling systems have stabilized the indoor environment.

A step up in cost also can buy you a prefinished floor that is stained, sealed, and ready to use as soon as it's installed. That's an advantage on jobs with tight schedules, and eliminates on-site sanding and finishing—a project that can take several days in warm, sticky weather when a polyurethane finish refuses to dry and you're waiting to move into the new space.

Most prefinished oak is thinner than the ¾-inch standard (some are just over ¼-inch thick), but built-in laminations are more resistant to shrinking and swelling than solid, unfinished wood. And because the boards, which range from 2¼- to 8-inch widths, arrive on site fully sealed, they have more resistance than raw wood to temperature and humidity swings in a partially sealed house still in the final phase of construction. Most prefinished products are too thin to stand up to nailing and generally are glued in place, which also cuts job time.

The ultimate in prefinishing is wood flooring with an acrylic-impregnated surface. Unlike most finishes that lie on top of the wood and seep only slightly into the grain, an acrylic finish is forced into the wood pores, which increases durability and reduces maintenance.

A good finish will protect the wood from drying out and shrinking to the point where seams crack open. It also helps to maintain indoor relative humidity at 30 to 50 percent. But don't be surprised to see seams open noticeably in wood that is close to a wood-stove or fireplace.

LAYING STRIP OAK

The complexity of the layout will relate to whether you use strip flooring throughout the house or in just one room. If the coverage is overall, then strips must run parallel and continuously through all areas with lengths following the long dimension of hallways and rooms. You are likely to have alignment problems when you encounter projections into a room, doorways, openings into closets, and so on.

Start by figuring how you are going to run the pieces, generally across the joists and in line with the long dimension of the house as a whole. Do a test run in a critical area (a hallway is good) by actually placing pieces of flooring loosely to see how they might lay out. By some trial and error, you can find where to make a start so strips can run as they should with minimum fuss on your part. In the very basic example in **26–9**, it is easy to see that strips started lengthwise in the hallway could move into rooms and remain parallel. Of course, all installations are not so simple, but the idea is there. Also, you can change the direction of the strips with a header piece of trim if you choose to, but it is wise to do that only as a last recourse.

Make a last inspection of the subfloor to be sure all nails are down and correctly seated. Sweep away dust and dirt or, preferably, do the job with a vacuum cleaner. Place a layer of double-weight building paper over the subfloor, lapping joints at least 4 inches, and

26–9

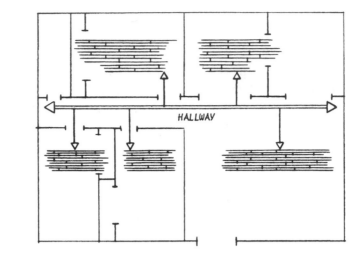

HALLWAY

then snap chalk lines to indicate the joist runs. Notice that the paper, like the joists, should run at right angles to the strips (**26–10**).

The type, size, and number of nails you use to secure the strips generally are specified by the flooring manufacturer. One of the most common is to maintain an 8-inch O.C. spacing. With joists 16 inches O.C., you would have a nail at each joist crossing and one between.

Start the first line of strips parallel to a wall, placing them as shown in **26–11**. Align these pieces carefully, as they will affect the placement of all pieces that follow. The surface nails you use to start with can be placed so they will be hidden later by the baseboard,

26–10

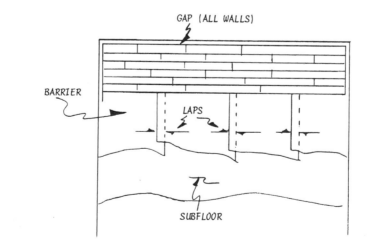

GAP (ALL WALLS)

BARRIER

LAPS

SUBFLOOR

26-11

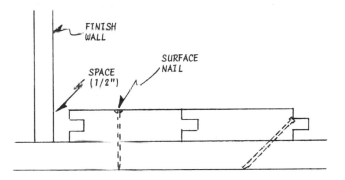

or you can set them and conceal them with a wood putty. Work with the longest pieces of flooring, saving shorter ones to end runs. Use cutoffs in closets and similar areas. After the first strip is down, place the next five or six lines loosely on the floor so you can judge positions of end joints, which should be staggered and not closer than 6 to 8 inches in succeeding courses. This is also the time to judge how adjacent strips (or courses) will blend in terms of grain patterns and color tones. Courses that follow the starter strips are blind-nailed by machine.

Work with a scrap piece of flooring and a hammer when you encounter pieces that won't fit tightly against those in preceding courses (**26-12**). If you find some are especially stubborn, tack-nail a piece of wood to the subfloor and then use another piece of wood or a wrecking bar as a lever to force the body into position until it is nailed. Use extra nails, if necessary, and only after drilling pilot holes to prevent splitting, to bring the ends into position (**26-13**).

26-12   **26-13**

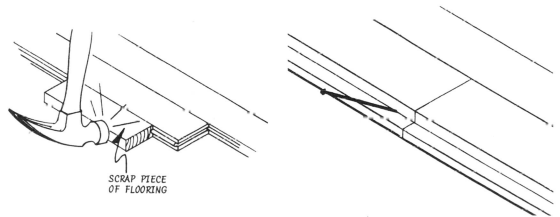

SCRAP PIECE
OF FLOORING

When you reach the opposite wall, rip the final strips to correct width and surface-nail them as you did the starters. Remember, there must be a space of about ½ inch between flooring and all walls.

WOOD OVER CONCRETE

To protect a wood floor in this situation, you need to cover the concrete with a reliable moisture barrier. Then you must provide joist substitutes (sleepers) to which you can nail the flooring. One solution is shown in **26–14**. The bottom sleepers are placed directly in asphaltic mastic, which must cover the slab completely. Spread the mastic uniformly with a toothed trowel. The top sleepers are nailed in place after the polyethylene film is laid down. Another system is to place the polyethylene film between two layers of mastic, and put 2 × 4 sleepers in the top layer of mastic as shown in **26–15**.

In all cases, the sleepers adjacent to the concrete should be secured with special hardened concrete nails spaced about 20 inches apart. You can drive them with a heavy hammer, or rent a power fastener that sinks the nails with explosive power. Use safety glasses, gloves, and full protective gear if you use a power fastener.

It's obvious that sleepers over concrete won't supply adequate support for thin-strip flooring; consider a minimum thickness of $25/32$ inch for your flooring . However, you can use an alternate method that will permit the use of any type of flooring. The slab is waterproofed and sleepers are placed as described above, but then a substantial subfloor of plywood is placed just as if you were working over conventional joists (**26–16**).

Some types of modern wood flooring materials, like the plank design in **26–17**, are

26–14

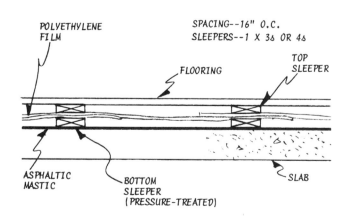

POLYETHYLENE FILM

SPACING--16" O.C.
SLEEPERS--1 X 3ʸ OR 4ʸ

FLOORING

TOP SLEEPER

ASPHALTIC MASTIC

BOTTOM SLEEPER (PRESSURE-TREATED)

SLAB

designed to be installed directly on concrete. Procedures for such products vary; make sure you understand the manufacturer's instructions, and follow them to the letter.

26-15

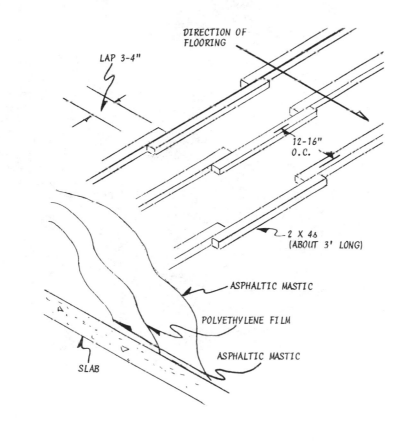

26-16

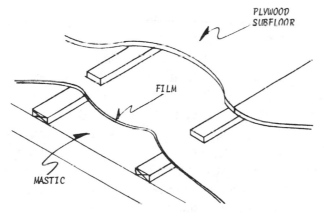

26–17

PARQUET FLOORING

There are dozens of types and patterns available, such as the two shown in **26–18** and **26–19**. Check installation specifics, especially regarding the adhesive recommended and to whether a vapor barrier is required; these may vary in different products.

A typical installation starts with a chalk line to mark the intersecting centerlines of the area (**26–20**). Then place loose blocks in both directions to see how they will end up at the walls. Make adjustments until, as shown in **26–21**, A and B are equal and at least one-half the width of a block. At this point, you can snap additional lines to show the position of the starters (**26–22**). Spread mastic from the centerpoint toward the area you will start to cover. It will probably be necessary to wait a bit for the adhesive to become tacky before you can place the blocks, but instructions on the container will explain this.

Start by placing blocks in pyramid fashion, as in **26–23**, until you have covered the

26–18

26–19

spread of mastic. Then continue in similar fashion until all but the blocks adjacent to the walls have been placed. At this point, work as shown in **26–24** so you can mark the border pieces correctly for cutting to width.

Design variations are possible when you place adjacent pieces so grain directions or designs are opposed (**26–25**). More impressive, and more complicated, departures from straightforward layouts are possible with a diagonal pattern (**26–26**). The actual installation of the blocks doesn't differ, but more planning, more cutting, and often more materials are required.

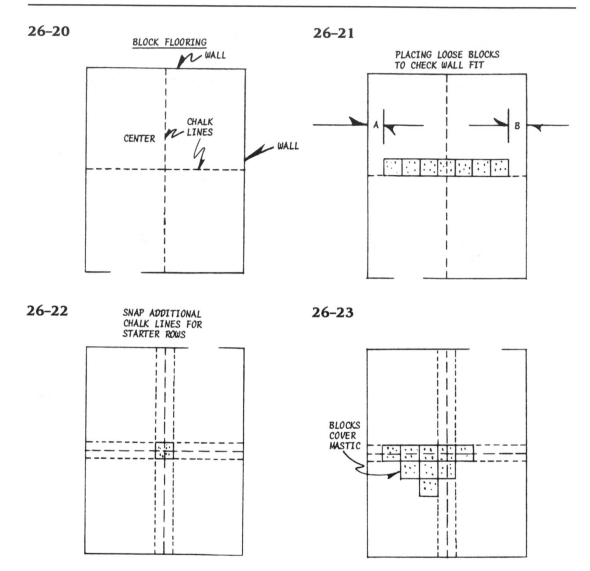

26–20

BLOCK FLOORING

WALL

CENTER

CHALK
LINES

WALL

26–21

PLACING LOOSE BLOCKS
TO CHECK WALL FIT

A

B

26–22

SNAP ADDITIONAL
CHALK LINES FOR
STARTER ROWS

26–23

BLOCKS
COVER
MASTIC

Figures 26–27 and **26–28** show two methods of making an attractive and unobtrusive joint when block flooring (or any wood flooring) abuts a carpet.

RESILIENT FLOORING

This type of floor cover is often used in kitchens and baths. You can use either tile or sheets, but both types must be installed over a sound, smooth underlayment. Even a small chip of wood can leave an impression (and eventually create a tear) in the thinner resilient sheet materials.

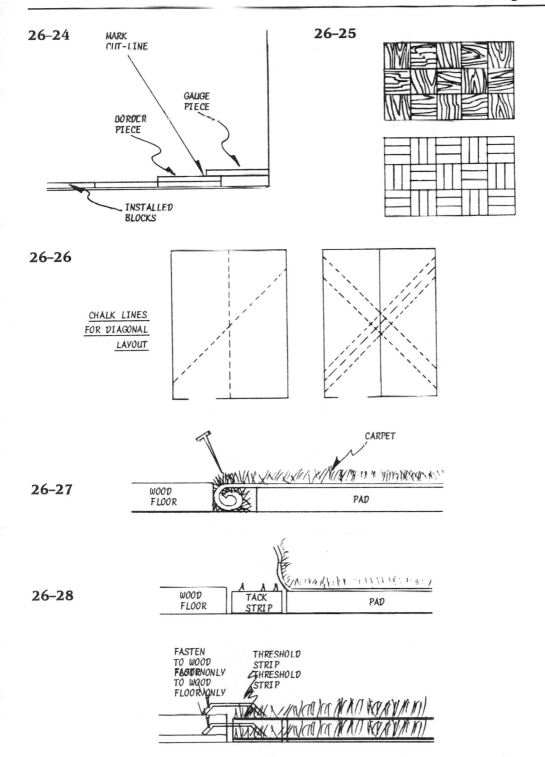

26–24

MARK
CUT-LINE

GAUGE
PIECE

BORDER
PIECE

INSTALLED
BLOCKS

26–25

26–26

CHALK LINES
FOR DIAGONAL
LAYOUT

26–27

CARPET

WOOD
FLOOR

PAD

26–28

WOOD
FLOOR

TACK
STRIP

PAD

FASTEN
TO WOOD
FLOOR ONLY

THRESHOLD
STRIP

THRESHOLD
STRIP

Most sheet flooring is installed in mastic. But there are some types, generally called floating floors, that do not require adhesive and are pinned at the edges by trim.

Vinyl tiles are installed with the same basic layout approach that you use on ceramic tiles. You need to find the center of the room and plan the job with equal-sized partial tiles at the edges.

Establish intersecting centerlines for the area as shown in **26–29**. This gets more complicated if the floor will have a pattern. The most foolproof way to go about a sheet installation is to make a full-size paper pattern.

Manufacturers will specify not only the type of adhesive to use, but also the application, which typically is made with a notched trowel to create even ribs of material. Place the first tiles carefully, being sure to follow the marked lines (**26–30**).

If you want to add some decorative detail, you can use ready-made feature strips that are placed along with the regular tiles and with the same adhesive (**26–31**). These are available in different colors so you can do combinations that will complement other colors in the room.

26–29

26–30

26–31

Finish the installation at walls or under cabinets with a ready-to-use cove base that is applied with the same adhesive used to stick down the tiles (**26–32**). This too is available in different colors, so you can work along with various decorating schemes. Tiles can be cut with snips when it is necessary to fit them around obstructions (**26–33**).

Clean over the area by working with a manufacturer-recommended solvent and a soft cloth. The cloth should be damp only; you don't want excess solvent to be sucked down between the joints in the tile.

To simplify the application, you might want to check out self-stick floor tiles. With these, the installation is a simple matter of removing the release paper from the back of the tile and then pressing the tile firmly into place (**26–34**). The floor is ready to use as soon as the last tile is down.

26–32

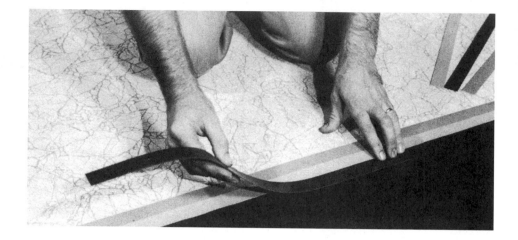

26–33

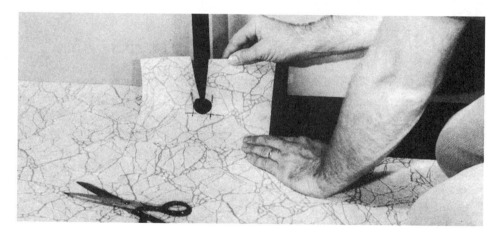

26–34

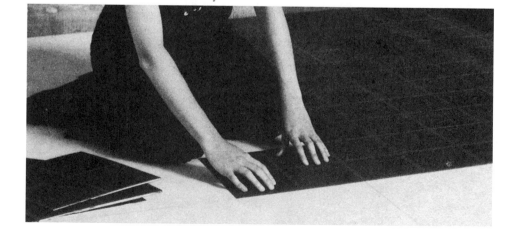

CERAMIC TILE BASICS

In the old days, ceramic tiles were placed over a thick reinforced bed of mortar supported by a solidly nailed subfloor or concrete slab. Because of the weight, extra-large joists or special bracing was often required, as in **26–35**. To maintain floor levels, tile can be installed on sunken framing (**26–36**). But transitions generally are handled with sills and thresholds.

Today, ceramic tile still needs a rigid subfloor, but is generally installed in a bed of organic adhesive spread with a notched trowel (**26–37**).

To make the floor rigid enough to prevent grout cracking, you typically add an extra layer of ⅝- or even ¾-inch plywood. For best results, use glue and screws to fasten the second layer. Then make a centered layout allowing for even partial tiles at the edges, and spread adhesive to the guidelines of your layout with a notched trowel. Remember to use the spreading method and notch size recommended by the tile manufacturer.

Check the working time of the adhesive, and spread only an area that will stay workable as you set the tiles. Some tiles have spacing lugs on the sides. If your tiles don't, you

26–35

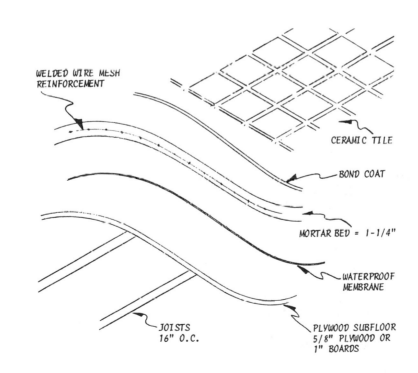

WELDED WIRE MESH REINFORCEMENT

CERAMIC TILE

BOND COAT

MORTAR BED = 1-1/4"

WATERPROOF MEMBRANE

JOISTS 16" O.C.

PLYWOOD SUBFLOOR 5/8" PLYWOOD OR 1" BOARDS

26–36

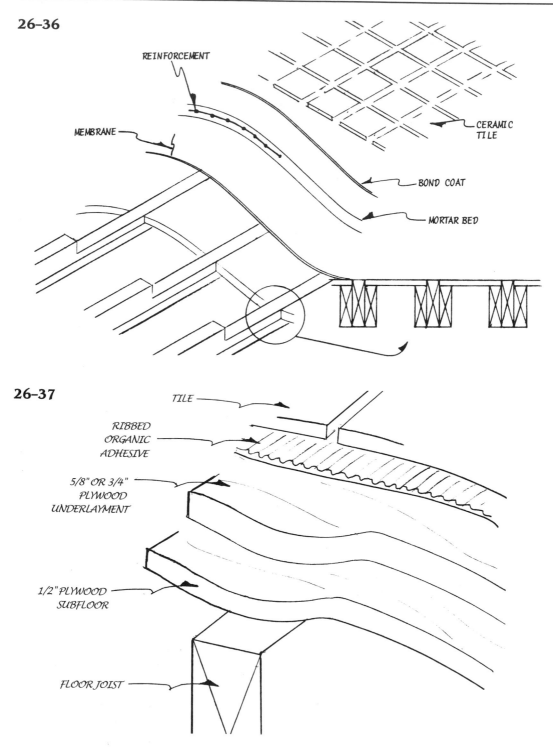

REINFORCEMENT

MEMBRANE

CERAMIC TILE

BOND COAT

MORTAR BED

26–37

TILE

RIBBED ORGANIC ADHESIVE

5/8" OR 3/4" PLYWOOD UNDERLAYMENT

1/2" PLYWOOD SUBFLOOR

FLOOR JOIST

can use small plastic spacers to maintain even grout joints. But even then, you should check the layout frequently with a straightedge or layout line.

To measure the cuts on partial tiles, set a loose tile directly on top of the full-size tile next to the space to be filled. Then set another loose tile on top of that one and slide it against the wall. Use the back edge of the uppermost tile as a guide and draw a line on the surface of loose tile below. This is the tile you cut. The only trick with this offset method is to allow room for a grout joint. Of course, if the room is square, you should be able to take several sample measurements along the wall, and then make all the cuts at once.

There are two tools that you can rent to handle the cutting. The most simple is called a snap cutter. It has guides and a cutting wheel that you draw across the tile by hand. Then you snap the tile along this score line by pressing down on the sides of the tile. On large projects you can rent a wet saw, which is basically a fixed circular saw lubricated with water. For odd cuts and curves, you need to chip away with a tile nipper.

CERAMIC TILE SHOWERS AND TUBS

This is the most difficult type of tile job, and generally should be left to a pro. That's because you need to install a waterproof pan in the tiled enclosure. It's not difficult if you use a prefab pan and only tile the walls, which should be covered in cement backer board with fiberglass-taped joints.

The framed shower enclosure must closely match the size of the pan, which means you need the pan on site before framing begins. You need to take measurements carefully so the pan fits snugly but without any buckling. Pressure on the pan, which typically is made of fiberglass, can cause cracking. The pan also has to line up exactly with the drain line. On most pans, you drive screws through the upper lip into the studs of the enclosure. The fasteners are covered by the cement board and tile.

Tiling the floor instead of installing a prefab is considerably more difficult. The key to waterproofing this installation is a rubberized base layer installed between the mortar, which must slope toward the drain, and the subflooring. It's the equivalent of a fiberglass or metal pan. The most common modern membranes are chlorinated polyethylene (CPE) and polyvinyl chloride (PVC). Both are flexible rubberlike sheets that you can cut easily with a utility knife.

To install the membrane, you first need to add blocking between the wall studs. The blocking provides support for the mortar bed and the membrane where it folds into edges of the floor and runs several inches up the wall. The membrane is folded over on itself in the corners, and around studs at the enclosure door opening. Tile and membrane suppliers offer specially molded patch pieces to provide extra waterproofing at these twists and turns.

GROUTING CERAMIC TILE

You can grout a floor after the tile adhesive is set, usually the day after installation. Start by sweeping out the seams to clear debris and to remove any spacers. Grout needs to fill the spaces between tiles.

Mix grout to a thick, soupy consistency following the manufacturer's directions, and use a sponge float or squeegee to work it back and forth across the joints. Use sweeping strokes on a diagonal to the grid pattern of tile, to feed material equally into all seams. When the grout sets up (the surface is firm but not yet hard), you can start to clean the floor. This process also requires many passes, but with a damp sponge, rinsing often to avoid respreading the grout residue. Use a clean, damp sponge to wipe off the final haze, which may not be visible until the surface dries completely.

After the floor is clean and dry, you can reduce ongoing maintenance and formations of mold and mildew by coating the grout with a silicone sealer.

OTHER TYPES OF FLOORING

How about a flagstone floor? **Figure 26–38** shows what I did in my studio over a concrete slab, but don't attempt it unless you are prepared for a good deal of labor. We purchased the material in bulk, which meant pieces had to be cut up with a hammer and chisel so they would fit together reasonably well (**26–39**). "Reasonably well" allows room for some

26–38

26–39

errors, since joints that are not perfectly uniform have an attractive rustic effect. One of the installation problems is caused by the unequal thickness of the bulk sheets. This can range from not much more than inch to over 1 inch, so the mortar bed must be carefully adjusted if the floor surface is to be smooth and even. The rewards are a distinctive floor that is very easy to maintain and will last indefinitely.

How about cut-and-loop sculptured shag that you can put down in the form of self-adhesive 12-inch squares? The material has a foam backing so you don't need the conventional padding (**26–40**).

To cover a porch floor or a completely outdoors area such as a patio or the deck around a swimming pool, consider indoor-outdoor carpeting that can take abuse and is easy to clean with a stream of water from a hose (**26–41**). Such materials come in sheet form in

26–40

26–41

6- and 12-foot widths. Usual colors are either green or brown, but new colors are cropping up, since the concept is beginning to become popular for indoor as well as outdoor areas. One type is available in self-adhesive 9-inch squares. We tried it in a small utility area and it's working fine.

27

INSTALLING TRIM

Before you add interior trim, rooms look a little ragged around the edges. They need that final touch to unify doors and windows, define space, and set architectural style. They also need dead-flat framing and drywall, or your trim joints won't close, even if you cut them accurately.

Rough-fitting 2 × 4s and protruding nails that don't hurt a building structurally can kill it cosmetically unless you take the time to flatten structural surfaces before you drywall. Plane down bulging timbers and set protruding nail heads, particularly around window and door openings where horizontal and vertical timbers are stacked, sometimes not very evenly.

It's also important to mark the locations of studs on the floor before walls are covered with drywall, and note the locations of in-wall braces you may need to secure trim around shelves, chair rails, or wall-mounted fixtures.

From a practical point of view, moldings that are used to cover gaps between door frames and walls and those used around windows like those in **27-1** are structural pieces.

27-1

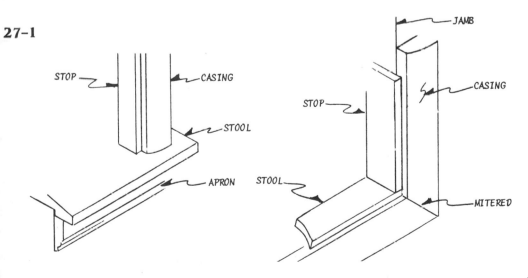

Yet the same moldings, or similar ones, can be used merely as decoration. **Figure 27-** shows how moldings can transform the blank look of flush doors.

A little-appreciated fact is that moldings provide clean lines to cover necessar spaces between construction elements, as baseboard does over a wood floor (**27-3** The baseboard also serves to protect the wall from damage when furniture is placed, o floors are cleaned. Planning for the use of moldings in particular areas also can reliev you of the chore of having to make a finished drywall joint, for example in wall-to-ceil ing corners.

27-2   DOOR MOLDINGS

27-3

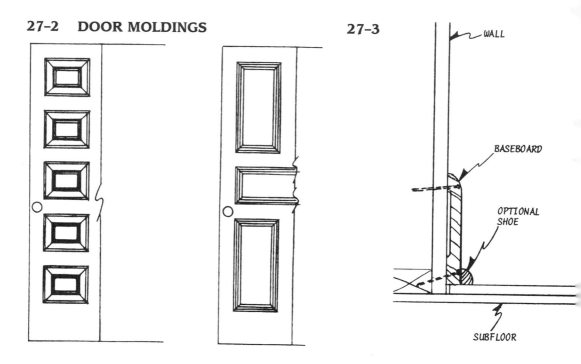

BUYING MOLDING

Most building-supply outlets stock common molding profiles in lengths running from 6 to 16 feet. When you determine molding lengths for your needs, always round off to the next highest foot. It's much better to end up with a cutoff than have to splice lengths to complete a run. Always add the amount of material required for miters. For example, if you are framing around a window, each piece will have a miter at each end. If the molding is 3 inches wide, you would add a minimum of 6 inches and then round off to the next even foot. This applies, of course, if you are getting moldings cut to specific lengths.

When you use bulk lengths, you cut pieces to accommodate only the extra material required for the miters.

TYPES OF MOLDING

The drawings in this section show standard ready-made moldings. All are available in different sizes, and some in different materials. While all were designed for a specific purpose, most are flexible enough to be used for decorative purposes as well as the intended structural applications. Many craftspeople use leftovers to do decorative things on cabinets and furniture and to make picture frames.

Casing is used to trim around doors and windows; baseboard is used at the bottom of walls (**27–4**). While each classification includes particular designs, there is enough overlap so the types are practically interchangeable.

A base shoe, shown in **27–5**, is designed for use where the baseboard and the floor meet. Base caps, shown in **27–6**, may be used to finish off the top of plain flat baseboards.

27–4   CASING DESIGNS

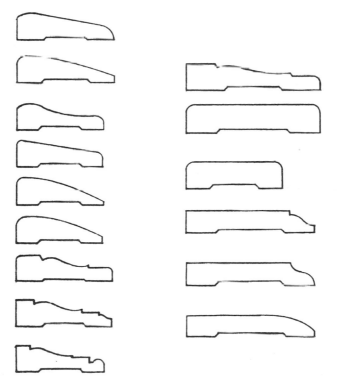

They end the job nicely and also serve to close any gap that might exist between the wa
and the baseboard.

Crown-and-bed moldings, shown in **27–7**, are used to soften the sharp lines wher
two planes meet. Usual applications are at corners where ceilings and walls meet, or out
side under eaves. Such moldings are very suitable for decorative trim work, around
mantel for example, or to make frames for pictures. The back areas are hollow, becaus
the moldings thus require less material to produce and are easier to install if the corner
they must cover do not meet at a true right angle.

Stop molding, shown in **27–8**, is nailed to jambs to stop the door when it is closed.

27–5   BASE SHOE

27–6   BASE CAP

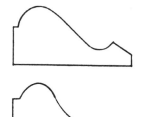

27–7   CROWN-AND-BED MOLDINGS

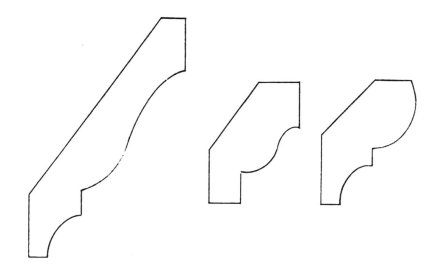

27-8   STOP MOLDINGS

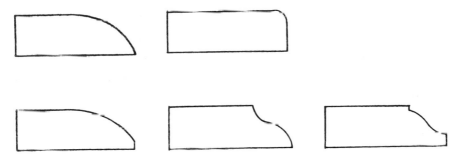

s also used on windows with sliding sash, and frequently selected for surface-mounting on cabinet doors when a raised-panel effect is desired.

Stools, shown in **27–9**, are used at the bottom of windows to provide a snug joint with the lowered sash. A saw cut to remove the bevel on the molding's undercut would make this an excellent material to finish off the edge of a table or counter.

Picture molding, shown in **27–10**, got its name because it was originally designed as

27–9   STOOLS

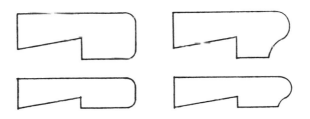

27–10   PICTURE MOLDING

perimeter trim from which pictures could be hung. It may still be used that way, but the modern application is as a substitute for crown molding.

Shelf edge or screen molding, shown in **27–11**, was originally designed to cover the raw edges of screening on doors or windows. It may also be used to decorate the edge of wood members like shelves, or to conceal exposed plywood edges. Because the moldings are thin, they may also be used as canvas-backed slats for tambour doors.

Corner guards, shown in **27–12**, do a good job of protecting and finishing outside corners, whether they are inside or outside the house.

Shingle molding, shown in **27–13**, makes a neat, decorative joint where the house siding abuts windowsills and overhangs. The strips are often used as shelf cleats and for decorative surface applications.

Brick molding, shown in **27–14**, is the trim used at the joint that occurs when an exterior wall is done partly in brick and partly in wood. It is also used if a wall is a stucco-wood combination.

27–11   SHELF-EDGE OR SCREEN MOLDING

27–12   CORNER GUARDS

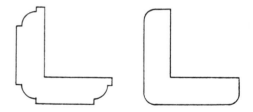

27–13   SHINGLE MOLDING

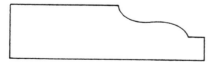

27–14   BRICK MOLDING

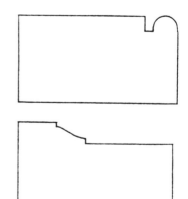

Drip caps, shown in **27–15**, are specially designed for use at top edges on the exterior side of doors and windows to prevent moisture from getting inside the walls.

Back bands, shown in **27–16**, are meant to be caps for baseboards and casings, but they may also be used as corner guards when only one edge of the material turning the corner is exposed.

Ply caps, shown in **27–17**, may be used at the top of wainscoting to supply a smooth finish. They are also effective for edging plywood and for framing any panel, especially if the panel will be used as a slab for, say, a tabletop.

Rounds are available as quarter-rounds, half-rounds, and full-rounds, as shown in **27–18**. Typical applications for full rounds are as closet poles, curtain rods, and banis-

27–15 DRIP CAPS   **27–16 BACK BAND**

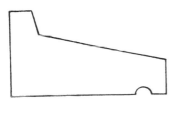

27–17 PLY CAP   **27–18 ROUNDS**

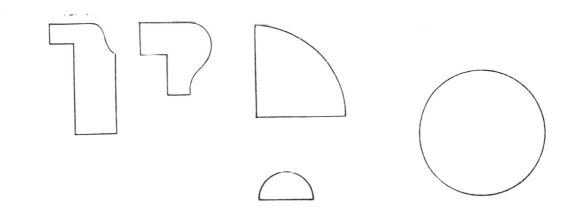

ters; for quarter-rounds, as decorative trim for inside corners and as shelf cleats; fc
half-rounds, as decorative surface trim or as seam covers.

A chair rail, shown in **27–19**, is applied to walls at particular heights to protect the wa.
from chair backs. It is not used so much today, but might still be a good idea in areas lik
playrooms.

Handrails, shown in **27–20**, are specially made for stairway applications.

27–19   CHAIR RAIL   **27–20   HAND RAILS**

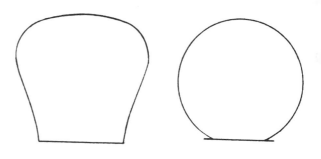

CUTTING AND JOINING

No matter what type of molding you select, installing it is the finishing touch that covers
rough edges and transitions between different materials, and often becomes the most
obvious sign of overall job quality. To achieve a superior finish with tight, clean-edged
joints, you need the basic carpentry skills of planning and measuring, and cutting tools
that may not be in the do-it-yourselfer's toolbox. Here are some of the options.

1. *Hand-powered trim saws.* The most common hand-powered cutting tool is a crosscut
   saw, either a 7- or 8-point model, which refers to the number of saw teeth per inch.
   It's good for general-purpose work around the house—cutting bookshelves and 2 × 4
   deck boards—but likely to make ragged edges on smooth-surfaced trim. One alternative, a full-size, 10-point finishing saw, will be cleaner, but unwieldy on small pieces
   of wood. Instead, consider a trim saw that is more compact and easier to use.

   The most practical is a backsaw, which is likely to have at least 12 and maybe more
   teeth per inch. Most have three helpful features. First, the saw is short, easy to draw
   back and forth, and stiff, with a reinforced upper edge that makes it easier to keep the

blade aligned while cutting. Second, although the saw is short, most have a full-scale handle that makes them comfortable and easy to control. Third, backsaws have little or no set, which refers to the splay in the teeth. Most saws have a set that makes a kerf, or channel, slightly wider than the saw blade itself. The set creates room for the blade and prevents binding. But teeth with a set remove extra material, and leave a rougher edge than teeth with no set. A no-set backsaw produces a furniture-quality joint, in soft or hard woods.

For very fine, small-scale work you could use a dovetail saw. It's smaller than a backsaw, with the same advantages except one. Most have a screwdriver-type handle. It's handy if you're flipping the blade around at angles to cut tiny dovetails, but unsteady over longer, straighter lines.

2. *Miter-box saws.* There are all kinds of miter boxes—frames in which you position pieces of trim to be cut, often at a 45-degree angle to make a corner joint. Some have saws built in. Good ones keep a very fine-toothed blade gliding across the wood under close control to produce accurate cuts. But they are expensive, specialized tools. Invest in one if you plan to do a lot of picture framing, or build furniture, but not for a few home improvement projects.

You can use a built-in model (**27–21**), or make a simple one as shown in **27–22**.

27–21

27–22 WOODEN MITER BOX

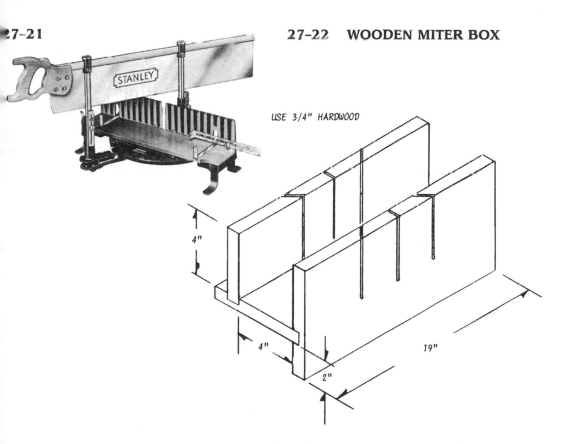

USE 3/4" HARDWOOD

4"

4"

2"

19"

Actually, even the simple type can be purchased ready-made, but may lack the lip that permits securing the unit with a clamp so it will hold steady as you saw (**27–23**). In addition to straight cuts and simple miters, the jig can be used to saw compound angles if you set it up properly (**27–24**). The width of the strip at the bottom determines the slope angle of the work.

27–23

27–24

3. *Shave trimmers.* These unique hand-powered tools—originally called Lion Trimmers, although there are now other brand names— also make sense only if you anticipate a lot of trim work. But they make finer cuts than any other trim tool hand- or electric-powered.

The business end is an oversize, sideways-sliding guillotine blade that shaves off slices of wood. It rides along an adjustable fence with stop positions like a miter box for standard angle cuts. You make a close cut with a saw, and then shave the piece until you get a joint with precisely the right fit. The device allows you to trim off a sixteenth of an inch, or a shaving thinner than tracing paper.

4. *Power trim saws.* Like a carpenter's crosscut handsaw, a standard circular-saw blade also is likely to leave rough edges—or burn marks if you crawl through the cut to prevent excessive splintering. If you want the speed that power provides, use a fine-toothed circular trim blade, preferably with carbide tips. Buying a good trim blade is an investment that makes sense. It's easy to switch with a crosscut blade, and you don't have to buy a new tool to power it.

Professionals generally don't have the time to cut by hand and use a cut-off saw. This tool, sometimes called a chop saw, is like a radial arm saw with a swiveling head, except it cuts down through the wood. It's a nice extra in a full-blown home shop, but not as versatile as a radial-arm saw.

5. *Slot cutters (biscuit jointers).* To make sure that miter seams between wide casings stay closed, particularly around doors with the extra stresses of opening and closing, you can reinforce the joints with biscuits, and install the casing on the door frame before setting the door in the wall. Slot-cutting power tools that make grooves for biscuits (biscuit jointers or jointers) used to be heavy-duty, high-priced, and for pros only. But several companies now offer basic, do-it-yourself tools for under $100.

To use one, fit the boards together, and draw a pencil line across the joint (try two lines for two biscuits on wide trim), so the opposing slots line up. Then adjust the cutter depth for the thickness of your wood so slots are mid-depth in each board, align the cutter with the mark, and pull the trigger. Finish the joint by applying glue to the biscuits, fitting them into the slots, and clamping the boards in place around them. You have to work quickly because the dry, compressed biscuits swell in contact with the glue—and when they set up in the joint, the joint stays flat and closed.

Whatever tool you use, in theory you should make a precisely plumb cut at 45 degrees to achieve a tight miter joint. But in the real world of slightly uneven framing and drywall joints, consider a standard carpentry procedure called undercutting. To close up a joint without resorting to wood filler, which can crack and often can't be concealed under clear finishes, the idea is to add just a few degrees of slope to the

cuts on mating trim pieces so the most visible front edges will meet first, just by a hair.
There are two ways to undercut. The most reliable is to make a plumb cut the way you normally would, without trying to tip the saw. Instead, tilt the trim just slightly in a clamp or miter box as you cut. A more heavy-handed method is to shave the cut face (everything except the front edge) with a block plane that's sharp enough to cut end grain smoothly. This is the kind of fine adjustment a trimmer handles with ease. With this approach, you tow the line on your 45-degree angle, but cheat on the straight-down, 90-degree cut.

COPES AND OTHER JOINTS

General molding rules are to miter all outside corners but to cope inside ones. The coped joint takes a little more work than a simple miter, but it's wise to do—for example, where baseboards meet at an inside corner—because nailing won't cause the joint to open, and shrinkage will not result in an obvious crack. Coping a joint merely means that you shape the end of one piece so it will conform to the profile of the piece it abuts (**27–25**).

27–25

COPE
CUT

You can do the job in one of two ways. You can transfer the profile of one piece to the end of the mating piece by using a compass (**27–26**). Then make the cut with a coping saw. With the second method, you cut a routine inside miter first and then follow the line of the miter with a coping saw, keeping the cut perpendicular to the back surface of the molding (**27–27**). It's a good idea to undercut a bit so you will be assured of a tight fit at the front edge of the moldings where they join.
Runs of molding are best made with single pieces, but if you must extend lengths it's

27–26   BUTTING MOLDINGS, USING A COMPASS

27–27   BUTTING MOLDINGS (ALTERNATE METHOD)

1. MAKE MITER CUT.

2. COPE CUT PERPENDICULAR TO MOLDING BACK.

3. BUTT SURFACES.

better to scarf the joint, as shown in **27–28**, instead of butting the ends. There is less likelihood that a scarfed joint will separate, especially if you apply some glue and drive a nail at an angle through the mating ends.

Butt joints will look good at first, although they are difficult to disguise under stain or paint, and have a tendency to open no matter how tight you make the connections initially. It helps to locate the joint out of sight, say, behind a radiator. If the trim is stained, try to match the grain so there won't be a noticeable change in texture from one board to another. Then join the boards with a scarf joint by cutting adjoining ends at complementary 45-degree angles so one board overlaps the other. This way, if the joint opens due to lumber shrinkage—as many new joints do, even if they are glued and nailed—you still see wood in the seam, not the black line of a gap.

If moldings intersect, you should let at least one piece run continuously. In the example shown in **27–29**, the cut pieces would be easy to shape by working with a coping saw and then smoothing with a drum sander. A butt block as shown in **27–30** is often used to provide a decorative detail or a transition point for intersecting dissimilar moldings.

27–28 SCARF JOINT

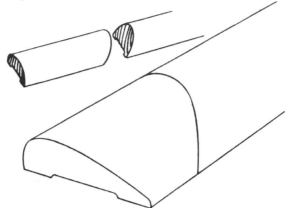

27–29 ONE PIECE CONTINUOUS   27–30 WITH BUTT BLOCK

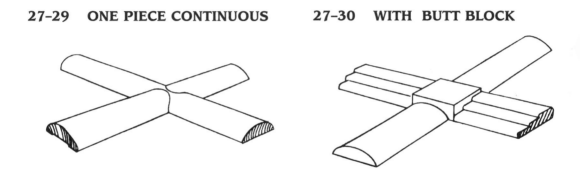

NAILING

Fasten moldings with either finishing or casing nails so that heads can be driven below the surface of the wood with a nail set and then concealed with wood putty. The size of nails depends on the thickness of the molding, but they must always be long enough to penetrate well into framing members such as studs, plates, trimmers, and headers. Don't forget to add the thickness of the wall cover when you choose a nail length.

Nails driven into profile corners will be easier to conceal (**27–31**). If you pre-tint the molding before you install it, the wood putty used to conceal the nail can be colored with the same stain. Prefinished moldings that may be supplied along with a paneling material should be attached with color-matched nails.

7-31

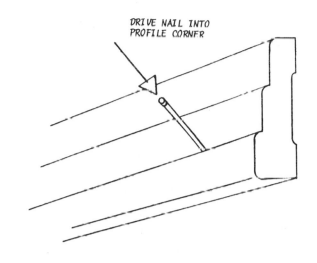

DRIVE NAIL INTO
PROFILE CORNER

SYNTHETIC MOLDINGS

Some people can't tolerate the idea of plastic trim on an otherwise wooden house. But despite the widespread prejudice, plastic foam trim products are used increasingly on new houses and remodeling jobs for several reasons.

While the supply of wood molding is limited, particularly wood trim with deep-relief and highly defined details, synthetics are available in hundreds of motifs in all major architectural styles from Victorian and Georgian to Neoclassical and Modern.

You can buy elaborate cornice moldings to ring rooms and pediments, crossheads to cap doors and windows, and components to make balustrades and railings, louvers, ceiling medallions, niches, and many other types of trim. Some have only a modest profile or a few shallow flutes; others are incredibly detailed with lifelike leaves and other decorations.

Several companies also offer porch posts and other structural components reinforced with PVC, fiberglass, or even steel to meet strength requirements of building codes. A Web search for architectural moldings should turn up several large manufacturers, such as Balmer, Fypon, Focal Point, and Style Solutions. Prices vary widely depending on the size and complexity of the piece. But a highly detailed, leafy, 15-inch ceiling medallion might cost $75, while ornate Victorian patterns in 36-inch units can cost $300.

Like wood, you can use most synthetics inside and outside. But wood can warp, shrink, rot, and become food for termites. And finding lumber that is straight and free of defects to use as decorative trim sometimes can be difficult. In contrast, most synthetic molding is made from closed-cell foam that prevents water penetration. That makes the material highly resistant to the seasonal shifting that's common with wood. And foam is more resistant to insects than wood.

High-density foam also has no grain, so there is no built-in bias to twist one way or the other. There are no splits or cracks or knots. Joints won't open the way they can on wood assemblies because most foam components are monolithic and have no joints.

While highly decorative wood moldings often are built up piece by piece, and joints are painstakingly matched, synthetics come out of the box ready to install. Even on a large pediment with angled tops and turned finials that can span a double door, there are no joints to fit.

The main advantage of synthetics comes in labor savings during the installation. Without layers of molding to apply and with no joints to cut on major pieces, you simply fasten sections to the house. Some products can be left as is with the smooth surface they have from the mold. Most pieces are factory-primed white. Some companies also offer metallic coatings, for some reason, and other special finishes.

Most synthetics can be worked like soft pine if you need to trim lengths to size. You can miter corners on cornice molding using a fine-toothed finishing saw to keep cuts smooth, and sand lightly as needed. But many firms offer special corner pieces so you don't have to cut miters or coped joints. You fasten the corner block in place and butt other trim sections against it with square-cut joints.

The lightweight material is installed with compatible adhesive (typically a polyurethane construction adhesive) and non-corrosive (typically galvanized) nails or screws. You can touch up holes with plastic wood filler. Adhesive and sometimes caulk is used at major joints in long runs. You also may need a bead of caulk where true lengths of molding meet an irregular existing surface.

You can paint smooth-surfaced urethanes the way you finish standard siding and trim. Some products also can be stained, which gets into the iffy territory of making plastic look like wood. But under a coat of paint (and particularly if the molding is up near the ceiling or edge of the roof), you won't know polymer from pine.

Metric Conversion Table

INCHES TO MILLIMETERS AND CENTIMETERS

MM—millimeters   *CM—centimeters*

Inches	MM	CM	Inches	CM	Inches	CM
⅛	3	0.3	9	22.9	30	76.2
¼	6	0.6	10	25.4	31	78.7
⅜	10	1.0	11	27.9	32	81.3
½	13	1.3	12	30.5	33	83.8
⅝	16	1.6	13	33.0	34	86.4
¾	19	1.9	14	35.6	35	88.9
⅞	22	2.2	15	38.1	36	91.4
1	25	2.5	16	40.6	37	94.0
1¼	32	3.2	17	43.2	38	96.5
1½	38	3.8	18	45.7	39	99.1
1¾	44	4.4	19	48.3	40	101.6
2	51	5.1	20	50.8	41	104.1
2½	64	6.4	21	53.3	42	106.7
3	76	7.6	22	55.9	43	109.2
3½	89	8.9	23	58.4	44	111.8
4	102	10.2	24	61.0	45	114.3
4½	114	11.4	25	63.5	46	116.8
5	127	12.7	26	66.0	47	119.4
6	152	15.2	27	68.6	48	121.9
7	178	17.8	28	71.1	49	124.5
8	203	20.3	29	73.7	50	127.0

INDEX